THE COMPLETE BOOK OF SOCCER

SECOND EDITION, FULLY REVISED

EDITED BY CHRIS HUNT

FIREFLY BOOKS

Dedicated to Cliff Hunt, a 'Gooner' until the end!

A Firefly Book

Published by Firefly Books Ltd. 2012

First printing

Publisher Cataloging-in-Publication Data (U.S.)

Hunt, Chris.
The complete book of soccer / edited by Chris Hunt.
2nd ed.
[400] p. : photos. (chiefly col.) ; cm.
Summary: Biographies of the greatest players, coaches and clubs in soccer history, and a detailed tournament-by-tournament history of the World Cup, the European Championship, as well as the worlds' major competitions at both club and international levels.
ISBN-13: 978-1-55407-688-8
1. Soccer – History. 2. Soccer players – Biography. I. Title.
796.334/2 dc22   GV942.5H868   2010

Library and Archives Canada Cataloguing in Publication

The complete book of soccer / edited by Chris Hunt. – 2nd ed.
Includes index.
ISBN-13: 978-1-55407-688-8
1. Soccer. I. Hunt, Chris, 1962-
GV943.C66 2010   796.334   C2010-906424-0

Published in the United States by
Firefly Books (U.S.) Inc.
P.O. Box 1338, Ellicott Station
Buffalo, New York 14205

Published in Canada by
Firefly Books Ltd.
66 Leek Crescent
Richmond Hill, Ontario L4B 1H1

All photography © Action Images Ltd

Printed in China

Developed by Hayden Media, Ashford, Middlesex, Great Britain

CONTENTS

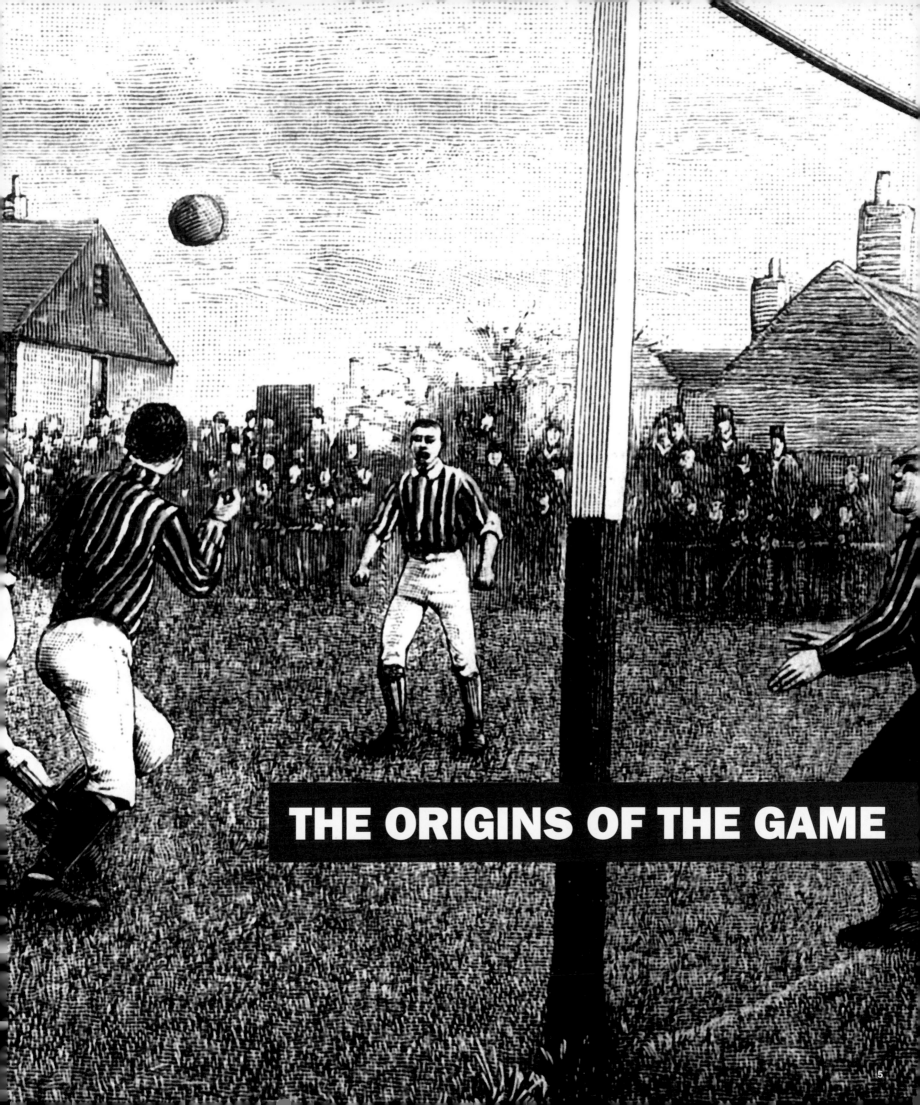

THE ORIGINS OF THE GAME

Above: Part of a 14th century misericord at Gloucester Cathedral depicts an early example of ball game players. Opposite: A game of 'mob football' on the streets of London in 1721.

THE ORIGINS OF THE GAME

TO WATCH FOOTBALL in the early decades of the 21st century is to watch a multimillion pound industry that creates global stars out of the most ordinary of people and stirs the emotions of billions of men, women and children around the world. In bars and cafés, homes and schools, from the Amazon to Zanzibar, the conversation is never far from 'the beautiful game'. Hours of television coverage are devoted not just to showing matches, but to talking about them, endlessly arguing over rules and their interpretation, over tactics, and the relative merits of the players. The world is obsessed with football.

But how did it get to this point? How did a game so apparently simple become the *raison d'être* for millions, a worldwide religion?

The only thing that can be said with any real certainty about the early origins of football is that a variety of games were played in countries around the world, which involved elements of today's football. Some featured little or no kicking, others lacked a competitive edge, but each embraced something recognisably part of the modern day game.

Recorded in a military manual dating back to the Han Dynasty (200-300 BC), it is usually said that the Chinese Tsu Chu is the earliest form of football known to man, though in truth it more closely resembles a fairground game than the

football we know today. Two nine-metre high bamboo canes were used to suspend a large piece of silk cloth with a hole 30cm-40cm in diameter cut into it. Competitors would then attempt to kick a leather ball filled with hair and feathers through the hole, sometimes with the added difficulty of being pressured by opponents. Tsu Chu, it seems, was played to celebrate the Emperor's birthday. The penalty for losing was death.

Less sinister, and certainly less fatal, was Kemari, a noncompetitive Japanese game dating from around the 5th century AD. Best described as 'keepie-uppies', Kemari was contested among a group of eight players standing in a circle and passing the ball to each other without allowing it to touch the ground. Further south, in the Malay states, they played Sepak Raga, a similar game in which you were permitted to use any part of your body apart from your hands to keep the ball in the air. In South America, in 400 AD, the Mayans played Poktapok, a game between two teams using rubber balls. Much later, the Aztecs had a similar game called Ullamatzli, while in North Africa there was Koura, a Berber ball game probably linked to fertility rights.

It is unlikely that there was any common link among these different games, rather that each civilisation invented its own game with its own rules uninfluenced by people living thousands of miles away. It is difficult, therefore, to sustain the Chinese claim to have

invented football, since the evidence that they took Tsu Chu to the world is at best threadbare. They may not even have invented the world's first ball game – there is actually evidence of ball games being played even earlier, in Greece, where the little-known Pheninda (or Episkyros) is mentioned in the writings of the Greek playwright Antiphanes, who lived in the 4th century BC. Adding weight to his words is a bas relief at the foot of a marble column in Athens, believed to date from 600 BC, which shows a figure playing a game that looks very much like football.

Episkyros probably did influence later games, not least as the forerunner of Harpastum. Used as a way of keeping the Roman army fit, Harpastum was played on a rectangular field with the aim of getting the ball over the opponents' boundary line. Kicking was limited and the game was probably more similar to rugby, but the growth of the Roman Empire took the game to new territories and it survived for 700 years. It may even have had some influence on the very early development of football in Britain: it is claimed that victory celebrations after a battle with the Romans in Derby in the 3rd century involved something resembling a game of football.

Yet despite the claims and counter-claims, none of these games was football as we know it. The game known around the world by that name did not really exist until the mid-19th century and its home was certainly England.

FOOTBALL MILESTONES

1848: First code of football rules compiled at Cambridge University. The 'Cambridge Rules' helped differentiate football from rugby.

1857 Sheffield FC, the world's oldest club, is formed after two keen cricket lovers, William Prest and Nathaniel Creswick, decided football would be the sport to keep their fitness levels up during the winter.

1862 Notts County, the Football League's oldest side, is founded as Nottingham Football Club.

1863 Football Association is formed in London.

1865 Tape is introduced between two posts of a goal.

1866 The offside rule altered to allow a player to be onside when three of opposing team are nearer their own goalline.

1867 Queen's Park, the oldest Scottish club, forms.

1869 Goal kicks introduced.

1871 The FA Cup competition is introduced and goalkeepers are first mentioned in the laws of the game.

1872 England and Scotland draw the first ever international 0-0 in Glasgow... The Scottish FA is formed... Wanderers win the first FA Cup final, beating Royal Engineers 1-0... Corner kicks are introduced... Le Havre are the first French team to be formed.

1874 Umpires are first mentioned in the laws of the game. Shinguards are also introduced.

1875 The FA make the crossbar obligatory after it had been used in the Sheffield Rules since 1870.

1876 Football Association of Wales is formed. Scotland play Wales for the first time.

1877 The London Association and Sheffield Association agree to use the same rules.

1878 The whistle is introduced by referees.

1879 First international between England and Wales takes place at Kennington Oval. England win 2-1.

1880 The Irish FA is formed.

1882 The two-handed throw-in is introduced.

1883 First British Home Championship is staged and won by Scotland.

1885 Professionalism is legalised in England. Arbroath beat Bon Accord 36-0, a record for a first-class match.

1886 The awarding of caps for international appearances is approved by the FA.

1887 Preston North End beat Hyde United 26-0 to record the highest FA Cup score… Football introduced in Russia.

1888 The Football League is formed.

1889 Preston North End win first league and cup 'double'. They complete the season without losing a game and are known as 'The Invincibles'.

1890 The Scottish League is formed.

1891 Devised by Liverpool engineer John Alexander Brodie, goal nets are introduced. The taking of penalties from a penalty line is also introduced.

1893 Genoa, Italy's oldest football club, is formed by British diplomat Sir Charles Alfred Payton and nine of his contemporaries. The club is originally named Genoa Football and Cricket Club.

1894 Scotland adopts professionalism. Referees are given complete control of the game… The first match is played in Brazil between employees of São Paulo railway and a local gas company, while the sport also makes its debut in Austria.

1895 The FA Cup trophy is stolen in Birmingham and not recovered… It is decided that players taking thrown-ins must be on the touchline.

1896 An unofficial football competition is played at the Athens Olympics, with teams from Denmark, Athens and Izmir taking part.

1897 The Players Union is formed for English and Scottish players… English club side Corinthians tour South America… Juventus are formed and play in pink shirts.

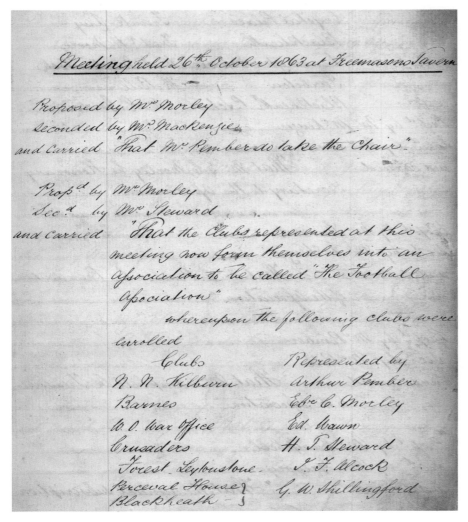

THE FOOTBALL ASSOCIATION RULES 1863

1. The maximum length of the ground shall be 200 yards, the maximum breadth shall be 100 yards, the length and breadth shall be marked off with flags; and the goal shall be defined by two upright posts, eight yards apart, without any tape or bar across them.

2. A toss for goals shall take place, and the game shall be commenced by a place kick from the centre of the ground by the side losing the toss for goals; the other side shall not approach within ten yards of the ball until it is kicked off.

3. After a goal is won, the losing side shall be entitled to kick off, and the two sides shall change goals after each goal is won.

4. A goal shall be won when the ball passes between the goal-posts or over the space between the goal-posts (at whatever height), not being thrown, knocked on, or carried.

5. When the ball is in touch, the first player who touches it shall throw it from the point on the boundary line where it left the ground in a direction at right angles with the boundary line, and the ball shall not be in play until it has touched the ground.

6. When a player has kicked the ball, any one of the same side who is nearer to the opponent's goal line is out of play and may not touch the ball himself, nor in any way whatever prevent any other player from doing so, until he is in play; but no player is out of play when the ball is kicked off from behind the goal line.

7. In case the ball goes behind the goal line, if a player on the side to whom the goal belongs first touches the ball, one of his side shall be entitled to a free-kick from the goal line at the point opposite the place where the ball shall be touched. If a player of the opposite side first touches the ball, one of his side shall be entitled to a free-kick at the goal only from a point 15 yards outside the goal line, opposite the place where the ball is touched, the opposing side standing within their goal line until he has had his kick.

8. If a player makes a fair catch, he shall be entitled to a free-kick, providing he claims it by making a mark with his heel at once; and in order to take such a kick he may go back as far as he pleases, and no player on the opposite side shall advance beyond his mark until he has kicked.

9. No player shall run with the ball.

10. Neither tripping nor hacking shall be allowed, and no player shall use his hands to hold or push his adversary.

11. A player shall not be allowed to throw the ball or pass it to another with his hands.

12. No player shall be allowed to take the ball from the ground with his hands under any pretext whatever while it is in play.

13. No player shall be allowed to wear projecting nails, iron plates, or gutta percha on the soles or heels of his boots.

THE ORIGINS OF the game in England are just as hazy as those elsewhere. Along with the story of the Romans in Derby, comes a tale from Chester of a game played with the severed head of a defeated Dane. Whether either is true is impossible to say, but what is clear is that from around the 12th century, ball games were a common sight in the towns and villages of the British Isles.

Often these games were for local pride, two teams in a village fighting it out for bragging rights, or neighbouring villages competing in an annual contest, usually staged on Shrove Tuesday (in northern France a similar game called La Soule was played on Shrove Tuesday, Sundays and Saints days, and it has been suggested that the Norman conquest of 1066 brought the tradition to England). However, local pride came at a cost, often counted in broken limbs and sometimes in fatalities.

The rules – if there were any – were vague. This was 'mob football', with no limit to the number of men on each side and virtually no method of play illegal. Nor was there necessarily much use of feet in contact with the ball. The general idea was to transport a ball (or pig's bladder) to one or other point within a village, but with so many players, games could last for days. (Annual games are still played today, albeit with less risk to life and limb, in places like Ashbourne in Derbyshire and Haxey in Lincolnshire, where they fight over a leather tube called a 'hood' rather than a ball.)

By the 14th century, these raucous street games were causing consternation among the authorities. So much so, in fact, that in 1314, King Edward II tried to ban them with the threat of jail. A proclamation was issued: 'For as much as there is great noise in the city caused by hustling over large balls, from which many evils arise, which God forbid; we command and forbid on behalf of the King, on pain of imprisonment, such game be used in the city in future.'

Yet Edward II was just the first of several monarchs to try – and fail – to clamp down on what was fast becoming the 'people's game'. When his son, Edward III, made his own attempt to ban football, he was not just concerned with public order issues but with the distraction football was causing at a time when England was at war with France. His subjects, he argued, should be focusing on more important business, like archery practice. However, despite his attempts – and those of monarchs to come – mob football continued to flourish in England (and Scotland) mainly due to the people's desire to play.

Meanwhile in Italy in the 14th century the game of Il Calcio had begun to be played in the main square in Florence on the feast day of St John the Baptist, the city's patron saint. With its roots in the Roman game of Harpastum, Il Calcio was nevertheless closer to modern day football than its ancient predecessor – to begin with, its name came from *calciare*, Italian for 'to kick'.

The game, with its teams dressed in bright colours, was certainly more civilised than its English counterpart. In 1580 a set of rules was published for the first time by Giovanni Bardi, and the game may even have had an influence on the development of football in Britain after a match was played in front of the British Consul. However, football in England remained firmly in the hands of the mobs (a character in Shakespeare's 1605 play *King Lear* refers to a 'base football player'). Rough, violent and a nuisance to the authorities, for several centuries no real progress was made in the development of the game.

The turning point came in the mid-19th

Top left: The minutes recording the formation of the Football Association.

Opposite top: A depiction of a football game at the turn of the 18th century.

Opposite bottom: A team from Harrow public school in the 19th century.

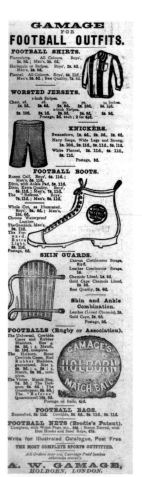
century. By then, football had long been played in the major public schools of England; the virtues of team play, discipline and exercise were noted by teachers, and the rough and tumble excesses were a joy to the pupils. By their nature more organised, these games allowed for a gradual refinement of the 'rules' to the point where a more sophisticated game was starting to be played.

There was still no uniformity. Different schools played by their own evolved regulations, dependent on, for example, the area of ground they had at their disposal for games or the whims of the master in charge. Other rules were added piecemeal over the years by each school, so that when two schools faced each other they would adopt the rules of one of the two teams, the other adapting as best they could, but there were too many problems to make this satisfactory.

There were irreconcilable differences, for example, in the degree to which handling was permitted. In some schools running with the ball in your hands was fine, while in others only minimal use of the hands was allowed. More controversial was the use of hacking, a technique which essentially involved kicking away at an opponent's shins if he had the ball.

It was not until a group of footballers from various public schools found themselves together at Cambridge University that the first attempt to draw up a uniform set of rules was made. Published in 1848, the 'Cambridge Rules' were by no means universally adopted, but the group of students behind them were to play an important part in raising awareness of the need for a standardised set

of rules and in persuading various schools and clubs to modify their own rules in order to develop unity.

Other rules were drawn up over the next 15 years (the best known being the 'Sheffield Rules' of 1857 and the 1862 'Rules for the Simplest Game' by JC Thring, a teacher at Uppingham School and one of the pioneers of the Cambridge Rules), but the breakthrough came in October 1863 when representatives from 11 clubs – Barnes, Blackheath, Blackheath School, Crusaders, Crystal Palace, Forest (later Wanderers), Kensington School, No Names Kilburn, Perceval House, Surbiton and War Office – met to form the Football Association.

Two months later, the Football Association rules were published [see previous page], and it was here that rugby and football went their separate ways and the football we know today really began to appear. Some clubs, Blackheath among them, opted to continue with their own game, based more on catching and passing the ball than kicking it, but those that stayed within the FA were determined that their 'football' should be played largely with the feet. For a while there was hope that the two groups – the rugby unionists and the association footballers as they became known – could be brought back under the same umbrella, but when, six years later, the FA banned all handling of the ball, the split became permanent and in 1871 the Rugby Football Union was formed.

The first FA laws were far from perfect – they did not, for example, stipulate the number of players on each side or the duration of the game – and to begin with, many schools and clubs continued to follow their own rules. Gradually

they began to be used all over the country and when, in 1878, the 'Sheffield Rules' were absorbed into a new set of FA rules, uniformity was fast approaching.

In 1886 overall responsibility for the laws of the game passed to the International Football Association Board comprising of one representative from each of the English, Scottish, Welsh and Irish football associations. (Since 1913 FIFA has also had a presence on the board, which now consists of four delegates, making up 50 per cent of any vote.)

As the FA grew bigger and stronger, there became a desire among the top teams to test themselves in organised competition. So, at the start of the 1871-2 season, the world's oldest cup competition, the FA Challenge Cup was launched. Based on a knockout competition – Cock House – and played at Harrow School, the inaugural FA Cup saw 15 entries; 13 from the London area, plus Donington School from Lincolnshire and Queen's Park from Glasgow, who were given a bye to the semi-finals because of the distance they had to travel. Sadly, having drawn their semi-final in London, the Scots decided they could not afford to return for the replay, so the first final, in 1872, pitted Royal Engineers against Wanderers, who won 1-0.

In October of the same year, England played Scotland in the first ever international match, a 0-0 draw in Glasgow. Just five months later, the Scottish FA was established at a meeting attended by Clydesdale, Dumbreck, Glasgow Eastern, Granville, Queen's Park, Rovers, Third Lanark and Vale Of Leven.

With football's popularity growing in England and attendances at matches rising,

it was not long before the potential financial rewards of football were noted. Spectators, it became apparent, could be charged for admission. And since, not surprisingly, the more successful teams attracted larger crowds, it was inevitable that ambitious clubs would look for ways to attract better players. There was little the FA could do to hold back the advent of professionalism. Having at first attempted to limit payments to players to 'wages lost' and 'expenses', in 1885 the FA gave in and permitted professional players.

Three years later, it was decided that the growing number of clubs warranted better organisation and the world's first Football League was established with 12 teams taking part: Accrington, Aston Villa, Blackburn Rovers, Bolton Wanderers, Burnley, Derby County, Everton, Notts County, Preston North End, Stoke, West Bromwich Albion and Wolverhampton Wanderers.

The FA was barely 25 years old yet English football had taken huge strides in the development of the game. In the FA Cup it had a glamorous knockout competition that drew large crowds, and it had a professional football league with a basic structure in place that would carry the game well into the 20th century. International football was under way too, with regular fixtures among the four home nations, England, Scotland, Wales and Ireland. But already football was far more than just a British sport. It was still a long way from becoming the most popular pastime in the world, but by the turn of the century, travelling British workers and businessmen had taken football to all four corners of the globe.

Top: Preston, the first double-winners in 1889. Above: Lord Kinnaird, who presided over the first ever international match.

THE FA CUP

MOST FOOTBALL-PLAYING nations have domestic knockout competitions – Spain's Copa Del Rey, for instance, or Italy's Coppa Italia – but none is older or more prestigious than England's FA Cup. The idea of a cup competition originated in London on July 20, 1871, with a proposal in the offices of *The Sportsman* by then FA honorary secretary Charles Alcock to establish 'a Challenge Cup… for which all clubs belonging to the Association should be invited to compete'. Fifteen clubs entered the inaugural FA Cup in the 1871-2 season, with Wanderers, a team of ex-public school and university players, making history as 1-0 winners of the first final against Royal Engineers at Kennington Oval. The match was played in front of a crowd of 2,000 who each paid one shilling for the privilege.

Since it was conceived as a 'challenge' cup, Wanderers simply defended the trophy the following year against Oxford University. A change of rules ushered in a more competitive tournament but Wanderers still dominated the early years, along with amateur side Old Etonians. Blackburn Rovers then became the dominant force until the turn of the century, when southern non-leaguers Tottenham Hotspur won in 1901.

For the first 50 years the trophy was played out in a number of venues, including the Oval and Crystal Palace, which hosted the final on 20 occasions, the last time being in 1914. The final moved to Old Trafford a year later, before the Great War forced its suspension.

Northern clubs held sway – notably Sheffield United, Bradford, Aston Villa and Newcastle United – until the great Arsenal side of the Thirties briefly made their mark. Manchester United registered a first win in 1909 (having first entered in 1886 as Newton Heath) but the club would have to wait until 1948 for a second win. United's triumph in 2004 was their 11th FA Cup win, a record in the competition. In all, 42 different clubs have won the cup.

In January 1922 building started on a permanent venue, Wembley Stadium. It cost £750,000 but it was completed too late to host that year's final. Instead, a year later Wembley began by hosting the famous 'White Horse Final' between Bolton Wanderers and West Ham United, when an over-capacity crowd spilt on to the pitch and were brought under control by a single mounted policeman and his white horse, Billy. Bolton emerged as 3-2 winners when order was restored.

All subsequent FA Cup finals were played at Wembley, excluding the war years (when there were unofficial competitions) until 2000, when the ground was knocked down. The Millennium Stadium in Cardiff staged the final for the next six years while a new arena was being built, with Chelsea's win over Manchester United in 2007 being the first final at the newly constructed Wembley Stadium.

The highest scoring final occurred in 1953 when Blackpool beat Bolton Wanderers 4-3 in a stunning comeback. It became known as 'The Matthews Final' after Blackpool's inspirational winger Stanley Matthews, though this is now regarded as rather unfair on Stan Mortensen who scored a hat-trick in the game.

There have been four actual trophies during the competition's existence. The original trophy, smaller than the present one, was stolen from a Birmingham shop window in 1895 and never recovered after Aston Villa had won the competition. The second trophy, an exact replica of the first, lasted until 1910 before being presented to FA president Lord Kinnaird. In 1911 it was replaced by a larger cup and fittingly the Bradford-made trophy was won by Bradford FC. The current cup, played for since 1992, is an exact replica of the third trophy.

FA Cup rules have differed little since World War II, though clubs higher up the league are given byes through the early rounds. Substitutes were finally allowed in 1966-7 and a replay was not necessary in the final until 1970, when the game at Wembley was drawn and to clinch the trophy Chelsea travelled to Old Trafford to beat Leeds United.

In 1991-2 penalty shoot-outs were introduced in order to settle replayed games that were still level after extra-time. Fortunately a shoot-out in the final itself did not occur until 2005, when Arsenal beat Manchester United 5-4. It was not a memorable final, as has become the case in recent years. However, some faith was restored in the FA Cup's ability to produce a thriller when West Ham and Liverpool met in 2006. Both teams played attacking football, producing a 3-3 draw with the game eventually settled by penalties in favour of Liverpool. It was easily the best final since 1987, when underdogs Coventry City beat Tottenham 3-2.

At the start of the 1994-5 season controversial

steps were taken to capitalise on the cup's appeal by introducing sponsorship. The competition remains titled the FA Cup, but AXA, Littlewoods and most recently E.On have paid for the rights to be associated with the world's oldest football cup. Such moves have made traditionalists uncomfortable, especially as the FA Cup has suffered from the dominance of league football in recent years, a symptom of the increased expectations of entering the Champions League and the power of the major Premier League sides in the English game.

The competition received a further blow in 1999 when, in an attempt to curry favour for a World Cup bid, the Football Association encouraged the withdrawal of holders Manchester United in order to travel abroad to compete in the World Club Championship.

Since a subsequent relaunch, there has been increased TV exposure, steps to stop clubs switching ties for financial gain to preserve the romance of David vs Goliath encounters, bigger prize money and a guaranteed Europa League place for the winners. In truth, it may never again possess quite the same glory, but with 600 teams entering annually, playing over 500 games on the way to a showcase final, the FA Cup still breeds romance and excitement like no other national cup competition anywhere in the world.

Above: An artist's impression of the 1891 FA Cup Final.

Left: Steven Gerrard of Liverpool lifts the FA Cup at the Millennium Stadium in Cardiff in 2006.

Opposite top: Queen Elizabeth and King George VI present the FA Cup to Sunderland captain Raich Carter in 1937.

Opposite centre: The original FA Challenge Cup trophy.

Opposite bottom: Newcastle captain Joe Harvey celebrates with the trophy in 1951.

Overleaf: West Ham and Bolton in action at the 1923 FA Cup Final at Wembley Stadium.

THE FOOTBALL LEAGUE

THE FOOTBALL ASSOCIATION had been in existence for 23 years before it was considered necessary to create an official league. Before then the nascent English game was strictly amateur, although unofficial payments were made to some players, with matches organised on an ad hoc, 'friendly' basis. The league's instigator was Scotsman William McGregor, an Aston Villa committee member who organised two meetings in London and Manchester in 1888 that brought together the 12 clubs that became the Football League's founder members: Accrington, Aston Villa, Blackburn Rovers, Bolton Wanderers, Burnley, Derby County, Everton, Notts County, Preston North End, West Bromwich Albion, Stoke and Wolverhampton Wanderers.

The idea was to create order and to lend structure to the game by guaranteeing fixtures, and revenue for a dozen professional teams, split equally between the north and the midlands, the south remaining predominantly amateur. Arsenal would become the first southern club to join the Football League in the 1893-4 season.

The first games played under Football League rules took place on September 8, 1888, with points awarded only for wins. This system was soon amended to include one point for a draw, remaining in place for the best part of a century until 1981-2, when to improve competition three points were awarded for a win.

Preston North End were the league's inaugural winners, also recording a league and cup 'double', a feat repeated by Aston Villa eight years later and then not achieved again until Tottenham in 1961. In all only seven different teams have won the 'double', the last being Chelsea in 2010.

The Football League acquired a 12-strong Second Division in the 1892-3 season, by taking over the rival Football Alliance, which featured Nottingham Forest and Crewe Alexandra amongst others. Promotion and relegation were settled with the top three teams from Division Two playing the bottom three from Division One. This rule was later simplified to stop anomalies.

A third division was established in 1920-1, then divided into regions the following year (Division Three North and Division Three South), creating four divisions. In 1958 it was decided to replace these with national third

and fourth divisions, with the top half of each regional division forming the new Division Three, and the bottom half becoming Division Four. This structure was to remain unchanged for 34 years.

The Football League proved to be a huge success, with attendances booming in the years up to World War I. Northern clubs held sway with Newcastle United, Blackburn and Sheffield Wednesday proving the dominant forces. Post-war, London clubs Chelsea and Arsenal joined the top flight but neither could break the northern stranglehold until the latter prised manager Herbert Chapman from powerful Huddersfield. He promptly took advantage of a change to the offside law to create a vibrant, attacking team in the 1930s that went on to win five league titles and four FA Cups.

Following another suspension for the Second World War, the Football League entered into another era of success, with the sport attracting massive attendances. Manchester United steadily asserted their influence but just as they appeared to be embarking on a period of domination after two consecutive league titles in 1954-5 and 1955-6, tragedy struck when an air crash robbed them of eight leading players, including captain Roger Byrne and rising star Duncan Edwards. The Munich air disaster occurred because United were returning from a European fixture with Red Star Belgrade. The previous season, despite great resistance from the Football League, United had been the first English club to enter a side in a European competition, reaching the quarter-finals.

The early part of the modern era saw the championship rotate regularly between clubs. A rare victory for London's Tottenham aside, the north continued to dominate. League football became increasingly attractive to business with regular televised coverage beginning on the BBC in 1964 (in the past it was confined to just European and FA Cup finals).

In the mid-Sixties, Liverpool began to establish themselves as a force under Bill Shankly and his successors, Bob Paisley and Joe Fagan, who brought about an unequalled period

of dominance. Liverpool's 1972-3 victory opened the way to 11 titles in 16 years and an overall total of 18, a feat finally equalled by Manchester United in 2009.

With Liverpool also taking the commercial lead by announcing a shirt sponsor in 1978, the league opened its doors to outside money. While there had been a few short-lived competitions like the Texaco Cup and the Watney Cup, the Football League took the next logical step with the announcement of a three-year deal with Canon in 1983. Further lucrative tie-ins followed. Another idea to generate money came with the revival of the concept of play-offs in 1986-7. Originally a means of helping to reduce Division One from 22 clubs to 20, play-offs proved so successful they still remain.

The 104-year history of the Football League received its greatest blow on February 20, 1992, when 22 clubs announced they were breaking away to form the FA Premier League from the beginning of the 1992-3 season. This was partly a way of revitalising the top flight, which had been damaged by a number of catastrophes in the Eighties, including 1985's Bradford fire, the carnage at the Heysel Stadium in Brussels, and 1989's Hillsborough disaster. Football

hooliganism was considered to be out of control, attendances were down, and the game's image was recognised as archaic.

After the birth of the Premier League, the remaining divisions of the Football League were renumbered, with automatic promotion and relegation continuing and the remaining 72 clubs governing themselves. In 2004-5 the Football League followed the Premiership example by rebranding itself, with the bigger clubs in Division One demanding more of the spoils. Coca-Cola announced a three-year sponsorship and the top tier became the Coca-Cola Championship with the other divisions becoming League One and League Two.

Since the establishment of the Premier League there has been a distinct fissuring between the clubs with the most money and those with lesser resources. Put simply, the richest dominate, with the title rotating between Manchester United, Arsenal and Chelsea. The only surprise in the Premiership era has been the triumph of Blackburn Rovers in 1994-5. Whether the title race in the top tier can ever be as open as it was is doubtful but England's four divisions have more strength in depth than any league in the world.

Above: Liverpool players run around the pitch after beating Arsenal 5-0 to win the league championship in 1964.

Left: Chelsea's John Terry lifts the Premier League trophy in 2010.

Opposite top: Winners of the 1897 league and FA Cup 'double', Aston Villa.

Opposite bottom: Ipswich Town captain Andy Nelson and his manager Alf Ramsey celebrate winning the title in 1962.

Above: France set sail for the inaugural 1930 World Cup, they were one of only four European teams to compete.

Opposite top: Henri Delaunay, the founder of the European Championship.

Opposite bottom: Leônidas and his Brazilian team-mates enjoy a kickabout while waiting for a train during the 1938 World Cup in France.

Right: FIFA president Jules Rimet, the man who established the World Cup and lent his name to its original trophy.

Overleaf: Uruguay and Argentina contest the 1930 World Cup Final in Montevideo.

THE WORLD GAME

IN 1930 URUGUAY hosted the first football World Cup, featuring 13 nations – France, Mexico, Chile, Argentina, Yugoslavia, Brazil, Bolivia, Romania, Peru, USA, Belgium, Paraguay and the hosts. Fifty years earlier the competition could not have been played; would not, in fact, have even been dreamed of. However, in the late 19th century, football had spread like wildfire, carried around the world by English sailors (to France), engineers (to Spain), schoolteachers (to Switzerland and

Germany), textile workers (to Holland), businessmen (to Argentina), students (to Portugal and Uruguay) and Scottish shipyard workers (to Sweden).

As early as 1866, British students were playing football in Portugal. By 1869 it had been introduced to Swiss schools and in 1872 a group of British sailors formed the Le Havre club in France. At around the same time their colleagues were playing the first football games half a world away in Brazil.

British influence can still be seen in the names of clubs around the world – AC Milan (rather than Milano), Athletic (not Atlético) Bilbao, Newell's Old Boys in Argentina, Young Boys of Berne, Corinthians of Brazil and Chile's Everton to name just a few.

Although they undoubtedly played the leading role, it was not just the British who helped the game to flourish worldwide. FC Barcelona, for example, who despite borrowing the club's colours from the old school of one of several English players who turned out in their first game, was founded by a Swiss, Joan Gamper, who had learned and loved the game at school. Internazionale of Milan (Inter Milan) chose their name because of the cosmopolitan make-up of their team. Yes, the British took football to the world, but it was not long before the world adopted football as its own.

In Brazil, Charles Miller, the son of an English father and a Brazilian mother, returned from studying in England with two footballs. Within the space of a year, the five teams Miller had organised for a São Paulo state championship had swelled to 70.

In neighbouring Argentina, River Plate was founded by an Englishman while an Irishman helped to inspire Boca Juniors, but it was the Italians who oversaw and pushed through the real growth of football there, as they did in Uruguay. Meanwhile, in Africa, colonialists – French, German and Portuguese, as well as English – played their part in introducing the game to the continent.

As football's popularity boomed around the world, so too did its organisation. In 1889, the Dutch and Danish football associations were established. By 1900, the associations of New Zealand, Argentina, Chile, Belgium, Italy, Germany, Switzerland and Uruguay were also up and running, and it was becoming increasingly apparent that, just as individual countries had football associations, so the sport would benefit from an organisation that could oversee the growth of the global game in the 20th century.

In May 1904, the Fédération Internationale de Football Association – FIFA – came into being, founded by representatives from France, Belgium, Holland, Spain, Sweden and

Switzerland. The English FA wrote to say that they could see no need for the new federation. (It would not be the last time that arrogance resulted in the English being missing at the start; in later years, the World Cup, European Cup and European Championship would all begin without the presence of English teams.)

Initially FIFA struggled to make a mark. Within a year the idea of a world championship had been raised, but when the first competition was arranged for 1906 in Switzerland, no-one entered. Yet despite this setback, there was a growing clamour for nations to test themselves against each other. The first opportunity had come at the Olympic Games of 1896, but since the teams taking part came from Denmark, Athens and Izmir, it could hardly be seen as a real international tournament.

The following two Olympics saw football played merely as a demonstration sport, but in 1908 in London the game was finally accepted, with England beating Denmark 2-0 in the final. The English repeated the trick four years later with a 4-2 win in Stockholm.

In those early years of the 20th century it was the European nations who led the way. However, by the mid-1920s Europe was being forced to take note of the increasing strength of South American football. Uruguay won the 1924 Olympic title, thrashing Switzerland in the final, and in 1928 they won the gold medal again, beating neighbours Argentina in a replay.

The South Americans had also organised their own international tournament, the Copa América. Initially beginning as an unofficial championship in 1910, featuring Argentina, Uruguay and Chile, the Copa América had developed into an annual opportunity for the major South American football-playing nations to test themselves against each other. The result was an improvement of standards throughout the continent and the development of tough, competitive teams.

The FIFA president, a Frenchman by the name of Jules Rimet, watched with growing interest. A long-time advocate of a world championship, Rimet now sensed an opportunity to finally get the project off the ground, and when Uruguay offered to host and fund the inaugural World Cup, his dream became reality. Little did Rimet know as he set out for South America with just four European countries agreeing to send teams, that his brainchild would become the biggest sporting event in the world.

FIFA HAD EXPERIENCED massive growth by the 1950s. Founded by the federations in Europe, in its first half-century football's world governing body had become truly global, its role much broader than initially envisaged, with the World Cup now established as the shining symbol of that development. With FIFA's attentions divided across Africa, Asia and the Americas, as well as Europe, the Europeans decided to create their own governing body to more carefully protect their interests and administer to their needs. In June 1954, at a meeting in Basle, Switzerland, UEFA was born.

Almost immediately, a plan was put in place for a national European Championship. The competition had actually been suggested nearly 30 years earlier by Henri Delaunay, a colleague of Jules Rimet at the French Federation, who considered the World Cup a bridge too far, arguing that the logical first step was to create a European Championship. However, the World Cup had captured FIFA's imagination and the European Championship was duly forgotten, though never by Delaunay.

In fact, Europe was a late starter in having its own international competition. By the time of the first European Championship final in

1957 The Confederation of African Football is founded and Egypt beat Ethiopia 4-0 to become the first African Nations Cup winners.

1958 Just Fontaine of France scores a record 13 goals in six games at the World Cup. Pelé is the youngest ever World Cup winner at 17 and scores twice in the final... Barcelona win the first Inter-Cities Fairs Cup, beating a London Select XI 8-2 on aggregate.

1960 The Soviet Union win the first European Championship, beating Yugoslavia 2-1 in the final... Uruguayan side Peñarol become the first winners of the Copa Libertadores... Real Madrid win the European Cup for the fifth consecutive time, beating Eintracht Frankfurt 7-3. They also win the first World Club Cup, beating Peñarol 5-1 on aggregate.

1961 CONCACAF founded in North and Central America... Juventus become the first Italian side to be awarded a gold star following their tenth title victory... Tottenham win England's first domestic 'double' of the 20th century... Fulham's Johnny Haynes becomes the first British player to earn £100 per week and the first British £100,000 transfer sees Denis Law move from Manchester City to Torino... Fiorentina win the first European Cup Winners' Cup, beating Rangers 4-1 on aggregate... Aston Villa are the first League Cup winners.

1963 The West German Bundesliga begins. Prior to this German football had been regional. Tottenham win the Cup Winners' Cup against Atlético Madrid... George Best makes his debut for Manchester United.

1964 Oryx Douala of Cameroon win the first African Champions Club Cup... Alfredo Di Stéfano scores his 49th European Cup goal.

1965 Stanley Matthews is first player to be knighted... Football League agrees to one substitute per team in event of injury... Arthur Rowley retires with a record 434 goals in the English league.

1960, a South American championship was well established; the first African Nations Cup had kicked-off in 1957, with Egypt beating Ethiopia in the final; the inaugural Asian Games had seen India victorious in 1951, with South Korea lifting the Asian Cup five years later; and the first CONCACAF Championship (North and Central America) had been won by Costa Rica back in 1941.

If the Europeans were slow to organise their first international championship, they were the pioneers of international club competitions. The godfather of international club football was an Austrian, Hugo Meisl, who hit upon the idea of a competition between the very best teams from Hungary, Czechoslovakia, Yugoslavia and Austria. He called his creation the Mitropa Cup, from the

German for central Europe – Mittel Europa. The format was simple, but ingenious: a two-legged (home and away) knockout with the winners progressing. The first competition, in 1927, was won by Sparta Prague, and in 1929 the Italians took part, adding to the prestige. Sadly, World War II halted the competition in mid-flight, and though it returned in the post-war years, in 1955 the bigger European competitions were already on their way, signalling the beginning of the end. (Amazingly the competition continued until 1991, when Torino lifted the trophy.)

The Mitropa Cup was crucial to the development of international club football (as was the Latin Cup, a competition involving teams from Spain, Italy, Portugal and France, which debuted in 1949). It was the forerunner

– in both concept and format – to the competition that would go on to become the richest and most glittering club competition in the world; the European Champions Cup.

The European Cup was actually born out of arrogance – the arrogance, once again, of the English. Their over-the-top response to Wolverhampton Wanderers' victory over Hungary's Honvéd at a waterlogged Molineux prompted the editor of France's *L'Equipe* to propose what he called a 'proper European club cup', pitching the champions of each country against each other in a knockout format based on the Mitropa Cup.

The English immediately banned champions Chelsea from taking part. Those more familiar with international club competitions, like Real Madrid, Milan and Sporting Lisbon, were enthusiastic, seeing the commercial and sporting benefits of playing against the top clubs from all over Europe. So, in 1955, the European Cup began, with immediate success.

In other circumstances Real Madrid's dominance – they won the first five finals – could have caused the competition to stagnate, but the manner of their victories and the wonderful football they played merely raised the stakes and European football was soon climbing to new heights.

Before long, two other notable European competitions had kicked-off: the Cup Winners' Cup (a knockout between domestic cup winners) and the Inter-Cities Fairs Cup (later to be replaced by the UEFA Cup), a competition that owed its origins to an age when industrial trade fairs were held in Europe's major cities. The idea was to arrange a competition that could be played between select teams of the cities that hosted these fairs. To begin with the matches were only played when the fairs were actually taking place, with the result that the first competition kicked off in June 1955 but did not finish until May 1958, when Barcelona defeated London in the very first final.

By the early 1960s all three competitions had become annual events and had cemented their places in the European football calendar, broadening the football experience and horizons of all who took part. Their success saw replicas spring up around the world. CONCACAF launched their own Champions Cup in 1962, with Mexico's Guadalajara taking the first honours, and the African Champions Cup arrived two years later, with Cameroon's Oryx Douala drawing first blood. The African Cup Winners' Cup followed in 1975 and the CAF Cup (essentially the African federation's version of the UEFA Cup) in 1992. In Asia, a club championship launched in 1967 but lasted just four years before falling apart (partly due to the huge geographical area covered). It returned in 1985 with South Korea's Daewoo Royals triumphant, and it also was joined by a Cup Winners' Cup in 1990.

The Europeans were also responsible for South America's Copa Libertadores. In the mid-Fifties, just as the European Cup was taking off, Henri Delaunay suggested a match between the club champions of Europe and those of South America. The South Americans liked the idea and despite the absence of Africa, Asia and the rest of the Americas, football's powerhouses of Europe and South America considered this a world championship. However, before it could take place they needed to establish who the South American champions were. For that, they needed a competition. They came up with the Copa Libertadores, won in its inaugural year, 1960, by Uruguay's Peñarol, who gleefully headed off for a money-spinning tie with the European champions, Real Madrid, in what was known as the Intercontinental Cup, or the World Club Cup.

BY THE MID-1960s, the fundamental structure of world and domestic football was established. FIFA was at the head of the global game, with UEFA (Europe), CONCACAF (Central and North America), CAF (Africa), CONMEBOL (South America), AFC (Asia) and OFC (Oceania) each taking control of their own geographical areas and running events such as the international club competitions and continental championships. The national football associations were then in charge of domestic football and their national teams.

In that sense little has changed, but although the structure remains familiar, football early in the new millennium is hardly recognisable from the game of 40 years ago. In the Sixties, local heroes mixed with fans on the way to matches, sharing buses, playing for the love of the game and earning a decent,

but far from spectacular living. When their careers ended, they would seek other work and many struggled to make ends meet. The history books are full of tragic stories of great footballers, like Brazil's World Cup winner Garrincha, whose lives ended in the gutter.

In contrast, today's football stars live a life of luxury, hidden away in palatial homes, treated like movie stars with flashy cars and bulging pay packets. When they retire in their 30s, many will never have to work again.

The move towards big wages actually began in South America as long ago as the

1940s, when the best players in the world, like Alfredo Di Stéfano, were lured to earn their fortunes in Colombia's super league. However, in 1951 Colombia (who had been expelled) rejoined FIFA on condition that the foreign players left. Rubbing their hands with glee, Europe's top clubs were quick to capitalise, not least Real Madrid, who led by a Spanish lawyer called Santiago Bernabéu, were determined to become the world's best club. Bernabéu offered the likes of Di Stéfano and Hector Rial up to £10,000 a year. Not surprisingly they took him up on that offer,

Above: Celtic's Jimmy Johnstone takes on Racing Club in the 1967 World Club Cup.

Opposite: Alfredo Di Stéfano, whose move to the unofficial Colombian super league was an early example of 'player power'.

Far left: Davie Provan of Rangers defends against Bayern Munich in the 1967 European Cup Winners' Cup Final.

Left: The programme from the second leg of the 1972 World Club Cup, which pitted Ajax against Independiente.

Right: The Inter Milan team enjoy the celebrations after winning the 2010 Champions League Final.

Opposite: When Real Madrid bought Cristiano Ronaldo in 2009 he became the most expensive player in the world.

laying the foundations for Madrid's early dominance of the European Champions Cup.

Italian clubs followed suit, paying their top players huge salaries in search of glory, but elsewhere in Europe players earned far less. It was not until Jimmy Hill led a revolution in 1961 that the English Football League abandoned its maximum wage for players, while in Germany and Belgium, footballers were not professional until the mid-Sixties.

However, even in the 1970s and 1980s, with wages theoretically limitless and hundreds of professional clubs watched by millions of fans, the idea of millionaire footballers was laughable. It was not until the 1990s that football, the world's most popular sport, finally became a big business.

Throughout the Seventies and Eighties, companies had increasingly used footballers to advertise their products, or made use of sponsorship opportunities to publicise their brand on club shirts or pitchside hoardings. The sport enjoyed a commercial awakening and transfer fees jumped to seven figures, with top players reaping the rewards. However, it was the involvement of television that changed football forever.

In the late Eighties and early Nineties, new TV stations across Europe sought to challenge the monopolies of the state channels and some of them – Rupert Murdoch's Sky in Britain, Silvio Berlusconi's Mediaset in Italy, and the Kirch group in Germany – saw football, 'the people's game', as the best way to do that. Off the back of a hugely successful 1990 World Cup in Italy, and with hopes that hooliganism was finally coming under control, football was enjoying a boom in popularity and these new television companies wanted a part of it.

The result was more and more television coverage of the game, with a resultant boost in exposure for any brands associated with clubs and players. What followed was an unseemly scramble as everyone from brewers to fast-food chains and mobile phone companies flocked to associate themselves with 'the beautiful game'.

The sudden commercial interest in the sport did not go unnoticed in football's corridors of power. In England, the chairmen of the top clubs saw their opportunity to seize power from the FA and control the rapidly increasing television revenues. In the 1992-3 season they launched the Premier League, with a restructuring of English football that not only revitalised the game but maximised the earning potential of the top clubs. This newly formed top division gained commercial independence from both the Football Association and the Football League, giving it license to negotiate its own broadcast and sponsorship agreements.

The first Sky television deal in Britain was worth £191 million over five seasons. By 2010 domestic television rights had risen to £1.782 billion for three seasons, with overseas rights delivering a further £1.4 billion. With the bulk of funds ending up with the biggest clubs, their ability to maintain their position as the dominant power has been hugely enhanced.

A year after the start of the English Premier

League, UEFA attempted to prevent the threats of a breakaway league by Europe's top clubs with the creation of the Champions League, a reformatted European Cup guaranteeing more matches, and therefore more TV coverage and money, for the continent's leading clubs.

In Deloitte's 2009 list of the world's biggest earning clubs, the top 20 were all European, underlining how real power in the world game now resides within the European Union's strongest and richest leagues: the English Premiership, Italy's Serie A, Spain's La Liga and Germany's Bundesliga.

This increase in wealth has flooded through the game, with increased wages and transfers fees the most obvious consequence. When Real Madrid shocked world football in 2001 by paying a world record £47 million for France's Zinédine Zidane it proved the height of the initial post Champions League boom. It would be eight more years until a player commanded a higher price, but in 2009 Real Madrid broke their own record twice in a month, first paying £56 million to AC Milan for Kaká and then £80 million to Manchester United for Cristiano Ronaldo, who they had openly courted for a number of years, against the wishes of his club.

With many of Europe's top players still earning in excess of £5 million a year, it has been warned that clubs are building up substantial debt or are reliant on wealthy owners to finance this kind of spending. With the huge sums of money involved in football it can surely only be a matter of time until the spending slows down, but as of 2010 there has been little sign of this happening.

It's all a far cry from medieval rabbles or public schoolboys making up the rules as they went along. Who then could have predicted what football would become, and who now can guess what the sport will be like in the next century?

Below: The money from television has changed the face of football.

1985 English clubs are banned from European competition following the Heysel stadium disaster.

1986 Two substitutes are allowed in FA Cup and League Cup matches.

1987 The two substitutes rule is approved by the Football League.

1990 The Taylor Report, issued in the light of the Hillsborough disaster, calls for all-seater stadia in England.

1991 Lothar Matthäus is voted FIFA's first World Player Of The Year.

1992 Late replacements Denmark win the European Championship. The European Cup is relaunched as the Champions League.

1993 Manchester United are the inaugural winners of the FA Premier League... The backpass rule is introduced to prevent defenders time wasting.

1994 The World Cup is decided on penalties for the first time as Brazil beat Italy.

1997 English goalkeeper Peter Shilton retires from football, following 1,005 first-class appearances.

1998 A record 32 teams compete in the World Cup finals in France.

1999 Lazio become the last winners of the European Cup Winners' Cup, as it merges with UEFA Cup.

2001 Zinédine Zidane smashes world transfer record when he joins Real Madrid from Juventus for £47 million.

2002 Real Madrid win the Champions League. It is their ninth European Cup triumph, a record for the competition.

2005 Raúl becomes the first player to score 50 European Cup goals.

2009 Cristiano Ronaldo is transferred from Manchester United to Real Madrid for a world record £80 million... The UEFA Cup becomes the Europa League

2010 The World Cup is staged on the African continent for the first time.

FOOTBALL DISASTERS

Right: Manchester United saw their first team squad decimated on a runaway in Munich in 1958.

1902: As Scotland play out a 1-1 draw with England, wooden planking gives way under the weight of 20,000 people in Ibrox's new West Stand – 25 fans die and hundreds are injured as the 40-foot high structure crashes to the ground.

1946: More than 65,000 fans are packed into Bolton's Burnden Park for an eagerly anticipated FA Cup sixth round tie with Stoke City. With another 20,000 milling around outside, many force their way into the ground, causing a crush barrier to collapse. Thirty-three people die from asphyxiation and more than 500 are injured, but the game restarts after just 26 minutes, with lifeless bodies still evident round the edge of the pitch.

1949: A plane carrying the entire Torino squad crashes into the Superga hills near Turin following a friendly match in Lisbon, Portugal. The crash is the biggest tragedy Italian sport has ever experienced. Torino had won the Serie A title for the previous four years and their team made up the bulk of Italy's national side. In total, 31 people die, including 18 players. Torino's youth team complete the season and receive the Serie A trophy.

1958: On February 6, Flight BE609, a British European Airways plane, crashes on its third attempt to take off in a blizzard from Munich-Riem airport. On board are the players and officials of Manchester United, plus a number of journalists and supporters. United are returning from a 3-3 draw with Red Star Belgrade which had earned them a place in the semi-finals, when the plane stops in Munich for a scheduled refuel. The pilot, Captain James Thain, tries to take off for the final leg of the journey but twice has to abort due to engine trouble. When the plane finally takes off at 3.04pm, it fails to reach the required height and crashes into a fence and a house: 23 of the 43 passengers die, including seven United players. Young star Duncan Edwards passes away some 15 days later. A build-up of slush, causing deceleration of the aircraft, is later blamed for the crash.

1964: The fierce South American rivalry between Peru and Argentina spills into the stands as a last minute Peruvian goal is ruled out in an Olympic qualifying match in Lima. The decision sparks mass rioting inside the National Stadium and 318 people are killed, with a further 500 injured. Martial law is put in place for 30 days.

1968: When fans of Boca Juniors drop lit torches on the rival fans of River Plate inside the Monumental Stadium, Buenos Aires, 74 people are killed and 113 are injured. Those at the front of the ensuing melee are crushed to death due to a closed passageway.

1969: El Salvador and Honduras go to war as a result of a World Cup tie in Mexico, which the Salvadorians won 3-2. Many Salvadorians living in Honduras are attacked and killed before the Salvador government launches a military attack.

1971: A disaster occurs at Ibrox on January 2 when, as a Rangers v Celtic match looks set to end in a goalless draw, Celtic take the lead, prompting a mass exodus of Rangers fans. Although Colin Stein then equalises, Stairway 13 at the ground gives way, resulting in the death of 66 fans. Initially it is speculated that fans trying to get back into the stadium are to blame and this myth is believed for many years.

1982: Some 340 people are killed as Spartak Moscow fans rush back into the Lenin Stadium following a late UEFA Cup equaliser against Dutch side Haarlem. While the incident is played down by police, who insist that just 61 people are dead, a report into the disaster seven years later reveals the real death toll.

1985: With Bradford City fans celebrating their Third Division title win, a loose cigarette end falls in to rubbish underneath Valley Parade's main stand. The wood and asbestos construction is quickly engulfed in flames and, with the exits at the back of the stand locked, 56 people lose their lives. The disaster leads to new legislation to increase safety in British football stadia.

1985: England is hit with a second tragedy in the same year when riots – started by English fans prior to Liverpool's European Cup final against Juventus – result in the death of 39 spectators inside the archaic Heysel Stadium in Brussels, Belgium. As the clashes intensify between the Liverpool section and the Juventus contingent in the 'neutral' block Z, Juve fans trying to escape the violence cower towards the corner flag at the front of the terracing. Under the intense pressure, a wall collapses and dozens of fans are either crushed or trampled underfoot. As a result, UEFA ban English clubs from European competition indefinitely.

1988: At least 93 fans are killed and more than 100 are injured in Kathmandu in Nepal, when a severe hailstorm leads to a stampede among fans at a game between Jankapur and Mukti Jodha. The fatalities occur because the stadium doors are locked.

Below left: The terraces of the Heysel Stadium, where 39 fans died before the 1985 European Cup Final.

Below right: A policeman helps an injured fan at Hillsborough Stadium in 1989, on a day when 96 died.

1989: Britain's worst sporting disaster occurs when Liverpool fans, eager to get into the ground to see their club's FA Cup semi-final with Nottingham Forest at Hillsborough, converge in a bottleneck outside the Leppings Lane end of the ground. With an estimated 5,000 trying to get in and an increasingly dangerous situation developing, the police decide to open a set of gates that do not have turnstiles. The result is hundreds of fans entering the ground through a narrow tunnel at the rear of the terrace and into two already overcrowded central pens. With security fences present, many at the front are crushed by the volume of people: 96 die and 766 are injured. As a result, the Taylor Report recommends that all fences are removed from grounds and stadia should become all-seater.

1991: Kaizer Chiefs score a goal against Orlando Pirates, which causes fighting and a stampede at the game in Orkney, near Johannesburg: 40 are killed and over 50 are injured.

1992: Just 15 minutes before Bastia play Marseille in a French Cup semi-final, a temporary metal stand in the Corsican town collapses, leading to the deaths of 15 people. The competition is cancelled for the season.

1993: A plane carrying the Zambian national squad crashes into the sea off Gabon on the way to a World Cup qualifier against Senegal. There are no survivors. The team's captain, Kalusha Bwalya, is not onboard as he was making his own way to the game from Holland.

1996: A stampede during the all-Central American clash between Guatemala and Costa Rica results in 84 deaths and 150 injuries in Guatemala City. The Stadio Meteo Flores held 45,000 but 60,000 were present on the day.

2001: Tragedy again strikes a Kaizer Chiefs v Orlando Pirates clash. A stampede outside the Ellis Park stadium in Johannesburg causes the death of 43 people inside, while 126 fans also die in the Accra Stadium in Ghana following a riot during the derby match between Hearts Of Oak and Asante Kotoko.

2009: A crush to get onto the terraces ahead of an Ivory Coast game against Malawi results in the deaths of 22 fans in Abidjan. The game is still played.

2010: A bus carrying Togo's national football team to the African Cup Of Nations in Angola is attacked by terrorist gunmen. Many passengers are wounded and three are killed, including assistant coach Amelete Abalo. It was reported that the team press officer died in the arms of Manchester City striker Emmanuel Adebayor. Togo withdraw from the competition at short notice and are banned from the next two African Cup of Nations tournaments, prompting angry protests.

Above: Celtic manager Jock Stein and Willie Waddell of Rangers lift a body on to a stretcher after the disaster at Ibrox in 1971.

Below: The funeral of Togo assistant coach Amalete Abalo, who died in a gun attack on the team bus en route to the 2010 African Nations Cup.

FOOTBALL SCANDALS

1900: Burnley goalkeeper Jack Hillman is the first British player suspended from football. He tries to bribe Nottingham Forest to lose. They win 4-0 and Hillman is banned for a year.

1904: Manchester City are fined £250 and their Hyde Road ground is shut for two games after they break transfer rules signing Glossop's Irvine Thornley and Frank Norgrove. Thornley is banned for a season.

1905: Middlesbrough, who have just bought Alf Common in the first £1,000 transfer, are fined £250 and 11 directors are suspended for three years after the club are found guilty of making illegal payments.

1905: Manchester City's Billy Meredith is banned for a season for attempting to bribe Aston Villa's Alec Leake while City are chasing the title.

1906: Some 17 current and former Manchester City players are fined a total of £900, suspended for six months and banned from playing for the club again after accepting illegal payments.

1909: Fulham's George Parsonage is banned for life after asking for a £50 signing on fee from Chesterfield.

1911: Middlesbrough chairman Thomas Poole and manager Andy Walker are banned for trying to fix a game against Sunderland.

1915: A football betting scandal erupts after a match between Manchester United and Liverpool is fixed in United's favour. An investigation reveals that players from both sides have been involved. Liverpool's Fred Pagnam is among the players refusing to take part and later he testifies against his team-mates. Seven players are banned for life.

1919: Leeds City are wound up by the FA after making illegal payments to players. Leeds United are formed.

1924: John Browning and Archibald Kyle are handed 60 days' hard labour for trying to fix games between Scottish Division Two clubs Bo'Ness and Lochgelly.

1927: Torino win the Scudetto, only to have their title annulled after allegations that Juventus defender Luigi Allemandi was bribed in a crucial game, even though he actually played quite well in the match. He is banned for life but the ban is rescinded and he wins the title with Inter Milan and the World Cup with Italy in 1934.

1930: At the 1930 World Cup, hosts Uruguay have a little help with the build-up to their third semi-final goal against Yugoslavia. The ball appears to go out of play, only to be kicked discretely back onto the pitch by a uniformed policeman.

1932: Former Montrose skipper Gavin Hamilton spends 60 days in jail after offering Montrose player David Mooney £50 to fix a home match with Edinburgh City.

1957: Sunderland are hit with a record £5,000 fine from the Football League for illegal payments to players.

1965: Sheffield Wednesday players Peter Swan, Tony Kay and David Layne are exposed for fixing a pools win and placing a £50 bet that correctly predicted their team would beat Ipswich Town 2-0. The scam, masterminded by Mansfield Town's Jimmy Gauld, results in ten players being found guilty of conspiracy to defraud. Gauld is jailed for four years, the others between four and 15 months. The Wednesday trio are also banned from football for life, which is overturned in 1972

1967: Millwall are fined £1,000 after fans attack referee Norman Burtenshaw at The Den.

1968: Port Vale are expelled from the Football League for illegal payments but are immediately re-elected.

1970: The England captain Bobby Moore is arrested in Bogota, Colombia, after being falsely accused of stealing a bracelet prior to the World Cup in Mexico. The England squad have to fly on to Mexico without him and he rejoins the team in time for the tournament.

1970: Derby County qualify for the Fairs Cup but are banned for administrative irregularities.

1971: Fifty-three players from seven West German clubs receive various punishments for match-fixing. Arminia Bielefeld are demoted to a regional league for their involvement, while Kickers Offenbach are stripped of their playing license for two years.

1973: Juventus are accused of using a go-between to try and bribe Francisco Marques Lobo, the referee for their European Cup semi-final game with Derby County.

1974: Polish players accuse their Italian opponents of offering cash incentives to lose a vital World Cup clash between the teams. Italy lose 2-1 and are eliminated.

1974: On the eve of the 1974 World Cup Final, German newspaper *Bild Zeitung* runs the unsubstantiated headline 'Cruyff, Champagne and Naked Girls', suggesting there was a 'naked party' in the swimming pool of the Dutch team's hotel during the competition, involving four Dutch players and two German girls. Legend has it that Johan Cruyff's wife keeps him on the phone late into the night before the final.

1977: Manchester United sack their manager Tommy Docherty following his affair with the wife of physio Laurie Brown.

1978: Scottish referee John Gordon and his two linesmen are suspended by the Scottish FA for accepting £1,000 presents from AC Milan prior to their UEFA Cup match with Levski Spartak. The Italian club are fined £8,000 by UEFA.

1978: It is alleged that Peru's game with Argentina at the 1978 World Cup was fixed by the Argentine military government, who shipped 35,000 tons of free grain to Peru, and possibly arms too, while the Argentine central bank unfroze $50 million in credits. Argentina won the game 6-0 and progressed to the World Cup final.

1980: Italy striker Paolo Rossi is banned for two years when it emerges that Perugia's 2-2 draw with Avellino the previous year, in which Rossi scored twice for the former, was fixed by a betting syndicate – 20 players are banned in the same investigation and AC Milan and Lazio are both relegated to Serie B for involvement in the bribery scam.

1982: Standard Liege manager Raymond Goethals and 13 players are banned for life for offering sweeteners to SV Thor Waterschei to ensure they won the Belgium League.

1985: Millwall fans riot at Kenilworth Road, prompting Luton to ban all away fans.

1986: Roma are banned from European competition for a season and president Dino Viola for four years after he tried to bribe the referee in a European Cup semi-final against Dundee United in 1982.

Below: An early legend of the game, Manchester City's Billy Meredith was banned for a year in 1905 after being implicated in a match-fixing scandal.

1988: Arsenal midfielder Paul Davis is banned for nine game for breaking the jaw of Southampton's Glenn Cockerill.

1989: Nottingham Forest boss Brian Clough receives a one-year touchline ban for striking a QPR spectator who had run on the pitch.

1990: Division One team Swindon are demoted to Division Three (Division Two on appeal) for irregular payments to players.

1990: Arsenal and Manchester United are deducted points following a brawl on the pitch.

1990: Bologna's Giuseppe Lorenzo is sent-off after just ten seconds for striking an opponent in a league game against Parma.

1991: Diego Maradona is banned from playing in Italy for 15 months after taking cocaine before a Napoli match. He is also handed a 14-month suspended jail sentence.

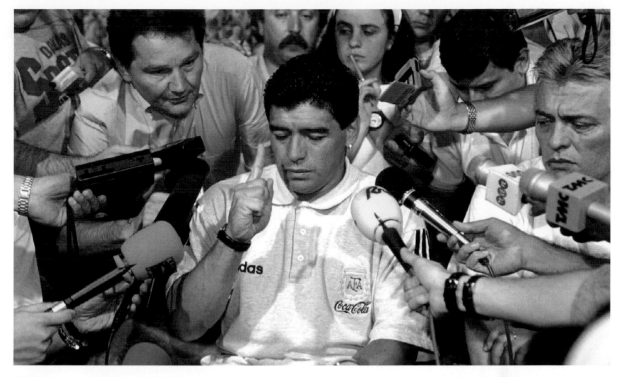

1993: Marseille chairman Bernard Tapie bribes opposition players from Valenciennes to guarantee that his club can rest first-team players for the upcoming European Cup final and still clinch the French title. Marseille are stripped of both wins. Tapie is sentenced to two years in prison.

1993: Former Manchester United player Mickey Thomas is jailed for 18 months for printing his own £10 notes.

1994: Diego Maradona is sent home from USA 94 for testing positive for weight loss drug ephedrine.

1995: Eric Cantona is banned from football for nine months following a two-footed, kung-fu attack on Crystal Palace fan Matthew Simmons.

1995: Arsenal sack George Graham after he is found guilty of accepting a £285,000 'bung' from agent Rune Hauge following the transfer of John Jensen to Highbury.

1997: Bruce Grobbelaar, John Fashanu and Hans Segers go on trial for match-fixing. Grobbelaar is accused of taking £40,000 to make sure Liverpool lost to Newcastle in 1993, while Segers and Fashanu's involvement concerns a Wimbledon defeat against Manchester United. All three are acquitted.

1997: Anderlecht admit that they gave the referee a £20,000 'loan' prior to the club's UEFA Cup semi-final victory over Nottingham Forest in 1984. Forest start court proceedings.

1999: Chelsea coach Graham Rix is sentenced to prison for having sex with a 15-year-old girl while on first-team duty with the club.

1999: A Malaysian-based betting syndicate is caught trying to install a remote-control device to sabotage the floodlights at Charlton Athletic. Investigations prove floodlight failures at West Ham and Crystal Palace in 1997 were caused by the syndicate.

2001: Dutch stars Jaap Stam, Edgar Davids and Frank de Boer receive bans for testing positive for the banned steroid nandralone.

2003: Faria Alam is dismissed from her job at the FA after it emerges she had affairs with chief executive Mark Palios and England coach Sven-Göran Eriksson.

2003: Manchester United defender Rio Ferdinand is banned for nine months from both club and international football after he fails to attend a drug test.

2004: Referee Ncedisile Zakhe is charged with the murder of Michael Sizani after the Young Tigers coach criticises his penalty decision

during a game with Mighty Eleven in South Africa. He is sentenced to four years in prison.

2005: German referee Robert Hoyzer is sentenced to two years and five months in prison, and banned from refereeing for life, following his bid to rig nine matches in a £1.3 million betting fraud in 2004.

2005: Brazilian referee Edilson Pereira de Carvalho is banned for life after being found guilty of taking money from a gambling ring to manipulate results – 11 championship games are declared null and void.

2005: Serie B champions Genoa demoted to Serie C1 after being found guilty of bribing Venezia in the final game of the season.

2006: Paolo di Canio is fined £7,000 for making a fascist salute after the Rome derby.

2006: The Juventus board resigns, as does the President of the Italian football federation, after serious allegations of match-fixing in the 2004-5 season. Juventus are punished with relegation to Serie B and are given a points deduction (they are also stripped of their last two titles). Fiorentina, Lazio and Milan are also given points deductions after appealing against relegation.

2009: Four Accrington Stanley players are banned after betting on opponents Bury in a game that Accrington lost 2-0.

2010: John Terry is stripped of the England captaincy after it is revealed that he has had an affair with the former girlfriend of international team-mate Wayne Bridge. As a consequence, Bridge withdraws from the England squad ahead of the World Cup.

Above: Argentina captain Diego Maradona faces the press in Dallas after failing a drug test at the 1994 World Cup.

Left: Manchester United's Eric Cantona attacks a Crystal Palace fan after being abused from the terraces in 1995.

THE WORLD CUP

THE WORLD CUP

Above from left to right: Brazil captain Cafu lifts the trophy in 2002; England's Alf Ramsey and Bobby Moore admire the trophy in 1966; the Italian team parade with the World Cup in 1982.

There is no other sporting event that captures the imagination across the globe quite like the World Cup. Ever since the first competition in Uruguay in 1930, the tournament has grown in popularity and prestige. However, that is not to say it has not been without its share of problems. Indeed, the origins of the tournament were so wrapped up in politics that it took 26 years for the idea of a World Cup to become a reality.

During its inaugural meeting in 1904, FIFA agreed that it had the sole right to organise a tournament that brought together the world's strongest national football teams. However, it was not until the 1920s that an idea nurtured by FIFA president Jules Rimet and French football administrator Henri Delaunay gained momentum. In the interim the Olympic football tournament had begun to establish itself as a credible competition, and such was its success that a FIFA commission was established in 1927 to examine the creation of a football World Cup. The recommendations struck a chord with FIFA's Executive Committee and at the 1928 congress, held at

the Amsterdam Olympics, FIFA voted in favour of a football World Cup.

Uruguay beat Argentina in 1928 to retain their Olympic title and proved they were the country most determined to host the inaugural World Cup. Not only did the Uruguayan government offer to build a magnificent new stadium in Montevideo capable of staging a showcase event but they offered to cover all the travel and accommodation costs of the visiting teams. Rivals Italy, Holland, Spain and Sweden were unprepared to match this offer and withdrew their bids, leaving Uruguay to stage the first World Cup.

The organisation of the tournament was not without its problems. At one stage it seemed that no European sides would make the two-week sea journey, but ultimately four signed on for the competition, although France, Romania, Belgium and Yugoslavia were hardly the major football nations of the continent.

On July 13, 1930, the first World Cup kicked-off amid the snow of a southern hemisphere winter, with France defeating Mexico and the USA beating Belgium in the opening games.

It was the only World Cup not to involve the modern system of qualifying rounds, with 13 invited teams competing for the 12-and-a-half-inch solid silver and goldplated prize. The original World Cup trophy was designed by French sculptor Abel Lafleur and based upon one of the great surviving masterpieces of Greek sculpture, Winged Victory Of Samothrace.

Since 1934 the 18 tournaments have seen only seven different winners. However, the World Cup has still been punctuated by some dramatic upsets that have helped create football history: the USA's defeat of England in 1950; North Korea beating Italy in 1966; Cameroon's opening match defeat of reigning champions Argentina in 1990; and Senegal's shock victory over holders France in 2002.

The early years of the competition were dogged by controversy. In 1934 holders Uruguay, still upset by the stay-away attitude of the European sides four years earlier, boycotted the tournament in Italy. Rumours also circulated about the many biased refereeing decisions in favour of the hosts. Sadly, not for the last time, the shadow of

1904: FIFA forms and says that no other organisation can stage a world championship.

1924: Jules Rimet is appointed President of FIFA and a world cup is debated at FIFA's Paris Congress.

1928: The World Cup is adopted at the Amsterdam Congress. Holland, Italy, Spain, Sweden and Uruguay bid to host it.

1930: Uruguay win first World Cup. The 13-team tournament includes just four European teams.

1936: France chosen ahead of Argentina to hosts the 1938 World Cup.

1948: World Cup officially named as the Jules Rimet Trophy.

1954: Hot favourites Hungary lose to West Germany in the final.

1905   1920   1925   1930   1935   1945   1950   1955

FIFA

1920: FIFA's Antwerp Congress: the idea of a World Cup is accepted in principle.

1926: Henri Delauney says international football can no longer be confined to the Olympics.

1929: Barcelona Congress: Uruguay is named as the host nation of the first World Cup.

1934: Uruguay refuse to defend their title in Italy. Italy win the 16-team knockout tournament.

1938: Italy successfully defend their world title.

1950: The format is changed and for the only time, the winners are decided by a final group stage.

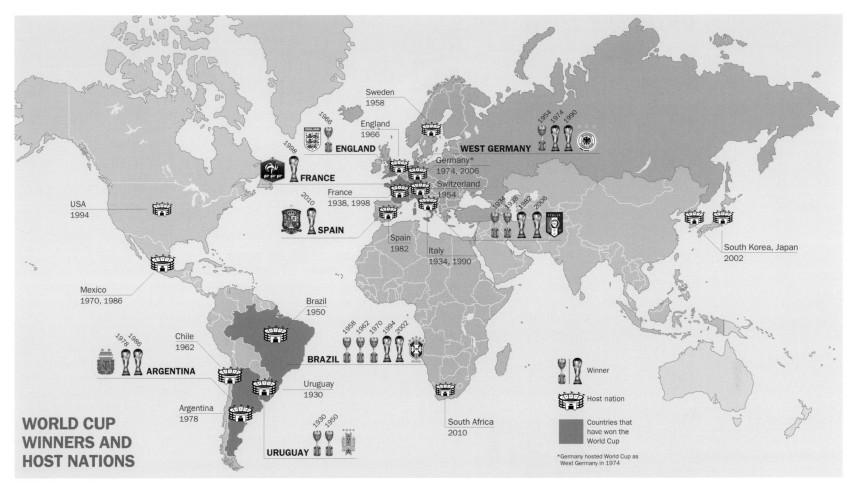

WORLD CUP WINNERS AND HOST NATIONS

Sweden 1958

England 1966

WEST GERMANY — Germany* 1974, 2006

Switzerland 1954

FRANCE — France 1938, 1998

USA 1994

SPAIN — Spain 1982

Italy 1934, 1990

South Korea, Japan 2002

Mexico 1970, 1986

Brazil 1950

Chile 1962

ARGENTINA

BRAZIL

Uruguay 1930

Argentina 1978

South Africa 2010

URUGUAY

Winner

Host nation

Countries that have won the World Cup

*Germany hosted World Cup as West Germany in 1974

world politics threatened to eclipse the event as Italian dictator Benito Mussolini used the World Cup as a showcase for his Fascist regime. A straightforward 16-team knockout format was used in 1934, while it was also the first World Cup to host games in more than one city.

The 1938 tournament was played under the clouds of impending conflict. Spain was in the middle of a bloody civil war, while Austria had been annexed by Germany and many of their best players persuaded to change allegiance.

The World Cup was contested three times in the 1930s before the Second World War put a 12-year stop to the competition. The trophy was renamed the Jules Rimet Cup in 1946, having survived World War II hidden in a shoebox under the bed of Dr Ottorino Barassi, the Italian vice-president of FIFA. In 1950, the World Cup made its comeback in Brazil. To host the event the country built the Maracanã, the largest stadium in the world. It was the first

time England entered the World Cup, although several other countries withdrew on the eve of the competition. This could have resulted in scheduling headaches but the original draw was retained, leaving a decidedly uneven competition: two groups consisting of four teams, one of three teams, and one of just two.

The World Cup format was rejigged again in 1954. Each group of four in the first round possessed two seeded teams who played only the two unseeded teams in their group. This increased the likelihood of sides ending up with the same number of points, and the need for play-offs meant that 26 games had to be played in just 19 days. It was a system that was never used again but the constant evolution of the format has not deterred interest.

Throughout its history the number of teams entering has continued to rise: just 38 nations started the 1954 campaign, while 205 nations entered the 2010 competition. In 1974 the World Cup had a new solid gold trophy as

three-time winners Brazil had retained the Jules Rimet Cup in 1970. In 1982, FIFA president João Havelange expanded the field from 16 teams to 24, opening the World Cup to the less established football nations. His expansionist philosophy saw the USA given the tournament in 1994, while in 1998 it was expanded further to include 32 finalists.

The 2002 competition in Japan and South Korea marked the first time the World Cup was held in Asia, and the first occasion it was staged by co-hosts, while in 2010 it visited yet another continent when the South Africans hosted.

It's been a long journey for the World Cup since its first tentative steps in 1930. Despite its many changes in format, such as the introduction of a second group stage between 1974 and 1982, and the use of the 'golden goal' in 1998, it still remains the biggest sporting event in the world, with viewing figures to match. However, the focus still remains the same: to raise aloft that glorious golden trophy.

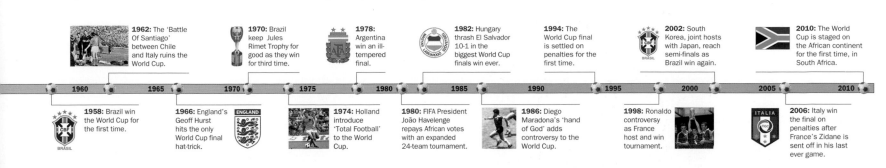

1962: The 'Battle Of Santiago' between Chile and Italy ruins the World Cup.

1970: Brazil keep Jules Rimet Trophy for good as they win for third time.

1978: Argentina win an ill-tempered final.

1982: Hungary thrash El Salvador 10-1 in the biggest World Cup finals win ever.

1994: The World Cup final is settled on penalties for the first time.

2002: South Korea, joint hosts with Japan, reach semi-finals as Brazil win again.

2010: The World Cup is staged on the African continent for the first time, in South Africa.

1960   1965   1970   1975   1980   1985   1990   1995   2000   2005   2010

1958: Brazil win the World Cup for the first time.

1966: England's Geoff Hurst hits the only World Cup final hat-trick.

1974: Holland introduce 'Total Football' to the World Cup.

1980: FIFA President João Havelange repays African votes with an expanded 24-team tournament.

1986: Diego Maradona's 'hand of God' adds controversy to the World Cup.

1998: Ronaldo controversy as France host and win tournament.

2006: Italy win the final on penalties after France's Zidane is sent off in his last ever game.

URUGUAY 1930

SEMI-FINALS
Argentina 6-1 USA
Uruguay 6-1 Yugoslavia

THIRD PLACE PLAY-OFF
Not held

TOP SCORERS
8 goals: Guillermo Stábile
(Argentina)
5 goals: Pedro Cea (Uruguay)
4 goals: Guillermo Subiabre (Chile)

FASTEST GOAL
1 minute: Adalbert Desu
(Romania v Peru)

TOTAL GOALS
70

AVERAGE GOALS
3.88 per game

🏆 FIFA had been trying to get a world championship off the ground since shortly after the beginning of the 20th century but it was not until Frenchman Jules Rimet ascended to the presidency of FIFA after World War I that plans for such a tournament started to take shape, finally receiving a stamp of approval from FIFA's governing congress in 1928. The following year five countries bid to host the tournament – Holland, Italy, Spain, Sweden and Uruguay – with the South Americans eventually winning the vote.

Thirteen countries (out of 41 that boasted FIFA membership) contested the inaugural tournament, with nine hailing from the Americas: Brazil, Bolivia, Mexico, Argentina, Chile, Peru, Paraguay, the United States and Uruguay. The remaining participants were made up of a rather disappointing turn-out from Europe: Yugoslavia, Belgium, France and Romania, who were coached by the country's reigning monarch, King Carol. Several European federations were undoubtedly

THE FINAL

URUGUAY (1) 4-2 (2) ARGENTINA

Date Wednesday July 30, 1930 **Attendance** 93,000
Venue Centenary Stadium, Montevideo

It was perhaps fitting that the tournament's first hosts should also end up as its first winners, in the country's centenary year. On top after 12 minutes through Pablo Dorado, Uruguay were nonetheless stunned when Carlos Peucelle brought the Argentinians level eight minutes later. Another setback for the hosts arrived in the 37th minute when Argentina took the lead through Stábile, the man who would end the tournament as its highest scorer with eight goals.

Uruguay rallied after the break with Pedro Cea equalising in the 57th minute and Santos Iriarte snatching a third 11 minutes later. Argentina were unlucky when Francisco 'Pancho' Varallo had a shot cleared off the line and their ill fortune was compounded a minute before the end when Hector Castro snatched the winner.

URUGUAY	
BALLESTRERO	
NASAZZI	
MASCHERONI	
ANDRADE	
GESTIDO	
FERNÁNDEZ	
SCARONE	
CEA	⚽
Goal: 57 mins	
DORADO	⚽
Goal: 12 mins	
CASTRO	⚽
Goal: 89 mins	
IRIARTE	⚽
Goal: 68 mins	

ARGENTINA	
BOTASSO	
DELLA TORRE	
PATERNÓSTER	
EVARISTO, J	
MONTI	
SUÁREZ	
VARALLO	
FERREIRA	
PEUCELLE	⚽
Goal: 20 mins	
STÁBILE	⚽
Goal: 37 mins	
EVARISTO, M	

Referee: Langenus (Belgium)

HOW THE TEAMS LINED UP

URUGUAY
COACH:
ALBERTO SUPPICCI

Ballesteros
Nasazzi · Mascheroni
Andrade · Fernández · Gestido
Dorado · Scarone · Castro · Cea · Iriarte

ARGENTINA
COACHES:
ULULAR OF TRAMUTOLA

Evaristo, M · Stábile · Peucelle
Ferreira · Varallo
Suárez · Monti · Evaristo, J
Paternóster · Della Torre
Botasso

Above: The opening ceremony of the 1930 World Cup at the Centenary Stadium in Montevideo, held five days after the start of the tournament. **Opposite top:** Uruguay goalkeeper Enrique Ballestrero watches the ball hit the back of the net in the final. **Opposite bottom:** Uruguay's one-armed striker Hector Castro in action in the World Cup final.

deterred by the great distance to Uruguay, then only negotiable by boat, while others fulminated that Italy had been overlooked as hosts. None of the British sides entered as they had withdrawn from FIFA in 1928 following a row over the definition of 'amateurism'.

The rather unwieldy number of teams was split into four pools: four teams in one and three in the rest. The draw did not take place until all the sides had arrived in Uruguay and the very first World Cup matches were staged on July 13, with two simultaneous kick-offs. The USA beat Belgium 3-0 in one, while France finished 4-1 winners over Mexico in the other, their first goal – and the first in the competition's history – scored by Lucien Laurent in the 19th minute. Disappointingly, neither game took place at the grand Centenary Stadium in Montevideo, as it was unfinished and would not be inaugurated for another five days.

The French were probably the European side most likely to win the tournament. They had even put their four goals past Mexico despite being reduced to ten men when their keeper went off injured in the first 20 minutes (no substitutes were allowed at the World Cup until 1970). However, any such ambitions came grinding to a halt in their next match, a controversial encounter with Argentina.

The South Americans were leading 1-0 but with the French slowly but surely getting on top it was an advantage that looked increasingly fragile. However, the Brazilian referee, Almeido Rego, blew the whistle for fulltime with six minutes still left on the clock and with France on the attack, provoking angry scenes and many accusations of foul play. Such was the furore that the referee eventually called the players back out to complete the final six minutes but by that stage the French had lost their rhythm and the game ended 1-0.

Argentina went on to qualify for the semi-finals at a canter. They defeated Chile 3-1, but

had been at their most impressive in their previous game, a 6-3 win over Mexico that had boasted three penalties and a hat-trick from young Argentine striker Guillermo Stábile.

Yugoslavia headed Pool 2 after wins over Brazil and Bolivia. They were the only one of the European entrants to make the semi-finals, as Uruguay and the United States took the honours in Pools 3 and 4 respectively. Uruguay did not concede a single goal as they despatched Peru and Romania, a feat matched by the Americans, who had little difficulty putting Belgium and Paraguay to the sword in two impressive 3-0 victories, the latter featuring three goals from Bertram Patenaude, the first hat-trick in World Cup history. For many years the official report attributed one of his goals to captain Thomas Florie until, in 2006, FIFA bowed to weight of evidence and agreed to amend their records.

Argentina and Uruguay ran up high scores against lesser opposition in the semi-finals, with Argentina winning 6-1 against the USA. Uruguay, meanwhile, started their showdown with Yugoslavia slowly, falling behind after just four minutes. The lead was short-lived as Pedro Cea equalised after 18 minutes and Pelegrin Anselmo scored twice before the interval to make it 3-1, although in the build-up to his second goal the ball had appeared to go out of play, only to be kicked discretely back onto the pitch by a uniformed policeman. Iriarte made it 4-1 with half an hour to play, and Cea completed an extraordinary hat-trick with goals in the 67th and 72nd minutes.

Uruguay and Argentina had met in the Olympic final in Amsterdam two years earlier. Uruguay, also Olympic champions in 1924, ran out 2-1 winners in that encounter, and were too strong again in the first World Cup final. Argentina may have been the reigning South American champions but they were unable to exact revenge on their great rivals, as Uruguay became the first world champions.

Above: The Brazilian entourage and their luggage arrive in Italy for the tournament. Opposite: Eventual winners Italy (top) edged past Spain 1-0 in Florence in the opening round thanks to a goal from Giuseppe Meazza (bottom).

ITALY 1934

Italian dictator Benito Mussolini hoped to use the first World Cup on European soil to further the cause of his fascist regime, but while the tournament can claim to have been a success it was not without controversy. Following the widespread European boycott of the 1930 tournament, the South American nations retaliated with holders Uruguay not even sending a team, and both Brazil and Argentina fielding under-strength sides.

With 32 nations competing, qualification was required before 16 teams reached the finals in Italy. Unlike the 1930 tournament that had been staged solely in Montevideo, eight cities across Italy hosted matches, with the first round kicking off simultaneously on May 27 in Genoa, Turin, Florence, Milan, Trieste, Rome, Naples and Bologna, although naturally it was to be Rome that would eventually stage the showpiece final.

Brazil, Argentina, USA and Egypt were the only non-European countries in the final 16 and all were making the long journey home after one game. Argentina's biggest stars had moved to play in the European leagues and not one member of their 1930 team appeared against Sweden in Bologna. However, they led twice before a late goal from Kroon sent the Swedes through 3-2. Brazil were barely in the game in Genoa before Spain took total control, leading 2-0 by the break. Brazil pulled one back but their fate was sealed by Langara's second goal of the match.

France took a shock lead against the second-favourites Austria in Turin, and although Matthias Sindelar levelled, it was not until extra-time that Austria's superiority showed. It took a blatant offside strike from Toni Schall to unsettle the French before Josef Bican decided the match for the Austrians. A late penalty for the French was nothing more than a consolation.

Germany turned around a 2-1 half-time deficit to beat Belgium 5-2 in Florence, with the victory owing much to a hat-trick in less than 20 minutes from Edmund Conen. The Dutch, meanwhile, crashed out of the competition 3-2 to Switzerland in Milan.

There were no such problems for favourites Italy against the USA. Angelo Schiavio netted a hat-trick in Rome as the hosts won 7-1. In Naples the first African challenge on the world stage succumbed in the second-half as Egypt, who had put 11 goals past Palestine to qualify for the finals, went out of the competition with a 4-2 defeat to Hungary.

In Trieste, highly-fancied Czechoslovakia struggled past Romania. Stefan Dobay had given the Romanians the lead shortly before the break, but the Czechs possessed the formidable forward pairing of Antonin Puc and Oldrich Nejedly, who both scored to line-up a quarter-final meeting with the Swiss.

Once again the Czechoslovakians did not have it all their own way, falling behind to an early goal from Leopold Kielholz before Frantisek Svoboda levelled the tie. Jiri Sobotka put the Czechs ahead early in the second-half, but Switzerland hit back and once again it needed Nejedly to find the target seven minutes from time to decide the see-saw match and put Czechoslovakia through to the semi-finals.

Germany and Austria disposed of Sweden and Hungary respectively but the most remarkable of the quarter-finals saw Italy triumph over Spain in Florence a full 24 hours after the game had kicked-off. The first encounter finished 1-1 and not even extra-time could separate the sides, so the first replay in World Cup history was arranged for the following day. The Spanish made seven changes and the Italians four but it was another close encounter. Ultimately settled in favour of the hosts by prolific Inter Milan marksman Giuseppe Meazza, who threw himself at the ball to head the winner in the 12th minute.

There was little respite for Vittorio Pozzo's side and just 48 hours later, having now moved on to Milan's San Siro stadium, they took on Austria's 'Wunderteam' in the semi-final. A first-half goal from Argentine-born winger Guaita was enough to take Italy through their fourth game in eight days.

The Czechs progressed through the other semi-final in Rome with a 3-1 victory over the Germans and Nejedly took centre stage once again, netting a hat-trick.

Four days later Germany did at least salvage some pride by winning the inaugural third place play-off with a 3-2 victory over Hugo Meisl's Austria. However, Mussolini and all of Italy had the dream they had longed for with the Azzurri in the final. For the second tournament running the hosts had gone all the way and now only Czechoslovakia stood before Pozzo's men and glory in Rome.

THE FINAL

ITALY (0) **2-1** (0) **CZECHOSLOVAKIA**
(aet; 1-1 at 90 mins)

Date Sunday June 10, 1934 **Attendance** 55,000
Venue Stadio del PNF, Rome

Czechoslovakia were less than ten minutes away from stunning the hosts and winning the World Cup in front of Mussolini. Antonin Puc, suffering with cramp, fired the Czechs ahead with little over 15 minutes remaining and an upset looked on the cards. However, Italy drew level though Raimundo Orsi in the 81st minute, and five minutes into extra-time Pozzo's men grabbed a deserved winner through Angelo Schiavio's fourth goal of the competition.

The final saw Italy's Luis Monti set a unique record, appearing in his second World Cup final but for different nations. Four years after finishing a runner-up with the country of his birth, Argentina, Monti was this time celebrating World Cup success with his adopted Italy.

HOW THE TEAMS LINED UP

ITALY
COACH:
VITTORIO POZZO

CZECHOSLOVAKIA
COACH:
KAREL PETRU

Combi
Monzeglio — Allemandi
Ferraris — Monti — Bertolini
Meazza — Ferrari
Guaita — Schiavio — Orsi
Puc — Sobotka — Junek
Nejedly — Svoboda
Krcil — Cambal — Kostálek
Ctyroky — Zenisek
Plánicka

Referee: Eklind (Sweden)

ITALY

COMBI
MONZEGLIO
ALLEMANDI
FERRARIS
MONTI
BERTOLINI
MEAZZA
FERRARI
GUAITA
SCHIAVIO ⚽
Goal: 95 mins
ORSI ⚽
Goal: 81 mins

CZECHOSLOVAKIA

PLÁNICKA
ZENISEK
CTYROKY
KOSTÁLEK
CAMBAL
KRCIL
SVOBODA
NEJEDLY
JUNEK
SOBOTKA
PUC ⚽
Goal: 71 mins

SEMI-FINALS
Czechoslovakia 3-1 Germany
Italy 1-0 Austria

THIRD PLACE PLAY-OFF
Germany 3-2 Austria

TOP GOALSCORERS
5 goals: Oldrich Nejedly (Czechoslovakia)
4 goals: Angelo Schiavio (Italy), Edmund Conen (Germany)

FASTEST GOAL
30 seconds: Ernst Lehner (Germany v Austria)

TOTAL GOALS
70

AVERAGE GOALS
4.12 per game

FRANCE 1938

The 1938 World Cup could boast Italy, one of the greatest teams of all time, and Leônidas, the Brazilian striker who emerged as the outstanding individual of the tournament. While nobody could argue with Italy's eventual triumph, thanks largely to their outstanding mix of tactical astuteness and pragmatic defending, it was hard luck on Leônidas, known as 'the Black Diamond', that he ended without even a place in the final. As top scorer with seven goals and with some magnificent performances, he was one of the earliest luminaries of the world game.

Yet Italy's all-round mix of resilience and flair was enough for a second consecutive triumph and confirmed Vittorio Pozzo as the foremost coach of his era. He had led the Italians to World Cup victory four years earlier and sandwiched the Olympic title in between. Who knows how great the Azzurri football dynasty could have been but for World War II?

Impending conflict in Europe cast a shadow over the tournament from the outset. Adolf Hitler's Germany had annexed Austria and

SEMI-FINALS
Italy 2-1 Brazil
Hungary 5-1 Sweden

THIRD PLACE PLAY-OFF
Brazil 4-2 Sweden

TOP GOALSCORERS
7 goals: Leônidas (Brazil)
6 goals: Gyula Zsengellér (Hungary)
5 goals: Gyorgy Sárosi (Hungary),
Silvio Piola (Italy)

FASTEST GOAL
35 seconds: Arne Nyberg
(Sweden v Hungary)

TOTAL GOALS
84

AVERAGE GOALS
4.67 per match

Above: The Germans, complete with controversial Nazi salute, line up against Switzerland. Opposite clockwise from top: The captains of Brazil and Poland exchange pennants; Belgian goalkeeper Badjou punches away the ball against France; the Belgian and French teams run out; the German keeper Raftl makes a save against Swiss striker Abbeglen.

THE FINAL

ITALY (3) 4-2 (1) HUNGARY

Date Sunday June 19, 1938 **Attendance** 45,000
Venue Stade Olympique de Colombes, Paris

Italy won by a two-goal margin but it was no contest. Pozzo's side were much stronger than Hungary and far more decisive in attack. Colaussi opened the scoring when he collected a Piola cross in the sixth minute and prodded home past Szabó from close range. Titkos immediately equalised but Hungarian hopes were dashed when Piola scored on 16 minutes, picking up a pass from Meazza to lash the ball high into the net. Colaussi added a third before half-time to put Italy in total control.

The reigning champions defended their lead in the second-half. Sárosi's goal put Hungary back in contention but when Piola scored with eight minutes remaining, Italy were certain of victory. They were in a class of their own.

ITALY	
OLIVIERI	
FONI	
RAVA	
SERANTONI	
ANDREOLO	
LOCATELLI	
MEAZZA	
FERRARI	
BIAVATI	
PIOLA	⚽⚽⚽
Goal: 16 mins, 82 mins	
COLAUSSI	⚽⚽
Goal: 6 mins, 35 mins	

HUNGARY	
SZABÓ	
POLGAR	
BIRÓ	
SZALAY	
SZÜCS	
LÁZÁR	
VINCZE	
ZSENGELLÉR	
SAS	
SÁROSI	⚽
Goal: 70 mins	
TITKOS	⚽
Goal: 8 mins	

Referee: Capdeville (France)

HOW THE TEAMS LINED UP

ITALY
COACH:
VITTORIO POZZO

HUNGARY
COACH:
KAROLY DIETZ

Olivieri
Foni — Rava
Serantoni — Andreolo — Locatelli
Meazza — Ferrari
Biavati — Piola — Colaussi

Titkos — Sárosi — Sas
Zsengellér — Vincze
Lázár — Szücs — Szalay
Biró — Polgar
Szabó

insisted the country's best players join the German side. Several did but others refused, notably star striker Matthias Sindelar, who would commit suicide a year later. Austria were forced to withdraw from the tournament and Spain too pulled out, racked by civil war.

Champions eight years earlier, Uruguay also stayed at home again, while Argentina pulled out over the decision to give the tournament to France. They had wanted to hold it themselves and felt FIFA should have alternated the venue between Europe and South America.

When the tournament finally kicked off, the three outstanding sides, Italy, Brazil and Hungary, were joined in the 16-team format by lesser nations such as Cuba and the Dutch East Indies. The competition was no less exciting for that. Italy needed a Silvio Piola goal in extra-time to win their opening match against Norway to reach the quarter-finals, while Cuba drew 3-3 with Romania and then stunned them by winning 2-1 in the replay. France beat Belgium 3-1 and Czechoslovakia knocked out Holland with a 3-0 win.

Switzerland, in a memorable clash, drew 1-1 with Germany and fell two goals behind in the replay but despite playing much of the game with only ten fit men after an injury to Aeby, shocked the Germans with four second-half goals to send them home early.

The game of the first round saw Brazil beat Poland 6-5, thanks mainly to Leônidas who even scored one of his goals barefoot, hitting the shot after his boot had come off in the mud. After 90 minutes the game was level at 4-4, but three minutes into extra-time Leônidas scored his second goal to put Brazil ahead. He completed his hat-trick in the 104th minute, although many records indicate that he scored four times. Such was the exceptional nature of his performance that it is often overlooked that just minutes later Polish striker Ernest Wilimowski did, in fact, score four goals, the first player to do so in a World Cup game.

Italy continued their fine form in the quarter-final by putting out hosts France with a 3-1 win at Colombes. Piola added two more goals to his tally in the game and captain Giuseppe Meazza dominated in midfield. It meant that for the first time the hosts would not win the World Cup.

Following their attacking exploits in the previous round Brazil showed an uglier side to their game in the clash with Czechoslovakia. A brawl and the sending-off of three players blighted the first match, which ended 1-1, but Brazil won the replay through goals from Leônidas and Roberto. In the other quarter-finals Hungary beat Switzerland 2-0, while Sweden crushed Cuba 8-0.

In the semi-final the Brazilians faced Italy but Brazil coach Adhemar Pimenta left out Leônidas, a decision that proved their undoing. Some say Leônidas was arrogantly rested for the final, others that he was simply unable to play because of injuries collected in the fierce clash with Czechoslovakia. Whatever the reason, Italy gained the advantage. Gino Colaussi scored shortly after half-time and Meazza added a penalty on the hour. Brazil managed only a consolation goal three minutes from time through Romeu.

In the other semi-final Hungary ended Sweden's run with a 5-1 triumph, despite conceding in the first minute. The Swedes' lead lasted 19 minutes before Hungary won through, thanks to goals from Titkos, Sárosi and a hat-trick from Gyula Zsengellér. The forward partnership between Zsengellér and Gyorgy Sárosi was perhaps the most thrilling in the tournament and revealed its power to devastating effect.

Leônidas returned for the third place play-off and Brazil fell two goals behind to Sweden before fighting back to win 4-2. He scored twice to finish top scorer with seven, while in the final the Italians confirmed their reputation as the most dominant football force of the era.

BRAZIL 1950

The 1950 World Cup was the oddest of tournaments: withdrawals dominated the build-up, only 13 teams turned up in Brazil, and no final was scheduled by the organisers, with the winners to be decided in a second league phase. Even the new Maracanã stadium, built specifically for the tournament, was not ready when the first game kicked-off. However, the chaotic preparations eventually gave way to some excellent football and the competition produced moments of pure drama and culminated in a game that will never be forgotten, one of the greatest clashes the World Cup has ever seen.

The draw itself looked lop-sided, with the opening round consisting of two groups of four, one of three and one of two. Argentina were among the many teams to pull out before the qualifiers, while Scotland and Turkey withdrew after booking a place in the finals. India refused to turn up, according to some reports, because FIFA insisted they wore boots.

All eyes were on Group 1, where the host nation and highly-fancied outsiders Yugoslavia impressed immediately. With a wonderfully entertaining line-up, boasting a trio of attackers who ranked among the finest in the world – Ademir, Jair and Zizinho – Brazil played skilful and inventive football and were favourites to lift the trophy for the first time in their history. They made a superb start beating Mexico 4-0 in their opener, with Ademir scoring twice. Yugoslavia kept pace with an impressive 3-0 win over Switzerland, maintaining their stunning form with a 4-1 win over Mexico in their second match.

Switzerland surprisingly held Brazil 2-2 but when the group leaders Brazil and Yugoslavia met in the Maracanã in front of 142,429 spectators, the hosts came out on top with a 2-0 win. Goals from Ademir and Zizinho ensured Brazil's safe passage to the final pool and with only one team to go through, it was harsh on the talented Yugoslavs who went home early.

In Group 2 England were the biggest attraction, taking part in their first World Cup. The team had lost star players Frank Swift and Tommy Lawton since the war but still boasted Billy Wright, Tom Finney and Stan Mortensen in their ranks. It was an impressive line-up and goals from Mortensen and Wilf Mannion secured a 2-0 win over Chile.

It looked as though England would cruise through to the next round but in their second game the United States inflicted one of the most embarrassing defeats in football history. Despite losing their opening game 3-1 to Spain, the Americans recorded a 1-0 win in Belo Horizonte on June 29, with Joe Gaetjens scoring the 38th minute winner. It was a major shock for the English, who had assumed their side would reach the final pool at the very least.

England's misery was doubled when Spain beat them 1-0 to reach the final pool with a 100 per cent record. Walter Winterbottom's team returned home thoroughly humiliated.

In Group 3, holders Italy, Sweden and Paraguay played each other, with Sweden earning an early advantage thanks to a 3-2 win over Italy. The Scandinavians' 2-2 draw with Paraguay in the next match was enough for them to clinch the top spot and Italy's 2-0 win over Paraguay was a mere consolation.

In the absurd two-team Group 4, Uruguay thrashed Bolivia 8-0 to make the final pool, with Juan Schiaffino catching the eye and Omar Miguez grabbing a hat-trick.

So to the final pool – the World Cup trophy would go to whoever topped the mini-league table. It could have been an anti-climax if one team had wrapped it up early but in the event it provided perhaps the most thrilling climax to any World Cup, with scorelines and scheduling throwing up an 'unofficial final' in front of the largest football crowd ever.

Certainly the hosts looked the best bet to win when the pool kicked-off, racking up a 7-1 win over Sweden, which included some of the finest attacking football ever seen. Ademir scored four goals in a truly blistering display as his understanding with Jair and Zizinho reached its peak. Next they thrashed Spain 6-1, with all three strikers getting on the scoresheet and winger Chico hitting the target twice. The hosts began to look unstoppable.

Uruguay kept in touch by starting with a 2-2 draw against Spain in a tough physical encounter, and then a 3-2 win over Sweden was enough to retain a slim chance of causing an upset. It meant the final group match, between Brazil and Uruguay, would decide who would win the World Cup. Uruguay needed to win, while the Brazilians needed only a draw.

As Brazil had played the better football and had home advantage, the result seemed a foregone conclusion but the unimaginable happened. Uruguay came from behind and hit a winner with just 11 minutes remaining to leave the crowd shellshocked. The 'Fateful Final' left a bitter feeling in Brazil that remains to this day and their white kit, deemed not patriotic enough, was replaced four years later by the yellow shirts they would make famous.

Above: A packed Maracanã hosts the World Cup. Opposite clockwise from top: Schiaffino equalises for Uruguay in the 'final' against Brazil; Uruguay celebrate; England in action against Chile; Brazil open the scoring against Uruguay.

FINAL POOL

	P	W	D	L	Pts
Uruguay	3	2	1	0	5
Brazil	3	2	0	1	4
Sweden	3	1	0	2	2
Spain	3	0	1	2	1

TOP GOALSCORERS

9 goals: Ademir Menezes (Brazil)

5 goals: Juan Schiaffino (Uruguay), Estanislao Basora (Spain)

FASTEST GOAL

2 minutes: Alfredo (Brazil v Switzerland)

TOTAL GOALS

88

AVERAGE GOALS

4.00 per game

THE FINAL POOL MATCH

URUGUAY (0) **2-1** (0) BRAZIL

Date Sunday July 16, 1950 **Attendance** 199,854

Venue Maracanã, Rio de Janeiro

Brazil had 30 shots on goal, the will of a nation behind them and 200,000 fans in the stadium, but Uruguay refused to read the script. During a goalless first-half the Uruguayans weathered the storm, with their defence doing everything to match the efforts of Brazil's famed attack, before they shocked in the second-half.

Friaça scored for Brazil two minutes after the break, making victory look inevitable, but on 66 minutes Juan Schiaffino swept in an equaliser. Uruguay stood firm and, on the break, Alcides Ghiggia attacked Barbosa's goal and scored from close range to seal a famous victory.

Uruguay had achieved the impossible and the home fans could hardly believe what they had seen. In the most dramatic circumstances, Brazil had failed to lift the World Cup.

HOW THE TEAMS LINED UP

URUGUAY
COACH: JUAN LOPEZ

BRAZIL
COACH: FLAVIO COSTA

Máspoli

Gonzáles, M   Tejera

Gambetta   Varela   Andrade

Ghiggia   Perez   Miguez   Schiaffino   Morán

Chico   Ademir   Friaça

Jair   Zizinho

Bigode   Danilo   Bauer

Juvenal   Augusto

Barbosa

URUGUAY
MÁSPOLI
GONZÁLES, M
ANDRADE
TEJERA
VARELA
GAMBETTA
PERÉZ
SCHIAFFINO ⚽
Goal: 66 mins
GHIGGIA ⚽
Goal: 79 mins
MIGUEZ
MORÁN

BRAZIL
BARBOSA
AUGUSTO
JUVENAL
BAUER
DANILO
BIGODE
ZIZINHO
JAIR
FRIAÇA ⚽
Goal: 47 mins
ADEMIR
CHICO

Referee: Reader (England)

SWITZERLAND 1954

🏆 Coming nearly ten years after the end of the Second World War, the 1954 World Cup may have been seen by a privileged few in flickering black and white television pictures for the first time, but it produced some of the most colourful attacking football in the competition's history, with 140 goals shared between 16 teams at an average of over five goals a game. The quarter-final between Austria and their Swiss hosts finished 7-5, still the highest aggregate for a game at the finals, and several other matches finished with scorelines that appear improbable today.

Switzerland was a logical choice to host the first post-war tournament to be held in Europe, and not simply because it had escaped the devastation sustained across the rest of the continent. FIFA's headquarters were situated in Zurich and 1954 represented the 50th anniversary of its formation.

The Swiss had been given the tournament at FIFA's first post-war congress in 1946, and they spent eight years building new stadia.

However, the finished football grounds had small capacities and were not really up to the requirements of such a tournament. Despite this, the competition was a financial success and the organisers even displayed early signs of grasping the World Cup's true marketing potential by minting and selling special commemorative coins.

The qualifying rounds featured the highest number of nations yet, with 38 entrants. Sweden and Spain failed to qualify, the latter being beaten by Turkey who automatically became seeds, a ruling that was to have particular significance as the competition unfolded. England and Scotland came through the Home Nations group, though the latter were to lose both their games and make a rapid return. Once again the Soviet Union and Argentina were notable absentees.

Almost inevitably FIFA tampered with the format, reverting to a complicated pool phase featuring 16 teams divided into four groups, with two seeded sides in each who would not play each other. The four group winners would then play each other in a knockout phase, as did the four runners-up, but the system was open to exploitation and under the direction of Sepp Herberger, the Germans did just that.

It was no surprise to find that Hungary, coached by Gusztáv Sebes, were favourites. This was the era of the 'Magical Magyars' and two years earlier they had been crowned Olympic champions. Now the Hungarians were at the peak of their powers, with a line-up crammed with stars, including the 'Galloping Major' Ferenc Puskás, striker Sándor Kocsis, dubbed 'The Man With The Golden Head', midfield dynamo József Bózsik and deep-lying centre-forward Nandor Hidegkuti.

This was the core of the side that destroyed English pretensions to superiority with a 6-3 win at Wembley in November 1953 (England's first home defeat to a continental side) and a 7-1 pasting in Budapest six months later. The Magyars hammered South Korea 9-0 in their opening game in Zurich and put eight past a deliberately weakened German side. By the end of the competition this potent side had scored a record 27 goals and Sándor Kocsis had won the Golden Boot with 11 goals, including two hat-tricks.

In the quarter-finals, Hungary's game against Brazil went down in football history for all the wrong reasons. Instead of the classic that it promised, the match degenerated into hand-to-hand combat, since dubbed the 'Battle Of Berne'. The bout was refereed by future British television personality Arthur Ellis, who sent-off three players, Hungary's József Bózsik and Brazil's Humberto Tozzi and Nilton Santos, after trouble broke out over a disputed penalty. The game degenerated into violence that continued in the changing rooms after the match, embroiling both managers and even the official delegations.

Above: Santos and Bózsik are sent off during the 'Battle of Berne'. Opposite top: Tom Finney gets a header in for England against Uruguay. Opposite bottom: Sandor Kocsis, whose goal put Hungary 2-0 up in their ill-fated final.

England, under Walter Winterbottom, topped a group featuring hosts Switzerland, Belgium and Italy. The side, featuring Billy Wright, Nat Lofthouse, Stanley Matthews and Tom Finney, should have gone further but came unstuck against Uruguay, losing 4-2 with goalkeeper Gil Merrick at fault for three goals. In the end the feeling was that their shattering 7-1 defeat at the hands of Hungary just weeks earlier had destroyed the team's confidence.

West Germany were admitted after their banishment following the Second World War and soon made a mockery of their non-seeding, beating Turkey 4-1, while France, another seeded side, lost to Yugoslavia. West German coach Sepp Herberger then exploited the play-off system by electing to send out a weak side against Hungary in the knowledge that the group winners would play Brazil in the knock-out phase, while the runners-up would face Korea or Turkey. His plan worked and Germany duly thrashed Turkey and squeezed past the Yugoslavs 2-0, scoring early on and holding out until a late goal sealed the victory. A 6-1 semi-final win over Austria sent out an ominous warning.

Hungary's semi-final against holders Uruguay was another memorable encounter that put paid to the South Americans' unbeaten record in the competition, with Hungary winning 4-2 in extra-time.

The final looked on paper to be a forgone conclusion. Unseeded West Germany faced the might of Hungary, who had not lost in 32 games and four years, but the form book was discarded in a fascinating see-saw encounter that saw the Germans come back from 2-0 down to win the trophy for the first time. Hungary were stunned and when the Soviet Union crushed the country's uprising two years later the squad broke up, effectively ending its dominance forever.

SEMI-FINALS

West Germany 6-1 Austria
Hungary 4-2 Uruguay
(aet: 2-2 at 90 mins)

THIRD PLACE PLAY-OFF

Austria 3-1 Uruguay

TOP GOALSCORERS

11 goals: Sándor Kocsis (Hungary)
6 goals: Max Morlock (West Germany), Josef Hügi (Switzerland), Erich Probst (Austria)

FASTEST GOAL

2 minutes: Mamat Suat
(Turkey v West Germany)

TOTAL GOALS

140

AVERAGE GOALS

5.38 per game

THE FINAL

WEST GERMANY (2) 3-2 (2) HUNGARY

Date Sunday July 4, 1954 **Attendance** 60,000
Venue Wankdorf Stadium, Berne

Though carrying an injury, Puskás put his side ahead after only six minutes when he followed up a Kocsis shot. Two minutes later Czibor latched on to a weak back pass to put them two up, but Morlock reduced the arrears after 11 minutes and a mistake by the Hungarian goalkeeper Grosics in the 18th minute allowed Rahn to equalise.

In the second-half Hidegkuti hit the post, Kocsis the bar, Kohlmeyer cleared off the line and Turek made a succession of great saves. Six minutes from time, winger Rahn picked up a half-hearted clearance, raced to the edge of the box and struck a low shot past Grosics, who appeared to slip. There was more drama when Puskás had a goal disallowed, with the Hungarians still arguing after the final whistle.

HOW THE TEAMS LINED UP

WEST GERMANY
COACH:
SEPP HERBERGER

HUNGARY
COACH:
GUSZTÁV SEBES

WEST GERMANY	
TUREK	
POSIPAL	
KOHLMEYER	
ECKEL	
LIEBRICH	
MAI	
MORLOCK	⚽
Goal: 11 mins	
WALTER, F	
RAHN	⚽⚽
Goal: 18 mins, 84 mins	
WALTER, O	
SCHÄFER	

HUNGARY	
GROSICS	
BUZÁNSZKY	
LANTOS	
BÓZSIK	
LÓRÁNT	
ZAKARIÁS	
KOCSIS	
PUSKÁS	⚽
Goal: 6 mins	
CZIBOR	
Goal: 9 mins	
HIDEGKUTI	
TÓTH, M	

Referee: Ling (England)

Above: One of Just Fontaine's record-breaking tally of 13 goals at the 1958 World Cup, this one part of his hat-trick against Paraguay. Opposite clockwise from top: Pelé beats the Swedish goalkeeper; John Charles of Wales helps his side edge out Hungary; a 17-year-old Pelé is overcome at the final whistle.

SWEDEN 1958

For fans of the beautiful game, the 1958 World Cup will always be remembered for the birth of a football nation and the introduction of Pelé to the world stage. Before the finals in Sweden, Brazil had never won the World Cup. It had been Uruguay that had forged a reputation as South America's finest side by twice lifting the trophy, but in 1958 the balance of power shifted as Brazil became world champions for the first time.

They did so by pioneering a style of play that, in an era when defenders could – and did – get away with kicking the opposition's best players into the crowd, had football writers everywhere purring at its grace and beauty. The first strains of what was to become known as 'Samba football' were born in Sweden. 'Where skill alone counted Brazil stood alone,' reported *The Times* newspaper. 'The way each daffodil shirt of theirs pulled the ball down out of the sky, tamed it with a touch of the foot, caressed it and stroked it away into an open space was a joy.'

Looking back, it is easy to over-romanticise about Brazil and to think that any team with so much skill, and with arguably the greatest ever player, was bound to succeed. But there was nothing inevitable about it. In the early decades of the World Cup, sides unfamiliar with foreign conditions did not travel well: until this tournament the winners had always been a team from the host continent. Brazil, third in 1938, spurned another great chance in 1950. This time, they meant business and even brought along a psychiatrist.

As for Pelé, while everyone knew he was a bit special, at 17 no-one knew how special. His mere selection remained in doubt, partly because of a niggling injury and partly because some believed he was not up to it.

The tournament was something of a watershed. Although there were plenty of feisty tackles, the finals in Sweden marked the last days of the more carefree, attack-minded post-war era of international football. In the 1960s, World Cup matches became increasingly cynical affairs characterised by defensive attitudes.

The finals began without some familiar names as two-time winners Uruguay and Italy both failed to qualify. For British football though, 1958 remains a high point, with all four nations qualifying for the only time. England, despite the Munich air disaster denying them such talents as Duncan Edwards, Tommy Taylor and Roger Byrne, were the favourites, particularly as they had never lost to any of the teams in their group. However, it was to prove a frustrating tournament for Walter Winterbottom's side. Creditable draws against the Soviet Union and Brazil – the first goalless match in World Cup finals history – meant they only had to beat eliminated Austria to advance, but the draws continued. It came down to a play-off with the Soviets, which England lost.

Scotland set the tone for future World Cups by also going out in the first round but Northern Ireland and Wales both advanced. The Irish, who had drawn 2-2 with West Germany in their group, beat Czechoslovakia in a play-off, a situation Wales were also catapulted into after drawing all three group matches. Inspired by John Charles, they came from behind to beat Hungary 2-1.

Charles was injured for the quarter-finals, when Wales met Brazil. For 70 minutes the Welsh dream lived on as Garrincha, Didi, Mazzola and Zagalo were continually thwarted but when Pelé scored the first of his 12 World Cup goals, it was all over.

The big guns were beginning to fire and in the same round France ended Irish resistance with a 4-0 thumping, West Germany sneaked home 1-0 against Yugoslavia and Sweden eliminated the Soviet Union 2-0.

Although West Germany, the defending champions, were still in the competition,

THE FINAL

BRAZIL (2) 5-2 (1) SWEDEN

Date Sunday June 29, 1958 **Attendance** 51,800
Venue Rasunda Stadium, Solna, Stockholm

Heavy rain and a passionate home crowd suggested now was not the time or place for South American flair, especially when Liedholm fired the hosts ahead after four minutes. Five minutes later Vavá equalised from Garrincha's cross, then Pelé struck the post and Vavá added a second. Suddenly Sweden were chasing shadows.

The second-half belonged to Pelé. His first goal in the 55th minute combined individual trickery with a rasping volley. Zagalo made it 4-1 before Simonsson restored hope for Sweden, but Pelé had the final word, heading home for a 5-2 win. The Brazilians were overcome, weeping openly. They sportingly paraded the Swedish flag around the pitch, bringing the stadium to its feet in acclaim.

BRAZIL	
GILMAR	
SANTOS, D	
BELLINI	
ORLANDO	
SANTOS, N	
DIDI	
ZITO	
GARRINCHA	
VAVÁ	⚽⚽
Goal: 9 mins, 32 mins	
PELÉ	⚽⚽
Goal: 55 mins, 90 mins	
ZAGALO	⚽
Goal: 68 mins	

SWEDEN	
SVENSSON	
BERGMARK	
AXDOM	
BORJESSON	
GUSTAVSSON	
PARLING	
GREN	
LIEDHOLM	⚽
Goal: 4 mins	
HAMRIN	
SIMONSSON	⚽
Goal: 80 mins	
SKOGLUND	

Referee: Guigue (France)

HOW THE TEAMS LINED UP

BRAZIL
COACH: VICENTE FEOLA

SWEDEN
COACH: GEORGE RAYNOR

Gilmar
Santos D   Bellini   Orlando   Santos N
Didi   Zito
Garrincha   Vavá   Pelé   Zagalo

Skoglund   Simonsson   Hamrin
Liedholm   Gren
Parling   Gustavsson   Borjesson
Axbom   Bergmark
Svensson

Sweden and Brazil had emerged as favourites. Sweden underlined their credentials in front of 53,000 fans in Gothenburg when they knocked out West Germany 3-1 in the semi-finals. The Germans had hung on until the last ten minutes when the home team scored twice to trigger wild celebrations. It was one of West Germany's darkest World Cup moments. Erich Juskowiak was sent-off for kicking and they were reduced to nine men for a time when Fritz Walter went off for treatment after a ferocious tackle by Sigvard Parling.

In the other semi-final in Stockholm, Brazil electrified the tournament with a 5-2 defeat of France, who had cruised through their quarter-final and were expected to pose a severe test. For half the match they did but they were blown away when Pelé netted a hat-trick in 23 unforgettable second-half minutes. French striker Just Fontaine had the consolation of scoring four times in the third place play-off against West Germany and taking his tournament to 13, a World Cup scoring record that looks unlikely to be broken.

The dream final had arrived and the era of Brazilian dominance was about to begin.

SEMI-FINALS
Brazil 5-2 France
Sweden 3-1 West Germany

THIRD PLACE PLAY-OFF
France 6-3 West Germany

TOP GOALSCORERS
13 goals: Just Fontaine (France)
6 goals: Pelé (Brazil), Helmut Rahn (West Germany)
5 goals: Vavá (Brazil), Peter McParland (Northern Ireland)

FASTEST GOAL
90 seconds: Vavá (Brazil v France)

TOTAL GOALS
126

AVERAGE GOALS
3.60 per game

CHILE 1962

SEMI-FINALS
Brazil 4-2 Chile
Czechoslovakia 3-1 Yugoslavia

THIRD PLACE PLAY-OFF
Chile 1-0 Yugoslavia

TOP GOALSCORERS
4 goals: Garrincha (Brazil),
Valentin Ivanov (Soviet Union),
Leonel Sánchez (Chile), Florian
Albert (Hungary), Drazen Jerkovic
(Yugoslavia), Vavá (Brazil)
* Garrincha awarded Top Scorer
prize, drawn by lot

FASTEST GOAL
15 seconds: Vaclav Masek
(Czechoslovakia v Mexico)

TOTAL GOALS
89

AVERAGE GOALS
2.78 per game

'We have nothing, that is why we must have the World Cup,' pleaded Carlos Dittborn, president of the Chilean Football Federation. FIFA had been looking for an alternative host following the devastating earthquake that caused serious damage and loss of life in Chile in May 1960 but Dittborn's pleas were heeded and Chile kept the World Cup, serving up a tournament of extremes, ranging from the appalling, brutal 'Battle Of Santiago' to the beautiful, crafted performances of the sublime Brazilians.

Local interest in the games wavered wildly, from disappointingly small attendances of under 6,000 at one extreme, to the crowds of over 60,000 who squeezed into the cauldron of Santiago. It was also a World Cup that witnessed the dawn of defensive football. This largely dismal football showpiece reached its nadir with the infamous 'Battle Of Santiago' between Italy and hosts Chile. Anti-Italian feeling had been whipped-up in Santiago as a result of the publication of derogatory articles about Chilean life by two Italian journalists. This was in addition to ill-feeling created by Italy's reputation for poaching South American players at both domestic and international level. Indeed, their line-up for the game included Argentinian Humberto Maschio and a veteran of Brazil's previous World Cup campaign, José 'Mazzola' Altafini.

The match, staged in front of a hostile over-capacity crowd in the Estadio Nacional, quickly descended into violence, which English referee Ken Aston failed to control. He did dismiss the Italian Giorgio Ferrini for retaliation after just eight minutes, although the player refused to leave the field for a further ten minutes and was eventually removed by FIFA officials and the police. A punch to Mario David by Leonel Sánchez, the son of a boxer, was overlooked, but when the Italian kicked Sánchez in the head, he too was sent off. The disgraceful violence continued until the final whistle, by which time Chile had won 2-0.

The group stages were dominated by defensive play and excessive violence. After three match days the Chilean press reported there had been 34 serious injuries. Among the casualties was 21-year-old Pelé, the result of a torn muscle from a groin injury sustained in a pre-tournament friendly – Pelé had refused to declare it because of fitness coach Paolo Amaral's 'don't train, don't play' policy.

The opening stages did feature the odd decent match, the most amazing being the Group 1 clash between the Soviet Union and first time qualifiers Colombia in Arica. Three goals in three minutes gave the Soviets a 3-0 lead by the 11th minute, with two goals from Ivanov sandwiching a single strike from Chislenko. The game looked over, and an Aceros goal ten minutes later did nothing to change that opinion, with Ponedelnik adding to Colombian woe with a fourth for the Soviets early in the second-half. However, Colombia staged a magnificent comeback to secure an amazing 4-4 draw, with Coll, Rada and Klinger all scoring. Indeed, Group 1 provided the most entertaining football of the early stages.

Outside of Santiago the games were poorly attended. The six Group 4 matches in Rancagua, for example, attracted an average crowd of just 7,000, the worst attended being England's dull 0-0 draw against Bulgaria.

The quickest goal was scored after just 15 seconds when Czechoslovakia's Vaclav Masek put the ball past Mexican keeper Carbajal, a veteran of three previous World Cups. Mexico won the game 3-1 but Czechoslovakia went on to reach the final despite finishing second to group winners and holders Brazil. They had built a team around the successful Dukla Prague club side, with a strategy built on defence. A cautious, counterattacking team, they had held Brazil to a goalless draw and beaten a disharmonious Spain 1-0 in the group, reaching the quarter-finals on goal

Above: Brazil's Garrincha goes past future World Cup winner Ray Wilson in their quarter-final with England. Opposite clockwise from top: Amarildo shows off his skills in the final; Chile's Rojas celebrates his country's last minute third place play-off win against Yugoslavia; Mauro lifts the Jules Rimet trophy after beating Chechoslovakia

average, which was being used for the first time at the World Cup. That they progressed further was in no small part down to Viliam Schrojf, the goalkeeper of the tournament. He was in magnificent form, particularly in the quarter-final and semi-final clashes with Hungary and Yugoslavia, with a series of magnificent saves keeping his opponents at bay in both games.

Brazil may have suffered the loss of Pelé after two games but they remained unfazed by the loss of their star, having unearthed Tavares Amarildo, who was quickly dubbed 'the white Pelé'. However, it was Garrincha who was Brazil's inspiration. The father of seven children, he was just as productive on the pitch when creating and scoring goals.

Brazil breezed through their quarter-final in Viña del Mar, outclassing England who had finished runners-up in Group 4. Garrincha, the smallest player on the field, opened the scoring with a header before later setting up Vavá and finding the net again in a 3-1 win.

The semi-final pitched the Brazilians against hosts Chile in an open game that was streaked with spite. Garrincha gave Brazil a 2-0 lead through a volley and a header, although a Toro free-kick halved the deficit for the hosts before the break.

A Garrincha free-kick was headed home by Vavá just after the interval, but Sánchez converted a penalty to keep Chile in touch. With 13 minutes remaining Zagalo dribbled through the Chilean defence and set up Vavá with another header. Shortly afterwards Chile's Landa was sent-off and only minutes later Garrincha followed, finally retaliating to one of the many kicks he had suffered during the game. Nevertheless, now firm favourites Brazil progressed to the final, where they beat Czechoslovakia 3-1 to retain the trophy.

THE FINAL

BRAZIL (1) 3-1 (1) CZECHOSLOVAKIA

Date Sunday June 17, 1962 **Attendance** 69,000
Venue National Stadium, Santiago

Brazil were able to name an unchanged side that even included Garrincha, despite his semi-final sending-off (FIFA had imposed one-match bans on the other five players dismissed during the tournament). The experienced Brazil side included eight members of the team that had won the World Cup in Sweden in 1958 but still they went 1-0 down to Masopust's opener.

Amarildo scored from an acute angle to equalise within two minutes and the match was closely-fought until the 69th minute when Amarildo's high pass was headed home by Zito.

The match was decided when keeper Schrojf allowed a Djalma Santos high ball to fall through his hands, enabling Vavá to stab home the loose ball for an unassailable 3-1 lead. It was the best match of the tournament.

BRAZIL	
GILMAR	
SANTOS, D	
MAURO	
ZÓZIMO	
SANTOS, N	
ZITO	⚽
Goal: 69 mins	
DIDI	
GARRINCHA	
VAVÁ	⚽
Goal: 77 mins	
AMARILDO	⚽
Goal: 17 mins	
ZAGALO	

CZECHOSLOVAKIA	
SCHROJF	
TICHY	
PLUSKAL	
POPLUHAR	
NOVAK	
KVASNAK	
MASOPUST	⚽
Goal: 16 mins	
SCHERER	
POSPICHAL	
KADRABA	
JELINEK	

Referee: Latychev (Soviet Union)

HOW THE TEAMS LINED UP

BRAZIL
COACH:
AYMORE MOREIRA

CZECHOSLOVAKIA
COACH:
RUDOLF VYTLACIL

Gilmar

Santos, D   Mauro   Zózimo   Santos, N

Zito   Didi   Zagalo

Garrincha   Vavá   Amarildo

Jelinek   Kadraba   Scherer   Pospichal

Masopust   Tichy

Novak   Popluhar   Pluskal   Tichy

Schrojf

ENGLAND 1966

Most England fans remember the 1966 World Cup as their country's greatest sporting triumph but the tournament itself was characterised by dour, often ugly defending, punctuated by occasional glimpses of brilliance and drama. Hosts England boasted players of the calibre of Bobby Moore, Bobby Charlton and Jimmy Greaves and expectations were high, particularly after coach Alf Ramsey had, on taking the job, promised the nation that his team would lift the trophy.

The draw pitted England against Uruguay, Mexico and France, but the opening game was an anticlimax with the negative Uruguayans blotting out England's sterile attack for a 0-0 draw. England followed this up with a still less than convincing 2-0 win against Mexico but progress to the second stage was sealed with a 2-0 win against France. After the game the FA had asked Ramsey to drop Nobby Stiles because of his fierce tackle on Jacky Simon, but the coach stood by his man.

In Group 2 West Germany got off to a flying start with a crushing 5-0 win over a Swiss team depleted by internal suspensions. The first surprise came when the physical Argentinians beat a Spanish side built around the players of the mighty Real Madrid. While Spain recovered to beat the Swiss, West Germany faced Argentina and were subjected to the kind of brutal tactics that saw the South Americans pick up a FIFA warning. It did not prevent Argentina progressing though, as they clinched their place in the next round after beating Switzerland in front of a hostile Hillsborough crowd. West Germany, meanwhile, qualified top after an Uwe Seeler goal put Spain out.

Group 3 favourites Brazil started well by beating Bulgaria 2-0 with two great strikes from Pelé and Garrincha, though the game was marred by a series of ugly challenges. Hungary, meanwhile, lost 3-1 to Portugal, with keeper Antal Szentmihályi at fault when the Portuguese took the lead. Hungary against Brazil, minus the injured Pelé, was to prove a classic match with the Hungarians showing a flair and skill rarely seen in the finals. Bene gave them the lead after three minutes, then Brazil equalised against the run of play. The second-half saw Hungary step up a gear, with Albert at the heart of their 3-1 win. Portugal finished top after beating Bulgaria and Brazil, and Hungary joined them in the quarter-finals.

Group 4 opened at Ayresome Park with the Soviet Union overpowering outsiders North Korea 3-0 and Italy beating Chile 2-0. The English fans warmed to the energetic North Koreans and inspired them to a draw with Chile in their next game. The meeting of the group heavyweights saw a curiously unbalanced Italy run ragged by the Soviets, who were not flattered by their 1-0 win.

Italy faced the North Koreans expecting to overcome their defeat to Russia and qualify in second place but Italian coach Fabbri picked his slowest defenders and the quick Koreans revelled in the occasion, scoring the winning goal after 42 minutes to knock Italy out.

England played Argentina in the first quarter-final, with Geoff Hurst coming in for the country's best striker Jimmy Greaves, injured in the game with France. Argentina continued their ugly approach and just before half-time the referee lost patience and sent-off Rattín, sparking ten minutes of mayhem as he initially refused to leave the field and then started abusing the crowd. Ten-man Argentina held

Above: Rattín is sent-off during Argentina's game with England. Opposite clockwise from top: England's Bobby Moore raises the trophy; Portugal's Eusébio leaves three Hungarians behind on his way to the Golden Boot; Soviet keeper Lev Yashin saves from Italy's Sandro Mazzola.

out until 13 minutes from time when a header from Hurst put England into the semi-finals. On the final whistle England manager Alf Ramsey was so furious with the performance of the Argentinians – who he later described as 'animals' – that he took to the field, physically preventing his players from exchanging shirts with the opposition.

The second quarter-final was equally unpleasant. Uruguay had looked the better side in an open first-half but after the interval the match descended into violence as the Germans reacted to provocation – Emmerich kicked Troche, only for the Uruguayan to respond with a kick to the stomach. Troche was sent-off and he slapped Uwe Seeler in the face as he left the field. Minutes later Uruguay were down to nine men and Germany cruised home with four goals in the last 20 minutes.

The third quarter-final saw the Soviet Union press the Hungarians into making mistakes, as twice goalkeeper Gelei blundered as the Hungarians went down 2-1.

The most exciting game of the round brought the North Koreans and Portugal together, and

unbelievably the Koreans were 3-0 up in just 25 minutes. Then, inspired by Eusébio (he would finish as the tournament's top scorer with nine goals), Portugal began their comeback, with their star scoring twice before half-time. After the break Eusébio scored two more before Augusto added a fifth.

The first semi-final saw West Germany beat the Soviet Union in another bruising encounter. Poor sportsmanship and violent conduct marred the game and the Soviets left the pitch a depleted force, with Chislenko sent-off and Sabo having to play on with an injury for much of the match.

The other semi-final was altogether different. Portugal struggled to breach England's resolute defence and Bobby Charlton was outstanding going forward, scoring in each half. A penalty pulled one back for Portugal but it was the English, who had controversially retained Hurst in the line-up over Greaves, who were in the final. Ramsey's team were about to fulfil the manager's prediction and Geoff Hurst, not even a first choice selection at the start of the tournament, was about to write himself into the football history books.

THE FINAL

ENGLAND (1) **4-2** (1) **WEST GERMANY**
(aet: 2-2 at 90 mins)

Date Saturday July 30, 1966 **Attendance** 93,000
Venue Wembley Stadium, London

The match got off to a poor start for the hosts as Haller scored to give the Germans a 12th minute lead, but six minutes later a fine header from Geoff Hurst made it 1-1. Both sides continued to press forward in the second-half until, with only 12 minutes left, Peters latched on to a poor clearance to give England the lead. In the final minute West Germany won a controversial free-kick and Weber equalised.

England went into extra-time on the attack and had already gone close twice when Hurst thumped a shot against the underside of the bar, with the linesman judging that the ball had bounced down over the line. In the final minute Hurst broke away to complete the only World Cup final hat-trick.

HOW THE TEAMS LINED UP

ENGLAND
COACH:
ALF RAMSEY

WEST GERMANY
COACH:
HELMUT SCHÖN

Banks

Cohen Charlton, J Moore Wilson

Ball Stiles Charlton, R Peters

Hunt Hurst

Emmerich Held Seeler

Overath Beckenbauer Haller

Schnellinger Weber Schulz Höttges

Tilkowski

ENGLAND

BANKS
COHEN
CHARLTON, J
MOORE
WILSON
STILES
CHARLTON, R
PETERS

Goal: 78 mins. Booked.

BALL
HUNT
HURST

Goal: 18 mins, 101 mins, 120 mins

WEST GERMANY

TILKOWSKI
HÖTTGES
SCHULZ
WEBER

Goal: 90 mins

SCHNELLINGER
HALLER

Goal: 12 mins

BECKENBAUER
OVERATH
SEELER
HELD
EMMERICH

Referee: Dienst (Switzerland)

MEXICO 1970

Against all the odds Mexico 70 turned into a feast of football and remains the most fondly remembered of all the World Cup competitions. However, in the build up, portents did not bode well. The problems of the extreme heat of the Mexican summer and the energy-sapping altitude threatened to stifle free-flowing, attacking football, especially in light of FIFA's decision to kick-off many games at midday to appease European broadcasters.

Pre-tournament fears of ultra-defensive and violent play, a worrying trend in the game, also threatened to put a negative stranglehold on the competition, but thanks to the colourful flamboyance and daring excellence of the multi-skilled, Pelé-inspired Brazilians, the beautiful game somehow managed to prosper like never before.

The first two qualifying groups saw the Soviet Union, Mexico, Italy and Uruguay come through without any surprises against lesser opposition. The ultra-cautious Italians qualified without conceding a goal, and scoring just

once, while the Soviet Union finished on top of their group above Mexico on goals scored.

The outstanding match of the group stage was between twice-champions Brazil and the holders England. In a wonderful end-to-end game, famed for Gordon Banks' incredible save from a downward goal-bound Pelé header, Brazil stole the honours with the only goal from the powerful Jairzinho, who was to score in all of Brazil's six matches. Both teams were to progress to the next stage.

In Group 4, despite an early struggle against a spirited Morocco, the West Germans gained maximum points with 'Der Bomber', Gerd Müller, in typically prolific form, knocking in hat-tricks against Peru and Bulgaria.

In León, England were matched against West Germany in the first quarter-final. With goals from Alan Mullery and Martin Peters, England were 2-0 up and in control early in the second-half. However, Alf Ramsey made a couple of rhythm-disturbing substitutions (Norman Hunter and Colin Bell for Bobby Charlton and Peters) and the Germans clawed themselves back into the game, with goals from Franz Beckenbauer and Uwe Seeler taking the tie to extra-time. A close-range volley from Müller past second-choice goalkeeper Peter Bonetti (Gordon Banks was ill with an upset stomach) finally eliminated the holders.

In the other quarter-finals, hosts Mexico lost out 4-1 to an atypically free-scoring Italy in Toluca, with the talented striker Gigi Riva scoring twice, while in Guadalajara Brazil continued their irrepressible form, getting the better of Peru in a six-goal thriller. In the lowest profile game of this stage, Uruguay narrowly defeated the Soviet Union with an extra-time goal by substitute Esparrago,

The match of the tournament came in Mexico City where the two European giants, Italy and West Germany, were pitted against each other in a thrilling semi-final. The Italians took the lead through Roberto Boninsegna

before withdrawing to protect their lead. It was a tactic that very nearly worked, but an equaliser in the third minute of injury-time from Karl-Heinz Schnellinger meant the game was not to be decided within the 90 minutes. Franz Beckenbauer famously remained on the field even with a dislocated shoulder, his arm in a sling strapped to his body. In extra-time the goals kept coming. Müller edged Germany into the lead, while Tarcisio Burgnich and Riva put Italy back in control at 3-2. Müller, the eventual Golden Boot winner, clawed it back to 3-3, before Rivera finally clinched one of the World Cup's most epic struggles for Italy.

The other semi-final pitted the old South American foes, Uruguay against Brazil, in Guadalajara. The Uruguayans took an early lead through Cubilla and immediately tried to shut up shop. Not an easy task against Mario Zagalo's side, and Brazil were on equal terms late in the first-half when right-half Clodoaldo powered in the equaliser. Despite aggressive tackling from Uruguay, the Brazilians took hold of the game in the second 45 minutes, and goals from Jairzinho and the fabulous Rivelino sealed a 3-1 victory. Late on Pelé almost hit the goal of the tournament, outrageously dummying Mazurkiewicz in the Uruguayan goal, before pulling his shot just wide.

Brazil were to play some of their most open and attacking football in the final, especially significant as Italy were the self-confessed masters of catenaccio, the most defence-minded style of play. The competition was also a personal victory for Pelé. Having threatened to quit football after his treatment at the 1966 tournament, his performances in 1970 stood as a permanent testament to his genius.

The 1970 World Cup was a triumph, and thanks, ironically, to television, a triumph on a global scale. How fitting that Mexico 70 was to be first tournament to be shown in colour, and thanks to the fantasy football of the Brazilians it was glorious technicolour.

SEMI-FINALS

Italy 4-3 West Germany (aet)
Brazil 3-1 Uruguay

THIRD PLACE PLAY-OFF

West Germany 1-0 Uruguay

TOP GOALSCORERS

10 goals: Gerd Müller (West Germany)
7 goals: Jairzinho (Brazil)
5 goals: Teófilo Cubillas (Peru)

FASTEST GOAL

3 minutes: Ladislav Petras (Czechoslovakia v Romania)

TOTAL GOALS

95

AVERAGE GOALS

2.97 per game

THE FINAL

BRAZIL (1) 4-1 (1) ITALY

Date Sunday June 21, 1970   **Attendance** 107,412
Venue Azteca Stadium, Mexico City

Pelé opened the scoring after 18 minutes, athletically getting his head on the end of Rivelino's cross. Against the run of play, Boninsegna pounced on a careless mistake by Clodoaldo to level the score but Italy were unable to match the Brazilians in terms of possession. Their skilful play left the Azzurri chasing shadows. In the 66th minute Gérson's left-footed cross-shot found the back of Albertosi's net, followed by Jairzinho's customary goal. The match winner was one of the most loved goals in football history: in a move where eight of Brazil's ten outfield players touched the ball, Jairzinho found Pelé and laid the ball off into the stride of captain Carlos Alberto, who thundered it low into the corner. The Jules Rimet Trophy was Brazil's to keep.

BRAZIL	
FÉLIX	
CARLOS ALBERTO	⚽
Goal: 87 mins	
BRITO	
PIAZZA	
EVERALDO	
JAIRZINHO	⚽
Goal: 71 mins	
CLODOALDO	
GÉRSON	⚽
Goal: 66 mins	
TOSTÃO	
PELÉ	⚽
Goal: 18 mins	
RIVELINO	🟨
Booked	
ITALY	
ALBERTOSI	
BURGNICH	🟨
Booked	
CERA	
BERTINI	▶
Subbed: 75 mins (Juliano)	
FACCHETTI	
ROSATO	
DOMENGHINI	
DE SISTI	
MAZZOLA	
BONINSEGNA	⚽ ▶
Subbed: 75 mins (Rivera)	
RIVA	
sub: JULIANO	▶
sub: RIVERA	▶

Referee: Glöckner (East Germany)

HOW THE TEAMS LINED UP

BRAZIL
COACH: MARIO ZAGALO

ITALY
COACH: FERRUCCIO VALCAREGGI

Félix
Carlos Alberto   Brito   Piazza   Everaldo
Clodoaldo   Gérson
Jairzinho   Tostão   Pelé   Rivelino

Riva   Boninsegna   Domenghini
De Sisti   Mazzola   Bertini
Facchetti   Rosato   Cera   Burgnich
Albertosi

Above: Gerd Müller in action against England. Opposite clockwise from top left: Germany and Italy in semi-final action; Pelé celebrates in the final; Carlos Alberto lifts the Jules Rimet Trophy; Pelé and Bobby Moore swap shirts.

WEST GERMANY 1974

The 1970 finals in Mexico had ended somewhat ignobly for the Europeans, with Italy on the receiving end of a 4-1 demolition from a seemingly unstoppable Brazil. However, this time European countries found themselves most definitely in the ascendancy and, at the tournament's end, Poland, Holland and West Germany were installed as the world's three best teams. The latter pair contested the final itself, which under a new system featuring 16 teams and two group stages, was the only proper 'knock-out' game of the tournament.

Although they had struggled slightly during qualification, Holland, under manager Rinus Michels and boasting a plethora of stars from the all-conquering Ajax club side, cut a swathe through the group stages. Their unique brand of 'Total Football', in which players switched positions and roles with astonishing versatility, saw them score 14 goals in six games, conceding just one.

They began their first group stage campaign with a comfortable 2-0 win over the very first world champions, Uruguay, both goals coming from Ajax star Johnny Rep. Michels' men followed it up with a goalless draw against Sweden but bounced back to record an impressive 4-1 rout of Bulgaria (including two penalties from another Ajax man, Johan Neeskens). This was enough for them to top the group and qualify for the last eight along with the Swedes.

A pre-tournament defeat of the West Germans had made Argentina seem a good 'dark horse' bet for glory at the finals but after only just edging out Italy for a place in the last eight they were effectively dismantled by the inspired Dutch in their opening second group stage game. Goals from Rep, Johan Cruyff (who scored twice) and Ruud Krol contributed to the 4-0 landslide. Holland's 2-0 win over the East Germans, who had beaten their West German neighbours earlier in the tournament, set up an all or nothing showdown with Brazil for a place in the final.

Without Pelé, who had by now retired, the Brazilians were clearly not the force they had once been. They had scraped through the first stage thanks to goalless draws with Yugoslavia and Scotland, and a 3-0 win over a hapless Zaïre side that had shipped nine against Yugoslavia. However, Brazil had started the second stage with something approaching their old swagger, beating East Germany 1-0, thanks to a second-half strike from Rivelino, and Argentina 2-1, with goals from Jairzinho and Rivelino again. However, despite improving form the Brazilians found it impossible to live with a Dutch side in peak

Above: Joe Jordan in action for Scotland during their win over Zaïre. Opposite clockwise from top: Holland captain Johan Cruyff; Gerd Müller fends off the Yugoslav Maric; Gerd Müller fires home against Poland; Franz Beckenbauer lifts the World Cup in Munich.

form. Two second-half goals, Cruyff's strike in the 65th minute following Neeskens' gorgeous lob in the 50th, saw Holland run out 2-0 winners. The self-destructing Brazilians finished with ten men after the dismissal of Luís Pereira. Holland, many assumed, were well on their way to a first and hugely deserved world championship.

In contrast West Germany started the tournament slowly. After a narrow win over Chile and an unimpressive 3-0 victory against Australia, Helmut Schön's men progressed to the last eight in second place after losing 1-0 to neighbours East Germany. However, a benefit of the shock result was that they avoided Brazil, Argentina and Holland in the next group stage and slowly but surely the West German team began to gel.

Spurred on by inspirational skipper Franz Beckenbauer, they started the second group stage impressively – beating Yugoslavia 2-0 thanks to goals from Paul Breitner and the prolific Gerd Müller. Even better followed in the shape of a 4-2 victory over Sweden. Finely balanced at 2-2 with 14 minutes left, Jürgen Grabowski and Uli Hoeness put the tie beyond doubt, setting up a crucial final group game with Poland in the process, a match the Germans only needed to draw to advance to their third World Cup final.

The Poles, who had surprisingly eliminated England during the qualifiers, were unbeaten thus far in the tournament and in Grzegorz Lato had a striker who would go on to become its highest scorer, with seven goals, including two in a 3-2 first stage victory over Argentina. He also scored a crucial second-half winner in the 2-1 victory over Yugoslavia that effectively brought Poland face-to-face with the West

THE FINAL

WEST GERMANY (2) 2-1 (1) HOLLAND

Date Sunday July 7, 1974 **Attendance** 75,200
Venue Olympic Stadium, Munich

Holland got off to the best possible start. After less than a minute Johan Cruyff was up-ended in the West German penalty area by Uli Hoeness. There had never been a penalty awarded in a World Cup final before but Johan Neeskens calmly slotted the ball past Sepp Maier to put Rinus Michels' side a goal up.

The Dutch continued to dominate but surrendered their lead cheaply in the 25th minute when a surging Bernd Hölzenbein run was bought to an abrupt end by a trip in the Holland penalty area. Paul Breitner converted the spot-kick and the Germans went on to snatch a decisive lead two minutes before half-time through Gerd Müller. Maier weathered the Dutch onslaught in the second-half and the West Germans were world champions again.

HOW THE TEAMS LINED UP

WEST GERMANY		
COACH: HELMUT SCHÖN		

HOLLAND		
COACH: RINUS MICHELS		

WEST GERMANY

MAIER	
VOGTS	
Booked: 3 mins	
SCHWARZENBECK	
BECKENBAUER	
BREITNER	⚽
Goal: 25 mins (pen)	
BONHOF	
HOENESS	
OVERATH	
GRABOWSKI	
MÜLLER	⚽
Goal: 43 mins	
HÖLZENBEIN	

HOLLAND

JONGBLOED	
SUURBIER	
RIJSBERGEN	▶
Subbed: 69 mins (De Jong)	
HAAN	
KROL	
JANSEN	
NEESKENS	⚽
Goal: 2 mins (pen). Booked: 39 mins	
VAN HANEGEM	
Booked: 22 mins	
REP	
CRUYFF	
Booked: 45 mins	
RENSENBRINK	▶
Subbed: 46 mins (Van De Kerkhof, R)	
sub: VAN DE KERKHOF, R	▶
sub: DE JONG	▶

Referee: Taylor (England)

Germans for a place in the World Cup final.

It was an exciting but incredibly nervy game for both sides, especially after the kick-off was delayed due to a waterlogged pitch. Poland's best chances came in the first half, with Robert Gadocha and the effervescent Lato forcing West Germany's goalkeeper Sepp Maier into a couple of excellent saves. In the second-half it was the turn of Maier's opposite number in the Polish goal, Jan Tomaszewski, to shine. He saved a penalty from Uli Hoeness but it was to prove in vain. West Germany snatched the winner 14 minutes from time when Hoeness's shot deflected into the path of Müller, who clinically buried it into the back of the net in typical fashion.

A 1-0 third place play-off victory over Brazil (the goal coming courtesy of Lato) was scant consolation for the Poles, who had surely been the tournament's biggest surprise package. The final was now to be contested between hosts West Germany, who had not won the tournament since 1954, and Holland, who hadn't even managed to qualify since 1938. Efficiency, organisation and hard work against versatility, vision and precocious talent.

SEMI-FINALS

Replaced by a second round group phase

THIRD PLACE PLAY-OFF

Poland 1-0 Brazil

TOP GOALSCORERS

7 goals: Gregorz Lato (Poland);
5 goals: Johan Neeskens (Holland), Andrzej Szarmach (Poland);
4 goals: Gerd Müller (Germany), Ralf Edström (Sweden), Johnny Rep (Holland)

FASTEST GOAL

80 seconds: Johan Neeskens (Holland v West Germany)

TOTAL GOALS

97

AVERAGE GOALS

2.55 per game

ARGENTINA 1978

SEMI-FINALS

Replaced by a second round group phase

THIRD PLACE PLAY-OFF

Brazil 2-1 Italy

TOP GOALSCORERS

6 goals: Mario Kempes (Argentina)

5 goals: Teófilo Cubillas (Peru), Rob Rensenbrink (Holland)

4 goals: Hans Krankl (Austria), Leopoldo Luque (Argentina)

FASTEST GOAL

31 seconds: Bernard Lacombe (France v Italy)

TOTAL GOALS

102

AVERAGE GOALS

2.68 per game:

When Daniel Passarella hoisted the World Cup aloft in Buenos Aires, it was one of the most romantic and tragic moments in football history. For Argentina, named as hosts back in 1966, just to have staged the event was an achievement given the political turmoil that had prompted several participants to talk of a boycott. To then win the trophy sent the nation ecstatic.

Yet for Holland, whose players endured the victory night celebrations cooped up in their hotel, defeat in the final for the second consecutive time was cruel beyond measure. The country that had illuminated Seventies football and had probably done more to create the modern game than any other, was destined to end the decade without a major honour.

The tournament itself, in the wake of the great Brazil team's performance of 1970 and the Beckenbauer/Cruyff head-to-head of 1974, was not a vintage. Mario Kempes emerged as

Argentina's hero but not to the extent that Diego Maradona would eight years later. While Argentina 78 lacked a true superstar or a great team, the extreme emotions it generated – not to mention the whiff of scandal – ensured its place in football folklore.

The threatened boycott in protest at General Videla's military regime never materialised and all 16 teams arrived, although Holland's enigmatic Cruyff stayed at home. Like 1974, there was no knockout stage. The top two teams in four groups would progress into a second group stage, with the winners going into the final.

Most of the football superpowers had qualified, with the exception of Euro 76 winners Czechoslovakia, the Soviet Union and, for the second consecutive finals, England. British interest centred on the Scottish, who assembled perhaps their greatest ever team, but their campaign degenerated into shambles and acrimony. Poor results, coupled with winger Willie Johnston failing a drugs test, ensured a shameful early exit for Scotland. Only then, when it was too late, did they show what they could do by beating Holland 3-2. Peru had proven they weren't the expected pushovers by topping the group, while doubts persisted whether second-placed Holland could mount a serious challenge without Johan Cruyff.

West Germany qualified in unimpressive style as runners-up to Poland in perhaps the weakest group. Brazil, under coach Claudio Coutinho, had gone from poetic to pragmatic. They too were far from convincing, managing only two goals in their first round group, but along with Austria they still squeezed through ahead of Spain and Sweden.

With so many big guns misfiring, the tournament appeared to be opening up. Italy, masters of the defensive approach that characterised football in this era, looked likely to prosper when they topped a group that also included Argentina, France and Hungary. Argentina's 2-1 defeat of France proved the decisive result for second place.

Despite their indifferent showings, all of the favourites had spluttered their way into a second round that fizzed with exciting match-ups. Group A featured European superpowers West Germany, Holland and Italy, plus a useful Austria side gorging itself on the goals of Hans Krankl. Group B included the less fancied Poles and Peru, plus arguably the fiercest rivals in world football – Argentina and Brazil.

When the two met in Rosario, the weight of history and the fear of defeat were too much for either side to bear and the match fizzled out into an ill-tempered goalless draw. With both sides having already recorded victories (Brazil had beaten Peru 3-0 and Argentina defeated Poland 2-0), providing both could win their last matches the finalist would be decided on goal difference. When Brazil overcame Poland 3-1, the balance of power appeared to have swung

Above: Scotland's Archie Gemmill scores his wonder goal against eventual finalists Holland. Opposite clockwise from top left: Daniel Passarella lifts the trophy; the ticker tape welcome as Argentina took to the pitch; top scorer Mario Kempes; Rob Rensenbrink of Holland in action.

their way but owing to some unfair scheduling, Argentina did not kick-off their final game against Peru in Rosario until 45 minutes after Brazil's game had finished. César Luis Menotti's side had the massive advantage of knowing they had to win by four clear goals to reach the final.

Peru, who had looked so accomplished early in the tournament, at first looked prepared for the challenge, even hitting the post. Then, in one of the most talked about matches in World Cup history, they rolled over and lost 6-0. Rumours had already circulated about some controversial decisions in Argentina's favour against France in the first round, and it was soon alleged that the match with Peru had been fixed by the country's ruling military junta. But when the dust settled, Argentina – 48 years after they had lost the first World Cup to Uruguay – had booked a ticket to the final of their own fiesta.

In the other group, Holland exploded into life with a 5-1 destruction of Austria to take an early stranglehold on the group, while Italy and West Germany drew 0-0. Holland strengthened their hand when, in a repeat of the 1974 final, goals from Haan and Rene Van De Kerkhof earned them a useful 2-2 draw with West Germany.

With Italy beating Austria 1-0, the Dutch knew that unless the West Germans could manage a landslide against Austria, a draw with Italy would be sufficient. West Germany, a shadow of their 1974 side, were put out of their misery when they lost 3-2 to the already-eliminated Austrians. Holland did all that was required and more by beating Italy 2-1.

In the third-place play-off, Brazil overcame Enzo Bearzot's Italy 2-1 to maintain the only unbeaten record of the tournament, but in some ways the victory only upset Brazilians even more. For the first time in the competition they had shed their inhibitions and played in the great Brazilian tradition, leaving many to wonder why they left it so late.

THE FINAL

ARGENTINA (1) 3-1 (1) HOLLAND
(aet; 1-1 at 90 mins)

Date Sunday June 25, 1978 **Attendance** 71,483

Venue River Plate Stadium, Buenos Aires

Argentina attempted to unnerve the Dutch by keeping them on the pitch for five minutes before their arrival to a sea of sky blue and white ticker tape. They then objected to a cast on Rene Van De Kerkhof's arm. When play began, high skill mingled with barely restrained violence. Rep wasted a great chance for Holland before Kempes put Argentina ahead on 37 minutes. The Dutch were growing feverish with frustration when, in the 81st minute, substitute Nanninga headed the ball into the net. Then with a minute to go, Rensenbrink struck the foot of the post.

Kempes, the tournament's top scorer, scrambled the hosts back into the lead a minute before the first period of extra-time ended and, with four minutes to go, Bertoni made the game safe.

HOW THE TEAMS LINED UP

ARGENTINA	
FILLOL	
OLGUIN	
GALVAN	
PASSARELLA	
TARANTINI	
ARDILES	
Booked: 40 mins. Subbed: 66 mins (Larossa)	
GALLEGO	
ORTIZ	
Subbed: 75 mins (Houseman)	
BERTONI	
Goal: 115 mins	
LUQUE	
KEMPES	
Goal: 37, 105 mins	
sub: LAROSSA	
Booked: 94 mins	
sub: HOUSEMAN	

HOLLAND	
JONGBLOED	
POORTVLIET	
Booked: 96 mins	
KROL	
Booked: 15 mins	
BRANDTS	
JANSEN	
Subbed: 73 mins (Suurbier)	
NEESKENS	
HAAN	
VAN DE KERKHOF, W	
VAN DE KERKHOF, R	
REP	
Subbed: 59 mins (Nanninga)	
RENSENBRINK	
sub: NANNINGA	
Goal: 82 mins	
sub: SUURBIER	
Booked: 94 mins	

Referee: Gonella (Italy)

ARGENTINA

COACH:
CÉSAR LUIS MENOTTI

Fillol

Olguin Galvan Passarella Tarantini

Ardiles Gallego Kempes

Bertoni Luque Ortiz

HOLLAND

COACH:
ERNST HAPPEL

Rensenbrink Rep v d Kerkhof, R

v d Kerkhof, W Neeskens Haan Jansen

Poortvliet Krol Brandts

Jongbloed

SPAIN 1982

There was a real sense of trepidation as the World Cup was awarded to Spain for the 1982 finals. Many doubted the country's ability to host such a global spectacular and those fears were heightened as the draw descended into chaos. To begin with the balls representing Peru and Chile were accidentally left in the draw when it was FIFA policy to keep them out initially in order to ensure the teams were kept apart from their more illustrious neighbours, Argentina and Brazil.

Scotland, meanwhile, found themselves mistakenly in Argentina's group instead of Belgium, before being moved into the correct grouping with Brazil. The confusion led to a halt in proceedings. Then to compound the situation, the cage containing the balls jammed and one split in half.

The critics were given further ammunition with the tournament's expansion to 24 teams. There was a fear that games would descend into a procession as the likes of Kuwait, Honduras and El Salvador took to the stage, while conversely there was every indication that such teams would stifle the opposition and defend for their lives. Thankfully, the inspirational opening ceremony and Belgium's subsequent 1-0 victory against champions Argentina allayed the fears and set the tone for a tournament that would promote the World Cup as a truly global affair.

Brazil were clear favourites. The flair and breathtaking skill – so absent four years earlier – had returned, while in Zico, Socrates, Falcão and Junior, they had a prowess that few could compete with. Their 4-1 victory against Scotland – in which David Narey had the audacity to score first – and a 4-0 win over New Zealand indicated their intention.

Their rivals did not have it so easy. Italy made a less than auspicious start, drawing against Poland and Peru, and their progress to the next round was only confirmed in a winner-takes-all game against Cameroon. A Graziani header ensured another draw but although he had secured safe passage on goal difference, Italy were being ridiculed back home.

West Germany, another thoroughbred, lost their opener to Algeria, then contributed to one of the most distasteful moments in World Cup history. Having scored against neighbours Austria, and knowing a 1-0 score would ensure the progress of both sides, the second-half descended into farce at the expense of Algeria, whose complaint to FIFA fell on deaf ears.

Spain were also left sweating on their progress to the next round, as a goal from Northern Ireland's Gerry Armstrong stunned the home support. However, the 1-0 result ensured both teams qualified, with Billy Bingham's side heading the group. The Irish also created history when their winger, Norman

Above: England captain Bryan Robson celebrates scoring the tournament's quickest goal. Opposite clockwise from top left: Argentina captain Daniel Passarella; Norman Whiteside on the ball for Northern Ireland; the victorious Argentina squad with the World Cup; Poland's Lato shoots against France in the third place play-off.

Whiteside, became the youngest player to appear in the finals, aged 17 years and 41 days.

Europe's other leading lights, France and England, were left to battle it out in Group 4. Aggrieved at England's seeding, the French were left to lick their wounds as Ron Greenwood's side put them to the sword with a 3-1 victory, kicked-off by a Bryan Robson goal in 27 seconds. Further wins against Czechoslovakia and Kuwait served to enhance England's reputation, while the French limped through, helped by a 4-1 defeat of Kuwait. It was a game remembered for coach Hidalgo's clash with police after a goal was disallowed because the Kuwaitis claimed they had stopped on hearing a whistle from the crowd.

With the second phase split into four groups of three, and with only the top side guaranteed a semi-final place, victory was imperative in the opening game, certainly in Group C, which contained Brazil, Argentina and Italy. The latter's flaccid displays had them installed as elimination fodder, yet goals from Tardelli and Cabrini ensured a 2-1 win against Argentina. With Brazil defeating their South American counterparts – a game that saw Maradona red-carded – the game between Brazil and Italy was billed as the clash of the tournament. The pendulum swung back and forth, yet it was the superlative finishing of Paolo Rossi that ensured Italy's 3-2 victory. His hat-trick, completed 15 minutes from time, created a hero and revitalised a nation.

England's progress, meanwhile, was halted by a lack of firepower. A sterile 0-0 draw against West Germany meant they had to beat Spain by two goals, but with the creativity of Kevin Keegan and Trevor Brooking still absent through injury, another 0-0 prevailed. Both players were desperately plunged into action with 27 minutes remaining but a clearly unfit Keegan fluffed a simple header that could have provided the impetus so desperately needed.

France and Poland made up the quartet, but it was Italy who had the easiest route to the

final against the Poles, who would sorely miss goalscorer Boniek. Rossi further enhanced his credentials with a goal in either half, and although the 2-0 win raised few eyebrows, the other semi was a classic.

With Platini in sparkling form for France, the game against West Germany finished 1-1 after 90 minutes. Further goals from Giresse and Tresor had the French dreaming of the final, yet Germany refused to quit. Coach Jupp Derwall gambled by introducing half-fit captain Rummenigge and after he pulled a goal back in the 106th minute, Fischer then equalised with an overhead kick. The resulting penalty shoot-out went to sudden death and Hrubesch saw the Germans home. The hero was keeper Schumacher, yet he should not have been on the pitch following an appalling challenge on Battiston, which had left the Frenchman unconscious for three minutes. The incident had won the Germans few admirers and with Italy on an upward spiral, there would be one winner and one hero...

THE FINAL

ITALY (0) **3-1** (0) **WEST GERMANY**

Date Sunday July 11, 1982 **Attendance** 77,260
Venue Santiago Bernabéu, Madrid

Italy were favourites to win their third World Cup but with midfielder Antognoni ruled out, their anxieties were heightened further when Graziani left the field with an injured shoulder inside the first ten minutes. Things then got even worse when Cabrini became the first player to miss a penalty in a World Cup final. Yet despite the setbacks Italy shaded a first-half dominated by fouls. The game finally came to life after 57 minutes when Paolo Rossi rose highest to connect with Gentile's pin-point cross.

Victory was secured 11 minutes later when Tardelli hit a superb left-footed shot from the edge of the area, and by the time Altobelli hammered home a Conti cross, the game had become a procession. Paul Breitner scored a late consolation but the Germans were left to pay a heavy price for their epic semi-final. Italy claimed their third crown and toasted Rossi, who had become an overnight sensation.

HOW THE TEAMS LINED UP

ITALY

ITALY	
ZOFF	
GENTILE	
SCIREA	
COLLOVATI	
BERGOMI	
CABRINI	
Missed pen: 25 mins	
ORIALI	
Booked: 73 mins	
TARDELLI	⚽
Goal: 69 mins	
CONTI	
Booked: 31 mins	
GRAZIANI	▶
Subbed: 8 mins (Altobelli)	
ROSSI	⚽
Goal: 57 mins	
sub: ALTOBELLI	⚽▶▶
Goal: 81 mins. Subbed: 88 mins (Causio)	
sub: CAUSIO	▶

WEST GERMANY	
SCHUMACHER	
KALTZ	
STIELIKE	
Booked: 73 mins	
FÖRSTER, K-H	
FÖRSTER, B	
LITTBARSKI	
Booked: 88 mins	
DREMMLER	▶
Booked: 61 mins. Subbed 63 mins (Hrubesch)	
BREITNER	⚽
Goal: 83 mins	
BRIEGEL	
FISCHER	
RUMMENIGGE	▶
Subbed: 70 mins (Muller H)	
sub: HRUBESCH	▶
sub: MULLER, H	▶

Referee: Coelho (Mexico)

ITALY
COACH:
ENZO BEARZOT

Zoff
Collovati   Scirea   Gentile   Cabrini
Oriali   Bergomi   Tardelli
Conti   Rossi   Graziani

WEST GERMANY
COACH:
JUPP DERWALL

Fischer   Rummenigge
Littbarski
Dremmler   Briegel   Breitner
Förster, B   Förster, K-H   Stielike   Kaltz
Schumacher

MEXICO 1986

SEMI-FINALS
Argentina 2-0 Belgium
West Germany 2-0 France

THIRD PLACE PLAY-OFF
France 4-2 Belgium
(aet: 2-2 at 90 mins)

TOP GOALSCORERS
6 goals: Gary Lineker (England)
5 goals: Emilio Butragueño
(Spain), Careca (Brazil), Diego
Maradona (Argentina)

FASTEST GOAL
63 seconds: Emilio Butragueño
(Spain v Northern Ireland)

TOTAL GOALS
132

AVERAGE GOALS
2.54 per game

When Colombia decided they no longer had the financial muscle to host the 1986 World Cup, Mexico stepped into the breach to become FIFA's saviour in what proved to be another troubled episode for the game's governing body. The Mexicans may have hosted an exemplary tournament in 1970, but with their own financial crisis and Mexican unemployment at record levels, the decision looked dubious given the stability provided by the rival USA bid.

When it was revealed that the tournament would be staged by Mexican television network Televisa, whose president was a friend of FIFA president João Havelange, it drew outrage from the Americans. A strained relationship ensued – bombs were even found outside the US Embassy – and to compound the problems, some 25,000 people were killed in a huge earthquake prior to the tournament.

Mexico simply had to deliver, yet little did they realise that a pint-sized genius from Argentina would play the trump card. Diego Maradona delighted fans everywhere while exorcising the ghosts of Spain 82, when a lunge on Brazilian defender Batista had ended his participation in the second round.

With a world record transfer fee of £6.9 million hanging over him, Maradona was a marked man and the succession of fouls inflicted by South Korea gave an indication of the fear he instilled. Yet he destroyed his opponents, setting up goals for Valdano and Ruggeri in a 3-1 Group A victory. A truer test came against champions Italy. No team knew the diminutive star better, yet he shone in a game of intrigue. In the 34th minute he eluded Napoli club team-mate Bagni, his low centre of gravity enabling him to score from an acute angle. The goal cancelled out Altobelli's penalty but both teams progressed.

Yet if Maradona created headlines for his on-field exploits, the enthusiasm of the home crowd proved unprecedented: 110,000 filled the Azteca for Mexico's opening win against Belgium and the 'Mexican Wave' phenomenon was born. Hero of the hour was Hugo Sanchez, whose feats were rivalling those of Maradona. Having scored in the win over Belgium, he was equally impressive against Paraguay and the consensus grew that the hosts could go far.

With the high altitude, European nations were given little chance. France were deemed a threat with Platini, Battiston and Bossis providing experience and guile, but a 1-0 win against Canada was less than convincing, while a 1-1 draw with an impressive Soviet Union side left the European champions sweating on their progress. However, their eventual qualification had more to do with the ineptitude of Canada and Hungary than their own creativity.

England also made heavy work of ensuring qualification as a 1-0 defeat against Portugal was followed by a sorry draw with Morocco. The 0-0 scoreline created a furore at home, and with captain Bryan Robson dislocating his shoulder and fellow midfielder Ray Wilkins being sent-off, victory against Poland was imperative. A Gary Lineker hat-trick saved the team as a 3-0 win kept manager Bobby Robson in a job and England in the competition.

Denmark appeared the European side best equipped to succeed in the tournament. An opening 1-0 win against Scotland was just an aperitif for the Michael Laudrup-inspired 6-1 demolition of Uruguay and a shock 2-0 victory over West Germany.

The second phase reverted to a knockout format for the first time since 1970. Brazil were looking a threat, having cruised through their opening group against Spain, Algeria and Northern Ireland. In the second round their 4-0 demolition of Poland saw a return to the flamboyance of old and Edinho's goal had the 45,000 Guadalajara crowd mesmerised.

Above: Golden Boot winner, England's Gary Lineker.
Opposite clockwise from top left: Argentina's Jorge Valdano fends off West Germany's Ditmar Jakobs; Diego Maradona celebrates victory against England; Bryan Robson about to dislocate his shoulder against Morocco; Uruguay's Jose Batista is sent-off against Scotland.

The expected nations progressed, with the exception of Denmark and Italy. The Danes had peaked and their emphatic 5-1 defeat at the hands of Spain is best remembered for Emilio Butragueño's four goals. The Italians, meanwhile, succumbed to a much-improved French team. Platini confirmed his class with a casual chip over Galli to set up a 2-0 win.

The French, playing as potential champions, would have to overcome Brazil in the quarter-finals if they had realistic ambitions, and with so much riding on the outcome, a game of cat and mouse ensued. Substitute Zico missed a crucial late penalty and the match was decided by a penalty shoot-out, France winning 4-3 thanks to Fernández's decider.

Shoot-outs decided three of the quarter-final ties, with West Germany edging past Mexico and Belgium overcoming Spain. The process of elimination led to calls for sudden death football. Yet if this was knee-jerk anger on the part of the losers, their pain was nothing compared to that felt by England following their exit at the hands of Argentina.

With the scores level at 0-0, a harmless backpass from Hodge was lobbed towards keeper Shilton, only for Maradona to seemingly head home. It appeared that the altitude had helped his elevation but replays proved he had punched the ball. 'A little of the hand of god and a little of the head of Maradona,' was how he would refer to it but his first goal only served to inspire his second, a fantastic solo effort six minutes later that put the game beyond doubt. Lineker's sixth goal of the tournament gave England hope, but the 'hand of God' goal would be the source of dispute between the two countries for many years.

A virtuoso semi-final performance against Belgium, which included two breathtaking second-half goals, restored faith in Maradona, and although West Germany eased past France 2-0, there was little stopping the Argentine. His hands were already on the cup.

THE FINAL

ARGENTINA (1) **3-2** (0) WEST GERMANY

Date Sunday June 29, 1986 **Attendance** 114,600
Venue Azteca Stadium, Mexico City

Argentina proved they were no one-man team as their superior skill and creativity came to the fore against the West Germans. With Burruchaga matching Maradona's performance, a 2-0 lead was established through Brown and Valdano. The Germans, who had so successfully stifled their opposition en route to the final, had no answer this time and Argentina were already dreaming of another ticker tape celebration back home.

Yet, even when trailing 2-0 the Germans could not be written off. As the game limped towards its conclusion, they finally showed the inventiveness that had been so absent. Two headers inside six minutes, from Rummenigge and Völler, brought the tie level with just ten minutes to play. But Maradona's inch-perfect pass found Burruchaga who beat the offside trap to power the ball past Schumacher, winning the World Cup for Argentina.

ARGENTINA

PUMPIDO	
Booked: 85 mins	
BROWN	⚽
Goal: 23 mins	
CUCIUFFO	
RUGGERI	
OLARTICOECHEA	
Booked: 77 mins	
GIUSTI	
BATISTA	
BURRUCHAGA	⚽ ▶
Goal: 83 mins. Subbed: 90 mins (Trobbiani)	
ENRIQUE	
Booked: 81 mins	
MARADONA	
Booked: 17 mins	
VALDANO	⚽
Goal: 56 mins	
sub: TROBBIANI	▶

WEST GERMANY

SCHUMACHER	
JAKOBS	
BERTHOLD	
FÖRSTER, K-H	
BRIEGEL	
Booked: 62 mins	
MATTHÄUS	
Booked: 21 mins	
BREHME	
MAGATH	▶
Subbed: 63 mins (Hoeness, D)	
EDER	
RUMMENIGGE	⚽
Goal: 74 mins	
ALLOFS	▶
Subbed: 46 mins (Völler)	
sub: HOENESS, D	▶
sub: VÖLLER	⚽ ▶
Goal: 80 mins	

Referee: Arppi Filho (Brazil)

HOW THE TEAMS LINED UP

ARGENTINA
COACH:
CARLOS BILARDO

Pumpido
Cuciuffo Brown Ruggeri
Giusti Batista Burruchaga Enrique Olarticoechea
Valdano Maradona

WEST GERMANY
COACH:
FRANZ BECKENBAUER

Allofs Rummenigge
Briegel Eder Magath Matthäus Berthold
Forster, K-H Jakobs Brehme
Schumacher

ITALY 1990

Italia 90 was the tournament where FIFA stepped up its campaign to turn the World Cup into a global marketing phenomenon, and no country was more suited to put on such a high profile football circus than Italy. As hosts for the second time, the Italians embarked on a major overhaul of ten stadiums and built two more in Turin and Bari in anticipation of the biggest tournament ever.

Sadly, the quality of play failed to live up to the vast hype and the carefully negotiated corporate endorsements. The competition was characterised by negativity, foul play and penalties, and the statistics only underline its sorry reputation: a mere 115 goals were scored at a ratio of 2.21 per game, yet there were a record 16 dismissals and 164 bookings.

The format remained the same as four years previous: 24 teams competed in six groups of four, with the top two teams and the four best third placed teams progressing through to a knockout second round, then quarter-finals, semi-finals and the final. Some strong teams were notably absent, including the 1986 semi-finalists France, coached by Michel Platini, and rising stars Denmark, but the Republic Of Ireland qualified for the first time.

Mexico were suspended for breaches of FIFA rules when fielding an ineligible player in a youth tournament, while Chile had failed to qualify after their goalkeeper Rojas attempted to fake an injury from a firecracker in a World Cup qualifier against Brazil. The match was abandoned and awarded to the Brazilians, while Chile were banned from entering the 1994 qualifying tournament.

Inevitably the hosts, under coach Azeglio Vicini, were hot favourites and their smooth progress only emphasised the feeling that their name was on the cup. They won all of their group games, against Austria, United States and Czechoslovakia, playing solid, attacking football without conceding a goal. The nation also discovered a new star in the shape of Palermo-born Salvatore 'Toto' Schillaci, a diminutive Juventus striker who rose from the substitute's bench to win the Golden Boot with six goals.

Italy also had Walter Zenga, who kept a clean sheet for a record 517 minutes, aided by a watertight defence superbly marshalled by Franco Baresi, but the Azzurri dream died against Argentina at the semi-final stage – not for the last time in a penalty shoot-out. Maradona had already attempted to divide the north and south of the country by appealing to Napoli fans to support his side. The hosts finished the tournament unbeaten but still had to settle for third place while the nation mourned.

Of the other possible contenders, both Brazil and Holland went out tamely in the second round. European champions the Dutch, featuring Ruud Gullit, Frank Rijkaard and Marco

Above: Roger Milla was one of the surprise stars of Italia 90. Opposite clockwise from top left: Jurgen Klinsmann and Guido Buchwald enjoy success against Holland; top-scorer Toto Schillaci; Maradona prays for Argentina; Paul Gascoigne in tears after England's semi-final exit.

Van Basten, were the biggest disappointments. Their encounter with old enemy West Germany is best remembered for Frank Rijkaard's rather too literal spat with Rudi Völler. Brazil topped a weak group featuring Sweden, Scotland and Costa Rica but lacked the firepower to finish off Argentina when they had the chance.

For a while it seemed Cameroon might make history by winning the World Cup. Despite being reduced to nine men, the 'Indomitable Lions' beat holders Argentina in a memorable tournament opener and they became the first African nation to reach the quarter-finals when they beat Colombia after extra-time.

Mixing some vibrant skills with a fairly strong physical presence, Cameroon's unquenchable spirit was embodied by Roger Milla, a goal-scoring talisman who danced around the corner flag after each of his four strikes as a substitute. Milla was then 38 years old and playing for JS Saint-Pierroise, a local team from Reunion Island, but he was persuaded to join the squad by the country's president. However, it was Cameroon's recklessness in the tackle that eventually proved their undoing when they allowed England to pull level and win their quarter-final in extra-time through two penalties.

The English had travelled to the World Cup more in hope than expectation, having just scraped through qualification as second best of the second-placed teams in the European groups. Bobby Robson's tenure as national coach had already involved the disastrous European Championship two years earlier and he was vilified by the British tabloid press for his team selections and tactics. However, in Gary Lineker England had a proven goalscorer, there was real creativity in a midfield that featured Chris Waddle and Paul Gascoigne, and in Peter Shilton they had a keeper who had not conceded

a goal in 540 minutes during qualification. But they made hard work of their group, progressing via two draws and a win, before stumbling past Belgium thanks to David Platt's memorable last minute volley. Their quarter-final defeat of Cameroon was a tense affair, with two penalties from Lineker seeing them into the semi-final.

England's finest performance was in a pulsating encounter with West Germany that remains one of the great World Cup semi-finals, but their failure in the subsequent penalty shoot-out was to leave some deep psychological scars and inspire at least one successful stage play.

Coached by Franz Beckenbauer, the West Germans were strong in all departments and had Lothar Matthäus and Jürgen Klinsmann both at the peak of their powers. However, for all their strengths, they did nothing to help Italia 90 finish on a high. Instead, the tournament got what it deserved in the final: stale, cynical football punctuated by fouls, histrionic diving and petulance. When a penalty against Argentina settled the final in West Germany's favour five minutes before time, the only sensation was relief that another 30 minutes would not have to be endured.

THE FINAL

WEST GERMANY (0) 1-0 (0) ARGENTINA

Date Sunday July 8, 1990 **Attendance** 73,603
Venue Olympic Stadium, Rome

Ranking as the worst final in World Cup history, the game was characterised by negativity and poor sportsmanship. Argentina arrived with a record of a foul every four minutes and were shorn of four players through suspension, but both teams were guilty of deeply cynical play.

West Germany held the upper hand for much of the game but the contest degenerated as Monzon became the first player to be sent-off in a World Cup final, following a wild lunge at Jurgen Klinsmann. It was no surprise when the match was settled by a spot-kick after a foul by Sensini on Völler. Argentina lost control and two minutes later Dezotti was also sent-off.

Maradona conducted his side's protests and the enduring image is not Matthäus holding aloft the cup but the Argentinian's tear-stained face.

HOW THE TEAMS LINED UP

WEST GERMANY
COACH:
FRANZ BECKENBAUER

Illgner
Berthold Kohler Buchwald Brehme
Augenthaler
Hässler Matthäus Littbarski
Völler Klinsmann

ARGENTINA
COACH:
CARLOS BILARDO

Dezotti Maradona
Lorenzo Troglio Burruchaga Basualdo Sensini
Serrizuela Simón Ruggeri
Goycoechea

WEST GERMANY

ILLGNER	
AUGENTHALER	
BERTHOLD	▶
Subbed: 75 mins (Reuter)	
KOHLER	
BUCHWALD	
BREHME	⚽
Goal: 85 mins (pen)	
HÄSSLER	
MATTHÄUS	
LITTBARSKI	
KLINSMANN	
VÖLLER	▯
Booked: 52 mins	
sub: REUTER	▶

ARGENTINA

GOYCOECHEA	
SIMÓN	
SERRIZUELA	
RUGGERI	▶
Subbed: 46 mins (Monzon)	
TROGLIO	
Booked: 84 mins	
SENSINI	
BURRUCHAGA	▶
Subbed: 54 mins (Calderon)	
BASUALDO	
LORENZO	
DEZOTTI	◼
Sent-off: 65 mins	
MARADONA	▯
Booked: 87 mins	
sub: MONZON	◼ ▶
Sent-off: 87 mins	
sub: CALDERON	▶

Referee: Codesal (Mexico)

SEMI-FINALS

Argentina 1-1 Italy
(aet: Argentina won 4-3 on penalties)
West Germany 1-1 England
(aet: West Germany won 4-3 on penalties)

THIRD PLACE PLAY-OFF

Italy 2-1 England

TOP GOALSCORERS

6 goals: Salvatore Schillaci (Italy)
5 goals: Tomás Skuhravy (Czechoslovakia)
4 goals: Míchel (Spain), Roger Milla (Cameroon), Gary Lineker (England), Lothar Matthäus (Germany)

FASTEST GOAL

4 minutes: Safet Susic (Yugoslavia v United Arab Emirates)

TOTAL GOALS

115

AVERAGE GOALS

2.21 per game

USA 1994

In light of their earlier snub in 1986, there was an air of inevitability when the USA were awarded the 1994 tournament. With rivals Morocco and Brazil unable to match the superior infrastructure, a lack of tradition was no barrier as FIFA used the competition to breach their final frontier.

There were concerns that the World Cup would fail to capture the public imagination in America and the excruciating opening ceremony penalty miss by singer Diana Ross cemented the apprehension. Yet the tournament would prove successful. Three points for a victory ended those lifeless group games, while the introduction of motorised carts for 'injured' players saw feigning decrease. Stadiums were full and only the actions of one player blighted the festival.

Diego Maradona came to America looking to play his third final and, on form, there was every chance the dream could become reality. However, after testing positive for five variants of the stimulant ephedrine, his aspirations and his career were at an end.

SEMI-FINALS
Brazil 1-0 Sweden
Italy 2-1 Bulgaria

THIRD PLACE PLAY-OFF
Sweden 4-0 Bulgaria

TOP GOALSCORERS
6 goals: Oleg Salenko (Russia), Hristo Stoichkov (Bulgaria)
5 goals: Kennet Andersson (Sweden), Roberto Baggio (Italy), Jürgen Klinsmann (Germany), Romario (Brazil)

FASTEST GOAL
2 minutes: Gabriel Batistuta (Argentina v Greece)

TOTAL GOALS
141

AVERAGE GOALS
2.71 per game:

THE FINAL

BRAZIL (0) 0-0 (0) ITALY
(aet: Brazil won 3-2 on penalties)

Date Sunday July 17, 1994 **Attendance** 94,194
Venue Pasadena Rose Bowl, Los Angeles

Although much was expected of the final, it was a disappointing display of defensive football, with Baresi at the heart of Italy's backline just three weeks after cartilage surgery. Normal time saw just one clear opportunity, when Pagliuca pushed Silva's effort on to a post, while Bebeto and Baggio spurned chances in extra-time.

The game went to penalties and Baresi's opening miss set the trend for the drama to follow. Santos missed for Brazil but after successful spot-kicks from Albertini and Evani for Italy and Romario and Branco for Brazil, the scores were level. Massaro saw his effort stopped by Taffarel, before Dunga converted for Brazil. This left Baggio needing to score but he shot over before bowing his head in despair.

HOW THE TEAMS LINED UP

BRAZIL
COACH:
CARLOS PARREIRA

Taffarel
Jorginho Aldair Marcio Santos Branco
Mazinho Mauro Silva Dunga Zinho
Bebeto Romario

ITALY
COACH:
ARRIGO SACCHI

Massaro Baggio, R
Donadoni Baggio, D Berti
Benarrivo Maldini Baresi Mussi
Pagliuca

BRAZIL	
TAFFAREL	
JORGINHO	▶
Subbed: 22 mins (Cafu)	
ALDAIR	
MARCIO SANTOS	
BRANCO	
MAZINHO	▯
Booked: 4 mins	
MAURO SILVA	
DUNGA	
ZINHO	▶
Subbed: 106 mins (Viola)	
BEBETO	
ROMARIO	
sub: **CAFU**	▯▶
Booked: 87 mins	
sub: **VIOLA**	▶

ITALY	
PAGLIUCA	
MUSSI	▶
Subbed: 34 mins (Apolloni)	
BARESI	
MALDINI	
BENARRIVO	
BERTI	
BAGGIO, D	▶
Subbed: 95 mins (Evani)	
ALBERTINI	▯
Booked: 42 mins	
DONADONI	
BAGGIO, R	
sub: **APOLLONI**	▯▶
Booked: 41 mins	
sub: **EVANI**	▶

Referee: Puhl (Hungary)

Above: Ray Houghton celebrates his strike against Italy. **Opposite clockwise from top left:** Brazil show off their spoils; Baggio and Taffarel experience differing emotions after the decisive penalty; Sweden salute their fans after semi-final defeat; Stoichkov's Bulgaria beat Germany.

The tournament began with Germany taking on Bolivia and a solitary goal from Jürgen Klinsmann spared his team from embarrassment, although it was overshadowed by the red carding of Bolivia's Marco Etcheverry four minutes after coming on as sub.

The early dismissal of defender Miguel Angel Nadal could have proved costly for Spain in the same group, as having taken a 2-0 lead against South Korea, the Spaniards conceded two late goals. With their match against Germany ending in stalemate, both superpowers teetered on the brink. However, Caminero hit a brace as Spain beat Bolivia and Klinsmann took his tally to four in a 3-2 win against the Koreans.

Group A proved equally fascinating. Having defeated Argentina 5-0 away in qualifying, Colombia were tipped to go far. Yet internal bickering and poor preparation caused their downfall, as a 3-1 defeat against Romania and a subsequent loss to the hosts sealed their fate. The USA result had tragic consequences for Colombia as Andrés Escobar, blamed for the defeat after scoring an own-goal, was murdered shortly after his return home.

Despite their tepid qualification form Brazil opened with a 2-0 victory against Russia, while Romario and Bebeto proved the catalysts in a 3-0 defeat of Cameroon. The Africans had arrived with high expectations following their exploits in 1990, yet they returned home after a 6-1 mauling by Russia, with Salenko scoring a record five goals. Sweden also booked their place in the next round with Brolin and Dahlin's Euro 92 momentum carrying them forward.

Prior to Maradona's positive drugs test, Argentina had the look of champions. A 4-0 defeat of Greece signalled Gabriel Batistuta's arrival with three goals and it was followed by victory over Nigeria. The Africans had their own hero in Yekini, who scored his country's first World Cup goal against Bulgaria. With Stoichkov scoring twice for Bulgaria against Greece, and Nigeria also beating them, Argentina limped into the second round in third place.

Led by Roberto Baggio's guile, Italy were the favourites in Group E. Yet after conceding Ray Houghton's solitary strike for the Republic Of Ireland, it meant that victory against Norway was imperative. The sending-off of keeper Pagliuca and injury to Baresi further troubled the Azzurri, yet Dino Baggio's goal ensured progress.

Bickering threatened Holland's chances in Group F. A spat between Ruud Gullit and coach Dick Advocaat led to the 32-year-old's omission, and a less than convincing 2-1 win against Saudi Arabia confirmed their troubles. The Saudis became the surprise package, beating Morocco 2-1 before Saeed Owairan, 'The Maradona Of The Arabs', ran 60 yards through the Belgian rearguard to secure victory and qualification.

The Germans continued their ominous march as Rudi Völler inspired a 3-2 second round win over Belgium, while Spain's emphatic defeat of Switzerland was closer than the 3-0 scoreline suggests. Two goals from Kennet Andersson enhanced his reputation as Sweden edged Saudi Arabia 3-1, while the tie of the round saw Argentina paired with Romania. Ariel Ortega did his best to fill Maradona's void, but it was Romanian playmaker, Gheorghe Hagi, who ran the midfield in a 3-2 victory. Argentina had ultimately been let down by their favourite son.

The heat of Orlando cost the Irish dearly and errors by Phelan and Bonner sealed their fate against Holland, while the USA's progress ended against Brazil, who had Leonardo sent-off for elbowing midfielder Tab Ramos so hard that he was later diagnosed with a fractured skull. Italy were rocked by Zola's red card against Nigeria but Roberto Baggio was the undisputed hero, with a last-minute equaliser against Nigeria and a subsequent extra-time penalty.

The final second round clash between Bulgaria and Mexico was delayed when a goalpost collapsed, but the Mexicans similarly collapsed when Aspe, Benal and Rodriguez missed kicks in the deciding penalty shoot-out.

Seven European sides from eight made the quarter-finals, with Italy in the ascendancy. Dino and Roberto Baggio's goals edged a thriller against Spain, while Brazil and Holland dished up a similarly scintillating show. Romario's drive and Bebeto's cool finish appeared to have won the game but Bergkamp and Winter replied to set up a grandstand finish, which Brazil won thanks to a free-kick from Branco. Bulgaria provided the biggest shock, beating Germany 2-1 with Stoichkov's free-kick and a text-book header by Letchkov, the tournament's star midfielder.

Sweden's quarter-final tussle with Romania went into extra-time. Stefan Schwarz's sending-off at 1-2 made progression for the Scandinavians unlikely but Andersson's goal took the game to penalties, where Ravelli saved from Belodedici to win the game for Sweden. Ravelli was once again inspired in the semi-final but Brazil beat them by a single Romario goal to reach the final. The Italians, meanwhile, had two goals from Baggio to thank for their own defeat of Bulgaria.

FRANCE 1998

After the sterile final of 1994, and a competition that failed to grip the imagination, France 98 came like a breath of fresh air, providing excitement, passion, drama and controversy. While it was the world's best footballer, Ronaldo, who would inflame the passions of the conspiracy theorists in the final, there was plenty of classic football action throughout the tournament.

The competition featured 32 teams, more than ever before, and that meant not only more games but more sides from Africa, Asia and other emerging regions. Four nations made a World Cup debut at the finals: Japan, Jamaica, South Africa and Croatia. There was also the introduction of the 'golden goal': if a game went into extra-time, the first goal scored would conclude the match immediately.

The hosts came into the tournament under pressure. They had failed to qualify for USA 94 and many claimed they had no strikers, but driven on by Zinédine Zidane and his fabulous midfield, goals did not seem a problem in their group as they dispatched South Africa 3-0, Saudi Arabia 4-0, and Denmark 2-1.

Scotland kept up another tradition by giving the good teams a run for their money and flopping against the lesser lights. A narrow defeat to Brazil in the opening match (2-1, with the winner coming from an own-goal by Tommy Boyd) was followed up by a 1-1 draw with Norway and a 3-0 defeat to Morocco. England fared better, stumbling through the group stage with a 2-0 victory over Tunisia, defeat to Romania after Dan Petrescu's last-minute goal, and a 2-0 win against Colombia.

In the other groups the major football nations emerged relatively unscathed, with one major exception. Always a favourite 'outsider' for any title given the exceptional talent within their domestic league, Spain again promised much but delivered very little. They lost a thriller with Nigeria 3-2, drew 0-0 with Paraguay, and despite a desperate effort in their last match, when they beat Bulgaria 6-1, the Spanish were out.

In the second phase, Brazil and Denmark were impressive, Italy and Croatia both crept through 1-0, Germany edged Mexico, the Dutch battled their way past Yugoslavia, and France's Laurent Blanc scored the World Cup's first ever 'golden goal' to pip Paraguay.

The match of the round brought together two old foes: England and Argentina. The first-half was simply brilliant, Gabriel Batistuta giving the South Americans an early lead through a penalty before Alan Shearer converted a spot-kick for England. Then came one of those moments that build a reputation, as 18-year-old striker Michael Owen controlled a long pass, raced towards the Argentine goal leaving defenders floundering, and beat Carlos

Roa with an unstoppable shot. England stayed ahead until just before the interval, when a clever free-kick routine saw Zanetti equalise.

The second-half saw drama of a different kind, and another of those defining moments. Within minutes of the restart, Diego Simeone brought down David Beckham. While on the ground, the Englishman kicked Simeone on the leg – hardly vicious, but certainly foolish – and the Argentinian went down, perhaps a little too easily. Beckham was sent-off and England had to play the rest of the second-half, and 30 minutes of extra-time, with ten men.

England held their own, even having an effort from Sol Campbell disallowed and a penalty appeal refused. In the deciding penalty shoot-out David Batty saw Roa save his spot-kick and England's dream was over, with the fans blaming Beckham rather than Batty.

In the quarter-finals Brazil and Denmark shared a pulsating duel, with Martin Jorgensen scoring for the Danes in the second minute. However, the South Americans played with confidence and won 3-2 thanks to a second goal from Rivaldo. Holland and Argentina were both reduced to ten men in their game, with Ariel Ortega red-carded for head-butting goalkeeper Edwin Van Der Sar in the dying minutes, and from the resulting free-kick the ball was eventually played upfield to Bergkamp who sealed a 2-1 win for the Dutch.

Croatia caused the upset of the round with a late goal from Davor Suker clinching a 3-0 win over Germany. Then the aristocracy of Europe played one of the dullest matches, as Italy and France failed to register a goal. The game went to penalties, and when Luigi di Biagio's effort hit the bar, the hosts were through.

The first semi-final saw the debutants from Croatia come up against the hosts. Suker opened the scoring before the team with no strikers once again relied on a defender to score, with Lilian Thuram netting twice to put France into the final. The other semi-final was also pure drama. Ronaldo's second-half goal looked enough until Kluivert scored a late equaliser for the Dutch. Neither side could

grab the winner and it went to penalties, with Brazil winning 4-2.

The dream final was on: the champions versus the hosts, Ronaldo versus Zidane, style versus substance. What could go wrong?

Above: The Romanian team celebrate progressing to the second round by dyeing their hair blond. Opposite clockwise from top left: Denmark's Brian Laudrup after scoring against Nigeria; France celebrate winning the World Cup on home soil; Michael Owen takes on Argentina's Jose Chamot; Holland's Edgar Davids in quarter-final action against Argentina.

SEMI-FINALS
Brazil 1-1 Holland
(aet: Brazil won 4-2 on penalties)
France 2-1 Croatia

THIRD PLACE PLAY-OFF
Croatia 2-1 Holland

TOP SCORERS
6 goals: Davor Suker (Croatia)
5 goals: Gabriel Batistuta (Argentina)

FASTEST GOAL
53 seconds: Celso Ayala (Paraguay v Nigeria)

TOTAL GOALS
171

AVERAGE GOALS
2.67 per game

THE FINAL

FRANCE (2) **3-0** (0) **BRAZIL**

Date Sunday July 12, 1998 **Attendance** 75,000
Venue Stade de France, Paris

The record will show the scoreline, the scorers and the fact that France's Marcel Desailly received his marching orders following a tackle on Cafu. What it will not show is the controversy which threatened to overshadow the final.

Brazil's World Player Of The Year, Ronaldo, was not named on coach Mario Zagalo's teamsheet when it was first handed in. An hour later his name was back on it again. It emerged that earlier in the day Ronaldo had suffered from convulsions and had been taken to hospital. Zagalo named the team without him but the striker declared himself fit to play.

Brazil – especially Ronaldo – looked lethargic, and Zinédine Zidane conducted the French orchestra to perfection, heading two goals, while Emmanuel Petit scored the breakaway third in the dying moments of the game. The country that had done so much to create the World Cup had finally won it – on home soil!

FRANCE
BARTHEZ
THURAM
DESAILLY
Booked: 48 mins. Sent-off (second booking) 68 mins
LEBOEUF
LIZARAZU
DESCHAMPS
Booked: 39 mins
ZIDANE
Goal: 27 mins, 45 mins
PETIT
Goal: 90 mins
KAREMBEU
Booked: 56 mins. Subbed: 56 mins (Boghossian)
DJORKAEFF
Subbed: 74 mins (Vieira)
GUIVARC'H
Subbed: 66 mins (Dugarry)
sub: BOGHOSSIAN
sub: DUGARRY
sub: VIEIRA

BRAZIL
TAFFAREL
CAFU
JUNIOR BAIANO
Booked: 33 mins
ALDAIR
ROBERTO CARLOS
CESAR SAMPAIO
Subbed: 57 mins (Edmundo)
LEONARDO
Subbed: 46 mins (Denilson)
DUNGA
RIVALDO
RONALDO
BEBETO
sub: DENILSON
sub: EDMUNDO

Referee: Belqola (Morocco)

HOW THE TEAMS LINED UP

FRANCE
COACH: AIME JACQUET

BRAZIL
COACH: MARIO ZAGALO

Barthez
Thuram Desailly Leboeuf Lizarazu
Karembeu Deschamps Petit
Zidane
Djorkaeff Guivarc'h
Bebeto Ronaldo
Rivaldo Dunga Cesar Sampaio Leonardo
Roberto Carlos Aldair Junior Baiano Cafu
Taffarel

KOREA/JAPAN 2002

The 17th World Cup finals in Japan and Korea were not only the first to be played in Asia, but also the first to be staged outside of Europe or the Americas. As if to signify a shift in the balance of global football dominance, from the very first game it was a competition full of shocks and surprise results. It was a tournament that saw many of the established nations and the biggest stars of the world game catching an early flight home, while it was also notable for the emergence of unfancied football nations, such as Senegal, Turkey and South Korea. Nevertheless, the final would ultimately be played out between the World Cup's two most successful sides.

It was World Cup debutantes Senegal who provided the biggest shock in the opening game, with Pape Bouba Diop scoring the goal that defeated the holders and favourites France. In a physical game, the Africans overpowered a jaded looking French team, clearly missing the talismanic presence of the injured Zinédine Zidane. Indeed, France failed to

SEMI-FINALS

Germany 1-0 South Korea
Brazil 1-0 Turkey

THIRD PLACE PLAY-OFF

Turkey 3-2 South Korea

TOP SCORERS

8 goals: Ronaldo (Brazil)
5 goals: Miroslav Klose (Germany); Rivaldo (Brazil)

FASTEST GOAL

10.8 seconds: Hakan Şükür (Turkey v South Korea)

TOTAL GOALS

161

AVERAGE GOALS

2.51 per game

THE FINAL

BRAZIL (0) **2-0** (0) **GERMANY**

Date Sunday June 30, 2002 **Attendance** 69,029
Venue International Stadium, Yokohama

Despite sharing seven World Cup titles between them, Brazil and Germany had never met in the final stages of the tournament. Brazil started as favourites but they would have to beat Oliver Kahn, who had conceded just one goal in the competition. A largely uneventful first half saw two bookings, while Kleberson hit the bar for Brazil and a couple of half-chances fell to Ronaldo. However, in the 67th minute Kahn spilt Rivaldo's shot into the path of the grateful Ronaldo, who pounced on the ball to score.

He was on the scoresheet again 12 minutes later, curling the ball past Kahn to make it 2-0. Shortly after the final whistle, skipper Cafu, playing in his third World Cup final, lifted the trophy to mark Brazil's record-breaking and wholly deserved fifth world title.

HOW THE TEAMS LINED UP

BRAZIL
COACH:
LUIZ FELIPE SCOLARI

GERMANY
COACH:
RUDI VÖLLER

Marcos

Lucio   Edmilson   Roque Junior

Cafu   Kleberson   Gilberto   Roberto Carlos

Ronaldinho

Rivaldo   Ronaldo

Klose   Neuville

Metzelder   Ramelow   Linke   Frings

Kahn

BRAZIL

MARCOS	
LUCIO	
EDMILSON	
ROQUE JUNIOR	
Booked: 6 mins	
CAFU	
KLEBERSON	
GILBERTO SILVA	
ROBERTO CARLOS	
RONALDINHO	▶
Subbed: 85 mins (Juninho)	
RIVALDO	
RONALDO	▶
Goal: 67 mins, 79 mins. Subbed: 90 mins (Denilson)	
sub: JUNINHO PAULISTA	▶
sub: DENILSON	▶

GERMANY

KAHN	
LINKE	
RAMELOW	
METZELDER	
FRINGS	
JEREMIES	▶
Subbed: 77 mins (Asamoah)	
HAMANN	
SCHNEIDER	
BODE	▶
Subbed: 84 mins (Ziege)	
NEUVILLE	
KLOSE	▶
Booked: 9 mins. Subbed: 74 mins (Bierhoff)	
sub: BIERHOFF	▶
sub: ASAMOAH	▶
sub: ZIEGE	▶

Referee: Collina (Italy)

Above: South Korea watch the penalty shoot-out that took them through to the semi-finals. Opposite clockwise from top left: Japan's Junichi Inamoto is mobbed by his team-mates after scoring against Russia; Roque Junior and Ronaldinho lift the World Cup; Senegal's goal celebrations after scoring against France; David Beckham gains revenge over Argentina.

score a single goal in three games and were out of the tournament earlier than anyone could have expected, the first reigning champions to exit at the group stage since Brazil in 1966.

Joint favourites Argentina also suffered the ignominy of early elimination. After a narrow win in their opening game against Nigeria, courtesy of a Gabriel Batistuta header, defeat to England and a draw against Sweden meant the hugely talented Argentine squad were to play no further part in the competition. The clash with England was one of the most eagerly anticipated games of the competition and saw David Beckham convert the match-winning penalty to gain revenge for his dismissal in the same fixture four years previous.

The much-fancied Portuguese side were the other high-profile first round casualties, losing out to both the USA and joint hosts South Korea, who topped their group despite never having won a match at the finals before.

An impressive Brazil, looking more assured and confident with every game, and perennial under-achievers Spain were the only two countries to qualify from their respective groups with 100 per cent records, while Slovenia, China and Saudi Arabia went home without a point. Germany's 8-0 demolition of Saudi Arabia was, by quite a margin, the most one-sided of all the games of the tournament. The other group winners were Denmark, Germany, Sweden, Mexico and Japan, much to the delight of an enthusiastic co-host nation.

With Germany and England securing routine wins against Paraguay and Denmark in the opening games of the second round, it was left to the South Koreans to provide the major upset of this stage. Some controversial refereeing decisions marred their 2-1 golden goal victory over the Italians, which saw Francesco Totti sent-off for diving, and an apparently good goal ruled out.

Despite the loss of captain Roy Keane, who walked out on the squad before they had even arrived at the World Cup, the Republic Of Ireland qualified for the knockout rounds, only to go out on penalties to Spain. The other games of this stage saw wins for the USA over Mexico, Senegal over Sweden and Brazil over Belgium, while a headed goal from Turkey's Umit Davala ended the dreams of Japan.

The quarter-final stage consisted of four established football nations (Brazil, Germany, England and Spain) and four inexperienced at this level of competition (USA, South Korea, Turkey and Senegal). Brazil beat England 2-1, countering an opportunistic Michael Owen strike with a defence-splitting goal from Rivaldo and a freak long-range strike from Ronaldinho. Germany were fortunate to get past the USA 1-0, especially after a blatant handball in their own penalty area had gone unnoticed. Turkey secured a 'golden goal' victory over an unlucky Senegal, and South Korea were once again up to their giant-killing antics. This time Guus Hiddink's superbly conditioned and well-drilled team got the better of Spain, but again the victory was not without controversy as the Spanish were furious that two perfectly good goals had been disallowed.

The semi-finals at last saw the established powers assert their dominance. Brazil eased past a spirited Turkey with a memorable goal from a rejuvenated Ronaldo. Germany narrowly got the better of the Koreans with a solitary goal from Michael Ballack, who got himself booked and missed the final.

Despite complaints over poor organisation in respect of ticket allocation, the World Cup was superbly staged, and the wide-eyed enthusiasm of the supporters of both host nations is sure to be considered one of the lasting memories of a successful tournament. No respecter of reputations, the 2002 World Cup in Korea/Japan will also be remembered as one when the smaller football nations fought back and nearly succeeded in overthrowing the existing global power base.

GERMANY 2006

After the shocks of the 2002 World Cup that saw outsiders South Korea and Turkey reach the semi-finals, Germany 2006 went some way to restoring the balance of power in favour of the established football nations. Only two of eight quarter-finalists had not previously won the competition, and even the hosts found they were a nation newly invigorated by this tournament after some years in relative decline.

Finding themselves paired in Group A with Ecuador, bitter rivals Poland, and opening game opponents Costa Rica, Germany surprised the doubters, proving an unstoppable force in attack. Philipp Lahm scored their opening goal just five minutes after the tournament had kicked-off and by the time the group stages were over, the Germans had racked up eight goals, progressing to the second round with a 100 per cent record.

Brazil cruised through the group stage but World Footballer Of The Year Ronaldinho seemed a shadow of his best, not benefiting from the defensive play of coach Carlos Alberto Parreira. Ronaldo also appeared out of shape and was even criticised by his country's president.

Under the guidance of the 2002 World Cup-winning coach Luiz Filipe Scolari, Portugal qualified for the second round without dropping a point. In doing so Scolari broke Vittorio Pozzo's 68-year-old record, becoming the first coach to win eight World Cup games in succession (the first seven he achieved with Brazil in 2002). Scolari would ultimately stretch this record to 11 games before the tournament was over.

Spain won all their games and qualified ahead of Ukraine, while Argentina appeared to be in unstoppable form. A 6-0 demolition of Serbia and Montenegro demonstrated their pace and class, with players as talented as Lionel Messi and Carlos Tevez having to settle for substitute appearances. But not all of the seeded nations had it their own way. England topped their group despite some lacklustre performances that even drew criticism from FIFA president Sepp Blatter. Italy's progress looked uncertain after a draw with the USA that saw the Italians lose one man to a red card and the Americans two. An early exit was prevented by victory over the Czechs, with Italy salvaging top spot ahead of Ghana.

French fans had called for coach Raymond Domenech to drop his ageing stars in favour of youngsters like Franck Ribéry, the 23-year-old Marseille midfielder with just three substitute appearances to his name. The coach stayed loyal to his stars but included Ribéry too, with France stumbling through as runners-up to the Swiss after coming alive in their game against Togo.

While the group stage had thrown up plenty of exciting games, the sudden death football of the second round brought a cautious approach. Argentina's clash with Mexico was an exception. The Mexicans took a sixth minute lead through Marquez, only to see Crespo equalise four

minutes later, but a thunderous left-foot volley from Maxi Rodriguez eight minutes into extra-time secured the win for Argentina.

In a limp encounter in Cologne the Swiss lost on penalties to Ukraine, becoming the first team to exit a World Cup without conceding a goal. A Beckham free-kick made all the difference in a pallid fixture between England and Ecuador, while Italy needed a controversial penalty to beat Australia with the last kick of the game. The hosts put in a workmanlike performance to see off Sweden, while Brazil brushed aside Ghana with little effort, Ronaldo becoming the World Cup's all-time leading scorer with his 15th goal.

In the 700th World Cup finals game, France needed a bit of self-made luck against Spain to be certain of a place in the last eight. Portugal edged through with a Maniche goal against Holland, but it was a fraught encounter that equalled the World Cup record for bookings (16) and broke the record for red cards: Portugal had Deco and Costinha dismissed, while Holland's Boulahrouz and Van Bronkhorst were sent-off.

The Germans were the first team to qualify for the semi-finals. They stunned Argentina with an 80th minute equaliser from Klose, before winning 4-2 in a penalty shoot-out. Portugal also needed penalties to beat ten-man England, who had Rooney sent-off early in the second-half. Italy stepped up a gear to defeat Ukraine 3-0, and in the biggest surprise of the round, Zinédine Zidane – who had retired from international football two years earlier – proved the inspiration his team needed to achieve victory over Brazil.

While the early exit of the holders created headlines, the first semi-final provided a greater shock. Under the shrewd tactical stewardship of Marcello Lippi, the Italians ended German hopes of winning the trophy in the best game of the tournament. Late in extra-time, with penalties just a minute away, defender Fabio Grosso hammered a magnificent first time shot into the back of the net. Just two minutes later, Gilardino played a sublime reverse pass into the path of Del Piero, who had run the length of the field to fire past Lehman with the last kick of the game.

A single Zidane penalty was enough to send France into the final at the expense of Portugal,

giving their World Cup winning veterans – Thuram, Barthez, Vieira and Zidane – one more chance to shine on the biggest stage.

France and Italy had started slowly but with both teams approaching top form at just the right time, the final would prove a dramatic encounter.

Above: Ghana celebrate victory over the Czechs. Opposite clockwise from top left: Marco Materazzi is butted by Zidane in the final; golden boot winner Miroslav Klose; England's Wayne Rooney sees red; Italy's Fabio Grosso with the World Cup.

THE FINAL

ITALY (1) **1-1** (1) **FRANCE**
(aet: Italy won 5-3 on penalties)

Date Sunday July 9 **Attendance** 69,000

Venue Olympic Stadium, Berlin

The 2006 World Cup final was destined to belong to Zinédine Zidane, playing his last game, but by the time the Italians lifted the trophy it was their defender Marco Materazzi who had made the most decisive impact. France took the lead with a seventh minute penalty after Materazzi fouled Malouda in the box and Zidane's chipped spot-kick ricocheted down from the underside of the bar. Just 12 minutes later Materazzi made amends when he rose to head home Pirlo's corner.

Italy remained the more threatening but in extra-time the best chance came to Zidane, his header pushed over the bar by Buffon. When the end came for Zidane it was not as expected: he received a red card for an off-the-ball assault on Materazzi, having knocked the Italian to the floor with a butt to the chest. David Trezeguet struck the only failed penalty of the shoot-out and the trophy was lifted by Italian captain Cannavaro.

HOW THE TEAMS LINED UP

ITALY
COACH:
MARCELLO LIPPI

FRANCE
COACH:
RAYMOND DOMENECH

Buffon
Zambrotta Cannavaro Materazzi Grosso
Pirlo Gattuso
Camoranesi Totti Perrotta
Toni

Henry
Malouda Zidane Ribéry
Vieira Makelele
Abidal Gallas Thuram Sagnol
Barthez

ITALY	
BUFFON	
GROSSO	
MATERAZZI	
Goal: 23 mins	
CANNAVARO	
ZAMBROTTA	
Booked: 5 mins	
PERROTTA	▶
Subbed: 60 mins (De Rossi)	
GATTUSO	
PIRLO	
CAMORANESI	▶
Subbed: 86 mins (Del Piero)	
TOTTI	
TONI	▶
Subbed: 60 mins (Iaquinta)	
sub: **IAQUINTA**	▶
sub: **DE ROSSI**	▶
sub: **DEL PIERO**	▶
FRANCE	
BARTHEZ	
ABIDAL	
GALLAS	
THURAM	
SAGNOL	
Booked: 12 mins	
MAKELELE	
Booked: 76 mins	
MALOUDA	
Booked: 111 mins	
VIEIRA	▶
Subbed: 56 mins (Diarra)	
RIBÉRY	▶
Subbed: 99 mins (Trezeguet)	
ZIDANE	
Goal: 7 mins (pen). Sent-off: 110 mins	
HENRY	▶
Subbed: 106 mins (Wiltord)	
sub: **DIARRA**	▶
Booked: 75 mins	
sub: **TREZEGUET**	▶
sub: **WILTORD**	▶
Referee: Elizondo (Argentina)	

SOUTH AFRICA 2010

Despite the scare stories and security issues that dogged the preparations for the 2010 World Cup, South Africa managed to stage a tournament that the country could be proud of, one that gave a divided nation a reason for its peoples to come together. The greatest shame was that the quality of the football failed to live up to expectations and that the most stellar names in the game failed to deliver performances worthy of their reputations.

Billed as the weakest hosts in World Cup history, South Africa kicked off the tournament to the excited drone of vuvuzelas, the controversial plastic trumpets that gave the competition its soundtrack. Despite playing second fiddle to Mexico for much of the opening game, they took a surprise lead when Tshabalala blasted into the net but Marquez's equaliser 12 minutes from time denied them a win. The South Africans went on to beat France in their final group game but they still became the first host nation to be knocked out in the opening round.

It was a more ignominious exit for the French who finished bottom of the table. However, they were the engineers of their own misfortune, with the players boycotting training before their final game in protest at the decision to send Nicolas Anelka home. With the French in disarray, Uruguay topped the group and the Mexicans followed them into the second round.

Poor morale and weak form also undermined England, who stuttered when Robert Green's goalmouth fumble gifted the USA a point. After Landon Donovan's last gasp goal against Algeria, it was the Americans who finished top, with the English stumbling through as runners-up. Reigning champions Italy were less fortunate. Their World Cup winning coach Marcello Lippi had returned but his team proved less than inspiring, drawing with both Paraguay and New Zealand. They contested a thriller with Slovakia but lost 3-2 and finished below outsiders New Zealand, who left the finals unbeaten. Paraguay went through in first place, followed by Slovakia.

Few had expected Joachim Löw's young team to offer a threat but Germany had the look of champions when they ripped Australia apart in their opening game, winning 4-0. They suffered a shock defeat to Serbia, who took a first-half lead shortly after Miroslav Klose had been harshly red carded, but they still topped the group following an entertaining victory over Ghana. The Africans scraped through as runners-up, finishing above Australia on goal difference.

Argentina and Holland both progressed from their groups with maximum points but favourites Spain had to endure a 1-0 defeat to Switzerland before edging Chile into the runners-up spot on goal difference. Despite predictions of a defensive style played under coach Dunga, Brazil looked imposing and qualified ahead of Portugal, whose 7-0 destruction of North Korea was easily the most one-sided contest of the tournament.

Uruguay ended South Korea's challenge in the first game of the knockout stages, Ghana's Asamoah Gyan fired home an extra-time winner to end the USA's campaign, and in one of the most anticipated clashes of the round Spain needed a 63rd-minute goal from David Villa to break the deadlock with Portugal.

Germany's lightning fast, counterattacking style made light work of England, although the match really turned on a moment of controversy in the 39th minute, when Frank Lampard's 20-yard shot bounced down from the bar a clear 12 inches over the line. It should have been the equaliser, England's second goal in two minutes, but the referee waved play on and in the second-half the Germans cruised to a 4-1 win. Refereeing decisions were again under the spotlight when Carlos Tevez headed Argentina into the lead against Mexico, despite being yards offside when the ball was played to him, and the Argentinians progressed to the quarter-finals with a 3-1 win.

The Dutch had Arjen Robben in the starting line-up for the first time as they stuttered past Slovakia 2-1, with goals from Robben and Wes Sneijder. Brazil comfortably brushed aside the challenge of Chile, who had looked impressive in the earlier stages, while in the only game of the round to go to penalties, Paraguay saw off Japan after a uninspiring 0-0 draw.

It was the quarter-finals that featured the most dramatic clashes. Robinho gave Brazil a first-half lead over Holland but Sneijder scored twice to cap an astonishing second-half comeback by the Dutch. In Cape Town Germany battered Argentina, with Klose scoring twice in the 4-0 win, while Spain had a late goal from David Villa to thank for beating Paraguay but both teams had earlier wasted good chances from the spot.

The Uruguayans got the better of Ghana but it took one of the competition's most controversial moments to help them through. In the dying seconds of injury time, with the scores level, Adiyiah's goalbound header was deliberately handled on the line by Luis Suárez. Asamoah Gyan missed the resulting penalty with the last kick of the game and Uruguay went on to win the deciding shoot-out, ending Ghana's dreams of becoming the first African side to reach the last four of the World Cup.

In the semi-finals the Dutch fended off the challenge of Uruguay. With two second-half goals in three minutes from Sneijder and Robben, they took a 3-1 lead and even Maxi Pereira's injury time strike failed to derail their path to the final. In the other semi-final Vicente Del Bosque took the brave decision to drop misfiring striker Fernando Torres and Spain's pretty possession football snuffed out the counterattacking threat of the Germans, who struggled to get back in the game after Carles Puyol's 73rd minute header.

Spain's performances across the tournament had not lived up to their billing, while the Dutch had reached the final despite being derided at home for abandoning the beautiful football so associated with the country's past. However, there was a real sense of excitement that the 2010 World Cup would certainly be won by a nation that had never before lifted the trophy.

Above: The Dutch celebrate against Slovakia. Opposite clockwise from top left: Ghana's Asamoah Gyan; David Villa with the World Cup; Siphiwe Tshabalala scores for South Africa; Uruguay's Diego Forlan.

SEMI-FINALS

Germany 0-1 Spain
Holland 3-2 Uruguay

THIRD PLACE PLAY-OFF

Germany 3-2 Uruguay

TOP SCORERS

5 goals: Thomas Müller (Germany), Wesley Sneijder (Holland), David Villa (Spain), Diego Forlan (Uruguay)
* Thomas Müller awarded the Golden Ball on 'assists'

FASTEST GOAL

2 mins 38 seconds: Thomas Müller (Germany v Argentina)

TOTAL GOALS

145

AVERAGE GOALS

2.27 per game

THE FINAL

SPAIN (0) 1-0 (0) HOLLAND
(aet: 0-0 at 90 mins)

Date Sunday July 11, 2010 **Attendance** 84,490

Venue Soccer City Stadium, Johannesburg

Holland's physical style did not win them any friends, resulting in a final that saw 14 yellow cards and one dismissal as the Dutch tried to prise the ball out of Spain's tight grip. Holland had their chances and Robben came close in the second-half but it was the Spanish who scored the only goal in extra-time. Iniesta received the ball from Fabregas and with his second touch drilled a right-footed shot across the keeper and into the net. Minutes earlier Heitinger had been sent-off after pulling back Iniesta.

Spain had won the World Cup scoring just eight times in their seven matches, less than any other winner in World Cup history. They abandoned their change strip for their famous red shirts to receive the trophy.

SPAIN

CASILLAS		
SERGIO RAMOS		
Booked: 23 mins		
PIQUÉ		
PUYOL		
Booked: 16 mins		
CAPDEVILA		
Booked: 67 mins		
BUSQUETS		
XABI ALONSO	▶	
Subbed: 87 mins (Fabregas)		
INIESTA		
Goal: 116 mins. Booked: 118 mins		
XAVI		
Booked: 120+1 mins		
RODRÍGUEZ	▶	
Subbed: 60 mins (Navas)		
VILLA	▶	
Subbed: 106 mins (Torres)		
Sub: **NAVAS**	▶	
Sub: **FABREGAS**	▶	
Sub: **TORRES**	▶	

HOLLAND

STEKELENBURG		
VAN DER WIEL		
Booked: 111 mins		
HEITINGA		
Booked: 57 mins. Sent-off: 109 mins		
MATHIJSEN		
Booked: 117 mins		
VAN BRONCKHORST	▶	
Booked: 54 mins. Subbed: 105 mins (Braafheid)		
VAN BOMMEL		
Booked: 22 mins		
DE JONG	▶	
Booked: 28 mins. Subbed: 99 mins (Van Der Vaart)		
ROBBEN		
Booked: 84 mins		
SNEIJDER		
KUYT	▶	
Subbed: 71 mins (Elia)		
VAN PERSIE		
Booked: 15 mins		
Sub: **ELIA**	▶	
Sub: **VAN DER VAART**	▶	
Sub: **BRAAFHEID**	▶	

Referee: Webb (England)

HOW THE TEAMS LINED UP

SPAIN

COACH:
VICENTE DEL BOSQUE

Casillas
Sergio Ramos — Piqué — Puyol — Capdevila
Busquets — Xabi Alonso
Iniesta — Xavi — Rodriguez
Villa

HOLLAND

COACH:
BERT VAN MARWIJK

Van Persie
Kuyt — Robben
Sneijder
De Jong — Van Bommel
Van Bronckhorst — Mathijsen — Heitinga — Van Der Wiel
Stekelenburg

WORLD CUP RESULTS

The Centenary Stadium in Montevideo was built especially for the 1930 World Cup Finals.

1930 URUGUAY

GROUP 1

France **4-1** Mexico
Argentina **1-0** France
Chile **3-0** Mexico
Chile **1-0** France
Argentina **6-3** Mexico
Argentina **3-1** Chile

	P	W	D	L	F	A	Pts
Argentina	3	3	0	0	10	4	6
Chile	3	2	0	1	5	3	4
France	3	1	0	2	4	3	2
Mexico	3	0	0	3	4	13	0

GROUP 2

Yugoslavia **2-1** Brazil
Yugoslavia **4-0** Bolivia
Brazil **4-0** Bolivia

	P	W	D	L	F	A	Pts
Yugoslavia	2	2	0	0	6	1	4
Brazil	2	1	0	1	5	2	2
Bolivia	2	0	0	2	0	8	0

GROUP 3

Romania **3-1** Peru
Uruguay **1-0** Peru
Uruguay **4-0** Romania

	P	W	D	L	F	A	Pts
Uruguay	2	2	0	0	5	0	4
Romania	2	1	0	1	3	5	2
Peru	2	0	0	2	1	4	0

GROUP 4

USA **3-0** Belgium
USA **3-0** Paraguay
Paraguay **1-0** Belgium

	P	W	D	L	F	A	Pts
USA	2	2	0	0	6	0	4
Paraguay	2	1	0	1	1	3	2
Belgium	2	0	0	2	0	4	0

SEMI-FINALS

Argentina **6-1** USA
Uruguay **6-1** Yugoslavia

THIRD PLACE PLAY-OFF

Not held

FINAL

Uruguay **4-2** Argentina

1934 ITALY

FIRST ROUND

Italy **7-1** USA
Czechoslovakia **2-1** Romania
Germany **5-2** Belgium
Austria **3-2** France
(aet)
Spain **3-1** Brazil
Switzerland **3-2** Holland
Sweden **3-2** Argentina
Hungary **4-2** Egypt

QUARTER-FINALS

Germany **2-1** Sweden
Austria **2-1** Hungary
Italy **1-1** Spain
(aet)
Italy **1-0** Spain
(replay)
Czechoslovakia **3-2** Switzerland

SEMI-FINALS

Czechoslovakia **3-1** Germany
Italy **1-0** Austria

THIRD PLACE PLAY-OFF

Germany **3-2** Austria

FINAL

Italy **2-1** Czechoslovakia
(aet)

1938 FRANCE

FIRST ROUND

Switzerland **1-1** Germany
(aet)
Switzerland **4-2** Germany
(replay)
Cuba **3-3** Romania
(aet)
Cuba **2-1** Romania
(replay)
Hungary **6-0** Dutch E. Indies
France **3-1** Belgium
Czechoslovakia **3-0** Holland
(aet)
Brazil **6-5** Poland
(aet)
Italy **2-1** Norway
(aet)
Sweden **w/o** Austria

QUARTER-FINALS

Sweden **8-0** Cuba
Hungary **2-0** Switzerland
Italy **3-1** France
Brazil **1-1** Czechoslovakia
(aet)
Brazil **2-1** Czechoslovakia
(replay)

SEMI-FINALS

Italy **2-1** Brazil
Hungary **5-1** Sweden

THIRD PLACE PLAY-OFF

Brazil **4-2** Sweden

FINAL

Italy **4-2** Hungary

1950 BRAZIL

POOL 1

Brazil **4-0** Mexico
Yugoslavia **3-0** Switzerland
Yugoslavia **4-1** Mexico
Brazil **2-2** Switzerland
Brazil **2-0** Yugoslavia
Switzerland **2-1** Mexico

	P	W	D	L	F	A	Pts
Brazil	3	2	1	0	8	2	5
Yugoslavia	3	2	0	1	7	3	4
Switzerland	3	1	1	1	4	6	3
Mexico	3	0	0	3	2	10	0

POOL 2

Spain **3-1** USA
England **2-0** Chile
USA **1-0** England
Spain **2-0** Chile
Spain **1-0** England
Chile **5-2** USA

	P	W	D	L	F	A	Pts
Spain	3	3	0	0	6	1	6
England	3	1	0	2	2	2	2
Chile	3	1	0	2	5	6	2
USA	3	1	0	2	4	8	2

POOL 3

Sweden **3-2** Italy
Sweden **2-2** Paraguay
Italy **2-0** Paraguay

	P	W	D	L	F	A	Pts
Sweden	2	1	1	0	5	4	3
Italy	2	1	0	1	4	3	2
Paraguay	2	0	1	1	2	4	1

POOL 4

Uruguay **8-0** Bolivia

	P	W	D	L	F	A	Pts
Uruguay	1	1	0	0	8	0	2
Bolivia	1	0	0	1	0	8	0

FINAL POOL

Uruguay **2-2** Spain
Brazil **7-1** Sweden
Uruguay **3-2** Sweden
Brazil **6-1** Spain
Sweden **3-1** Spain
Uruguay **2-1** Brazil*

	P	W	D	L	F	A	Pts
Uruguay	3	2	1	0	7	5	5
Brazil	3	2	0	1	14	4	4
Sweden	3	1	0	2	6	11	2
Spain	3	0	1	2	4	11	1

THIRD PLACE

Sweden

FINAL (DECIDING MATCH)

Uruguay **2-1** Brazil*

* the last game of the Final Pool decided the World Cup.

1954 SWITZERLAND

POOL 1

Yugoslavia **1-0** France
Brazil **5-0** Mexico
France **3-2** Mexico
Brazil **1-1** Yugoslavia
(aet)

	P	W	D	L	F	A	Pts
Brazil	2	1	1	0	6	1	3
Yugoslavia	2	1	1	0	2	1	3
France	2	1	0	1	3	3	2
Mexico	2	0	0	2	2	8	0

POOL 2

Hungary **9-0** South Korea
West Germany **4-1** Turkey
Hungary **8-3** West Germany
Turkey **7-0** South Korea

	P	W	D	L	F	A	Pts
Hungary	2	2	0	0	17	3	4
West Germany	2	1	0	1	7	9	2
Turkey	2	1	0	1	8	4	2
South Korea	2	0	0	2	0	16	0

PLAY OFF FOR 2ND GROUP PLACE

West Germany **7-2** Turkey

POOL 3

Austria **1-0** Scotland
Uruguay **2-0** Czechoslovakia
Austria **5-0** Czechoslovakia
Uruguay **7-0** Scotland

	P	W	D	L	F	A	Pts
Uruguay	2	2	0	0	9	0	4
Austria	2	2	0	0	6	0	4
Czechoslovakia	2	0	0	2	0	7	0
Scotland	2	0	0	2	0	8	0

POOL 4

England **4-4** Belgium
(aet)
England **2-0** Switzerland
Switzerland **2-1** Italy
Italy **4-1** Belgium

	P	W	D	L	F	A	Pts
England	2	1	1	0	6	4	3
Switzerland	2	1	0	1	2	3	2
Italy	2	1	0	1	5	3	2
Belgium	2	0	1	1	5	8	1

PLAY-OFF FOR 2ND GROUP PLACE

Switzerland **4-1** Italy

QUARTER-FINALS

West Germany **2-0** Yugoslavia
Hungary **4-2** Brazil
Austria **7-5** Switzerland
Uruguay **4-2** England

SEMI-FINALS

West Germany **6-1** Austria
Hungary **4-2** Uruguay
(aet)

THIRD PLACE PLAY-OFF

Austria **3-1** Uruguay

FINAL

West Germany **3-2** Hungary

1958 SWEDEN

POOL 1

West Germany **3-1** Argentina
Northern Ireland **1-0** Czechoslovakia
West Germany **2-2** Czechoslovakia
Argentina **3-1** Northern Ireland
West Germany **2-2** Northern Ireland
Czechoslovakia **6-1** Argentina

Fritz Walter scores West Germany's fifth goal in the 1954 semi-final against Austria.

Pelé, unable to play in the 1962 final because of injury, hugs replacement Amarildo.

	P	W	D	L	F	A	Pts
West Germany	3	1	2	0	7	5	4
Northern Ireland	3	1	1	1	4	5	3
Czechoslovakia	3	1	1	1	8	4	3
Argentina	3	1	0	2	5	10	2

PLAY-OFF FOR 2ND GROUP PLACE
Northern Ireland **2-1** Czechoslovakia
(aet)

POOL 2
France **7-3** Paraguay
Yugoslavia **1-1** Scotland
Yugoslavia **3-2** France
Paraguay **3-2** Scotland
France **2-1** Scotland
Yugoslavia **3-3** Paraguay

	P	W	D	L	F	A	Pts
France	3	2	0	1	11	7	4
Yugoslavia	3	1	2	0	7	6	4
Paraguay	3	1	1	1	9	12	3
Scotland	3	0	1	2	4	6	1

POOL 3
Sweden **3-0** Mexico
Hungary **1-1** Wales
Wales **1-1** Mexico
Sweden **2-1** Hungary
Sweden **0-0** Wales
Hungary **4-0** Mexico

	P	W	D	L	F	A	Pts
Sweden	3	2	1	0	5	1	5
Wales	3	0	3	0	2	2	3
Hungary	3	1	1	1	6	3	3
Mexico	3	0	1	2	1	8	1

PLAY-OFF FOR 2ND GROUP PLACE
Wales **2-1** Hungary

POOL 4
England **2-2** Soviet Union
Brazil **3-0** Austria
England **0-0** Brazil
Soviet Union **2-0** Austria
Brazil **2-0** Soviet Union
England **2-2** Austria

	P	W	D	L	F	A	Pts
Brazil	3	2	1	0	5	0	5
Soviet Union	3	1	1	1	4	4	3
England	3	0	3	0	4	4	3
Austria	3	0	1	2	2	7	1

PLAY-OFF FOR 2ND GROUP PLACE
Soviet Union **1-0** England

QUARTER-FINALS
France **4-0** Northern Ireland
West Germany **1-0** Yugoslavia
Sweden **2-0** Soviet Union
Brazil **1-0** Wales

SEMI-FINALS
Brazil **5-2** France
Sweden **3-1** West Germany

THIRD PLACE PLAY-OFF
France **6-3** West Germany

FINAL
Brazil **5-2** Sweden

1962 CHILE

GROUP 1
Uruguay **2-1** Colombia
Soviet Union **2-0** Yugoslavia
Yugoslavia **3-1** Uruguay
Soviet Union **4-4** Colombia
Soviet Union **2-1** Uruguay
Yugoslavia **5-0** Colombia

	P	W	D	L	F	A	Pts
Soviet Union	3	2	1	0	8	5	5
Yugoslavia	3	2	0	1	8	3	4
Uruguay	3	1	0	2	4	6	2
Colombia	3	0	1	2	5	11	1

GROUP 2
Chile **3-1** Switzerland
West Germany **0-0** Italy
Chile **2-0** Italy
West Germany **2-1** Switzerland
West Germany **2-0** Chile
Italy **3-0** Switzerland

	P	W	D	L	F	A	Pts
West Germany	3	2	1	0	4	1	5
Chile	3	2	0	1	5	3	4
Italy	3	1	1	1	3	2	3
Switzerland	3	0	0	3	2	8	0

GROUP 3
Brazil **2-0** Mexico
Czechoslovakia **1-0** Spain
Brazil **0-0** Czechoslovakia
Spain **1-0** Mexico
Brazil **2-1** Spain
Mexico **3-1** Czechoslovakia

	P	W	D	L	F	A	Pts
Brazil	3	2	1	0	4	1	5
Czechoslovakia	3	1	1	1	2	3	3
Mexico	3	1	0	2	3	4	2
Spain	3	1	0	2	2	3	2

GROUP 4
Argentina **1-0** Bulgaria
Hungary **2-1** England
England **3-1** Argentina
Hungary **6-1** Bulgaria
Argentina **0-0** Hungary
England **0-0** Bulgaria

	P	W	D	L	F	A	Pts
Hungary	3	2	1	0	8	2	5
England	3	1	1	1	4	3	3
Argentina	3	1	1	1	2	3	3
Bulgaria	3	0	1	2	1	7	1

QUARTER-FINALS
Yugoslavia **1-0** West Germany
Brazil **3-1** England
Chile **2-1** Soviet Union
Czechoslovakia **1-0** Hungary

SEMI-FINALS
Brazil **4-2** Chile
Czechoslovakia **3-1** Yugoslavia

THIRD PLACE PLAY-OFF
Chile **1-0** Yugoslavia

FINAL
Brazil **3-1** Czechoslovakia

1966 ENGLAND

GROUP 1
England **0-0** Uruguay
France **1-1** Mexico
Uruguay **2-1** France
England **2-0** Mexico
Uruguay **0-0** Mexico
England **2-0** France

	P	W	D	L	F	A	Pts
England	3	2	1	0	4	0	5
Uruguay	3	1	2	0	2	1	4
Mexico	3	0	2	1	1	3	2
France	3	0	1	2	2	5	1

GROUP 2
West Germany **5-0** Switzerland
Argentina **2-1** Spain
Spain **2-1** Switzerland
Argentina **0-0** West Germany
Argentina **2-0** Switzerland
West Germany **2-1** Spain

	P	W	D	L	F	A	Pts
West Germany	3	2	1	0	7	1	5
Argentina	3	2	1	0	4	1	5
Spain	3	1	0	2	4	5	2
Switzerland	3	0	0	3	1	9	0

GROUP 3
Brazil **2-0** Bulgaria
Portugal **3-1** Hungary
Hungary **3-1** Brazil
Portugal **3-0** Bulgaria
Portugal **3-1** Brazil
Hungary **3-1** Bulgaria

	P	W	D	L	F	A	Pts
Portugal	3	3	0	0	9	2	6
Hungary	3	2	0	1	7	5	4
Brazil	3	1	0	2	4	6	2
Bulgaria	3	0	0	3	1	8	0

GROUP 4
Soviet Union **3-0** North Korea
Italy **2-0** Chile
Chile **1-1** North Korea
Soviet Union **1-0** Italy
North Korea **1-0** Italy
Soviet Union **2-1** Chile

	P	W	D	L	F	A	Pts
Soviet Union	3	3	0	0	6	1	6
North Korea	3	1	1	1	2	4	3
Italy	3	1	0	2	2	2	2
Chile	3	0	1	2	2	5	1

QUARTER-FINALS
England **1-0** Argentina
West Germany **4-0** Uruguay
Portugal **5-3** North Korea
Soviet Union **2-1** Hungary

SEMI-FINALS
West Germany **2-1** Soviet Union
England **2-1** Portugal

THIRD PLACE PLAY-OFF
Portugal **2-1** Soviet Union

FINAL
England **4-2** West Germany
(aet)

1970 MEXICO

GROUP 1
Mexico **0-0** Soviet Union
Belgium **3-0** El Salvador
Soviet Union **4-1** Belgium
Mexico **4-0** El Salvador
Soviet Union **2-0** El Salvador
Mexico **1-0** Belgium

	P	W	D	L	F	A	Pts
Soviet Union	3	2	1	0	6	1	5
Mexico	3	2	1	0	5	0	5
Belgium	3	1	0	2	4	5	2
El Salvador	3	0	0	3	0	9	0

GROUP 2
Uruguay **2-0** Israel
Italy **1-0** Sweden
Uruguay **0-0** Italy
Sweden **1-1** Israel
Sweden **1-0** Uruguay
Italy **0-0** Israel

	P	W	D	L	F	A	Pts
Italy	3	1	2	0	1	0	4
Uruguay	3	1	1	1	2	1	3
Sweden	3	1	1	1	2	2	3
Israel	3	0	2	1	1	3	2

GROUP 3
England **1-0** Romania
Brazil **4-1** Czechoslovakia
Romania **2-1** Czechoslovakia
Brazil **1-0** England
Brazil **3-2** Romania
England **1-0** Czechoslovakia

	P	W	D	L	F	A	Pts
Brazil	3	3	0	0	8	3	6
England	3	2	0	1	2	1	4
Romania	3	1	0	2	4	5	2
Czechoslovakia	3	0	0	3	2	7	0

England's Bobby Charlton in full flight against France at Wembley Stadium during the 1966 World Cup.

WORLD CUP RESULTS

Rivelino of Brazil takes the game to Italy in the 1970 final at the Azteca Stadium.

GROUP 4

Peru **3-2** Bulgaria
West Germany **2-1** Morocco
Peru **3-0** Morocco
West Germany **5-2** Bulgaria
West Germany **3-1** Peru
Morocco **1-1** Bulgaria

	P	W	D	L	F	A	Pts
West Germany	3	3	0	0	10	4	6
Peru	3	2	0	1	7	5	4
Bulgaria	3	0	1	2	5	9	1
Morocco	3	0	1	2	2	6	1

QUARTER-FINALS

West Germany **3-2** England (aet)
Brazil **4-2** Peru
Italy **4-1** Mexico
Uruguay **1-0** Soviet Union (aet)

SEMI-FINALS

Italy **4-3** West Germany (aet)
Brazil **3-1** Uruguay

THIRD PLACE

West Germany **1-0** Uruguay

FINAL

Brazil **4-1** Italy

1974 WEST GERMANY

GROUP 1

West Germany **1-0** Chile
East Germany **2-0** Australia
West Germany **3-0** Australia
East Germany **1-1** Chile
Australia **0-0** Chile
East Germany **1-0** West Germany

	P	W	D	L	F	A	Pts
East Germany	3	2	1	0	4	1	5
West Germany	3	2	0	1	4	1	4
Chile	3	0	2	1	1	2	2
Australia	3	0	1	2	0	5	1

GROUP 2

Brazil **0-0** Yugoslavia
Scotland **2-0** Zaïre
Brazil **0-0** Scotland
Yugoslavia **9-0** Zaïre
Yugoslavia **1-1** Scotland
Brazil **3-0** Zaïre

	P	W	D	L	F	A	Pts
Yugoslavia	3	1	2	0	10	1	4
Brazil	3	1	2	0	3	0	4
Scotland	3	1	2	0	3	1	4
Zaïre	3	0	0	3	0	14	0

GROUP 3

Holland **2-0** Uruguay
Bulgaria **0-0** Sweden
Holland **0-0** Sweden
Bulgaria **1-1** Uruguay
Holland **4-1** Bulgaria
Sweden **3-0** Uruguay

	P	W	D	L	F	A	Pts
Holland	3	2	1	0	6	1	5
Sweden	3	1	2	0	3	0	4
Bulgaria	3	0	2	1	2	5	2
Uruguay	3	0	1	2	1	6	1

GROUP 4

Italy **3-1** Haiti
Poland **3-2** Argentina
Argentina **1-1** Italy
Poland **7-0** Haiti
Argentina **4-1** Haiti
Poland **2-1** Italy

	P	W	D	L	F	A	Pts
Poland	3	3	0	0	12	3	6
Argentina	3	1	1	1	7	5	3
Italy	3	1	1	1	5	4	3
Haiti	3	0	0	3	2	14	0

SECOND ROUND GROUP A

Brazil **1-0** East Germany
Holland **4-0** Argentina
Holland **2-0** East Germany
Brazil **2-1** Argentina
East Germany **1-1** Argentina
Holland **2-0** Brazil

	P	W	D	L	F	A	Pts
Holland	3	3	0	0	8	0	6
Brazil	3	2	0	1	3	3	4
East Germany	3	0	1	2	1	4	1
Argentina	3	0	1	2	2	7	1

SECOND ROUND GROUP B

Poland **1-0** Sweden
West Germany **2-0** Yugoslavia
Poland **2-1** Yugoslavia
West Germany **4-2** Sweden
Sweden **2-1** Yugoslavia
West Germany **1-0** Poland

	P	W	D	L	F	A	Pts
West Germany	3	3	0	0	7	2	6
Poland	3	2	0	1	3	2	4
Sweden	3	1	0	2	4	6	2
Yugoslavia	3	0	0	3	2	6	0

THIRD PLACE PLAY-OFF

Poland **1-0** Brazil

FINAL

West Germany **2-1** Holland

1978 ARGENTINA

GROUP 1

Argentina **2-1** Hungary
Italy **2-1** France
Argentina **2-1** France
Italy **3-1** Hungary
Italy **1-0** Argentina
France **3-1** Hungary

	P	W	D	L	F	A	Pts
Italy	3	3	0	0	6	2	6
Argentina	3	2	0	1	4	3	4
France	3	1	0	2	5	5	2
Hungary	3	0	0	3	3	8	0

GROUP 2

West Germany **0-0** Poland
Tunisia **3-1** Mexico
Poland **1-0** Tunisia
West Germany **6-0** Mexico
Poland **3-1** Mexico
West Germany **0-0** Tunisia

	P	W	D	L	F	A	Pts
Poland	3	2	1	0	4	1	5
West Germany	3	1	2	0	6	0	4
Tunisia	3	1	1	1	3	2	3
Mexico	3	0	0	3	2	12	0

GROUP 3

Austria **2-1** Spain
Sweden **1-1** Brazil
Austria **1-0** Sweden
Brazil **0-0** Spain
Spain **1-0** Sweden
Brazil **1-0** Austria

	P	W	D	L	F	A	Pts
Austria	3	2	0	1	3	2	4
Brazil	3	1	2	0	2	1	4
Spain	3	1	1	1	2	2	3
Sweden	3	0	1	2	1	3	1

GROUP 4

Peru **3-1** Scotland
Holland **3-0** Iran
Scotland **1-1** Iran
Holland **0-0** Peru
Peru **4-1** Iran
Scotland **3-2** Holland

	P	W	D	L	F	A	Pts
Peru	3	2	1	0	7	2	5
Holland	3	1	1	1	5	3	3
Scotland	3	1	1	1	5	6	3
Iran	3	0	1	2	2	8	1

SECOND ROUND GROUP A

Italy **0-0** West Germany
Holland **5-1** Austria
Italy **1-0** Austria
Holland **2-2** West Germany
Holland **2-1** Italy
Austria **3-2** West Germany

	P	W	D	L	F	A	Pts
Holland	3	2	1	0	9	4	5
Italy	3	1	1	1	2	2	3
West Germany	3	0	2	1	4	5	2
Austria	3	1	0	2	4	8	2

SECOND ROUND GROUP B

Argentina **2-0** Poland
Brazil **3-0** Peru
Argentina **0-0** Brazil
Poland **1-0** Peru
Brazil **3-1** Poland
Argentina **6-0** Peru

	P	W	D	L	F	A	Pts
Argentina	3	2	1	0	8	0	5
Brazil	3	2	1	0	6	1	5
Poland	3	1	0	2	2	5	2
Peru	3	0	0	3	0	10	0

THIRD PLACE PLAY-OFF

Brazil **2-1** Italy

FINAL

Argentina **3-1** Holland (aet)

1982 SPAIN

GROUP 1

Italy **0-0** Poland
Peru **0-0** Cameroon
Italy **1-1** Peru
Poland **0-0** Cameroon
Poland **5-1** Peru
Italy **1-1** Cameroon

	P	W	D	L	F	A	Pts
Poland	3	1	2	0	5	1	4
Italy	3	0	3	0	2	2	3
Cameroon	3	0	3	0	1	1	3
Peru	3	0	2	1	2	6	2

GROUP 2

Algeria **2-1** West Germany
Austria **1-0** Chile
West Germany **4-1** Chile
Austria **2-0** Algeria
Algeria **3-2** Chile
West Germany **1-0** Austria

	P	W	D	L	F	A	Pts
West Germany	3	2	0	1	6	3	4
Austria	3	2	0	1	3	1	4
Algeria	3	2	0	1	5	5	4
Chile	3	0	0	3	3	8	0

GROUP 3

Belgium **1-0** Argentina
Hungary **10-1** El Salvador
Argentina **4-1** Hungary
Belgium **1-0** El Salvador
Belgium **1-1** Hungary
Argentina **2-0** El Salvador

	P	W	D	L	F	A	Pts
Belgium	3	2	1	0	3	1	5
Argentina	3	2	0	1	6	2	4
Hungary	3	1	1	1	12	6	3
El Salvador	3	0	0	3	1	13	0

West Germany's Littbarski tackles Urquiaga of Spain during the 1982 World Cup.

GROUP 4

England **3-1** France
Czechoslovakia **1-1** Kuwait
England **2-0** Czechoslovakia
France **4-1** Kuwait
France **1-1** Czechoslovakia
England **1-0** Kuwait

	P	W	D	L	F	A	Pts
England	3	3	0	0	6	1	6
France	3	1	1	1	6	5	3
Czechoslovakia	3	0	2	1	2	4	2
Kuwait	3	0	1	2	2	6	1

GROUP 5

Spain **1-1** Honduras
Northern Ireland **0-0** Yugoslavia
Spain **2-1** Yugoslavia
Northern Ireland **1-1** Honduras
Yugoslavia **1-0** Honduras
Northern Ireland **1-0** Spain

	P	W	D	L	F	A	Pts
Northern Ireland	3	1	2	0	2	1	4
Spain	3	1	1	1	3	3	3
Yugoslavia	3	1	1	1	2	2	3
Honduras	3	0	2	1	2	3	2

GROUP 6

Brazil **2-1** Soviet Union
Scotland **5-2** New Zealand
Brazil **4-1** Scotland
Soviet Union **3-0** New Zealand
Scotland **2-2** Soviet Union
Brazil **4-0** New Zealand

	P	W	D	L	F	A	Pts
Brazil	3	3	0	0	10	2	6
Soviet Union	3	1	1	1	6	4	3
Scotland	3	1	1	1	8	8	3
New Zealand	3	0	0	3	2	12	0

SECOND ROUND GROUP A

Poland **3-0** Belgium
Soviet Union **1-0** Belgium
Soviet Union **0-0** Poland

	P	W	D	L	F	A	Pts
Poland	2	1	1	0	3	0	3
Soviet Union	2	1	1	0	1	0	3
Belgium	2	0	0	2	0	4	0

SECOND ROUND GROUP B

West Germany **0-0** England
West Germany **2-1** Spain
England **0-0** Spain

	P	W	D	L	F	A	Pts
West Germany	2	1	1	0	2	1	3
England	2	0	2	0	0	0	2
Spain	2	0	1	1	1	2	1

Scotland's Graeme Souness on the ball against West Germany at the 1986 finals.

SECOND ROUND GROUP C

Italy **2-1** Argentina
Brazil **3-1** Argentina
Italy **3-2** Brazil

	P	W	D	L	F	A	Pts
Italy	2	2	0	0	5	3	4
Brazil	2	1	0	1	5	4	2
Argentina	2	0	0	2	2	5	0

SECOND ROUND GROUP D

France **1-0** Austria
Northern Ireland **2-2** Austria
France **4-1** Northern Ireland

	P	W	D	L	F	A	Pts
France	2	2	0	0	5	1	4
Austria	2	0	1	1	2	3	1
Nothern Ireland	2	0	1	1	3	6	1

SEMI-FINALS

Italy **2-0** Poland
West Germany **3-3** France
(aet)
West Germany won 5-4 on penalties

THIRD PLACE PLAY-OFF

Poland **3-2** France

FINAL

Italy **3-1** West Germany

1986 MEXICO

GROUP A

Bulgaria **1-1** Italy
Argentina **3-1** South Korea
Italy **1-1** Argentina
Bulgaria **1-1** South Korea
Argentina **2-0** Bulgaria
Italy **3-2** South Korea

	P	W	D	L	F	A	Pts
Argentina	3	2	1	0	6	2	5
Italy	3	1	2	0	5	4	4
Bulgaria	3	0	2	1	2	4	2
South Korea	3	0	1	2	4	7	1

GROUP B

Mexico **2-1** Belgium
Paraguay **1-0** Iraq
Mexico **1-1** Paraguay
Belgium **2-1** Iraq
Paraguay **2-2** Belgium
Mexico **1-0** Iraq

	P	W	D	L	F	A	Pts
Mexico	3	2	1	0	4	2	5
Paraguay	3	1	2	0	4	3	4
Belgium	3	1	1	1	5	5	3
Iraq	3	0	0	3	1	4	0

GROUP C

Soviet Union **6-0** Hungary
France **1-0** Canada
Soviet Union **1-1** France
Hungary **2-0** Canada
France **3-0** Hungary
Soviet Union **2-0** Canada

	P	W	D	L	F	A	Pts
Soviet Union	3	2	1	0	9	1	5
France	3	2	1	0	5	1	5
Hungary	3	1	0	2	2	9	2
Canada	3	0	0	3	0	5	0

GROUP D

Brazil **1-0** Spain
Northern Ireland **1-1** Algeria
Spain **2-1** Northern Ireland
Brazil **1-0** Algeria
Spain **3-0** Algeria
Brazil **3-0** Northern Ireland

	P	W	D	L	F	A	Pts
Brazil	3	3	0	0	5	0	6
Spain	3	2	0	1	5	2	4
Northern Ireland	3	0	1	2	2	6	1
Algeria	3	0	1	2	1	5	1

GROUP E

West Germany **1-1** Uruguay
Denmark **1-0** Scotland
Denmark **6-1** Uruguay
West Germany **2-1** Scotland
Scotland **0-0** Uruguay
Denmark **2-0** West Germany

	P	W	D	L	F	A	Pts
Denmark	3	3	0	0	9	1	6
West Germany	3	1	1	1	3	4	3
Uruguay	3	0	2	1	2	7	2
Scotland	3	0	1	2	1	3	1

GROUP F

Morocco **0-0** Poland
Portugal **1-0** England
England **0-0** Morocco
Poland **1-0** Portugal
England **3-0** Poland
Morocco **3-1** Portugal

	P	W	D	L	F	A	Pts
Morocco	3	1	2	0	3	1	4
England	3	1	1	1	3	1	3
Poland	3	1	1	1	1	3	3
Portugal	3	1	0	2	2	4	2

SECOND ROUND

Mexico **2-0** Bulgaria
Belgium **4-3** Soviet Union
(aet)
Brazil **4-0** Poland
Argentina **1-0** Uruguay
France **2-0** Italy
West Germany **1-0** Morocco
England **3-0** Paraguay
Spain **5-1** Denmark

QUARTER-FINALS

France **1-1** Brazil
(aet)
France won 4-3 on penalties
West Germany **0-0** Mexico
(aet)
West Germany won 4-1 on penalties
Argentina **2-1** England
Spain **1-1** Belgium
(aet)
Belgium won 5-4 on penalties

SEMI-FINALS

Argentina **2-0** Belgium
West Germany **2-0** France

THIRD PLACE PLAY-OFF

France **4-2** Belgium

FINAL

Argentina **3-2** West Germany

1990 ITALY

GROUP A

Italy **1-0** Austria
Czechoslovakia **5-1** USA
Italy **1-0** USA
Czechoslovakia **1-0** Austria
Italy **2-0** Czechoslovakia
Austria **2-1** USA

	P	W	D	L	F	A	Pts
Italy	3	3	0	0	4	0	6
Czechoslovakia	3	2	0	1	6	3	4
Austria	3	1	0	2	2	3	2
USA	3	0	0	3	2	8	0

GROUP B

Cameroon **1-0** Argentina
Romania **2-0** Soviet Union
Argentina **2-0** Soviet Union
Cameroon **2-1** Romania
Argentina **1-1** Romania
Soviet Union **4-0** Cameroon

	P	W	D	L	F	A	Pts
Cameroon	3	2	0	1	3	5	4
Romania	3	1	1	1	4	3	3
Argentina	3	1	1	1	3	2	3
Soviet Union	3	1	0	2	4	4	2

GROUP C

Brazil **2-1** Sweden
Costa Rica **1-0** Scotland
Brazil **1-0** Costa Rica
Scotland **2-1** Sweden
Brazil **1-0** Scotland
Costa Rica **2-1** Sweden

	P	W	D	L	F	A	Pts
Brazil	3	3	0	0	4	1	6
Costa Rica	3	2	0	1	3	2	4
Scotland	3	1	0	2	2	3	2
Sweden	3	0	0	3	3	6	0

GROUP D

Colombia **2-0** UAE
West Germany **4-1** Yugoslavia
Yugoslavia **1-0** Colombia
West Germany **5-1** UAE
West Germany **1-1** Colombia
Yugoslavia **4-1** UAE

	P	W	D	L	F	A	Pts
West Germany	3	2	1	0	10	3	5
Yugoslavia	3	2	0	1	6	5	4
Colombia	3	1	1	1	3	2	3
UAE	3	0	0	3	2	11	0

GROUP E

Belgium **2-0** South Korea
Uruguay **0-0** Spain
Belgium **3-1** Uruguay
Spain **3-1** South Korea
Spain **2-1** Belgium
Uruguay **1-0** South Korea

	P	W	D	L	F	A	Pts
Spain	3	2	1	0	5	2	5
Belgium	3	2	0	1	6	3	4
Uruguay	3	1	1	1	2	3	3
South Korea	3	0	0	3	1	6	0

GROUP F

England **1-1** Rep. Of Ireland
Holland **1-1** Egypt
England **0-0** Holland
Egypt **0-0** Rep. Of Ireland
England **1-0** Egypt
Holland **1-1** Rep. Of Ireland

	P	W	D	L	F	A	Pts
England	3	1	2	0	2	1	4
Rep. Of Ireland	3	0	3	0	2	2	3
Holland	3	0	3	0	2	2	3
Egypt	3	0	2	1	1	2	2

SECOND ROUND

Cameroon **2-1** Colombia
(aet)
Czechoslovakia **4-1** Costa Rica
Argentina **1-0** Brazil
West Germany **2-1** Holland
Rep. Of Ireland **0-0** Romania
(aet)
Rep. Of Ireland won 5-4 on penalties
Italy **2-0** Uruguay
Yugoslavia **2-1** Spain
(aet)
England **1-0** Belgium
(aet)

QUARTER-FINALS

Argentina **0-0** Yugoslavia
(aet)
Argentina won 3-2 on penalties
Italy **1-0** Rep. Of Ireland
West Germany **1-0** Czechoslovakia
England **3-2** Cameroon
(aet)

SEMI-FINALS

Argentina **1-1** Italy
(aet)
Argentina won 4-3 on penalties
West Germany **1-1** England
(aet)
West Germany won 4-3 on penalties

THIRD PLACE PLAY-OFF

Italy **2-1** England

FINAL

West Germany **1-0** Argentina

1994 USA

GROUP A

USA **1-1** Switzerland
Colombia **1-3** Romania
USA **2-1** Colombia
Romania **1-4** Switzerland
USA **0-1** Romania
Switzerland **0-2** Colombia

	P	W	D	L	F	A	Pts
Romania	3	2	0	1	5	5	6
Switzerland	3	1	1	1	5	4	4
USA	3	1	1	1	3	3	4
Colombia	3	1	0	2	4	5	3

GROUP B

Cameroon **2-2** Sweden
Brazil **2-0** Russia
Brazil **3-0** Cameroon
Sweden **3-1** Russia
Russia **6-1** Cameroon
Brazil **1-1** Sweden

	P	W	D	L	F	A	Pts
Brazil	3	2	1	0	6	1	7
Sweden	3	1	2	0	6	4	5
Russia	3	1	0	2	7	6	3
Cameroon	3	0	1	2	3	11	1

GROUP C

Germany **1-0** Bolivia
Spain **2-2** South Korea
Germany **1-1** Spain
South Korea **0-0** Bolivia
Bolivia **1-3** Spain
Germany **3-2** South Korea

	P	W	D	L	F	A	Pts
Germany	3	2	1	0	5	3	7
Spain	3	1	2	0	6	4	5
South Korea	3	0	2	1	4	5	2
Bolivia	3	0	1	2	1	4	1

England's Paul Gascoigne takes on Cameroon in the 1990 World Cup quarter-final.

WORLD CUP RESULTS

The USA's Roy Wegerle chases Mazinho of Brazil in 1994.

GROUP D

Argentina **4-0** Greece
Nigeria **3-0** Bulgaria
Argentina **2-1** Nigeria
Bulgaria **4-0** Greece
Greece **0-2** Nigeria
Argentina **0-2** Bulgaria

	P	W	D	L	F	A	Pts
Nigeria	3	2	0	1	6	2	6
Bulgaria	3	2	0	1	6	3	6
Argentina	3	2	0	1	6	3	6
Greece	3	0	0	3	0	10	0

GROUP E

Italy **0-1** Rep. Of Ireland
Norway **1-0** Mexico
Italy **1-0** Norway
Mexico **2-1** Rep. Of Ireland
Rep. Of Ireland **0-0** Norway
Italy **1-1** Mexico

	P	W	D	L	F	A	Pts
Mexico	3	1	1	1	3	3	4
Rep. Of Ireland	3	1	1	1	2	2	4
Italy	3	1	1	1	2	2	4
Norway	3	1	1	1	1	1	4

GROUP F

Belgium **1-0** Morocco
Holland **2-1** Saudi Arabia
Belgium **1-0** Holland
Saudi Arabia **2-1** Morocco
Morocco **1-2** Holland
Belgium **0-1** Saudi Arabia

	P	W	D	L	F	A	Pts
Holland	3	2	0	1	4	3	6
Saudi Arabia	3	2	0	1	4	3	6
Belgium	3	2	0	1	2	1	6
Morocco	3	0	0	3	2	5	0

SECOND ROUND

Germany **3-2** Belgium
Spain **3-0** Switzerland
Saudi Arabia **1-3** Sweden
Romania **3-2** Argentina
Holland **2-0** Rep. Of Ireland
Brazil **1-0** USA
Nigeria **1-2** Italy
(aet)
Mexico **1-1** Bulgaria
(aet)
Bulgaria won 3-1 on penalties

QUARTER-FINALS

Italy **1-1** Spain
Holland **2-3** Brazil
Germany **1-2** Bulgaria
Sweden **2-2** Romania
(aet)
Sweden won 5-4 on penalties

SEMI-FINALS

Brazil **1-0** Sweden
Italy **2-1** Bulgaria

THIRD PLACE PLAY-OFF

Sweden **4-0** Bulgaria

FINAL

Brazil **0-0** Italy
(aet)
Brazil won 3-2 on penalties

1998 FRANCE

GROUP A

Brazil **2-1** Scotland
Morocco **2-2** Norway
Brazil **3-0** Morocco
Scotland **1-1** Norway
Brazil **1-2** Norway
Scotland **0-3** Morocco

	P	W	D	L	F	A	Pts
Brazil	3	2	0	1	6	3	6
Norway	3	1	2	0	5	4	5
Morocco	3	1	1	1	5	5	4
Scotland	3	0	1	2	2	6	1

GROUP B

Italy **2-2** Chile
Austria **1-1** Cameroon
Chile **1-1** Austria
Italy **3-0** Cameroon
Chile **1-1** Cameroon
Italy **2-1** Austria

	P	W	D	L	F	A	Pts
Italy	3	2	1	0	7	3	7
Chile	3	0	3	0	4	4	3
Austria	3	0	2	1	3	4	2
Cameroon	3	0	2	1	2	5	2

GROUP C

Saudi Arabia **0-1** Denmark
France **3-0** South Africa
France **4-0** Saudi Arabia
South Africa **1-1** Denmark
France **2-1** Denmark
South Africa **2-2** Saudi Arabia

	P	W	D	L	F	A	Pts
France	3	3	0	0	9	1	9
Denmark	3	1	1	1	3	3	4
South Africa	3	0	2	1	3	6	2
Saudi Arabia	3	0	1	2	2	7	1

GROUP D

Paraguay **0-0** Bulgaria
Spain **2-3** Nigeria
Nigeria **1-0** Bulgaria
Spain **0-0** Paraguay
Nigeria **1-3** Paraguay
Spain **6-1** Bulgaria

	P	W	D	L	F	A	Pts
Nigeria	3	2	0	1	5	5	6
Paraguay	3	1	2	0	3	1	5
Spain	3	1	1	1	8	4	4
Bulgaria	3	0	1	2	1	7	1

GROUP E

South Korea **1-3** Mexico
Holland **0-0** Belgium
Belgium **2-2** Mexico
Holland **5-0** South Korea
Belgium **1-1** South Korea
Holland **2-2** Mexico

	P	W	D	L	F	A	Pts
Holland	3	1	2	0	7	2	5
Mexico	3	1	2	0	7	5	5
Belgium	3	0	3	0	3	3	3
South Korea	3	0	1	2	2	9	1

GROUP F

Germany **2-0** USA
Yugoslavia **1-0** Iran
Germany **2-2** Yugoslavia
USA **1-2** Iran
Germany **2-0** Iran
USA **0-1** Yugoslavia

	P	W	D	L	F	A	Pts
Germany	3	2	1	0	6	2	7
Yugoslavia	3	2	1	0	4	2	7
Iran	3	1	0	2	2	4	3
USA	3	0	0	3	1	5	0

GROUP G

England **2-0** Tunisia
Romania **1-0** Colombia
Colombia **1-0** Tunisia
Romania **2-1** England
Romania **1-1** Tunisia
Colombia **0-2** England

	P	W	D	L	F	A	Pts
Romania	3	2	1	0	4	2	7
England	3	2	0	1	5	2	6
Colombia	3	1	0	2	1	3	3
Tunisia	3	0	1	2	1	4	1

GROUP H

Argentina **1-0** Japan
Jamaica **1-3** Croatia
Japan **0-1** Croatia
Argentina **5-0** Jamaica
Argentina **1-0** Croatia
Japan **1-2** Jamaica

	P	W	D	L	F	A	Pts
Argentina	3	3	0	0	7	0	9
Croatia	3	2	0	1	4	2	6
Jamaica	3	1	0	2	3	9	3
Japan	3	0	0	3	1	4	0

SECOND ROUND

Italy **1-0** Norway
Brazil **4-1** Chile
France **1-0** Paraguay
(aet)
France won with golden goal
Nigeria **1-4** Denmark
Germany **2-1** Mexico
Holland **2-1** Yugoslavia
Romania **0-1** Croatia
Argentina **2-2** England
(aet)
Argentina won 4-3 on penalties

QUARTER-FINALS

Italy **0-0** France
(aet)
France won 4-3 on penalties
Brazil **3-2** Denmark
Holland **2-1** Argentina
Germany **0-3** Croatia

SEMI-FINALS

Brazil **1-1** Holland
(aet)
Brazil won 4-2 on penalties
France **2-1** Croatia

THIRD PLACE PLAY-OFF

Holland **1-2** Croatia

FINAL

Brazil **0-3** France

2002 KOREA/JAPAN

GROUP A

France **0-1** Senegal
Uruguay **1-2** Denmark
Denmark **1-1** Senegal
France **0-0** Uruguay
Senegal **3-3** Uruguay
Denmark **2-0** France

	P	W	D	L	F	A	Pts
Denmark	3	2	1	0	5	2	7
Senegal	3	1	2	0	5	4	5
Uruguay	3	0	2	1	4	5	2
France	3	0	1	2	0	3	1

GROUP B

Paraguay **2-2** South Africa
Spain **3-1** Slovenia
Spain **3-1** Paraguay
South Africa **1-0** Slovenia
South Africa **2-3** Spain
Slovenia **1-3** Paraguay

	P	W	D	L	F	A	Pts
Spain	3	3	0	0	9	4	9
Paraguay	3	1	1	1	6	6	4
South Africa	3	1	1	1	5	5	4
Slovenia	3	0	0	3	2	7	0

Argentina's Matias Almeyda holds off Dennis Bergkamp of Holland in 1998.

GROUP C

Brazil **2-1** Turkey
China **0-2** Costa Rica
Brazil **4-0** China
Costa Rica **1-1** Turkey
Costa Rica **2-5** Brazil
Turkey **3-0** China

	P	W	D	L	F	A	Pts
Brazil	3	3	0	0	11	3	9
Turkey	3	1	1	1	5	3	4
Costa Rica	3	1	1	1	5	6	4
China	3	0	0	3	0	9	0

GROUP D

South Korea **2-0** Poland
USA **3-2** Portugal
South Korea **1-1** USA
Portugal **4-0** Poland
Portugal **0-1** South Korea
Poland **3-1** USA

	P	W	D	L	F	A	Pts
South Korea	3	2	1	0	4	1	7
USA	3	1	1	1	5	6	4
Portugal	3	1	0	2	6	4	3
Poland	3	1	0	2	3	7	3

GROUP E

Rep. Of Ireland **1-1** Cameroon
Germany **8-0** Saudi Arabia
Germany **1-1** Rep. Of Ireland
Cameroon **1-0** Saudi Arabia
Cameroon **0-2** Germany
Saudi Arabia **0-3** Rep. Of Ireland

	P	W	D	L	F	A	Pts
Germany	3	2	1	0	11	1	7
Rep. Of Ireland	3	1	2	0	5	2	5
Cameroon	3	1	1	1	2	3	4
Saudi Arabia	3	0	0	3	0	12	0

GROUP F

Argentina **1-0** Nigeria
England **1-1** Sweden
Sweden **2-1** Nigeria
Argentina **0-1** England
Sweden **1-1** Argentina
Nigeria **0-0** England

	P	W	D	L	F	A	Pts
Sweden	3	1	2	0	4	3	5
England	3	1	2	0	2	1	5
Argentina	3	1	1	1	2	2	4
Nigeria	3	0	1	2	1	3	1

GROUP G

Croatia **0-1** Mexico
Italy **2-0** Ecuador
Italy **1-2** Croatia
Mexico **2-1** Ecuador
Mexico **1-1** Italy
Ecuador **1-0** Croatia

	P	W	D	L	F	A	Pts
Mexico	3	2	1	0	4	2	7
Italy	3	1	1	1	4	3	4
Croatia	3	1	0	2	2	3	3
Ecuador	3	1	0	2	2	4	3

GROUP H

Japan **2-2** Belgium
Russia **2-0** Tunisia
Japan **1-0** Russia
Tunisia **1-1** Belgium
Tunisia **0-2** Japan
Belgium **3-2** Russia

	P	W	D	L	F	A	Pts
Japan	3	2	1	0	5	2	7
Belgium	3	1	2	0	6	5	5
Russia	3	1	0	2	4	4	3
Tunisia	3	0	1	2	1	5	1

2ND ROUND

Germany **1-0** Paraguay
Denmark **0-3** England
Sweden **1-2** Senegal
(aet)
Senegal won with golden goal
Spain **1-1** Rep. Of Ireland
(aet)
Spain won 3-2 on penalties
Mexico **0-2** USA
Brazil **2-0** Belgium
Japan **0-1** Turkey
South Korea **2-1** Italy
(aet)
South Korea won with golden goal

QUARTER-FINALS

England **1-2** Brazil
Germany **1-0** USA
Spain **0-0** South Korea
(aet)
South Korea won 5-3 on penalties
Senegal **0-1** Turkey
(aet)
Turkey won with golden goal

SEMI-FINALS

Germany **1-0** South Korea
Brazil **1-0** Turkey

THIRD PLACE MATCH

South Korea **2-3** Turkey

FINAL

Germany **0-2** Brazil

2006 GERMANY

GROUP A

Germany **4-2** Costa Rica
Poland **0-2** Ecuador
Germany **1-0** Poland
Ecuador **3-0** Costa Rica
Costa Rica **1-2** Poland
Ecuador **0-3** Germany

	P	W	D	L	F	A	Pts
Germany	3	3	0	0	8	2	9
Ecuador	3	2	0	1	5	3	6
Poland	3	1	0	2	2	4	3
Costa Rica	3	0	0	3	3	9	0

GROUP B

England **1-0** Paraguay
Trinidad & Tobago **0-0** Sweden
Sweden **1-0** Paraguay
England **2-0** Trinidad & Tobago
Paraguay **2-0** Trinidad & Tobago
Sweden **2-2** England

	P	W	D	L	F	A	Pts
England	3	2	1	0	5	2	7
Sweden	3	1	2	0	3	2	5
Paraguay	3	1	0	2	2	2	3
Trinidad & Tobago	3	0	1	2	0	4	1

GROUP C

Argentina **2-1** Ivory Coast
Serbia & Mont. **0-1** Holland
Holland **2-1** Ivory Coast
Argentina **6-0** Serbia & Mont.
Holland **0-0** Argentina
Ivory Coast **3-2** Serbia & Mont.

	P	W	D	L	F	A	Pts
Argentina	3	2	1	0	8	1	7
Holland	3	2	1	0	3	1	7
Ivory Coast	3	1	0	2	5	6	3
Serbia & Mont.	3	0	0	3	2	10	0

Italy's Fabio Grosso celebrates scoring the winning penalty in the 2006 final.

GROUP D

Mexico **3-1** Iran
Angola **0-1** Portugal
Mexico **0-0** Angola
Portugal **2-0** Iran
Portugal **2-1** Mexico
Iran **1-1** Angola

	P	W	D	L	F	A	Pts
Portugal	3	3	0	0	5	1	9
Mexico	3	1	1	1	4	3	4
Angola	3	0	2	1	1	2	2
Iran	3	0	1	2	2	6	1

GROUP E

Italy **2-0** Ghana
USA **0-3** Czech Republic
Italy **1-1** USA
Czech Republic **0-2** Ghana
Czech Republic **0-2** Italy
Ghana **2-1** USA

	P	W	D	L	F	A	Pts
Italy	3	2	1	0	5	1	7
Ghana	3	2	0	1	4	3	6
Czech Republic	3	1	0	2	3	4	3
USA	3	0	1	2	2	6	1

GROUP F

Australia **3-1** Japan
Brazil **1-0** Croatia
Brazil **2-0** Australia
Japan **0-0** Croatia
Croatia **2-2** Australia
Japan **1-4** Brazil

	P	W	D	L	F	A	Pts
Brazil	3	3	0	0	7	1	9
Australia	3	1	1	1	5	5	4
Croatia	3	0	2	1	2	3	2
Japan	3	0	1	2	2	7	1

GROUP G

South Korea **2-1** Togo
France **0-0** Switzerland
France **1-1** South Korea
Togo **0-2** Switzerland
Togo **0-2** France
Switzerland **2-0** South Korea

	P	W	D	L	F	A	Pts
Switzerland	3	2	1	0	4	0	7
France	3	1	2	0	3	1	5
South Korea	3	1	1	1	3	4	4
Togo	3	0	0	3	1	6	0

GROUP H

Spain **4-0** Ukraine
Tunisia **2-2** Saudi Arabia
Spain **3-1** Tunisia
Saudi Arabia **0-4** Ukraine
Saudi Arabia **0-1** Spain
Ukraine **1-0** Tunisia

	P	W	D	L	F	A	Pts
Spain	3	3	0	0	8	1	9
Ukraine	3	2	0	1	5	4	6
Tunisia	3	0	1	2	3	6	1
Saudi Arabia	3	0	1	2	2	7	1

2ND ROUND

Germany **2-0** Sweden
Argentina **2-1** Mexico
England **1-0** Ecuador
Portugal **1-0** Holland
Italy **1-0** Australia
Switzerland **0-0** Ukraine
(aet)
Ukraine won 3-0 on penalties
Brazil **3-0** Ghana
Spain **1-3** France

QUARTER-FINALS

Germany **1-1** Argentina
(aet)
Germany won 4-2 on penalties
Italy **3-0** Ukraine
England **0-0** Portugal
(aet)
Portugal won 3-1 on penalties
Brazil **0-1** France

SEMI-FINALS

Germany **0-2** Italy
Portugal **0-1** France

THIRD PLACE PLAY-OFF

Germany **3-1** Portugal

FINAL

Italy **1-1** France
(aet)
Italy won 5-3 on penalties

2010 SOUTH AFRICA

GROUP A

South Africa **1-1** Mexico
Uruguay **0-0** France
South Africa **0-3** Uruguay
France **0-2** Mexico
France **1-2** South Africa
Mexico **0-1** Uruguay

	P	W	D	L	F	A	Pts
Uruguay	3	2	1	0	4	0	7
Mexico	3	1	1	1	3	2	4
South Africa	3	1	1	1	3	5	4
France	3	0	1	2	1	4	1

GROUP B

South Korea **2-0** Greece
Argentina **1-0** Nigeria
Argentina **4-1** South Korea
Greece **2-1** Nigeria
Nigeria **2-2** South Korea
Greece **0-2** Argentina

	P	W	D	L	F	A	Pts
Argentina	3	3	0	0	7	1	9
South Korea	3	1	1	1	5	6	4
Greece	3	1	0	2	2	5	3
Nigeria	3	0	1	2	3	5	1

GROUP C

England **1-1** USA
Algeria **0-1** Slovenia
Slovenia **2-2** USA
England **0-0** Algeria
Slovenia **0-1** England
USA **1-0** Algeria

	P	W	D	L	F	A	Pts
USA	3	1	2	0	4	3	5
England	3	1	2	0	2	1	5
Slovenia	3	1	1	1	3	3	4
Algeria	3	0	1	2	0	2	1

GROUP D

Serbia **0-1** Ghana
Germany **4-0** Australia
Germany **0-1** Serbia
Ghana **1-1** Australia
Ghana **0-1** Germany
Australia **2-1** Serbia

	P	W	D	L	F	A	Pts
Germany	3	2	0	1	5	1	6
Ghana	3	1	1	1	2	2	4
Australia	3	1	1	1	3	6	4
Serbia	3	1	0	2	2	3	3

GROUP E

Holland **2-0** Denmark
Japan **1-0** Cameroon
Holland **1-0** Japan
Cameroon **1-2** Denmark
Denmark **1-3** Japan
Cameroon **1-2** Holland

	P	W	D	L	F	A	Pts
Holland	3	3	0	0	5	1	9
Japan	3	2	0	1	4	2	6
Denmark	3	1	0	2	3	6	3
Cameroon	3	0	0	3	2	5	0

GROUP F

Italy **1-1** Paraguay
New Zealand **1-1** Slovakia
Slovakia **0-2** Paraguay
Italy **1-1** New Zealand
Paraguay **0-0** New Zealand
Slovakia **3-2** Italy

	P	W	D	L	F	A	Pts
Paraguay	3	1	2	0	3	1	5
Slovakia	3	1	1	1	4	5	4
New Zealand	3	0	3	0	2	2	3
Italy	3	0	2	1	4	5	2

GROUP G

Ivory Coast **0-0** Portugal
Brazil **2-1** North Korea
Brazil **3-1** Ivory Coast
Portugal **7-0** North Korea
North Korea **0-3** Ivory Coast
Portugal **0-0** Brazil

	P	W	D	L	F	A	Pts
Brazil	3	2	1	0	5	2	7
Portugal	3	1	1	0	7	0	5
Ivory Coast	3	1	1	1	4	3	4
North Korea	3	0	0	3	1	12	0

GROUP H

Honduras **0-1** Chile
Spain **0-1** Switzerland
Chile **1-0** Switzerland
Spain **2-0** Honduras
Switzerland **0-0** Honduras
Chile **1-2** Spain

	P	W	D	L	F	A	Pts
Spain	3	2	0	1	4	2	6
Chile	3	2	0	1	3	2	6
Switzerland	3	1	1	1	1	1	4
Honduras	3	0	1	2	0	3	1

ROUND 2

Uruguay **2-1** South Korea
USA **1-2** Ghana
(aet)
Germany **4-1** England
Argentina **3-1** Mexico
Holland **2-1** Slovakia
Brazil **3-0** Chile
Paraguay **0-0** Japan
(aet)
Paraguay won 5-3 on penalties
Spain **1-0** Portugal

QUARTER-FINALS

Holland **2-1** Brazil
Uruguay **1-1** Ghana
(aet)
Uruguay won 4-2 on penalties
Argentina **0-4** Germany
Paraguay **0-1** Spain

SEMI-FINALS

Uruguay **2-3** Holland
Germany **0-1** Spain

THIRD PLACE PLAY-OFF

Uruguay **2-3** Germany

FINAL

Holland **0-1** Spain
(aet)

Andrés Iniesta celebrates scoring the winner in the 2010 World Cup Final.

THE EUROPEAN CHAMPIONSHIP

THE EUROPEAN CHAMPIONSHIP

The European Championship is the most prestigious continental competition for national teams, and falls second in significance only to the World Cup in the football pecking order. It is contested every four years, and the finals are staged two years apart from the World Cup. The championship is open to all members of UEFA.

As early as 1927 Henri Delaunay, head of the French football association, proposed the idea of a championship involving the top European countries – he was also a driving force behind the foundation of the World Cup. However, after the creation of UEFA on June 15, 1954, the idea was raised once again, and two years later the planning got underway for the competition Delaunay had dreamed of. Sadly, he passed away in 1955, but in his honour the trophy played for will forever hold his name.

The first qualifying matches for the European Nations Cup were played in 1958. The format for the early tournaments remained in place until 1980, and consisted of four finalists who would contest the semi-finals and final in a host

country, with games to be played over a week. Qualification for the earliest tournaments was through a series of knockout preliminary rounds, but a qualifying group phase was introduced for the 1968 competition.

In the summer of 1960 the first finals were held in Delaunay's native France. Just like the World Cup, the inaugural competition could not remain unspoilt by world politics. The quarter-finals drew the Soviet Union against Spain, whose fascist dictator Franco refused the Communist side entry to his country, and in so doing forfeited the tie. This worked in the Soviet Union's favour, as they finished winners under the inspirational leadership of keeper Lev Yashin, beating Yugoslavia 2-1 in the first final.

By 1968 the tournament had undergone a change of name from the unwieldy European Nations Cup to the European Championship. Hosts Spain and Italy were winners in 1964 and 1968, a sequence that was broken by West Germany in 1972, but even then they were given a scare by hosts Belgium in a close semi-final.

In 1976 the tournament was held in an Eastern Bloc country for the first time, with Yugoslavia hosting. Yet another first was created in the final when a spirited Czech side held the holders West Germany to a draw, and the game was decided by a penalty shoot-out. The Czechs held their nerve and ran out 5-3 winners, with Antonin Panenka famously dinking his penalty over a stranded Sepp Maier to claim the trophy.

The 1980 competition saw the final stage format change, as the semi-final was jettisoned in favour of eight teams competing in two mini-leagues, with the winners of both groups advancing directly to the final. Once again the strength of West Germany saw them through, where they narrowly defeated Belgium with a late goal from match-winner Horst Hrubesch.

Forever tinkering with the format, UEFA reintroduced the semi-final stage to the tournament in 1984, with the top two teams from each group playing for a place in the final. France, under the inspirational captaincy of Michel Platini, swept all other teams aside, and

Above from left to right: France's Sylvain Wiltord kisses the trophy after victory over Italy in 2000; Czechoslovakia enjoy their 1976 win after beating West Germany on penalties; Holland's Adri Van Tiggelen and Frank Rijkaard celebrate in 1988.

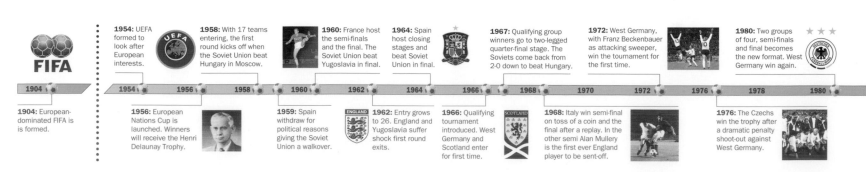

FIFA

1954: UEFA formed to look after European interests.

1958: With 17 teams entering, the first round kicks off when the Soviet Union beat Hungary in Moscow.

1960: France host the semi-finals and the final. The Soviet Union beat Yugoslavia in final.

1964: Spain host closing stages and beat Soviet Union in final.

1967: Qualifying group winners go to two-legged quarter-final stage. The Soviets come back from 2-0 down to beat Hungary.

1972: West Germany, with Franz Beckenbauer as attacking sweeper, win the tournament for the first time.

1980: Two groups of four, semi-finals and final becomes the new format. West Germany win again.

| 1904 | 1954 | 1956 | 1958 | 1960 | 1962 | 1964 | 1966 | 1968 | 1970 | 1972 | 1976 | 1978 | 1980 |

1904: European-dominated FIFA is is formed.

1956: European Nations Cup is launched. Winners will receive the Henri Delaunay Trophy.

1959: Spain withdraw for political reasons giving the Soviet Union a walkover.

1962: Entry grows to 26. England and Yugoslavia suffer shock first round exits.

1966: Qualifying tournament introduced. West Germany and Scotland enter for first time.

1968: Italy win semi-final on toss of a coin and the final after a replay. In the other semi Alan Mullery is the first ever England player to be sent-off.

1976: The Czechs win the trophy after a dramatic penalty shoot-out against West Germany.

EUROPEAN CHAMPIONSHIP WINNERS & HOST NATIONS

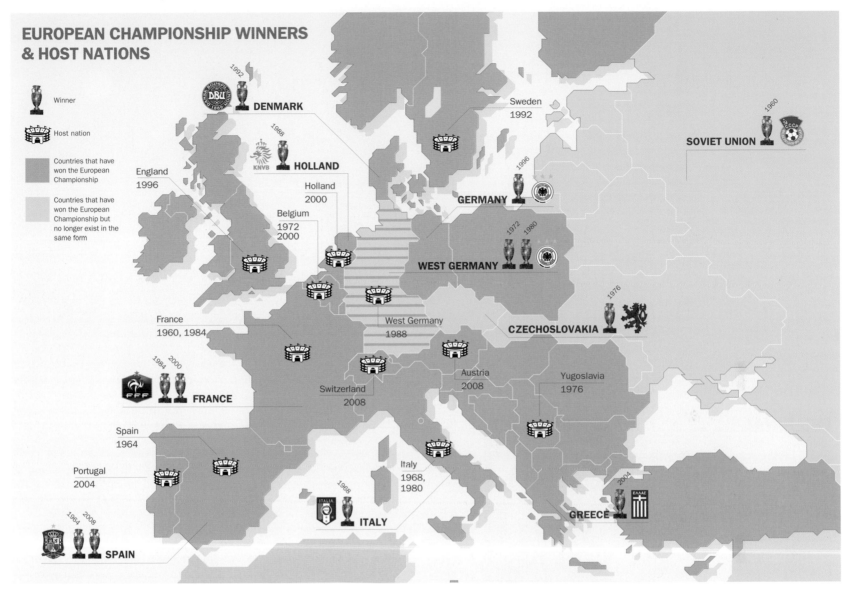

- Winner
- Host nation
- Countries that have won the European Championship
- Countries that have won the European Championship but no longer exist in the same form

DENMARK

Sweden 1992

SOVIET UNION 1960

England 1996

HOLLAND 1988

Holland 2000

Belgium 1972 2000

GERMANY 1996

WEST GERMANY 1972 1980

CZECHOSLOVAKIA 1976

West Germany 1988

Austria 2008

Yugoslavia 1976

France 1960, 1984

FRANCE 1984 2000

Switzerland 2008

Spain 1964

Portugal 2004

Italy 1968, 1980

ITALY 1968

GREECE 2004

SPAIN 1964 2008

for the third time in seven tournaments it was the hosts who claimed victory.

The format for the final stages of the 1988 and 1992 competition remained unaltered. The tournaments are best remembered for Dutch master Marco Van Basten's wonderstrike in the final against the Soviet Union in 1988, and for Denmark literally coming from nowhere to defeat the Germans in the 1992 final. Having initially failed to qualify, the Danes were only playing as last-minute replacements for the Yugoslavians, who had been suspended.

The increased success of the tournament saw a further expansion in 1996, with 16 teams competing in four leagues to produce eight quarter-finalists. This was the tournament when football came home to England, and the success of Euro 96 went a long way to rehabilitating the reputation of English football, both on and off the pitch. Despite this, it was still the Germans who claimed the trophy. A close final against the Czech Republic was notable for Oliver Bierhoff's 94th minute strike – it was the first time that a 'golden goal' winner had decided the outcome of a major international competition.

Four years later France's David Trezeguet repeated the trick against Italy, concluding another wonderful European Championship final with a 'golden goal'. It was only the second time that a nation simultaneously reigned as European and world champions.

The 2004 competition in Portugal provided international football with its biggest shock, when outsiders Greece beat the hosts to lift their first major trophy, while in 2008 the finals came to a thrilling conclusion with the Spanish claiming the cup for the first time in 44 years.

With Euro 2012 to be split between Poland and Ukraine, the tournament continues to grow in prestige. It also continues to grow in size, as from 2016 the finals will see the number of competing nations increase from 16 to 24.

Details of red and yellow cards for the European Championships prior to the 1984 tournament are not available.

1984: Michel Platini and France win a magnificent tournament.

1988: Ruud Gullit and Marco Van Basten goals win the trophy for Holland.

1995: Holland and Belgium announced as joint-hosts of the 2000 tournament.

1999: Portugal announced as Euro 2004 hosts.

2004: Greece shock world football when they become European champions.

2012: Poland and Ukraine are due to stage the finals.

| 1982 | 1984 | 1986 | 1988 | 1990 | 1992 | 1994 | 1996 | 1998 | 2000 | 2002 | 2004 | 2006 | 2008 | 2012 | 2016 |

1983: Spain thump Malta 12-1 to conveniently qualify on goal difference at the expense of Holland.

1987: Holland thrash Cyprus 8-0 in qualification but have to replay behind closed doors after a firework hits the Cyprus goalkeeper.

1992: Denmark, late replacements for Yugoslavia, win the trophy in Sweden.

1996: Germany win Euro 96 final with 'golden goal' in an expanded tournament of 16 teams.

2000: France win the final to jointly hold the World Cup and the European Championship.

2008: Spain beat Germany in Vienna to win the 2008 final.

2016: To be staged in France, the tournament will grow in size to 24 teams.

FRANCE 1960

SEMI-FINALS

Soviet Union 3-0 Czechoslovakia
Yugoslavia 5-4 France

THIRD PLACE PLAY-OFF

Czechoslovakia 2-0 France

TOP GOALSCORERS

2 goals: François Heutte (France),
Valentin Ivanov (Soviet Union),
Victor Ponedelnik (Soviet Union),
Milan Galic (Yugoslavia), Drazen
Jerkovic (Yugoslavia)

FASTEST GOAL

11 minutes: Milan Gallic
(Yugoslavia v France)

TOTAL GOALS

17

AVERAGE GOALS

4.25 per game

As France has provided the game of football with some of its greatest visionaries, it is no real surprise to discover that it was a Frenchman, Henri Delaunay, head of the French Football Federation, who came up with the idea for a tournament between Europe's top nations.

The European Championship, or the European Nations Cup as it was originally called, was finally established at the third UEFA Congress in Stockholm on June 6, 1958, but Delaunay had actually conceived the idea as far back as 1927. However, at that time getting the World Cup off the ground was the priority. It was Delaunay who chaired the original commission set up by Jules Rimet in 1927 to look into a world football tournament and this took precedence.

When UEFA was created in 1954 Delaunay became its general secretary and rapidly installed two competitions, one for club teams and one for national sides. His aim was to bring into a single competition the three

Above: Hosts France take a 4-2 lead in their semi-final with Yugoslavia, only to be undone by three goals in the last 15 minutes. Opposite: The Soviet Union and Yugoslavia contest the first European Championship final under floodlights.

THE FINAL

SOVIET UNION (0) 2-1 (1) YUGOSLAVIA

(aet; 1-1 at 90 minutes)

Date Sunday July 10, 1960 **Attendance** 18,000

Venue Parc Des Princes, Paris

Played under floodlights in persistent drizzle on a heavy pitch, the inaugural European Nations Cup final was a credit to both sides. The conditions favoured the more technical skills of the Yugoslavs and they started strongly, eventually taking the lead in the 43rd minute as Galic nodded home after a cross by Jerkovic.

The Yugoslavs should have capitalised on several more opportunities, but Lev Yashin made some spectacular saves. Four minutes into the second-half the Soviets equalised through Metreveli and the match became increasingly tactical until the final whistle found both teams locked at 1-1. The Soviets proved stronger in extra-time and in the 113th minute, Ponedelnik headed home from Meskhi's cross.

HOW THE TEAMS LINED UP

SOVIET UNION
COACH:
GABRIEL KATCHALINE

YUGOSLAVIA
COACH:
ALEKSANDAR TIRNANIC

	Yashin	
Chokheli		Maslenkin
Krutikov	Voinov	Netto
Ivanov, V		Bubukin
Metreveli	Ponedelnik	Meskhi
Kostic	Galic	Jerkovic
Matus		Sekularac
Perusic	Miladinovic	Zanetic
Jusufi		Durkovic
	Vidinic	

SOVIET UNION

YASHIN
CHOKHELI
MASLENKIN
KRUTIKOV
VOINOV
NETTO
IVANOV, V
BUBUKIN
METREVELI
Goal: 49 mins
PONEDELNIK
Goal: 114 mins
MESKHI

YUGOSLAVIA

VIDINIC
DURKOVIC
JUSUFI
ZANETIC
MILADINOVIC
PERUSIC
SEKULARAC
MATUS
JERKOVIC
GALIC
Goal: 41 mins
KOSTIC

Referee: Ellis (England)

regional tournaments that already existed: the British Home Championship, the Nordic Cup and the Central European Championship. Sadly, Delaunay died in 1955 before he could see his scheme fulfilled but his son Pierre took over the reins and the trophy was named in his father's honour.

It was agreed to hold the tournament once every four years, in between the World Cups, but UEFA initially struggled to find enough countries who were willing to compete and much behind the scenes negotiating went on to ensure that there was a competitive first tournament. The cause was not helped by the British teams; fearing the end of the Home International Championship, they refused to participate. Also refusing to enter were the 1958 World Cup hosts and runners-up Sweden, along with West Germany and Italy.

In the end 17 out of 33 countries affiliated to UEFA agreed to take part, and after a two-legged eliminator between Ireland and Czechoslovakia had whittled the number of sides down to an even 16 for the qualifiers, the first match in the European Nations Cup was played between the Soviet Union and Hungary.

The remaining 14 nations to enter the qualifying phase were Austria, Bulgaria, Czechoslovakia, Denmark, France, East Germany, Greece, Norway, Poland, Portugal, Romania, Spain, Turkey, and Yugoslavia. The entry fee was £50 and it was agreed that gate receipts would be split 50-50 between FIFA and UEFA. The initial structure of the competition was very different from the European Championship as we know it today. Teams played home and away matches, the losing team being eliminated, and the winner proceeding to the next round.

There were further problems, too, when Spain were drawn against the Soviet Union. Under Helenio Herrera, and with stars like Di Stéfano, Suarez and Gento in their squad, the Spanish would have been strong contenders. However, Spain's fascist dictator, General Franco, refused to allow his nation to play against the Communists, resulting in Spain losing by default and putting the Soviets through to the semi-finals. Thus four games (the semi-finals, the third place play-off and the final) constituted the tournament proper and were played over five days between July 6 and 10 in Paris and Marseilles.

The hosts had to qualify in the same manner as the other sides, beating Austria convincingly to go through to a semi-final against Yugoslavia, a game that proved to be the most emotionally charged tie of the tournament. The French, third in the 1958 World Cup, were without Raymond Kopa and Golden Boot winner Just Fontaine, but put on a good performance to come back from an early deficit to lead Yugoslavia 4-2 just 15 minutes before the final whistle. However, Tomislav Knez started the comeback and two goals from Drazan Jerkovic were enough to knock France out and stun the fans of the host nation.

The Soviet Union proved much too strong for Czechoslovakia in the other semi-final, with Victor Ponedelnik, a formidable goalmouth poacher, scoring twice as the Soviets eased to a 3-0 win that brought them face to face with Yugoslavia in the final.

The match was a repeat of the 1956 Olympic Games gold medal match in Melbourne, which had been won 1-0 by the USSR. Whether this gave them a psychological advantage as the teams lined-up in the early evening at the Parc Des Princes is unclear, but the Soviets were to prove too strong for their opponents once more. They became the first team to lift the Henri Delaunay trophy after coming through in extra-time to win 2-1 and claim their first and only major tournament victory.

Above: Spain celebrate winning the European Nations Cup on home soil. Opposite: Soviet Union keeper Lev Yashin concedes the opening goal in the final at the Bernabéu.

SEMI-FINALS
Spain 2-1 Hungary
(aet: 1-1 at 90 mins)
Soviet Union 3-0 Denmark

THIRD PLACE PLAY-OFF
Hungary 3-1 Denmark
(aet: 1-1 at 90 mins)

TOP GOALSCORERS
2 goals: Jesus Maria Pereda (Spain), Ferenc Bene (Hungary), Dezso Novák (Hungary)

FASTEST GOAL
6 minutes: Jesus Maria Pereda (Spain v Soviet Union)

TOTAL GOALS
13 goals

AVERAGE GOALS
3.25

SPAIN 1964

The European Championship was still in its infancy and struggling to make its mark in the international calendar. In 1963, however, one result in the qualifying stages captured the headlines and made Europe sit up and take notice. Luxembourg, with a population of just 300,000, produced a remarkable performance over two legs, beating Holland to achieve the greatest victory in their history and the first real upset of the fledgling competition.

Luxembourg's triumph fired the public imagination, but to make matters worse for the humiliated Dutch, both legs were played in their own country. The first, in Amsterdam in September 1963, ended in a 1-1 draw as Nuninga gave the Holland the lead after five minutes, with May equalising half an hour later. The second leg, played in Rotterdam, saw a host of changes in the Dutch line-up but Dimmer gave Luxembourg a shock lead. After Kruiver equalised the outsiders survived an onslaught before Dimmer grabbed an unexpected second 23 minutes from time to seal a famous victory.

Amazingly Luxembourg nearly repeated the feat against Denmark in the quarter-finals, drawing 3-3 and 2-2 before losing the play-off 1-0, a game played, ironically, on neutral territory in Amsterdam. They may have been knocked out but they had created a sensation and achieved the biggest success in their history. Elsewhere, France crushed England over two legs, while Italy also lost out.

Despite earlier shocks the latter stages had a familiar look, as Spain, Hungary, the Soviet Union and Denmark won through to the last four, with the finals to be played in Spain over four days in June 1964. While the football was

of a decent standard, the competition failed to grab the attention in the way the World Cup did. Luxembourg's giant-killing acts were entertaining at the time but the spread of matches over a lengthy period did little to concentrate the minds of fans across Europe, and with only four teams making the finals it had little mass appeal.

There were still players to admire. Spain were favourites thanks to home advantage and the wing skills of Luis Suarez, while the Soviet Union had the best goalkeeper in the world in Lev Yashin. Hungary also had centre-forward Florian Albert, later a European Footballer Of The Year, who was a superbly balanced striker able to give hope to his ageing side.

In the semi-final Spain met Hungary in Madrid in front of a crowd of 125,000 and Jose Villalonga's side did enough in extra-time to make it through to the final. Pereda gave them a first-half lead from Suarez's cross, before Bene struck an equaliser six minutes before full-time. It took an Amancio goal in the 115th minute to decide the outcome.

In the other semi-final, the Soviet Union saw off outsiders Denmark with a comfortable 3-0 victory in the Nou Camp to set up a final that would see if Spain could finally match the club achievements of Real Madrid with a triumph for the national team.

They did, and with it came Spain's first major trophy. It was a fitting tribute to the country that had dominated club football for half a decade, but the national team was not moulded in the same style. They lacked the flair, the grace and the sheer dazzling brilliance of the famous Madrid team in white. Despite offering flashes of skill from Suarez and Amancio, both among the best players in the world at the time, the Spanish generation of 1964 would not go down in history as one of the country's greatest sides.

THE FINAL

SPAIN (1) **2-1** (1) **SOVIET UNION**

Date Sunday June 21, 1964 **Attendance** 79,115
Venue Santiago Bernabéu, Madrid

The largest ever crowd to watch a European Championship final turned up to see the home side lift the trophy. They did, but only just. It was a tense affair, although in front of dictator General Franco the Spanish got off to a dream start with a sixth-minute goal from Pereda. Khusainov struck back two minutes later and the Soviets packed their defence, with inside-left Korneyev playing as an extra defender.

All the talk in the build-up about Lev Yashin facing the deft skills of the Spanish attack came to little on the big day, although Suarez was in outstanding form. Spain finally found a way through, with Zaragoza centre-forward Marcelino scoring the winner with a diving header from Pereda's cross in the 84th minute. The Soviets, with so little time to come back, were beaten.

HOW THE TEAMS LINED UP

SPAIN
COACH: JOSE VILLALONGA

SOVIET UNION
COACH: KONSTANTIN BESKOV

Iribar
Rivilla — Olivella
Calleja — Zoco — Fuste
Pereda — Suarez
Amancio — Marcelino — Lapetra
Khusainov — Ponedelnik — Chislenko
Korneyev — Ivanov, V
Anichkin — Voronin — Mudrik
Shesternyov — Shustikov
Yashin

SPAIN
IRIBAR
RIVILLA
OLIVELLA
CALLEJA
ZOCO
FUSTE
PEREDA
Goal: 6 mins
SUAREZ
AMANCIO
MARCELINO
Goal: 84 mins
LAPETRA

SOVIET UNION
YASHIN
SHUSTIKOV
SHESTERNYOV
MUDRIK
VORONIN
ANICHKIN
IVANOV, V
KORNEYEV
CHISLENKO
PONEDELNIK
KHUSAINOV
Goal: 8 mins

Referee: Holland (England)

ITALY 1968

The competition to win the Henri Delaunay Trophy underwent a change of name and format in 1968, as the European Nations Cup became the European Football Championship. The original two-legged knockout qualification was dropped and for the first time replaced with eight qualifying groups totalling a record 31 teams, including newcomers Scotland and West Germany. The eight group winners qualified for the quarter-finals, which were played over two legs.

The big tie of the quarter-finals pitched World Cup winners England against the defending European champions Spain. Bobby Charlton scored the only goal of the first leg at Wembley, and in the return England won 2-1 in Madrid with goals from Martin Peters and Norman Hunter.

Italy were named hosts of the latter stages of the tournament and they qualified after a 4-3 aggregate win over Bulgaria's best-ever side, one that featured Hristo Bonev and Petar Jekov. It was Jekov who clinched the winner in a five-goal thriller in Sofia, but in Naples a fortnight later Italy won 2-0 with goals from Prati and Domenghini, becoming the first team to reach the semis.

Yugoslavia's young and energetic team easily overcame France. After a 1-1 draw in Marseille they thrashed the French 5-1 in Belgrade, with two goals each from Petkovic and Musemic, and a single strike from Dzajic.

The best performance of the quarter-final stage was by the Soviet Union, who overturned

Above: The Soviets before their play-off with England. Opposite clockwise from top left: Italy dominated the final replay; Facchetti celebrates winning the decisive toss after the USSR semi; England's Bobby Charlton; Italy before the final replay.

a 2-0 defeat by Hungary in Budapest with a magnificent home performance in Moscow, running out 3-2 aggregate winners. It was a tremendous comeback against a team who later the same year would be crowned Olympic champions.

The Soviet Union's reward was a semi-final clash with hosts Italy in Naples. A hard enough challenge in itself, but team selection was made even harder by circumstances when winger Igor Chislenko and half-back Murtaz Khurtzilava sustained injuries in an Olympic qualifier against Czechoslovakia just days earlier. It meant that manager Mikhail Yakushin arrived in Italy with an injury-decimated squad.

The 75,000 crowd in the San Paolo Stadium were forced to witness a dreadful game, played in appalling weather conditions, between

a makeshift Soviet side and an Italian team with a mortal fear of losing. The Soviets did dominate the first-half, but they squandered the few good chances they created. After the break Rivera returned to the pitch following an enforced first-half absence caused by a collision with the Soviet fullback Afonin, and an impatient Italian crowd saw their team improving to get the better of the second-half.

However, this time it was the turn of the Soviet defence to hold firm. The closing minutes saw Italy produce attack after attack, during which Domenghini hit the post, but even extra-time brought no goals. So a place in the 1968 European Championship Final was decided in the dressing room with the spin of a 1916 French ten franc coin. The hosts won the toss and it was Italy who progressed to the final.

The other semi-final in Florence between favourites England and the gifted young Yugoslav side was equally dismal. Played in a humid, thundery atmosphere, one reporter described the match as a technical dirge. It was a frustrating game involving uncompromising tackling from both sides. After just five minutes England's Norman Hunter had inflicted an ankle injury on Yugoslavian playmaker Ivica Osim, making him virtually a passenger for the rest of the game. It set the tone for the remainder of the contest and there were a staggering 49 free-kicks awarded.

The decisive action took place in the 85th minute when the excellent Dragan Dzajic beat goalkeeper Gordon Banks with an exquisite volley that proved to be the winning goal. It got worse for England before the final whistle when Alan Mullery, after being ruthlessly brought down by Trivic, retaliated with a blatant kick on his assailant. He became the first England player ever to be sent-off, and that in 96 years of international football.

England, without the suspended Mullery, the injured Alan Ball, and hayfever sufferer Colin Bell, recovered to win an entertaining Third Place Play-Off clash with the Soviet Union. Goals from Bobby Charlton and Geoff Hurst gave England a deserved 2-0 win.

SEMI-FINALS

Italy 0-0 Soviet Union
(aet: Italy won on toss of coin)
Yugoslavia 1-0 England

THIRD PLACE PLAY-OFF

England **2-0** Soviet Union

TOP GOALSCORER

2 goals: Dragan Dzajic (Yugoslavia)

FASTEST GOAL

11 mins: Gigi Riva
(Italy v Yugoslavia replay)

TOTAL GOALS

7

AVERAGE GOALS

1.4 per game

FINAL GAME
ITALY
ZOFF
BURGNICH
FACCHETTI
FERRINI
GUARNERI
CASTANO
DOMENGHINI
Goal: 80 mins
JULIANO
LODETTI
ANASTASI
PRATI
YUGOSLAVIA
PANTELIC
FAZLAGIC
DAMJANOVIC
PAVLOVIC
PAUNOVIC
HOLCER
TRIVIC
ACIMOVIC
PETKOVIC
MUSEMIC
DZAJIC
Goal: 39 mins
Referee: Dienst (Switzerland)

THE FINAL

ITALY (0) 1-1 (1) YUGOSLAVIA (aet)

Date Saturday June 8, 1968 **Attendance** 69,000
Venue Olympic Stadium, Rome

Italy were favourites but Yugoslavia dominated. Goalkeeper Dino Zoff kept Italy in the game but was unable to stop Dzajic scoring in the 39th minute. The inability to beat Zoff again proved Yugoslavia's undoing. With ten minutes to go Domenghini's 25-yard free-kick crashed in. Extra-time saw no goals.

REPLAY

ITALY (2) 2-0 (0) YUGOSLAVIA

Date Monday June 10, 1968 **Attendance** 50,000
Venue Olympic Stadium, Rome

Italy made five changes, bringing in Rosato, Salvadore, Mazzola, De Sisti and Riva. The transformed team dominated and Yugoslavia never recovered after Italy's magnificent start. Riva scored with a great left-foot shot early on and after 32 minutes Anastasi fired on the turn to make it 2-0.

REPLAY
ITALY
ZOFF
BURGNICH
FACCHETTI
SALVADORE
GUARNERI
ROSATO
DOMENGHINI
MAZZOLA
DE SISTI
ANASTASI
Goal: 32 mins
RIVA
Goal: 11 mins
YUGOSLAVIA
PANTELIC
FAZLAGIC
DAMJANOVIC
PAVLOVIC
PAUNOVIC
HOLCER
TRIVIC
LAUKUNU
HOSIC
MUSEMIC
DZAJIC
Referee: Ortiz de Mendibil (Spain)

HOW THE TEAMS LINED UP

ITALY
COACH: FERRUCCIO VALCAREGGI

YUGOSLAVIA
COACH: RAJKO MITIC

Above: The Soviet Union line up before the final. Below right: Paul Van Himst of Belgium on the ball against West Germany. Opposite clockwise from top: Gerd Müller lifts the trophy after West Germany's 3-0 victory; West Germany charge forward; Müller nets one of his two goals; the West Germans inspect the trophy.

BELGIUM 1972

It may not be remembered as one of the great international football tournaments of all time, but the 1972 European Championship was significant for one reason: it saw West Germany pick up their first major international trophy since the 1954 World Cup, beginning a golden era of almost 25 years that would see the Germans become the most powerful nation in world football.

To be fair to the Germans, the success had been coming. Finishing a creditable third behind the greatest Brazilian team of all time at the 1970 World Cup had indicated there was something special to come, but 1972 saw the new young team built by coach Helmut Schön truly come of age.

Qualifying for the tournament had begun in 1970, with 32 European nations involved. Italy and West Germany were among the favourites, as both had come into the tournament off the back of promising World Cup campaigns, finishing as runners-up and third respectively. England, meanwhile, were also still considered to be a major football power, despite failing to live up to expectations in Mexico.

In the first qualifying phase, these three each finished top of their groups and remained unbeaten, while the Soviet Union also came through impressively without losing a single game, making them serious contenders for a place in the final.

The quarter-finals saw Hungary eliminate Romania 2-1 in a play-off, with the original encounters finishing 3-3 on aggregate. The Soviets cruised through 3-0 against Yugoslavia, their vanquished opponents from the first ever European Championship final. A physical Belgian outfit muscled past Italy, winning 2-1 on aggregate, but the big tie of the round was undoubtedly West Germany against England.

West Germany travelled to Wembley in April 1972 and completed an impressive 3-1 away win in the first leg – it was the first time Germany had beaten the English on their home soil. This result was enough to see them through as the return match ended in a scoreless draw.

The Belgians were voted hosts for the final stages and they were drawn against the West Germans, who had now emerged as clear favourites. Home advantage counted for little for Belgium as so many German fans made the relatively short trip to Antwerp to cheer on their team. Belgium started well enough, containing the German threat, but a great header from Müller gave the favourites the lead going in at half-time. The Belgians, to their credit, threw men forward in the second period and brought some great saves out of German keeper Sepp Maier, but the game turned decisively in West Germany's favour in the 71st minute when Müller put his side two up. Belgium pulled a goal back late on but it was to no avail.

While a crowd of nearly 60,000 had watched the hosts lose the first semi-final, the live televising of the game meant that only 2,000 fans were at the Parc Astrid in Brussels to witness a the other simultaneously played contest, a disappointing display between two of Eastern Europe's top football nations. The skilful Hungarians faced the Soviet Union, a nation with an impressive record in the tournament, but with neither side threatening in the first-half, the game only came to life when Konkov blasted the Soviets in front after the break. Hungary rallied but failed to equalise, even missing a late penalty.

Before the final came the third place play-off. Another disappointing crowd of only 10,000 saw Belgium live up to their physical reputation, grinding out a 2-1 win over the Hungarians. Three days later at the Heysel Stadium in Brussels, West Germany, playing in front of

THE FINAL

WEST GERMANY (1) **3-0** (0) SOVIET UNION

Date Sunday June 18, 1972 **Attendance** 43,437
Venue Heysel Stadium, Brussels

The West Germans were on the offensive from the start, mounting wave after wave of attack. Netzer controlled the midfield and was impressively supported by sweeper Beckenbauer, while Gerd Müller ran the Soviet defence ragged. Soviet keeper Rudakov kept the Germans at bay until late in the first-half when Müller met a cross with his chest, brought the ball down and slotted home.

The Germans raised their game after the break, limiting the Soviets to just three shots in the game. The excellent Wimmer played a one-two with Heynckes, before crashing the ball home to put daylight between the two sides. Five minutes later Müller wrongfooted the goalkeeper to score the third goal of the game. It made him the tournament's top scorer.

WEST GERMANY	
MAIER	
HÖTTGES	
BECKENBAUER	
SCHWARZENBECK	
BREITNER	
HOENESS, U	
WIMMER	⚽
Goal: 52 mins	
NETZER	
HEYNCKES	
MÜLLER, G	⚽⚽
Goal: 27 mins, 58 mins	
KREMERS, E	

SOVIET UNION	
RUDAKOV	
DZODZUASHVILI	
ISTOMIN	
KHURTSILAVA	
KAPLICHNY	
KOLOTOV	
TROSHKIN	
BAIDACHNY	
BANISHEVSKY	▶
Subbed: 66 mins (Kozinkevich)	
KONKOV	▶
Subbed: 46 mins (Dolmatov)	
ONISHCHENKO	
sub: **KOZINKEVICH**	▶
sub: **DOLMATOV**	▶

Referee: Marschall (Austria)

HOW THE TEAMS LINED UP

WEST GERMANY
COACH:
HELMUT SCHÖN
★ ★ ★

Maier

Höttges Schwarzenbeck Beckenbauer Breitner

Wimmer Hoeness, U Netzer

Heynckes Müller, G Kremers, E

SOVIET UNION
COACH:
ALEKSANDR PONOMAREV

Onishchenko Banishevsky Baidachny

Konkov Troshkin Kolotov

Istomin Kaplichny Khurtsilava Dzodzuashvili

Rudakov

a largely German crowd, faced the Soviet Union as clear favourites. Beckenbauer and his team-mates did not disappoint, lifting the trophy with a comprehensive 3-0 victory.

The tournament's best team had won and it would not be the last time a German side would return from a major international competition brandishing silverware. Despite it only being the very beginning of a long and successful spell, many critics now believe that this was the best of all the great German sides, even better than the team who went on to lift the World Cup two years later.

SEMI-FINALS

West Germany 2-1 Belgium
Soviet Union 1-0 Hungary

THIRD PLACE PLAY-OFF

Belgium 2-1 Hungary

TOP GOALSCORER

4 goals: Gerd Müller (West Germany)

FASTEST GOAL

24 mins: Raul Lambert (Belgium v Hungary); Gerd Müller (West Germany v Belgium)

TOTAL GOALS

10

AVERAGE GOALS

2.5 per game

YUGOSLAVIA 1976

If you were to imagine the most unlikely conclusion to a major final, it would probably involve the world champions losing with the last kick of the tournament. However, in 1976, that's exactly what happened.

In a brief but exhilarating competition, restricted to only four teams and four days, Czechoslovakia lifted the Henri Delaunay Trophy when the usually nerveless West German team suffered an uncharacteristic outbreak of penalty shoot-out jitters. However, the 1976 championship was about so much more than Uli Hoeness's hoof over the bar. At the peak of a golden era of European football, brilliant, attacking play dominated throughout and the underdog prevailed.

Yugoslavia 76 was one of the most closely fought major tournaments ever staged. Every match, both semi-finals, the final and third-place play-off went into extra-time. The quality of play throughout was both exhilarating and, for those not involved, a chilling reminder of how far the game had moved on, led by Dutch 'Total Football' and the powerful athleticism of West Germany. For some traditional football

Above: The victorious Czech team. Opposite clockwise from top left: The final was a close affair between the Czechs and West Germany; the Czechs lift the cup after a penalty shoot-out; an exhausted Franz Beckenbauer; Ivo Viktor celebrates.

powers, Yugoslavia 76 rudely showed how far the game had changed and how far they were being left behind. Italy, World Cup finalists just six years earlier, only finished third in their group during qualification.

England, world champions ten years earlier, also failed to progress beyond the group stages, although typically false promise came before the fall. In the opening match of their qualification group, Don Revie's team trounced the eventual winners of the tournament 3-0 at Wembley. Defeat in the return fixture, coupled with an inability to beat Portugal either home or away, spelled elimination as group runners-up one point behind the Czechs.

Qualification for the quarter-finals was a straightforward battle for supremacy across eight groups. Of the British nations, only Wales made it this far after overcoming a group containing Hungary, Austria and Luxembourg. Quarter-finals over two legs then determined which four teams would receive their exclusive invites to the midsummer festival of football.

Yugoslavia made sure they would not miss the party by beating Wales 2-0 at home, then drawing 1-1 in Cardiff. The other bright spot for the British teams was Don Givens, whose eight goals for Northern Ireland in the qualification phase was not bettered during the entire competition.

Joining the hosts in the last four were West Germany, the outrageously talented Holland and neat but lightly fancied Czechoslovakia. Such a brief tournament needed to catch fire immediately, and in a sensational opening game three players were sent-off as Holland crashed out. For Johan Cruyff and his team-mates, this tournament, sandwiched between their two World Cup final appearances, should have been payback time for their 1974 World

Cup Final defeat to West Germany, but instead they again paid the price for overconfidence, ending their game against Czechoslovakia with nine men. Their opponents scored two goals in extra-time to run out 3-1 winners.

Holland's exit appeared to pave the way for West Germany. They duly earned their place in the final courtesy of a 4-2 defeat of the hosts, although it was much closer than the score suggested. In one of the competition's classic encounters, watched by 70,000 fans in Belgrade, Yugoslavia raced into a two-goal lead with little more than 30 minutes played. They were still a goal to the good with ten minutes remaining when West Germany brought on Dieter Müller. Within two minutes he had equalised to send the match into extra-time and he netted twice more to complete his hat-trick and Yugoslavia's misery.

Utterly deflated, the Yugoslavs did well to force the third place play-off against Holland into extra-time, where Geels scored the winning goal to enable the Dutch to edge the game 3-2 and gain some small consolation in front of a crowd of just 7,000.

All eyes now focused on Belgrade: could the Czechoslovakians, a talented but hardly feared football power, possibly match the might of the confident, powerful world champions? Franz Beckenbauer was at the height of his powers and his side contained incredible talent, even by the high standards of the mid-Seventies.

Dieter Müller's three goals in the semi-final were enough to retain his place in the German starting line-up, but in Viktor, crowd favourites Czechoslovakia boasted the goalkeeper of the tournament. He was kept busy in a final match that proved worthy of this wonderful tournament, and one that eventually resulted in a surprise win for the Czechoslovakians.

SEMI-FINALS

Czechoslovakia 3-1 Holland
(aet: 1-1 at 90 mins)

West Germany 4-2 Yugoslavia
(aet: 2-2 at 90 mins)

THIRD PLACE PLAY-OFF

Holland 3-2 Yugoslavia
(aet: 2-2 at 90 mins)

TOP GOALSCORER

4 goals: Dieter Müller (West Germany)

FASTEST GOAL

8 mins: Jan Svehlík (Czechoslovakia v West Germany)

TOTAL GOALS

19

AVERAGE GOALS

4.75 per game

THE FINAL

CZECHOSLOVAKIA (2) 2-2 (1) WEST GERMANY
(aet: Czechoslovakia won 5-3 on penalties)

Date Sunday June 20, 1976 **Attendance** 35,000

Venue Red Star Stadium, Belgrade

The highly-fancied Germans were stunned by Czechoslovakia's attacking start, and after 25 minutes they were 2-0 down to goals from Svehlík and Dobiás. Dieter Müller grabbed one back straight away, but the Czechs looked to be holding on. Wave after wave of West German attacks finally paid off with a dramatic equaliser in the final minute. It appeared that nothing could deny Beckenbauer another trophy in his 100th international appearance, but the Czechs were kept alive in extra-time by keeper Viktor and the game was settled by penalties. When Hoeness blasted over and Panenka slotted home, the trophy was on its way to Prague.

CZECHOSLOVAKIA		
VIKTOR		
PIVARNÍK		
ONDRUS		
CAPKOVIC		
GÖGH		
DOBIÁS		⚽▶
Goal: 25 mins. Subbed: 94 mins (Vesely)		
MÓDER		
PANENKA		
MASNY		
SVEHLÍK		⚽▶
Goal: 8 mins. Subbed: 79 mins (Jurkemik)		
NEHODA		
sub: JURKEMIK		▶
sub: VESELY		▶

WEST GERMANY		
MAIER		
VOGTS		
SCHWARZENBECK		
BECKENBAUER		
DIETZ		
WIMMER		▶
Subbed: 46 mins (Flohe)		
BONHOF		
BEER		▶
Subbed: 80 mins (Bongartz)		
HOENESS, U		
MÜLLER, D		⚽
Goal: 28 mins		
HÖLZENBEIN		⚽
Goal: 89 mins		
sub: FLOHE		▶
sub: BONGARTZ		▶

Referee: Gonella (Italy)

HOW THE TEAMS LINED UP

CZECHOSLOVAKIA

COACH:
VACLAV JEZEK

WEST GERMANY

COACH:
HELMUT SCHÖN

Viktor

Pivarník Ondrus Capkovic Gögh

Dobiás Móder Panenka

Masny Svehlík Nehoda

Hölzenbein Müller, D Hoeness, U

Bonhof Beer Wimmer

Dietz Beckenbauer Schwarzenbeck Vogts

Maier

ITALY 1980

With the 1976 European Championship in Yugoslavia hailed as an undoubted success, full of skill, technique and drama, the tournament played out some four years later was nothing short of disastrous.

Negative football, poor refereeing and hooliganism were the abiding memories of Euro 80, while the depressing statistic of just 1.93 goals per game no doubt contributed to attendances that dropped as low as 9,000 for the Czechoslovakia v Greece game. Even the opening fixture between West Germany and the Czechs attracted just 11,000 fans in Rome. In hindsight, staying away was a wise choice considering the fear-riddled game that was settled by a Rummenigge header.

With the competition split into two groups of four teams, and the winners of each group contesting the final, the formula was a disaster waiting to happen. Teams that lost their opening fixture invariably had a mountain to climb and therefore played out meaningless ties, while those in contention for the top spot approached games in a chess-like fashion rather than expressing their true capabilities.

Indeed, it explained why Greece, in their first major tournament, were regarded as the most expressive team in Group One, despite losing their opening games against Holland and the Czechs. A creditable stalemate with West Germany secured their fate, but the fact that a team that ended up with one point were the most talked about of the competition spoke volumes for the entertainment on show.

England, again, flattered to deceive and their opening fixture against Belgium in Turin was shrouded in controversy and disgrace. With 15 minutes to play and the game poised at 1-1, German referee Aldinger disallowed a perfectly valid goal by Woodcock for offside, prompting clashes between fans and riot police on the terraces. The game had already been halted for three minutes in the first-half, following Ceulemans' equaliser, which left England keeper Clemence needing treatment for the effects of tear gas.

With the hosts drawing their opening fixture 0-0 against Spain, and all four teams in Group B with a point apiece, Italy's clash with England was a war of attrition, both on and off the terraces. Yet while the visiting fans remained calm, the players received a battering by an Italian team determined to stay in the competition at all costs. In a game of cat and mouse played out in front of 59,000 supporters, a rare slip by Liverpool fullback Phil Neal proved costly as Tardelli headed home with just 11 minutes remaining.

Although England went on to beat Spain 2-1 in Naples, it was left to Belgium and Italy to fight out a place in the final. Having beaten Spain 2-1, Guy Thys's side knew that a draw

Above: Hosts Italy finished fourth. Opposite clockwise from top left: Horst Hrubesch scored both goals in West Germany's final win; Karl Heinz Rummenigge clears; Schuster takes on the Belgian defence; West Germany celebrate.

against the Italians would see them progress on goal difference, thus causing one of the all-time tournament shocks. With a vociferous 60,000 crowd behind them in Rome the Italians failed spectacularly in a game riddled with bookings and defensive football. The 0-0 stalemate was enough to see Belgium through. Italy were undone by their defensive instincts, scoring just one goal in three games.

With Holland and West Germany winning their opening games in Group One, it was assumed that both would fight it out for a place in the final, yet the famous Dutch stars of 'Total Football' failed to rise to their final challenge and were put to the sword in their pivotal second game against the Germans. The 3-2 scoreline flattered the Dutch and only in their final group game against Czechoslovakia did the real Holland emerge, but by then the 1-1 draw was too little too late and they even failed to reach the third place play-off.

West Germany's final points tally of five indicated their dominance in a group that rarely saw them break sweat. Without the likes of Beckenbauer, Bonhof and Müller, they still reached the final by playing only 60 minutes of top quality football against Holland, in a game where they established a 3-0 lead before taking their foot off the pedal. Safe in the knowledge that a place in the final was assured, West Germany played out a 0-0 draw in their final group game against the Greeks.

The hope was that the final would be the tournament's saving grace, and the omens were good as the third place play-off preamble proved an exciting affair in Naples. With extra-time banished in the hope of more attacking football, Czechoslovakia took the lead against the hosts when Jurkemik scored in the 53rd minute from a Panenka corner. The strike prompted the Italians to emerge from their tournament slumber and they were finally rewarded when a Causio free-kick was headed home by Graziani with 17 minutes remaining.

The Czechs should have wrapped the game up when Nehoda's shot was brilliantly saved by Zoff late in the game, but Barmos silenced the home side with the winner in a tense 9-8 penalty shoot-out victory.

THE FINAL

WEST GERMANY (1) **2-1** (0) BELGIUM

Date Sunday June 22, 1980 **Attendance** 47,864
Venue Olympic Stadium, Rome

Belgium's refusal to play the bridesmaid ensured that a lacklustre ten days of football were brought to an exciting climax. The pattern was set as early as the tenth minute, when an inch-perfect pass from Schuster was met by 20-year-old Hamburg striker Horst Hrubesch, who rounded Millecamps before sliding his shot into the corner of the net. The goal woke the Belgians up, but the West Germans should have doubled their lead when Schuster and Allofs brought fine saves out of Pfaff before the break.

Belgium drew level with Vandereycken's penalty, awarded for a challenge from Stielike on Van Der Elst that was clearly outside the box. However, with a minute remaining Hrubesch met Karl-Heinz Rummenigge's corner to win the game for the West Germans.

HOW THE TEAMS LINED UP

WEST GERMANY
COACH:
JUPP DERWALL

BELGIUM
COACH:
GUY THYS

Schumacher

Kaltz Förster, K-H Stielike Dietz

Briegel Schuster Müller, H

Rummenigge, K-H Hrubesch Allofs, K

Ceulemans Van der Elst

Mommens Van Moer Vandereycken Cools

Renquin Meeuws Millecamps, L Gerets

Pfaff

WEST GERMANY
SCHUMACHER
KALTZ
FÖRSTER, K-H
STIELIKE
DIETZ
BRIEGEL
Subbed: 55 mins (Cullmann)
SCHUSTER
MÜLLER, H
ALLOFS, K
RUMMENIGGE, K-H
HRUBESCH
Goal: 10 mins, 88 mins
sub: CULLMANN

BELGIUM
PFAFF
GERETS
MILLECAMPS, L
MEEUWS
RENQUIN
COOLS
VANDEREYCKEN
Goal: 72 mins (pen)
VAN MOER
MOMMENS
VAN DER ELST
CEULEMANS

Referee: Rainea (Romania)

FRANCE 1984

For the French, the 1984 European Championship represented nothing less than a date with destiny. The country was in danger of becoming famous for instigating major football tournaments without ever actually winning them. Two years earlier, at the World Cup, they had exuded quality before being physically battered by West Germany in Seville and losing their nerve in a semi-final they should have won. Now they were desperate to make amends and fulfil their promise. As hosts for the second time, they knew they might never have a better opportunity.

Against this background the 1984 European Championship produced some of the finest football the tournament has ever seen. The final competition was restricted to just eight teams, making qualification a reasonably tight affair, and by the opening game in June 1984 there were some notable absentees, including World Cup holders Italy, who finished a dreadful qualifying campaign second from bottom of their group. Also absent were Holland, Sweden

SEMI-FINALS

France 3-2 Portugal
(aet: 1-1 at 90 mins)

Spain 1-1 Denmark
(aet: Spain won 5-4 on penalties)

THIRD PLACE PLAY-OFF

Did not take place

TOP GOALSCORER

9 goals: Michel Platini (France)

FASTEST GOAL

3 mins: Michel Platini
(France v Belgium)

TOTAL GOALS

41

AVERAGE GOALS

2.73 per game

THE FINAL

FRANCE (0) 2-0 (0) SPAIN

Date Wednesday June 27, 1984 **Attendance** 47,368
Venue Parc Des Princes, Paris

The 1984 final started with some robust play from the Spaniards that had the home crowd whistling but it was no doubt designed to unsettle the hosts. The Czech referee, Christov, quickly clamped down and play began to flow from end to end. Giresse had a shot as early as the first minute, but nevertheless there was no score at half-time. When the second-half started the French began to look edgy as they attempted to break the Spanish down, and it took a bad mistake from goalkeeper Arconada to settle Gallic nerves when he let a Platini free-kick squeeze past him. Spain held on and searched for an equaliser, but as they committed more men forward, in the closing moments Bellone was able to break clear and chip over the goalkeeper to seal the game.

FRANCE

BATS	
BATTISTON	
Subbed: 72 mins (Amoros)	
LE ROUX	■
Sent-off: 85 mins	
BOSSIS	
DOMERGUE	
TIGANA	
FERNANDEZ	
PLATINI	⚽
Goal: 57 mins	
GIRESSE	
LACOMBE	
Subbed: 80 mins (Genghini)	
BELLONE	⚽
Goal: 90 mins	
sub: **AMOROS**	
sub: **GENGHINI**	

SPAIN

ARCONADA	
URQUIAGA	
SALVA	
Subbed: 85 mins (Roberto)	
GALLEGO	▢
Booked.	
SENOR	
FRANCISCO	
VICTOR	
CAMACHO	
JULIO ALBERTO	
Subbed: 77 mins (Sarabia)	
SANTILLANA	
CARRASCO	▢
Booked.	
sub: **ROBERTO**	▢
sub: **SARABIA**	

Referee: Christov (Czechoslovakia)

HOW THE TEAMS LINED UP

FRANCE
COACH:
MICHEL HIDALGO

SPAIN
COACH:
MIGUEL MUNOZ

France: Bats; Battiston, Le Roux, Bossis, Domergue; Tigana, Fernandez, Platini, Giresse; Lacombe, Bellone

Spain: Arconada; Urquiaga, Salva, Gallego, Senor; Carrasco, Santillana; Julio Alberto, Camacho, Victor, Francisco

Above: Michel Platini opens the final scoring from this free-kick. Opposite clockwise from top left: Platini on the attack again; Platini lifts the Henri Delaunay Trophy, France's first major honour; the French team celebrate the final whistle with joy; mixed emotions as Spanish keeper Luis Arconada allows Platini's free-kick to slip through his grasp.

and the Soviet Union, while the failure of England, Scotland, Northern Ireland and Wales to get through to the finals made it a disastrous clean sweep for the British Isles.

England were largely in transition under new manager Bobby Robson. They came second in their group behind Denmark after a 1-0 defeat at home. As the cream of Europe assembled in France that June they went off to play a friendly tournament in South America, ironically throwing up one of the enduring images of English football when John Barnes scored a wonderful solo effort in the Maracanã.

There was no great shame in losing to Denmark as it turned out, because they were an emerging football nation with world class talents like Preben Elkjaer and Michael Laudrup in their ranks. The Danes would go as far as the semi-finals.

In the build up it was clear that France and the World Cup runners-up, West Germany, were the joint favourites. Under Michel Hidalgo 'Les Bleus' were, if anything, an even stronger outfit than they had been two years previous – particularly with the addition of Luis Fernández in midfield and Joel Bats in goal, probably the country's finest ever goalkeeper. They also boasted a tight defence that was still being carefully orchestrated by the dependable Maxime Bossis. That, in turn, sat behind possibly the best midfield in the world, even if they were nearly all in their thirties. The only question mark hung over the team's lack of true strike power, which is where Platini's presence was to prove crucial.

Once the tournament got under way France eased through Group A, winning all of their games, which included a 5-0 thumping of neighbours Belgium. Platini was already hitting form, scoring two perfect hat-tricks (left foot, right foot, header) in succession. Denmark qualified for the semi-finals behind them in second place.

The real shock of the competition came in Group B, with holders West Germany failing to make the semi-finals. Even though they were held to a draw by Portugal, the Germans were still tipped to progress to the later stages. However, a last-minute header by Antonio Maceda in their final group showdown with Spain sent them home stunned and cost unpopular coach Jupp Derwall his job. Spain, who also missed a penalty in that match, took their place in the last four, with Portugal completing the semi-final line-up.

The first semi-final, on June 23, paired France with Portugal in the Stade Vélodrome in a match now regarded as a classic. After a slow start to the game France scored first through a Jean-François Domergue free-kick, before being pegged back to 1-1 by a Jordao header with 16 minutes remaining. The home side then conceded a second goal in extra-time before Domergue, on his 27th birthday, scored again. With the prospect looming of a penalty shoot-out, one that France surely would have lost if recent form was anything to go by, Platini lashed home a Jean Tigana cross to put them through to the final with just 64 seconds remaining on the clock.

The other semi-final between Denmark and Spain was just as tight, if a little less open, and with the two sides locked at 1-1 it was the Danish who buckled under the pressure of the penalty shoot-out, with Preben Elkjaer knocking the decisive fifth kick over the bar.

Nothing now was going to deny Les Bleus from seizing their moment. The European Championship trophy was named after a Frenchman, and now the name of the French team appeared likely to be engraved on it. Despite the weight of expectation, Platini's nerve held and he led his team to victory with his ninth goal in five games. The final proved to be one of his quieter matches, but he was quite rightly named the player of the tournament.

Above: Joy for the Dutch as they pose with the trophy. Opposite clockwise from top left: Goalscorers Gullit and Van Basten celebrate in the final; Lineker of England; Brehme celebrates Germany's semi win; Roberto Mancini takes on Denmark.

WEST GERMANY 1988

A decade after consecutive World Cup finals ended in bitterness and defeat, Holland achieved redemption in one of the most exciting tournaments of the 1980s. Dutch football had been plagued by a sense of unfulfilled potential since the twin losses of 1974 and 1978. In banishing the old demons, they closed that chapter of their history and ushered in a new golden era, centred on superstars such as Van Basten, Gullit and Rijkaard.

Holland were undoubtedly the best team of Euro 88, a tournament that produced possibly the finest football in these championships since 1976. Only eight teams contested the finals again and this time, with all the leading countries except defending champions France booking their places, fireworks were guaranteed.

Group 1, featuring hosts West Germany, Italy, Spain and Denmark, appeared to be the stronger of the two, and few thought that both eventual finalists would emerge from Group 2, made up of Holland, the Soviet Union, the Republic Of Ireland and England. However, this group crackled with tension until the final moments when a late goal ended Ireland's adventure and sparked Holland's tournament into life.

By that point the competition had long gone sour for England. Strongly fancied after their World Cup quarter-final appearance in Mexico two years earlier, they suffered a shock 1-0 loss in their opening match against the Irish. The defeat, to a team coached by Englishman Jack Charlton, was a blow from which Bobby Robson's side never recovered. They capitulated 3-1 to Holland, in a match best remembered for Marco Van Basten's stunning hat-trick, and by the same score to the fast-improving Soviets.

For the Irish, beating England was the catalyst for an unlikely crusade into unknown territory, battering and bettering supposedly superior sides. Denied by a late equaliser in their next match against the Soviet Union, they headed into their final game against Holland knowing a draw would be enough for a place in the semi-finals. The Soviets, meanwhile, had beaten Holland in their opening match, and having scraped a draw against the Irish they required only a point against a dispirited England in their last game to qualify.

Despite their impressive showing against England, the Dutch were in danger of paying for their opening defeat: they had to beat the Irish. While the improving Soviets cruised past England, Holland struggled to make any impact on the solid, organised Irish, who came closest to scoring when McGrath headed against the post. With Charlton's men eight minutes away from the semi-finals, luck came to Holland's rescue when Ronald Koeman mishit a shot that Kieft was on hand to guide in.

In Group 1, a draw between West Germany and Italy enabled Spain to steal a march on their rivals by beating Denmark 3-2. However, the old superpowers went on to reassert their dominance; the Germans brushed aside the Danes 2-0 and Italy squeezed past Spain with a single goal. Italy completed their advance with a routine 2-0 defeat of the already-eliminated Danes, while West Germany clinically disposed of Spain by the same scoreline. The group was going according to expectations, with many experts believing the opening encounter between the hosts, World Cup finalists two years earlier, and the Italians, who were building a talented side for Italia 90, had been a dress rehearsal for the final.

The semi-finals threw up arguably the fiercest rivalry in European football as West Germany met Holland. The match inevitably provoked memories of 1974, when West Germany wore down the Cruyff-inspired Dutch. Holland's manager then was Rinus Michels, the man credited with creating Total Football. In a delicious twist of fate, he was back in charge of his national side.

In a match worthy of the final, Holland took the early initiative in Hamburg only for Matthäus to fire West Germany ahead from the penalty spot in the 53rd minute. The Dutch fell apart and as their play grew ragged, the spectre of indiscipline returning to haunt them – until the 73rd minute, when the referee levelled the score by awarding them a disputed penalty. Koeman equalised and in the last minute of normal time Van Basten, out of favour early in the tournament, scored his fourth goal of the competition to derail the hosts and send Holland into the final.

In the other semi-final, the Soviets added a rugged approach to their fast, neat game and managed to beat Italy 2-0 in Stuttgart. Quietly and effectively the Soviet Union had earned the right to contest the final for a fourth time.

Valery Lobanovsky, their manager, was as much a pioneer of the modern game as Dutch coach Michels, the man he would be pitting his wits against in the final. Lobanovsky had led Dynamo Kiev to seven championships before taking over the national side. Would he be the man to end his country's 28-year wait for a second major trophy, or would Michels, 14 years after the disappointment of losing the World Cup final, lead Holland to glory?

THE FINAL

HOLLAND (1) 2-0 (0) SOVIET UNION

Date Saturday June 25, 1988 **Attendance** 72,308
Venue Olympic Stadium, Munich

The final will always be remembered for Marco Van Basten's wonder goal ten minutes into the second-half, but until that point the destiny of the trophy was far from certain. The Soviet Union started brightly and had the better of the opening 20 minutes, but gradually the Dutch began to draw their sting. Gullit took control of the midfield, the 37-year-old Mühren started hitting probing passes, and Holland, who had the longer period to recover from their semi-final, suddenly looked to be in the ascendancy.

Twelve minutes before half-time Gullit headed Holland in front and Van Basten's vicious volley, which made him the tournament's top scorer with five, doubled the lead in the 54th minute. Van Breukelen saved a late penalty and Holland at last had the silverware they deserved.

HOW THE TEAMS LINED UP

HOLLAND
COACH: RINUS MICHELS

SOVIET UNION
COACH: VALERY LOBANOVSKY

Van Breukelen

Van Aerle Koeman, R Rijkaard Van Tiggelen

Vanenburg Wouters Koeman, E Mühren, A

Gullit Van Basten

Belanov Protasov

Gotsmanov Mikhailichenko Zavarov Litovchenko

Rats Aleinikov Demianenko Khidiatullin

Dasayev

HOLLAND	
VAN BREUKELEN	
VAN AERLE	
Booked: 49 mins	
KOEMAN, R	
RIJKAARD	
VAN TIGGELEN	
VANENBURG	
WOUTERS	
KOEMAN, E	
MÜHREN, A	
GULLIT	⚽
Goal: 33 mins	
VAN BASTEN	⚽
Goal: 54 mins	

SOVIET UNION	
DASAYEV	
KHIDIATULLIN	🟨
Booked: 42 mins	
DEMIANENKO	🟨
Booked: 31 mins	
ALEINIKOV	
RATS	
LITOVCHENKO	🟨
Booked: 34 mins	
ZAVAROV	
MIKHAILICHENKO	
GOTSMANOV	▶
Subbed: 69 mins (Baltacha)	
PROTASOV	▶
Subbed: 72 mins (Pasulko)	
BELANOV	
sub: BALTACHA	▶
sub: PASULKO	▶

Referee: Vautrot (France)

SEMI-FINALS
West Germany 1-2 Holland
Soviet Union 2-0 Italy

THIRD PLACE PLAY-OFF
Did not take place

TOP GOALSCORER
5 goals: Marco Van Basten (Holland)

FASTEST GOAL
3 mins: Sergei Aleinikov (England v Soviet Union)

TOTAL GOALS
34

AVERAGE GOALS
2.26 per game

SWEDEN 1992

Euro 92 was an extraordinary tournament for a host of reasons. The redrawing of Europe's political map, following the fall of Communism, had a significant effect on international football, with the former Soviet Union competing as the Commonwealth Of Independent States (CIS), and East and West Germany present as a single unified country. Further political intrigue had seen Yugoslavia disqualified from the tournament in line with United Nations sanctions against Serbia. That meant a last minute call-up for Denmark, runners-up in Yugoslavia's qualifying group by just a single point.

No-one gave Richard Moller Nielsen's team much chance of making an impact as the squad had barely a fortnight to prepare for the competition and many players had been recalled from their summer holidays. In true fairytale style, the Danes went on to prove their doubters spectacularly wrong.

Eight countries, split into two groups of four, contested the finals. Sweden, Denmark, France

SEMI-FINALS

Sweden 2-3 Germany

Holland 2-2 Denmark

(aet: Denmark won 5-4 on penalties)

THIRD PLACE PLAY-OFF

Did not take place

TOP GOALSCORERS

3 goals: Dennis Bergkamp (Holland), Tomas Brolin (Sweden), Henrik Larsen (Denmark), Karlheinz Riedle (Germany)

FASTEST GOAL

2 mins: Frank Rijkaard (Holland v Germany)

TOTAL GOALS

32

AVERAGE GOALS

2.13 per game

Above: John Jensen opens the scoring for Denmark in the final. Below: Hässler and German team-mates enjoy a semi-final goal. Opposite clockwise from top left: Eventual winners Denmark open with a 0-0 draw against England; Brian Laudrup kisses the trophy; Hosts Sweden equalise against England; Scotland fall at the first stage.

THE FINAL

DENMARK (1) **2-0** (0) **GERMANY**

Date Friday June 26, 1992 **Attendance** 37,800

Venue Nya Ullevi Stadium, Gothenburg

Germany started the final well as Denmark struggled to come to terms with the absence of suspended midfielder Henrik Andersen. However, having successfully soaked up the early pressure the Danes took the lead in the 18th minute, when John Jensen rifled the ball past German goalkeeper Bodo Illgner.

Germany tried to reassert themselves but were twice denied by Peter Schmeichel before the interval. The same pattern continued after the break with Vogts' men having the best of the chances. However, Germany soon became frustrated at their inability to score and lost their discipline. With 12 minutes left Denmark sealed a famous win when Kim Vilfort made it 2-0, although the Germans who argued that he controlled the ball with his hand had a point.

DENMARK

SCHMEICHEL	
SIVEBAEK	▶
Subbed: 65 mins (Christensen)	
NIELSEN, K	
OLSEN, L	
CHRISTOFTE	
JENSEN	⚽
Goal: 18 mins	
POVLSEN	
LAUDRUP, B	
PIECHNIK	▢
Booked: 32 mins	
LARSEN	
VILFORT	⚽
Goal: 78 mins	
CHRISTENSEN	▶

GERMANY

ILLGNER	
REUTER	▢
Booked: 55 mins	
BREHME	
KÖHLER	
BUCHWALD	
HÄSSLER	▢
Booked: 38 mins	
RIEDLE	
HELMER	
SAMMER	▶
Subbed: 46 mins (Doll)	
EFFENBERG	▶ ▢
Booked: 35 mins. Subbed: 78 mins (Thom)	
KLINSMANN	▢
Booked: 88 mins	
DOLL	▶ ▢
Booked: 83 mins	
THOM	▶

Referee: Galler (Switzerland)

HOW THE TEAMS LINED UP

DENMARK

COACH:
R MOLLER NIELSEN

Schmeichel

Sivebaek   Nielsen, K   Olsen, L   Christofte

Jensen   Povlsen   Laudrup, B   Piechnik

Larsen   Vilfort

GERMANY

COACH:
BERTI VOGTS

Klinsmann   Effenberg

Sammer   Helmer   Riedle   Hässler

Buchwald   Köhler   Brehme   Reuter

Illgner

and England were in Group A, producing only nine goals between them in six games. Sweden finished top of the group, thanks to wins against Denmark (1-0) and England (2-1, with the prolific Tomas Brolin hitting a terrific winner six minutes from time). The Danes followed them into the semi-finals despite winning only one of their games, 2-1 over France, then managed by the legendary Michel Platini. Injury-ravaged England had once again disappointed on the big stage, returning home with only a single David Platt goal to their name just two years after a penalty shoot-out defeat against West Germany had denied them a place in the World Cup final.

Group B proved a little livelier, although predictably it was Germany and Holland who qualified for the semi-finals at the expense of Scotland and the hodgepodge of nations that made up the CIS. Indeed, the Dutch became red-hot favourites to retain the Henri Delaunay Trophy after squashing Germany 3-1, thanks to goals from Frank Rijkaard, Rob Witschge and Ajax's Dennis Bergkamp, making his first major international tournament appearance. Bergkamp also grabbed Holland's early winner against Scotland in a 1-0 victory. The Germans, meanwhile, were living dangerously and had Thomas Hässler not struck a last minute equaliser against the CIS in their opening game, it is doubtful they would have made it through to the last four at all.

The tournament really sprang into life at the semi-final stage with two memorable matches. World champions Germany lived up to their prodigious reputation in a tough game against injury-depleted Sweden, with Hässler giving Berti Vogts' side an early lead before Karl-Heinz Riedle added a second with just over half an hour to go. However, the hosts pulled one back when the irrepressible Brolin converted a penalty five minutes later, and even when Riedle added a third two minutes from time after a fine through ball from Thomas Helmer, it failed to kill the off the Swedes, who reduced

the deficit immediately. It set up a nail-biting finale, which eventually saw the Germans hold on for the 3-2 win.

The semi-final between Denmark and Holland was even more dramatic, with the still unfancied Danes a goal up through Henrik Larsen after just five minutes following some good work down the right from Brian Laudrup. Bergkamp's equaliser for the Dutch, midway through the first-half, provided short-lived relief as Larsen netted a second just past the half-hour mark. Rinus Michels' side threw everything they had at the Danes in the second-half, and their pressure finally told five minutes from the final whistle when Rijkaard grabbed a second equaliser from a corner.

Somehow the shattered Danes pulled themselves together and kept Holland at bay during extra-time, meaning the tie had to be decided on penalties. It was Marco Van Basten, without a single goal in the tournament, who missed the vital spot-kick as Denmark stunned European football by triumphing 5-4 in the lottery of the penalty shoot-out.

The Danes had ridden their luck and eagerly grasped every opportunity that had come their way, but surely this team could not win a tournament that they had not even originally qualified for. Could they?

ENGLAND 1996

The 'golden goal' rule was used to decide the outcome of a successful European Championship, as Germany claimed the trophy from the Czech Republic in a repeat of the 1976 final. However, the tournament will be remembered for much more than Oliver Bierhoff's late strike, as a great English summer saw three weeks of fantastic goals, enthusiastic support and tense penalty shoot-outs.

Held in England for the first time, it was important for the hosts not only to play well, but also to reconstruct their hooligan-tarnished image in front of the eyes of the football world. Under the shrewd management of Terry Venables England opened the tournament against Switzerland, but after a promising start they ran out of ideas and were held 1-1. Group A's other participants were Scotland and Holland, who played out a 0-0 draw.

The so-called Battle of Britain was one of the most eagerly awaited confrontations of the group stages and the dramatic end-to-end action of the game did not disappoint. England took the lead with Alan Shearer's second goal of the tournament, and then came the passage of play that was to settle the contest. Scotland were awarded a second-half penalty, which David Seaman was fortunate to keep out from Gary McAllister via his elbow and the crossbar. From the resulting corner, England broke down the pitch and, latching on to a through ball, Paul Gascoigne deftly flicked the ball over Colin Hendry before volleying one of the best goals of the tournament, and creating a much-loved moment in English football history.

The team's confidence was at a high, and in another wonderful display of attacking football they defeated a complacent Holland side 4-1. The consolation goal was to prove valuable, as Patrick Kluivert's strike ensured qualification for the Dutch ahead of Scotland on goal difference.

Group B saw France finish top and go forward to the quarter-finals along with Spain, at the expense of the Eastern European representatives Bulgaria and Romania. In a low-scoring series of contests, no game was decided by more than one goal. Old war horses Hristo Stoichkov and Gheorghe Hagi both failed to inspire their teams to get the better of a couple of sides blessed with a new generation of world-class talent.

Many tournaments produce one group packed with a seeming imbalance of strong sides, the so-called Group of Death, and Euro 96 was no exception. Italy, Russia, the Czech Republic and Germany were matched against each other, and something had to give. That something turned out to be Italian participation in the competition, and despite possessing arguably the most talented squad, in many ways they managed to engineer their own

departure. A confident victory over Russia in the first game saw the Italians make changes to the starting line-up against the underrated Czechs, who snatched a 2-1 victory. In the final game Italy needed to defeat the already-qualified Germans to go through, but a 0-0 draw and the Czech Republic's point against Russia conspired against them.

Group D saw Portugal and newcomers Croatia grab the honours, with Denmark and Turkey knocked out of the tournament. The game of this group was won by Croatia against holders Denmark and will be remembered for Davor Suker's exquisite chipped finish against Peter Schmeichel.

After the open play of the group stages, the quarter-finals turned out to be tense affairs. England got the better of Spain via a penalty shoot-out, and France eliminated Holland in the same manner. England's shoot-out was notable for the redemption of left-back Stuart Pearce, who laid the ghost of his 1990 World Cup miss to rest after emphatically burying his spot-kick past Zubizarreta in the Spanish goal.

The clash between Germany and Croatia turned out to be the most spiteful of the whole tournament, and despite possessing an array of world-class talent in their side, including Davor Suker and Zvonimir Boban, Croatia temporarily put quality football on hold and attempted to kick lumps out of their German opponents. Jürgen Klinsmann and his side limped out 2-1 winners.

Thanks to mop-topped Karel Poborsky's wonderful, improvised lob over Portugal's Vitor Baia, the Czechs continued their impressive run. They secured a place in the final after a 0-0 draw with France at Old Trafford resulted in yet another semi-final penalty shoot-out failure for the French.

The other semi-final between the hosts England and old foes Germany also went to penalties, but not before an epic struggle in the game of the tournament. England made the start they wanted, with the eventual Golden Boot winner Alan Shearer heading them in front in the third minute, but they were unable to press home the advantage and

Germany, through Stefan Kuntz, levelled the score. In extra-time England came agonisingly close to claiming a spot in the final through Darren Anderton and Gascoigne, while Kuntz had a headed goal disallowed. In a repeat of the events of 1990, once again England failed to see off the Germans. It fell to Gareth Southgate to miss the vital penalty and leave the hosts as nothing more than spectators for the final.

Above left: England's Stuart Pearce after his penalty shoot-out spot-kick in the quarter-final with Spain. Above right: Oliver Bierhoff celebrates scoring in the final. Opposite clockwise from top left: The Czech team after their semi-final victory; German goal machine Jürgen Klinsmann; England congratulate Paul Gascoigne on his goal against Scotland; Italy's Pierluigi Casiraghi.

SEMI-FINALS

France 0-0 Czech Republic
(aet: Czechs won 6-5 on penalties)
England 1-1 Germany
(aet: Germany won 6-5 on penalties)

THIRD PLACE PLAY-OFF

Did not take place

TOP GOALSCORERS

5 goals: Alan Shearer (England)
3 goals: Jürgen Klinsmann (Germany); Brian Laudrup (Denmark), Hristo Stoichkov (Bulgaria)

FASTEST GOAL

3 mins: Alan Shearer (England v Germany); Hristo Stoichkov (Bulgaria v Romania)

TOTAL GOALS

64 goals

AVERAGE GOALS

2.06 per game

THE FINAL

GERMANY (0) **2-1** (0) **CZECH REPUBLIC**
(aet: 1-1 at 90 mins)

Date Sunday June 30, 1996 **Attendance** 73,611
Venue Wembley Stadium, London

Despite the exit of the hosts, the enthusiastic spirit of Euro 96 continued into the final in front of a full house at Wembley. Germany went into the game as favourites, and coach Berti Vogts' side were determined not to lose back-to-back European Championship finals. The underdog tag did not deter the fast-improving Czech Republic side, who took the lead in the 59th minute with star player Patrik Berger converting a penalty past goalkeeper Andreas Köpke.

Substitute Oliver Bierhoff brought Germany back into the game only four minutes after coming on, and it was the tall striker who made football history by scoring the first ever 'golden goal' in a major tournament final with just four minutes of extra-time played.

GERMANY

KÖPKE	
BABBEL	
SAMMER	
Booked: 69 mins	
HELMER	
Booked: 62 mins	
STRUNZ	
HÄSSLER	
EILTS	▶
Subbed: 46 mins (Bode)	
SCHOLL	▶
Subbed: 69 mins (Bierhoff)	
ZIEGE	
Booked: 91 mins	
KLINSMANN	
KUNTZ	
sub: BODE	▶
sub: BIERHOFF	▶ ⚽⚽
Goal: 73 mins, 95 mins	

CZECH REPUBLIC

KOUBA	
SUCHOPAREK	
KADLEC	
HORNAK	
Booked: 47 mins	
RADA	
POBORSKY	▶
Subbed: 88 mins (Smicer)	
NEDVED	
NEMEC	
BERGER	⚽
Goal: 59 mins (pen)	
BEJBL	
KUKA	
sub: SMICER	▶

Referee: Pairetto (Italy)

HOW THE TEAMS LINED UP

GERMANY
COACH: BERTI VOGTS

CZECH REPUBLIC
COACH: DUSAN UHRIN

Köpke

Babbel · Sammer · Helmer · Strunz

Hässler · Eilts · Scholl · Ziege

Klinsmann · Kuntz

Kuka · Bejbl

Berger · Nemec · Nedved · Poborsky

Rada · Hornak · Kadlec · Suchoparek

Kouba

BELGIUM/HOLLAND 2000

SEMI-FINALS

Portugal 1-2 France
(aet: 1-1 at 90 mins)

Italy 0-0 Netherlands
(aet: Italy won 3-1 on penalties)

THIRD PLACE PLAY-OFF

Did not take place

TOP GOALSCORERS

5 goals: Patrick Kluivert (Holland),
Savo Milosevic (Yugoslavia)

4 goals: Nuno Gomes (Portugal)

FASTEST GOAL

3 mins: Paul Scholes
(England v Portugal)

TOTAL GOALS

85 goals

AVERAGE GOALS

2.74 per game

Above: Italy clinch a place in the final. **Opposite clockwise from top left:** Alan Shearer against Germany; Didier Deschamps lifts the cup; Luis Figo and Nuno Gomez of Portugal; Holland's Patrick Kluivert celebrates.

It was a tournament for purists, full of attacking flair, defensive ingenuity and high drama, most notably in the games played by the Dutch, but Euro 2000 will be remembered for the extension of French football dominance, and the grace and guile of Zinédine Zidane. The midfielder, along with Portugal's Luis Figo, was undoubtedly the star of the tournament, entertaining fans with an armoury of tricks, flicks and defence-splitting passes. While Figo and Portugal were the surprise package of the tournament, it was Zidane's France who extended their superiority following their World Cup win in 1998.

The opening game was indicative of how the tournament was to continue, mixing controversy with exciting football. However, that drama would come at a cost, especially for Belgian goalkeeper Filip De Wilde. Eight minutes into the second-half, with Belgium leading Sweden 2-0, he trod on the ball while trying to control a backpass, allowing Swedish striker Johan Mjallby to stroll past him and sweep the ball into the net. Belgium still managed to hang on for a deserved win.

England's campaign started with equally catastrophic defensive incidents in Group A. After taking a two-goal lead against Portugal, Kevin Keegan's men were torn apart by Figo and conceded three goals. England went on to defeat arch-rivals Germany 1-0, but a defensive blunder from Phil Neville against Romania led to the penalty that knocked them, along with defending champions Germany, out of the tournament.

Almost immediately Keegan's coaching credentials were criticised by the English press, as well as by a number of his senior players, including first-team defender Martin Keown. The Arsenal centre-half accused the team of being inept tactically and claimed individual and collective errors had prevented England from beating teams they should have swept aside easily. The writing was already on the wall and Keegan's reign as England manager was to be short-lived. Meanwhile, Germany's failure to make it past the first round, almost unthinkable a few years earlier, was seen as indicative of a waning of their power.

Hosts Holland struggled to get out of first gear in their opening Group D game, defeating the Czech Republic by a single penalty and demolishing Denmark 3-0 to cruise into the quarter-finals. It was here that Patrick Kluivert and his team-mates quickly upped the ante, firing six goals past a bemused Yugoslavian team in a performance that was pure perfection. However, in their semi-final clash with the Italians, who had defeated a strong Romanian side 2-0 in the quarter-finals, drama struck.

Having been reduced to just ten men after Gianluca Zambrotta was sent-off for a second bookable offence, Italy sat back and defended, with goalkeeper Francesco Toldo commanding his area admirably. Even with two penalty kicks in their favour, Holland, having been unable to convert either, failed to defeat the Italians. Worse was to come and after the 'golden goal' period failed to produce a result, Holland missed the first three penalties of the shoot-out to gift the Italians victory. 'I think they could have played for the whole day shooting at our goal and they would never have scored', said Italian keeper Toldo. Dutch striker Dennis Bergkamp was more damning. 'We only have ourselves to blame,' he said, 'I don't know why Holland can't win a penalty shoot-out.'

Italy, who had infuriated both fans and opponents alike with their ultra-defensive football in Group B, had ground their way to the final. Their qualifying group rivals Turkey were later knocked out of the quarter-finals by the Portuguese 2-0.

The French were ruthless in Group D, easing their way into the quarter-finals without ever looking stretched: a 3-2 defeat at the hands of the Dutch was played at half pace. They dispensed with Spain 2-1 to progress into the semi-finals with goals from Zidane and Djorkaeff; Spain had responded with a converted spot-kick from Mendieta, but minutes before the final whistle Raúl had missed the game's second penalty, and with it the chance to take the game into extra-time. That the Spanish were unable to make it past the quarter-final stage in yet another major competition was proof that the tag of perennial underachievers was hanging heavy.

Still, Spain had provided the game of the tournament when, in their final Group C clash against Yugoslavia, they had come back from 3-2 down to score two goals in stoppage time and win the tie 4-3. At this stage in the competition many felt that the Spanish, with Raúl of Real Madrid and Valencia's Gaizka Mendieta hitting top form in attack, were likely contenders for the title.

The French clearly had other ideas and, after sweeping aside Spain, they defeated the Portuguese in the semi-finals with an extra-time penalty 'golden goal', slotted home by Zidane after Abel Xavier had controversially been adjudged to have handled in the area. The battle between the tournament's two stars, Zidane and Figo, had gone in favour of the Frenchman. The final set-up a mouth watering battle between the attacking force of France and Italy's resolute defence, but much more drama was to come.

THE FINAL

FRANCE (0) **2-1** (0) **ITALY**
(aet: 1-1 at 90 mins)

Date Sunday July 2, 2000 **Attendance** 50,000

Venue De Kuip Stadium, Rotterdam

Many would have preferred to see the attacking play of Holland against France, rather than the defensive Italians, but nevertheless the climax to Euro 2000 was a fascinating affair.

Having gone a goal down in the 54th minute to Marco Delvecchio, France threw on Sylvain Wiltord and David Trezeguet with 15 minutes to play and with full-time approaching, fortune favoured the French. Wiltord broke through in injury time to fire the ball beneath the body of Toldo and send the game into extra-time.

The first period was a typically cagey affair until Robert Pires hit a low cross into the Italian penalty area and Trezeguet fired the ball into the roof of the net for the 'golden goal' that would end the game and hand France victory.

HOW THE TEAMS LINED UP

FRANCE
COACH:
ROGER LEMERRE

ITALY
COACH:
DINO ZOFF

FRANCE	
BARTHEZ	
THURAM	
Booked: 58 mins	
BLANC	
DESAILLY	
LIZARAZU	
Subbed: 86 mins (Pires)	
DESCHAMPS	
VIEIRA	
DJORKAEFF	▶
Subbed: 76 mins (Trezeguet)	
ZIDANE	
DUGARRY	▶
Subbed: 57 mins (Wiltord)	
HENRY	
sub: **WILTORD**	▶ ⚽
Goal: 90 mins	
sub: **TREZEGUET**	▶ ⚽
Goal: 103 mins	

ITALY	
TOLDO	
CANNAVARO	
Booked: 41 mins	
NESTA	
IULIANO	
PESSOTTO	
ALBERTINI	
DI BIAGIO	▶
Booked: 30 mins, Subbed: 66 mins (Ambrosini)	
FIORE	▶
Subbed: 53 mins (Del Piero)	
MALDINI	
TOTTI	
Booked: 90 mins	
DELVECCHIO	⚽ ▶
Goal: 54 mins, Subbed: 86 mins (Montella)	
sub: **AMBROSINI**	▶
sub: **DEL PIERO**	▶
sub: **MONTELLA**	▶

Referee: Frisk (Sweden)

PORTUGAL 2004

Never has a European Championship victory attracted so much debate. When Greece lifted the famous trophy in front of a largely heartbroken crowd in Lisbon, they had pulled off one of world football's biggest upsets. An Angelos Charisteas header on 57 minutes was enough to put hosts Portugal to the sword, making the Werder Bremen striker a modern-day God in his homeland. Greece had ended the tournament as they had started it, humbling hosts Portugal into submission.

The victory sent shockwaves across Europe. Greece's last venture on to the world stage had been an unmitigated disaster: they lost all three of their 1994 World Cup games, conceding ten goals and scoring none. Even their victorious 2004 team had no star names to speak of, and they were coached by an ageing German who the average Greek fan believed was merely looking for a final payday. But 65-year-old Otto Rehhagel had other ideas. While the brawn of his side fuelled further debate about the merits of Greece's success, his workmanlike system proved to be a winning formula.

Portugal, who came so close to victory in their home country, had started the competition among the favourites. Coached by Luiz Felipe Scolari, who had led Brazil to World Cup success in 2002, the Portuguese went into the tournament with a squad crammed with talent, boasting players of the calibre of Deco and Ricardo Carvalho, the youthful exuberance of Cristiano Ronaldo and the experience of Luis Figo, but as the hosts trudged off the Estadio do Dragao pitch on June 12 after an opening day defeat to Greece, the significance of the result would only become apparent after the tournament was over.

Even with this surprise victory under their belts, Greece only progressed to the next round in second place on goal difference, ahead of group favourites Spain. A 1-1 draw with the Spanish had helped their cause, but a 2-1 defeat to Russia – in which Dmitri Kirichenko scored the fastest goal in European Championship history after just 68 seconds – did not suggest the glorious performances that lay ahead.

Fate had dealt Rehhagel's men a fortuitous hand, and how they grasped it. Reigning champions France were eliminated in the quarter-finals thanks to a second-half Charisteas header, while the Czech Republic were dispatched in similar style in the semi-finals, the Greeks stifling their technically-gifted opponents before winning the game thanks to a silver goal from defender Traianos Dellas.

While Greece's indomitable style thrust them into the spotlight, there were other highlights to an illuminating competition. England's opening Group B clash with the French had been much vaunted in the international football press. Given the rivalry between the countries

Above: Milan Baros scores for the Czech Republic. Opposite clockwise from top left: England celebrate a goal against Croatia; Henrik Larsson of Sweden; a dejected Cristiano Ronaldo following the final; Greece lift the trophy.

and the number of Gallic players in the English Premiership, it was signposted as the match of the tournament from the moment the draw had taken place. Frank Lampard gave England a deserved 1-0 lead in the 38th minute, while the talents of 18-year-old Wayne Rooney were unveiled to a global audience for the first time. David Beckham missed a 73rd minute penalty but as the game ebbed to its conclusion, England committed football suicide.

With 90 minutes on the clock Emile Heskey gave away a free-kick, which Zinédine Zidane disposed of with ruthless efficiency. Three minutes later a poor back pass from Steven Gerrard was intercepted by Thierry Henry, who was upended by on-rushing keeper David James. Up stepped Zidane to take the resulting penalty kick, and despite twice throwing up while cueing the ball, he slotted home to clinch the most unlikely of victories.

For the neutral observer the most thrilling game saw the Czech Republic come from two down to beat Holland 3-2 in their Group D encounter. Wilfred Bouma and Ruud Van Nistelrooy had put the Dutch 2-0 up inside 20 minutes, only for Milan Baros and Jan Koller to turn the game on its head. Dick Advocaat's men were rattled, and to compound their frustration Johnny Heitinga was sent-off with 15 minutes remaining. Vladimir Smicer's 88th minute winner had an inevitable ring to it, with the Liverpool man tapping in from close range.

The prequel to this Group D encounter ended 0-0 but was no less captivating as Latvia battled the might of Germany. As surprise qualifiers, the Baltic minnows bowed out with this solitary point, but their celebrations at the final whistle would only be bettered by the Greeks on July 4.

The Germans tumbled out of the 'group of death' following defeat against the Czechs, knowing their decidedly anonymous squad needed much surgery. Holland progressed to the quarter-finals beating Sweden on penalties before crashing out to Portugal. The Czech Republic were emerging as favourites, having dispatched of Denmark 3-0 to set up their

semi-final with Greece. But all eyes were on the hosts, who had battled back from their opening-game debacle to reach a quarter-final clash with England. An early Michael Owen goal should have inspired Sven-Göran Eriksson's men, but following Rooney's departure through injury after 27 minutes it signalled a rearguard action that would prove costly. Postiga equalised on 83 minutes, Sol Campbell had a goal disallowed by ref Urs Meier on the stroke of 90 minutes, and extra-time goals from Rui Costa and Frank Lampard set-up a penalty shoot-out. Inevitably England bowed out, with Darius Vassell failing to convert the all-important kick.

The hosts went on to beat the Dutch 2-1 in the semi-final, but there was a consolation for England with the emergence of Rooney. For many, the 18-year-old was the player of the tournament following his four goals, but it was an adversary from across Liverpool's Stanley Park – Milan Baros – who ended up with the Golden Boot. The Greeks, meanwhile, prepared for the Euro 2004 final as the biggest underdogs in the competition's 44 year history, proving that in this wonderful game of football, anything can happen.

THE FINAL

GREECE (0) 1-0 (0) PORTUGAL

Date Sunday July 4, 2004 **Attendance** 62,865
Venue Estadio da Luz, Lisbon

As they had done for much of the tournament, Greece adopted a safety-first policy, inviting the hosts to break down a rock solid defence. The Portuguese certainly took the early initiative, with Miguel forcing Antonios Nikopolidis into action with a 13th minute drive, while Maniche saw a shot from the edge of the area flash inches wide.

It was not unusual to see the Greeks with ten men behind the ball, and once Angelos Charisteas hit the back of the net on 57 minutes with a trademark header from an Angelos Basinas corner, there would be only one winner. Ronaldo missed a guilt-edged chance, lifting his shot over the bar after being put clean through, and Luis Figo also saw a late shot deflected wide before referee Markus Merk blew time to signal this unlikeliest of victories.

GREECE

NIKOPOLIDIS	
SEITARIDIS	
Booked: 64 mins	
KAPSIS	
DELLAS	
FISSAS	
Booked: 66 mins	
ZAGORAKIS	
KATSOURANIS	
BASINAS	
Booked: 45 mins	
GIANNAKOPOULOS	▶
Subbed: 76 mins (Venetidis)	
VRYZAS	▶
Subbed: 81 mins (Papadopoulos)	
CHARISTEAS	⚽
Goal: 73 mins	
sub: VENETIDIS	▶
sub: PAPADOPOULOS	▶
Booked: 84 mins	

PORTUGAL

RICARDO	
MIGUEL	▶
Subbed: 43 mins (Ferreira)	
ANDRADE	
RICARDO CARVALHO	
NUNO VALENTE	
Booked: 90 mins	
MANICHE	
COSTINHA	▶
Booked: 11 mins. Subbed: 60 mins (Rui Costa)	
RONALDO	
DECO	
FIGO	
PAULETA	▶
Subbed: 74 mins (Nuno Gomes)	
sub: FERREIRA	▶
sub: RUI COSTA	▶
sub: NUNO GOMES	▶

Referee: Merk (Germany)

HOW THE TEAMS LINED UP

GREECE
COACH:
OTTO REHHAGEL

Nikopolidis
Seitardis Delias Fissas
Zagorakis Kapsis Katsouranis Basinas
Giannakopoulos Vryzas Charisteas

PORTUGAL
COACH:
LUIZ FELIPE SCOLARI

Pauleta
Figo Deco Maniche Ronaldo
Costinha
Nuno Valente Carvalho Andrade Miguel
Ricardo

AUSTRIA/ SWITZERLAND 2008

SEMI-FINALS
Germany 3-2 Turkey
Russia 0-3 Spain

THIRD PLACE PLAY-OFF
Did not take place

TOP GOALSCORERS
4 goals: David Villa (Spain)
3 goals: Lukas Podolski (Germany), Roman Pavlyuchenko (Russia), Hakan Yakin (Switzerland), Semih Senturk (Turkey)

FASTEST GOAL
4 minutes: Luka Modric (Croatia v Austria)

TOTAL GOALS
77 goals

AVERAGE GOALS
2.48 goals per game

A thrilling tournament packed with giddying highs and tear inducing lows, by the time it was over Euro 2008 had managed to provide the final outcome that many neutrals craved. The fluent and intelligent football of the Spanish ultimately triumphed over the pragmatism of the Germans, but the competition was not without its surprises and it did not follow strictly to the form guide. Along with the two finalists, Portugal, France and Italy had also been rated as a good bet, but not all of Europe's football superpowers lived up to their billing.

The Germans were ranked among the favourites despite having qualified for the finals as runners-up to the Czech Republic, and once the competition was underway they suffered the embarrassment of defeat to Croatia in their second game. Darijo Srna opened the scoring for the Czechs when his outstretched boot beat Marcell Jansen to the ball, and they doubled

their lead when a deflected cross ricocheted off the post for Ivica Olic to tap into an empty net. Podolski pulled a goal back, but an injury time red card for Bastian Schweinsteiger ended Germany's hopes of forcing an equaliser. Croatia progressed with maximum points, while the Germans followed, thanks to victories over Poland and Austria.

The Spanish arrived at the tournament unbeaten in 16 games, but veteran coach Luis Aragones was playing down their chances. He had jettisoned experienced stalwart Raúl from his squad, but with a talented young team featuring David Villa, Fernando Torres, Xavi and Andres Iniesta, he had enough strength in depth to give Spain a good shot at a first tournament victory in 44 years. They progressed from their group with maximum points after beating Russia, Sweden and Greece, while the Russians joined them despite playing without suspended striker Andrei Arshavin for their first two games.

Much was expected of the Italians. Not only were they the reigning world champions but in Gianluigi Buffon they could claim the best keeper on the continent. Drawn with France and Holland, plus group makeweights Romania, it was still felt that Roberto Donadoni's team had what it took to dominate the 'group of death'. However, it was the Dutch, under coach Marco van Basten, who proved to be in the most devastating form, crushing the Italians 3-0 with a compelling display of counter-attacking football.

Holland employed the same tactic to inflict a 4-1 defeat on France in their second game and finished the group with a 100 per cent record. With both the Italians and the French failing to earn more than a point each out of Romania, a place in the quarter-finals was at stake when the teams met in the deciding game. However, France lost Franck Ribéry to an early injury and Eric Abidal to a red card midway through the first-half. Andrea Pirlo converted the resulting penalty and Daniele De Rossi scored with a 30-yard free-kick, eliminating the French.

Portugal topped the remaining group above Turkey on goal difference but lost their final game after fielding an understrength team against Switzerland, with two strikes from Hakan Yakin preventing them from finishing with maximum points. Turkey clinched the remaining quarter-final place with a 3-2 win over the Czech Republic after fighting back from 2-0 down, with Nihat Kahveci dramatically scoring twice in the dying minutes. As the game lurched into injury time the contest became increasingly ill-tempered and Turkish keeper Volkan Demirel was sent-off for a foul on Jan Koller.

In the first of the quarter-finals Portugal proved incapable of dealing with the aerial threat of Miroslav Klose and Michael Ballack and the Germans won 3-2, with coach Joachim Löw watching from the stands after an earlier

Above: Cesc Fabregas after the quarter-final. Opposite clockwise from top left: Holland's Ooijer and Robben against France; Spain's Fernando Torres; Arshavin and Zyrianov of Russia get the better of Sweden; Germany's Michael Ballack scores against Austria.

suspension. Despite having impressed in the group stage, the Portuguese were always second best in a rousing game and Helder Postiga's late strike did nothing more than make the score respectable.

It took penalties for Turkey to win their quarter-final although Croatia had looked the most likely to progress after Ivan Klasnic headed the first goal with just a minute of extra-time remaining. However, after Semih Senturk equalised with the last kick of the game, keeper Rustu saved from Mladen Petric in the penalty shoot-out to put Turkey into the semi-finals.

In the biggest shock of the competition the Russians marked the Dutch strikers out of the game, winning 3-1 thanks to an outstanding performance from Arshavin, who scored the winner in the 116th minute. It took penalties for Spain to get the better of the Italians, with keeper Iker Casillas saving from Daniele de Rossi and Antonio di Natale in the shoot-out.

In a rollercoaster semi-final the Germans overcame a Turkish side that had been ravaged by suspensions and injuries, yet it was the Turks that had the best of the chances, opening the scoring midway through the first-half when Ugur Boral stabbed the ball into the net after a fortuitous rebound off the crossbar. After Schweinsteiger and Klose gave the Germans the advantage, Senturk once again scored a late equaliser. But this time it was not enough and Philipp Lahm cut open the defence with a well-played one-two and hit a last minute winner for Germany.

In the other semi-final Spain comfortably defeated Russia in their second meeting of the tournament, thanks to three second-half goals. An injury to David Villa meant they would be without the tournament's leading goalscorer in the final, yet the stylish and elegant Spaniards were still expected to put an end to their nation's reputation as football's great underachievers. Only the Germans, football's most resilient grafters, stood in their way.

THE FINAL

SPAIN (1) 1-0 (0) GERMANY

Date Saturday June 29, 2008 **Attendance** 51,428
Venue Ernst Happel Stadium, Vienna

Throughout the tournament the Spanish had played beautiful, attacking football, and even minus the injured David Villa in the final they always looked the side most likely to take the lead. It was Fernando Torres who scored the goal that won them the game in the 33rd minute. Running onto a defence-splitting pass from Xavi that Lahm should have cleared, Torres lifted the ball over the advancing Jens Lehmann from just inside the area.

German captain Michael Ballack was unable to inspire his team to rise to the challenge, and although the slender lead came under threat, Spain defended well and always looked the most threatening. When the final whistle sounded, the team celebrated as if a huge weight had been lifted.

SPAIN
CASILLAS
Booked: 43 mins
RAMOS
MARCHENA
PUYOL
CAPDEVILA
SENNA
INIESTA
XAVI
FABREGAS ▶
Subbed: 63 mins (Alonso)
SILVA ▶
Subbed: 66 mins (Cazorla)
TORRES
Goal: 33 mins. Booked: 74 mins.
Subbed: 78 mins (Guiza)
sub: ALONSO ▶
sub: CAZORLA ▶
sub: GUIZA ▶

GERMANY
LEHMANN
FRIEDRICH
MERTESACKER
METZELDER
LAHM ▶
Subbed: 46 mins (Jansen)
FRINGS
HITZLSPERGER ▶
Subbed: 58 mins (Kuranyi)
SCHWEINSTEIGER
BALLACK
Booked: 43 mins
PODOLSKI
KLOSE ▶
Subbed: 79 mins (Gomez)
sub: JANSEN ▶
sub: KURANYI ▶
Booked: 88 mins
sub: GOMEZ ▶

Referee: Rosetti (Italy)

HOW THE TEAMS LINED UP

SPAIN
COACH:
LUIS ARAGONÉS

Casillas
Ramos Marchena Puyol Capdevila
Senna
Iniesta Xavi Fabregas Silva
Torres

GERMANY
COACH:
JOACHIM LÖW

Klose
Podolski Ballack Schweinsteiger
Hitzlsperger Frings
Lahm Metzelder Mertesacker Friedrich
Lehmann

EUROPEAN CHAMPIONSHIP RESULTS

1960 FRANCE

SEMI-FINALS

Soviet Union **3-0** Czechoslovakia

Yugoslavia **5-4** France

THIRD PLACE PLAY-OFF

Czechoslovakia **2-0** France

FINAL

Soviet Union **2-1** Yugoslavia
(aet)

1964 SPAIN

SEMI-FINALS

Spain **2-1** Hungary
(aet)

Soviet Union **3-0** Denmark

THIRD PLACE PLAY-OFF

Hungary **3-1** Denmark
(aet)

FINAL

Spain **2-1** Soviet Union

1968 ITALY

SEMI-FINALS

Italy **0-0** Soviet Union
(aet)
Italy won on toss of a coin

Yugoslavia **1-0** England

THIRD PLACE PLAY-OFF

England **2-0** Soviet Union

FINAL

Italy **1-1** Yugoslavia
(aet)

REPLAY

Italy **2-0** Yugoslavia

1972 BELGIUM

SEMI-FINALS

West Germany **2-1** Belgium

Soviet Union **1-0** Hungary

THIRD PLACE PLAY-OFF

Belgium **2-1** Hungary

FINAL

West Germany **3-0** Soviet Union

1976 YUGOSLAVIA

SEMI-FINALS

Czechoslovakia **3-1** Holland
(aet)

West Germany **4-2** Yugoslavia
(aet)

THIRD PLACE PLAY-OFF

Holland **3-2** Yugoslavia
(aet)

FINAL

Czechoslovakia **2-2** West Germany
(aet)
Czechoslovakia won 5-3 on penalties

1980 ITALY

GROUP 1

West Germany **1-0** Czechoslovakia

Holland **1-0** Greece

West Germany **3-2** Holland

Czechoslovakia **3-1** Greece

Czechoslovakia **1-1** Holland

West Germany **0-0** Greece

The England team managed third place in the 1968 European Championship, just two years after their World Cup win.

	P	W	D	L	F	A	Pts
West Germany	3	2	1	0	4	2	5
Czechoslovakia	3	1	1	1	4	3	3
Holland	3	1	1	1	4	4	3
Greece	3	0	1	2	1	4	1

GROUP 2

Belgium **1-1** England

Spain **0-0** Italy

Spain **1-2** Belgium

Italy **1-0** England

Spain **1-2** England

Italy **0-0** Belgium

	P	W	D	L	F	A	Pts
Belgium	3	1	2	0	3	2	4
Italy	3	1	2	0	1	0	4
England	3	1	1	1	3	3	3
Spain	3	0	1	2	2	4	1

THIRD PLACE PLAY-OFF

Czechoslovakia **1-1** Italy
(no extra time)
Czechoslovakia won 9-8 on penalties

FINAL

West Germany **2-1** Belgium

1984 FRANCE

GROUP 1

France **1-0** Denmark

Belgium **2-0** Yugoslavia

France **5-0** Belgium

Denmark **5-0** Yugoslavia

France **3-2** Yugoslavia

Denmark **3-2** Belgium

France's Bruno Bellone at Euro 84.

	P	W	D	L	F	A	Pts
France	3	3	0	0	9	2	6
Denmark	3	2	0	1	8	3	4
Belgium	3	1	0	2	4	8	2
Yugoslavia	3	0	0	3	2	10	0

GROUP 2

West Germany **0-0** Portugal

Spain **1-1** Romania

West Germany **2-1** Romania

Portugal **1-1** Spain

West Germany **0-1** Spain

Portugal **1-0** Romania

	P	W	D	L	F	A	Pts
Spain	3	1	2	0	3	2	4
Portugal	3	1	2	0	2	1	4
West Germany	3	1	1	1	2	2	3
Romania	3	0	1	2	2	4	1

SEMI-FINALS

France **3-2** Portugal
(aet)

Spain **1-1** Denmark
(aet)
Spain won 5-4 on penalties

THIRD PLACE PLAY-OFF

Not held

FINAL

France **2-0** Spain

1988 WEST GERMANY

GROUP 1

West Germany **1-1** Italy

Denmark **2-3** Spain

West Germany **2-0** Denmark

Italy **1-0** Spain

West Germany **2-0** Spain

Italy **2-0** Denmark

	P	W	D	L	F	A	Pts
West Germany	3	2	1	0	5	1	5
Italy	3	2	1	0	4	1	5
Spain	3	1	0	2	3	5	2
Denmark	3	0	0	3	2	7	0

GROUP 2

England **0-1** Rep. Of Ireland

Holland **0-1** Soviet Union

England **1-3** Holland

Rep. Of Ireland **1-1** Soviet Union

England **1-3** Soviet Union

Rep. Of Ireland **0-1** Holland

	P	W	D	L	F	A	Pts
Soviet Union	3	2	1	0	5	2	5
Holland	3	2	0	1	4	2	4
Rep. Of Ireland	3	1	1	1	2	2	3
England	3	0	0	3	2	7	0

SEMI-FINALS

West Germany **1-2** Holland

Soviet Union **2-0** Italy

THIRD PLACE PLAY-OFF

Not held

FINAL

Holland **2-0** Soviet Union

1992 SWEDEN

GROUP A

Sweden **1-1** France

Denmark **0-0** England

France **0-0** England

Sweden **1-0** Denmark

Sweden **2-1** England

France **1-2** Denmark

	P	W	D	L	F	A	Pts
Sweden	3	2	1	0	4	2	5
Denmark	3	1	1	1	2	2	3
France	3	0	2	1	2	3	2
England	3	0	2	1	1	2	2

GROUP B

Holland **1-0** Scotland

Germany **1-1** CIS

Germany **2-0** Scotland

Holland **0-0** CIS

Scotland **3-0** CIS

Holland **3-1** Germany

	P	W	D	L	F	A	Pts
Holland	3	2	1	0	4	1	5
Germany	3	1	1	1	4	4	3
Scotland	3	1	0	2	3	3	2
CIS	3	0	2	1	1	4	2

SEMI-FINALS

Sweden **2-3** Germany

Holland **2-2** Denmark
(aet)
Denmark won 5-4 on penalties

THIRD PLACE PLAY-OFF

Not held

FINAL

Denmark **2-0** Germany

1996 ENGLAND

GROUP A

England **1-1** Switzerland

Holland **0-0** Scotland

Switzerland **0-2** Holland

Scotland **0-2** England

Scotland **1-0** Switzerland

Holland **1-4** England

	P	W	D	L	F	A	Pts
England	3	2	1	0	7	2	7
Holland	3	1	1	1	3	4	4
Scotland	3	1	1	1	1	2	4
Switzerland	3	0	1	2	1	4	1

GROUP B

Spain **1-1** Bulgaria

Romania **0-1** France

Bulgaria **1-0** Romania

France **1-1** Spain

France **3-1** Bulgaria

Romania **1-2** Spain

	P	W	D	L	F	A	Pts
France	3	2	1	0	5	2	7
Spain	3	1	2	0	4	3	5
Bulgaria	3	1	1	1	3	4	4
Romania	3	0	0	3	1	4	0

Stefan Kuntz celebrates Oliver Bierhoff's winning 'golden goal' in the Euro 96 final.

Didier Deschamps lifts the trophy in Rotterdam after France's triumph at Euro 2000.

GROUP C

Germany **2-0** Czech Republic
Italy **2-1** Russia
Czech Republic **2-1** Italy
Russia **0-3** Germany
Russia **3-3** Czech Republic
Italy **0-0** Germany

	P	W	D	L	F	A	Pts
Germany	3	2	1	0	5	0	7
Czech Republic	3	1	1	1	5	6	4
Italy	3	1	1	1	3	3	4
Russia	3	0	1	2	4	8	1

GROUP D

Denmark **1-1** Portugal
Turkey **0-1** Croatia
Portugal **1-0** Turkey
Denmark **0-3** Croatia
Croatia **0-3** Portugal
Denmark **3-0** Turkey

	P	W	D	L	F	A	Pts
Portugal	3	2	1	0	5	1	7
Croatia	3	2	0	1	4	3	6
Denmark	3	1	1	1	4	4	4
Turkey	3	0	0	3	0	5	0

QUARTER-FINALS

England **0-0** Spain
(aet)
England won 4-2 on penalties
France **0-0** Holland
(aet)
France won 5-4 on penalties
Germany **2-1** Croatia
Portugal **0-1** Czech Republic

SEMI-FINALS

France **0-0** Czech Republic
(aet)
Czech Republic won 6-5 on penalties
England **1-1** Germany
(aet)
Germany won 6-5 on penalties

THIRD PLACE PLAY-OFF

Not held

FINAL

Germany **2-1** Czech Republic
(aet)
Germany won with golden goal

2000 BELGIUM/HOLLAND

GROUP A

Germany **1-1** Romania
Portugal **3-2** England
Romania **0-1** Portugal
England **1-0** Germany
England **2-3** Romania
Portugal **3-0** Germany

	P	W	D	L	F	A	Pts
Portugal	3	3	0	0	7	2	9
Romania	3	1	1	1	4	4	4
England	3	1	0	2	5	6	3
Germany	3	0	1	2	1	5	1

GROUP B

Belgium **2-1** Sweden
Turkey **1-2** Italy
Italy **2-0** Belgium
Sweden **0-0** Turkey
Turkey **2-0** Belgium
Italy **2-1** Sweden

	P	W	D	L	F	A	Pts
Italy	3	3	0	0	6	2	9
Turkey	3	1	1	1	3	2	4
Belgium	3	1	0	2	2	5	3
Sweden	3	0	1	2	2	4	1

GROUP C

Spain **0-1** Norway
Yugoslavia **3-3** Slovenia
Slovenia **1-2** Spain
Norway **0-1** Yugoslavia
Yugoslavia **3-4** Spain
Slovenia **0-0** Norway

	P	W	D	L	F	A	Pts
Spain	3	2	0	1	6	5	6
Yugoslavia	3	1	1	1	7	7	4
Norway	3	1	1	1	1	1	4
Slovenia	3	0	2	1	4	5	2

GROUP D

France **3-0** Denmark
Holland **1-0** Czech Republic
Czech Republic **1-2** France
Denmark **0-3** Holland
France **2-3** Holland
Denmark **0-2** Czech Republic

	P	W	D	L	F	A	Pts
Holland	3	3	0	0	7	2	9
France	3	2	0	1	7	4	6
Czech Republic	3	1	0	2	3	3	3
Denmark	3	0	0	3	0	8	0

QUARTER-FINALS

Portugal **2-0** Turkey
Italy **2-0** Romania
Holland **6-1** Yugoslavia
France **2-1** Spain

SEMI-FINALS

Portugal **1-2** France
(aet)
France won with golden goal
Italy **0-0** Holland
(aet)
Italy won 3-1 on penalties

THIRD PLACE PLAY-OFF

Not held

FINAL

France **2-1** Italy
(aet)
France won with golden goal

2004 PORTUGAL

GROUP A

Portugal **1-2** Greece
Spain **1-0** Russia
Greece **1-1** Spain
Russia **0-2** Portugal
Russia **2-1** Greece
Spain **0-1** Portugal

	P	W	D	L	F	A	Pts
Portugal	3	2	0	1	4	2	6
Greece	3	1	1	1	4	4	4
Spain	3	1	1	1	2	2	4
Russia	3	1	0	2	2	4	3

GROUP B

Switzerland **0-0** Croatia
France **2-1** England
England **3-0** Switzerland
Croatia **2-2** France
Switzerland **1-3** France
Croatia **2-4** England

	P	W	D	L	F	A	Pts
France	3	2	1	0	7	4	7
England	3	2	0	1	8	4	6
Croatia	3	0	2	1	4	6	2
Switzerland	3	0	1	2	1	6	1

GROUP C

Denmark **0-0** Italy
Sweden **5-0** Bulgaria
Bulgaria **0-2** Denmark
Italy **1-1** Sweden
Italy **2-1** Bulgaria
Denmark **2-2** Sweden

	P	W	D	L	F	A	Pts
Sweden	3	1	2	0	8	3	5
Denmark	3	1	2	0	4	2	5
Italy	3	1	2	0	3	2	5
Bulgaria	3	0	0	3	1	9	0

GROUP D

Czech Republic **2-1** Latvia
Germany **1-1** Holland
Latvia **0-0** Germany
Holland **2-3** Czech Republic
Holland **3-0** Latvia
Germany **1-2** Czech Republic

	P	W	D	L	F	A	Pts
Czech Republic	3	3	0	0	7	4	9
Holland	3	1	1	1	6	4	4
Germany	3	0	2	1	2	3	2
Latvia	3	0	1	2	1	5	1

QUARTER-FINALS

Portugal **2-2** England
(aet)
Portugal won 6-5 on penalties
France **0-1** Greece
Sweden **0-0** Holland
(aet)
Holland won 5-4 on penalties
Czech Republic **3-0** Denmark

SEMI-FINALS

Portugal **2-1** Holland
Greece **1-0** Czech Republic
(aet)
Greece won with silver goal

FINAL

Portugal **0-1** Greece

2008 AUSTRIA/SWITZERLAND

GROUP A

Switzerland **0-1** Czech Republic
Portugal **2-0** Turkey
Czech Republic **1-3** Portugal
Switzerland **1-2** Turkey
Switzerland **2-0** Portugal
Turkey **3-2** Czech Republic

Spain's Cesc Fabregas at Euro 2008

	P	W	D	L	F	A	Pts
Portugal	3	2	0	1	5	3	6
Turkey	3	2	0	1	5	5	6
Czech Republic	3	1	0	2	4	6	3
Switzerland	3	1	0	2	3	3	3

GROUP B

Austria **0-1** Croatia
Germany **2-0** Poland
Croatia **2-1** Germany
Austria **1-1** Poland
Poland **0-1** Croatia
Austria **0-1** Germany

	P	W	D	L	F	A	Pts
Croatia	3	3	0	0	4	1	9
Germany	3	2	0	1	4	2	6
Austria	3	0	1	2	1	3	1
Poland	3	0	1	2	1	4	1

GROUP C

Romania **0-0** France
Holland **3-0** Italy
Italy **1-1** Romania
Holland **4-1** France
Holland **2-0** Romania
France **0-2** Italy

	P	W	D	L	F	A	Pts
Holland	3	3	0	0	9	1	9
Italy	3	1	1	1	3	4	4
Romania	3	0	2	1	1	3	2
France	3	0	1	2	1	6	1

GROUP D

Spain **4-1** Russia
Greece **0-2** Sweden
Sweden **1-2** Spain
Greece **0-1** Russia
Greece **1-2** Spain
Russia **2-0** Sweden

	P	W	D	L	F	A	Pts
Spain	3	3	0	0	8	3	9
Russia	3	2	0	1	4	4	6
Sweden	3	1	0	2	3	4	3
Greece	3	0	0	3	1	5	0

QUARTER-FINALS

Portugal **2-3** Germany
Croatia **1-1** Turkey
(aet)
Turkey won 3-1 on penalties
Holland **1-3** Russia
(aet)
Spain **0-0** Italy
(aet)
Spain won 4-2 on penalties

SEMI-FINALS

Germany **3-2** Turkey
Russia **0-3** Spain

FINAL

Germany **0-1** Spain

Dabizas, Zagorakis and Venetidis of Greece celebrate winning Euro 2004.

INTERNATIONAL COMPETITIONS

OLYMPIC GAMES

OLYMPIC GAMES FINAL RESULTS

1908 LONDON
England **2-0** Denmark

1912 STOCKHOLM
England **4-2** Denmark

1920 ANTWERP
Belgium **2-0** Czechoslovakia
(Match abandoned after 78 mins. Czechoslovakia disqualified and Spain awarded silver)

1924 PARIS
Uruguay **3-0** Switzerland

1928 AMSTERDAM
Uruguay **1-1** Argentina (aet)
Uruguay **2-1** Argentina Replay

1932 LOS ANGELES
No Tournament

1936 BERLIN
Italy **2-1** Austria (aet)

1948 LONDON
Sweden **3-1** Yugoslavia

1952 HELSINKI
Hungary **2-0** Yugoslavia

1956 MELBOURNE
Soviet Union **1-0** Yugoslavia

1960 ROME
Yugoslavia **3-1** Denmark

1964 TOKYO
Hungary **2-1** Czechoslovakia

1968 MEXICO CITY
Hungary **4-1** Bulgaria

1972 MUNICH
Poland **2-1** Hungary

1976 MONTREAL
East Germany **3-1** Poland

1980 MOSCOW
Czechoslovakia **1-0** East Germany

1984 LOS ANGELES
France **2 - 0** Brazil

1988 SEOUL
Soviet Union **2-1** Brazil (aet)

1992 BARCELONA
Spain **3-2** Poland

1996 ATLANTA
Nigeria **3-2** Argentina

2000 SYDNEY
Cameroon **2-2** Spain (aet)
(Cameroon win 5-3 on penalties)

2004 ATHENS
Argentina **1-0** Paraguay

2008 BEIJING
Argentina **1-0** Nigeria

Football at the Olympics has gone through three distinct phases, evolving from a sport that had not convinced the International Olympic Committee of its popularity, before eventually becoming an essential ingredient to making any Olympic Games a success. More spectators than any other sporting discipline, including athletics, now watch the Olympic football tournament. This has led to an uneasy partnership between the IOC and FIFA over the status of the Olympic football tournament.

There were unofficial tournaments at the first three Olympics, although some historians dispute the veracity of the evidence for the 1896 games. However, gold medals have been awarded retrospectively for the 1900 and 1904 Olympics. The first official tournament was at the 1908 London Games. Six purely amateur teams competed, including French 'A' and 'B' teams. The two French sides were knocked out by Denmark, who thrashed the 'B' team 9-0 and, in a game that included a ten-goal haul for Sophus Nielsen, the 'A' team 17-1. After such prolific success, the Danes ultimately lost the final to England 2-0.

The IOC were uncertain as to the popularity of football and actually questioned whether the sport warranted a place in the games in 1912, a competition that was again won by England. From 1920 to 1928 the Olympic football tournament was regarded as a world championship and was organised by FIFA, but because they allowed 'broken time' payments to players to compensate for loss of earnings, debate raged between national associations about the definition of 'amateurism' at a time when the Olympics did not allow professionals.

Belgium hosted and won the 1920 event held in Antwerp, beating Czechoslovakia 2-0 in the final, but the record books do not always mention that after Larnoe netted Belgium's second goal in the 78th minute, the Czech team walked off

the pitch incensed by what they perceived as refereeing bias.

Football from South America dominated the Olympics of both 1924 and 1928 through the thrilling play of the Uruguayans, who won both tournaments. The World Cup was finally born two years later and from that point the two events would rival one another until 1950, when the World Cup established itself as football's premier event.

The post-war years brought the second phase of the Olympic football tournament. The Olympics still held firm to its amateur ethos, which was perfectly circumvented by the rising Communist Bloc countries of Eastern Europe. Under Communist regimes football was a leisure activity but the players were paid by, and deemed to work for, whatever national institution or industry their club was affiliated to, enabling the pretence of amateurism. Between 1952 and 1980 every Olympic football final was won by an East European team: Hungary (1952, 1964, 1968), the Soviet Union (1956), Yugoslavia (1960), Poland (1972), East Germany (1976) and Czechoslovakia (1980). Each final in

this period, except for 1960, featured just East European teams.

The sequence was ended when France beat Brazil 2-0 in the 1984 gold medal match, but it was only because there had been a Communist Bloc boycott of the Los Angeles Olympic Games in retaliation for the Western-led boycott of the Moscow Olympics four years earlier. For that tournament FIFA had already sought to address the problem and had ruled that any European or South American player who had played in a competitive game became ineligible.

However, the Soviet Union carefully planned its Olympic ambitions in conjunction with its European and World Cup hopes. The Soviets had a hot property in 19-year-old Igor Dobrovolski, who had five full caps for his country, all won in friendlies. Potentially he could have played at the European Championship in 1988, but he was redirected to the Olympics. It was well worth the gamble as Dobrovolski was excellent, helping the Soviet Union to a gold medal after beating Brazil 2-1 in the final. Brazil were the only non-European side to make it as far as the semi-finals that year, but in Romario they produced the tournament's star player.

The competition also saw one of the greatest shocks in the history of the Olympics. Italy had been so determined to win the gold medal that they had gone as far as delaying the start of the country's domestic season to accommodate the Olympic football tournament, but the Italians were comprehensively beaten 4-0 by Zambia, with Kalusha Bwalya scoring a hat-trick.

Professional sport was now becoming an integral part of the Olympics and the IOC wanted the football tournament to reflect that, with big names and big teams. FIFA, on the other hand, did not want a rival to the World Cup. To the consternation of the IOC, FIFA decreed the tournament could only be an Under-23 event, with teams allowed to include just three over-aged players.

Spain hosted and won the event in 1992, beating Poland 3-2 in a thrilling and dramatic final that attracted 95,000 spectators. In 1996 the final was played in Athens, Georgia, some 70 miles north west of the Olympic host city of Atlanta. Nevertheless, a staggering 1.36 million paying spectators witnessed the competition, culminating in Nigeria's 3-2 defeat of Argentina in the final. African success continued four years later in Australia, with Cameroon's victory over Spain after a penalty shoot-out. It was Cameroon's first Olympic gold medal in any sport, proving that the Olympics needs football, whatever its status.

In 2004 Argentina saw off the threat of Paraguay to win the country's first Olympic gold medal in 52 years, thanks to an 18th minute Carlos Tevez goal, his eighth of the competition. The Argentinians did not concede a goal during the tournament and found the going made easier in the second half of the final when Paraguay had both Emilio Martinez and Diego Figueredo sent-off. However, the most talked about match of the competition was played out for the bronze medal, when Italy had to take to the field against Iraq, the tournament's biggest surprise package. It was an emotional game played just hours after it emerged that a kidnapped Italian journalist had been murdered in Iraq in the aftermath of the war in the country. Alberto Gilardino scored the only goal as Italy won the bronze medal and ended Iraq's spectacular run.

In 2008 the Argentinians survived the heat of Beijing to retain the Olympic title as they beat Nigeria 1-0, with Benfica striker Angel di Maria beautifully chipping the keeper from 18 yards after running onto a Lionel Messi pass played from his own half. The Nigerians had their chances but the game was stopped twice to allow players to take on water as temperatures reached 42°c. Both coaches criticised the decision to play the game in the midday sun. Nevertheless, over two million spectators attended the competition, the highest number yet, confirming once again the ever-growing popularity of the Olympic football tournament.

COPA AMÉRICA
(SOUTH AMERICAN CHAMPIONSHIP)

The South American Championship is the oldest continental title in the world, having been staged 42 different times, including eight that are deemed unofficial. It has been played under various names and in varying formats, but since 1975 it has been known as the Copa América. There have been seven different winners of the championship over the years, but for the most part the competition has been dominated by the national sides of Argentina and Uruguay.

Argentina gave birth to the event in 1910, hosting and winning a triangular tournament that also involved Uruguay and Chile. Six years later, as part of the centenary celebrations to mark the country's independence from

Spain, a second tournament was organised with the addition of Brazil, but this time the cup was won by Uruguay. Both events were actually unofficial, as the Confederación Sudamericana de Futbol (CONEMBOL) was only founded during the 1916 tournament.

The first official tournament took place in Uruguay just over a year later and was contested by the same four teams, with Uruguay winners again. The championships were played on a league basis with all of the games staged in one host city (with the exception of 1949) until 1975. During the 1920s the South American Championship was an annual event, but the rise of professionalism led to a hiatus of six years, when an unofficial professional championship was staged in Peru in 1935. The success of this tournament led to a revival in interest, and a plethora of sanctioned and unsanctioned tournaments were staged during the Forties and Fifties. These competitions were invariably won by Argentina or Uruguay, except in 1939, 1949 and 1953, when Peru, Brazil and Paraguay triumphed respectively.

By the 1960s the championship began to suffer because of the increased popularity of the international club game, and in particular the Copa Libertadores. Played just twice in the decade, in 1963 and 1967, after being staged 30 times the South American Championship disappeared from the football calendar for eight years. When it did return in 1975, all ten members of CONEMBOL entered for the first time. The format was revamped and played on a home and away basis. The winners from three groups of three teams joined holders Uruguay in two-legged semi-finals. The final

was contested by Peru and Colombia, with each team winning a match before Peru clinched a play-off victory 1-0 in Caracas.

In 1987 the Copa América reverted to being staged by a single host country. This was the ideal logistical solution. However, fans of the various host nations were notoriously fickle and attendances suffered as a consequence. In Argentina that year only 500 fans bothered to turn up to watch Colombia play Bolivia, and in 1995 less than 100 fans watched Paraguay's clash with Venezuela in Uruguay, which at least did have the mitigating circumstances of being played in a torrential downpour.

It also has to be said that most tournaments have not produced good football. The 1987 event was dire and witnessed 14 players sent-off in 13 games. The final between Uruguay and Chile was a foul-riddled affair that saw four players dismissed. The Uruguayans, as holders, had been given a bye to the semi-finals, and therefore had successfully defended the title by playing just two games.

The next tournament saw Brazil win their first major honour since the 1970 World Cup victory some 19 years earlier. The competition featured two groups of five teams, leading to a final round of four teams – that resulted in a schedule of 26 games in 16 days, with teams playing every other day to bring in the much needed television revenues and gate receipts. CONEMBOL justified this as preparation for the 1990 World Cup, but as one player – Uruguay's Pablo Bengochea – failed a drugs test that revealed more than the permitted amount of caffeine in his urine, it was a schedule too gruelling for some.

The other problem facing teams was that

Above: Brazil celebrate after defeating Argentina in the 2007 Copa América Final.

Right: The victorious Argentinian team after winning the Copa América in 1993.

Bottom: United States keeper Kasey Keller parades with the Gold Cup in 2005.

COPA AMÉRICA
WINNERS

1910: Argentina*
1916: Uruguay*
1917: Uruguay
1919: Brazil
1920: Uruguay
1921: Argentina
1922: Brazil
1923: Uruguay
1924: Uruguay
1925: Argentina
1926: Uruguay
1927: Argentina
1929: Argentina
1935: Uruguay*
1937: Argentina
1939: Peru
1941: Argentina*
1942: Uruguay
1945: Argentina*
1946: Argentina*
1947: Argentina
1949: Brazil
1953: Paraguay
1955: Argentina
1956: Uruguay*
1957: Argentina
1959: Argentina
1959: Uruguay*
1963: Bolivia
1967: Uruguay
1975: Peru
1979: Paraguay
1983: Uruguay
1987: Uruguay
1989: Brazil
1991: Argentina
1993: Argentina
1995: Uruguay
1997: Brazil
1999: Brazil
2001: Colombia
2004: Brazil
2007: Brazil

* Unofficial Tournaments

many of the European-based players were absent from the competition, while the best of the talent on display would invariably end up Europe-bound after catching the attention of scouts during the tournament. It was to become a problem that was further aggravated by CONEMBOL's decision to create a fixture-heavy World Cup qualifying programme. To earn the television money, teams played up to 18 qualifying matches. The Copa América became a secondary concern to many teams, who fielded understrength sides.

A desire to revitalise the event, plus a need for increased TV revenues, led CONEMBOL to invite guest teams from other areas of the world to take part. So far Mexico (finalists in 1993 and 2001), the USA, Costa Rica, Japan and Honduras have all participated. The Canadians were invited in 2001 but when the event in Colombia looked set to be postponed they withdrew, along with Argentina.

The Argentinians won their 15th title in 1993, beating Mexico 2-1 in the final, while Uruguay's 14th trophy was won in 1995 following a penalty shoot-out win over Brazil. In 1997 Bolivia's Juan Baldivieso scored the Copa América's 2,000th goal, but it was the Brazilians who lifted the trophy that year, as they did again in 1999. Colombia became the seventh nation to win the Copa América when they hosted the 41st competition in 2001.

The 2004 Copa América competition was a battle between Brazil and Argentina, the two undisputed giants of South American football in recent times. Staged in Peru, the tournament could hardly have come to a more exciting conclusion, with Brazil snatching the advantage with the last kick of the game, when Adriano's injury-time equaliser resulted in a 2-2 final scoreline and took the game to penalties. The Brazilians converted their first four penalties to win the shoot-out 4-2, leaving the Argentinian team devastated.

The battle continued four years later when both teams reached the final in Venezuela, but it was a pragmatic and counterattacking Brazil side that triumphed once again. Favourites Argentina fielded players of the calibre of Carlos Tevez and Lionel Messi, but they were unable to prevent the Brazilians winning the competition for the eighth time, with goals from Julio Baptista and Daniel Alves, and an unfortunate own-goal from Argentina defender Roberto Ayala.

GOLD CUP
(CONCACAF CHAMPIONSHIP)

When Jack Warner was elected as President of CONCACAF in April 1990 he insisted on setting up an equivalent to the international competitions that existed in Africa, Asia, Europe and South America. Previous incarnations such as the CCCF Championship, run by the Confederación Centroamericana y del Caribe de Fútbol between 1941 and 1961, and the CONCACAF Championship, which ran from 1963 to 1989 had been limited successes. Mexico did not enter until 1963 and initially did not take the competition that seriously. The United States was another notable absentee.

In 1991 the CONCACAF Gold Cup was born. Twenty-six teams entered, chasing the eight final places. The inaugural tournament was hosted by the USA, as have been all subsequent competitions, although in 1993 and 2003 they co-hosted the event with Mexico.

Under coach Bora Milutinovic, the USA won the first Gold Cup. Recording a 2-0 win over the Mexicans in the semi-final, it was their first victory over their near neighbours in 11 years, which led the Mexico coach Manuel Lapuente to resign. The final against Honduras was played at the Coliseum in Los Angeles and after a goalless game the destination of the trophy was decided on penalties. Sixteen spot-kicks were taken, with the USA's goalkeeper Tony Meola, who was

voted the tournament's Most Valuable Player, saving three of them. Spot-kick number 15 saw Clavijo convert to put the USA 4-3 ahead, before Espinoza of Honduras fired the ball over the bar to give the Americans victory.

Two years later the Mexicans got their revenge in a competition of eight teams. Despite being co-hosts, Mexico had originally submitted a 'B' team, but it was rejected by CONCACAF secretary Chuck Blazer. A full strength Mexico blew away most of the opposition, thrashing Martinique 9-0 (including seven goals for Zaguinho), Canada 8-0, and Jamaica 6-1 in a game that saw keeper Jorge Campos switch to centre-forward when the reserve keeper came on as a substitute in the second-half. In front of 120,000 screaming fans in Mexico City, the Mexicans, under coach Miguel Meija Baron, comprehensively beat USA 4-0 in the final.

A switch of dates from July in odd years to January and February in even years began with the third tournament in 1996. There was a further change with the addition of an invited team, Brazil, who sent their Olympic Under-23 side but still managed to reach the final where they faced Mexico, who were now under ex-USA coach Bora Milutinovic. Backed by the majority of the 88,155 crowd in the Los Angeles Coliseum, and playing in appalling conditions directly after the third place play-off match was contested at the same venue, Mexico were cynically determined to win. They committed 38 fouls on the way to a 2-0 victory.

In 1998 the tournament featured ten teams. Brazil were once again invited to take part and allowed to play their games in Miami, despite California being firmly established as the home of the Gold Cup. This was connected to the revenue from television, as Los Angeles was some six hours ahead of Brazil, while Miami offered just a three-hour time difference. In a rain-affected tournament, one tie between Jamaica and El Salvador was postponed because of the weather. There was a low turn-out of 11,234 for the competition's opening fixture between hosts USA and Cuba (the first meeting between the two countries since 1949), but in the semi-finals USA went on to record their first ever win

over Brazil at full international level, thanks to a goal from Preki. The real hero of the game was goalkeeper Kasey Keller who was magnificent under relentless Brazilian pressure. However, it was Mexico, back under the stewardship of Manuel Lapuente, who completed a hat-trick of Gold Cup titles, beating the USA by a single Luis Hernandez goal in the final.

In 2000 12 teams battled for the £100,000 prize money, including guests Peru, South Korea and Colombia. It was also the tournament that revealed just how financially dependent the competition was on Mexican success. Mexico were knocked-out at the quarter-final stage by a 'golden goal' from Canada's Richard Hastings, and with hosts USA going out on penalties to Colombia at the same stage, attendance figures subsequently plummeted. The final between Canada and Colombia attracted just 6,197 spectators inside the Los Angeles Coliseum. Canada, who had earlier progressed through the group on the toss of a coin at the expense of South Korea, won 2-0 with a headed goal from Jason De Vos and a Carlo Corazzin penalty.

In 2002 the 12 teams included guests Ecuador, who were knocked-out at the group stage by a draw of lots that allowed Canada and Haiti through. Mexico sent a 'B' team, under pressure from the clubs back home not to select their best players, but they still managed to increase the disappointing crowds to an average of 18,500 for the event, which climaxed with the USA's 2-0 defeat of Costa Rica with goals from Josh Wolff and Jeff Agoos. Mexico clinched a record fourth Gold Cup title in 2003. A 'golden goal' from Daniel Osorno in the 97th minute defeated favourites Brazil in the final.

In 2005 the format of the competition's first stage changed from four groups of three teams to three groups of four, with the top two in each group and the two best third-placed teams progressing to the quarter-finals. Again several teams fielded second-string squads, including guests Colombia and South Africa, while the region's strongest teams, Mexico and USA, were missing at least half of their usual starting line-ups. Matches in Miami were postponed because of Hurricane Dennis, but the biggest shock of the competition was Panama's success in reaching the final for the first time. Their path included a penalty shoot-out victory over South Africa in the quarter-finals, but penalties could not save them again in the final. After a scoreless game, the USA won the shoot-out 3-1, with Brad Davis slotting home the decisive kick.

The Americans retained their title in 2007 in one of the most exciting, end-to-end Gold Cup matches in memory, although they had been lucky to reach the final having received a fortunate refereeing decision in the semi-final that ruled out an equalising goal from Canada.

Once in the final against Mexico, in front of a sell-out crowd of 60,000 (many of them Mexicans) at Soldier Field in Chicago, they trailed to an Andrés Guardado goal at half-time.

However, Landon Donovan equalised from the penalty spot in the 62nd minute, and shortly afterwards Benny Feilhaber hit a beautiful volley into the net from 22 yards to win the game for the Americans.

Mexico's coach Hugo Sanchez felt cheated by the result but he was unable to lead the team to revenge after losing his job the following year. It was under Javier Aguirre that the Mexicans again faced the USA in the 2009 final, staged at the Giants Stadium in New Jersey, and they managed to beat the tournament favourites 5-0, despite coming off the pitch second best after a scoreless first-half. Five goals after the interval sealed a momentous victory for the Mexicans.

ASIAN CUP

The second oldest continental competition in the world, the Asian Cup is played once every four years and has run uninterrupted since 1956, involving a qualifying competition from the outset. The first three Asian Cups were contested in a four-team league and won by South Korea in both 1956 and 1960, and Israel – who had been runners-up at the first two tournaments – in 1964. The latter competition was notable for its lack of skilled football and for its poor sportsmanship.

The Iranians made their Asian Cup debut in 1968, both hosting and winning the tournament. Iran's success was significant because it boosted the game of football in Arabic countries, where it had previously been banned for religious reasons. The five-team finals marked the last appearance of Israel, while North Korea, the Asian heroes of the 1966 World Cup, bizarrely did not even enter.

Semi-finals and a final were added to the six-team league stage in 1972, with Iran dominating the revamped competition and lifting the trophy following a 2-1 victory over South Korea after extra-time, with Khalani scoring the 107th minute winner in Bangkok. The Iranians completed a hat-trick of triumphs in 1976 when, as hosts, they beat Kuwait 1-0.

Iran went 17 successive Asian Cup games without defeat, with their magnificent run ultimately ended by Kuwait in the semi-finals of the 1980 competition. Kuwait went on to win the trophy in one of the most entertaining tournaments in the history of the Asian Cup: 76 goals were scored in the 24 games.

The number of entrants increased as the competition progressed, but in a politically volatile region there were inevitably withdrawals. However, the Asian Cup increased in prestige, helped by the gradual rise of professionalism. Saudi Arabia beat China in the 1984 final and successfully defended the title four years later in a competition dominated by the Middle Eastern sides, with seven out of the ten finalists originating from that region.

Japan were victorious at the 1992 Asian Cup, a tournament that was hit by political problems, with only 23 out of the 37 members entering. The finals were marred by violent play on the pitch, with eight players sent-off and 49 booked. Iran were the worst culprits, with three players facing one-year bans and another two receiving match bans.

At the 40th anniversary tournament in 1996 Iran won the Fair Play Award, as well as boasting both the highest goalscorer in Ali Daei and the Player Of The Tournament, Khodadad Azizi. The host nation lost a final for the very first time, when Saudi Arabia beat the United Arab Emirates in a penalty shoot-out to win the 12-team tournament. This was an impressive display, as three key Saudi players had been suspended for breaking Islamic Sharia Law.

Japan beat Saudi Arabia 1-0 in Beirut to win the 2000 tournament, with a goal from Shigeyoshi Mochizuki, only playing in the final because Junichi Inamoto had been suspended. Earlier in the competition Japan had thrashed Uzbekistan 8-1, the highest scoring game in the competition's history.

In 2004 China hosted the biggest Asian

Above: The Mexican squad celebrate beating the United States in 2009 Gold Cup Final.

THE CONCACAF CHAMPIONSHIP
WINNERS

1941: Costa Rica
1943: El Salvador
1946: Costa Rica
1948: Costa Rica
1951: Panama
1953: Costa Rica
1955: Costa Rica
1957: Haiti
1960: Costa Rica
1961: Costa Rica
1963: Costa Rica
1965: Mexico
1967: Guatemala
1969: Costa Rica
1971: Mexico
1973: Haiti
1977: Mexico
1981: Honduras
1985: Canada
1989: Costa Rica

GOLD CUP
WINNERS

1991: USA
1993: Mexico
1996: Mexico
1998: Mexico
2000: Canada
2002: USA
2003: Mexico
2005: USA
2007: USA
2009: Mexico

Above: Victory for Iraq in the 2007 Asian Cup.

Bottom: Bilal Mohammed of Qatar is mobbed by team-mates after scoring in the 2006 Asian Games gold medal match.

THE ASIAN CUP WINNERS

1956:	South Korea
1960:	South Korea
1964:	Israel
1968:	Iran
1972:	Iran
1976:	Iran
1980:	Kuwait
1984:	Saudi Arabia
1988:	Saudi Arabia
1992:	Japan
1996:	Saudi Arabia
2000:	Japan
2004:	Japan
2007:	Iraq

THE ASIAN GAMES WINNERS

1951:	India
1954:	Taiwan
1958:	Taiwan
1962:	India
1966:	Burma
1970:	Burma & South Korea *(title shared)*
1974:	Iran
1978:	South Korea & North Korea *(title shared)*
1982:	Iraq
1986:	South Korea
1990:	Iran
1994:	Uzbekistan
1998:	Iran
2002:	Iran
2006:	Qatar

Cup tournament yet, with 16 teams competing. The hosts reached their first final in 20 years, inspiring a home television audience of 250 million to tune in to the deciding game with Japan, making it the most watched sporting event in Chinese TV history. The hosts made the better start, but in the 22nd minute they found themselves behind to a Takashi Fukunishi goal scored against the run of play. Despite a first-half equaliser from China's Li Ming, Japan went on to win 3-1 through goals from Koji Nakata and Keiji Tamada. The home fans, who had booed the Japanese national anthem before the game, demonstrated their anger at the final whistle while Japan picked up the trophy.

To avoid clashes with the Olympics and the European Championship, the next Asian Cup was contested a year early. Co-hosted by Indonesia, Malaysia, Thailand and Vietnam, the 2007 tournament gave the Iraq team its first taste of triumph, with team captain Younes Mahmoud heading a 72nd minute corner past floundering Saudi Arabia keeper Yasser Al Mosailem to win the match.

The Iraqis celebrated the final whistle with unbridled joy, but there had been sadness earlier in the competition. After the team's victory over South Korea in the semi-final, thousands of celebrating fans took to the streets back home in Iraq and more than 50 were killed in a series of terrorist bombings targeting the crowds.

ASIAN GAMES

Football has always been part of the multi-sport Asian Games since the inaugural event was held in India in 1951. Six teams entered the first tournament, playing matches of 80 minutes in duration, but the standard was not particularly high. The hosts beat Iran 1-0 in the final.

From such humble beginnings the football tournament has increased in size, with Taiwan, mainly represented by players from Hong Kong, winning the finals in 1954 and 1958, beating South Korea on both occasions. The latter competition was marred by accusations of biased and incompetent refereeing.

In political terms the participation of both Taiwan and Israel were a problem in 1962 and hosts Indonesia rescinded the invitations to both teams. In 1974 both North Korea and Kuwait refused to play Israel, so after a 3-0 win over Burma, the Israelis found themselves in the final, where they lost to Iran by an own-goal.

On two occasions the gold medal has been shared. In both 1970 and 1978 South Korea were held to 0-0 draws, firstly by Burma and then by North Korea. South Korea finally won the gold medal outright in 1986, a competition noted for a quarter-final round decided entirely by penalty shoot-outs.

Iran has been the dominant nation at the Asian Games since 1990, winning three times in four tournaments. Goalkeeper Ahmadreza Abedzadeh was the hero in Beijing in 1990, saving two penalties in a 4-1 shoot-out victory over North Korea. That tournament was played in the shadow of the Iraqi invasion of Kuwait. The Kuwaiti team went on to reach the quarter-finals, while the Iraqis were banned and both India and Indonesia withdrew.

Iran won the gold medal again in 1998, beating Kuwait 2-0 in the first final between West Asian sides. Despite having Mehdi Mahdavikia sent-off late in the game, Iran outplayed a depleted Kuwait, with first-half goals from Ahmed Karimi and Karim Bagheri. By this point the tournament had become a 24-team event (although Saudi Arabia withdrew) and was played over three weeks.

By the 2002 Asian Games, the football tournament had been revamped and turned into an Under-23 competition, with each team allowed to field up to three over-age players. The idea was to prepare Asian teams for the Olympics. However, this revamp seemed to have a detrimental effect on attendances. Held in South Korea after the World Cup, the cream of Asian youth seemed a massive turn-off to Korean fans who had become accustomed to the big names of world football, and many of the games were played in half-empty stadiums.

When South Korea were knocked out by Iran in the semi-finals, fans attempted to get refunds for their final tickets. Dissatisfied with their team's performance, the South Korean football association immediately sacked coach Park Hang-Seo for delivering just the bronze medal. He had been assistant to Guus Hiddink at the World Cup and he managed to last only two months in the top job.

Iran became the first team to retain the title outright in 2002, beating Japan 2-1. The tournament marked the return of Afghanistan after an 18-year absence, but they lost all three games and conceded 32 goals.

In 2006 Qatar won the football gold medal for the first time, doing so as hosts in front of a partisan home crowd in Doha. Despite having finished second to Uzbekistan in the group stage, the home team achieved solid victories over Thailand and Iran in the knockout rounds, before dominating Iraq to win the competition. Rumours before the final had suggested that the Iraqis were far from unified, with the country's sectarian divide mirrored by dissatisfaction within the squad. The team did little to allay these fears during the match, not managing a shot on target. However, it was only a headed goal from Bilal Mohammed in the 65th minute that secured the gold medal for Qatar.

AFRICAN NATIONS CUP

The first African Nations Cup was held in Sudan in 1957 between Egypt, Ethiopia, South Africa and Sudan, the founder members of the Confédération Africaine de Football (CAF). However, the South Africans were forced to withdraw when they refused to send a multi-racial team. They offered only an all-white or an all-black team, neither of which was acceptable to the other CAF members. South Africa did not return to the African Nations Cup until they hosted and won the 1996 tournament.

In the Khartoum Stadium on February 16, 1957, the first African Nations Cup was decided when Egypt defeated Ethiopia 4-0, with all the goals scored by Al-Diba. It was appropriate that Egypt should be the first winners, since the trophy was named after Abdel Aziz Abdallah Salem, the first president of CAF and an Egyptian. The competition has since developed from a small three-team tournament to a 16-team event that is televised around the world.

The 1960s saw the rise of Ghana, winners of the tournament in 1963 and 1965, runners-up in 1968 and 1970. Ghana had drawn on the experience of a number of European coaches and even embarked on a European tour in 1962, proving themselves to be far and away the best team in Africa at the time. Although successive Nations Cup triumphs were just 23 months apart, only one player, Odametey, played in both finals. Ghana finally won the original African Nations Cup trophy outright in 1978.

For the 1968 tournament there was a qualifying round for the first time, and that year's final, when Congo-Kinshasa (later known as Zaïre) beat favourites Ghana 1-0 with a goal from Kalala, was the first African Nations Cup match to be televised. In 1970 Sudan beat Ghana in the final, but it was Ivory Coast who broke the record for the biggest win at the tournament with a 6-1 thrashing of Ethiopia. Laurent Pokou also scored five goals in that game and both records still stand.

The Nations Cup finally came of age in the Eighties. Nigeria, buoyant through oil money, staged a magnificent tournament in 1980, with state-of-the-art facilities and enormous spectator support. A total of 735,000 fans attended the 16 games, including an 80,000 capacity crowd in the National Stadium in Surulere for a final that saw Nigeria beat Algeria 3-0.

A new dimension was brought to the competition in Libya in 1982, when all the games were played on artificial pitches. Technically it was a good tournament but goals were at a premium. The final itself was resolved by a penalty shoot-out, with Ghana overcoming the hosts 7-6 on penalties after a 1-1 draw.

The Ivory Coast was consumed by football fever when staging the tournament in 1984, but national pride – and local interest in the competition – was severely dented when the hosts went out in the first round. The crowds stayed away from the latter stages and the organisers were forced to give tickets away to get a capacity crowd for the final, which saw Cameroon come from a goal down to beat Nigeria 3-1. This tournament was the first to seriously arouse the interest of European scouts following the impressive performance of the African nations at the 1982 World Cup. This proved the start of the plundering of the continent's talent by the leading clubs of Europe, a problem for the tournament in later years.

The refusal of European clubs to release their players in 1990 contributed to a poor tournament. In 1992 CAF responded by switching the event to January and increasing the number of finalists to 12. Of the 263 players on call, some 83 were professionals from the European leagues. It was nations from western Africa that dominated the tournament, which for the first time had comprehensive television coverage. Sadly it was not a great tournament, although the final produced a dramatic climax. After a goalless draw, the match was settled with a 20-minute penalty shoot-out involving 24 spot-kicks. Ivory Coast ultimately won 11-10 when Ghana's Tony Baffoe saw his kick saved after Kouame Ake had converted with his second penalty of the shoot-out.

The 1994 final was one of the best in the history of the competition. Zambia faced Nigeria, just a year after the air crash that had wiped out the Zambian national team. Litana put them ahead after just three minutes but Emmanuel Amunike equalised two minutes later and then scored the winner in the 47th minute. It had been his first appearance at the tournament, making him the 19th squad player used by Nigeria in the finals.

At the 1998 tournament Mahmoud Al-Gohari became the first man to win the African Nations Cup as both a player (1959) and a coach, when he guided Egypt to glory in Burkina Faso. However, it was Cameroon that were the dominant side of the first tournaments of the 21st century and they became the first team in 37 years to win consecutive competitions after lifting the trophy in both 2000 and 2002.

In 2004, under the direction of French coach Roger Lemerre, Tunisia won the cup for the very first time. They had taken the lead in the final after just four minutes through Dos Santos, but Youssef Mokhtari equalised for Morocco with a header shortly before half-time. It was a mistake by Morocco keeper Khalid Fouhami that gifted striker Ziad Jaziri the winner six minutes into the second-half, enabling the hosts to win.

In 2006 hosts Egypt beat Ivory Coast 4-2 on penalties to win the competition. Although the match had finished goalless in front of a crowd of 75,000 in Cairo, the Egyptians had their chances during the match, including a disallowed goal with seven minutes of normal time remaining and a missed penalty in extra-time. However, Egypt's hero was keeper Essam Al Hadary, who saved spot-kicks from Ivory Coast captain Didier Drogba and Bakary Kone in the deciding shoot-out.

It would prove to be the first of a hat-trick of wins in consecutive tournaments for the Egyptians, who lifted the trophy again in 2008 after defeating Cameroon in Accra, Ghana. The Egyptians had the better of the chances but they did not take the lead until the 77th minute when Mohamed Aboutrika managed to find the net after team-mate Mohamed Zidan pick-pocketed Cameroon captain Rigobert Song on the edge of the penalty area.

Two years later the Egyptians were confirmed as the strongest force in African football when they won their seventh African Nations Cup title, some small consolation for their devastating failure to reach the World Cup finals in South Africa just weeks earlier. When Egypt's captain Ahmed Hassan lifted the trophy it was an incredible personal achievement for the player, having won the competition four times.

The Egyptians were easily the best team at the tournament, but they did not manage to fully overpower a young Ghanaian team in the final and they needed their very own super sub to win the game. Mohamed Nagy, better known as Gedo, came on as a 70th minute substitute and after playing a one-two with Mohamed Zidan, he curled a shot beyond keeper Richard Kingson. It was his fifth goal of the tournament, all scored after coming on from the bench, and it was enough to make him the competition's leading goalscorer. After the game Egypt retained the trophy permanently, having won it three times since it was first introduced in 2001.

Despite ending with jubilant celebrations, the 2010 Nations Cup had been shrouded in controversy after a bus carrying Togo's team had been attacked by terrorists days before the competition kicked off. Numerous passengers were wounded and three were killed, including assistant coach Amelete Abalo. As a result, Togo withdrew from the competition and left Ivory Coast, Ghana and Burkina Faso to play on in a reduced group. Controversially CAF suspended Togo from the two subsequent tournaments as punishment for their withdrawal.

Above: Egypt's players enjoy victory in the African Nations Cup final in 2010.

AFRICAN NATIONS CUP WINNERS

1957: Egypt
1959: Egypt
1962: Ethiopia
1963: Ghana
1965: Ghana
1968: Congo-Kinshasa
1970: Sudan
1972: Congo
1974: Zaïre
1976: Morocco
1978: Ghana
1980: Nigeria
1982: Ghana
1984: Cameroon
1986: Egypt
1988: Cameroon
1990: Algeria
1992: Ivory Coast
1994: Nigeria
1996: South Africa
1998: Egypt
2000: Cameroon
2002: Cameroon
2004: Tunisia
2006: Egypt
2008: Egypt
2010: Egypt

5

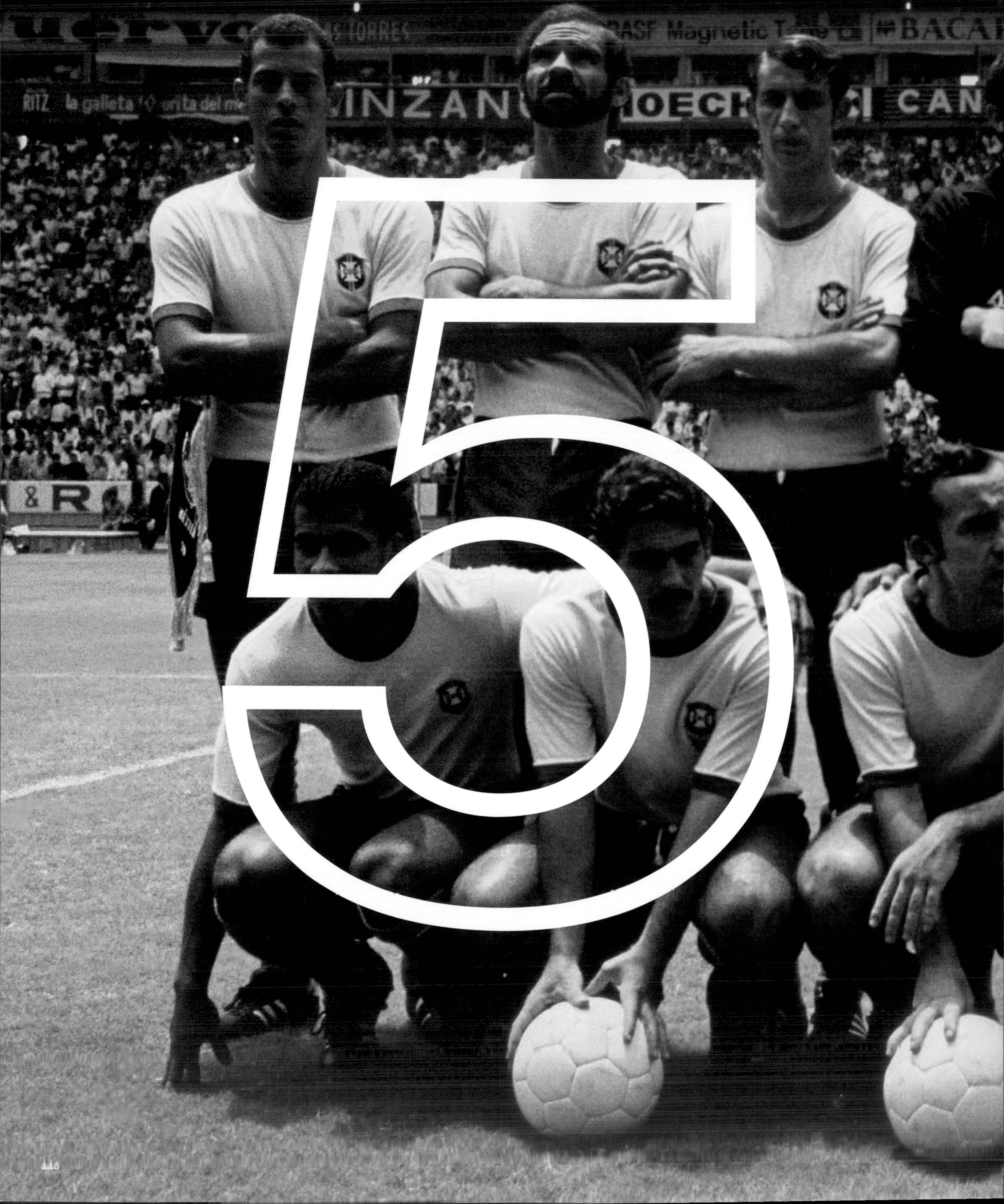

FOOTBALL NATIONS OF THE WORLD

THE COUNTRIES AND CONFEDERATIONS OF WORLD FOOTBALL

FIFA FÉDÉRATION INTERNATIONALE DE FOOTBALL ASSOCIATION

Founded: 1904 **Headquarters:** Zurich, Switzerland **Members:** 208

International Competitions: World Cup, Under-20 World Cup, Under-17 World Cup, Confederations Cup

Club Competitions: Club World Cup

Women's Competitions: Women's World Cup, Women's Club World Cup, Women's Under-20 World Cup, Women's Under-17 World Cup

The FIFA World Rankings in this chapter are as they stood after the World Cup in July 2010.

CONCACAF
CONFEDERATION OF NORTH, CENTRAL AMERICAN AND CARIBBEAN ASSOCIATION FOOTBALL

Founded: 1961

Headquarters: New York, USA

Members: 40

International Competitions: Gold Cup, Under-20 Championship, Under-17 Championship

Club Competitions: Champions League

Women's Competitions: Women's Gold Cup, Women's Under-20 Championship, Women's Under-17 Championship

Seats On FIFA Executive

UEFA	👤👤👤👤👤👤👤👤
AFC	👤👤👤👤
CAF	👤👤👤👤
CONMEBOL	👤👤👤
CONCACAF	👤👤👤
FIFA	👤👤
OFC	👤

CONMEBOL
CONFEDERACIÓN SUDAMERICANA DE FÚTBOL

Founded: 1916

Headquarters: Asunción, Paraguay

Members: 10

International Competitions: Copa América, South American Under-20 Football Championship, South American Under-17 Football Championship, South American Under-15 Football Championship

Club Competitions: Copa Libertadores, Copa Sudamericana, Recopa Sudamericana

Women's Competitions: Sudamericano Femenino, South American Under-20 Women's Championship, South American Under-17 Women's Championship

ICELAND

FAROE ISLANDS

DENMARK
GERMANY
SCOTLAND
NORTHERN IRELAND
HOLLAND
REPUBLIC OF IRELAND
ENGLAND
BELGIUM
WALES
LUXEMBOURG
FRANCE
LIECHTENSTEIN
SWITZERLAN

ANDORRA
PORTUGAL
SPAIN
TUNIS

MOROCCO

ALGERIA

CAPE VERDE
MAURITANIA
SENEGAL
MALI
GAMBIA
BURKINA FASO
GUINEA
GUINEA-BISSAU
SIERRA LEONE
IVORY COAST
BENIN
LIBERIA
GHANA
NIGERIA
TOGO
CAMEROON
SAO TOMÉ & PRÍNCIPE
EQUATORIAL GUINEA
GABON

CANADA

UNITED STATES OF AMERICA

BERMUDA

BAHAMAS
TURKS AND CAICOS ISLANDS
ANGUILLA
BRITISH AND US VIRGIN ISLANDS
CUBA
DOMINICAN REPUBLIC
ST KITTS AND NEVIS
MEXICO
CAYMAN ISLANDS
PUERTO RICO
ANTIGUA AND BARBUDA
MONTSERRAT
DOMINICA
BELIZE
ST LUCIA
JAMAICA
HAITI
NETHERLANDS ANTILLES
ST VINCENT AND THE GRENADINES
GUATEMALA
NICARAGUA
ARUBA
BARBADOS
GRENADA
COSTA RICA
TRINIDAD AND TOBAGO
EL SALVADOR
GUYANA
HONDURAS
PANAMA
VENEZUELA
SURINAM

COLOMBIA

ECUADOR

BRAZIL

PERU

BOLIVIA

CHILE
PARAGUAY

ARGENTINA
URUGUAY

UEFA
UNION OF EUROPEAN FOOTBALL ASSOCIATIONS

Founded: 1954

Headquarters: Nyon, Switzerland

Members: 53

International Competitions: European Championship, Under-21 Football Championship, Under-19 Football Championship, Under-17 Football Championship

Club Competitions: European Champions League, Europa League, Intertoto Cup, European Super Cup

Women's Competitions: UEFA Women's Championship, Women's Under-19 Football Championship, Under-17 Football Championship, UEFA Women's Champions League

OFC
OCEANIA FOOTBALL CONFEDERATION

Founded: 1966

Headquarters: Auckland, New Zealand

Members: 11

International Competitions: Oceania Nations Cup, Olympic Qualifying Tournament, Under-20 Qualifying Tournament, Under-17 Qualifying Tournament

Club Competitions: Oceania Champions League

Women's Competitions: Women's Championship, Women's Olympic Qualifying Tournament, Women's Under-20 Qualifying Tournament, Women's Under-17 Qualifying Tournament

AFC
ASIAN FOOTBALL CONFEDERATION

Founded: 1954

Headquarters: Kuala Lumpur, Malaysia

Members: 46

International Competitions: Asian Cup, Challenge Cup, Asian World Cup Qualifying Tournament, Asian Olympic Qualifying Tournament, Under-19 Championship, Under-16 Championship

Club Competitions: Champions League, AFC Cup, President's Cup

Women's Competitions: Women's Asian Cup, Under-19 Women's Championship, Under-17 Women's Championship

CAF
CONFÉDÉRATION AFRICAINE DE FOOTBALL

Founded: 1957

Headquarters: Cairo, Egypt

Members: 55

International Competitions: African Cup Of Nations, African Nations Championship, African Youth Championship, African Under-17 Championship

Club Competitions: Champions League, Confederations Cup, Super Cup

Women's Competitions: Women's Championship, Women's Under-17 Championship, Women's Under-20 Championship

AFGHANISTAN

Federation: Afghanistan Football Federation
Founded: 1933
Joined FIFA: 1948
Confederation: AFC
FIFA world ranking: 193 (joint)

ALBANIA

Federation: Federata Shqiptare e Futbolit
Founded: 1930
Joined FIFA: 1932
Confederation: UEFA
FIFA world ranking: 71

Football arrived in Albania at the turn of the century but the ruling Turks actively prevented the locals playing the sport. Independence in 1912 saw the game flourish and in 1930 the Football Association of Albania (FSF) was formed, along with the Albanian league championship. However, between 1938 and 1944 football activities ceased, with the country first under the control of Mussolini's Fascists and then the Soviet-backed Communists.

Football returned after World War II and Albania claimed their only title as Balkan Cup winners in 1946. A period of self-imposed isolation followed and between 1954 and 1963 Albania played just one international. In the 1960s Albania began to compete at both club and national level for the first time. They remain one of Europe's football minnows, with a poor record. During the 1980s, for example, the national team won just two matches. On the domestic scene in Albania, the game is dominated by the Tirana clubs.

ALGERIA

Federation: Fédération Algérienne de Football
Founded: 1962
Joined FIFA: 1963
Confederation: CAF
FIFA world ranking: 33
Honours: African Nations Cup 1990

Arguably the greatest moment in Algerian football history was the shock 2-1 defeat of the mighty West Germany at the 1982 World

Cup. Algeria, under coach Mahieddine Khalef, gave a resolute defensive performance against the attacking Germans, with goals from Rabah Madjer and Lakhdar Belloumi earning the landmark victory. However, Algeria were cheated out of a second round place by 'The Great Gijón Swindle', when a convenient 1-0 win for West Germany over Austria sent both nations through at Algeria's expense. In 1990 the Algerians finally experienced success when they hosted and won the African Nations Cup for the first time, an Oudjani goal beating Nigeria 1-0 in the final.

It was the French who introduced the game to Algeria at the turn of the century. By the 1920s the Muslim Algerians embraced the game and football quickly became the focus of a rising nationalist sentiment that was to lead to the country's independence from France in 1962. The first Algerian national league season culminated in 1963 with USM Algeria winning the title. JS Kabylie (aka JE Tizi-Ouzou), the Berber region team, have been the most successful Algerian side both at home and in the modern African game, having won a hat-trick of CAF Cups in 2000, 2001 and 2002.

AMERICAN SAMOA

Federation: Football Federation American Samoa
Founded: 1984
Joined FIFA: 1998
Confederation: OFC
FIFA world ranking: 202 (joint)

ANDORRA

Federation: Federació Andorrana de Fútbol
Founded: 1994
Joined FIFA: 1996
Confederation: UEFA
FIFA world ranking: 201

In October 2004 Andorra recorded a first competitive win after eight years of trying, beating Macedonia 1-0 in a World Cup qualifier. Their previous two victories were friendly wins over Belarus in 2000 and Albania in 2002. The Principality of Andorra boasts an open eight-club top division vying for a fan-base from its 70,000 inhabitants.

ANGOLA

Federation: Federação Angolana de Futebol
Founded: 1977
Joined FIFA: 1980
Confederation: CAF
FIFA world ranking: 86

For a country that has been blighted by over 30 years of bloody civil war, Angola's first World Cup qualification in 2006, under coach Luís Oliveira Gonçalves who took over in 2003, was nothing short of incredible. The 'Palancas Negras' (the Black Impalas) had only previously appeared in three African Nations Cup tournaments, winning just one match and never getting past the first phase, but they had won the regional COSAFA Cup on three occasions, in 1999, 2001 and 2004. Many Angolan-born players have been raised in Portugal and the Federação Angolana de Futebol searches for European-based talent for the national team. The domestic Angolan league is dominated by club sides AS Aviacao and Petro Atletico.

ANGUILLA

Federation: Anguilla Football Association
Founded: 1990
Joined FIFA: 1996
Confederation: CONCACAF
FIFA world ranking: 202 (joint)

ANTIGUA AND BARBUDA

Federation: Antigua and Barbuda Football Association
Founded: 1928
Joined FIFA: 1970
Confederation: CONCACAF
FIFA world ranking: 129

THE COUNTRIES OF UEFA

ICELAND

NORWAY

FINLAND

FAROE ISLANDS

SWEDEN

HOLLAND

ESTONIA

SCOTLAND

BELGIUM

RUSSIA

DENMARK

LITHUANIA

LATVIA

NORTHERN IRELAND

ENGLAND

BELARUS

GERMANY

REPUBLIC OF IRELAND

POLAND

KAZAKHSTAN

CZECH REPUBLIC

UKRAINE

SLOVAKIA

WALES

LUXEMBOURG

SLOVAKIA

ROMANIA

AUSTRIA

MOLDOVA

FRANCE

HUNGARY

GEORGIA

SERBIA

TURKEY

CROATIA

BULGARIA

PORTUGAL

SWITZERLAND

SLOVENIA

GREECE

ARMENIA

LIECHTENSTEIN

SPAIN

CYPRUS

ITALY

MONTENEGRO

ANDORRA

SAN MARINO

ALBANIA

MACEDONIA

AZERBAIJAN

MALTA

BOSNIA & HERZEGOVINA

ISRAEL

ARGENTINA

Federation: Asociación del Fútbol Argentina
Founded: 1893
Joined FIFA: 1912
Confederation: CONMEBOL
FIFA world ranking: 5
Honours: World Cup 1978, 1986; Copa América 1910, 1921, 1925, 1927, 1929, 1937, 1941, 1945, 1946, 1947, 1955, 1957, 1959, 1991, 1993; Olympics 2004, 2008; Confederations Cup 1993

Argentina's football history can be traced back to 1867, when immigrant English rail workers organised the country's first recorded match on a cricket field in Buenos Aires. The same Englishmen had just founded Buenos Aires FC, which was not only the country's first football club but one of the first outside of the British Isles. The sport continued to be played by the British community in Argentina, resulting in the founding of several of the country's oldest clubs, such as Rosario Central and Quilmes.

The Argentine league was contested for the first time in 1893, following a one off league organised by Alexander Watson Hutton two years earlier. It is the oldest league outside of Great Britain and ten of the first 20 championships were claimed by Alumni, a team of former students of The English High School, founded by Alexander Watson Hutton.

The early years of the 20th century saw the league's reputation grow with the formation of the Buenos Aires 'Big Five', clubs that still dominate the championship to this day: River Plate (founded by the English), Racing Club (French), Boca Juniors (Italians), Independiente and San Lorenzo. After World War I the number of clubs in the top division steadily rose, hitting a peak in the late 1920s with 36 clubs.

Argentina took part in the first international game played outside of Britain, beating Uruguay 3-2 in Montevideo in May 1901. The first unofficial South American Championship was also hosted and won by the country nine years later, although the tournament consisted of just two other teams, Uruguay and Chile.

The national team impressed at the inaugural World Cup in 1930, losing to hosts Uruguay 4-2 in the final. This success led to the beginning of Argentine football's professional era in 1931, with Boca Juniors setting the pace with three championship victories in the first five seasons. River Plate and Independiente also enjoyed extended spells of dominance, with the former enjoying a purple patch of five titles in six years during the Fifties.

It was within the first three decades of the formation of the professional league that the country established itself as a superpower in

Above: The Argentina players celebrate winning the Copa América after their victory over Mexico in Ecuador in 1993.
Opposite: Diego Maradona capped a series of fine performances in 1986 by lifting the World Cup.

world football. In this period attendances grew and the national team won eight of its 14 Copa América titles, but the World Cup remained out of reach. However, a league-restructuring programme in 1967 had a positive effect. The formation of two regional competitions, the Metropolitano and the Nacional, cut down on travelling times and expenses, leaving clubs to flourish. This was reflected in the next ten years by the World Club Cup triumphs of Racing Club, Estudiantes, Independiente and Boca Juniors.

Boca's victory in 1977 was followed a year later by the thing the country wanted most of all: World Cup success for Argentina on home soil. Coach César Luis Menotti led his team to the final, where they beat pre-tournament favourites Holland 3-1 in a politically charged clash. Menotti's team were greeted onto the pitch by a ticker tape welcome and two goals from Mario Kempes made him more popular than the country's president. Yet while Kempes had secured a place in Argentine football history, his star would soon be cast into the shadows by the emerging talent of a certain Diego Maradona.

The 17-year-old Maradona had only missed out on a place in Argentina's 1978 World Cup squad on the eve of the tournament, but when he was finally thrust onto the world stage at the 1982 finals in Spain, the world's most expensive player showed off both his unrivalled ball control and his suspect temperament. His World Cup ended with a red card for a rash kick at Brazil substitute Batista, but this was not to be the competition that would cement Maradona's legend.

Bowing out in second round proved to be a temporary blip for Argentinian football and having reverted to a single national league in 1985, Independiente's World Club Cup victory over Liverpool in 1984 and River Plate's success against Steaua Bucharest two years later only

emphasised the buoyancy that carried itself through to the 1986 World Cup Finals, where Maradona reigned supreme.

Fans of Pelé might argue otherwise but never in a World Cup had one player made such an impact. The contribution of team-mate Jorge Valdano can not be underestimated but it was Maradona who took teams apart single-handedly, as both Belgium and England would confirm. The English may have been left with rumblings of discontent following his 'Hand of God' goal, but his second strike against Bobby Robson's side is still regarded as one of the greatest goals ever scored. Although the skipper did not reach his usual dizzy heights in the 3-2 win against West Germany in the final, few would argue that he deserved to lift the trophy for Argentina at the very peak of his career.

Maradona led Argentina to the final again in 1990 but the team's unsightly mix of roughhouse play and safety-first tactics won them few friends as they lost to the Germans. Maradona's positive drugs test at the tournament four years later further blemished Argentina's reputation, allowing arch-rivals Brazil to gain the ascendancy in the world game.

The new century has seen a resurgence in the Argentine game. Boca Juniors have contested five Copa Libertadores finals since 2000, winning four of them, while Estudiantes also lifted the trophy in 2009. The national team won the Olympic title in 2004 with a team featuring Carlos Tevez, who was voted South American Player Of The Year three years running, and they won it again with Lionel Messi in 2008. Yet even with both of these stars in a side controversially coached by Diego Maradona, Argentina were unable to get further than the quarter finals of the 2010 World Cup, knocked out by Germany at this stage for the second consecutive tournament.

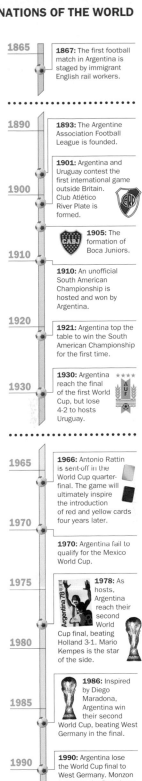

1865

1867: The first football match in Argentina is staged by immigrant English rail workers.

1890

1893: The Argentine Association Football League is founded.

1900

1901: Argentina and Uruguay contest the first international game outside Britain. Club Atlético River Plate is formed.

1905: The formation of Boca Juniors.

1910

1910: An unofficial South American Championship is hosted and won by Argentina.

1920

1921: Argentina top the table to win the South American Championship for the first time.

1930

1930: Argentina reach the final of the first World Cup, but lose 4-2 to hosts Uruguay.

1965

1966: Antonio Rattin is sent-off in the World Cup quarter-final. The game will ultimately inspire the introduction of red and yellow cards four years later.

1970

1970: Argentina fail to qualify for the Mexico World Cup.

1975

1978: As hosts, Argentina reach their second World Cup final, beating Holland 3-1. Mario Kempes is the star of the side.

1980

1986: Inspired by Diego Maradona, Argentina win their second World Cup, beating West Germany in the final.

1985

1990: Argentina lose the World Cup final to West Germany. Monzon becomes the first player to be sent-off in a World Cup final, followed by Dezotti.

1990

1993: Argentina beat tournament guests Mexico to win their 14th South American Championship.

1995

2000

2004: Argentina win the Olympic gold medal. They win again in 2008.

2005

2009: Lionel Messi becomes the first Argentine to be crowned World Player Of The Year.

2010

ARMENIA

Federation: Football Federation of Armenia
Founded: 1992
Joined FIFA: 1992
Confederation: UEFA
FIFA world ranking: 96 (joint)

Since the country's football separated from the Soviet Union in 1992, Yerevan-based Pyunik have been the most dominant force, winning nine league titles in the first decade of the 21st century. The Armenian Premier League consists of just eight teams.

ARUBA

Federation: Arubaanse Voetbal Bond
Founded: 1932
Joined FIFA: 1988
Confederation: CONCACAF
FIFA world ranking: 197

AUSTRALIA

Federation: Football Federation Australia
Founded: 1961
Joined FIFA: 1963
Confederation: AFC
FIFA world ranking: 20
Honours: Oceania Nations Cup 1980, 1996, 2000, 2004

Football in Australia was overhauled with the instigation of the A-League in 2005, which is contested by ten Australian teams and one from New Zealand (a 12th team will be added in 2011). The switching of confederations from Oceania to Asia in 2006, and a federation revamp that dropped the word 'soccer', have also help to rebrand the sport in Australia.

The club gaining the most points in the season is accorded the title of 'Premiers', while the 'Champions' are deemed to be the winners of the Grand Final, played between the table toppers and the runners-up. Despite finishing second behind Central Coast Mariners, the first A-League 'Champions' were Sydney, coached by Pierre Littbarski and inspired on the field by Dwight Yorke and in the boardroom by actor Anthony LaPaglia. Attendances more than doubled after the revamp but the clubs suffered financial problems when television and sponsorship revenues were not realised.

From 2007 the 'Champions' and 'Premiers' participated in the Asian Champions League (Adelaide United were runners-up in the 2008), while the national team joined the Asian Cup. Australia had previously dominated the Oceania Cup, winning it four times, while their clubs won the first four outings of Oceania Club Championship.

Australia qualified for the 2006 and 2010 World Cups, having reached the finals only once before. The team depends on players employed overseas and of the 2006 and 2010 squads only two players at each competition were with clubs at home, compared with the entirely Australian-based squad in 1974.

AUSTRIA

Federation: Österreichischer Fussball-Bund
Founded: 1904
Joined FIFA: 1905
Confederation: UEFA
FIFA world ranking: 60

On October 12, 1902, the first international football match between European nations outside of Britain was staged when Austria defeated Hungary 5-0 in Vienna, a city that became the centre of football excellence in central Europe. In Vienna, the emphasis was placed on the kind of skill, short passing and innovative tactics that wowed the rest of Europe. In 1911 the Austrian league was formed (albeit exclusively with Vienna-based clubs), followed eight years later by the Austrian Cup, with both competitions dominated by FK Austria Vienna (initially as Amateur-SV) and SK Rapid Vienna.

The 1930s saw the country's 'Wunderteam' establish a formidable reputation in international football. With a side including the celebrated Matthias Sindelar, between April 1931 and May 1934 Austria were defeated just twice in a 30-game run that saw them score 101 goals. They were also World Cup semi-finalists in 1934, losing to Italy 1-0, and Olympic runners-up in 1936. Austria looked set to dominate the European game but when the country was absorbed by Hitler's Germany in 1938, Austrian football ceased to exist.

In the Fifties the national team experienced a brief renaissance under coach Walter Nausch, reaching the semi-finals of the 1954 World Cup. The side included Ernst Ocwirk and Gerhard Hanappi and will be best remembered for an incredible 7-5 quarter-final victory over hosts Switzerland. Subsequently Austrian football influence began to fade and the team did not qualify for the World Cup again until 1978.

At both club and international level the game had become quite ordinary, and despite unearthing such talents as Hans Krankl and Herbert Prohaska, the nadir was reached with a 1-0 defeat by the Faroe Islands in 1990. Austria did qualify for the 1990 and 1998 World Cups but exited at the group stage both times.

AZERBAIJAN

Federation: Association of Football Federations of Azerbaijan
Founded: 1992
Joined FIFA: 1994
Confederation: UEFA
FIFA world ranking: 106

The Azerbaijan Premier League replaced the previous competition in 2007. Since independence from the Soviet Union in 1991, the most successful clubs have been Neftchi Baku, Gäncä, Inter Baku, Shamkir and Baku. The national team had to play its Euro 96 home qualifiers in Turkey, but subsequently matches have been largely played in Baku at the Tofik Bakhramov Stadium, named after the famous 1966 World Cup Final linesman.

Left: Armenia fail to stop Cesc Fabregas in a World Cup qualifier in 2009.

Below: Australia's Brett Holman celebrates scoring against Ghana at the 2010 World Cup.

BAHAMAS

Federation: Bahamas Football Association
Founded: 1967
Joined FIFA: 1968
Confederation: CONCACAF
FIFA world ranking: 179

BANGLADESH

Federation: Bangladesh Football Federation
Founded: 1972
Joined FIFA: 1974
Confederation: AFC
FIFA world ranking: 153

BELARUS

Federation: Football Federation of the Republic of Belarus
Founded: 1989
Joined FIFA: 1992
Confederation: UEFA
FIFA world ranking: 77

BAHRAIN

Federation: Bahrain Football Association
Founded: 1957
Joined FIFA: 1966
Confederation: AFC
FIFA world ranking: 69

BARBADOS

Federation: Barbados Football Association
Founded: 1910
Joined FIFA: 1968
Confederation: CONCACAF
FIFA world ranking: 128

Opposite centre: Van Himst of Belgium in action in 1972.

Below: Belgium's Eric Gerets takes on Franz Beckenbauer in the final of the 1980 European Championship.

Dinamo Minsk were the leading Belorussian side in the Soviet league and dominated the early years of the Belarus championship, established in 1992. However, in the first decade of the 21st century BATE Borisov have been the most successful club, winning the title six times in the 11 seasons since their top flight debut in 1998. The national team have not yet managed to qualify for the finals of a major tournament, while Alexander Hleb has been the country's most successful player of recent times.

BELGIUM

Federation: Belgian Football Association
Formed: 1895
Joined FIFA: 1904
Confederation: UEFA
FIFA world ranking: 48
Honours: Olympics 1920

Belgians loved football from the sport's earliest days and their contribution to the game is too often overlooked. The Royal Antwerp club was formed in 1880, the Belgian league began in 1896, and the national team played for the first time against France in 1904. Founder members of FIFA, the Belgians promoted the nascent World Cup to the extent that they were one of only four European sides to travel to Uruguay in 1930 for the first tournament. Indeed, the referee for the inaugural World Cup final was a Belgian, Jean Langenus.

This unfettered enthusiasm saw the amateur game flourish. Semi-professionalism was reluctantly accepted later but it was not until 1972 that club football turned professional. During the Seventies and beyond, Anderlecht established a reputation as Belgium's most successful club side and they represented the country with distinction on the continental stage, lifting the European Cup Winners' Cup in both 1976 and 1978 (they were runners-up in the intervening year), and the UEFA Cup in 1983. Club Brugge further enhanced the reputation of the Belgian game by finishing

BELIZE

Federation: Football Federation of Belize
Founded: 1980
Joined FIFA: 1986
Confederation: CONCACAF
FIFA world ranking: 182 (joint)

BENIN

Federation: Fédération Béninoise de Football
Founded: 1962
Joined FIFA: 1964
Confederation: CAF
FIFA world ranking: 61

BERMUDA

Federation: Bermuda Football Association
Founded: 1928
Joined FIFA: 1962
Confederation: CONCACAF
FIFA world ranking: 159

BHUTAN

Federation: Bhutan Football Federation
Founded: 1983
Joined FIFA: 2000
Confederation: AFC
FIFA world ranking: 198

BOLIVIA

Federation: Federación Boliviana de Fútbol
Founded: 1925
Joined FIFA: 1926
Confederation: CONMEBOL
FIFA world ranking: 53
Honours: Copa América 1963

as runners-up in the 1978 European Cup.

Between 1982 and 2002 the national side qualified for every World Cup, reaching the semi-final in 1986 and losing to a Maradona-inspired Argentina. They were runners-up in the European Championship in 1980 and have twice hosted the tournament, in 1972 and as co-hosts in 2000.

The most significant influence on the modern game was caused by a Belgian, when the 'Bosman Ruling' shook football to its roots. Jean-Marc Bosman brought a court case that led to freedom of movement for foreign players within Europe and gained legal rights for footballers, allowing them to leave a club once their contract had expired without the need for a transfer fee.

Bolivia is a modest football nation but on the international stage its players can count on enormous home advantage due to the altitude at La Paz, which is 12,000 feet above sea level. The team's only Copa América success was in

1963 when they hosted the tournament. They have reached the World Cup just three times: in 1930 when invited, in 1950 with a walk-over, and in 1994 when qualifying second to Brazil in their group. Historically the domestic game in all its incarnations – La Paz League (1914), National Championship (1926) and the National League (1977) – has been dominated by three clubs: The Strongest, Jorge Wilsterman and Bolivar.

Above right: Erwin Sanchez of Bolivia fends of Germany's Thomas Berthold at the 1994 World Cup.

Above left: Djiman Koukou of Benin (left) fends of a challenge from Paito of Mozambique at the 2010 African Nations Cup.

BOSNIA-HERZEGOVINA

Federation: Football Federation of Bosnia-Herzegovina
Founded: 1992
Joined FIFA: 1996
Confederation: UEFA
FIFA world ranking: 57

Bosnia's independence did not provide a unified football scene. Initially there were separate leagues for Muslims, Croats and Serbians but in 2002-3 Bosnia's national league was extended to include clubs from all areas of the country. Similarly, non-Muslim players have only been selected for the national team since 1999.

BOTSWANA

Federation: Botswana Football Association
Founded: 1970
Joined FIFA: 1978
Confederation: CAF
FIFA world ranking: 93

BRAZIL

Federation: Confederação Brasileira de Futebol

Founded: 1914

Joined FIFA: 1923

Confederation: CONMEBOL

FIFA world ranking: 3

Honours: World Cup 1958, 1962, 1970, 1994, 2002; Copa América 1919, 1922, 1949, 1989, 1997, 1999, 2004, 2007; Confederations Cup 1997, 2005, 2009

Some believe that football was brought to Brazil by British and Dutch sailors in the second half of the 19th Century, yet the accepted consensus is that Charles Miller, who was born in Brazil but educated in Southampton, returned to his birthplace in 1894 with two footballs, a rule book and a set of playing kit to teach the locals of São Paulo the laws of the beautiful game.

The first recorded football match in Brazil was organised by Miller and took place the following year between employees of the local gas company and São Paulo Railways, which the latter side won 4-2. The game created fervent interest in the sport and within just a few years the first club sides were springing up in São Paulo and beyond, such as the São Paulo Athletic Club, Mackenzie Athletic Association, Germania, Internacional and Paulistino.

In 1901 the São Paulo League was formally established, Rio de Janeiro following suit and in 1914 the Brazilian national team played its first official international fixture, losing 3-0 to neighbours Argentina. The Brazilian Confederation Of Sport was formed in 1914 and football became far more organised, yet competitions were still only staged within individual states and the game did not begin to resemble a professional sport until 1933.

With many teams touring Europe, there was a real danger of a player exodus. Certainly Leônidas da Silva had achieved international acclaim by showing off his famed bicycle kick, while Arthur Friedenreich, a prolific striker, was said to have scored more than a thousand goals. It was imperative that suitable financial incentives were put in place to keep such players in Brazil, but this idea was originally met with stiff resistance from clubs who wished to remain amateur. As a result it was an understrength Brazil that participated in the first two World Cups of 1930 and 1934.

The internal bickering among the regions continued and it was not until 1960 and the birth of the Copa Libertadores (South America's answer to the European Cup) that Brazil were prompted into forming the nationwide Taca do Brazil cup competition, while the national league (the Brasileiro) was created as late as 1971.

Above: Pelé scores in the 1970 World Cup Final. Opposite clockwise from top right: Rivaldo with the World Cup in 2002; Kaká at the 2010 World Cup; the 2004 Copa América winners; Socrates at the 1982 World Cup.

Both competitions were formed during a purple period in the history of Brazilian football. Having hosted the 1950 World Cup and built the famous Maracanã Stadium, finishing second to Uruguay was devastating but it was also an indication that the country was fast emerging as a major force in world football. Eight years later Brazil were hailed world champions in a tournament that saw the arrival of 17-year-old Pelé in a side that also included Garrincha, Zagalo and Gilmar. In 1962, with the majority of the same team, Brazil retained the World Cup, defeating Czechoslovakia 3-1 in the final.

Dominance at international level was also reflected on the domestic front, as Pelé's team, Santos, won the World Club Cup in 1962 and 1963, defeating Benfica and Milan respectively. However, it would be 18 years until a Brazilian team, the Zico-inspired Flamengo, would again emerge victorious in the competition.

On the international stage Brazil continued to impress and the World Cup winning side of 1970 is regarded by many as the greatest team in the history of the sport. With Pelé at his peak, his team-mates Rivelino, Jairzinho and Carlos Alberto also became household names as the team swept all before them. The finals, held in Mexico, were also the first to be televised in colour, bringing another dimension to the samba flair on offer. Certainly Carlos Alberto's emphatic strike in the 4-1 final win against Italy remains an enduring image.

After Pelé's international retirement the country continued to be a source of great talent, yielding the likes of Paulo Cesar, Zico, Falçao, Socrates and Cerezo, but the national team failed to deliver on the world stage for 24 years.

So highly regarded had Brazilian players become that a player drain abroad was inevitable. What remained was a weak national league

that saw teams with ever-changing sides. In the first 20 seasons of the league 13 different clubs won the title, and to this day it remains a fragile competition, with attendances reflecting the level of entertainment on offer. The average attendance across the league in 2009 was just under 18,000, which was approximately half the figure of that season's English Premier League.

For all the problems of the domestic league, the national team experienced a renaissance in the Nineties. Brazil had won silver medals at the 1984 and 1988 Olympics, and players from those teams provided the stars of the 1994 World Cup squad. Keeper Taffarel, defender Jorginho, and strikers Romario and Bebeto stepped up from the 1988 side, while captain Dunga was a veteran from 1984, and together their potential came to fruition with a penalties victory over Italy in the 1994 World Cup Final.

With a new sense of belief restored to the national team, young players such as Ronaldo, Rivaldo and Denilson helped Brazil reach the 1998 World Cup Final, this time facing hosts France. A mysterious illness to Ronaldo on the morning of the game put paid to any chances of victory, but four years later the player made amends as an exciting and attacking Brazil side triumphed at the 2002 World Cup. Ronaldo scored eight goals in the competition and four years later, despite Brazil's surprise exit in the quarter-finals, he became the World Cup's all-time top scorer, breaking Gerd Müller's record.

Dunga coached Brazil to success in the Copa América in 2007 and led the team to the 2010 World Cup, controversially omitting some of the country's big name stars and adding a solid defence to the team. However, despite playing like potential champions, a shock defeat to Holland in the quarter-final ended Brazil's campaign and Dunga's stint as coach.

BRITISH VIRGIN ISLANDS

Federation: British Virgin Islands Football Association
Founded: 1974
Joined FIFA: 1996
Confederation: CONCACAF
FIFA world ranking: 191 (joint)

BRUNEI DARUSSALAM

Federation: Football Federation of Brunei Darussalam
Founded: 1959
Joined FIFA: 1969
Confederation: AFC
FIFA world ranking: 187

Below: Velizar Dimitrov of Bulgaria celebrates with Dimitar Berbatov after scoring against Romania in 2007.

BULGARIA

Federation: Bulgaria Football Union
Founded: 1923
Joined FIFA: 1924
Confederation: UEFA
FIFA world ranking: 43

Communism was good for the development of football in Bulgaria. Although the game was played, prior to 1944 it was not very well organised. The national team had even failed to win a game in the first six years after debuting in 1924. The arrival of Soviet troops brought wholesale changes to Bulgarian life and football was completely overhauled.

A new national league was put in place, with promotion and relegation throughout. Clubs became affiliated to official organisations – CSKA were allied to the Army, Levski to the Interior Ministry and Lokomotiv Sofia to the railways – and players were professionals in all but name. While working for these companies

or departments, workers embarked on a full-time regime of football training known in the Communist bloc as 'The System'.

The quality of Bulgarian football improved immeasurably and none benefited more than CSKA (then known by a succession of names, including CDNA). Inspired by the goals of Ivan Kolev, between 1951 and 1962 the club were crowned national champions 11 times, a trend that made the domestic game predictable. They were unpopular, mainly because the army club could pick players simply by drafting them. They also provided the bulk of the national team and Bulgaria were one of Europe's top sides of the era, becoming World Cup regulars from 1962 and winning Olympic bronze in 1956 and silver in 1968.

The fall of communism forced clubs to become financially independent, which led to the sale of players. Ironically this helped the national team as their top stars gained experience abroad and Bulgaria reached the 1994 World Cup semi-final, with Barcelona's Hristo Stoichkov becoming the tournament's joint top scorer. Together with Levski, CSKA remain one of Bulgaria's strongest sides.

BURKINA FASO

Federation: Fédération Burkinabé de Foot-Ball
Founded: 1960
Joined FIFA: 1964
Confederation: CAF
FIFA world ranking: 45

BURUNDI

Federation: Fédération de Football du Burundi
Founded: 1948
Joined FIFA: 1972
Confederation: CAF
FIFA world ranking: 141

CAMBODIA

Federation: Cambodian Football Federation
Founded: 1933
Joined FIFA: 1953
Confederation: AFC
FIFA world ranking: 180 (joint)

CAMEROON

Federation: Fédération Camerounaise de Football
Founded: 1959
Joined FIFA: 1962
Confederation: CAF
FIFA world ranking: 40
Honours: African Nations Cup 1984, 1988, 2000, 2002; Olympics 2000

The Cameroon team are known as the 'Indomitable Lions' and their roar was first heard on the world stage in 1982, when they made an unbeaten debut at the World Cup, drawing their three group games against Peru, Poland and Italy. However, it was eight years later at the World Cup in Italy that Cameroon took the African game to the next level. After defeating reigning champions Argentina 1-0 in their opening match, a rugged team inspired by veteran substitute Roger Milla went on a run to within ten minutes of a semi-final place before they were defeated 3-2 by England.

Although Cameroon's subsequent World Cup appearances have not reached the same giddy heights, there have been successes in the African Nations Cup. They became the first side in 37 years to win successive cups in 2000 and 2002, and they also won Olympic gold in 2000 after beating Spain in the final. All three triumphs came after penalty shoot-outs.

Football was played in both British and French protectorates of the pre-independence country, but it did not really thrive until business began running the clubs in the Forties. Independence saw the formation of a cup competition in 1960 and a national league in 1960-1. For many years these competitions were dominated by the two Yaoundé clubs, Canon and Tonnerre, along with Union Douala. However, in recent years they have been eclipsed by the dominance of Cotonsport, who won six consecutive league titles between 2003 and 2008. Oryx Douala were the first African Cup winners in 1964, an achievement later matched three times by Canon Yaoundé and once by Union Douala.

A number of Cameroonian players have been voted African Player Of The Year: Roger Milla (1976 and 1990), Thomas N'Kono (1979 and 1982), Jean Manga-Onguene (1980), Theophile Abega (1984), Patrick Mboma (2000). More recently Samuel Eto'o won the award three times (2003, 2004 and 2005).

Above: Roger Milla on the ball against England in the quarter-final of the 1990 World Cup.

Above left: Lauren leads the celebrations as Cameroon win Olympic gold in 2000.

CANADA

Federation: Canadian Soccer Association
Founded: 1912
Joined FIFA: 1913
Confederation: CONCACAF
FIFA world ranking: 100
Honours: Olympics 1904; CONCACAF Championship 1985, 2000

In a land where ice hockey dominates, football has struggled to make any kind of impact, despite Olympic Games gold in 1904 courtesy of Galt FC. Canada competed at the 1986 World Cup with a largely part-time squad coached by former England keeper Tony Waiters, who had taken them to the quarter-finals of the Olympics two years earlier. It had been hoped that the World Cup appearance would finally inspire a permanent league but it was not to be. Toronto FC currently compete in the American MLS and will be joined in 2011 by Vancouver Whitecaps and in 2012 by Montreal Impact.

CAPE VERDE ISLANDS

Federation: Federação Caboverdiana de Futebol
Founded: 1982
Joined FIFA: 1986
Confederation: CAF
FIFA world ranking: 108

CAYMAN ISLANDS

Federation: Cayman Islands Football Association
Founded: 1966
Joined FIFA: 1992
Confederation: CONCACAF
FIFA world ranking: 173 (joint)

CENTRAL AFRICAN REP

Federation: Fédération Centrafricaine de Football
Founded: 1961
Joined FIFA: 1963
Confederation: CAF
FIFA world ranking: 202 (joint)

Centre: Canada celebrate with the Gold Cup in 2000.

CHAD

Federation: Fédération Tchadienne de Football
Founded: 1962
Joined FIFA: 1988
Confederation: CAF
FIFA world ranking: 124 (joint)

CHILE

Federation: Federación de Fútbol de Chile
Founded: 1895
Joined FIFA: 1913
Confederation: CONMEBOL
FIFA world ranking: 10

Valaparaiso FC became Chile's first football club in 1889 and others, mainly British in origin, followed. The second oldest football federation in South America was founded in Chile in 1895, while the national team debuted in 1910, although they did not win a game until 1926 when they defeated Bolivia 7-1.

Chilean football improved after David Arellano founded Colo Colo in 1925. The club became a driving force behind the success of the new professional national league in 1933, although they were pipped to the first title after defeat to Magallanes in a play-off after tying on points. Nevertheless, they went on to became the country's most successful and popular club. Historically the league was a fairly open competition but Colo Colo have been the most dominant side since the 1970s. They also won the country's first continental club honour when they lifted the Copa Libertadores in 1991.

Chile have appeared in the World Cup with limited success, save for the 1962 competition when as hosts they finished third. The feat was marred by the appalling spectacle against Italy known as the 'Battle of Santiago'. The national team were banned from the 1994 World Cup after Chilean keeper Roberto Rojas faked an injury in a qualifier against Brazil in 1989. In more recent times Chile have taken impressive sides to the 1998 and 2010 World Cups but were unfortunate to come up against Brazil in the first knockout round on both occasions.

CHINA

Federation: Football Association of the People's Republic of China
Founded: 1924
Joined FIFA: 1931-58, 1979
Confederation: AFC
FIFA world ranking: 78

China played in the first international match in Asia at the Far Eastern Games in Manila in February 1913, losing 2-1 to the Philippines. China joined FIFA in 1931 and took part at the 1936 and 1948 Olympics, but they did not enter the World Cup. In 1958 China withdrew from FIFA in protest at the membership of Taiwan. This self-imposed exile did little for the domestic game, even though a national league ran sporadically from 1951 to 1966. It was not until 1976 that China rejoined FIFA. Soon afterwards the national league was resurrected and cultural and sporting ties were brokered. The quality of football was poor, although there were occasional highlights, such as Liaoning winning the Asian Champions Cup in 1990, and China finishing runners-up in the Asian Cup in 1984 and the Asian Games in 1994.

The advent of professionalism, with its foreign player imports and sponsorship gave the league a major boost, as did rebranding the top division as the Chinese Super League in 2004. The league was enlarged from 12 to 14 clubs in 2005 and to 16 clubs in 2006, with the introduction of promotion and relegation for the first time. Dalian Shide have been the most successful club of the professional era.

In 2002 China qualified for the World Cup and hosted the 2004 Asian Cup, losing to Japan in the final, much to the displeasure of the home fans. The Chinese game has improved, with several leading players making careers abroad.

CHINESE TAIPEI

Federation: Chinese Taipei Football Association
Founded: 1924
Joined FIFA: 1954
Confederation: AFC
FIFA world ranking: 166

COLOMBIA

Federation: Federación Colombiana de Fútbol
Founded: 1924
Joined FIFA: 1936-50, 1954
Confederation: CONMEBOL
FIFA world ranking: 39
Honours: Copa América 2001

Colombia has had a dark and controversial football history, but illuminating the darkness have been flamboyant players who have produced breathtaking moments, ranging from the spectacular goals of Carlos Valderrama to the astonishing 'scorpion' save of goalkeeper Rene Higuita in a friendly against England.

In 1948 a wealthy independent professional league (the DiMayor) put Colombian football on the map, and among the 18 wealthy clubs was Deportivo Municipal, who became known as 'Los Millonarios', because they were bankrolled by two extremely rich Bogotá businessmen. In its four-year existence this new league became

Above: Rodrigue Dikaba (right) in action for the Democratic Republic of Congo against Egypt in 2008.

COMOROS

Federation: Federation Comorienne de Football
Founded: 1979
Joined FIFA: 2005
Confederation: CAF
FIFA world ranking: 172

CONGO

Federation: Fédération Congolaise de Football
Founded: 1962
Joined FIFA: 1962
Confederation: CAF
FIFA world ranking: 107
Honours: African Nations Cup 1972

CONGO DR

Federation: Fédération Congolaise de Football Association
Founded: 1919
Joined FIFA: 1962
Confederation: CAF
FIFA world ranking: 124 (joint)
Honours: African Nations Cup 1968, 1974

In 1974, as Zaïre, the Democratic Republic of Congo became the first sub-Saharan (and black African) team to qualify for the World Cup. Heavily influenced by European football, and by the Belgians in particular who had introduced the game to the country, Zaïre were a major force in African football from the mid-Sixties to the mid-Seventies, winning the African Nations Cup twice.

COOK ISLANDS

Federation: Cook Islands Football Association
Founded: 1971
Joined FIFA: 1994
Confederation: OFC
FIFA world ranking: 193 (joint)

COSTA RICA

  (crest)

Federation: Federación Costarricense de Fútbol
Founded: 1921
Joined FIFA: 1927
Confederation: CONCACAF
FIFA world ranking: 49
Honours: CONCACAF Championship 1941, 1946, 1948, 1953, 1955, 1960, 1961, 1963, 1969, 1989

The formal birth of Costa Rican football was in 1921, the year their federation was founded and the inaugural league championship kicked-off. CS Herediano were the dominant club before the war, while Deportivo Saprissa were the runaway team of the Sixties and Seventies, a period when the Costa Rican national team were the strongest in the region, winning seven of ten CCCF Championships and three of the subsequent CONCACAF titles before the tournament was again revamped in 1991. Despite such an impressive record Costa Rica shunned the World Cup until 1958. They have since qualified three times: in 1990, when they reached the second round under Bora Milutinovic, 2002 and 2006. They narrowly missed out on qualification to the 2010 finals, losing 2-1 on aggregate to Uruguay in a play-off.

CROATIA

(flag)

Federation: Croatian Football Federation
Founded: 1912, 1991
Joined FIFA: 1941, 1992
Confederation: UEFA
FIFA world ranking: 15

Although Croatia did have its own league and national team under German occupation during the Second World War, for the much of the century Croatia formed a part of Yugoslavia, and its players and clubs were among the powerhouses of Yugoslav football

known as the 'El Dorado' period, as star players from all over South America and Europe were lured to Colombia with offers of lucrative wages and signing-on fees. This was possible because the league was operating outside of FIFA jurisdiction and Colombian clubs were refusing to pay transfer fees. They attracted players of the calibre of Alfredo Di Stéfano, Nestor Rossi and Neil Franklin, but by the time Colombia was readmitted to FIFA in 1954, the huge fees had smashed the Colombian game.

In the mid-Sixties a rival organisation challenged the incumbent football association and this political infighting led to FIFA taking on the running of Colombian football until the current FCF was formed. It was not the last football problem to confront the country. Colombia was due to host the 1986 World Cup but was forced to withdraw after being unable to provide sufficient facilities and communications for a 24-team tournament.

In the Eighties and Nineties Colombian league football was an exciting spectator sport but off the pitch it had become dogged by allegations of money-laundering by drug cartels and of high stake bets and bribes. Players, officials and investigators were brutally murdered during this period. In one of the more notorious incidents, defender Andrés Escobar was shot dead after returning from the 1994 World Cup, having inadvertently scored an own-goal against the USA.

There have been times when the Colombian league has been suspended and the national side has refused to play at home, but in 2001 the country had a chance to celebrate when the national team won the Copa América for the first time, beating Mexico in the final.

Right: Croatia's Igor Stimac, Zvonimir Boban and Davor Suker celebrate victory over Holland in the 1998 World Cup third place play-off match.

prior to real independence in 1991 and official FIFA recognition the following year. Clubs such as Dinamo Zagreb and Hajduk Split were regular challengers to the Belgrade-based clubs, while in 1967 Dinamo Zagreb became the first Croatian (and Yugoslavian) club to lift a European trophy when they won the Fairs Cup.

Great players such as Zvonimir Boban, Robert Jarni and Robert Prosinecki (half-Croat) were part of the Yugoslavian team that qualified for the European Championship in 1992, but by then Croatia had declared independence and as a result their clubs had withdrawn from the Yugoslav league. Croatian players were also banned from playing for Yugoslavia, who were then forced to withdraw from Euro 92.

In the shadow of civil war and grave economic problems, the Croatian league kicked-off in the 1992-3 season without the country's biggest stars, many having chosen to play their club football abroad. However, the Croatian game has gained in popularity because of the exploits of the national side, who made a startling impact at the 1996 European Championship by reaching the quarter-finals, and later going on to finish third at the 1998 World Cup in France. They also beat Germany in the group stage of Euro 2008 but were eliminated by Turkey on penalties in the quarter-finals.

CUBA

Federation: Asociación de Fútbol de Cuba
Founded: 1924
Joined FIFA: 1932
Confederation: CONCACAF
FIFA world ranking: 114

CYPRUS

Federation: Cyprus Football Association
Founded: 1934
Joined FIFA: 1948
Confederation: UEFA
FIFA world ranking: 63

Football was introduced to Cyprus by British servicemen in the late 1870s, although it was not until 1934 that an association was formed. League and cup competitions were created the same year, with Trast AC finishing the season as the winner of both titles. With a population of mainly Greek Cypriots, the most successful teams were of Greek origin, while Çetin Kaya were the only Turkish Cypriot side to win the national title, in 1951. Following the

division of the island in 1974, teams from both communities found themselves displaced and although the Turkish Republic of Northern Cyprus has a league, it is not recognised by FIFA. In the 1990s the Cypriot league grew stronger, with Anorthosis Famagusta becoming the most prominent side. The national team took its biggest scalp in 1998, beating Spain 3-2 in a Euro 2000 qualifier.

CZECH REPUBLIC

Federation: Ceskomoravsky Fotbalovy Svaz
Founded: 1901
Joined FIFA: 1907-16, 1994
Confederation: UEFA
FIFA world ranking: 31
Honours: European Championship 1976; Olympics 1980 *(both as Czechoslovakia)*

From the 1993-4 season, FIFA recognised both the Czech Republic and Slovakia as the joint successors to Czechoslovakia's historic records in world football, and although both have had limited success on the world stage, it was initially the Czech Republic that made the biggest impact. Not only did they qualify for Euro 96, but they reached the final before losing to Germany by a golden goal. The Czech Republic's biggest stars, such as Patrik Berger, Pavel Nedved and Petr Cech, have all performed at the highest level, following in the tradition of former Czechoslovakian greats like Josef Masopust and Frantisek Plánicka.

Football had been played in the region since the 1890s, although the area was then known as Bohemia, a province of the Austro-Hungarian empire. Club sides Slavia and Sparta were both formed in Prague during that decade, while a Bohemian league and a football association were founded, and a national team existed until Czechoslovakia declared independence in 1918. Seven years later, the regions of Bohemia, Monravia and Slovakia formed a new, professional Czechoslovakian league.

Czechoslovakia soon became a strong football nation. They reached the 1920 Olympic final but walked off the pitch in the second-half, complaining of refereeing bias. They also finished the 1934 World Cup as runners-up, losing to hosts Italy in the final

Before the Second World War Slavia and Sparta dominated Czechoslovakian league and cup competitions, but in 1945 Communist rule led to the affiliation of both clubs to state organisations and as a consequence they were eclipsed by the army team, Dukla Prague. Dukla provided the core of the national side in the Sixties, when Czechoslovakians often came close to glory without ever winning the biggest prizes. They finished third in the 1960 European Championship and were runners-up at the 1962 World Cup (to Brazil) and at the 1964 Olympics (to Hungary).

The late Seventies saw another resurgence, with Czechoslovakia winning the European Championship in 1976 after beating West Germany in a dramatic penalty shoot-out. Four years later they were also Olympic champions. At home Dukla's star began to fade even before independence and Sparta and Slavia again dominated the Czech game in a free market.

Below: Substitute Vladimir Smicer of the Czech Republic celebrates scoring the winning goal against Holland at Euro 2004.

Above: Denmark shocked world football by winning the 1992 European Championship.

DENMARK

Federation: Dansk Boldspil-Union
Founded: 1889
Joined FIFA: 1904
Confederation: UEFA
FIFA world ranking: 29
Honours: European Championship 1992

Denmark caused one of the biggest shocks in world football in 1992 by winning the European Championship despite initially failing to qualify for the tournament. Just a week before the competition many of their players were already sunning themselves on the beach when the call came that offered them the chance to become last-minute replacements for Yugoslavia. With no time for preparation the squad went on to win the trophy, beating Germany 2-0 in the final with goals from John Jensen and Kim Vilfort.

This was undoubtedly the finest 90 minutes in Denmark's football history.

The triumph followed a period in the 1980s when the Danish game had gained recognition and plaudits for its thrilling style. The Danes could boast a talented crop of players, most notably brothers Brian and Michael Laudrup, Jesper Olsen, Jan Molby, John Sivebaek and Soren Lerby. These players took Denmark to their first World Cup in 1986 where they beat Scotland, West Germany and hit six past Uruguay to reach the second round, only to meet an in-form Spain who beat them 5-1. For the European Championship triumph, the squad also included Peter Schmeichel, Henrik Larsen and Flemming Povlsen.

The first truly great Danish player was Allan Simonsen, who was voted European Player Of The Year in 1977. To succeed he had left the country's purely amateur domestic game in 1972 to ply his trade for Borussia Mönchengladbach and later for Barcelona. However, the tide was turning and the selection of professionals for the national team had been allowed since 1971.

Danish domestic football had been amateur ever since the formation of the country's first club, KB Copenhagen, in 1876. Among the early amateur players of the Danish game had been Niels Bohr, who later won the Nobel Prize for Physics. However, the introduction of professionalism finally came in 1978 and the first professional club were Brondby, who helped turn Danish football from a pastime into a national success story. The other significant change that helped the development of Danish football came in 1991 when the Superliga switched from a summer season to a winter season, in line with the major leagues of Europe.

Although the national team failed to qualify for USA 94 as reigning European champions, the Danes recaptured some form at the 1998 World Cup with a run to the quarter-finals. However, despite taking an early lead against Brazil, they lost 3-2. They also impressed at the finals in 2002 when they helped to eliminate holders France at the group stage, but they failed to reach the finals four years later and were knocked out at the first stage in 2010.

DJIBOUTI

Federation: Fédération Djiboutienne de Football
Founded: 1979
Joined FIFA: 1994
Confederation: CAF
FIFA world ranking: 191 (joint)

DOMINICA

Federation: Dominica Football Association
Founded: 1970
Joined FIFA: 1994
Confederation: CONCACAF
FIFA world ranking: 180 (joint)

DOMINICAN REPUBLIC

Federation: Federación Dominicana de Fútbol
Founded: 1953
Joined FIFA: 1958
Confederation: CONCACAF
FIFA world ranking: 185

EAST TIMOR

Federation: Federação Futebol Timor Leste
Founded: 2002
Joined FIFA: 2005
Confederation: AFC
FIFA world ranking: 200

ECUADOR

Federation: Federación Ecuatoriana De Fútbol
Founded: 1925
Joined FIFA: 1926
Confederation: CONMEBOL
FIFA world ranking: 58

Ecuador, under Hernan Dario Gomez, qualified for the World Cup for the first time in 11 attempts in 2002 after finishing runners-up to Argentina in the ten-strong CONMEBOL group. Notably, this magnificent achievement also included their first ever win over Brazil. Luis Fernando Suarez repeated the feat, including another win over Brazil, when he guided Ecuador to the finals in Germany in 2006, where they reached the knockout stages after victories over Poland and Costa Rica. Prior to 2006, the team had played just three matches in Europe.

Barcelona and El Nacional have been the most successful clubs in the league, sharing 26 titles between them since 1957. Barcelona have also twice reached the Copa Libertadores final, in 1990 and 1998, but it was LDU Quito who became the first Ecuadorian club to lift South America's premier club trophy after a penalty shoot-out victory over Fluminense in 2008.

In 2005 the country's league briefly adopted the Apertura (opening) and Clausura (closing) format popular in South America, splitting the season into two campaigns with a champion for each. However, after just one year using this system the league reverted to the tradition season-long format.

EGYPT

Federation: Egyptian Football Association
Founded: 1921
Joined FIFA: 1923
Confederation: CAF
FIFA world ranking: 9
Honours: African Nations Cup 1957, 1959, 1986, 1998, 2006, 2008, 2010

Egypt are Africa's most successful football nation and ever since the sport first arrived in the country it has been an extremely popular pastime. In 1907 native Egyptians got behind the newly-formed Al-Ahly, an exclusive all-Egyptian sporting club and a beacon for nationalist pride. Al-Ahly developed into Egypt's most popular and successful club, dominating the Egyptian Cup from soon after its inception in 1921-2. The presence in the country of allied forces during World War II also boosted the already well-organised domestic game and inspired a championship, which Al-Ahly won nine times in a row after it first kicked off in 1948-9.

Egypt were the initial trailblazers for African football: they were the continent's first team to play in the Olympics in 1928 and the first to reach the World Cup finals in 1934. A founder member of the Confederation Africaine de Football (CAF) in 1957, Egypt also provided the organisation with its first president, Abdel Aziz Abdullah Salem, who the original African Nations Cup trophy was named after. Indeed, the national team were the earliest recipients of this trophy, winning the first two tournaments in 1957 and

Above: The Egypt players celebrate after winning the African Nations Cup in 2010.

1959. Although they have appeared in only two World Cups, 'The Pharaohs' have won the African Nations Cup a record seven times and have played at the finals of 22 tournaments, four times as host. They recorded the competition's first hat-trick of wins after picking up the trophy in 2006, 2008 and 2010.

Al-Ahly is still Africa's best club side of recent years. Having won the African Champions League four times in the first decade of the 21st century, the club also clinched six Egyptian championships in the same period, topping the table by a staggering 31-point margin in 2005 after completing the season unbeaten. Al-Ahly's nearest rivals are five times African Champions League winners Zamalek, who went 52 league games without defeat between December 2002 and November 2004.

EL SALVADOR

Federation: Federación Salvadoreña de Fútbol
Founded: 1935
Joined FIFA: 1938
Confederation: CONCACAF
FIFA world ranking: 90
Honours: CONCACAF Championship 1943

The El Salvador team have qualified for the World Cup just twice, causing a war and suffering the worst defeat in World Cup finals history. In 1969 the team were involved in a controversial three-game second round qualifying clash with neighbouring Honduras. Border infractions and rioting followed the first two games, and when El Salvador finally defeated Honduras 3-2 in neutral Mexico, the result inflamed an already tense border situation, causing El Salvador's Army to invade Honduras to protect its citizens from persecution. The action sparked war between the two countries. At the World Cup the following year the team lost all three group games.

At the finals of 1982 El Salvador were beaten 10-1 by Hungary, the biggest defeat experienced by any team at the World Cup finals.

1860

1863: The Football Association forms at the Freemason's Tavern in London on October 26.

1870

1871: The FA Cup begins, contested by 15 teams, including Glasgow's Queen's Park.

1880

1872: Wanderers win the first FA Cup and England play Scotland in the first international match.

1890

1888: The first league begins with 12 clubs taking part. Preston are the first champions.

1925

1923: With 250,000 fans in a stadium built for 127,000, the first FA Cup final at Wembley turns to chaos.

1950

1950: England enter the World Cup for the first time but are shocked by a 1-0 defeat to the USA in Brazil.

1955

1958: Manchester United are decimated when a plane crash in Munich claims 23 lives.

1960

1966: England win the World Cup as hosts. Geoff Hurst scores a hat-trick as West Germany are beaten 4-2 after extra-time.

1965

1970

1968: England's first European Cup winners are Manchester United after victory over Benfica at Wembley.

1975

1977: Liverpool win the European Cup. They are followed by Nottingham Forest and Aston Villa as the trophy stays in England until 1982.

1980

1985

1985: 56 fans die in a fire at Bradford City. English clubs are banned from Europe following the events at the Heysel Stadium.

1990

1989: England's worst sporting tragedy sees 95 Liverpool fans die during the FA Cup semi-final at Hillsborough.

1995

1990: England reach the World Cup semi-final, losing out to West Germany on penalties.

2000

1999: Manchester United win the Champions League. They are the first English club to lift the European Cup trophy in 15 years.

2005

2010

2010: England crash out of the 2010 World Cup after defeat to Germany.

ENGLAND

Federation: The Football Association
Founded: 1863
Joined FIFA: 1905-20, 1924-28, 1946
Confederation: UEFA
FIFA world ranking: 7
Honours: World Cup 1966

England enjoys a lofty status as the home of football because the modern game was fashioned by the English in the mid 19th century, before it was exported all over the world. The Football Association was founded as early as 1863, the first FA Cup final was contested in 1872, and the basic structure of English football was pretty much in place by 1888, when the Football League was established with 12 members. To this day the country's football clubs remain enshrined in its local communities and they still provide a focus for millions of people each week.

Having first developed the game, the English inevitably had a head start in the early days. Teams initially played 2-3-5 before a 1925 change to the offside rule inspired Arsenal's Herbert Chapman to turn it into the classic 'WM formation', a system that dominated the English game well into the 1950s. During this period the national team may have regularly defeated foreign opponents whenever they deigned to play them, but a classically insular island approach, together with an overbearing sense of superiority, meant that the English repeatedly stood apart from the game's most significant developments.

When FIFA pioneered a world tournament in the 1920s the Football Association declined to take part. It then resigned from FIFA in 1928 and did not rejoin until 1946, nor enter a World Cup until 1950. The Football League had a similar stance and advised champions Chelsea not to take part in the inaugural European Cup in 1955. For these reason a talented generation of players, including Billy Wright, Stanley Matthews and Tom Finney, were starved of the kind of competition that could have elevated their play.

The English game remained oblivious to any thoughts of modernisation. Defeat to the USA at the 1950 World Cup was deemed a freak result, but it was a 6-3 defeat by Hungary at Wembley in 1953 that finally exploded the myth of English superiority. Yet, in 1958 when UEFA launched the European Nations Cup (later the European Championship), England still refused to take part on the basis that it would undermine the British Home International Championship.

After yet another disastrous World Cup campaign in 1962, it took the appointment of Alf Ramsey as England manager to shake up the way the national team was both selected and coached. Vindication for Ramsey's tactical innovations finally arrived in 1966 when his

Above: Duncan Edwards clears against Scotland in 1957. Opposite top: England's stars of 1966 celebrate with the World Cup. Opposite bottom from left to right: Stanley Matthews, Gary Lineker and Wayne Rooney.

'wingless wonders' defeated West Germany 4-2 to win the World Cup on home soil, with the help of a hat-trick from Geoff Hurst.

Yet there was a failure to capitalise on the resultant euphoria. At the World Cup four years later, with arguably a better squad, England were eliminated in a disastrous quarter-final confrontation with West Germany, ushering in a period of upheaval from which it took years to recover. England failed to qualify for successive World Cups in the Seventies and were hamstrung by technical shortcomings through the following decade. Even reaching the semi-finals of Italia 90, with a side that included Gary Lineker and Paul Gascoigne, failed to inspire a new era. It was followed by a poor Euro 92, and failure to qualify for the 1994 World Cup or progress beyond the quarter-finals ever since.

The England team's uneven history is belied by the achievements of its clubs in continental competition. Manchester United would surely have won the European Cup long before their breakthrough in 1968 but for the tragedy of the 1958 Munich air disaster. The national team may have struggled in the late Seventies and early Eighties, but it proved to be a golden era for English club football, with four European Cup wins for Liverpool, one for Aston Villa and back-to-back trophies for Nottingham Forest. However, the country's dominance of European football ended abruptly in the wake of the 1985 Heysel tragedy, when a pitched battle between Liverpool and Juventus fans resulted in 39 deaths and a six-year European ban for English clubs.

Hooliganism had been an unpleasant feature of English football and it took a heavy toll in the Eighties. Gate receipts declined and other disasters – the 1985 Bradford fire and the 1989 Hillsborough tragedy – only served to underline the fact that the game's structure needed a radical overhaul. The 1990 Taylor Report and the consequent move to all-seater stadia helped usher in a new era for English football in the

Nineties. Money flooded into the sport via television and corporate sponsorship, and the advent of the Premier League in 1992 further revamped the game's image. Domestic English football has subsequently thrived at the top level, and although financial pressures have threatened clubs in every tier of the football pyramid in recent years, the country continues to support four fully professional nationwide divisions.

Liverpool and Manchester United remain the country's most successful clubs, with 18 league titles each. Liverpool were strongest in the Seventies and Eighties, having built on the revival overseen by Bill Shankly in the previous decade. However, Manchester United are the country's richest and most successful club of recent times, and they have won 11 of their league titles – and two of their three European Cups – since the onset of the Premier League era in 1992-3, all under the shrewd guidance of Alex Ferguson.

Only two clubs have challenged Manchester United in this period. Arsenal maintained a consistent threat around the turn of the century, winning three league titles under Arsene Wenger, two of them as part of league and cup 'doubles', while Chelsea have also tested United's dominance thanks to the multimillion pound investment of Roman Abramovich. As a result, in 2005 Chelsea won the league title for the first time for 50 years and retained the trophy the following season, winning it again in 2010.

The buoyancy of English football is now dependent on record-breaking television and sponsorship deals. However, the success of the Premier League is built upon the talents of many top quality foreign imports, not on homegrown players. As a result the national team has consistently struggled to emulate the achievements of the country's best club sides, whose dominance of the latter stages of the Champions League peaked in 2009, when for the third consecutive season England supplied three of the competition's four semi-finalists.

EQUATORIAL GUINEA

Federation: Federación Ecuatoguineana de Fútbol
Founded: 1960
Joined FIFA: 1986
Confederation: CAF
FIFA world ranking: 147 (joint)

ERITREA

Federation: Eritrean National Football Federation
Founded: 1992
Joined FIFA: 1998
Confederation: CAF
FIFA world ranking: 158

ESTONIA

Federation: Eesti Jalgpalli Liit
Founded: 1921, 1992
Joined FIFA: 1923, 1992
Confederation: UEFA
FIFA world ranking: 95

Estonia became the first Baltic side to play an international when they were thrashed 6-0 by Finland in 1920. The game marked the start of an undistinguished 20-year record, including a failed attempt to qualify for the 1938 World Cup, that ran until Estonia was absorbed by the Soviet Union. Independence in 1991 saw a revival of both the national team and the domestic league. Estonia's strongest clubs since then have been Tallinn sides Flora and Levadia. The most notable player of recent times has been keeper Mart Poom, six-times Estonian Player Of The Year.

ETHIOPIA

Federation: Ethiopian Football Federation
Founded: 1943
Joined FIFA: 1953
Confederation: CAF
FIFA world ranking: 146
Honours: African Nations Cup 1962

FAROE ISLANDS

Federation: Fotboltssamband Føroya
Founded: 1979
Joined FIFA: 1988
Confederation: UEFA
FIFA world ranking: 117

The Faroe Islands had a sensational debut on the international football stage. In their first competitive match in September 1990, the part-time players of the Faroe Islands beat Austria 1-0 in Sweden, thanks to scorer Allan Morkore and bobble-hatted keeper Martin Knudsen. Football has been played on the islands for more than a century, with a league since 1942 and a cup competition since 1955. International matches were played against teams like Iceland and the Shetland Islands as early as 1930, but only games after 1988 are classed as official.

Local weather and a lack of pitches forced them to host their international matches in Sweden, but a grass pitch was soon laid to allow the Faroes to play at home and a national stadium was built in Tórshavn in 1999. The leading club sides are the Tórshavn clubs, HB and B36, as well as KI Klaksvik and GÍ Gotu.

FIJI

Federation: Fiji Football Association
Founded: 1938
Joined FIFA: 1963
Confederation: OFC
FIFA world ranking: 130 (joint)

FINLAND

Federation: Suomen Palloliito
Founded: 1907
Joined FIFA: 1908
Confederation: UEFA
FIFA world ranking: 51

Football was first brought to Finland in the 1890s by English sailors and a Finnish league has been in existence since 1908, although as a spectator sport football continues to play second fiddle to ice hockey. The national team played their first match in 1911, but unlike their Scandinavian neighbours the Finns have made little impact on the international stage in the subsequent 100 years.

The top flight of Finnish football is the Veikkausliiga. It is made up of 14 clubs and in recent times the most successful have been HJK Helsinki and Haka Valkeakoski. Traditionally Finnish teams struggle in the early rounds of the European competitions but Kuusysi did reach the European Cup quarter-finals in 1986. Many Finnish players have plied their trade abroad but Sami Hyppia and Jari Litmanen remain the most successful, both having won the European Cup.

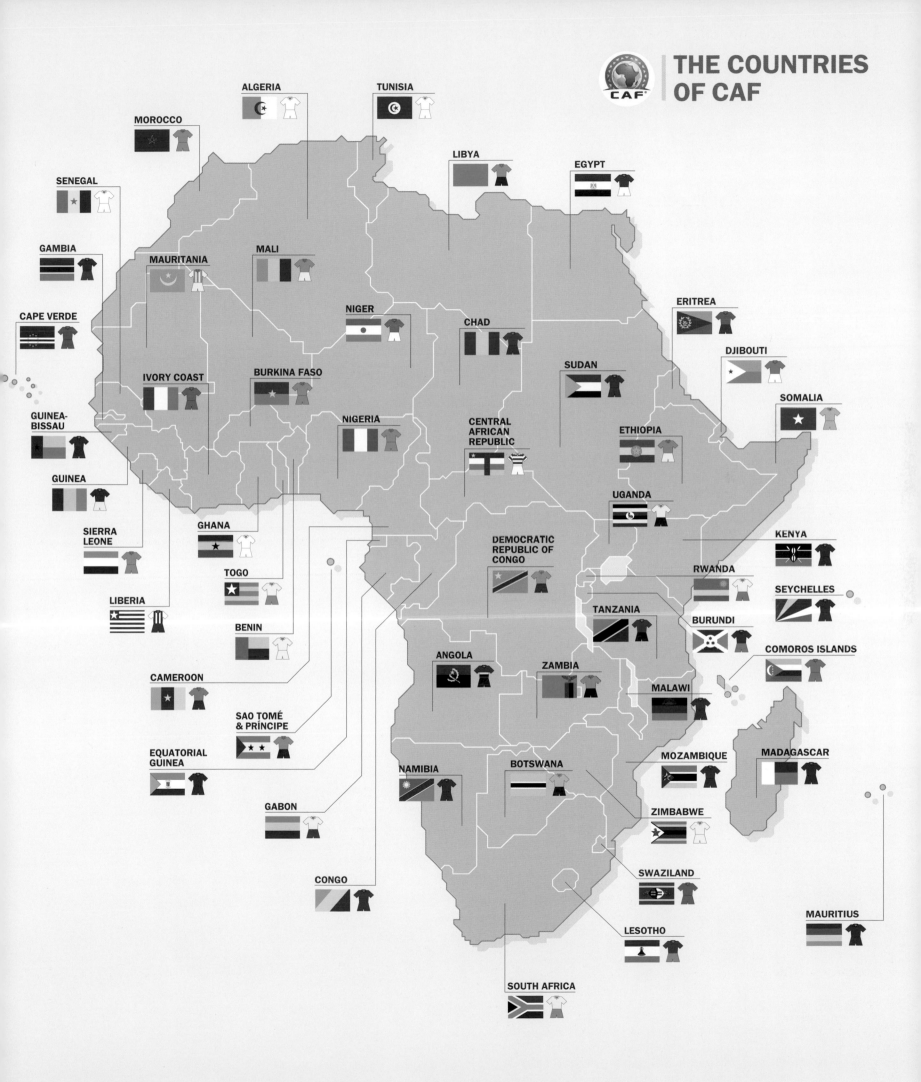

THE COUNTRIES OF CAF

FRANCE

Federation: Fédération Française de Football
Founded: 1919
Joined FIFA: 1904
Confederation: UEFA
FIFA world ranking: 21
Honours: World Cup 1998; European Championship 1984, 2000; Olympics 1984

The French have played a key role in the history of football's development: the World Cup was launched in 1930 by Frenchman Jules Rimet; the first FIFA president, Robert Guérin, was French; Gabriel Hanot, a former international and editor of France's leading sports paper *L'Equipe*, was the driving force behind the European Cup; and the European Championship trophy is still named in honour of its founder, Henri Delaunay. Yet in the early days of the game the French national team were seen as outsiders and they struggled to make the breakthrough on the pitch that would match their role off it.

Lille won the country's first professional league title in 1932-3, although Sochaux, backed by Peugeot, were one of the most prominent teams of the era. France hosted the World Cup in 1938 and the tournament was considered a success, despite the home team going down 3-1 in a quarter-final defeat to eventual winners Italy.

After the Second World War the introduction of continental club competition gave the French an opportunity to flourish. They did so thanks to Reims, who made a significant mark in the earliest days of the European Cup under coach Albert Batteux. Reims reached the final of the first competition in 1956, losing 4-3 to Real Madrid in Paris. The sides met three years later with the same outcome, by which time Reims had become the greatest French team of the era.

Raymond Kopa was the biggest French star of the day, playing for Reims before switching to Real Madrid to play alongside Ferenc Puskás and Alfredo Di Stéfano. An outside-right or centre-forward, he had a leading role in the French run to the semi-finals at the 1958 World Cup Finals. France finished in third place as Kopa formed a brilliant partnership with Just Fontaine, who scored 13 goals, a World Cup record that looks unlikely to be beaten. However, the Sixties saw a decline in the country's football fortunes and to improve standards a national youth training programme was introduced by George Boulogne, with the aim of producing better-skilled professional players. This training system would later bear fruit remarkably.

In the meantime the success of Saint-Etienne filled the void, as the club became the country's premier force in the Seventies. They challenged for major honours, winning the league and cup four times each in the decade and losing out in

Above: Michel Platini at the 1986 World Cup. Opposite top: Didier Deschamps lifts the trophy after victory over Italy at Euro 2000. Opposite bottom: World Cup success on home soil in 1998.

the 1976 European Cup Final to Bayern Munich.

Their success barely hinted at the exciting times to come for the French national team. In the 1980s a generation of such talent and flair emerged that they were dubbed the 'Blue Brazil'. Michel Platini was the leading player as France reached the 1982 World Cup semi-final, where they were beaten on penalties by West Germany after a thrilling 3-3 draw. However, the match is as much remembered for the brutal foul on defender Patrick Battiston by German keeper Harald Schumacher.

This skilful French team was devastating to watch and two years later, under coach Michel Hidalgo, the players were finally rewarded when they won the 1984 European Championship on home soil. Platini scored nine goals in five matches and, aided by the likes of Jean Tigana and Alain Giresse, he led Hidalgo's team as they beat Spain 2-0 in the final.

Platini's retirement in 1987 led to a slump for the national side but Marseille came along as the new heroes of French football. A dazzling side, they left the rest of French football trailing in their wake as they became a genuine European superpower. Marseille won four league titles between 1989 and 1992, playing open and attacking football with a team boasting Chris Waddle, Abedi Pele and Jean-Pierre Papin.

Marseille had impressive European Cup runs in 1989-90 (when they lost in the semi-finals on the away goals rule) and in 1990-1 (when they finished runners-up), but they finally became the first French club to lift the trophy in 1993, when a side captained by Didier Deschamps and featuring Marcel Desailly and Fabien Barthez beat Milan in Munich. However, triumph soon turned to scandal when it emerged that club president Bernard Tapie had fixed a domestic league match against Valenciennes shortly before the final. It tainted their European triumph and plunged French football into misery.

In the 1990s French players moved abroad in greater numbers because of the Bosman ruling and the national team improved dramatically, as key players gained confidence from their experience of other leagues. Coach Aimé Jacquet built a solid team for the 1998 World Cup around the sublime skills of playmaker Zinédine Zidane. They had not been expected to win by the French public but the team grew in strength as the tournament progressed and deservedly beat Brazil 3-0 in the final. Zidane scored twice and the nation celebrated with more than one million supporters pouring onto the Champs-Elysées.

The French had found a winning formula and triumphed at the European Championship two years later with an even higher standard of play. Thierry Henry led a more potent attack, and Zidane produced some majestic midfield displays. They failed show the same flair in 2002, when they became the first reigning champions to be eliminated from a World Cup at the group stage since 1966.

In 2006 this golden generation were once again inspired to the World Cup final by Zidane, who had been talked out of his earlier international retirement. However, they lost to Italy on penalties and Zidane, playing in his last ever game, was red-carded for headbutting Marco Materazzi. Four years later the tournament ended even more ignominiously for the French after the players went on strike following the sending home of Nicolas Anelka, contributing to a surprise elimination at the group stage.

Since the beginning of the 21st century the French league has been dominated by Lyon, who won seven successive league titles between 2001 and 2008. The domestic game still loses its best talent to the more attractive leagues in Italy and England. However, for the French there is always hope as the country still has a thriving youth academy programme, which continues to provide talent for the national team.

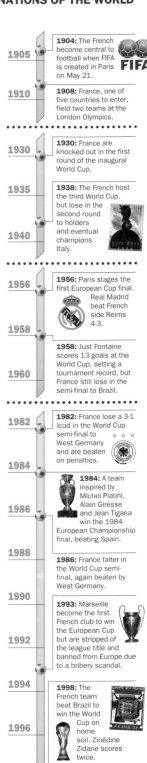

1905

1904: The French become central to football when FIFA is created in Paris on May 21.

1910

1908: France, one of five countries to enter, field two teams at the London Olympics.

1930

1930: France are knocked out in the first round of the inaugural World Cup.

1935

1938: The French host the third World Cup, but lose in the second round to holders and eventual champions Italy.

1940

1956

1956: Paris stages the first European Cup final. Real Madrid beat French side Reims 4-3.

1958

1958: Just Fontaine scores 13 goals at the World Cup, setting a tournament record, but France still lose in the semi-final to Brazil.

1960

1982

1982: France lose a 3-1 lead in the World Cup semi-final to West Germany and are beaten on penalties.

1984

1984: A team inspired by Michel Platini, Alain Giresse and Jean Tigana win the 1984 European Championship final, beating Spain.

1986

1986: France falter in the World Cup semi-final, again beaten by West Germany.

1988

1990

1993: Marseille become the first French club to win the European Cup but are stripped of the league title and banned from Europe due to a bribery scandal.

1992

1994

1998: The French team beat Brazil to win the World Cup on home soil. Zinédine Zidane scores twice.

1996

1998

2000: France prove their class at Euro 2000 when they beat Italy in a tense final.

2000

2002: Holders France go out in the first round of the Japan/Korea World Cup without scoring a goal.

2002

2006: Zidane inspires France to the World Cup final, but he is sent-off before Italy win the trophy on penalties.

2004

2006

2010: France crash out of the World Cup at the group stage after infighting in the squad.

2010

145

Right: Fritz Walter clutches the Jules Rimet Cup after West Germany win the 1954 World Cup Final.

GABON

Federation: Fédération Gabonaise de Football
Founded: 1962
Joined FIFA: 1963
Confederation: CAF
FIFA world ranking: 34

GAMBIA

Federation: Gambia Football Association
Founded: 1952
Joined FIFA: 1966
Confederation: CAF
FIFA world ranking: 102

GEORGIA

Federation: Georgian Football Federation
Founded: 1990
Joined FIFA: 1992
Confederation: UEFA
FIFA world ranking: 111

Dinamo Tbilisi were Georgia's leading team in the Soviet Supreme League, winning the championship in 1964 and 1978, and lifting the European Cup Winners' Cup in 1981. They have maintained their dominance, being crowned champions in 13 of the first 20 seasons after Georgian independence, but Torpedo Kutaisi and Olimpi Rustavi have offered a serious challenge in recent years.

Below: Daniel Cousin of Gabon fends off a Tunisian Challenge at the 2010 African Nations Cup.

GERMANY

Federation: Deutscher Fussball-Bund
Founded: 1900
Joined FIFA: 1904
Confederation: UEFA
FIFA world ranking: 4
Honours: World Cup 1954, 1974, 1990; European Championship 1972, 1980, 1996 (*all except 1996 won as West Germany*)

Germany's outstanding tournament record is all the more remarkable given their late start in the game. They enjoyed barely any success before the Second World War, and afterwards had virtually no international relations until 1950. It was a modest beginning for one of the modern era's football superpowers. Yet since those difficult early days the Germans have won trophies at every level and earned a reputation as one of the authentic masters of the game.

The nation has produced an array of great players, including arguably the world's greatest defender, Franz Beckenbauer, and the deadliest goalscorer, Gerd Müller. Three times World Cup winners, finalists on four further occasions, and three times European champions, the nation's record is unequalled in Europe.

While success at international level runs deep, the country's clubs have also made a lasting impact. Bayern Munich are one of the richest and most successful clubs in the world and they have lifted the European Cup four times, finishing as runners-up on a further four occasions. Borussia Mönchengladbach, Eintracht Frankfurt, Hamburg, Borussia Dortmund and Bayer Leverkusen have also graced the final, with Hamburg winning in 1983 and Dortmund in 1997.

German teams have developed an uncanny ability to rise to the occasion, no matter what the circumstances. They are noted, and envied, for making the most of their talents and on occasion becoming greater than the sum of their parts. The German mix of skill, tactical nous and unshakeable self-belief goes beyond levels other nations attain. They have found a winning formula, yet their humble origins mean success is not taken for granted.

The West Germans emerged from the post-war doldrums to score their first major triumph when they won the World Cup against the odds in 1954, defeating Hungary, the outstanding team of the era, in the final. The start of the Bundesliga in 1963 saw the standard of domestic football improve following more than half a century of regionalised leagues, and during the Sixties the West Germans became a force to be reckoned with, reaching the World Cup final again in 1966 before losing 4-2 in extra-time to hosts England.

The pattern for success was set. In 1972 they became European champions for the first time, beating the Soviet Union in the final. Two years later, on home soil, they ran out World Cup winners for a second time when Gerd Müller scored the winner in a 2-1 victory over Holland in the newly-built Olympic Stadium in Munich.

Franz Beckenbauer was the German star of his era, thanks to his revolutionary style of play. A midfielder at the 1966 World Cup, in the Seventies he became a free-moving defender who operated behind the markers and attacked from deep positions. The man nicknamed 'Der Kaiser' wooed crowds with his elegance on the ball and his counter-attacking instincts.

Müller, the ultimate poacher, was equally important, creating little outside the box but scoring an astonishing total of 68 goals in 62 internationals. His stocky build and deceptive pace made him a nightmare for defenders to handle, and alongside Beckenbauer he helped

Bayern Munich to a hat-trick of European Cup victories from 1974 to 1976. Both players deservedly picked up European Footballer Of The Year awards during the decade.

In 1980 West Germany became European champions once again with the help of Bernd Schuster, while in the World Cup final two years later the fast and powerful Karl-Heinz Rummenigge captained the side to a 3-1 defeat to Italy. As the decade progressed German football became increasingly built around the 3-5-2 formation, utilising a sweeper, wing-backs and central strikers at both national and international level. This style became intrinsically linked with the German game and it proved to be a success for them. Under coach Franz Beckenbauer the team reached the final of both the 1986 and 1990 World Cups, losing to Argentina in the former and beating them in the later thanks to an Andreas Brehme penalty.

The 1990 triumph was their last trophy prior to the country's reunification, with Lothar Matthäus the driving force of the team behind the potent attacking duo of Jürgen Klinsmann and Rudi Völler. Their next success came thanks to a former East German star, Matthias Sammer, who was Player Of The Tournament when a united Germany won Euro 96. He was the best example of a sweeper since Beckenbauer and he inspired Dortmund to an unlikely European Cup triumph 12 months later.

Euro 96 aside, after reunification German football struggled by its own high standards, failing to meet expectations in a series of competitions. Bayern Munich won a fourth European Cup in 2001, needing penalties to beat Valencia, yet the 5-1 defeat to England in a World Cup qualifier in Munich in 2001 marked arguably the lowest point in the history of the national team. However, Rudi Völler's side made it to the tournament through the play-offs and defied the critics to reach the final, thanks to the extraordinary goalkeeping of Oliver Kahn. They lost the trophy to Brazil, but Kahn was voted Player Of The Tournament.

In 2006 Germany hosted the World Cup. Coach Jürgen Klinsmann brought his progressive coaching techniques and love of attacking football to the national team and defied expectations by reaching the semi-finals. Miroslav Klose ended the tournament as its highest scorer but the team were unlucky to be knocked out by Italy with two goals in the last two minutes of extra-time.

Under Klinsmann's assistant Joachim Löw, the Germans reached the final of Euro 2008 and the semi-final of the 2010 World Cup, losing to Spain on both occasions. The future can only be bright though, as Löw's exciting young World Cup team thrilled fans with their counter-attacking play, while 20-year-old Bayern Munich striker Thomas Müller won the Golden Boot and was voted the tournament's Best Young Player. It seems that Germany can never be written off.

Top: Franz Beckenbauer in action. Bottom: The Germans unite in victory over the Czech Republic at Euro 96.

1900: The Deutscher Fussball Bund is founded in 1900.

1904: The Germans are one of the original members of FIFA.

1934: Germany finish third on their World Cup debut.

1954: West Germany shock the world by defeating the invincible Hungarians to win the World Cup.

1960: Eintracht Frankfurt lose 7-3 to Real Madrid in the greatest ever European Cup final.

1966: West Germany reach the World Cup final, but lose to hosts England after a disputed goal.

1972: One of the greatest West German sides win the European Championship.

1974: After defeat in the first round to the East Germans, West Germany win the World Cup as hosts, beating Holland in the final.

1980: Inspired by Bernd Schuster, West Germany collect another European Championship.

1990: West Germany win the World Cup in a poor final with Argentina.

1996: The newly unified German team win Euro 96, with Bierhoff's golden goal beating the Czechs.

1997: Borussia Dortmund win the Champions League.

2001: Bayern beat Valencia to win the Champions League.

2002: Germany reach the final of the World Cup, losing to Brazil.

2010: Thomas Müller is voted Best Young Player at the World Cup and wins the Golden Boot.

1900
1905
1935
1955
1960
1965
1970
1975
1980
1985
1990
1995
2000
2005
2010

GHANA

Federation: Ghana Football Association
Founded: 1957
Joined FIFA: 1958
Confederation: CAF
FIFA world ranking: 23
Honours: African Nations Cup 1963, 1965, 1978, 1982

The 'Black Stars' of Ghana were the first team to win the African Nations Cup four times. By the late Seventies and early Eighties they looked like the African team destined to make the biggest impact on the world stage, but Ghana's first World Cup would not come until 2006 and it would not be until 2010 that they would really make a mark on the tournament.

The country had long since built a reputation for producing talented footballers. The most impressive have included Ibrahim Sunday and Karim Abdul Razak, voted African Player Of The Year in 1971 and 1978 respectively. Abedi Pele also won that honour for three successive seasons between 1991 and 1993.

The new century has seen Ghana boast another truly world-class talent in Michael Essien, who was part of the generation of players that had helped the country to the final

of the 2001 World Youth Championship, where they lost 3-0 to Argentina, and to the 2006 World Cup, where they finished second in their group to Italy and were eliminated in the first knockout round by Brazil.

Although injury deprived Ghana of the services of Michael Essien at the 2010 World Cup, his generation of Ghanaian stars, such as Asamoah Gyan, Stephen Appiah, John Mensah, Sulley Muntari and Richard Kingson, all helped the national team to the quarter-finals of the 2010 World Cup, where they were just a last-minute, goal-line handball away from becoming the first African nation to reach the semi-final. Asamoah Gyan missed the resulting penalty and moments later Ghana lost to Uruguay in a penalty shoot-out.

The Ghanaian Premier League is currently made up of 16 teams and the country's two most successful clubs are Hearts Of Oak and Asante Kotoko, who have dominated the domestic game since the league began in 1958. The two teams contested the first African Confederation Cup final in 2004, with Hearts Of Oak winning the all-Ghanaian affair 8-7 on penalties. Both clubs have also won the more illustrious African Champions Cup, with Asante triumphing in 1970 and 1983, while Hearts Of Oak lifted the trophy for the first time in 2000.

Football was introduced to Ghana by the British in the days when the territory went under the name of the Gold Coast, playing its first international in 1950. The British influence

continued for many years, to the extent that Stanley Matthews guested for Hearts Of Oak in 1957, the same year that Ghana gained independence from Britain.

GREECE

Federation: Hellenic Football Federation
Founded: 1926
Joined FIFA: 1927
Confederation: UEFA
FIFA world ranking: 12
Honours: European Championship 2004

Greece's European Championship triumph in 2004 was one of the biggest shocks in the history of football. Yet despite the massive popularity of the sport in Greece, for many years football was amateur and full-time professionalism did not arrive until 1979, making Panathinaikos's 1971 European Cup Final appearance against Ajax at Wembley an even greater achievement. The game remains the only occasion that a Greek club has reached a major European final.

A national league kicked-off in 1959 and it has since been dominated by three teams: Olympiakos, Panathiniakos and AEK Athens. The previous Greek championship began in 1928 and was the product of regional leagues

Below: Ghana celebrate Sulley Muntari's goal against Uruguay in the 2010 World Cup quarter-final.

with deciding play-offs, but it was dominated by the same three teams.

In the first half of the 20th century the country's football development stalled in the face of great adversity. Civil war, Balkan conflict, political instability and the Second World War all played their part in preventing the growth of the sport. After professionalism was introduced to the domestic game in 1979, hooliganism blighted Greek football through the Eighties, but the game survived and the hooligan problem has lessened over the years.

It was under German coach Otto Rehhagel that the Greeks enjoyed their greatest moment with a team that had been instilled with a self-belief lacking from previous national sides. They defeated hosts Portugal 2-1 in their Euro 2004 opener and next drew with Spain, despite having a player sent-off in each game. Those results were enough to send them through to the quarter-finals, where a goal from Angelos Charisteas knocked out holders France and then an extra-time strike from Traianos Dellas eliminated the Czech Republic.

In the final Greece faced hosts Portugal once again, but a 57th minute header from Charisteas was enough for them to be crowned European champions, with captain Theo Zagorakis lifting the trophy.

Greece's European victory was a reward for fans who have always kept the game popular despite the team only reaching the finals of the European Championship (1980) and the World Cup (1994) once each before their triumph in 2004. Even as European champions they did not qualify for the 2006 World Cup. However, although they reached the 2010 tournament they were knocked out in the group stage after finishing behind Argentina and South Korea.

Above: Greece enjoy the moment after their shock win over hosts Portugal to win Euro 2004.

GRENADA

Federation: Grenada Football Association
Founded: 1924
Joined FIFA: 1978
Confederation: CONCACAF
FIFA world ranking: 133

GUAM

Federation: Guam Football Association
Founded: 1975
Joined FIFA: 1996
Confederation: AFC
FIFA world ranking: 193 (joint)

GUATEMALA

Federation: Federación Nacional de Fútbol de Guatemala
Founded: 1919
Joined FIFA: 1946
Confederation: CONCACAF
FIFA world ranking: 118
Honours: CONCACAF Championship 1967

GUINEA

Federation: Fédération Guinéenne de Football
Founded: 1960
Joined FIFA: 1962
Confederation: CAF
FIFA world ranking: 101

GUINEA-BISSAU

Federation: Federação de Futebol da Guiné-Bissau
Founded: 1974
Joined FIFA: 1986
Confederation: CAF
FIFA world ranking: 188 (joint)

GUYANA

Federation: Guyana Football Federation
Founded: 1902
Joined FIFA: 1968
Confederation: CONCACAF
FIFA world ranking: 119 (joint)

HAITI

Federation: Fédération Haïtienne de Football
Founded: 1904
Joined FIFA: 1933
Confederation: CONCACAF
FIFA world ranking: 130 (joint)
Honours: CONCACAF Championship 1957, 1973

Haiti first entered the World Cup in 1934 but did not reach the finals until 1974, a year after winning a second CONCACAF Championship. The Haitians claimed to be using voodoo as a secret weapon at the World Cup, and striker Emmanuel Sanon made the audacious claim that he would score twice against Italy. He did score but just once, and Haiti lost 3-1. Disturbingly, Ernst Jean-Joseph failed a drug test and was beaten up by his own officials. With low morale the team were eliminated and they have since been eclipsed in their region by the dominance of Mexico and the rise of the USA.

HOLLAND

Federation: Koninklijke Nederlandse Voetbal Bond

Founded: 1889

Joined FIFA: 1904

Confederation: UEFA

FIFA world ranking: 2

Honours: European Championship 1988

The Dutch were the architects of 'Total Football' and they have given the game some of its most talented players, yet they were also one of the sport's late developers. One of the first countries outside of Britain to pick up on the appeal of football, Holland's first club, Haarlemsche FC, was founded in 1879 and its football association was set up ten years later. But while the insistence on adhering to strictly amateur, Calvinist principles yielded some return at the Olympics in the Twenties, it eventually proved to be a barrier to progress. In the post-war era it was evident that the Dutch were lagging behind tactically and they regularly failed to make it through qualification for major championships.

The exodus of the top players, such as Cor Van Der Hart and Faas Wilkes, to foreign clubs forced the KNVB to usher in professionalism in 1954. Ten years later the decision began to pay dividends as Dutch football accelerated into a new era, uncluttered by old traditions.

The real breakthrough came in the mid-Sixties when the concept of Total Football took hold at Ajax under coach Rinus Michels and with the young Johan Cruyff, Holland's most talented footballer. It relied on every player being comfortable on the ball, willing to play fluidly and move into space constantly. It proved a hugely influential system and it characterised the way the Dutch played the game for many years.

Ajax served notice that Dutch football had emerged from the dark ages with a memorable 5-1 thrashing of Bill Shankly's Liverpool in 1966. Three years later they made their first appearance in a European Cup final when they lost to Milan, before winning the trophy on three successive occasions between 1971 and 1973, beating Panathiniakos 2-0 at Wembley, Inter Milan 2-0 in Rotterdam and Juventus 1-0 in Belgrade.

At the 1974 World Cup the Dutch emerged as a real force on the international stage, but despite going 1-0 up in the first two minutes of the final against hosts West Germany, the team's over-confidence proved to be their downfall and they eventually lost 2-1. This psychological blow hung over Dutch football for a generation, but four years later, minus Cruyff, the national team again succeeded in reaching the World Cup final. However, they were undone by the hosts for a second time, with Argentina winning 3-1.

The ghost was partially laid to rest in 1988

Above: Captain Johan Cruyff with the Dutch team. Opposite clockwise from top left: Ruud Van Nistelrooy in 2005; Johnny Rep at the 1978 World Cup; Ruud Gullit picks up the trophy at Euro 88; Mark Van Bommel in the 2010 World Cup Final.

when the most talented Dutch team since the mid-Seventies, a side built around Ruud Gullit, Frank Rijkaard and Marco Van Basten, won the European Championship playing thrilling, attacking football. They also had the added satisfaction of gaining revenge over their German hosts in the semi-final.

In domestic football, the Dutch Eredivisie only came into existence in 1956 and it has been dominated by three clubs ever since: Ajax, who won the inaugural title, PSV and Feyenoord. The lack of competition has contributed to the country's best players regularly seeking more challenging climes abroad. In 1973 Cruyff headed for Barcelona, while Rijkaard, Gullit and Van Basten became the bedrock for Milan's success in the early Nineties.

Amsterdam-based Ajax remain one of the most famous clubs in the world. Founded in 1900, the team began their early domination of Dutch football under Englishman Jack Reynolds, who enshrined the club's reputation for attacking play. They have won the league more times than any other club and in 1995 a single goal from Patrick Kluivert added the Champions League to their three European Cup victories of the 1970s.

Amsterdam is effectively a one-club city and Ajax's bitterest rivals can be found in the port of Rotterdam, where Feyenoord became the team who first put Dutch football on the map when they picked up the European Cup in 1970. While Feyenoord fans still harbour an inferiority complex about their rivals, the club has had its fair share of success. It has won the league title on 14 occasions and the UEFA Cup twice, lifting the trophy in home stadium De Kuip in both 1974 and 2002. The stadium also annually hosts the final of cup competition, the KNVB Cup.

The third club in Holland's 'big three' is based in Eindhoven, home to industrial giant Philips, which also bankrolls Philips Sport Vereniging,

the football club founded in 1913. PSV are the richest club in the Holland, although only the second most successful with 21 championship wins, seven of which came in the first decade of the 21st century. The club's greatest achievement came in 1988, when a team coached by Guus Hiddink and featuring Ronald Koeman and Eric Gerets and Wim Kieft beat Benfica on penalties to lift the European Cup.

Hooliganism became an unpleasant feature of Dutch football in the Nineties and a compulsory membership scheme for fans was introduced in 1996. The rivalry between leading Dutch clubs is so fierce that in 2010, when Ajax and Feyenoord were due to contest the KNVB Cup for the first time in 30 years, security fears resulted in the traditional one-off final at De Kuip being changed to a two-legged final, played home and away.

Clubs have struggled with debt in recent years. In 2010 the Dutch football association announced that the 37 professional clubs had made a combined loss of £90 million, with only six of them being deemed financially healthy. It came not long after one of Holland's oldest clubs, HFC Haarlem, were declared bankrupt.

If the new realities are starting to hit Dutch football, at least the league has had its most open period in a generation, with AZ and Twente winning the title in 2009 and 2010 respectively, shaking up the dominance of the big three for the first time since AZ were champions in 1981.

The new era brought with it a more pragmatic approach by the national team, who reached the final of the 2010 World Cup in the face of much criticism for their 'un-Dutch' style. A victory in the final against Spain could have made the criticism disappear, but the aggressive manner of their extra-time defeat, described by Johan Cruyff as 'ugly, vulgar, hard', did not endear them to football fans, who prefer to remember the beautiful *oranje* football of the past.

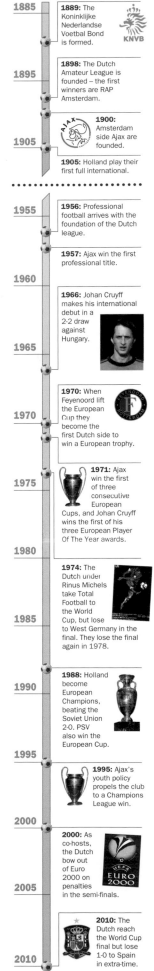

1885

1889: The Koninklijke Nederlandse Voetbal Bond is formed.

1895

1898: The Dutch Amateur League is founded – the first winners are RAP Amsterdam.

1905

1900: Amsterdam side Ajax are founded.

1905: Holland play their first full international.

1955

1956: Professional football arrives with the foundation of the Dutch league.

1957: Ajax win the first professional title.

1960

1966: Johan Cruyff makes his international debut in a 2-2 draw against Hungary.

1965

1970: When Feyenoord lift the European Cup they become the first Dutch side to win a European trophy.

1970

1971: Ajax win the first of three consecutive European Cups, and Johan Cruyff wins the first of his three European Player Of The Year awards.

1975

1974: The Dutch under Rinus Michels take Total Football to the World Cup, but lose to West Germany in the final. They lose the final again in 1978.

1980

1985

1988: Holland become European Champions, beating the Soviet Union 2-0. PSV also win the European Cup.

1990

1995: Ajax's youth policy propels the club to a Champions League win.

1995

2000: As co-hosts, the Dutch bow out of Euro 2000 on penalties in the semi-finals.

2000

2005

2010: The Dutch reach the World Cup final but lose 1-0 to Spain in extra-time.

2010

151

HONDURAS

Federation: Federación National Autónoma de Fútbol de Honduras
Founded: 1951
Joined FIFA: 1951
Confederation: CONCACAF
FIFA world ranking: 46
Honours: CONCACAF Championship 1981

The early 1980s saw the heyday of football in Honduras. The nation won the CONCACAF Championship in 1981 and qualified for the 1982 World Cup in Spain. Drawing with the hosts and Northern Ireland, Honduras could have qualified for the second stage but they lost to a late penalty against Yugoslavia.

Below: Hungary captain Ferenc Puskás congratulates Fritz Walter, holding the Jules Rimet Cup, on West Germany's victory in the 1954 World Cup final.

HONG KONG

Federation: Hong Kong Football Association
Founded: 1914
Joined FIFA: 1954
Confederation: AFC
FIFA world ranking: 135

The former British colony was at the forefront of football development on the Asian continent. Hong Kong was a founder members of the Asian Football Confederation in 1954 and hosted the inaugural Asian Cup in 1956. The Hong Kong league was the first professional league on the continent, drawing players from abroad, especially British players. It began in 1946 and was first won by the Royal Air Force team. An older league had existed since 1909 but it is not recognised by the Hong Kong FA.

Hong Kong's most successful club have been South China, who have won the most league championships and who also won four titles in a row between 2007 and 2010. In the 21st century they have seen off the challenge of Sun Hei, who won all four domestic trophies in 2005, the first club to do so since South China in 1991, and Happy Valley, who were relegated in 2010, just four years after winning their most recent title.

HUNGARY

Federation: Magyar Labdarúgó Szövetség
Founded: 1901
Joined FIFA: 1907
Confederation: UEFA
FIFA world ranking: 62
Honours: Olympics 1952, 1964, 1968

Once among the game's most innovative football cultures, Hungary have long since ceased to be a force in the game. Great promise failed to yield trophies, talent drained away and sociopolitical decline left the country financially crippled and the national team struggling to compete.

The Hungarian football association was founded early in the 20th century, but a national, professional league did not arise until 1926. Prior to that the league only contained teams from Budapest, but MTK, a club evolving from the Jewish community, proved such a strong force under the coaching of Scotsman Jimmy Hogan that the need for some kind of organised league became apparent.

Prior to the Second World War Hungarian football began to display the kind of ability and cohesion needed to challenge the hegemony of established football giants. The national side even reached the final of the 1938 World Cup where they lost 4-2 to Italy, but it was during the post-war era of the 'Magical Magyars' when the Hungarians really rewrote the way that the game was played, producing a clutch of football legends in the Fifties that included József Bózsik, Sandor Kocsis, Nandor Hidegkuti and Ferenc Puskás. Their impact was vividly underlined in 1953 when they became the first non-British team to beat England at Wembley, with a resounding 6-3 victory.

In 51 games played between May 1950 and February 1956, Hungary lost just once – agonisingly that defeat occurred in the 1954 World Cup Final, when they threw away an early 2-0 lead over West Germany. The team's promise ended abruptly with the Soviet invasion in 1956, when many of the players were out of the country on tour with Honvéd and chose not to return. Kocsis and Zoltan Czibor headed for Barcelona, while Puskás opted for Real Madrid.

Within six years a talented new side had emerged, with striker Florian Albert helping Hungary to the quarter-finals of both the 1962 and 1966 World Cups, but it was to be their last hurrah. Despite winning Olympic gold in 1964 and 1968, Hungary failed to qualify for the 1970 World Cup and have not been present at the tournament since 1986, where they managed a first round victory against Canada, but suffered heavy defeats to the Soviet Union and France. A fourth place finish in the 1972 European Championship remains their best showing in the modern era, when the team lost to a solitary goal in the semi-final against the Soviet Union.

At club level Hungarian football has rarely matched the brilliance of its national team. Budapest-based Ferencváros beat Juventus to win the Fairs Cup in 1965 and were runners-up in 1968. Újpest also reached the final the following year and Videoton lost the UEFA Cup final to Real Madrid in 1985.

While the national team continues to struggle to qualify for the World Cup, a revival remains a long way off. Yet there is hope for the future after a third place finish in the 2009 Under-20 World Cup. It was Hungary's first medal of significance in nearly half a century.

ICELAND

Federation: Knattspyrnumsamband Island
Founded: 1947
Joined FIFA: 1947
Confederation: UEFA
FIFA world ranking: 79

The Icelandic league, played between May and September, has been dominated by the Reykjavik clubs, such as KR, Valur, Fram and

Vikingur, but ÍA and FH have enjoyed success in recent years, with FH winning five league titles in the first decade of the 21st century.

INDIA

Federation: All India Football Federation
Founded: 1937
Joined FIFA: 1948
Confederation: AFC
FIFA world ranking: 132

Football was introduced to India by the British. Although it has grown in popularity, historically the Indian population has shown little interest in the game, instead preferring cricket and hockey. The early Calcutta league was strictly British, but Indian teams such as Mohammedan Sporting, East Bengal and Mohun Bagan did spring up to challenge the British dominance. In 1989, to mark the club's centenary, Mohun Bagan were named 'The National Football Team of India'.

The country's most famous players have included Jumma Khan, the first Indian to play in boots, Syed Abdus Samad, 'the Indian Stanley Matthews', who played until he was 52, and imposing defender Gostha Pal, who was known as 'the Great Wall Of China'.

INDONESIA

Federation: Persatuan Sepak Bola Seluruh Indonesia
Founded: 1930
Joined FIFA: 1952
Confederation: AFC
FIFA world ranking: 138

IRAN

Federation: Football Federation of the Islamic Republic of Iran
Founded: 1920
Joined FIFA: 1945
Confederation: AFC
FIFA world ranking: 64
Honours: Asian Cup 1968, 1972, 1976

Iranian football rose to prominence in the Sixties and Seventies with the national team winning a hat-trick of Asian Cups and making the Olympic quarter-finals in 1976. The highlight of the period was a deserved 1-1 draw with Scotland at the 1978 World Cup. However, football became somewhat less of a priority after the Islamic Revolution the following year.

In the Nineties Iran re-emerged from a period of instability, qualifying for the 1998 World Cup with a campaign that had opened with a 17-0 defeat of the Maldives. It was the widest margin in World Cup qualification history at the time and Karim Bagheri scored seven goals. At the subsequent tournament they recorded their first World Cup win with a defeat of the USA.

In the modern era Iran has established a reputation for playing good football and is one of Asia's leading sides. In 2004 striker Ali Daei became the first man to score 100 international goals, while Ali Karimi was voted Asian Player Of The Year. They are two of a handful of Iranian players to have forged successful careers in Germany's Bundesliga.

Only two Iranian clubs have achieved success in the Asian Champions League. Esteghlal won it in 1970, when the club was known as Taj, and again in 1991. PAS Tehran also won it in 1993.

IRAQ

Federation: Iraq Football Association
Founded: 1948
Joined FIFA: 1950
Confederation: AFC
FIFA world ranking: 104
Honours: Asian Cup 2007

Iraqi football enjoyed its best period during the 1980s, when the national team won gold at the 1982 Asian Games. They also qualified for the 1986 World Cup under Brazilian coach Evaristo de Macedo, but they lost all three of their group games and it remains their only World Cup.

In the post-Saddam Hussein era the national team have experienced a revival, despite being unable to play at home for security reasons. They reached the 2004 Olympic semi-final before finishing in fourth place and won the 2007 Asian Cup, beating Saudi Arabia in the final. The team have struggled to capitalise on this success as government interference in Iraqi sporting bodies has resulted in FIFA bans.

Competitive club football resumed in the 2004-5 season and since then the Kurdish team Arbil have dominated the domestic league.

ISRAEL

Federation: Israel Football Association
Founded: 1928
Joined FIFA: 1929
Confederation: UEFA
FIFA world ranking: 37
Honours: Asian Cup 1964

Israel were once a strong force in the Asian Football Confederation. They were runners-up in the Asian Cups of 1956 and 1960, before lifting the trophy in 1964. They also represented the confederation at the 1970 World Cup. However, the political situation meant that Israel were never fully welcome in Asian football and they were grouped with teams from the Far East to separate them from their Arab neighbours.

In 1976 Arab disquiet resulted in Israel being thrown out of the AFC and they were shunted first into Europe and then Oceania, even facing South American teams in World Cup play-offs. As a consequence Israel have played World Cup qualifiers on every continent. Israel were given a permanent football home in UEFA in 1991.

Above: The Iranian and American teams prepare for their game at the 1998 World Cup.

1895

1898: The Italian football federation is formed. It organises the first Italian championship, played in just one day and won by Genoa.

1905

1910: The national team debuts with a 6-2 win over France in Milan.

1910

1930

1930: Italy decide against entering the first World Cup.

1934: Italy win the World Cup. They lift the trophy again in 1938 after winning Olympic gold in 1936.

1935

1949: After dominating Italian football since the war, Torino's plane crashes in the fog, killing the entire squad.

1950

1955

1957: Fiorentina make it to the second European Cup final but lose 2-0 to Real Madrid.

1960

1963: Milan become the first Italian side to win the European Cup.

1965

1968: Italy are crowned champions of Europe.

1970

1970: Italy lose the World Cup final to Brazil.

1975

1980: A bribery scandal is revealed in Italy involving top players and officials. Paolo Rossi is banned for two years.

1980

1982: The head of Italy's football federation resigns on the eve of the World Cup after a betting scandal. Paolo Rossi returns to help Italy win the World Cup.

1985

1990

1990: Italy host the World Cup, but only manage to finish third.

1995

1994: Italy are beaten on penalties by Brazil in the World Cup final.

2000

2006: Italy win the World Cup and Juventus are stripped of the title after a match-fixing scandal.

2005

2010: Inter Milan win the Champions League.

2010

ITALY

Federation: Federazione Italiana Giuoco Calcio
Founded: 1898
Joined FIFA: 1905
Confederation: UEFA
FIFA world ranking: 11
Honours: World Cup 1934, 1938, 1982, 2006; European Championship 1968; Olympics 1936

Although a nationwide, professional league did not begin in Italy until the 1929-30 season, there had been a football association and a national championship since 1898. Italy's biggest clubs – Juventus, AC Milan and Internazionale – were established in a period between 1897 and 1908, but they exert a powerful influence on football to this day and have all played a part in dominating the European game in the modern era.

The national side has enjoyed a similar position in the game since debuting with a 6-2 home victory over France in 1910. Indeed, Italy were the dominant force in international football in the mid 1930s, despite having passed on the opportunity to play at the first World Cup in 1930. They were hosts four years later, and led by coach Vittorio Pozzo the Italians started their campaign with a 7-1 win over the USA. They found Spain a much tougher nut to crack in the quarter-final, and they had a controversial equaliser to thank for taking a bruising tie to a replay, which they duly won. Italy defeated Austria 1-0 in the semi-final and, cheered on by Italy's Prime Minister Benito Mussolini, came from behind to overcome Czechoslovakia with two late goals in the final.

To underline their superiority the Italians went on to win gold at the Berlin Olympics in 1936. They defeated Austria 2-1 in the final and were no doubt glad to put to rest the conspiracy theories about the nature of their World Cup victory two years earlier, as some had accused Mussolini of engineering victory in the tournament.

The first European team to lift the Jules Rimet Trophy soon became the first nation to retain it. Pozzo took a remodelled squad to the 1938 World Cup, with only Giuseppe Meazza and Giovanni Ferrari remaining from the team that won the final in 1934. His side featured several of the stars of the Olympic winning team, but they found opening round opponents Norway trickier than expected to beat. A fine display from keeper Aldo Olivieri and an extra-time winner from Silvio Piola saw Pozzo's attack-minded side progress.

France were dispatched 3-1 in the quarter-final, and two second-half goals put paid to Brazil in the semi-final (Meazza scored the second from the spot as he struggled to hold up his shorts after the elastic snapped). Hungary were the opponents in the final, but Italy won 4-2 with Piola and Gino Colaussi scoring twice each.

Above: Vittorio Pozzo and his 1934 World Cup winners. Opposite clockwise from top left: Sandro Mazzola in 1974; coach Marcello Lippi and the victorious Italian World Cup team of 2006; Paolo Rossi; Roberto Baggio in action at France 98.

With the clouds of war gathering, the victory had been trumpeted as a victory for fascism. However, when football resumed in the post-war era, Italy were among the defeated nations and had to endure a short spell in the international wilderness. Even when they were competing again and just a year away from defending their world title at the 1950 World Cup, the heart was ripped out of the national side when the entire first-team squad of reigning champions Torino were killed in a plane crash. Six members of the national team who had played in Italy's previous game died in the disaster.

Italy failed to make it past the first round at the two subsequent World Cups, but they missed out altogether in 1958 and had to endure the humiliation of losing to Chile in 1962 and to North Korea in 1966. Italian football finally got back on track when the country hosted – and won – the 1968 European Championship, although they had to rely on the toss of a coin to defeat the Soviet Union in the semi-final and they needed a replay to beat Yugoslavia in the final. Coach Ferruccio Valcareggi built on that success, taking his side all the way to the final of the 1970 World Cup, where they were heavily defeated by Brazil.

Coached by Enzo Bearzot the Italians finished fourth at the Argentina finals in 1978, but won the World Cup for a third time in 1982. They did it the hard way, drawing all of their first round games, before beating reigning champions Argentina and favourites Brazil in the second group phase. The latter match, a 3-2 win, was memorable for an astonishing hat-trick from 25-year-old Paolo Rossi, who had only recently returned to football following a two-year ban for match-fixing. He hit two more in the semi-final against Poland and scored Italy's first goal in a 3-1 final triumph over West Germany in the final.

Italy finished third when hosting the World Cup in 1990, losing to Argentina on penalties in the semi-final. They were beaten on penalties again in the 1994 final by Brazil, but finally claimed their fourth title in 2006. Captained by Fabio Cannavaro and coached by Marcello Lippi, they beat France 5-3 on penalties after at 1-1 draw

at Berlin's Olympic Stadium to become Europe's most successful nation in the World Cup.

Italian club sides have also enjoyed sustained success and have dominated significant periods of the modern era. The two Milan clubs, Inter and AC Milan, won the European Cup twice each during the Sixties, while in the Eighties and Nineties the top Italian clubs lavished money on expensive foreign players and consequently ruled European football. Milan won the European Cup in 1989 and 1990, and again in 1994 when it had become the Champions League. Juventus did likewise in 1996 and eight out of 11 UEFA Cup finals between 1989 and 1999 were won by Italian sides, four of them being all-Italian affairs.

While Italy can boast some of the biggest names in European club football, controversy has never been far from the domestic game and in 2006 many of the country's most powerful clubs were caught up in a match-fixing scandal that became known as 'calciopoli'. It was revealed that Juventus general manager Luciano Moggi had been influencing the appointment of referees and eventually other clubs were implicated, resulting in the relegation of Juventus to Serie B and the deduction of points from Fiorentina, Lazio, Reggina and Milan. Juventus were also stripped of the 2005 and 2006 league titles. Runners-up Inter Milan were awarded the 2006 title instead and they promptly filled the void created by the punishment of their rivals, winning the next four league titles and the 2010 Champions League Final.

While the scandal was a setback, it is the excess of the 1990s that continues to weigh down Italian football. Many of the clubs who failed to deliver glory in exchange for unrealistic spending have been paying the price for their over-ambition for many years. However, the desire to improve the balance sheets of the leading clubs ultimately led to a significant restructuring of Italian football. The clubs of Serie A broke away from the old league system at the beginning of the 2010-11 season and took control of their own destiny. It remains to be seen whether this will be for the benefit of the Italian game.

IVORY COAST

Federation: Fédération Ivoirienne de Football
Founded: 1960
Joined FIFA: 1961
Confederation: CAF
FIFA world ranking: 26
Honours: African Nations Cup 1992

The French introduced football to the Ivory Coast. The West African nation has one of the best-organised and richest leagues on the continent, but strength at home has not often been turned into success in the international arena. The national team's only major trophy came under coach Yeo Martial, when they won the African Nations Cup in dramatic fashion in 1992. They beat Ghana 11-10 in a penalty shoot-out that saw every player on the pitch take a penalty. Kouame Aka scored to give the Ivorians the edge, before the team's legendary keeper Alain Gouamene, who was to play in a record seven African Nations Cups, made a decisive save, having already scored.

It was not until 2006 that the 'Elephants' reached the World Cup for the first time, thanks to French coach Henri Michel and a new group of stars, such as Didier Drogba and Kolo Toure. The side were also runners-up at the African Nations Cup the same year, losing to hosts Egypt on penalties. En route to the final they triumphed over Cameroon in a shoot-out that took 24 spot-kicks to decide. Coach Sven-Göran Eriksson led the team to the 2010 World Cup, but they failed to progress to the second round.

In club football Stade Abidjan won the African Champions Cup in 1966 and ASEC Mimosas won the competition in 1998. Historically ASEC Mimosas are the Ivory Coast's most successful club and they have developed a very successful youth academy that has produced numerous international stars. Since 1990 they have only failed to win the championship four times.

JAMAICA

Federation: Jamaica Football Federation
Founded: 1910
Joined FIFA: 1962
FIFA world ranking: 83
Confederation: CONCACAF

Jamaica has had a football federation, care of its former British colonial rulers, since 1910, although it does not have much history as an organised sport. The rise of the 'Reggae Boyz' in the late Nineties saw the Jamaicans make their World Cup debut under Brazilian coach Rene Simoes, having recruited players of Jamaican descent from English football, such as Fitzroy Simpson, Frank Sinclair, Robbie Earle, Marcus Gayle, Paul Hall and Deon Burton. At the finals they secured a 2-1 victory over Japan in their last group game, but heavy defeats to Croatia and Argentina ensured the adventure went no further. Jamaica were the inaugural winners of the Caribbean Cup in 1991, lifting the trophy again in 1998, 2005 and 2008.

JAPAN

Federation: Japan Football Association
Founded: 1921
Joined FIFA: 1929-45, 1950
Confederation: AFC
FIFA world ranking: 32
Honours: Asian Cup 1992, 2000, 2004

The first Japanese football club, Tokyo Shukyu-dan, was founded in 1917, the same year that the national team made its debut, but although attempts were made to start a championship, usually in cup format, a football league did not exist until the formation of the Japanese Soccer League in 1965. Three years later Japan won bronze at the 1968 Olympics, but the league's amateur status hindered further development of the game and in 1993 it was replaced by the J.League, a revamp that saw $20 million invested in a professional league. It even attracted stars from abroad, such as Gary Lineker and Zico, who was to stay at Kashima Antlers as player and coach for 15 years.

The game was also given a boost in 2002 when the country co-hosted the World Cup. Since then the J.League has thrived, growing from just ten clubs in 1993 to a record 37 clubs in 2010, with 18 clubs in the top flight and 19 in the second division. In the intervening period the league's rules have gradually become more traditional, with the introduction of the points system (in its earliest seasons, only the number of wins counted towards league position) and the dispensing of extra-time, golden goals and penalty shoot-outs to decide league games.

The changes have given the game a boost in popularity after the poor attendances of the late 1990s, when the existence of some clubs was under threat. Crowds have steadily increased, from an average of 11,000 a game in 1999 to 19,000 ten years later. The emphasis during this period has been on developing community ties, youth schemes and a restrained financial budget to prevent overspending.

The J.League has retained many leading Japanese players, helping the development of the national side. Under Zico Japan won the Asian Cup for the third time in 2004, beating China 3-1 in Beijing. Philip Troussier led Japan to the second round of the 2002 World Cup and Takeshi Okada repeated the feat in 2010.

Opposite: Didier Drogba in action for the Ivory Coast at the 2010 World Cup.

JORDAN

Federation: Jordan Football Association
Founded: 1949
Joined FIFA: 1958
FIFA world ranking: 98 (joint)
Confederation: AFC

KAZAKHSTAN

Federation: Football Federation of Kazakhstan
Founded: 1914
Joined FIFA: 1994
FIFA world ranking: 126
Confederation: UEFA

KENYA

Federation: Kenya Football Federation
Founded: 1960
Joined FIFA: 1960
FIFA world ranking: 115
Confederation: CAF

KUWAIT

Federation: Kuwait Football Association
Founded: 1952
Joined FIFA: 1962
Confederation: AFC
FIFA world ranking: 85
Honours: Asian Cup 1980

Kuwait's one major trophy came in 1980 when they hosted and won the Asian Cup. However, the abiding memory of Kuwaiti football came when Prince Fahid called his team off the pitch in protest at a refereeing decision at the 1982 World Cup. Outside influence remains a problem and Kuwait have twice been suspended from FIFA since 2007 due to government interference in the sport.

Above: Martin Buechel of Liechtenstein evades the attention of Russia's Roman Pavlyuchenko.

KYRGYZSTAN

Federation: Football Federation of Kyrgyz Republic
Founded: 1992
Joined FIFA: 1994
Confederation: AFC
FIFA world ranking: 165

LAOS

Federation: Lao Football Federation
Founded: 1951
Joined FIFA: 1952
Confederation: AFC
FIFA world ranking: 182

LATVIA

Federation: Latvijas Futbola Federacija
Founded: 1921
Joined FIFA: 1922, 1991
Confederation: UEFA
FIFA world ranking: 50

Between 1922 and 1949 Latvia were the strongest of the Baltic states but remained a minnow in football terms. They came close to qualifying for the 1938 World Cup but lost 2-1 to Austria in a play-off. Soviet occupation eventually led to the demise of the Latvian national team, but after independence in 1991 they took part in the qualifying stages for the 1994 World Cup and the 1996 European Championship. Since their return to international football, Latvia have yet to make any impression on either

Right: Libya's Abdusalam Nader (right) fights Zimbabwe's Thabani Kamusoko for the ball in 2009.

competition. Latvia's most successful club has been Skonto Riga, who won the championship 14 successive times after it was revived in 1991. In recent years the league has also been won by Liepajas Metalurgs and FK Ventspils.

LEBANON

Federation: Federation Libanaise de Football Association
Founded: 1933
Joined FIFA: 1935
Confederation: AFC
FIFA world ranking: 151

LESOTHO

Federation: Lesotho Football Association
Founded: 1932
Joined FIFA: 1964
Confederation: CAF
FIFA world ranking: 154

LIBERIA

Federation: Liberia Football Association
Founded: 1936
Joined FIFA: 1962
Confederation: CAF
FIFA world ranking: 156 (joint)

Liberian football has never been strong but in former World Player Of The Year, George Weah, the country has produced one truly great footballer. He has provided enormous support to the game in Liberia, but the national team have only twice qualified for the African Nations Cup and have never appeared at the World Cup.

LIBYA

Federation: Libyan Football Federation
Founded: 1962
Joined FIFA: 1963
Confederation: CAF
FIFA world ranking: 96 (joint)

LIECHTENSTEIN

Federation: Liechtensteiner Fussball-Verband
Founded: 1934
Joined FIFA: 1974
Confederation: UEFA
FIFA world ranking: 140

The Liechtenstein team debuted in 1982 and they gained a first competitive point against the Republic Of Ireland in 1995 in a Euro 96 qualifier. They earned their first World Cup qualifying point by drawing 2-2 at home to Portugal in 2004 and then recorded their first ever competitive wins with 4-0 and 3-0 victories over Luxembourg in the same 2006 World Cup qualifying group. There is no national league in Liechtenstein, with the country's clubs playing in the lower divisions of the Swiss league.

LITHUANIA

Federation: Lietuvos Futbolo Federacija
Founded: 1922
Joined FIFA: 1923, 1992
Confederation: UEFA
FIFA world ranking: 52

The Lithuanians played their first international in 1923, but after being absorbed into the Soviet Union it proved to be the weakest of the Baltic states. Its clubs barely made an impact on Soviet football until Zalgiris Vilnius won promotion to the Supreme Soviet League in 1982, finishing third in 1987. Sigitas Jakubauskas became the first Lithuanian to play for the Soviet Union when he won his only cap in 1985, and Arminas Narbekovas was an Olympic gold medal winner with the Soviets in 1988 despite never winning

a full cap. FBK Kaunas and Ekranas Panevezys have been the strongest Lithuanian clubs in recent years, dominating a league that regularly exports its best players.

LUXEMBOURG

Federation: Fédération Luxembourgeoise de Football
Founded: 1908
Joined FIFA: 1910
Confederation: UEFA
FIFA world ranking: 116

In a huge shock to world football, Luxembourg beat Holland to reach the quarter-final of the European Championship in 1964. However, the country's part-time footballers have one of the poorest records in Europe and their clubs have suffered the worst aggregate defeats in European football: Stade Dudelange lost 18-0 over two legs to Benfica in the European Cup in 1966, Jeunesse Hautcharage were defeated 21-0 on aggregate by Chelsea in the Cup Winners' Cup in 1971, as were US Rumelange by Feyenoord in the UEFA Cup in 1972.

MACAU

Federation: Associação de Futebol de Macau
Founded: 1939
Joined FIFA: 1978
Confederation: AFC
FIFA world ranking: 196

MACEDONIA FYR

Federation: Football Federation of Macedonia
Founded: 1948
Joined FIFA: 1994
Confederation: UEFA
FIFA world ranking: 66 (joint)

The national team of the Former Yugoslav Republic Of Macedonia debuted in 1994 and their highlights have included an away draw with England in 2002. When part of Yugoslavia, Vardar Skopje were the only Macedonian club to lift trophies, winning the Yugoslav Cup in 1961. They also won the league title in 1987, helped by the fact that ten rival teams went into the league campaign carrying a six point deduction.

MADAGASCAR

Federation: Fédération Malagasy de Football
Founded: 1961
Joined FIFA: 1962
Confederation: CAF
FIFA world ranking: 144

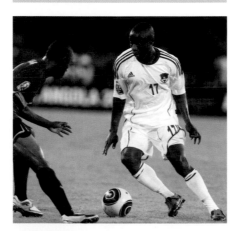

MALAWI

Federation: Football Association of Malawi
Founded: 1966
Joined FIFA: 1967
Confederation: CAF
FIFA world ranking: 74

MALAYSIA

Federation: Persatuan Bolasepak Malaysia
Founded: 1933
Joined FIFA: 1956
Confederation: AFC
FIFA world ranking: 142

MALDIVES

Federation: Football Association of Maldives
Founded: 1982
Joined FIFA: 1986
Confederation: AFC
FIFA world ranking: 145

MALI

Federation: Fédération Malienne de Football
Founded: 1960
Joined FIFA: 1962
Confederation: CAF
FIFA world ranking: 55

MALTA

Federation: Malta Football Association
Founded: 1900
Joined FIFA: 1959
Confederation: UEFA
FIFA world ranking: 152

Football was introduced to Malta in the earliest days of the sport as a means of entertainment for British soldiers stationed on the island, but a formal league was not introduced until the 1909-10 season, when won by Floriana. Malta did not join FIFA until 1959 and only then with the permission of the English FA, to whom they had been affiliated since 1913. They did not enter the World Cup until 1974 and have since had very limited success. One of Europe's smallest football nations, the strongest teams in the Maltese league in recent years have been Sliema Wanderers, Valletta and Birkirkara.

MAURITANIA

Federation: Fédération de Foot-Ball de la Républic Islamique de Mauritanie
Founded: 1961
Joined FIFA: 1964
Confederation: CAF
FIFA world ranking: 168

MAURITIUS

Federation: Mauritius Football Association
Founded: 1952
Joined FIFA: 1962
Confederation: CAF
FIFA world ranking: 177 (joint)

Centre: Jimmy Zakazaka of Malawi on the ball in 2010.

MEXICO

Federation: Federación Mexicana De Fútbol Asociación
Founded: 1927
Joined FIFA: 1929
Confederation: CONCACAF
FIFA world ranking: 24
Honours: CONCACAF Championship 1965, 1971, 1977, 1993, 1996, 1998, 2003, 2009; Confederations Cup 1999

Mexico have regularly appeared at the World Cup, having reached the finals on 14 occasions. They also took part in one of the two simultaneously played games that opened the first ever tournament in 1930. Their strongest showings came in 1970 and 1986 when they progressed to the quarter-finals, both times as hosts. In 1986, it took a penalty shoot-out with eventual finalists West Germany to eliminate the team led by the great Hugo Sanchez, the most famous Mexican player of recent times. Sanchez, known for his extravagant and often over-the-top goal celebrations, was a familiar figure in Europe, having plied his trade very successfully for many years with both Atlético Madrid and Real Madrid.

Some critics argue that Mexican football has suffered internationally due to a lack of meaningful competition in the Central and North American region. Only in the recent era, with the rise of the United States as a credible football force, have the Mexicans experienced a serious local rival. For many years it was argued that Mexico would enjoy more testing competition by joining the South American championship, the Copa América, and in 1993, together with the United States, they were invited to do so for the first time as guests.

It proved a wise move as Mexico reached the Copa América final at the first attempt, only losing to Argentina 2-1 after a late Gabriel Batistuta strike. Subsequently they have continued to take part in the competition and have become one of the strongest nations, finishing third in 1997, 1999 and 2007, and finishing runners-up again in 2001.

After the near miss of the 1986 World Cup, Mexico qualified for the 1990 tournament in Italy but did not attend because they were banned from all international competitions after fielding an ineligible player in the qualifying stages for the 1988 Olympic Games. In 1999 further controversy surrounded the Mexicans when accusations were made of drug-taking among the players following the team's impressive third place in the Copa América.

Football was first introduced to Mexico by Cornish miners at the end of the 19th century. Although the country had its own five-team football league by 1902, the sport did not turn fully professional until 1943. Currently the Primera División is made up of 18 clubs, but the league itself has undergone significant changes since it first began, most recently in 1993 when it split the season into two competitions, a system popular in many countries in South America. The Apertura (opening) season now runs from August to December and the Clausura (closing) season runs from January to May, resulting in two champions each year. Relegation also differs from traditional systems, being based on performance over a number of seasons rather than just the current campaign.

The country's glamour club is América from Mexico City. Bought in 1959 by broadcasting company Televisa and heavily promoted through the purchase of overseas stars and widespread television exposure, América developed a nationwide following, becoming the strongest force in Mexican football in the Eighties.

América are one of only two clubs to have stayed in Mexico's top division continuously since it was founded in 1943. The other club is Guadalajara, who are often referred to by their nickname 'Chivas', and who famously only select Mexican players for their team.

Below: The Mexico team celebrate winning the Gold Cup in 2009.

MOLDOVA

Federation: Federatia Moldoveneasca de Fotbal
Founded: 1990
Joined FIFA: 1994
Confederation: UEFA
FIFA world ranking: 89

When Burevestnik Kishinev finished sixth in 1956, it was the best performance by a Moldovan club in the Soviet league. After a series of name changes, the club became Zimbru Chisinau, by far the strongest team in the first decade after the launch of the Moldovan league in 1992. Subsequently they have been eclipsed by Sheriff Tiraspol, who celebrated their tenth consecutive league title in 2010.

MONGOLIA

Federation: Mongolian Football Federation
Founded: 1959
Joined FIFA: 1998
Confederation: AFC
FIFA world ranking: 182 (joint)

MONTENEGRO

Federation: Fudbalski Savez Crne Gore
Founded: 1931
Joined FIFA: 2007
Confederation: UEFA
FIFA world ranking: 72

Formerly part of Yugoslavia, after the country's disintegration in 1991, Montenegro played alongside Serbia as Yugoslavia until the country was renamed Serbia and Montenegro in 2003. After qualifying for the 2006 World Cup under that name, the people of Montenegro declared independence just weeks before the tournament, but the two nations still competed jointly at the finals before separating immediately afterwards.

MONTSERRAT

Federation: Montserrat Football Association
Founded: 1994
Joined FIFA: 1996
Confederation: CONCACAF
FIFA world ranking: 202 (joint)

MOROCCO

Federation: Fédération Royale Marocaine de Football
Founded: 1955
Joined FIFA: 1960
Confederation: CAF
FIFA world ranking: 82
Honours: African Nations Cup 1976

Morocco became the first African team to progress to the second round of the World Cup in 1986. They topped their group after 0-0 draws with England and Poland, and a 3-1 win over Portugal. They faced West Germany but were beaten by a last minute goal.

When Morocco debuted at the World Cup in 1970, they shocked their German opponents by taking the lead before losing 2-1. Despite their success in reaching the second round at the 1986 competition, at the 1994 World Cup they lost all three games by a single goal. Four years later a 2-2 draw with Norway and a 3-0 win over Scotland was impressive enough but still failed to take them through to the next round.

It was the French who introduced football to Morocco and several Moroccan-born players have featured for the French national team, including Larbi Ben Barek and Just Fontaine. Independence from France in 1956 brought a remarkably robust and open league. Three Moroccan sides – FAR Rabat in 1985, Raja Casablanca in 1989, 1997, 1999 and Wydad Casablanca in 1992 – have won the African Champions Cup, while Ahmed Faras (1975), Mohamed Timoumi (1985), Badou Zaki (1986) and Mustapha Hadji (1998) have been voted African Player Of The Year.

MOZAMBIQUE

Federation: Federação Mocambicana de Futebol
Founded: 1976
Joined FIFA: 1980
Confederation: CAF
FIFA world ranking: 80

MYANMAR

Federation: Myanmar Football Federation
Founded: 1947
Joined FIFA: 1952
Confederation: AFC
FIFA world ranking: 143

NAMIBIA

Federation: Namibia Football Association
Founded: 1990
Joined FIFA: 1992
Confederation: CAF
FIFA world ranking: 119 (joint)

NEPAL

Federation: All Nepal Football Federation
Founded: 1951
Joined FIFA: 1970
Confederation: AFC
FIFA world ranking: 156 (joint)

NETHERLANDS ANTILLES

Federation: Nederlands Antilliaanse Voetbal Unie
Founded: 1921
Joined FIFA: 1932
Confederation: CONCACAF
FIFA world ranking: 150

NEW CALEDONIA

Federation: Fédération Calédonienne de Football
Founded: 1928
Joined FIFA: 2004
Confederation: OFC
FIFA world ranking: 162

Below: Namibian defender Richard Gariseb takes on the Kenyans during a World Cup qualifier in 2008.

Above: North Korea celebrate their amazing victory over Italy at the 1966 World Cup.

NIGERIA

Federation: Nigeria Football Federation
Founded: 1945
Joined FIFA: 1960
Confederation: CAF
FIFA world ranking: 30
Honours: African Nations Cup 1980, 1994; Olympics 1996

The formation of a football association in 1945 and the subsequent launch of the Governor's Cup (later renamed the FA Challenge Cup in 1954) saw the formal birth of football in Nigeria after it had been introduced by the British. However, it was not until the 1970s that Nigerian football, despite its popularity, began to develop thanks to huge investment from petrol dollars.

A national league was formed in 1972 with just six teams, and a combination of stability and investment began to reap rewards, most notably when Nigeria hosted and won the 1980 African Nations Cup, beating Algeria 3-0 in the final. More significant was the 1985 Under-16 World Cup victory, which saw Nigeria beat West Germany 2-1 with goals from Jonathan Akpoborie and Victor Igbinoba. It was the first world title won by an African nation.

This was to provide the springboard that helped Nigeria's 'Super Eagles' to qualify for three successive World Cups in 1994, 1998 and 2002. They also lifted the African Nations Cup a second time in 1994, and won Olympic gold in 1996. The improvement in the quality of Nigerian football also resulted in a series of individual awards, and Rashidi Yekini (1993), Emmanuel Amunike (1994), Nwankwo Kanu (1996 and 1999) and Victor Ikpeba (1997) have all been voted African Footballer Of The Year.

The Nigerian league was relaunched as the Professional League in 1990, ruled by strict guidelines to aid the modernisation of the game. It later changed its name to the Premier League and Enyimba have been the most successful club of recent times, winning two African Champions League titles, five Nigerian championships and two Nigerian Cups between 2001 and 2010.

The constant improvement in the quality of domestic football has meant that Nigerian players have become in demand all over the world and are often snapped up by European clubs at a young age. This experience helped the Olympic team win silver at the 2008 games in Beijing and contributed to steady development of the national team. However, a poor showing at the 2010 World Cup caused controversy when the country's president announced that he would be withdrawing the national team from international competition for two years following their early elimination. The ban was later rescinded under pressure from FIFA.

NORTH KOREA

Federation: DPR Korea Football Association
Founded: 1945
Joined FIFA: 1958
Confederation: AFC
FIFA world ranking: 103

Prior to the 1960s, football in the Democratic People's Republic of Korea was strictly a domestic sport, with any contact at international level limited to just the Communist countries. However, in 1966 North Korea entered the World Cup for the first time, qualifying for the finals after beating Australia in a play-off. The team astounded the world with their skill and sportsmanship, with Pak Doo Ik scoring a winning goal against the mighty Italy to take the Koreans into the quarter-finals against Portugal. North Korea took a 3-0 lead over the Portuguese through Park Seung-Zin, Li Dong Woon and Yang Sung Kook but ended up losing 5-3.

They did not qualify for the World Cup again until 2010, when they were impressive in defeat to Brazil but were beaten 7-0 by Portugal.

NORTHERN IRELAND

Federation: Irish Football Association
Founded: 1880
Joined FIFA: 1911
Confederation: UEFA
FIFA world ranking: 59

The Irish FA is the fourth oldest football federation in the world. Until 1923 it controlled the game throughout Ireland, competing under that name until 1953, when FIFA ruled that the team should become known as Northern Ireland to differentiate from the Republic Of Ireland, both of whom had entered the 1950 World Cup under the name Ireland.

In the early days they only played England, Scotland and Wales, usually in the annual Home International Championship that ran from 1884 to 1984, although they were far from successful, winning it outright just three times (in 1914, 1980 and 1984). They did not meet non-British opposition until 1951, soon after they stopped picking players from southern Ireland.

World Cup qualification in 1982 and 1986 showcased a talented generation that included Martin O'Neill, Gerry Armstrong, Pat Jennings, Sammy McIlroy and Norman Whiteside. However, the country's best World Cup performance was in 1958, when Danny Blanchflower led the team to the quarter-finals.

NEW ZEALAND

Federation: Soccer New Zealand
Founded: 1891
Joined FIFA: 1948
Confederation: OFC
FIFA world ranking: 117 (joint)
Honours: Oceania Nations Cup 1973, 1998, 2002, 2008

New Zealand's football team are known as the 'All Whites' to distinguish themselves from the dominant Rugby Union 'All Blacks'. They are now the leading force in the Oceania region following Australia's defection to the AFC. They have reached the World Cup twice, in 1982 and 2010, achieving their best ever result at the latter, holding reigning champions Italy to a draw.

NICARAGUA

Federation: Federación Nicaraguense de Fútbol
Founded: 1931
Joined FIFA: 1950
Confederation: CONCACAF
FIFA world ranking: 161

NIGER

Federation: Fédération Nigerienne de Football
Founded: 1967
Joined FIFA: 1967
Confederation: CAF
FIFA world ranking: 147 (joint)

THE COUNTRIES OF AFC

AFC — Asian Football Confederation

MONGOLIA

LEBANON

SYRIA

IRAN

IRAQ

JORDAN

KUWAIT

PALESTINE

SAUDI ARABIA

YEMEN

TURKMENISTAN

UZBEKISTAN

AFGHANISTAN

PAKISTAN

BAHRAIN

QATAR

UAE

OMAN

KYRGYSTAN

TAJIKISTAN

NEPAL

INDIA

MALDIVES

SRI LANKA

BANGLADESH

BHUTAN

MYANMAR

THAILAND

SINGAPORE

NORTH KOREA

SOUTH KOREA

CHINA

LAOS

MACAU

CHINESE TAIPEI

HONG KONG

CAMBODIA

VIETNAM

BRUNEI

MALAYSIA

JAPAN

GUAM

PHILIPPINES

INDONESIA

EAST TIMOR

AUSTRALIA

THE COUNTRIES OF OFC

VANUATU

SAMOA

AMERICAN SAMOA

SOLOMON ISLANDS

PAPUA NEW GUINEA

FIJI

TONGA

COOK ISLANDS

TAHITI

NEW CALEDONIA

NEW ZEALAND

There has been a league contested since 1891 but club football is semi-professional, with the best players leaving for careers in England and Scotland. There is also a sectarian element to football in Northern Ireland, with clubs such as Linfield and Cliftonville regarded as Protestant and Catholic respectively. George Best is still regarded as the country's greatest player, despite never having had the opportunity to represent his country at a major tournament.

NORWAY

Federation: Norges Fotballforbund
Founded: 1902
Joined FIFA: 1908
Confederation: UEFA
FIFA world ranking: 22

Football has been played in Norway since the 1890s. The oldest club, Odds BK of Skein, was formed in 1894 and a federation and cup competition were started in 1902. The national team debuted with an 11-3 away defeat by Sweden in 1908 and they did not win a game for ten years. They achieved success at the 1936 Olympics, beating Germany 2-0 in front of Adolf Hitler to pick up the bronze medal. However, it took the Norwegians a long time to achieve a breakthrough on the international stage.

After watching neighbours Denmark and Sweden make an impact on the game, Norway's national team started to get noticed in the 1990s, with qualification for the 1994 and 1998 World Cups. They even managed a 2-1 win over Brazil in the group stage of the 1998 finals, before losing to Italy in the next round.

This improvement coincided with an increase in the number of Norwegians making their name abroad. This was initially because they were proving cheaper to sign in the Eighties and Nineties, but it gave players such as Erik Thorstvedt, Stig Inge Bjornebye, Ole Gunnar

Below: Paraguay celebrate beating Japan on penalties at the 2010 World Cup.

Solksjaer and Tore Andre Flo the opportunity to win a host of honours.

Ironically, the domestic game in Norway has shifted from an open championship to being dominated by Rosenborg. The Trondheim club won the Norwegian title a record 13 successive times between 1992 and 2004 and have regularly featured in the Champions League.

OMAN

Federation: Oman Football Association
Founded: 1978
Joined FIFA: 1980
Confederation: AFC
FIFA world ranking: 81

PAKISTAN

Federation: Pakistan Football Federation
Founded: 1947
Joined FIFA: 1948
Confederation: AFC
FIFA world ranking: 163 (joint)

PALESTINE

Federation: Palestine Football Federation
Founded: 1928, 1962
Joined FIFA: 1998
Confederation: AFC
FIFA world ranking: 171

PANAMA

Federation: Federación Panameña de Fútbol
Founded: 1937
Joined FIFA: 1938
Confederation: CONCACAF
FIFA world ranking: 94
Honours: CONCACAF Championship 1951

Panama's national team entered the World Cup for the first time for the 1978 competition, but they have never come close to reaching the finals. They enjoyed success in 1951, when they

won the CCCF Championship, a forerunner of the Gold Cup. They had to wait until 2005 for another chance to be crowned champions of their region, when coach Jose Hernandez took them to the final of the Gold Cup. However, they lost 3-1 on penalties to the USA after a 0-0 draw.

PAPUA NEW GUINEA

Federation: Papua New Guinea Football Association
Founded: 1962
Joined FIFA: 1963
Confederation: OFC
FIFA world ranking: 202 (joint)

PARAGUAY

Federation: Asociacion Paraguaya de Futbol
Founded: 1906
Joined FIFA: 1925
Confederation: CONMEBOL
FIFA world ranking: 16
Honours: Copa América 1953, 1979

One of the stronger football nations of South America, Paraguay remain among the poorest and least glamorous. However, the national side can be proud of several successes. The Paraguayans have twice won the South American championship, in 1953 and 1979, and have featured at eight World Cups, including the 2010 finals in South Africa, when they reached the quarter-final before losing narrowly to Spain.

Five Paraguayan footballers have been voted South American Player Of The Year: Julio Cesar Romero (1985), Raul Vicente Amarilla (1990), Jose Luis Chilavert (1996), Jose Cardozo (2002), the national team's record goalscorer, and Salvador Cabañas (2007). Carlos Gamarra holds the country's international appearance record and in 2005 he became the first Paraguayan to win 100 caps.

The Paraguayan League with its 12-team Apertura and Clausura championships is played between February and December, with a hiatus during July. It is dominated by the Asuncion-based clubs, with Cerro Porteño, Guarani, Libertad, Nacional and Olimpia all hailing from the capital. Olimpia may not be the force they once were, but they have three Copa Libertadores triumphs (1979, 1990 and 2002) to add to their 38 Paraguayan league titles and their World Club Cup victory in 1980.

In recent years Argentine Gerardo Martino has been the most influential coach in the country. He claimed the league title several times between 2002 and 2006, with Libertad and Cerro Porteño, before leading the national team through their most successful World Cup campaign in 2010.

PERU

Federation: Federacion Peruana De Futbol
Founded: 1922
Joined FIFA: 1924
Confederation: CONMEBOL
FIFA world ranking: 38
Honours: Copa América 1939, 1975

Peru entered the international arena with a 4-0 defeat to Uruguay at the 1927 South American Championship. It was to be a forgettable start for the Peruvians, who went on to concede 26 goals in their first seven games. They did go on to win the tournament in 1939, and again in 1975, the first win of the Copa América era.

On the world stage Peru have only been a strong force in one period, qualifying for the World Cups of 1970, 1978 and 1982. Coached by former Brazil star Didi, the team reached the quarter-finals in 1970. The 1978 side included several memorable players, such as the eccentric keeper Ramon Quiroga, Hector Chumpitaz, and the real star of the side, Teófilo Cubillas. He inspired the team to the second phase of the tournament, successfully negotiating a group that included Iran, a talented Scotland side, and eventual runners-up Holland. Cubillas was particularly impressive in his side's 3-1 defeat of the Scots, scoring twice in the last 20 minutes.

The Peruvian capital has always been the heart of the nation's club football. The Lima-based league was traditionally the strongest in the country until a national championship was set up in 1966. Club football today continues to be dominated by the Lima teams Alianza, Universitario and Sporting Cristal, although another Lima side, Universidad San Martín, have also won the title in recent years.

Peruvian club have still to achieve success in the Copa Libertadores, although Universitario and Sporting Cristal have been runners-up, in 1971 and 1997 respectively.

PHILIPPINES

Federation: Philippine Football Federation
Founded: 1907
Joined FIFA: 1930
Confederation: AFC
FIFA world ranking: 167

POLAND

Federation: Polski Zwiazek Pilki Noznej
Founded: 1919
Joined FIFA: 1923
Confederation: UEFA
FIFA world ranking: 56
Honours: Olympics 1972

The Polish played their first international game in 1921 but had to wait 50 years for their team to come of age. Polish football peaked in the Seventies and early Eighties, with a stylish brand of attacking play that produced Olympic gold in 1972 and a series of excellent World Cup campaigns. The team registered third place at the World Cup of 1974 in West Germany after famously eliminating England in qualification, and again finished third in Spain in 1982.

During this golden era they could boast players of the calibre of Grzegorz Lato and Kazimierz Deyna, although injury ruled the nation's top scorer, Wlodzimierz Lubanski, out of the 1974 squad. By the 1982 World Cup only Lato, Marek Kusto, Andrzej Szarmach, and Wladyslaw Zmuda remained from the squad of 1974, but with the team including new Juventus signing Zbigniew Boniek, they were unlucky not to progress further than the semi-finals. However, they had to play the decisive match against Italy without Boniek, who had been suspended after a needless booking two minutes from the end of their previous game.

By the mid-Eighties Polish football had slid into decline, blighted by hooliganism and corruption. The national side failed to reach any tournament in the Nineties, and after finally qualifying for the 2002 and 2006 World Cups, the team performed poorly. Their results in 2002 so enraged one fan that he attempted to sue vocalist Edyta Gorniak for singing the national anthem too slowly and failing to inspire the team prior to their game with South Korea.

The first recorded football game in Poland was played in Lwow in 1894, while the sport really started to take off in the mining regions of Silesia in the early 20th Century. The country's first clubs, Lechia Lwow and Czarni Lwow, were formed in 1903, while Wisla Krakow and Cracovia (famous for being the team supported by Pope John Paul II) both formed in 1906.

After several seasons when a championship was organised as the culmination of a series of regional competitions, a nationwide league finally began in 1927, when it was won by Wisla Krakow. The league's most successful side has been Gornik Zabrze, while in the era of the Soviet bloc, army side Legia Warsaw and Widzew Lodz have been the only Polish teams to reach the semi-finals of the European Cup, in 1970 and 1983 respectively. Wisla Krakow are the country's most successful club of recent times, having won the league six times in the first decade of the 21st century.

Match-fixing and violence have continued to plague the game. In 2005 authorities began an investigation into the corruption within the game, resulting in numerous arrests, while a series of security initiatives were introduced in 2009 to try and rid the game of hooliganism.

PORTUGAL

Federation: Federação Portuguesa de Futebol
Founded: 1914
Joined FIFA: 1923
Confederation: UEFA
FIFA world ranking: 8

For a nation with such a passion for football and the ability to produce players of exceptional talent, Portugal's record on the international stage has been poor and it has only been in the 21st century that the Portuguese have finally become tournament regulars.

Football started to gain popularity in the country in the late 19th century, although a fully functioning national league did not begin until 1938. Prior to that the Portuguese champions had been decided by a cup competition. The national team played for the first time in December 1921, but it was not until 1966 that the Portuguese finally qualified for the finals of the World Cup, despite entering every tournament since 1934.

With a side featuring Eusébio, who scored nine goals at the 1966 finals, Portugal were unfortunate to be eliminated by hosts England. They finished third after beating the Soviet Union in the play-off, but rather than build on this success, it took the Portuguese 20 years to make another appearance. However, at the 1986 World Cup they failed at the first round stage, their players refusing to train at one point after a dispute with the federation. As a consequence Portugal attempted to qualify for the 1988 European Championship with their youth side.

Back-to-back World Youth Championship wins in 1989 and 1991 ushered in a group of young players, including Luis Figo, Rui Costa and Paulo Sousa, who were rapidly hailed as the 'Golden Generation'. Figo would later become World Player Of The Year and for a while the most expensive footballer on the planet. Once again, however, performances failed to outstrip expectations, although the team did progress to the semi-final of the European Championship in 2000, when a handball decision in sudden-death extra-time went against them and prompted acrimonious scenes. When the team finally qualified for another World Cup in 2002, inconsistency saw elimination by hosts South Korea and further displays of bad sportsmanship.

Euro 2004 offered the 'Golden Generation' a chance for redemption and under Brazilian World Cup winning coach Luiz Felipe Scolari they reached the final as hosts. However, in one of the biggest shocks in world football, they were beaten by Greece. Two years later Scolari took them to the semi-finals of the World Cup but they lost to France. Portugal have since struggled to match their potential, even with the world's most expensive player, Cristiano Ronaldo.

Domestic football is a tale of two cities and no club outside of Lisbon and Porto has ever won the league. In the capital Benfica figure largest in the game's history. Founded in 1904, 'The Eagles' have won the league title on more than 30 occasions and lifted the European Cup twice, in 1961 and 1962, inspired in the latter by the country's greatest player, Eusébio, whose statue stands outside the Stadium Of Light.

Sporting are the capital's other great side, but along with Benfica they have been playing second fiddle to FC Porto, who dominated Portuguese football in the first decade of 21st century, culminating in a UEFA Cup win in 2003 and Champions League success in 2004 (they had also won the European Cup in 1987). To underline the city's new found status, even Boavista managed a first ever league title in 2001.

Above: Robbie Keane of the Republic Of Ireland in 2009.

QATAR

Federation: Qatar Football Association
Founded: 1960
Joined FIFA: 1970
Confederation: AFC
FIFA world ranking: 76

REPUBLIC OF IRELAND

Federation: Football Association Of Ireland
Founded: 1921
Joined FIFA: 1923
Confederation: UEFA
FIFA world ranking: 36

PUERTO RICO

Federation: Federación Puertorriqueña de Fútbol
Founded: 1940
Joined FIFA: 1960
Confederation: CONCACAF
FIFA world ranking: 170

The Football Association Of Ireland was founded in 1921 following the division of the country into two separate entities, and it first entered a team into the World Cup in 1934, competing as the Irish Free State. After 1936 separate 'Ireland' teams were fielded by both the FAI in the south and by the Irish Football Association in the north,

Opposite: Portugal's Eusébio, takes on the Hungarian keeper during the 1966 World Cup.

167

with each organisation claiming to represent the whole of Ireland. Both Ireland teams contested qualification for the 1950 World Cup and both drew on players from the entire territory, including four players who represented both associations during the course of the campaign. To avoid this confusion, in 1953 FIFA ruled that the two associations should field players based on their political borders and that the FAI team should be known as the Republic Of Ireland.

The first internationals played by the Irish Free State were at the 1924 Olympics in Paris, and in 1949 they became the first non-British team to defeat England at home – a 2-0 win at Goodison Park. Although Ireland had entered all but the inaugural World Cup, they consistently failed to reach the finals, despite going close on at least a couple of occasions, and their record in the European Championship was similarly anaemic, although they had made it to the quarter-finals in 1964.

Ireland's fortunes changed with the arrival of Jack Charlton as manager in February 1986. Charlton scoured the English divisions looking for players with a family link strong enough to entitle them to play for the Republic (at least one grandparent of Irish extraction). Soon he had recruited players of the calibre of John Aldridge, Kevin Sheedy and Ray Houghton, and had steered the Irish to the finals of Euro 88 in West Germany. Although they were eliminated at the group stage, they did beat England 1-0, thanks to an early goal from Houghton and some inspired goalkeeping from Celtic's 'Packie' Bonner.

Ireland qualified for their first ever World Cup finals two years later and, having beaten Romania in a heart-stopping penalty shoot-out in the second round, reached the quarter-finals. It took a goal from the tournament's top scorer, Italy's Toto Schillaci, to halt their ambitions. They got their revenge at the 1994 World Cup by beating the Italians 1-0, but they were knocked out in the second round by Holland.

Charlton stepped down as manager in 1995 after failure to qualify for the following year's European Championship and was replaced by Mick McCarthy. Having negotiated a difficult qualification group that included both Portugal and Holland, Ireland overcame Iran in the play-offs to book their place at the 2002 World Cup. Unfortunately, their tournament was overshadowed by an ill-tempered spat between McCarthy and his captain, Roy Keane, who walked out on the team en route to the finals.

Keane returned home and announced his retirement from international football. Ireland went on to reach the second round, before being eliminated in a penalty shoot-out by Spain. Since then the Irish have failed to qualify for any major tournament.

The Irish league season runs from March to November and has benefited from the recent introduction of professionalism at the top level. Bohemians and Shelbourne have been the two powerhouses of recent times, each winning the title four times in the first decade of the 20th century. Cork City and Drogheda United have also enjoyed recent league success.

RUSSIA

Federation: Russian Football Union
Founded: 1912
Joined FIFA: 1912
Confederation: UEFA
FIFA world ranking: 17
Honours: European Championship 1960; Olympics 1956, 1988

After the break-up of the Soviet Union in 1991, Russia was recognised by FIFA as successor to the USSR's records and heritage in the game. The Soviets had produced some of the finest football teams that Europe had seen, winning the inaugural European Championship in 1960, finishing runners-up three times, and picking up Olympic gold in 1956 and 1988. They could also claim some of the world's greatest football talents and three Soviet players were voted European Footballer Of The Year: Lev Yashin in 1963, considered by many to be the finest goalkeeper of all time, plus Ukrainian forwards Oleg Blokhin (1975) and Igor Belanov (1986).

Domestically the Soviet game was dominated by Moscow clubs in the first half of the century and it was not until 1961 that a team from outside the capital won the title. It was Ukrainian side Dynamo Kiev who celebrated that year and by the dissolution of the Soviet Union in 1991, they

Below: Romania's Gheorghe Hagi during Euro 96.

ROMANIA

Federation: Federatia Romana de Fotbal
Founded: 1909
Joined FIFA: 1923
Confederation: UEFA
FIFA world ranking: 42

After playing at the first three World Cups, Romania failed to qualify again until 1970. However, in the Eighties and Nineties the country became a potent force, notably through Steaua Bucharest, their leading club, and Gheorghe Hagi, their most outstanding player.

Historically the army team, Steaua were founded in 1947 as ASA Bucharest and won their first trophies under a succession of names. They earned the right to be placed among the great clubs of Europe in the Eighties, lifting the European Cup in 1986 after beating Barcelona on penalties. The game may be remembered as a dour and goalless affair, but no-one in Bucharest was complaining. With Hagi added to the team, Steaua reached the final again in 1989 but lost heavily to Milan.

After the Romanian Revolution of 1989 and the fall of communist dictator Nicolae Ceausescu, Romanian players moved abroad in increasing numbers during the Nineties. Gheorghe Popescu was an elegant defender who starred for Barcelona among others, and striker Florin Raducioiu played in all five major European leagues, but the star was Hagi, a wonderfully gifted midfielder with a wicked left foot. Nicknamed the 'Maradona of the Carpathians', he was the driving force behind Romania's development and he helped them to all three World Cups in the Nineties, reaching the quarter-finals in 1994.

Hagi briefly retired from international football after the 1998 World Cup but returned to help the team to the quarter-finals of Euro 2000. However, the Romanian game has been in decline ever since, with the national team failing to qualify for a succession of tournament. Although they reached Euro 2008, they were knocked out in the group stage.

The domestic game has been dominated by Bucharest clubs Steaua, Dinamo and Rapid, but a breakthrough was made by outsiders CFR Cluj after major investment helped them gain promotion to the top flight in 2004. They have since won the league twice and celebrated a hat-trick of Romanian Cup victories.

ST LUCIA

Federation: St Lucia Football Association
Founded: 1979
Joined FIFA: 1988
Confederation: CONCACAF
FIFA world ranking: 188 (joint)

Left: Aleksandr Zavarov shoots for the Soviet Union at the 1988 Euro Championship final. Since the break up of the Soviet Union, Russia have struggled to make the same impact.

ST VINCENT AND THE GRENADINES

Federation: Saint Vincent and The Grenadines Football Federation
Founded: 1979
Joined FIFA: 1988
Confederation: CONCACAF
FIFA world ranking: 160

SAMOA

Federation: Football Federation Samoa
Founded: 1968
Joined FIFA: 1986
Confederation: OFC
FIFA world ranking: 176

SAN MARINO

Federation: Federazione Sammarinese Giuoco Calcio
Founded: 1931
Joined FIFA: 1988
Confederation: UEFA
FIFA world ranking: 202 (joint)

had won more league titles than any other club. Dynamo Moscow, meanwhile, became the first Soviet side to reach a European final, losing 3-2 to Rangers in the 1972 Cup Winners' Cup.

The Soviets had established a formidable reputation by that stage. Their 1960 European Championship triumph did not go unnoticed, even though the competition had not yet acquired profile that it would latter achieve. In the final they beat Yugoslavia 2-1 after extra-time, and they went on to reach the World Cup quarter-final in 1962 and the semi-final in 1966. Yashin was the undisputed star of the era and was the first Soviet player to attract worldwide recognition.

In 1975, with Oleg Blokhin at the peak of his powers, Dynamo Kiev beat Ferencváros 3-0 in the European Cup Winners' Cup final to earn Soviet club football its first continental trophy. A year later he was voted European Footballer Of The Year and he would have undoubtedly been a huge success in the major European leagues had he been allowed to leave his homeland.

Georgian club Dinamo Tbilisi also won the Cup Winners' Cup in 1981 and it was this generation of Soviet footballers that were most pleasing on the eye. Igor Belanov starred for both Dynamo Kiev and the Soviet Union in 1986, scoring late in the final of the Cup Winners' Cup to help his club beat Atlético Madrid. He also inspired the Soviets to impressive displays at the World Cup, hitting a hat-trick in the 4-3 second round defeat to Belgium. Aleksandr Zavarov was his able midfield deputy for both club and country at the time, while Rinat Dassayev was a worthy successor to Yashin in the Soviet goal.

In the Seventies and Eighties, Ukrainian-born coach Valery Lobanovsky was the mastermind behind the greatest performances of the Soviet team. He won bronze at the 1976 Olympics during the first of several spell in charge and he later took the team to the 1988 European Championship Final before losing to Holland. However, since the break-up of the Soviet Union, when the country's once powerful football structure disintegrated into 15 separate competing nations, the Russians have yet to match the kind of impact made by the Soviets on the world stage, even facing serious regional rivalry from Ukraine.

There have been highlights though. Although Russia failed to qualify for the 2010 World Cup, they did reach the semi-finals of Euro 2008 before losing to eventual winners Spain. In club football, Rubin Kazan have helped to break up the Moscow dominance of the league in recent times, while CSKA Moscow and Zenit Saint Petersburg have enjoyed success in the UEFA Cup, winning in 2005 and 2008 respectively. Exports such as Roman Pavlyuchenko and Andrei Arshavin have continued to impress.

RWANDA

Federation: Fédération Rwandaise de Football Association
Founded: 1972
Joined FIFA: 1978
Confederation: CAF
FIFA world ranking: 113

ST KITTS & NEVIS

Federation: St Kitts and Nevis Football Association
Founded: 1932
Joined FIFA: 1992
Confederation: CONCACAF
FIFA world ranking: 147 (joint)

Davide Gualteri holds the record for the quickest goal in international football, taking the lead for San Marino after 8.3 seconds against England in a World Cup qualifier in 1993. They went on to lose 7-1 and they have only ever won one game, a 2004 friendly against Liechtenstein. The Most Serene Republic Of San Marino, located within Northern Italy, has run a national amateur league and cup since 1985, featuring teams such as Tre Fiori, Murata and Domagnano, yet it is Gualteri's goal that remains the nation's highlight to date.

Opposite: Scotland's Willie
Johnstone in 1977.

SAO TOMÉ AND PRINCIPE

Federation: Federação Santomense de Futebol
Founded: 1975
Joined FIFA: 1986
Confederation: CAF
FIFA world ranking: –

SAUDI ARABIA

Federation: Saudi Arabia Football Federation
Founded: 1959
Joined FIFA: 1959
Confederation: AFC
FIFA world ranking: 68
Honours: Asian Cup 1984, 1988, 1996

Saudi Arabia is the greatest exporter of oil in the world and it is from this influx of wealth that football got the kickstart it needed in the Seventies. Millions of dollars were invested in state-of-the-art facilities, and clubs such as Al-Hilal, Al-Nasr and Al-Ahli began to thrive. Foreign coaches were lured to the country by the large salaries and in 1975 the first nationwide Saudi Arabian league championship began.

This investment began to pay dividends, as the Saudis won the Asian Cup in 1984 after beating China 2-0 in Singapore, with goals from Majed Abdullah and record goalscorer Shaye Al-Nafisa. They retained the trophy four years later, defeating South Korea 4-3 on penalties.

After winning the Under-17 World Cup in 1989, Saudi Arabian football relied on the best of this generation to inspire its future successes.

Below: Saudi Arabia players
celebrate a goal against Kuwait
in the 2009 Gulf Cup semi-final.

Four World Cups followed but none would be more eventful than the first in 1994, when they beat Morocco in the first ever all-Arab World Cup clash. Saeed Owairan also scored the best goal of the tournament against Belgium. In the round of 16 Fahad Al-Ghesheyan hit an impressive late consolation but Sweden finished 3-1 winners.

Goalkeeper Mohammed Al-Deayea holds the world international appearance record, having played 181 times for his country. He retired from international football after the 2006 World Cup.

SCOTLAND

Federation: Scottish Football Association
Founded: 1873
Joined FIFA: 1910-20, 1924-28, 1946
Confederation: UEFA
FIFA world ranking: 41

Scotland's first football clubs were formed in the 1860s and its football association was founded in 1873, making it the second oldest in world football. The national side were also involved in the first match in the history of international football. It was at home against England on November 30, 1872, and it began one of the world's great sporting rivalries. There had been several clashes between the two countries prior to that but as they were played in London using only London-based Scottish players, they have never been deemed official by the Scottish FA.

The first game ended goalless but unlike rivals England, the Scots never went on to taste glory at the highest level. Despite consistently qualifying for the World Cup, Scotland have often underperformed against teams they should have beaten, while performing heroically against far stronger opposition.

The Scots qualified for their first ever World Cup in 1950 after finishing runners-up in the British Home Internationals tournament but they chose not to attend, insisting they would only want to go to Brazil as British champions.

Perhaps the Scotland team that should have had most impact on the international stage was the one that went to the World Cup in Argentina under Ally MacLeod in 1978. A decent outside bet, it was a side packed with talented players, many based in the English top flight, such as Kenny Dalglish, Graeme Souness, Joe Jordan, Archie Gemmill, Don Masson and Bruce Rioch.

MacCleod recklessly promised that Scotland would bring the World Cup home, a bold claim he would live to regret. Scotland disappointed, both on and off the field, losing to Peru and scraping a draw with Iran before beating eventual finalists Holland and almost, but not quite, qualifying for the second stage. To make matters worse, winger Willie Johnston was sent home in disgrace after failing a dope test.

The country's most celebrated win came not in a major tournament but in 1967 against the 'Auld Enemy', England. The world champions, undefeated since lifting the trophy the previous year, were beaten 3-2 by the skill and guile of Scottish legends Jim Baxter, Billy Bremner and Denis Law, allowing fans to proclaim their team 'unofficial world champions'.

Recent times have seen the rapid demise of Scottish football at international level. The main reason often cited for this decline is that there are too many foreign players preventing young, local talent from getting top-flight experience.

At club level, Scottish football has historically been dominated by the 'Old Firm' of Celtic and Rangers, possibly the fiercest rivalry in club football anywhere in the world. Other clubs have had brief stays at the top, notably Edinburgh sides Hibernian and Hearts in the Fifties and Sixties, while in the early Eighties it seemed that the 'New Firm' of Aberdeen and Dundee United had broken the stranglehold. Aberdeen won three league titles, four Scottish Cups and a European Cup Winners' Cup in a six year period, while Dundee United won their first title in 1983. Normal service was resumed by the 'Old Firm' in the second half of the decade and ever since it has been either Celtic or Rangers carving up the league title between them.

In European competition both sides have struggled to replicate their domestic success. Celtic made history in 1967 when they became the first British side to lift the European Cup, beating Inter Milan. They were runners up in 1970 and they also reached the final of the UEFA Cup in 2003. Rangers' only European triumph came in the 1972 Cup Winners' Cup.

SENEGAL

Federation: Fédération Sénégalaise de Football
Founded: 1960
Joined FIFA: 1962
Confederation: CAF
FIFA world ranking: 91

Under French coach Bruno Metsu, Senegal caused a sensation with their first appearance at the World Cup finals in 2002, beating holders France 1-0 in the tournament's opening game. Midfielder Pape Bouba Diop beat France's galaxy of stars to score the first goal, but it was striker El Hadji Diouf who would receive the most accolades. Earlier the same year, the 'Lions of Teranga' had reached the final of the African Nations Cup, losing to Cameroon on penalties. The success owed much to Metsu's predecessor Peter Schnittger, who had been appointed in 1995 to structure a development programme for both the national team and the club game.

SERBIA

Federation: Football Association of Serbia
Founded: 1919
Joined FIFA: 1923
Confederation: UEFA
FIFA world ranking: 13 (joint)
Honours: Olympics 1960 *(as Yugoslavia)*

Following the break-up of Socialist Federal Republic of Yugoslavia in 1991, the present day Serbia was the football nation nominated by FIFA as the direct descendant of Yugoslavia's national team. The country's other constituent parts, Bosnia-Herzegovina, Croatia, Macedonia and Slovenia each formed separate international teams, none of which lay claim to Yugoslavia's heritage in the game. Initially both Serbia and Montenegro played on as the Federal Republic of Yugoslavia, qualifying for the 2002 World Cup. The country was officially renamed Serbia and Montenegro in 2003 and although they competed under that name at the 2006 World Cup, the two nations separated immediately afterwards, leaving Serbia to play on alone.

In their day, Yugoslavia had one of the most exciting teams in Europe. They were serious contenders to win Euro 92 but by the time the finals were due to kick-off the country was in the midst of a bloody civil war and most of the non-Serbian players had refused to take part, leading UEFA to expel them from the competition.

The country of Yugoslavia did not exist until after the First World War, but several clubs in Serbia did, and a Yugoslav championship began in 1923. However, it was not until after the Second World War, with the country under communist rule, that the league began to take real shape, with Serbian clubs Red Star Belgrade and Partizan Belgrade often dominating. In 1991, Red Star became the first and only Yugoslav side to win the European Cup when they beat Marseille 5-3 on penalties after a goalless draw.

Yugoslavia were one of only four European sides to play at the first World Cup in 1930, although they fielded a predominantly Serbian team after Croatian players refused to take part. They contested the football final at the Olympic Games on four successive occasions but won only once, in 1960, when they beat Denmark 3-1. They reached the World Cup semi-final twice (1930 and 1962), the quarter-finals on three occasions (1954, 1958 and 1990), and in 1968 they also reached the European Championship final, but lost to hosts Italy after a replay.

Since 2006 Serbia have competed as an independent nation, often needing to rely on solid teamwork rather than the flair players of the Yugoslav era. They pulled off their biggest shock at the 2010 World Cup, beating Germany in a group game. However, they still finished bottom of their group. The domestic league in Serbia continues to be dominated by the Belgrade clubs, Red Star and Partizan.

SEYCHELLES

Federation: Seychelles Football Federation
Founded: 1979
Joined FIFA: 1986
Confederation: CAF
FIFA world ranking: 177 (joint)

SIERRA LEONE

Federation: Sierra Leone Football Association
Founded: 1967
Joined FIFA: 1967
Confederation: CAF
FIFA world ranking: 139

SINGAPORE

Federation: Football Association of Singapore
Founded: 1892
Joined FIFA: 1952
Confederation: AFC
FIFA world ranking: 121 (joint)

SLOVAKIA

Federation: Slovenský Futbalový Zväz
Founded: 1993
Joined FIFA: 1907, 1994
Confederation: UEFA
FIFA world ranking: 27

Between 1939 and 1944 Slovakia competed as an independent state and ran a short-lived league. It was won four times by Slovan Bratislava, who were one of the region's strongest teams in the subsequent Czechoslovakian league up until 1992. Since then teams such as Kosice and MSK Zilina have also taken the honours. Slovakia qualified for the 2010 World Cup, losing to Holland in the second round.

SLOVENIA

Federation: Nogometna Zveza Slovenije
Founded: 1920
Joined FIFA: 1992
Confederation: UEFA
FIFA world ranking: 19

Slovenian clubs made no impact on the league in Yugoslavia but since independence in 1992, the national team has defied the odds to qualify for the finals of the European Championship in 2000 and the World Cups of 2002 and 2010.

Below: Serbia's Milos Krasic shoots against Australia at the 2010 World Cup.

SOLOMON ISLANDS

Federation: Solomon Islands Football Federation
Founded: 1978
Joined FIFA: 1988
Confederation: OFC
FIFA world ranking: 169

SOMALIA

Federation: Somalia Football Federation
Founded: 1951
Joined FIFA: 1960
Confederation: CAF
FIFA world ranking: 173 (joint)

SOUTH AFRICA

Federation: South African Football Association
Founded: 1892, 1991
Joined FIFA: 1952-76, 1992
Confederation: CAF
FIFA world ranking: 66 (joint)
Honours: African Nations Cup 1996

Football has been played in South Africa since the 1870s but the progress of the game was hindered for many years by the existence of apartheid, which resulted in a succession of FIFA suspensions and bans. In 1992 South Africa returned to international football and with the formation of the new, multi-racial South African Football Association, the country was readmitted to FIFA. They subsequently won the African Nations Cup in 1996, finished runners-up the following year, and qualified for the 1998 and 2002 World Cups, although they failed to reach the second round on both occasions.

After controversially losing out to Germany in their attempt to stage the 2006 World Cup, South Africa benefited from FIFA's short-lived policy of rotating the tournament between the confederations when they were chosen to host the 2010 competition from an African-only shortlist that also included Morocco and Egypt. The tournament proved to be a success for the country and although they failed to reach the second round once again, Siphiwe Tshabalala scored the World Cup's opening goal against Mexico and the team provided one of the shocks

of the tournament when they finished above France in their group after beating Les Bleus 2-1.

Domestic football in South Africa has had a long and convoluted history. The all-white National Football League kicked-off in 1959, while the highly successful but non-white National Professional Soccer League was formed in the early Seventies. The two leagues merged in 1978, but the domestic game was dogged by disputes and splits until the formation of the Premier Soccer League in 1996. Mamelodi Sundowns and SuperSport United have been the most successful club in the PSL era.

SOUTH KOREA

Federation: Korea Football Association
Founded: 1928
Joined FIFA: 1948
Confederation: AFC
FIFA world ranking: 44
Honours: Asian Cup 1956, 1960

South Korea gave Asian football a huge boost by finishing fourth at the 2002 World Cup, a competition that they co-hosted with Japan. This was an amazing feat for a country that had failed to win a single match in their five previous World Cups. Backed by stunning home support, and coached by Dutchman Guus Hiddink, the

Koreans overcame their inferiority complex and all of the pre-tournament predictions to top their group with a 1-0 defeat of Portugal, in a game that was estimated to have been watched on television by 75 per cent of Korean households. A sensational 2-1 second round win over Italy followed and a tense 5-3 penalty shoot-out overcame Spain, but it was the Germans who finally put paid to the dream in the semi-final.

In comparison South Korea were somewhat disappointing at the finals four years later, failing to progress beyond the group stage. However, they reached the second round again at the 2010 World Cup before losing to Uruguay.

The South Koreans have long been a force in Asian football, although not always as winners. They produce many talented young players and have won the Asian Under-19 title on 11 occasions. The creation of a professional league in 1983 (later the K-League) lifted Korean football and accounted for a development of the game that resulted in qualification for seven successive World Cups from 1986 onwards.

Investment from business has helped clubs and it is evident in team names such as Suwon Samsung Bluewings and Jeonbuk Hyundai Motors. However, this financial backing has not always translated into high wages and many star players have moved abroad.

South Korea's greatest player was Hong Myung-Bo, who played in four successive World Cups and won a host of domestic honours, while Kim Joo-Sung was voted Asian Player Of The Year three times in a row.

Above: South Africa's winning team celebrate victory in the African Nations Cup with Nelson Mandela in 1996.

1889: Recreativo de Huelva is founded as Huelva Recreation Club, making it Spain's first and oldest football club.

1902: The Spanish Cup is established.

1904: Spain become a founding member of FIFA.

1913: The Real Federacion Española de Futbol is formed, with King Alfonso XIII as honorary president.

1928: The modern league championship emerges with ten teams competing.

1929: Barcelona win the first-ever Spanish league title, Real Madrid are runners-up.

1936-39: La Liga is suspended during the Spanish Civil War.

1956: Real Madrid win the first of five consecutive European Cups.

1960: In the European Championship, Spain draw the Soviet Union, but General Franco withdraws his side for political reasons.

1964: Spain win the European Championship in front of 125,000 fans in Madrid.

1982: A talented Spanish side fail to get past the second round of the World Cup on home soil.

1984: Spain reach the final of the European Championship but lose to France.

1992: Barcelona win their first European Cup, beating Sampdoria 1-0.

2006: Barcelona win the Champions League final in Paris.

2008: A goal from Fernando Torres wins the European Championship for Spain during a record unbeaten run stretching 35 games.

2010: The Spanish win the World Cup for the first time after beating Holland in extra-time.

SPAIN

Federation: Real Federación Española de Fútbol
Founded: 1913
Joined FIFA: 1904
Confederation: UEFA
FIFA world ranking: 1
Honours: World Cup 2010; European Championship 1964, 2008; Olympics 1992

Football came to Spain in the late 19th century through British shipyard workers and miners operating in the country, particularly around the northern ports. Bilbao, the industrial port closest to England, became one of the first places associated with the game in Spain and the city's flagship side, Athletic Bilbao, display their English roots to this day in the club's colours.

The game spread quickly among students in the port towns and industrial cities. In the early years Barcelona, Irun, Gijon, Seville, La Coruna and Valencia could all boast teams but Recreativo de Huelva hold the honour of being the first club, as they were formed in Andalucia by British miners in 1889. They played Spain's first recorded football match against a side from Seville the same year, although only two players on the pitch were Spanish.

Real Madrid, known simply as Madrid FC, and Atlético Madrid were formed in the capital just after the turn of the century but with the exception of Real, the game failed to make the same kind of impact in the Spanish interior that it was making in the port towns.

It was as late as 1913, under the honorary presidency of King Alfonso XIII, that a number of regional associations consolidated to form the nationwide Real Federación Española de Fútbol. Yet thanks to the representatives of Madrid FC, Spain had already become a founding member of FIFA, while the Spanish Cup, which had started 11 years earlier, was already thriving.

Indeed, it was predicted the cup would have greater longevity than a league given the amount of time it took to get one organised. After the emergence of several regional championships, a nationwide league did not begin in its modern form until the 1928-9 season, and although professionalism had been introduced to the Spanish game several years earlier, when the league began just ten clubs were selected by the Spanish football federation to compete for the main prize. Barcelona overtook their Madrid rivals on the last day of the season to win the first championship by just two points.

By this time Madrid FC had been gifted the prefix 'Real', meaning 'royal', by King Alfonso. The most ambitious club in the league, Real Madrid invested heavily in chasing the championship and won it for the first time in 1932, having signed former Barcelona keeper

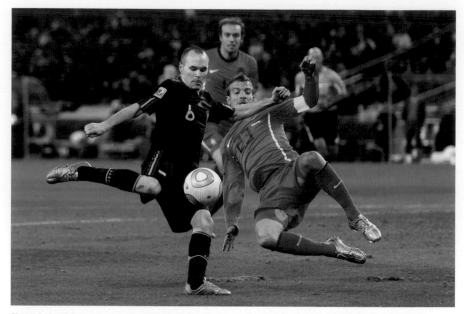

Above: Andres Iniesta scores in the 2010 World Cup Final. Opposite clockwise from top left: Emilio Butragueno; Cesc Fabregas lift the trophy at Euro 2008; Raul at the 2002 World Cup; Carles Puyol with the World Cup trophy in 2010.

Ricardo Zamora the previous season for the kind of price tag more commonplace in the financially buoyant English league. Adding another former Barcelona star, Pepe Samitier, the following year, Real retained the title in 1933.

The Spanish Civil War between 1936 and 1939 ravaged the country and political divisions were even evident in the football arena in the bitter rivalry that had grown between Barcelona and Real Madrid. As the flagship side of Catalonia, a region seeking independence from Spain, Barcelona associated their rivals with fascist dictator General Franco, a Real supporter, and once the league resumed in 1939, matches between the two sides proved to be bruising affairs. To further fuel the antipathy, teams from the Basque provinces also had their own agenda, and to this day Athletic Bilbao will only employ players with a direct connection to the region.

The disdain between clubs only served to establish the Spanish league as one of the most competitive in Europe and by the Fifties Barcelona and Real Madrid were leading the way with seven titles in the decade between them. Both were also regularly achieving crowds approaching the 100,000 mark and with their dominance unrivalled, the logical step was to test themselves against the continent's finest clubs, with Real proving the most successful.

Following the inception of the European Cup in 1956, Real Madrid won the competition five times in succession, with Alfredo Di Stéfano scoring in all five finals, including a hat-trick in the 7-3 victory over Eintracht Frankfurt in the 1960 game (he was outdone by Ferenc Puskás, who scored four). Although Barcelona won the Fairs Cup in 1958, they would not win the European Cup until 1992, when a Ronald Koeman free-kick defeated Sampdoria 1-0. Despite winning the trophy twice more, their tally is dwarfed by the nine European Cup and Champions League titles boasted by Real.

Today, the Spanish league is widely regarded as one of the best in Europe and this is not only reflected in the exciting football on display but also by the contribution its clubs have made to the Champions League in recent times. Real Madrid won three of the five finals between 1998 and 2002, Barcelona won the trophy in 2006 and 2009, while Valencia finished runners-up in both the 2000 and 2001 finals.

Despite a flourishing league, it has only been late in the first decade of the 21st century that the national team has finally been able to justify Spanish pretensions to being one of the world's strongest football powers. For many years Spain were the great underachievers of the international game, with their 1964 European Championship victory against the Soviet Union standing testament to their only success, and even that was achieved with home advantage. Although they reached the final once more in 1984, when they were defeated by France, the Spanish would not lift the trophy again until 2008, when coach Luis Aragonés led a talented side to victory over Germany.

Vicente Del Bosque took over from Aragonés after the final and continued Spain's unbeaten run, which he stretched to 35 games, equalling Brazil's world record in the quarter-final of the Confederations Cup in 2009. However, the run ended with a shock defeat to the United States in the following game. The team still qualified for the 2010 World Cup with a 100 per cent record, scoring nearly three goals a game.

At the tournament in South Africa they were shocked by a 1-0 defeat to Switzerland in their opening game but thanks to their attractive possession football they would only concede one more goal in the competition. They beat Holland in the final, thanks to an extra-time strike from Andrés Iniesta, and became only the third side to hold both the World Cup and the European Championship at the same time.

SRI LANKA

Federation: The Football Federation of Sri Lanka
Founded: 1939
Joined FIFA: 1952
Confederation: AFC
FIFA world ranking: 155

SUDAN

Federation: Sudan Football Association
Founded: 1936
Joined FIFA: 1948
Confederation: CAF
FIFA world ranking: 121 (joint)

SURINAM

Federation: Surinaamse Voetbal Bond
Founded: 1920
Joined FIFA: 1929
Confederation: CONCACAF
FIFA world ranking: 123

SWAZILAND

Federation: National Football Association of Swaziland
Founded: 1968
Joined FIFA: 1978
Confederation: CAF
FIFA world ranking: 134

SWEDEN

Federation: Svenska Fotbollförbundet
Founded: 1904
Joined FIFA: 1904
Confederation: UEFA
FIFA world ranking: 35
Honours: Olympics 1948

In football terms, Sweden – with a population in 2009 of nine million and a domestic game that turned professional very late – have always punched above their weight on the international stage. The Swedish FA formed in 1904 and it was a founding member of FIFA. The national team qualified for the World Cup for the first time in 1934 and shocked Argentina 3-2 on the way to the quarter-finals, where they were edged out 2-1 by Germany. They went one better in 1938, reaching the semi-finals, where they were defeated 5-1 by Hungary, before going down 4-2 to Brazil in the third-place play-off.

In 1948 Englishman George Raynor was appointed national team coach, and he led the Swedes to a gold medal at the 1948 London Olympics. However, success was costly for Swedish football, as several of the country's top players turned professional to play in Italy's lucrative Serie A. With strict rules barring players if they made their living abroad, Raynor was missing many of his Olympic champions for the 1950 World Cup in Brazil, yet the newly remodelled team pulled off a major surprise by beating Italy's professional stars 3-2. Despite a crushing 7-1 defeat by Brazil in the Final Pool, the Swedes went on to pip Spain to third place.

Despite the continuing player drain, Raynor coached the team to a bronze medal at the 1952 Olympics in Helsinki but by the time they took part in the 1958 World Cup Finals as hosts, the Swedish FA had finally amended its selection rules. As a result Raynor was able to field what many claim to be Sweden's best ever team, with previously barred veterans such as Gunnar Gren and Nils Liedholm returning to international action, along with young professionals such as and Kurt Hamrin. Buoyed by home advantage and a strong team spirit, they finished as runners-up, defeating Hungary and the Soviet Union along the way. They beat ten-man West Germany in the semi-final but were cut down to size by Brazil in the final, losing 5-2.

Since those heady days Sweden have regularly qualified for the World Cup without the same level of success, although under highly-regarded coach Tommy Svensson they shocked many observers by finishing third at the 1994 World Cup before losing out to eventual winners Brazil in the semi-final by a single goal.

Sweden have only qualified for the finals of the European Championship on four occasions:

Below: Sweden celebrate a penalty shoot-out victory over Romania in the 1994 World Cup semi-final.

Left: Gelson Fernandes on the ball as Switzerland beat Spain at the 2010 World Cup.

in 1992, 2000, 2004 and 2008. As hosts they were semi-finalists in 1992, losing 3-2 to Germany, and they were quarter-finalists in 2004 before losing to Holland on penalties.

For many years domestic football in Sweden was predominantly amateur. Since a nationwide league was first introduced in 1925, the most successful clubs have been IFK Gothenburg and Malmö. Gothenburg were the country's most dominant side in the Eighties and Nineties and represented Sweden in Europe, winning the UEFA Cup in 1982 and 1987, while Malmö were runners-up in the European Cup and the World Club Cup in 1979.

SWITZERLAND

Federation: Schweizerischer Fussballverband
Founded: 1895
Joined FIFA: 1904
Confederation: UEFA
FIFA world ranking: 18

Switzerland is the home to both the European and world governing bodies of football, UEFA and FIFA, and the Swiss were influential in the formation of each organisation. They had plenty of experience, having been introduced to football by the English as early as the 1860s. The first club to be formed was St Gallen in 1879 and although a Swiss championship was contested as early as 1898, a national league did not kick-off until 1934. Switzerland played internationals from 1905 and in the first half of the century had a strong team, winning an Olympic silver medal in 1924 and reaching the World Cup quarter-finals in 1934 and 1938.

Tactics were revolutionised in the Thirties by Switzerland's Austrian coach, Karl Rappan, when he devised the 'Swiss Bolt', a forerunner of the sweeper system, but after the war the Swiss

game went into decline. The national side was not helped by the rivalry between the French, German and Italian communities of the country, who historically have accused coaches of bias.

The Swiss reached the second round of the 1994 World Cup under Roy Hodgson, while at the 2006 finals they were only knocked out in the round of 16 after a penalty shoot-out defeat to Ukraine. They became the first team to exit a World Cup without conceding a single goal, having never kept a clean sheet in 22 World Cup games prior to 2006. Their run continued at the 2010 finals but ended moments after they had broken the World Cup record for the most consecutive minutes without conceding a goal.

Switzerland hosted the 1954 World Cup but were knocked out 7-5 by Austria in the quarter-finals, and together with Austria, co-hosted the 2008 European Championship.

SYRIA

Federation: Syrian Arab Federation for Football
Founded: 1936
Joined FIFA: 1937
Confederation: AFC
FIFA world ranking: 92

TAHITI

Federation: Fédération Tahitienne de Football
Founded: 1989
Joined FIFA: 1990
Confederation: OFC
FIFA world ranking: 188 (joint)

TAJIKISTAN

Federation: Tajikistan National Football Federation
Founded: 1936
Joined FIFA: 1994
Confederation: AFC
FIFA world ranking: 137

TANZANIA

Federation: Tanzania Football Federation
Founded: 1930
Joined FIFA: 1964
Confederation: CAF
FIFA world ranking: 112

THAILAND

Federation: Football Association of Thailand
Founded: 1916
Joined FIFA: 1925
Confederation: AFC
FIFA world ranking: 105

Below: Thailand's Suchao Nutnum holds off a Jordan player in 2010.

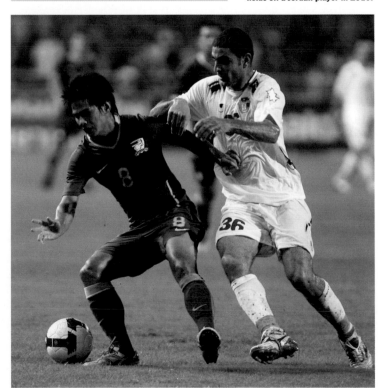

Above: Emmanuel Adebayor (left) of Togo attempts to get past an Angola player in 2009.

TONGA

Federation: Tonga Football Association
Founded: 1965
Joined FIFA: 1994
Confederation: OFC
FIFA world ranking: 186

TRINIDAD AND TOBAGO

Federation: Trinidad and Tobago Football Federation
Founded: 1908
Joined FIFA: 1963
Confederation: CONCACAF
FIFA world ranking: 76

With a population of 1.2 million, Trinidad and Tobago became the smallest country to qualify for the World Cup in 2006, having already come close in 1974, 1990 and 2002. The 'Soca Warriors' have won the Caribbean Cup on eight occasions, while club side Defence Force have won the CONCACAF Champions Cup twice, in 1978 (shared) and 1985.

Football was amateur on the islands until 1996 when a semi-pro league was created. Since the Professional Football League came into being in 1999, the title has been won by Defence Force, Williams Connection, San Juan Jabloteh, North East Stars and Joe Public. The number of teams in the league has varied, but in 2010 it was contested by ten teams from the island of Trinidad and one from Tobago.

TUNISIA

Federation: Fédération Tunisienne de Football
Founded: 1956
Joined FIFA: 1960
Confederation: CAF
FIFA world ranking: 65
Honours: African Nations Cup 2004

Tunisia won the African Nations Cup for the first time in 2004, beating Morocco 2-1 in the final. They had previously been losing finalists in 1965 and 1996. Under coach Roger Lemerre, who guided France to the European Championship in 2000, Tunisia maintained their position as one of Africa's leading football nations and in 2006 qualified for their third successive World Cup, their fourth in all. Tunisia were the first African team to win a match at the World Cup when they beat Mexico 3-1 in 1978.

Tunisian sides Club Africain and Esperance have both won the African Champions Cup, in 1991 and 1994 respectively, while Étoile Sahel won the competition in 2007 when it had been renamed the Champions League. The country's clubs have also enjoyed considerable success in the CAF Confederation Cup, as well as former continental competitions the CAF Cup and the African Cup Winners' Cup.

In domestic football Esperance have been the most successful club side and they won all but three league titles between 1998 and 2010. Many Tunisian players have established careers in Europe, particularly in France, but despite the country's reputation for producing talented players, only one Tunisian has been voted African Player Of The Year: Tarak Dhiab in 1977.

TURKEY

Federation: Turkiye Futbol Federasyonu
Founded: 1923
Joined FIFA: 1923
Confederation: UEFA
FIFA world ranking: 28

Football had a hard time in establishing itself in Turkey as the rulers of the Ottoman Empire disliked a game that had been introduced by the British. However, once Turkey was declared a republic in 1923, a football federation was formed, regional competition was launched, and the national team debuted the same year.

A nationwide, professional league began in 1959 but despite being able to claim a fiercely contested domestic championship, it was not until the Nineties that Turkish teams began to make an impact on a wider stage. The first real indication of this came in 2000 when Galatasaray, Turkey's leading club alongside Besiktas and Fenerbahçe, won the UEFA Cup.

The national team managed to qualify for their first European Championship in 1996, and in 2002 they also made it to the World Cup after an absence of 48 years, finishing a creditable third. They were unable to build on this success, failing to qualify for the finals of 2006 and 2010.

Turkish fans have been known to create one of the most intimidating atmospheres in football and on occasion this has been mirrored by tensions on the field. Such a situation occurred after play-off defeat to Switzerland ended the team's 2006 World Cup ambitions. As a result Turkey were ordered to play all of their home Euro 2008 qualifiers behind closed doors. However, this did not prevent them reach the semi-finals of the tournament before losing to Germany through a last minute goal.

TOGO

Federation: Fédération Togolaise de Football
Founded: 1960
Joined FIFA: 1962
Confederation: CAF
FIFA world ranking: 75

A national holiday was called when Togo reached the 2006 World Cup. The West African nations were shock qualifiers from a continent where they are not considered major players. However, they went into their first match at the finals having just persuaded coach Otto Pfister to return to his post after walking out a few days earlier. When they finally took to the pitch Togo took an early lead against South Korea but exited the tournament after losing all three games.

Nicknamed the 'Sparrow Hawks', they had previously appeared at six African Nations Cup tournaments and had never gone beyond the first round. Qualifying for the World Cup was by far Togo's greatest football success, with the 1987 African Youth Cup Final appearance and Emmanuel Adebayor's 2008 African Player Of The Year Award the other most significant football achievements for the country.

In January 2010 the Togo squad were the victims of a terrorist attack while en route to the 2010 African Nations Cup. A bus carrying the team came under gunfire and three passengers were killed, including assistant coach Amelete Abalo. Togo withdrew from the competition but were suspended from the two subsequent tournaments as punishment for their withdrawal. In protest, Emmanuel Adebayor retired from international football.

AC Semassi have been the most successful team in the history of Togo's league, although they have not won the championship since 1999. At the end of the 2000s, ASKO Kara won successive title when coached by Amelete Abalo.

TURKS & CAICOS ISLANDS

Federation: Turks and Caicos Islands Football Association
Founded: 1996
Joined FIFA: 1998
Confederation: CONCACAF
FIFA world ranking: 182 (joint)

TURKMENISTAN

Federation: Football Federation of Turkmenistan
Founded: 1992
Joined FIFA: 1994
Confederation: AFC
FIFA world ranking: 136

UGANDA

Federation: Federation of Uganda Football Associations
Founded: 1924
Joined FIFA: 1959
Confederation: CAF
FIFA world ranking: 70

UKRAINE

Federation: Football Federation of Ukraine
Founded: 1991
Joined FIFA: 1992
Confederation: UEFA
FIFA world ranking: 25

Until independence in 1991 Ukraine was one of the strongest football territories of the Soviet Union and its most talented players often formed the backbone of the Soviet team. However, in the early years of independence many Ukrainian stars, such as Viktor Onopko and Andrei Kanchelskis, opted to play for Russia, which had been nominated as the natural successor to the Soviet team.

Without their stars Ukraine initially struggled. Although continuing to produce players of the calibre of Sergei Rebrov and Andriy Shevchenko, they faltered in the play-offs for both the 1998 and 2002 World Cups, but their fortunes took an upturn when they reached the quarter-final of the 2006 finals.

Dynamo Kiev are Ukraine's most successful club, having won 16 Soviet league titles, the European Cup Winners' Cup in 1975 and 1986, and dominated the Ukrainian league since its inception in 1992. Only Shakhtar Donetsk have provided a serious challenge, breaking Dynamo's domination with a series of title wins in the first decade of the 21st century. They also lifted the UEFA Cup in 2009.

Three Ukrainians have been voted European Footballer Of The Year. Oleg Blokhin, the coach who took the national team to the 2006 World Cup, received the award in 1975, and Igor Belanov repeated the feat in 11 years later. Andriy Shevchenko, in 2004, is the only Ukrainian to have been honoured since independence.

UNITED ARAB EMIRATES

Federation: United Arab Emirates Football Association
Founded: 1971
Joined FIFA: 1972
Confederation: AFC
FIFA world ranking: 88

Until the formation of the United Arab Emirates in 1971, football was not taken seriously in the region. As the sport developed, many leading coaches were enticed to the country by the financial rewards. Don Revie was among the recruits but it was under Brazilian World Cup winner Mario Zagalo that the UAE qualified for the 1990 World Cup. However, he was sacked before the tournament after making disparaging remarks about the team's chances and it was another Brazilian, Carlos Alberto Parreira, who led the team to the finals. They lost all of their games and have not qualified since.

UNITED STATES

Federation: United States Soccer Federation
Founded: 1913
Joined FIFA: 1914
Confederation: CONCACAF
FIFA world ranking: 13
Honours: CONCACAF Championship 1991, 2002, 2005, 2007

A form of 'soccer' was introduced in the USA in Boston as early as 1862 but in its formative years it resembled rugby. In 1884 the American Football Association was formed, in affiliation with the English FA, to bring the game into line with the rules played in England. European immigrants filled most teams, mainly on the eastern seaboard, and leagues appeared and disappeared with regularity.

The formation in 1913 of the American Amateur Football Association (much later to become the US Soccer Federation) saw affiliation to FIFA and the beginnings of an American Soccer League. The national team even reached the semi-final of the inaugural World Cup in 1930 but the sport still failed to capture the imagination of a country brought up on American football and baseball.

Few eyebrows were raised when the American Soccer League folded in 1933. Regional leagues continued but even the national team's famous 1-0 victory against England at the 1950 World Cup failed to stir much interest in the game.

The formation of the North American Soccer League in 1968 brought the game to the mainstream and in the Seventies the league attracted numerous big name stars in the twilight of their careers, such as Pelé, Franz Beckenbauer and Johan Cruyff. Attendances boomed, yet when these football legends hung up their boots, the crowds tailed-off. The league may have been disbanded in 1984 but the NASL had succeeded in making football one of most popular youth participation sports in the country.

FIFA awarded the 1994 World Cup to the USA, making the creation of a professional, nationwide league a precondition. Major League Soccer was founded the year before the finals and since hosting the 1994 World Cup, football in the United States has thrived. The national team

Below: USA's Kasey Keller and Frankie Hejduk hold up the Gold Cup in 2005.

Above: Uruguay's Diego Forlan scores against South Africa from the penalty spot during the 2010 World Cup.

decide the champions. It ended up in an all-or-nothing showdown with hotly fancied hosts Brazil in front of a packed Maracanã stadium and despite falling behind early in the second-half, Uruguay clinched their second World Cup in 20 years with goals from Juan Schiaffino and Alcides Ghiggia.

They reached the semi-finals in both 1954 and 1970, and the quarter-finals in 1966, but there was no doubting that Uruguay's World Cup star was on the wane as their appearances at the finals became far less frequent. They even failed to qualify for the 2006 finals after losing to outsiders Australia on penalties in a play-off.

They would finally revitalise their tarnished reputation at the 2010 World Cup in South Africa. Although they needed the backdoor of the play-offs to reach the finals, the draw favoured the Uruguayans, and coached by Oscar Tabárez they progressed to the semi-finals, with the goals of Diego Forlan and Luis Suárez helping to put the country back on the football map. They had a controversial last minute goal-line handball from Suárez to thank for victory against Ghana in the quarter-final, but they ultimately fell to defeat against Holland in the next round. They lost a rollercoaster third place play-off to Germany but could take pride in the fact that Diego Forlan had finished the tournament as its joint highest scorer and he was also voted its best player.

Uruguay have an excellent record in the South American Championship and they had won the title seven times before World War II. Although they have appeared in the final less frequently during the Copa América era, they last won the title in 1995, when they beat Brazil on penalties.

have qualified for every World Cup since and have lifted CONCACAF Gold Cup four times. They also pulled off a shock defeat of Spain in the semi-final of the 2009 Confederations Cup but lost to Brazil in the final after leading 2-0.

In recent years the profile of the MLS has been raised by a new generation of star name imports, such as David Beckham, and in 2011 the league will expand to 18 clubs, with the introduction of new franchises from Vancouver and Portland. DC United dominated the early seasons of the league but subsequently the MLS has produced an open championship, with the title being won by Chicago Fire, Kansas City Wizards, San Jose Earthquakes, Los Angeles Galaxy, Houston Dynamo, Columbus Crew and Real Salt Lake.

URUGUAY

Federation: Asociacıon Uruguaya de Fútbol
Founded: 1900
Joined FIFA: 1923
Confederation: CONMEBOL
FIFA world ranking: 6
Honours: World Cup 1930, 1950; Copa América 1916, 1917, 1920, 1923, 1924, 1926, 1935, 1942, 1956, 1959, 1967,1983, 1987,1995; Olympics 1924, 1928

The tiny South American nation was arguably the strongest force in world football in the first half of the 20th century. Uruguay won Olympic gold medals in both 1924 and 1928, when the competition doubled as a world championship, and they also won the World Cup in both 1930 and 1950. Not only were they very successful but the Uruguayans were also stylish, playing imaginative pass-and-move football that stood in stark contrast to the physicality then prevalent elsewhere in the world game.

Uruguay had been the first South American country to enter the football tournament at the Olympic Games and they made an immediate impact on the 1924 competition in Paris. Europeans had rarely encountered skills such as those displayed by legendary midfielder Jose Leandro Andrade, who wowed the huge crowds that turned up to see them in the latter stages of their campaign. The team cantered to the final, where goals from Pedro Petrone, Pedro Cea and Angel Romano gave them an easy 3-0 victory over Switzerland. Four years later they returned to the Olympics to defend their title in Amsterdam and they beat Argentina 2-1 to win gold after a replay.

Uruguay's Olympic success resulted in an offer to host the first World Cup in 1930 and they continued their excellent run of form by becoming the first winners of the Jules Rimet Trophy. Again it was neighbours and rivals Argentina who Uruguay put to the sword in the final, this time 4-2, with their last goal coming from one-armed forward Hector Castro.

Deterred by the distance, many European countries had stayed away from the tournament. Four years later Uruguay retaliated by declining the opportunity to defend their world title in Italy and although they did not compete in the finals again until 1950, the wait proved more than worth it. They thumped Bolivia 8-0, with Omar Miguez scoring a hat-trick, before joining Brazil, Spain and Sweden in a 'mini league' to

US VIRGIN ISLANDS

Federation: US Virgin Islands Soccer Federation
Founded: 1992
Joined FIFA: 1998
Confederation: CONCACAF
FIFA world ranking: 191 (joint)

UZBEKISTAN

Federation: Uzbekistan Football Federation
Founded: 1946
Joined FIFA: 1994
Confederation: AFC
FIFA world ranking: 87

VANUATU

Federation: Vanuatu Football Federation
Founded: 1934
Joined FIFA: 1988
Confederation: OFC
FIFA world ranking: 163 (joint)

VENEZUELA

Federation: Federación Venezolana de Fútbol
Founded: 1926
Joined FIFA: 1952
Confederation: CONMEBOL
FIFA world ranking: 47

Venezuela are one of the weakest football nations in South America, where the sport ranks behind baseball in popularity. Professional football arrived in 1957 and Caracas FC are the country's most successful club, despite only being formed in 1967. The country hosted the Copa América for the first time in 2007, winning their first ever Copa América game on the way to the quarter-finals.

VIETNAM

Federation: Vietnam Football Federation
Founded: 1962
Joined FIFA: 1964
Confederation: AFC
FIFA world ranking: 127

WALES

Federation: Football Association of Wales
Founded: 1876
Joined FIFA: 1910-20, 1924-28, 1946
Confederation: UEFA
FIFA world ranking: 84

Football in Wales has always been a poor second in popularity to Rugby Union, despite the existence of a national team since March 1876 and a national cup competition since 1877. What Wales lacked was a national league, which

did not arrive until 1993, although its semi-professional status did not attract the country's strongest sides. Cardiff City, Swansea City and Wrexham have all played in the English league since the 1920s, while Cardiff even won the English FA Cup in 1927.

This situation, along with the plundering of the best of Welsh talent by English clubs, has left domestic football in Wales as a poor product. Nevertheless, the national side qualified for the 1958 World Cup and famously reached the quarter-final. They were narrowly eliminated by eventual winners Brazil after having to play without the team's one truly world-class player, John Charles, who had been injured in the previous round. They also won the British Championship outright on seven occasions.

The Welsh have produced a host of great players over the years, including Billy Meredith, Ivor Allchurch, Ryan Giggs, Ian Rush and Mark Hughes. However, the 1958 World Cup remains the only time the national team has qualified for the finals of a major tournament.

YEMEN

Federation: Yemen Football Association
Founded: 1962
Joined FIFA: 1980
Confederation: AFC
FIFA world ranking: 109

ZAMBIA

Federation: Football Association of Zambia
Founded: 1929
Joined FIFA: 1964
Confederation: CAF
FIFA world ranking: 73

In April 1993 Zambian football was in the ascendence when tragedy struck. A plane carrying the national team crashed into the Atlantic, killing 18 players and five officials. At the time Zambia had looked likely to qualify for the 1994 World Cup, but although their hastily reassembled team ultimately failed, they still reached the final of the African Nations Cup the following year before losing to Nigeria.

One of the greatest moments in Zambian football occurred five years before the crash, when the country reached the quarter-finals of the Olympic tournament after thrashing Italy 4-0, in a game that saw African Player Of The Year Kalusha Bwalya score a hat-trick. Captain of the national team, Bwalya was not on the fateful

plane in 1993, as he was travelling separately from Holland where he played with PSV, but he played a major part in the rebuilding of the team.

In club football Nkana FC reached the final of the African Champions Cup in 1990 and Power Dynamos won the African Cup Winners' Cup in 1991, becoming the first Zambian team to win a continental trophy, but since the air disaster, the country has failed to hit such heights again.

Above: Gentle giant John Charles (left) leads Wales onto the pitch to face Scotland in 1962.

ZIMBABWE

Federation: Zimbabwe Football Association
Founded: 1965
Joined FIFA: 1965
Confederation: CAF
FIFA world ranking: 110

The apartheid policies of the former Rhodesia kept the country out of the international arena until the 1970 World Cup qualifiers. However, CAF did not accept the country until its independence in 1980 and the instigation of black majority rule. Despite producing players of the calibre of Bruce Grobbelaar and Peter Ndlovu, Zimbabwe's national team have yet to make an impact, although they came within one game of reaching the 1994 World Cup.

CLUB COMPETITIONS OF THE WORLD

EUROPEAN CUP & CHAMPIONS LEAGUE

The Champions League is the world's foremost club cup competition, but the origins of the European Cup, or the European Champions Clubs' Cup to give its more precise name, came into being following a boast by the English press that champions Wolverhampton Wanderers were the best club side in world football. The outlandish claim was the result of a 3-2 friendly victory in 1954 against Hungarian side Honvéd under the new Molineux floodlights. It was also a knee-jerk reaction from Fleet Street journalists, who had witnessed the England national team comprehensively beaten the previous year by Hungary's 'Magical Magyars' – 6-3 at Wembley and then 7-1 in Budapest six months later.

With the Hungarians inspired by the skill and tactical awareness of Puskás, Czibor and Kocsis, both results finally buried the myth that England remained the best exponents of the beautiful game. The pride of a nation had been dented, yet the result at Molineux – and the subsequent 4-0 victory by Wolves against Spartak Moscow – saw some pride restored to a bruised ego.

The boast fell on deaf ears on the continent. Gabriel Hanot, editor of French sports newspaper *L'Equipe* and a former French international, was particularly aggrieved by the claims from England. In response to the *Daily Mail*'s comment that Wolves were 'the best team in the world', Hanot suggested that a new European tournament – devised for teams from nominated countries played on a home-and-away basis – should be implemented to determine the best team on the continent.

His observations received a somewhat lukewarm reaction from a number of football associations, with the English FA particularly concerned at the impact that a new competition would have on their own domestic campaign. Yet, following a meeting in Paris on April 2, attended by 15 of Europe's leading clubs, it was decided that Hanot's format should be presented to FIFA for it to receive international recognition.

Within four weeks, the world's governing body gave the competition its seal of approval and handed responsibility for its smooth running to UEFA. The European Champions Clubs' Cup saw its very first match kick-off between Sporting Lisbon and Partizan Belgrade on September 4, 1955. In total, 16 countries had teams represented in the inaugural competition, but English league champions Chelsea were conspicuous by their absence. Pressured into withdrawing from the competition by Alan Hardaker, the anti-European secretary of the Football League, Chelsea's place went instead to Polish side Gwardia Warsaw.

Although these were humble beginnings, 38,000 fans attended the first final between Real Madrid and Stade de Reims, and so was born a tournament that has thrilled and excited for over 50 years. The amazing final of 1960, which saw Real Madrid run out 7-3 victors against Eintracht Frankfurt, is now widely regarded as the greatest spectacle of club football ever seen.

Other highlights include Celtic's shock win against Inter Milan in Lisbon in 1967, the dominance of the Johan Cruyff inspired Ajax sides of the early 1970s, and the stranglehold

that English clubs seemed to have on the competition towards the end of that decade and into the early Eighties. If England had little to do with the competition upon its inception, the nation has been intrinsically linked with the European Cup ever since, and not always for the happiest of reasons. For Manchester United, February 6, 1958 marks the darkest day in the club's illustrious history after eight of the fabled 'Busby Babes' were tragically killed on a Munich runway on the way back from their 5-4 aggregate quarter-final win against Red Star Belgrade.

Having stopped to refuel, the freezing conditions caused two aborted takeoffs and on the third attempt the plane failed to gain altitude, hit a house and burst into flames. Roger Byrne, Geoff Bent, Mark Jones, David Pegg, Liam Whelan, Eddie Colman and Tommy Taylor died instantly, while the game's biggest rising star – Duncan Edwards – passed away two weeks later. Manager Sir Matt Busby survived, but it took him another ten years to rebuild his team into European champions.

Yet the darkest moment in the competition's history came on May 29, 1985, when drunken Liverpool 'fans' went on the rampage inside the Heysel Stadium, Brussels, prior to the club's appearance in the final against Juventus. Italian supporters came under a hail of missiles and were faced with a spontaneous charge behind the goal. As they cowered in the corner of Block Z, a wall gave way under the pressure and 39 people were crushed to death, while hundreds were injured. This wanton act of barbarism brought shame on English football and, more

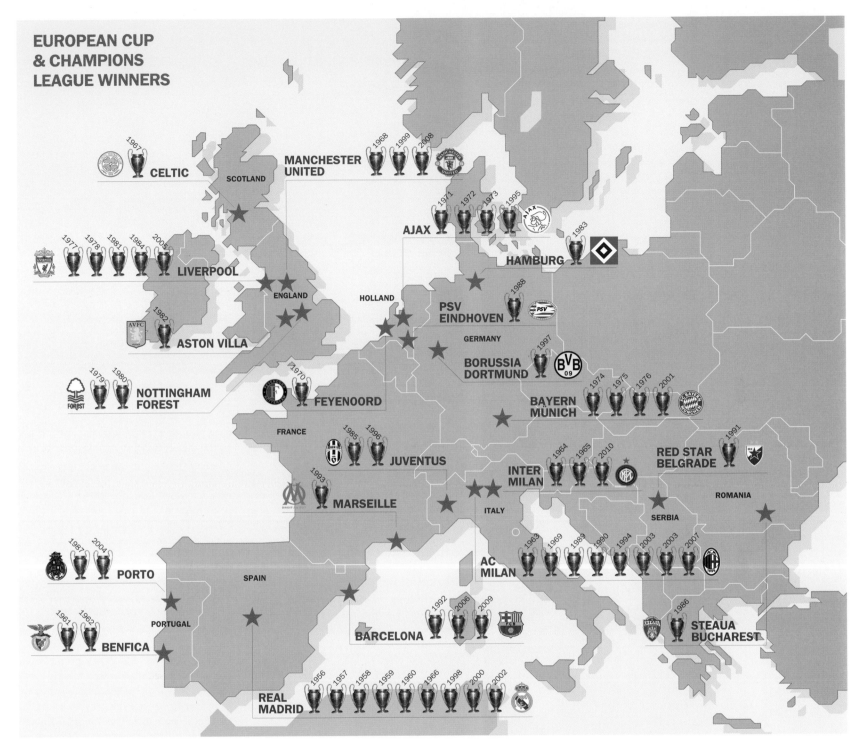

EUROPEAN CUP & CHAMPIONS LEAGUE WINNERS

importantly, prompted UEFA to ban English clubs 'indefinitely' from all European club competitions. It would be another six years before the country would be represented in the European Cup.

On their return English teams would find a very different competition. With commercialism beginning to exert a much stronger influence on the sport, the bigger clubs were looking for more financial revenue from the competition, while the breakdown of the Eastern Bloc meant more quality teams and therefore a more exploitable overall package had been created.

In 1991-2 the format changed. The first and second rounds continued as normal, but the third round consisted of two mini leagues of four teams, with the winners meeting in the final. The league format met with widespread approval and guaranteed a cash windfall for those teams participating in the latter stages. The following season UEFA formalised the changes, rebranding the competition as the Champions League.

In 1993-4 UEFA revamped the competition again, adding a semi-final phase for the top two teams in each group. The following season the tournament grew even more, with the first two rounds replaced by a larger group phase: the holders and the seven top seeded teams would progress to four league groups, each containing four clubs, with the other clubs coming from a round of preliminary ties. The top two teams in

each group progressed to the quarter-finals. As the seasons have passed further changes have been implemented so that several of the highest-placed finishers in certain domestic leagues are now guaranteed a place in the competition, and such is the windfall that many teams now bank on qualification to ensure financial stability.

The model is now in place for a European Super League to evolve, consisting of only the most elite. While these big name clubs ultimately aspire to take control of the competition, for the time being it remains in the hands of UEFA. Whoever runs Europe's premier club competition in the future, the likelihood is that a Wolves or Honvéd will never again claim to be the continent's dominant club.

Right: AC Milan won Italy's first European Cup, beating Benfica at Wembley in 1963.

1956: REAL MADRID

PARC DES PRINCES, PARIS June 13

Real Madrid **4-3** Stade de Reims
(Spain)   (France)

With a vociferous crowd behind them, Reims took a 2-0 lead through Michel Leblond and Jean Templin, but favourites Real Madrid soon found their composure and stamped their mark on the game. Alfredo Di Stéfano scored from the edge of the box and Rial's headed equaliser set up a storming second-half. A goal from Real winger Joseito was disallowed shortly after the break and Reims took advantage when Michel Hidalgo headed in Raymond Kopa's free-kick to edge them back in front. Real's 67th minute equaliser came when a Marquitos shot was deflected into the net, and with ten minutes remaining Rial scored again to win the game.

1957: REAL MADRID

BERNABÉU STADIUM, MADRID May 30

Real Madrid **2-0** Fiorentina
(Spain)   (Italy)

Real Madrid's second final was played in front of a partisan 124,000 crowd, and although the Italians possessed skilful Brazilian Julinho and Argentine striker Miguel Montuori, they were no match for the Spaniards. The game was a stale affair until the 70th minute when Real winger Enrique Mateos was fouled and Alfredo Di Stéfano converted the penalty. Six minutes later Paco Gento found himself with the keeper to beat and held his nerve to secure victory.

Below: Real Madrid's 1960 win over Eintracht Frankfurt was perhaps the greatest game ever.

1958: REAL MADRID

HEYSEL STADIUM, BRUSSELS May 28

Real Madrid **3-2** AC Milan (aet)
(Spain)   (Italy)
2-2 at 90 minutes

With Milan marshalled by Cesare Maldini, in an edgy match the Italians kept Di Stéfano and Kopa at bay until the 59th minute when Schiaffino put Milan into the lead. Di Stéfano equalised in the 74th minute, only for Grillo to put Milan back in front minutes later. Within 60 seconds Rial levelled the game, and although Liedholm came close for the Italians, hitting the bar in the dying moments, the match went to extra-time and Madrid made it three successive wins when Gento scored at the second attempt.

1959: REAL MADRID

NECKAR STADIUM, STUTTGART June 3

Real Madrid **2-0** Stade de Reims
(Spain)   (France)

In a dour affair, the French were criticised for a lack of adventure as Real won at a canter. The pattern was set as early as the second minute when Mateos shot past Colonna and, shortly after the restart, Di Stéfano scored the second to continue his record of scoring in every final. After the game, Real's Raymond Kopa moved back to Reims but French football would not see another team in the final until 1976.

1960: REAL MADRID

HAMPDEN PARK, GLASGOW May 18

Real Madrid **7-3** Eintracht Frankfurt
(Spain)   (West Germany)

Quite possibly the greatest attacking game of football ever staged, Frankfurt were blown away by the flair and imagination of Real.

A near post volley from Kress put the Germans into the lead, but Di Stéfano netted twice before Puskás crashed in a left-foot shot to make it 3-1 at half-time. Ten minutes after the break Puskás scored a penalty, then followed up with a header from Gento's cross. He scored his fourth with a shot on the turn, before a Stein goal 15 minutes from time gave the Germans some respectability. Yet almost immediately a Puskás pass set up Di Stéfano for his hat-trick before Stein scored again following a Madrid defensive blunder.

1961: BENFICA

WANKDORF STADIUM, BERNE May 31

Benfica **3-2** Barcelona
(Portugal)   (Spain)

Barcelona's attack of Kubala, Kocsis and Czibor was rightly feared, but opponents Benfica, with the likes of Augusto, Coluna and Germano, were fast becoming the best team on the continent. The Spaniards took the lead through a Kocsis header on 19 minutes but were on the back foot after Benfica scored twice in two minutes, through captain José Aguas and an own-goal by keeper Antoni Ramallets. In the 55th minute Benfica scored their third with a Coluna volley before a Barça onslaught saw Czibor get one back. Czibor, Kocsis and Kubala all hit the post but it was Benfica that celebrated.

1962: BENFICA

OLYMPIC STADIUM, AMSTERDAM May 2

Benfica **5-3** Real Madrid
(Portugal)   (Spain)

Another classic encounter saw Puskás score three times inside 38 minutes for Madrid, becoming the only player to have scored hat-tricks in two European Cup finals. Benfica cut back the deficit by half-time through José Aguas and Domiciano Cavem. With Di Stéfano pulling the strings for Real a tactical switch was made and he was man-marked by Cavem in the second-half. As a consequence the game swung in Benfica's favour. Coluna pounced on a slip by Puskás to level the scores and the stage was set for 19-year-old Eusébio to weave his magic. Having won a penalty, he slammed the kick past Araquistain in the 65th minute, and three minutes later he connected with a pass from Coluna to secure victory.

1963: AC MILAN

WEMBLEY STADIUM, LONDON May 22

AC Milan **2-1** Benfica
(Italy) (Portugal)

A half-full Wembley witnessed a no-nonsense display by Milan. The plan was to stifle Benfica captain Mario Coluna but the strategy played into Eusébio's hands as he left Trapattoni in his wake to score in the 18th minute. Milan's determination shone through in the second-half and when Rivera found Altafini, the centre-forward fired home. With Coluna a passenger following Pivatelli's crude challenge, there would be only one winner and that came via Altafini who, having picked up the ball on the halfway line, ran half the length of the pitch before firing past Pereira at the second attempt.

1964: INTER MILAN

PRATER STADIUM, VIENNA May 27

Inter Milan **3-1** Real Madrid
(Italy) (Spain)

Having conceded just four goals in the competition, Inter were favourites to win the final in Vienna. Sandro Mazzola rocked Real when he scored from 25 yards in the 43rd minute, and a 61st minute mistake by keeper Vicente let in Milani to put the Italians 2-0 ahead. Although Puskás hit a post, the writing was on the wall for Real. Felo cut the deficit with a 70th minute header but just six minutes later Mazzola pounced on a bad clearance to secure victory for Inter Milan.

1965: INTER MILAN

SAN SIRO, MILAN May 27

Inter Milan **1-0** Benfica
(Italy) (Portugal)

Prior to the final Benfica complained to UEFA that hosting the game at Inter's home ground gave the Italians an unfair advantage and threatened to field their youth team. They finally backed down when made fully aware of the financial benefits, but in hindsight their youngsters might have made a better job of it. Played in pouring rain, the players struggled with their footing and the match was settled when Jair's shot slithered through the hands of Costa Pereira in the 42nd minute.

1966: REAL MADRID

HEYSEL STADIUM, BRUSSELS May 11

Real Madrid **2-1** Partizan Belgrade
(Spain) (Yugoslavia)

Although the club was contesting its eighth European Cup final, it was an inexperienced Real side that faced the Yugoslavs and victory looked to be slipping away when Vasovic headed in Pirmajer's cross in the 56th minute. Real's response was to launch an all-out attack and in the 70th minute Amancio met a through pass from Grosso to shoot past Soskic. The Real players were stung into action, and with Partizan's star striker Galic struggling with injury, Serena curled home from 25 yards to wrap the game up for Madrid.

1967: CELTIC

ESTÁDIO NACIONAL, LISBON May 25

Celtic **2-1** Inter Milan
(Scotland) (Italy)

Celtic turned the Portuguese stadium into a sea of green and white, a sight that spurred Jock Stein's side into action against their much-fancied and defensively-organised opponents. A good start was a necessity but when Jim Craig felled Cappellini after six minutes, referee Tschenscher pointed to the spot and Mazzola sent Simpson the wrong way. Lesser teams could have crumbled, but Celtic went for broke and when Auld and Gemmell both hit the bar, it gave an indication of the Scots' dominance.

They were finally rewarded in the 62nd minute when left-back Gemmell hit a 20-yard rocket into the corner of Sarti's net. The Inter defence was rattled and in the 83rd minute a Murdoch shot appeared to be going wide before Stevie Chalmers intercepted to guide the ball home.

Above: Archie Gemmell turns away after scoring Celtic's first goal in the 1967 European Cup Final in Lisbon.

1968: MANCHESTER UNITED

WEMBLEY STADIUM, LONDON May 29

Manchester United **4-1** Benfica (aet)
(England) (Portugal)
1-1 at 90 minutes

The first-half was a scrappy affair with chances at a premium and with United's ingenious playmaker George Best being tightly marked by Cruz and Humberto. David Sadler came closest to breaking the deadlock with two half-chances but it was not until the second-half, when Ashton began to cause problems down the left flank, that United looked dangerous. They were finally rewarded when Bobby Charlton headed home a Dunne cross in the 52nd minute, but 1-0 never looked a scoreline that would be enough to secure victory.

When Graça equalised with nine minutes to go, Benfica proved that the match was anything but over. Eusébio failed with a great chance to win the game in the dying seconds and it proved to be the defining moment, as Best waltzed round two defenders to put United back in the lead early in extra-time. The goal demoralised Benfica and strikes from Kidd and Charlton finally laid to rest the ghosts of 1958.

Above: Allan Clarke is fouled by Bayern's Franz Beckenbauer in the 1975 European Cup Final but to the anger of Leeds United no penalty is given.

1969: AC MILAN

BERNABÉU STADIUM, MADRID May 28

AC Milan **4-1** Ajax
(Italy)   (Holland)

In a move rarely associated with Italian sides, Milan attacked from the start against an inexperienced Ajax, with Prati hitting the post in the first minute. They opened the scoring as early as the sixth minute when Prati's looping header sailed over Bals' goal, and despite Ajax's best intentions, the lead was doubled when Prati's shot flew in from the edge of the box. After Keizer was fouled by Lodetti just inside the penalty area, Vasovic's spot-kick gave Ajax hope on the hour. Sormani put away Milan's third just five minutes later and Prati completed his hat-trick after 74 minutes to seal the win.

1970: FEYENOORD

SAN SIRO, MILAN May 6

Feyenoord **2-1** Celtic (aet)
(Holland)   (Scotland)
1-1 at 90 minutes

With Feyenoord billed as underdogs, Celtic reverted to a 4-2-4 formation, believing an offensive action would win them the game. That assumption appeared to be correct when, in the 29th minute, Gemmell swept home from 25 yards. But within three minutes the Dutch equalised when Hasil's free-kick was lofted over a static Celtic defence for captain Israel to head home. Feyenoord completely dominated the second-half but somehow Celtic made it to

extra-time and keeper Williams kept them in the game with fine saves from Kindvall and Wery. However, he could do nothing when Kindvall took advantage of McNeill's slip to steer home the winner with four minutes remaining.

1971: AJAX

WEMBLEY STADIUM, LONDON June 2

Ajax **2-0** Panathinaikos
(Holland)   (Greece)

Puskás's love affair with the European Cup continued as he guided the Greek club to the final, this time as a manager. His team started as underdogs against the Total Football of Ajax, who took a grip on the game as early as the fifth minute, when Keizer whipped in a left-wing cross for Van Dijk to head clinically past Oeconomopoulos. The Greek keeper then pulled off a number of fine saves, most notably from the impressive Cruyff, and although the Dutch seemed content to sit on their one goal advantage, Panathinaikos failed to seize the initiative. The game was won in the 87th minute when Haan finished off Cruyff's mazy run, his shot deflecting into the net off Kapsis.

1972: AJAX

DE KUIP STADIUM, ROTTERDAM May 31

Ajax **2-0** Inter Milan
(Holland)   (Italy)

The Italians adopted their defensive 'catenaccio' tactics in an attempt to overcome the Dutch masters, but it was clear from kick-off that they

were fighting a losing battle as Ajax played with the flair and imagination that had won them a domestic 'double' back in Holland. The loss of centre-half Giubertoni after 12 minutes did not help Inter's cause, but the deadlock was not broken until the 47th minute when Cruyff pounced on a mix-up between Bordon and Burgnich to stroke home. The goal forced the Italians to attack and Sandro Mazzola had a good chance to equalise before European Footballer Of The Year, Johan Cruyff, made the game safe in the 77th minute.

1973: AJAX

RED STAR STADIUM, BELGRADE May 30

Ajax **1-0** Juventus
(Holland)   (Italy)

In a mirror image of the previous year's final, Dutch artistry overcame Italian stubbornness as Ajax became only the second team in history to win the cup three years in succession. On a humid night in Yugoslavia, Ajax went for an early kill and were rewarded when a deep cross from Blankenburg was met by wonderkid Johnny Rep, who rose above Marchetti to head home. Again Cruyff teased the opposition, and although his team-mates could not take advantage, the result was never in doubt as the masters nonchalantly played possession football as the game drew to a close.

1974: BAYERN MUNICH

HEYSEL STADIUM, BRUSSELS May 15

Bayern Munich **1-1** Atlético Madrid (aet)
(West Germany)   (Spain)
0-0 at 90 minutes

In a closely-fought encounter Atlético had the better of the early exchanges, with their flair and passing catching the West Germans offguard. Bayern upped the tempo in the second-half but, although Gerd Müller and Uli Hoeness looked dangerous, the game went to extra-time. The deadlock was broken when a delightful Aragones free-kick beat Sepp Maier, and with seven minutes remaining the cup appeared to be heading to Spain. Yet, in typical fashion, the Germans rose from the ashes and with just seconds remaining, Schwarzenbeck unleashed a shot from 35 yards that flew past Miguel Reina. The title would be decided by a replay.

REPLAY

HEYSEL STADIUM, BRUSSELS May 17

Bayern Munich **4-0** Atlético Madrid

With playmaker Javier Irureta suspended and centre-half skipper Adelardo later substituted through injury, Atlético were on the back foot and the match proved to be a one-sided affair. Although the score was just 1-0 at half-time, thanks to Hoeness's 28th minute strike, the Germans turned the screw after the break and doubled their lead when Müller volleyed home

Kapellmann's cross. A delicate lob from Gerd Müller made it three, and with eight minutes remaining Hoeness scored his second by rounding the goalkeeper.

1975: BAYERN MUNICH

PARC DES PRINCES, PARIS May 28;

Bayern Munich **2-0** Leeds United
(West Germany)   (England)

With their physical, no-nonsense approach, Leeds bossed the game in the opening half and had two legitimate appeals for a penalty turned down when Beckenbauer appeared to intercept a pass to Lorimer with his hand and later tripped Allan Clarke inside the box. It simply was not going to be United's night, which was confirmed when Lorimer volleyed into the roof of the net after 67 minutes, only for the goal to be disallowed for offside. This decision caused rioting by a section of the Leeds fans and they were further riled when Roth scored in the 72nd minute following good work from Gerd Müller. Although Leeds continued to throw men forward, the Germans wrapped the game up with eight minutes remaining as Müller ghosted past Madeley and beat Stewart at his near post.

1976: BAYERN MUNICH

HAMPDEN PARK, GLASGOW May 12

Bayern Munich **1-0** Saint-Etienne
(West Germany)   (France)

Although the scoreline suggests a tight game, it was anything but as Saint-Etienne's imagination was matched by Bayern's counter-attacking football. The Germans were denied a goal in the second minute when Gerd Müller was deemed offside as he slotted the ball past Curkovic, but television replays proved he had been onside. The decision galvanised the French, who saw Bathenay and Santini hit the woodwork, but 12 minutes into the second-half Bayern landed the killer blow when a Beckenbauer free-kick was lashed home by Franz Roth.

1977: LIVERPOOL

OLYMPIC STADIUM, ROME May 25

Liverpool **3-1** Borussia
Mönchengladbach
(England)   (West Germany)

Liverpool's creativity was rewarded in the 27th minute when Steve Heighway's cross was met by McDermott and his shot flew past Borussia keeper Wolfgang Kneib. Yet within six minutes of the restart, Simonsen intercepted a poor Case back-pass and his left-foot shot beat Clemence emphatically. The goal lifted the Germans and the England goalkeeper was called into action on a number of occasions after that.

Having ridden the storm, Liverpool imposed themselves again and another Heighway cross was met by Tommy Smith, who rose quickest

to make it 2-1. With Kevin Keegan – in his last game for the club – running rings round the Germans, defender Vogts scythed him down and Phil Neal converted the resulting spot-kick.

1978: LIVERPOOL

WEMBLEY STADIUM, LONDON May 10

Liverpool 1-0 Club Brugge
(England)   (Belgium)

In total contrast to the previous year's final, Liverpool retained their crown in a totally uninspiring game. With the influential Lambert and Courant both absent through injury, Brugge's defence-first policy stifled Liverpool, themselves below par after another intense domestic season. A Jimmy Case free-kick was the closest either side came to scoring in the first-half, but 'The Reds' finally broke the deadlock in the 66th minute when Dalglish latched on to a through ball from Souness to delightfully chip over advancing keeper Birger Jensen. Liverpool became the first English team to win the European Cup twice, ample consolation for losing the championship and League Cup to Nottingham Forest.

1979: NOTTINGHAM FOREST

OLYMPIC STADIUM, MUNICH May 30

Nottingham Forest **1-0** Malmö
(England)   (Sweden)

Another poor final, as Malmö were missing influential defenders Larsson, Andersson and skipper Tapper, while Forest were without Gemmill and O'Neill. However, they did have £1 million man Trevor Francis in their ranks, and he scored the only goal of the game on the stroke of half-time when he met Robertson's cross with a far post header. Robertson also hit the post himself after the break, and Birtles

missed a sitter with just goalkeeper Jan Möller to beat. An Anders Ljungberg free-kick proved to be Malmö's only clear attempt at goal.

1980: NOTTINGHAM FOREST

BERNABÉU STADIUM, MADRID May 28

Nottingham Forest **1-0** Hamburg
(England)   (West Germany)

With Trevor Francis absent with an Achilles injury and goalkeeper Peter Shilton struggling with a calf problem, Hamburg took the game to Forest, with fullback Kaltz and midfielder Memering keen to feed Kevin Keegan whenever possible. Yet as they pushed forward, Forest broke on the counterattack, a move that worked to perfection in the 19th minute when Robertson played a neat one-two with Birtles before striking home from the edge of the box. Reimann had a goal disallowed for offside on the half-hour mark and although Keegan and captain Peter Nogly went close, Forest held on.

1981: LIVERPOOL

PARC DES PRINCES, PARIS May 27

Liverpool **1-0** Real Madrid
(England)   (Spain)

With Real defenders Camacho and Cortes shadowing Souness and Dalglish, and the team's playmaker Uli Stielike hustled off his game by Liverpool's Sammy Lee, an extremely tense first-half saw chances at a premium. Yet as the second-half got underway, Real skipper Camacho was clean through only to see his shot sail over the bar. It acted as a wake-up call to Liverpool, who then took hold of the game. With eight minutes remaining a Ray Kennedy throw-in was chested down by Alan Kennedy, who skipped past a tackle from Cortes before driving home from an acute angle. Liverpool held on and Bob Paisley became the first coach to win the European Cup three times.

Left: Trevor Francis enjoys Nottingham Forest's first European Cup win in 1979.

Below: Phil Neal and Alan Kennedy celebrate their third European Cup success, this time in 1981 against Real Madrid.

Above: Tony Morley lifts the cup after Aston Villa defeat Bayern Munich in 1982.

Rummenigge, inspiring his team-mates to fight back. In the 67th minute, Tony Morley's bobbling cross was met by Withe, who spooned the ball home past Manfred Müller.

1983: HAMBURG

OLYMPIC STADIUM, ATHENS May 25

Hamburg **1-0** Juventus
(West Germany) (Italy)

With six of Italy's World Cup-winning team in their ranks, including Paolo Rossi, plus French midfield maestro Michel Platini, a Juventus victory was seen as a formality. Yet it was West German industry that reigned supreme, and within eight minutes Hamburg were ahead, as Felix Magath's looping shot fooled the 41-year-old keeper Dino Zoff. Platini and Rossi were poor throughout and the only Juventus player to emerge with any credit was Zbigniew Boniek, whose runs were a constant torment. However, there was no denying Hamburg their victory and Juventus were left to rue the hype that had surrounded the team in the build-up.

1984: LIVERPOOL

OLYMPIC STADIUM, ROME May 30

Liverpool **1-1** Roma (aet)
(England) (Italy)
1-1 at 90 minutes; Liverpool won 4-2 on penalties

The Italians may have been spurred on by a vociferous home crowd, but Liverpool managed to silence them after just 15 minutes when keeper Franco Tancredi lost the ball under pressure and Phil Neal gratefully stroked it home. Within seconds Souness scored but was ruled offside, and 'The Reds' were left to rue the decision as Pruzzo headed home Conti's cross on 38 minutes. Liverpool keeper Bruce Grobbelaar made key saves from Falção and Tancredi, and after extra-time stalemate the game went to penalties. In front of the Roma fans Nicol missed the opening kick and Di Bartolomei scored. Neal hit the net while Conti, distracted by the leg-wobbling antics of Grobbelaar, missed. Souness, Righetti and Rush all scored before Graziani hit the crossbar. It was left to Alan Kennedy to wrap the game up and he converted with consummate ease.

1985: JUVENTUS

HEYSEL STADIUM, BRUSSELS May 29

Juventus **1-0** Liverpool
(Italy) (England)

The on-field events at Heysel were completely overshadowed by rioting on the terraces, which resulted in the deaths of 39 Juventus fans. Prior to kick-off a group of Liverpool fans charged at their Italian rivals behind the goal and, as the Juve fans fled the barrage of missiles being aimed in their direction, a wall collapsed under the pressure. The enormity of the disaster became apparent as kick-off approached,

with many fans being pulled out unconscious or dead. There is little doubt the crumbling stadium and lack of organisation was partly to blame, but it was at the ugly face of English hooliganism that UEFA vented their fury. As a result English club sides were banned from all European competition for five years, while Liverpool were banned for six. Juventus won the game thanks to Platini's 56th minute penalty.

1986: STEAUA BUCHAREST

SÁNCHEZ PIZJUÁN STADIUM, SEVILLE May 7

Steaua Bucharest **0-0** Barcelona (aet)
(Romania) (Spain)
Steaua Bucharest won 2-0 on penalties

After a manic start that saw referee Michel Vautrot hand out cards like confetti, the game settled down and Steaua Bucharest took control through their playmakers Balint and Balan. Yet it was Terry Venables' Barcelona who went closest to breaking the deadlock with a Bernd Schuster header on the half-hour. With the match goalless at half-time, the Romanian rearguard shone in the second-half and Barça's closest effort came from Steve Archibald, who headed over the crossbar. Extra-time failed to separate the sides and the game went to penalties. The first four were saved, but as Lacatus and Balint converted, Barcelona's saw their two saved, handing Steaua success.

1987: PORTO

PRATER STADIUM, VIENNA May 27

Porto **2-1** Bayern Munich
(Portugal) (West Germany)

The West Germans took a controversial lead when Porto's Jaime Magalhaes was illegally ordered back from a Bayern throw-in. As he retreated the ball was deflected off his head to Kögl, who headed home himself. The injustice unsettled Porto as Rummenigge and Matthäus also went close, but the second-half was a contrasting affair as Sousa began pulling the strings in midfield. The equaliser came in the 77th minute when Madjer cheekily backheeled the ball past Pfaff, and two minutes later Juary connected with Madjer's cross to seal victory.

1988: PSV EINDHOVEN

NECKAR STADIUM, STUTTGART May 25

PSV Eindhoven **0-0** Benfica (aet)
(Holland) (Portugal)
PSV won 6-5 on penalties

With PSV boasting four players from the Dutch national team that would win the European Championship that summer, they were clear favourites. Their chances were further boosted when Benfica skipper Diamantino was ruled out with injury, but as the Portuguese side launched a damage limitation exercise, the game petered out into a boring spectacle. Vanenburg and Gillhaus went close for PSV after the break,

1982: ASTON VILLA

DE KUIP STADIUM, ROTTERDAM May 26

Aston Villa **1-0** Bayern Munich
(England) (West Germany)

With a strong team that included German internationals Rummenigge and Hoeness, Bayern were clear favourites to lift the trophy in 1982, but it was Villa who started brightest, going close through both Peter Withe and Alan Evans. However, the early promise threatened to be undone when keeper Jimmy Rimmer was taken off with an injured neck and replaced by 23-year-old Nigel Spink after just nine minutes. Any nerves that the youngster might have been experiencing were settled with two fantastic saves from Bernd Durnberger and Karl-Heinz

Left: PSV Eindhoven had to rely on a penalty shoot-out to beat Benfica to the cup in 1988.

while Nielsen missed an open goal, but extra-time proved equally dreary and only penalties lifted the gloom that had descended around the stadium. All of the penalties were expertly taken until PSV keeper Hans Van Breukelen pushed out Antonio Veloso's weak effort.

1989: AC MILAN

NOU CAMP, BARCELONA May 24

AC Milan **4-0** Steaua Bucharest
(Italy)   (Romania)

With Ruud Gullit, Marco Van Basten, Frank Rijkaard and Paolo Maldini in their ranks, Milan confirmed their status as Europe's top side with a total demolition of Steaua. The passing and movement was a joy to behold, and although Lacatus and Hagi were early threats, the Romanians were soon under pressure. Milan took the lead after 18 minutes when Bumbescu fluffed a clearance and Gullit was on hand to tuck the ball home. Eight minutes later Van Basten rose to head home Tassotti's cross. As the half drew to a close, Gullit received a pass from Donadoni and in one movement swivelled to volley past Lung. It would have been easy to shut up shop but within 60 seconds of the restart Van Basten received Rijkaard's through ball to score the fourth.

1990: AC MILAN

PRATER STADIUM, VIENNA May 23

AC Milan **1-0** Benfica
(Italy)   (Portugal)

Milan adopted a more defensive approach than the previous year, due in part to Benfica's very lively forward line of Magnusson and Valdo. Indeed, the Portuguese side made most of the running in the first-half, but it was Milan who came closest to breaking the deadlock when Marco Van Basten's shot was well-saved by Silvino. The match was settled in the 68th

minute by the best move of the game, involving Alessandro Costacurta, Filippo Galli and Van Basten, whose through ball was coolly tucked home by Rijkaard. Gullit had a chance to make the final 15 minutes more comfortable, but despite a scare from José Carlos, Milan held on.

1991: RED STAR BELGRADE

SAN NICOLA STADIUM, BARI May 29

Red Star Belgrade **0-0** Marseille (aet)
(Yugoslavia)   (France)
Red Star won 5-3 on penalties

With both sides famous for their attacking instincts, it was somehow inevitable that the game would become a tedious affair. Red Star played with a lone striker in Pancev, a defensive midfield and an uncompromising defence, which meant the flair of Marseille's Jean-Pierre Papin and Chris Waddle were given little space or time to shine. The first-half was forgettable, but at least the French side took the game to their opponents after the break and Waddle went close in the 75th minute with a header that flashed wide. Papin also had a chance but it was Prosinecki who almost won the game for Red Star, his late free-kick shaving the post. Waddle passed on the penalty shoot-out, unable to shake the memory of his World Cup semi-final miss of the previous year. Instead it was Amoros who handed Red Star victory after his kick was saved.

1992: BARCELONA

WEMBLEY STADIUM, LONDON May 20

Barcelona **1-0** Sampdoria (aet)
(Spain)   (Italy)
0-0 at 90 minutes

Barcelona took to the field in an unfamiliar orange kit, and although they showed more attacking instincts than their edgy opponents, coach Johan Cruyff's side were nearly caught on the break when Lombardo's shot was well

held by Zubizarretta. The pace picked up in the second-half, with Vialli missing two guilt-edged chances, while Barça striker Stoichkov saw his shot rebound off a post. As the clock ticked, anxiety set in and a melee followed Bakero's poor tackle on Cerezo. Mancini had a chance to win with the ensuing free-kick but the game went into extra-time. In the 110th minute, Barcelona controversially took the lead after the referee wrongly judged that Invernizzi had fouled Eusebio Sacristán on the edge of the box. From the resulting free-kick, Koeman's ferocious strike beat Pagliuca to secure victory.

1993: MARSEILLE

OLYMPIC STADIUM, MUNICH May 26

Marseille **1-0** AC Milan
(France)   (Italy)

In the first Champions League final it was all change for Milan, who left Ruud Gullit on the bench, while Jean-Pierre Papin was sacrificed for Marco Van Basten, who was making only

Below: Hristo Stoichkov helped Barcelona to get hold of the European Cup for the very first time in 1992.

Right: Edgar Davids of Ajax lifts the trophy alongside Finidi George, Jari Litmanen and Nwankwo Kanu in 1995.

his third appearance following ankle surgery. Marseille had their own problems with rumours of match-fixing threatening to overshadow their very existence. Milan dominated the opening half-hour and could have been 2-0 up if Massaro had shown more composure, but the French gradually clawed their way back into the game. Völler went close with a shot that rebounded off goalkeeper Rossi's legs, while Alen Boksic also saw an effort shave the bar. The breakthrough finally came on the stroke of half-time when Boli rose to powerfully head home Abedi Pele's corner for Marseille.

The second-half was one-way traffic as Milan pushed for an equaliser, but although Papin and Massaro both went close, they were left to rue Van Basten's shocking 48th minute miss from just eight yards out. Following the game, Marseille were found guilty of match fixing in the league, banned from European football and relegated to the French Second Division.

1994: AC MILAN

OLYMPIC STADIUM, ATHENS May 18

AC Milan **4-0** Barcelona
(Italy)   (Spain)

With Barcelona possessing the attacking prowess of Stoichkov, Romario and Sergi, it was anticipated that the Italians would implement 'catenaccio' to the highest degree, yet the game was turned on its head as Milan displayed their own brand of breathtaking, offensive football. They showed their intentions from the start when Panucci's header was disallowed in the ninth minute, and although Romario forced a good save from keeper Rossi, Massaro broke the deadlock from Savicevic's cross in the 22nd minute. He added a second on the stroke of half-time following good work from Donadoni, and the game was all but sealed in the 47th minute when Savicevic chipped the ball over Zubizarretta from 20 yards. Desailly, playing in midfield, scored a fourth and Savicevic had time to hit the post twice before the final whistle put Barcelona out of their misery.

Below: Milan celebrate putting four goals past Barcelona in the 1994 European Cup final.

1995: AJAX

ERNST HAPPEL STADIUM, VIENNA May 24

Ajax **1-0** AC Milan
(Holland)   (Italy)

Although coach Louis Van Gaal's young side had beaten Milan twice earlier in the competition, by the time of the final Milan had not conceded a goal for five European matches and were clear favourites. As the first-half progressed Milan took a hold of the game, and although they failed to create much, they were bossing the midfield. With a defence packed with talent, Milan were comfortably dealing with the threat of Ajax forwards Jari Litmanen, Finidi George and Marc Overmars.

The first real chance of the game came via a Desailly shot on 41 minutes, while Van Der Sar saved from Simone on the stroke of half-time. Ajax were happy to return to the dressing room on level terms and Van Gaal then played a masterstroke by bringing on young strikers Kanu and Kluivert, who helped turn the game around with their pace and trickery. The winner came in the 85th minute, when Rijkaard's through ball found Kluivert and, at 18 years and 327 days, he became the youngest ever European Cup final goalscorer.

1996: JUVENTUS

OLYMPIC STADIUM, ROME May 22

Juventus **1-1** Ajax (aet)
(Italy)   (Holland)
1-1 at 90 minutes; Juventus won 4-2 on penalties

Although missing the injured Overmars, Ajax were everybody's tip to retain the trophy, but a defensive mix up between Frank De Boer and goalkeeper Van Der Sar on 12 minutes let in Juventus striker Fabrizio Ravanelli to score from the acutest of angles. Both sides had chances as the half progressed – most notably Musampa for Ajax and Del Piero for Juve – but in the 41st minute a foul by Vierchowod on Kanu resulted in a De Boer

free-kick being turned home by Litmanen for Ajax. Vialli and Del Piero had chances to win the game for Juventus in the second-half, but extra-time was required. Del Piero had a great chance at the death but shot straight at Van Der Sar. There was a feeling that it wasn't to be for the Italians, but they held their nerve in the shoot-out with Angelo Peruzzi saving from Edgar Davids and Sonny Silooy.

1997: BORUSSIA DORTMUND

OLYMPIC STADIUM, MUNICH May 28

Borussia Dortmund **3-1** Juventus
(Germany)   (Italy)

With the Germans containing four ex-Juventus players – Kohler, Möller, Paulo Sousa and Reuter – Dortmund had an added incentive to do well, but what followed was one of the biggest upsets in European Cup history. For the first half-hour Juventus attacked with purpose through Boksic and Vieri, but it was the Germans who struck first when Lambert's chip was met by Riedle, who rifled the ball home. Within five minutes, Riedle had doubled Dortmund's lead, heading home Möller's cross.

The game was far from over for Juve, who saw Zidane hit the post and Vieri have a goal disallowed before half-time. Throwing caution to the wind, Marcello Lippi replaced defender Porrini with Del Piero and it was a move that appeared to pay off when the substitute scored after 64 minutes. Far from perturbed, Borussia scored a third when Ricken spotted Peruzzi off his line and lobbed the keeper from 35 yards.

1998: REAL MADRID

AMSTERDAM ARENA, AMSTERDAM May 20

Real Madrid **1-0** Juventus
(Spain)   (Italy)

With 21 internationals on the pitch and a further six on the bench, this game was billed as a clash of the giants, but although both teams started brightly enough, neither side could make their pressure pay. Edgar Davids and Roberto Carlos were both booked as frustrations grew and Mijatovic, causing constant problems down the left, was a target of some uncompromising Juventus defending.

Raúl missed a golden opportunity to open the scoring on the stroke of half-time, while Inzaghi repeated the feat for Juventus soon after the restart, following good work from Davids. However, just as fans were beginning to consider the possibility of extra-time, Real Madrid took the lead with less than 20 minutes remaining. Seedorf crossed from the right and although Carlos's shot was saved, Mijatovic was on hand to slot the ball home from a tight angle.

1999: MANCHESTER UNITED

NOU CAMP, BARCELONA May 26

Manchester United **2-1** Bayern Munich
(England)　　　(Germany)

With Roy Keane and Paul Scholes suspended, the odds were against United lifting the trophy for the first time in 31 years and their chances looked even more remote after a shaky start. As early as the sixth minute Johnsen fouled Jancker, and from the resulting free-kick Basler fired the ball over Schmeichel and into the net. United's creative force of Giggs and Blomqvist were contained, Effenberg and Jeremies had control of the midfield, while Andy Cole and Dwight Yorke were given little opportunity to show their obvious talent. Indeed, as the game wore on and United became more desperate, they left themselves open and Effenberg went close while Scholl hit the bar.

As the game entered its 90th minute, with the Bayern fans already celebrating their team's success, United keeper Peter Schmeichel went up for a last-gasp Beckham corner. He failed to connect but the ball fell to Giggs, whose shot was intercepted by substitute Teddy Sheringham, who fired the ball into the back of the net. The Bayern Munich players were clearly distraught and before they had managed to rediscover their composure, Beckham sent in another corner, which was flicked on by Sheringham and diverted home by substitute Ole Gunnar Solskjaer.

2000: REAL MADRID

STADE DE FRANCE, PARIS May 24

Real Madrid **3-0** Valencia
(Spain)　　　(Spain)

In the first final between two teams from the same country, Madrid completely dominated with their brand of attacking football and breathtaking skill. With Steve McManaman pulling the strings in midfield, wing-backs Roberto Carlos and Michel Salgado marauding forward at every opportunity, and Raúl a constant threat in attack, there was only ever going to be one winner. The only surprise was that it took 39 minutes for Real to open

the scoring. A Roberto Carlos free-kick was deflected into the path of Anelka, whose ball found Morientes unmarked at the far post.

In the 63rd minute McManaman was rewarded as he crashed home through a pack of players to put the game beyond Valencia's reach, but the best was saved until last as Raúl ran 70 yards before rounding Canizares and tucking the ball home.

2001: BAYERN MUNICH

SAN SIRO, MILAN May 23

Bayern Munich **1-1** Valencia (aet)
(Germany)　　　(Spain)
1-1 at 90 minutes; Bayern won 5-4 on penalties

In a game of penalties, Valencia opened the scoring as early as the second minute when Mendieta's shot was adjudged to have hit Patrick Andersson on the arm and the Spanish playmaker stepped up to convert the penalty kick himself. Incredibly, referee Jol awarded another spot-kick just five minutes later when Angloma scythed Effenberg down, but Scholl's kick was saved by the legs of Canizares.

The early edge, both psychological and in terms of goals, would not last for the Spaniards as Bayern enjoyed plenty of possession, with Lizarazu and Salihamidzic causing problems down the left. Scholl went close with a free-kick and Carew could have made it 2-0 to Valencia with a header that flashed wide, but it was the introduction of Jancker that proved crucial.

Within five minutes of coming on, the big striker's challenge on Carboni forced the Italian defender to handle the ball and Effenberg stepped up to send keeper Santiago Canizares the wrong way. In extra-time Canizares blocked a close range shot from Elber and Scholl fired a free-kick tamely wide. The Valencia keeper also kept out an angled drive by Salihamidzic, but the Germans held their nerve to win a tense penalty shoot-out.

2002: REAL MADRID

HAMPDEN PARK, GLASGOW May 15

Real Madrid **2-1** Bayer Leverkusen
(Spain)　　　(Germany)

Zidane's breathtaking volley in the final minute of the first-half is the enduring image of a game that saw Real's class overcome Leverkusen's stubbornness. The French star, who had contributed little in the previous 44 minutes, met a left-wing cross from Roberto Carlos and let fly from the edge of the area with a waist-high volley that flew past goalkeeper Butt.

Earlier Raúl had struck in the ninth minute from a move that began with a long throw by Roberto Carlos, and Brazilian defender Lucio had headed the leveller in the 14th minute from a Schneider free-kick. However, Zidane apart, the star of the show was young Real goalkeeper Casillas, who replaced the injured César Sánchez in the 67th minute before making fine saves from a Bastürk header and Berbatov's injury-time strike. The result meant that Madrid, beaten in the league and Spanish Cup final after being on course for the treble, finally won the biggest prize of all in their centenary year.

2003: AC MILAN

OLD TRAFFORD, MANCHESTER May 28

AC Milan **0-0** Juventus (aet)
(Italy)　　　(Italy)
Milan won 3-2 on penalties

In the first all-Italian final in the 48-year history of the competition, Juventus faced Milan minus suspended Czech midfielder Pavel Nedved. Without him the team lacked midfield urgency as Milan had three good scoring chances in the first 45 minutes. Shevchenko had the ball in the Juventus net in the eighth minute, but Rui Costa was adjudged offside, while Inzaghi went close with a diving header that was spectacularly saved by Buffon. Six minutes before the break

Below: The celebrations start for Bayern Munich in 2001.

Above: Steven Gerrard inspired Liverpool's fantastic comeback from 3-0 down to win the Champions League in 2005.

another chance fell to Rui Costa when Pirlo found him in front of goal, but the Portuguese midfielder pulled his shot wide of Buffon's right-hand post. An effort from Trezeguet and a Del Piero shot on the stroke of half-time were Juve's best of the half and, indeed, the game.

The second-half degenerated into a game of defensive mastery. Extra-time and penalties were inevitable, but even the shoot-out proved disappointing, and it was left to Shevchenko to score the winner and make up for his earlier disappointment.

2004: PORTO

ARENA AUFSCHALKE, GELSENKIRCHEN May 26

Porto **3-0** AS Monaco
(Portugal)   (France)

José Mourinho's disciplined Porto side ended their surprising campaign by becoming European champions for the first time since 1987. Monaco started brightly and looked the better of the two sides, but after injury robbed them of their captain and playmaker, Ludovic Giuly, midway through a sterile first-half, Porto took the initiative. A 38th minute volley from Brazilian teenager Carlos Alberto put the Portuguese champions in the lead, but Monaco continued to press forward and constantly looked the more threatening of the two sides.

Porto proved dangerous on the counter-attack with Brazilian playmaker Deco breaking from the halfway line and receiving a return pass from substitute Dmitri Alenitchev before scoring a delightful chipped goal with 20 minutes left. Moments later the veteran Russian

Right: Arsenal goalkeeper Jens Lehmann sees red in 2006. He became the first player to be sent off in a European Cup final.

star Alenitchev scored Porto's third, firing home a deflected pass from Derlei Silva. Monaco had been punished ruthlessly on the break, enabling Porto to add the Champions League trophy to the UEFA Cup they had won the previous year.

2005: LIVERPOOL

ATATÜRK STADIUM, ISTANBUL May 25

Liverpool **3-3** AC Milan (aet)
(England)   (Italy)
3-3 at 90 mins; Liverpool won 3-2 on penalties

In an unprecedented comeback at this level, Liverpool became champions of Europe for a fifth time with three goals in six incredible second-half minutes. Outclassed before the break, 'The Reds' found themselves 3-0 down by half-time, with Paolo Maldini putting Milan in front inside the first minute. Harry Kewell limped off injured after just 22 minutes, and two goals from Hernan Crespo at the close of the first-half compounded Liverpool's problems.

Steven Gerrard threw the English club a lifeline in the 54th minute, heading home a John Arne Riise's cross, and within six minutes the scores were level. The tie was taken into extra-time thanks to goals from Smicer and Alonso, who had followed up his own saved penalty to score. After extra-time the game was settled by a dramatic penalty shoot-out. Andriy Shevchenko, scorer of the winning penalty in the 2003 final, was this time denied by Jerzy Dudek, whose goal-line antics conjured up memories of Bruce Grobbelaar in 1984.

2006: BARCELONA

STADE DE FRANCE, PARIS May 17

Barcelona **2-1** Arsenal
(Spain)   (England)

A final that had all the potential to be the most exciting in years, the match exploded in to life from the kick-off, with Arsenal's Thierry Henry coming close twice in the opening exchanges. However, after just 18 minutes of free-flowing,

end-to-end football, the game took a sensational turn that altered the flavour of the tie and settled the destination of the trophy. Ronaldinho played a ball through to Samuel Eto'o, but the Cameroon forward was caught on the edge of the box by the onrushing Jens Lehmann. The ball fell to Giuly, who tapped it home, but the referee disallowed the goal, awarded a free-kick to Barcelona and red-carded the Arsenal keeper, who became the first player to be sent-off in a European Cup final.

With Almunia replacing Lehmann in goal, Arsenal absorbed the pressure and snatched the lead through a 37th minute Sol Campbell header. Arsenal held their own, with Henry spurning his fair share of chances before Eto'o scored with just 14 minutes remaining. 'The Gunners' tired in the heavy rain and as Barcelona surged forward, Belletti scored the winner in the 80th minute.

2007: AC MILAN

OLYMPIC STADIUM, ATHENS May 23

AC Milan **2-1** Liverpool
(Italy)   (England)

In a rematch of the 2005 final, Milan exacted revenge for the penalty shoot-out defeat that Liverpool had inflicted on them two years earlier, thanks to two goals from Pippo Inzaghi. It was a much-anticipated contest with tickets exchanging hands on the black market for substantial sums, but there were chaotic scenes before the match as Greek police denied entry to genuine ticket holders on the grounds that the stadium was already full.

Once the match was underway Liverpool dominated much of the early play but seconds before the interval they conceded an unexpected goal when Andrea Pirlo's free-kick caught a freak deflection off Inzaghi and wrong-footed keeper Pepe Reina. Steven Gerrard missed a solid chance for Liverpool in the second-half, but as the game edged into its final ten minutes Inzaghi made a perfectly timed run onto Kaká's

smartly played through ball into the box and rounded the keeper before slotting comfortably into the net from a wide angle.

Liverpool clawed a goal back through a header from lone striker Dirk Kuyt, scored with just a minute remaining, but any thoughts that this would inspire another comeback proved unfounded when the final whistle blew.

2008: MANCHESTER UNITED

LUZHNIKI STADIUM, MOSCOW May 21

Manchester United **1-1** Chelsea (aet)
(England) (England)
1-1 at 90 minutes; Manchester United won 6-5 on penalties

It was perhaps fitting that 50 years after the Munich air disaster it should be Manchester United that claimed the trophy, winning after a thrilling final was settled by a tense penalty shoot-out in the heavy rain of Moscow.

It was United's young Portuguese starlet Cristiano Ronaldo who opened the scoring midway through the first-half when he rose above a stranded Michael Essien to head home Wes Brown's 26th-minute cross. United continued to attack and keeper Petr Cech frustrated them with a magnificent double save from Tevez and Carrick. Frank Lampard pulled 'The Blues' back into the game after capitalising on a defensive mix-up before the interval and he celebrated by dedicating the goal to his mother, who had died the previous month.

Although United had the greater share of the first-half chances, both Lampard and Didier Drogba hit the woodwork before the end of the match, although Chelsea finished extra-time with just ten men after Drogba was sent-off for a slap to Nemanja Vidic.

In a seesaw penalty shoot-out Chelsea initially held the advantage after Ronaldo missed with United's third spot-kick, but captain John Terry slipped in his run-up and hit the post with the shot that would have settled the game in Chelsea's favour. The shoot-out went to sudden death and it was United keeper Edwin Van Der Sar who became the hero when he saved from Nicholas Anelka. A sobbing John Terry had to be consoled by coach Avram Grant while United received the trophy.

2009: BARCELONA

OLYMPIC STADIUM, ROME May 27

Barcelona **2-0** Manchester United
(Spain) (England)

It was the dream final that so many neutral fans had hoped for, but a strangely lacklustre display from Manchester United saw Barcelona comfortable winners. The English club started the final well, with Cristiano Ronaldo looking like he would pose the biggest threat in the earliest exchanges. However, with just ten minutes on the clock Samuel Eto'o powered into the United box, beating Nemanja Vidic before slotting the ball under keeper Van Der Sar.

With Andrés Iniesta and Xavi dominating the midfield for Barcelona, United made little impact on the game and with 20 minutes remaining Lionel Messi nipped into the box between John O'Shea and Rio Ferdinand and rose completely unopposed to head home a pinpoint cross from Xavi.

United fought back immediately but after Victor Valdés stopped a shot from Ronaldo, United all but capitulated. In just his first season as Barcelona coach, Pep Guardiola completed a dream 'treble', adding the Champions League trophy to his Spanish league and cup 'double'.

2010: INTER MILAN

BERNABÉU STADIUM, MADRID May 22

Inter Milan **2-0** Bayern Munich
(Italy) (Germany)

There was little question that José Mourinho's immaculately prepared Inter Milan side had the measure of Bayern Munich. From the kick-off they were well drilled and perfectly capable of snuffing out any threat offered up by their opponents. They were also able to break like lightning on the counterattack. They may have offered little ingenuity in the first half an hour as Arjen Robben inspired an expansive Bayern to bring the game to the Italian side, but the contest looked dead and buried once Diego Milito ran on to a smartly played through ball from Wesley Sneijder and fired past Hans-Jörg Butt on 34 minutes.

Although the Bayern players raised their game early in the second half, it was Milito who scored again with 20 minutes remaining, collecting a pass from Samuel Eto'o and turning the Real defence inside out before impeccably placing the ball past the stranded keeper. The Argentine striker gained his own special

standing ovation when he was replaced in the dying seconds of the game, making substitute Marco Materazzi Inter Milan's only Italian player of the night.

Despite the fact that it was the first time in 45 years that an Inter team had laid hands on the European Cup, and that they had also become the first Italian side ever to win the 'treble', it was really Mourinho's triumph. In his last game in charge of Inter, he had become became only the third coach to lift the European Cup with two different clubs.

Above: John Terry's slip during the 2008 penalty shoot-out hands the trophy to Manchester United.

Below: After the 2010 final, Inter Milan celebrate winning the European Cup for the first time in 45 years.

FAIRS CUP, UEFA CUP & EUROPA LEAGUE

Above from left to right: The 1992 Ajax side celebrate after beating Torino on away goals; Mick Mills of Ipswich lifts the trophy in 1981; Porto beat Celtic to win the UEFA Cup in 2003.

Opposite clockwise from top left: Atlético Madrid win the first Europa League final in 2010; Parma start the celebrations after defeating Marseille in 1999; Billy Bremner and the Leeds United team party with the Fairs Cup trophy in 1971; CSKA Moscow's big moment in 2005.

The Europa League is Europe's second most prestigious international club competition, rebranded under this name for the 2009-10 season after more than three decades known as the UEFA Cup. However, when it came into being in the 1971-2 season, it was itself first introduced as a replacement for the Fairs Cup, a competition that had been running since 1955. UEFA does not include the Fairs Cup in the statistics and records of the competitions that succeeded it, as it was not staged under the auspices of the organisation, but it would be unfair to tell the story of the Europa League without tracing the roots of the competition back to the beginnings of the Fairs Cup.

The Inter-Cities Fairs Cup began life as something of an anomaly. It was dreamt up in 1955, shortly after the inception of the European Cup, by future FIFA president, Sir Stanley Rous, and two future FIFA vice-presidents, Switzerland's Ernst Thommen and Italy's Ottorino Barassi. Their idea was to hold a competition for European cities that regularly organised trade fairs. Entry was unrelated to a club's league placing, which threw up some insignificant teams early on, as well as some peculiar representative sides featuring players from several clubs, like the London Select XI that starred in the first campaign.

The first Fairs Cup involved teams from Barcelona, Basle, Birmingham, Copenhagen, Frankfurt, Lausanne, Leipzig, London, Milan and Zagreb. Originally conceived as a two-year tournament, it actually lasted for three, during which time 23 games were played in a clumsy group system complicated by withdrawals. The final was contested over two legs by Barcelona, using players exclusively from FC Barcelona, and the London Select XI, which included Arsenal goalkeeper Jack Kelsey, Tottenham's Danny Blanchflower, Fulham's Johnny Haynes and Jimmy Greaves of Chelsea. The London XI, who had played several of their games under floodlights at Wembley Stadium, held Barcelona 2-2 in front of 45,000 fans at Stamford Bridge, but they were routed 6-0 in the return two months later.

Two years on the format was altered, limiting participation to 16 professional club sides from cities that held trade fairs. Barcelona held onto the trophy, beating Birmingham City, who went on to lose two finals in a row after defeat the following year to AS Roma, the only Italian club who would lift the 'Coppa Delle Fiere'.

Following this brief Italian interlude, Spanish clubs returned to their position of predominance in the competition. Between 1962 and 1964 the final was an all Spanish affair, with Valencia winning twice in succession before losing in the third consecutive year to Real Zaragoza in a one-legged confrontation at Barcelona's Nou Camp stadium. Hungarians Ferencváros finally broke the Mediterranean hegemony in 1965, before Barcelona reclaimed the title again a year later.

There were more changes in 1967 when the competition was renamed the European Fairs Cup and increased to 48 entrants, the first of a succession of expansions that saw 64 sides competing in the 1969-70 season, by which time it was unofficially known as the 'runners-up cup'. Never was a title more merited than in 1968 when Don Revie's Leeds United lifted the trophy. They had earned the status of 'nearly men' in English football and had been the beaten finalists the previous season, losing to Dinamo Zagreb. However, they shook off their 'bridesmaid' image, progressing smoothly past AC Spora, Partizan Belgrade, Hibernian, Rangers and Dundee, before holding onto a narrow 1-0 first leg lead against Ferencváros.

Leeds United's first victory opened the door for English clubs to dominate the competition, with Newcastle picking up the trophy the following season. The Magpies had finished tenth in the First Division but qualified thanks to a one-city, one-team rule. They demonstrated their worth by seeing off the challenge of Sporting Lisbon, Real Zaragoza and Rangers before a 6-2 victory over an Újpest Dozsa side that featured six Hungarian internationals.

In 1970 Arsenal beat Anderlecht to win the club's first European trophy despite finishing 12th in the league that season. Facing a 3-1 deficit from the away leg, Arsenal looked set to notch up an unenviable record of three final defeats in succession, having lost the two previous League Cup finals, but the 'Gunners' romped to a 3-0 win at Highbury, ending a run of 17 years without a trophy.

Leeds returned to prominence in 1971, winning the last ever Fairs Cup by beating Juventus on away goals, a rule used for the first time in the competition's history. It took three matches to settle the tie, as a replay of the first leg in Italy was needed after the original game

was abandoned due to an unplayable pitch.

With UEFA taking over the competition the following season, the name was changed to the UEFA Cup, the trophy replaced and the format altered. Leeds and Barcelona, as the two sides with the best overall playing record in the competition, contested a specially organised play-off on September 22, 1971. Barcelona won 2-1 and the trophy now resides permanently at the Nou Camp. The first winners of the new trophy, a silver cup on a yellow marble plinth designed and crafted by the Bertoni workshops in Milan, were Tottenham, who won an all English affair in 1972, beating Wolverhampton Wanderers 3-2 on aggregate.

Liverpool's first UEFA Cup win the following year was the culmination of eight consecutive seasons of continental action, a record that no other English club could boast. The two-legged final against Borussia Mönchengladbach was an epic that included an abandoned first leg due to a waterlogged pitch at Anfield. Bill Shankly used the opportunity to rejig his side, replacing Brian Hall with John Toshack the following evening – a move that saw 'The Reds' post a 3-0 win that Borussia could not match in the return.

The 1974 competition was notable for the outbreak of crowd trouble at the final after Spurs fans went on the rampage following a 2-0 defeat to Feyenoord in Rotterdam, a display that led to the club being banned from the competition for two years. However, it was not Tottenham's last problem with hooliganism in the competition. Ten years later a fan died in rioting and 200 arrests were made after the Londoners beat Anderlecht in the first UEFA Cup penalty shoot-out, with keeper Tony Parks writing his name in the club's history books.

After Liverpool's 1976 victory over Belgian side Club Brugge, it would be another five years before an English side again lifted the UEFA Cup, with Juventus, PSV Eindhoven, Borussia Mönchengladbach and Eintracht Frankfurt passing the trophy around in the intervening period. Bobby Robson's Ipswich

Town restored English pride in 1981, with Frans Thijssen and Arnold Mühren squaring up to fellow Dutchmen AZ 67 Alkmaar and emerging 5-4 aggregate winners. The cup went to a Scandinavian side for the first time the following year, with Gothenburg overcoming Hamburg. The Swedish club would lift the trophy again in 1987, beating Dundee United.

Tottenham's 1984 triumph over Anderlecht effectively saw the end of England's dominance, as English clubs were banned from European competition for five years following the disaster at Heysel before the European Cup final. No English side would compete in the competition again until the Aston Villa team were allowed to enter in September 1990. It was 11 years before an English team actually lifted the cup again, when Liverpool beat Spanish side Alaves in a 5-4 thriller decided by an own 'golden goal', though Arsenal did reach the final against Galatasaray in 2000, an occasion that resulted in further fan violence and the first ever UEFA Cup win for a Turkish team.

The late Eighties saw Italian clubs make a significant mark. Maradona's Napoli broke the country's 12-year drought in the competition, beating Stuttgart in 1989 and opening the door for Serie A clubs to dominate in a six-year run broken only by Ajax in 1992. Juventus and Inter were the main beneficiaries, with three of the finals all-Italian affairs.

After consecutive wins for German clubs Bayern and Schalke, the 1998 UEFA Cup again featured two Italian sides in the final, with Milan beating Lazio 3-0 in Paris. By then the expansion of the Champions League had resulted in a further raft of changes: those clubs failing to qualify for the Champions League group stages received a bye into the next round of the UEFA Cup. In the 1999-2000 season the competition was effectively merged with the European Cup Winners' Cup and further qualification routes were opened up to the three 'winners' of the Intertoto Cup and three clubs from UEFA's Fair Play League.

In 2003 Porto became Portugal's first

winners of the competition, beating Celtic in Seville. The following year Valencia secured the club's first European trophy since 1980, beating Marseille 2-0 in Gothenburg, but the team were helped when the French had keeper Fabien Barthez sent-off just before half-time.

The format of the competition was given a significant overhaul for the 2004-5 season. After the first round, the 40 surviving teams entered a group phase, featuring eight pools of five, where each club played just two games at home and two away. The top three in each group progressed to the next round, where they were joined by the eight third-placed teams from the Champions League group phase. From this point, the UEFA Cup returned to its traditional format: a two-legged knockout competition with a one-off final.

CSKA Moscow were the first winners using this format. With the final played in Lisbon, home advantage helped Sporting to an early lead but CSKA won 3-1 to take the UEFA Cup to Russia for the first time. Sevilla were also first-time winners in 2006, beating Middlesbrough 4-0 in the club's centenary year. They retained the cup a year later after beating Espanyol. Zenit Saint Petersburg and Shakhtar Donetsk won in subsequent seasons, before the UEFA Cup underwent another a major reinvention.

In an attempt to increase the prestige of the competition, it was rebranded as the Europa League at the beginning of 2009-10 and the intake was increased to 48 teams, drawn into 12 groups of four. After playing each other on a home and away basis, the top two sides in each group progress to the next round, where they are joined in a knockout stage by the teams eliminated from the Champions League. The first Europa League final was between Fulham and Atlético Madrid, with the Spanish side winning their first European trophy in 48 years.

It remains to be seen whether the rebranding of the competition will raise its profile once again, as the continual aggrandisement of the Champions League has only served to diminish the status of the Europa League.

THE WINNERS OF THE FAIRS CUP/UEFA CUP/EUROPA LEAGUE

FAIRS CUP

1958: BARCELONA
1ST LEG March 5
London Select XI **2-2** Barcelona
(England)   (Spain)
2ND LEG May 1
Barcelona **6-0** London Select XI
Barcelona won 8-2 on aggregate

1960: BARCELONA
1ST LEG March 29
Birmingham City **0-0** Barcelona
(England)   (Spain)
2ND LEG May 4
Barcelona **4-1** Birmingham City
Barcelona won 4-1 on aggregate

1961: AS ROMA
1ST LEG September 27
Birmingham City **2-2** AS Roma
(England)   (Italy)
2ND LEG October 11
AS Roma **2-0** Birmingham City
AS Roma won 4-2 on aggregate

1962: VALENCIA
1ST LEG September 8
Valencia **6-2** Barcelona
(Spain)   (Spain)
2ND LEG September 12
Barcelona **1-1** Valencia
Valencia won 7-3 on aggregate

1963: VALENCIA
1ST LEG June 12
Dynamo Zagreb **1-2** Valencia
(Yugoslavia)   (Spain)
2ND LEG June 26
Valencia **2-0** Dynamo Zagreb
Valencia won 4-1 on aggregate

1964: REAL ZARAGOZA
NOU CAMP, BARCELONA June 25
Real Zaragoza **2-1** Valencia
(Spain)   (Spain)

1965: FERENCVÁROS
COMUNALE, TURIN June 23
Ferencváros **1-0** Juventus
(Hungary)   (Italy)

1966: BARCELONA
1ST LEG September 14
Barcelona **0-1** Real Zaragoza
(Spain)   (Spain)
2ND LEG September 21
Real Zaragoza **2-4** Barcelona (aet)
Barcelona won 4-3 on aggregate

1967: DYNAMO ZAGREB
1ST LEG August 30
Dynamo Zagreb **2-0** Leeds United
(Yugoslavia)   (England)
2ND LEG September 6
Leeds United **0-0** Dynamo Zagreb
Dynamo Zagreb won 2-0 on aggregate

1968: LEEDS UNITED
1ST LEG August 7
Leeds United **1-0** Ferencváros
(England)   (Hungary)
2ND LEG September 11
Ferencváros **0-0** Leeds United
Leeds United won 1-0 on aggregate

1969: NEWCASTLE UNITED
1ST LEG May 29
Newcastle United **3-0** Újpest Dozsa
(England)   (Hungary)
2ND LEG June 11
Újpest Dozsa **2-3** Newcastle United
Newcastle United won 6-2 on aggregate

1970: ARSENAL
1ST LEG April 22
Anderlecht **3-1** Arsenal
(Belgium)   (England)
2ND LEG April 28
Arsenal **3-0** Anderlecht
Arsenal won 4-3 on aggregate

1971: LEEDS UNITED
1ST LEG May 26
Juventus **0-0** Leeds United
(Italy)   (England)
Match abandoned after 51 mins waterlogged pitch
1ST LEG REPLAY May 28
Juventus **2-2** Leeds United
2ND LEG June 3
Leeds United **1-1** Juventus
Leeds United won on away goals rule

The Fairs Cup was replaced by The UEFA Cup in the 1971-72 season

UEFA CUP

1972: TOTTENHAM HOTSPUR
1ST LEG May 3
Wolverhampton **1-2** Tottenham
Wanderers   Hotspur
(England)   (England)
2ND LEG May 17
Tottenham **1-1** Wolverhampton
Hotspur   Wanderers
Tottenham Hotspur won 3-2 on aggregate

1973: LIVERPOOL
1ST LEG May 9
Liverpool **0-0** Borussia
      Mönchengladbach
(England)   (West Germany)
Match abandoned after 27 mins waterlogged pitch
1ST LEG REPLAY May 10
Liverpool **3-0** Borussia
      Mönchengladbach
2ND LEG May 23
Borussia **2-0** Liverpool
Mönchengladbach
Liverpool won 3-2 on aggregate

1974: FEYENOORD
1ST LEG May 21
Tottenham **2-2** Feyenoord
Hotspur
(England)   (Holland)
2ND LEG May 29
Feyenoord **2-0** Tottenham
      Hotspur
Feyenoord won 4-2 on aggregate

1975: B. MÖNCHENGLADBACH
1ST LEG May 7
Borussia **0-0** FC Twente
Mönchengladbach
(West Germany)   (Holland)
2ND LEG May 21
FC Twente **1-5** Borussia
      Mönchengladbach
Borussia Mönchengladbach won 5-1 on aggregate

1976: LIVERPOOL
1ST LEG April 28
Liverpool **3-2** Club Brugge
(England)   (West Germany)
2ND LEG May 19
Club Brugge **1-1** Liverpool
Liverpool won 4-3 on aggregate

1977: JUVENTUS
1ST LEG May 4
Juventus **1-0** Athletic Bilbao
(Italy)   (Spain)
2ND LEG May 18
Athletic Bilbao **2-1** Juventus
Juventus won on away goal rule

1978: PSV EINDHOVEN
1ST LEG April 26
SC Bastia **0-0** PSV Eindhoven
(France)   (Holland)
2ND LEG May 9
PSV Eindhoven **3-0** SC Bastia
PSV Eindhoven won 3-0 on aggregate

1979: B. MÖNCHENGLADBACH
1ST LEG May 9
Red Star Belgrade **1-1** Borussia
      Mönchengladbach
(Yugoslavia)   (West Germany)
2ND LEG May 23
Borussia **1-0** Red Star Belgrade
Mönchengladbach
Borussia Mönchengladbach won 2-1 on aggregate

1980: EINTRACHT FRANKFURT
1ST LEG May 7
Borussia **3-2** Eintracht
Mönchengladbach   Frankfurt
(West Germany)   (West Germany)
2ND LEG May 21
Eintracht **1-0** Borussia
Frankfurt   Mönchengladbach
Eintracht Frankfurt won on away goal rule

1981: IPSWICH TOWN
1ST LEG May 6
Ipswich Town **3-0** AZ 67 Alkmaar
(England)   (Holland)
2ND LEG May 20
AZ 67 Alkmaar **4-2** Ipswich Town
Ipswich Town won 5-4 on aggregate

1982: IFK GOTHENBURG
1ST LEG May 5
IFK Gothenburg **1-0** Hamburg
(Sweden)   (West Germany)
2ND LEG May 19
Hamburg **0-3** IFK Gothenburg
IFK Gothenburg won 4-0 on aggregate

1983: RSC ANDERLECHT
1ST LEG May 4
Anderlecht **1-0** Benfica
(Belgium)   (Portugal)
2ND LEG May 18
Benfica **1-1** Anderlecht
RSC Anderlecht won 2-1 on aggregate

1984: TOTTENHAM HOTSPUR
1ST LEG May 9
Anderlecht **1-1** Tottenham
      Hotspur
(Belgium)   (England)
2ND LEG May 23
Tottenham **1-1** Anderlecht (aet)
Hotspur
Tottenham Hotspur won 4-3 on penalties

1985: REAL MADRID
1ST LEG May 8
Videoton **0-3** Real Madrid
(Hungary)   (Spain)
2ND LEG May 22
Real Madrid **0-1** Videoton
Real Madrid won 3-1 on aggregate

1986: REAL MADRID
1ST LEG April 30
Real Madrid **5-1** Köln
(Spain)   (West Germany)
2ND LEG May 6
Köln **2-0** Real Madrid
Real Madrid won 5-3 on aggregate

1987: IFK GOTHENBURG
1ST LEG May 6
IFK Gothenburg **1-0** Dundee United
(Sweden)   (Scotland)
2ND LEG May 20
Dundee United **1-1** IFK Gothenburg
IFK Gothenburg won 2-1 on aggregate

1988: BAYER LEVERKUSEN
1ST LEG May 4
Espanyol **3-0** Bayer Leverkusen
(Spain)   (West Germany)
2ND LEG May 18
Bayer Leverkusen **3-0** Espanyol (aet)
Beyer Leverkusen won 3-2 on penalties

1989: NAPOLI
1ST LEG May 3
Napoli **2-1** Vfb Stuttgart
(Italy)   (West Germany)
2ND LEG May 17
Vfb Stuttgart **3-3** Napoli
Napoli won 5-4 on aggregate

1990: JUVENTUS
1ST LEG May 2
Juventus **3-1** Fiorentina
(Italy)   (Italy)
2ND LEG May 16
Fiorentina **0-0** Juventus
Juventus won 3-1 on aggregate

1991: INTER MILAN
1ST LEG May 8
Inter Milan **2-0** AS Roma
(Italy)   (Italy)
2ND LEG May 22
AS Roma **1-0** Inter Milan
Inter Milan won 2-1 on aggregate

1992: AJAX
1ST LEG April 29
Torino **2-2** Ajax
(Italy)   (Holland)
2ND LEG May 13
Ajax **0-0** Torino
Ajax won on away goals rule

1993: JUVENTUS
1ST LEG May 5
Borussia **1-3** Juventus
Dortmund
(Germany)   (Italy)
2ND LEG May 19
Juventus **3-0** Borussia
      Dortmund
Juventus won 6-1 on aggregate

1994: INTER MILAN
1ST LEG April 26
Austria Salzburg **0-1** Inter Milan
(Austria)   (Italy)
2ND LEG May 11
Inter Milan **1-0** Austria Salzburg
Inter Milan won 2-0 on aggregate

1995: PARMA
1ST LEG May 3
Parma **1-0** Juventus
(Italy)   (Italy)
2ND LEG May 17
Juventus **1-1** Parma
Parma won 2-1 on aggregate

1996: BAYERN MUNICH
1ST LEG May 1
Bayern Munich **2-0** Bordeaux
(Germany)   (France)
2ND LEG May 15
Bordeaux **1-3** Bayern Munich
Bayern Munich won 5-1 on aggregate

1997: FC SCHALKE 04
1ST LEG May 7
FC Schalke 04 **1-0** Inter Milan
(Germany)   (Italy)
2ND LEG May 21
Inter Milan **1-0** FC Schalke 04
(aet)
FC Schalke 04 won 4-1 on penalties

1998: INTER MILAN
PARC DES PRINCES, PARIS May 6
Inter Milan **3-0** Lazio
(Italy)   (Italy)

1999: PARMA
LUZHNIKI, MOSCOW May 12
Parma **3-0** Marseille
(Italy)   (France)

2000: GALATASARAY
PARKEN, COPENHAGEN May 17
Galatasaray **0-0** Arsenal (aet)
(Turkey)   (England)
Galatasaray won 4-1 on penalties

2001: LIVERPOOL
WESTFALEN, DORTMUND May 16
Liverpool **5-4** Alavés (aet)
(England)   (Spain)

2002: FEYENOORD
DE KUIP, ROTTERDAM May 8
Feyenoord **3-2** Borussia
      Dortmund
(Holland)   (Germany)

2003: PORTO
OLIMPICO, SEVILLE May 21
Porto **3-2** Celtic (aet)
(Portugal)   (Scotland)

2004: VALENCIA
NYA ULLEVI, GOTHENBURG May 19
Valencia **2-0** Marseille
(Spain)   (France)

2005: CSKA MOSCOW
JOSÉ ALVALADE, LISBON May 18
CSKA Moscow **3-1** Sporting Lisbon
(Russia)   (Portugal)

2006: SEVILLA
PSV STADIUM, EINDHOVEN May 10
Sevilla **4-0** Middlesbrough
(Spain)   (England)

2007: SEVILLA
HAMPDEN PARK, GLASGOW May 16
Sevilla **2-2** Espanyol
(Spain)   (Spain)
Sevilla won 3-1 on penalties

2008: ZENIT ST PETERSBURG
CITY OF MANCHESTER STADIUM, MANCHESTER May 14
Zenit St Petersburg **2-0** Rangers
(Russia)   (Scotland)

2009: SHAKHTAR DONETSK
SUKRU SARACOGLU STADIUM, ISTANBUL May 20
Shakhtar Donetsk **2-1** Werder Bremen
(Ukraine)   (Germany)

UEFA EUROPA LEAGUE

2010: ATLÉTICO MADRID
VOLKSPARK STADIUM, HAMBURG May 12
Atlético Madrid **2-1** Fulham
(Spain)   (England)

EUROPEAN CUP WINNERS' CUP

 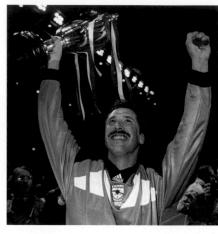 

Above from left to right: Barcelona celebrate in 1997; Arsenal's David Seaman lifts the cup in 1994; Real Zaragoza enjoy the moment after victory over Arsenal in 1995.

Opposite clockwise from top left: Dinamo Tbilisi celebrate in 1981; Lazio, winners of the last ever final in 1999; Ron Harris and the Chelsea team bring the cup home to their fans in 1971; Willie Miller leads the Aberdeen players on a lap of honour.

When Lazio's Pavel Nedved struck home the winning goal against Mallorca in the 81st minute of the 1999 European Cup Winners' Cup final at Villa Park, he was not only ensuring the win for the Rome side, he was also entering the history books as the last ever player to score in the tournament. After 39 years the competition was discontinued, and swallowed up by the expanded UEFA Cup. This was due in the most part to the increased importance of the Champions League, and pressure on UEFA to streamline its European club fixtures. The final nail in the competition's coffin could be said to be Barcelona's decision to play in the Champions League rather than defend their title in 1998.

The European Cup Winners' Cup was launched in 1960 and organised to run in parallel with the UEFA Cup. Based on the same format as the European Cup, with home and away knockout ties up to the final, the participants in the competition were generally the winners of their domestic cup, as well as the previous season's holders. However, if the cup winners were identical to the winners of the national championship (who would therefore be competing in the European Cup), the runners-up in the cup competition would take part. At the time the tournament was established many European countries did not possess a domestic cup competition, but the promise of qualification and extra revenue meant they soon acquired one.

The first Cup Winners' Cup tournament attracted teams from ten countries. Inspired by legendary Swedish winger Kurt Hamrin, the trophy was lifted by Fiorentina – the first piece of European silverware to be won by an Italian side. They overcame Rangers 4-1 on aggregate in a final played over two legs (the format changed to a one-off game the following year). Rangers themselves had reached the final after disposing of Wolverhampton Wanderers in a keenly contested all-British semi-final.

With the competition deemed a success, the following year saw a far larger pool of entrants, with some 23 countries now taking part. The final again saw Fiorentina involved, but this time they were deprived of the distinction of retaining their title by Atlético Madrid, who lifted the cup after a 3-0 replay win. Curiously, the replay was played nearly four months after the original game.

In 1963 the holders once again had the opportunity to retain their trophy by making it to the final, but this time Atlético fell at the last hurdle. Their conquerors were Bill Nicholson's 'double' winning Tottenham side, and the result was an emphatic 5-1 result, with the prolific Jimmy Greaves and Terry Dyson getting on the scoresheet twice each. The victory made Tottenham the first English club to get their hands on a European trophy.

Over the course of its 39 years the Cup Winners' Cup saw many British clubs making it to the final. In 1965, in front of a 100,000 capacity Wembley crowd, West Ham United brought the trophy back to London with their 2-0 defeat of TSV 1860 Munich. Neighbours Chelsea made it a hat-trick for sides from the English capital in 1971 with their stunning Peter Osgood-inspired replay victory over the mighty Real Madrid. A year earlier, northern pride had been restored with Manchester City's victory over Górnik Zabrze of Poland. The silverware headed to Maine Road thanks to goals by Neil Young and Francis Lee.

Scotland's Rangers also had success in the competition, and over the course of the 1972 final they narrowly got the better of Dynamo Moscow, coming out of the game 3-2 winners after leading 3-0 for much of the game. This was third time lucky for the Glasgow side, who were on the wrong end of two final defeats in 1960 and 1967.

It was not always plain sailing for the English clubs that made the final either. In the 1966 Liverpool were unlucky to lose out to Borussia Dortmund after extra-time, and a similar fate befell Leeds United (1973), West Ham (1976) and Arsenal (1980 and 1995) in subsequent finals. Arsenal's 1980 defeat was against Valencia, and after a 0-0 draw the match was the first European club final to be decided on penalties. It was former England midfielder Graham Rix's failure from the spot that gave the Spaniards the trophy.

After an 11 year gap without any British success it was left to Alex Ferguson's Aberdeen to heroically recapture the Cup Winners' Cup in 1983, and they achieved it at the expense of Real Madrid. Played in atrocious weather conditions, the match was settled by substitute John Hewitt's diving header in extra-time and was a famous victory for the Scottish side.

Right: Parma's Lorenzo Minotti at Wembley in 1993.

Far right: West Ham's Bobby Moore shows the cup to the fans outside the Town Hall in 1965.

Opposite top: Youri Djorkaeff of Paris Sant-Germain in action in the 1996 final.

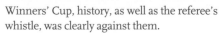

Opposite bottom: Rangers keeper Billy Ritchie saves a shot from Fiorentina's Kurt Hamrin in the first leg of the final in 1961.

Below: Terry Dyson and Jimmy Greaves of Tottenham give a victory thumbs-up. They scored two goals each in the 1963 final.

Since Aberdeen's triumph there have been four other British successes. In 1985 Howard Kendall's Everton disposed of Rapid Vienna with a clinical 3-1 win, with goals from Andy Gray, Trevor Steven and Kevin Sheedy. It was to be the last time English clubs participated in European competition until 1991, following their ban in the wake of the Heysel tragedy. This was the year that saw Manchester United take the honours from Barcelona.

In 1994 Arsenal finally got their name on the trophy with a 1-0 victory, courtesy of an Alan Smith goal against the much-fancied Parma. The following year they were to suffer heartache as former Tottenham midfielder Nayim, now playing for Real Zaragoza, famously chipped David Seaman from nearly the halfway line. The last English side to win the trophy were Chelsea, who secured the title for a second time in 1998 with their narrow win against Stuttgart in Stockholm, thanks to an opportunistic strike from Gianfranco Zola. The Italian had only come on a minute earlier as a substitute and found the roof of the net with his first touch.

Other clubs to win the Cup Winners' Cup on more than one occasion were Milan (1968 and 1973), Anderlecht (1976 and 1978), and Dynamo Kiev (1975 and 1986). However, if there was one club that could lay claim to being the team of the tournament over its entire history, then it would have to be Barcelona. The Catalan side lifted the trophy four times – ironic then, that their refusal to play in the tournament in 1998 would indirectly lead to the discontinuance of the competition.

Their first success was in the 1979 final when they edged out Fortuna Düsseldorf 4-3 in extra-time in one of the great finals of the competition's history. The 1982 final saw them storm to victory over Standard Liege in front of 100,000 fans in their own stadium, while a 2-0 victory over Italian side Sampdoria in 1989 at the Wankdorf Stadium in Berne, Switzerland, saw them complete a hat-trick of victories. The string of successes was rounded off in the 1997 final when Ronaldo's 37th minute penalty was enough to defeat Paris Saint-Germain. The French side were the holders of the trophy, and with no side ever managing to retain the Cup

Winners' Cup, history, as well as the referee's whistle, was clearly against them.

Throughout the history of the tournament many high-profile sides had laid claim to the trophy. However, part of the event's charm lay in the fact that some of the lesser known clubs were also able to compete against the major teams of European football, something that rarely happened in the UEFA Cup, and was even scarcer in the European Cup. In 1981, arguably the greatest ever shock of the Cup Winners' Cup came about when Welsh Cup winners Newport County somehow managed to reach the quarter-finals, one round further than the holders Valencia. Newport were in the fourth tier of English football at the time.

Smaller clubs to go all the way to the final have included Slovan Bratislava, who in 1969 saw off the challenge of Barcelona to lift the trophy in a famous 3-2 victory for the Slovak side. In 1974 FC Magdeburg of East Germany held the trophy aloft after beating a star-studded Milan side 2-0 in Rotterdam. Georgia's Dinamo Tbilisi ran out winners in 1981, and Belgium's Mechelen also added their name to the roll of honour in 1988 with a win over Dutch giants Ajax.

Always the third tournament behind the European Cup and the UEFA Cup in terms of prestige in the European club calendar, nevertheless the Cup Winners' Cup packed a lot of passion, spectacle and great football into its 39 year history. Nedved's winning goal in 1999 ensures that Lazio will be the holders of the trophy in perpetuity, but such giants of the game as Barcelona, Milan, Manchester United and Juventus all have fond memories of a trophy that, for a period of time, proudly occupied a special place in their trophy cabinets.

THE WINNERS OF THE EUROPEAN CUP WINNERS' CUP

1961: FIORENTINA

1ST LEG May 17

Rangers **0-2** Fiorentina
(Scotland)   (Italy)

2ND LEG May 27

Fiorentina **2-1** Rangers
Fiorentina won 4-1 on aggregate

1962: ATLÉTICO MADRID

HAMPDEN PARK, GLASGOW May 10

Atlético Madrid **1-1** Fiorentina
(Spain)   (Italy)

REPLAY: NECKAR, STUTTGART
September 5

Atlético Madrid **3-0** Fiorentina

1963: TOTTENHAM HOTSPUR

DE KUIP, ROTTERDAM May 15

Tottenham **5-1** Atlético Madrid
Hotspur
(England)   (Spain)

1964: SPORTING LISBON

HEYSEL, BRUSSELS May 13

Sporting Lisbon **3-3** MTK Budapest
(aet)
(Portugal)   (Hungary)

REPLAY: BOSUIL, ANTWERP
May 15

Sporting Lisbon **1-0** MTK Budapest

1965: WEST HAM UNITED

WEMBLEY, LONDON May 19

West Ham United **2-0** 1860 Munich
(England)   (West Germany)

1966: BORUSSIA DORTMUND

HAMPDEN PARK, GLASGOW May 5

Borussia **2-1** Liverpool (aet)
Dortmund
(West Germany)   (England)

1967: BAYERN MUNICH

FRANKEN, NÜREMBERG May 31

Bayern Munich **1-0** Rangers (aet)
(West Germany)   (Scotland)

1968: AC MILAN

DE KUIP, ROTTERDAM May 23

AC Milan **2-0** Hamburg
(Italy)   (West Germany)

1969: SLOVAN BRATISLAVA

ST JAKOB, BASLE May 21

Slovan Bratislava **3-2** Barcelona
(Czechoslovakia)   (Spain)

1970: MANCHESTER CITY

PRATER, VIENNA May 29

Manchester City **2-1** Górnik Zabrze
(England)   (Poland)

1971: CHELSEA

KARAISKAKIS, PIRAEUS May 19

Chelsea **1-1** Real Madrid (aet)
(England)   (Spain)

REPLAY: KARAISKAKIS, PIRAEUS May 21

Chelsea **2-1** Real Madrid

1972: RANGERS

NOU CAMP, BARCELONA May 24

Rangers **3-2** Dynamo Moscow
(Scotland)   (Soviet Union)

1973: AC MILAN

KAFTANTZOGLIO SALONICA May 16

AC Milan **1-0** Leeds United
(Italy)   (England)

1974: FC MAGDEBURG

DE KUIP, ROTTERDAM May 8

FC Magdeburg **2-0** AC Milan
(East Germany)   (Italy)

1975: DYNAMO KIEV

ST JAKOB, BASLE May 14

Dynamo Kiev **3-0** Ferencváros
(Soviet Union)   (Hungary)

1976: ANDERLECHT

HEYSEL, BRUSSELS May 5

Anderlecht **4-2** West Ham United
(Belgium)   (England)

1977: HAMBURG

OLYMPISCH, AMSTERDAM May 11

Hamburg **2-0** Anderlecht
(West Germany)   (Belgium)

1978: ANDERLECHT

PARC DES PRINCES, PARIS May 3

Anderlecht **4-0** Austria Vienna
(Belgium)   (Austria)

1979: BARCELONA

ST JAKOB, BASLE May 16

Barcelona **4-3** Fortuna
Düsseldorf (aet)
(Spain)   (West Germany)

1980: VALENCIA

HEYSEL, BRUSSELS May 14

Valencia **0-0** Arsenal (aet)
(Spain)   (England)
Valencia won 5-4 on penalties

1981: DINAMO TBILISI

RHEINSTADION, DÜSSELDORF May 13

Dinamo Tbilisi **2-1** FC Carl-Zeiss
Jena
(Soviet Union)   (East Germany)

1982: BARCELONA

NOU CAMP, BARCELONA May 12

Barcelona **2-1** Standard Liège
(Spain)   (Belgium)

1983: ABERDEEN

NYA ULLEVI, GOTHENBURG May 11

Aberdeen **2-1** Real Madrid (aet)
(Scotland)   (Spain)

1984: JUVENTUS

ST JAKOB, BASLE May 16

Juventus **2-1** FC Porto
(Italy)   (Portugal)

1985: EVERTON

DE KUIP, ROTTERDAM May 15

Everton **3-1** Rapid Vienna
(England)   (Austria)

1986: DYNAMO KIEV

GERLAND, LYON May 2

Dynamo Kiev **3-0** Atlético Madrid
(Soviet Union)   (Spain)

1987: AJAX

OLYMPIC, ATHENS May 13

Ajax **1-0** Lokomotive
Leipzig
(Holland)   (East Germany)

1988: KV MECHELEN

MEINAU, STRASBOURG May 11

KV Mechelen **1-0** Ajax
(Belgium)   (Holland)

1989: BARCELONA

WANKDORF, BERNE May 10

Barcelona **2-0** Sampdoria
(Spain)   (Italy)

1990: SAMPDORIA

NYA ULLEVI, GOTHENBURG May 9

Sampdoria **2-0** Anderlecht (aet)
(Italy)   (Belgium)

1991: MANCHESTER UNITED

DE KUIP, ROTTERDAM May 15

Manchester **2-1** Barcelona
United
(England)   (Spain)

1992: WERDER BREMEN

ESTADIO DA LUZ, LISBON May 6

Werder Bremen **2-0** Monaco
(Germany)   (France)

1993: PARMA

WEMBLEY, LONDON May 12

Parma **3-1** Royal Antwerp
(Italy)   (Belgium)

1994: ARSENAL

PARKEN, COPENHAGEN May 4

Arsenal **1-0** Parma
(England)   (Italy)

1995: REAL ZARAGOZA

PARC DES PRINCES, PARIS May 10

Real Zaragoza **2-1** Arsenal (aet)
(Spain)   (England)

1996: PARIS SAINT-GERMAIN

KING BAUDOUIN, BRUSSELS May 8

Paris Saint- **1-0** Rapid Vienna
Germain
(France)   (Austria)

1997: BARCELONA

DE KUIP, ROTTERDAM May 14

Barcelona **1-0** Paris Saint-
Germain
(Spain)   (France)

1998: CHELSEA

RASUNDA, STOCKHOLM May 13

Chelsea **1-0** Stuttgart
(England)   (Germany)

1999: LAZIO

VILLA PARK, BIRMINGHAM May 19

Lazio **2-1** Mallorca
(Italy)   (Spain)

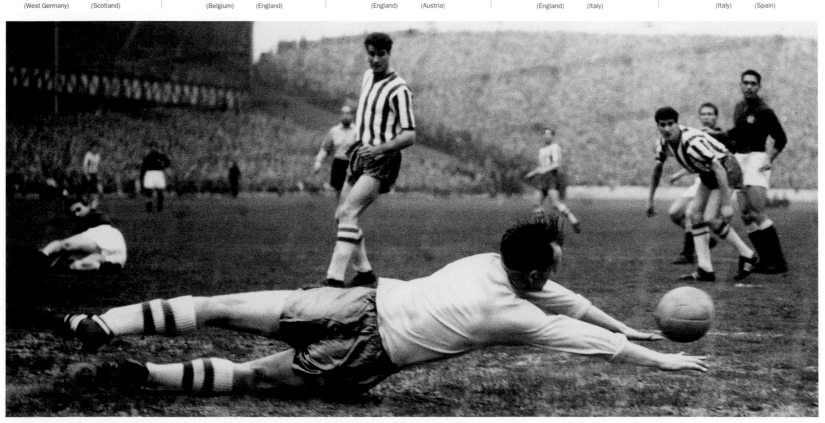

COPA LIBERTADORES

(THE SOUTH AMERICAN CLUB CUP)

The Copa Libertadores is the premier club competition in South America, and it has been played between the continent's top sides on an annual basis since its inception in 1960. Very much the equivalent of the Champions League, it was sparked into life when UEFA proposed that the champions of Europe should play against the South American champions for a world title (the Intercontinental Cup, or the World Club Cup as it also became known).

Seven national league winners competed home and away on a knockout basis in the inaugural tournament and it was Uruguay's Peñarol who were first to lift the trophy, beating Olimpia of Paraguay 1-0 in the first leg and drawing 1-1 in the second. Rather than winning on goal aggregate they were deemed to have won on points, having a win and a draw to Olimpia's one draw and a defeat. This system continued until 1988 when goal aggregate was introduced to decide the winners.

The competition was not without historical precedent, as in 1948 a similar tournament had been held in Chile, staged by Santiago's leading club, Colo Colo. The event was won by Brazil's Vasco Da Gama, but proved to be such a financial disaster for all involved that it was not staged again. It was with such an uncertain legacy that the current Copa Libertadores was launched. The tournament has not only survived but flourished, and despite format changes and many moments of controversy, it has become the most important date in the South American football calendar, far exceeding the Copa América in terms of popularity.

In 1962 Pelé, by then a star on the global stage, gave the competition's profile a much needed image boost as his Santos side got the better of Peñarol, still the champions having retained their title in 1961. Although the first leg in Montevideo had been played without incident, resulting in a 2-1 win for Santos, the second leg was far more unsavoury and the game was suspended shortly after half-time as the referee had been knocked unconscious by a stone thrown from the crowd. After a lengthy delay the game was restarted with Peñarol ahead 3-2, only for a linesman to endure the same fate, just as Peñarol were on the verge of adding to their lead. The game was abandoned and awarded to the Uruguayans, forcing a play-off that saw Santos run out 3-0 winners.

The following year Santos retained the trophy after beating Boca Juniors convincingly, with Pelé scoring a vital late goal in the second leg. It would be another 13 years until a Brazilian side won the Copa Libertadores again. This was due, in part, to the strong Argentinian teams taking the event more seriously, but also to a four-year Brazilian boycott from 1966 to 1970, after an amendment to the competition's format allowed the entry of league runners-up. The extra fixtures not only caused disruption to the Brazilian national league but reduced the tournament's financial rewards.

The boycott opened the door for Peñarol to claim another title, this time snatching victory from River Plate with a 4-2 win after a replay. Two of the goals were scored by Alberto Spencer, one of the tournament's most prolific

marksmen. Sadly, the event was again spoilt by controversy, as two former Peñarol players in the River Plate side, Cubilla and Matosas, were accused of deliberately 'throwing' the game.

In 1969, two of the strongest Argentine clubs, Velez Sarsfield and River Plate, followed Brazil's example and played no part in the tournament in protest over fixture congestion. This action inevitably led to CONMEBOL streamlining the competition by reducing the number of group matches and the following year the teams of both countries joined as normal.

In the early Seventies it was Buenos Aires club Independiente that dominated the competition, with a remarkable run of four consecutive titles. In 1972 'The Red Devils' got the better of Universitario de Deportes of Peru, while Colo Colo were the club's victims the following year in a closely fought play-off game. The 1974 final could not be decided over two legs, but the Independiente players held their nerve in another play-off to claim a 1-0 victory over São Paulo. The club's fantastic run culminated with a win over Unión Española in 1975, when the cup was again decided by a play-off game, with Independiente winning 2-0, with goals from Ruiz Moreno and Daniel Bertoni. The club still holds the record for the most titles, with seven wins.

Independiente's run of success was finally brought to an end in 1976 when the title was won by Cruzeiro of Brazil, who included veteran Jairzinho in their side. However, with the notable exception of a Zico-inspired Flamengo in 1981, it was to be teams from Argentina and

Above: Internacional celebrate defeating Guadalajara Chivas in 2010 to lift the trophy.

Right: Carlos Tevez of Boca Juniors kisses the trophy after beating Santos of Brazil in 2003.

Uruguay that continued to dominate the Copa Libertadores in the late Seventies and through the Eighties. Boca Juniors won the trophy in 1977 and 1978, with River Plate, Argentinos Juniors and Independiente also savouring victory during a rich period for Argentinian football. For Uruguay, both Peñarol (1982 and 1987) and Nacional (1980 and 1988) were crowned champions. However, Nacional's 1988 win was to be the last time a Uruguayan side would pick up the cup.

The smaller nations were at last beginning to challenge the long-established monopoly of South America's major football nations. The first team from outside of Brazil, Argentina or Uruguay to succeed were Olimpia of Paraguay in 1979; they defeated the mighty Boca Juniors 2-0 in their home leg, and managed to secure a 0-0 draw in Buenos Aires to claim the trophy.

From 1985 to 1987, Colombian side América de Cali competed in three consecutive finals but were unfortunate to be runners-up each time. A similar fate was suffered by Cobreloa of Chile, who lost in both 1981 and 1982. However, the less celebrated nations were not to be denied: Colombia's Atlético Nacional narrowly defeated Olimpia in 1989, and the following year the runners-up made it to the final again, this time defeating Ecuador's Barcelona.

In 1991 the pattern continued and major sides were once again frozen out when Colo Colo of Chile claimed the trophy for the first time. These successes coincided with a format change in 1988, with more home and away knockout rounds introduced after the group phase. The final would also be decided by aggregate scores or extra-time and penalties rather than a play-off.

Considering the country's dominance on the international stage, the record of Brazilian sides was a relatively poor one coming into the Nineties. However, this was all set to change. In 1992, with talented midfielder Raí pulling the strings in midfield, São Paulo beat Newell's Old Boys 3-2 on penalties. The following year, with a team including international players such as Cafu, Palhinha and Müller among their ranks, they defeated Chile's Universidad Catolica 5-3 on aggregate. Brazilian sides then won four of the next six titles, with separate wins for Grêmio, Cruzeiro, Vasco da Gama and Palmeiras.

Trends never last in the Copa Libertadores though, and the new millennium saw a resurgence in the fortunes of Argentine giants Boca Juniors. With a talented side coached by Carlos Bianchi, the club claimed back-to-back titles in 2000 and 2001, with penalty shoot-out victories against Palmeiras and Cruz Azul (clubs from Mexico were first invited to play in 1998). Indeed, 2001 saw the competition relaunched with another new format, plus a lucrative TV deal and sponsorship. Where only five sides had previously been eliminated at the group stages, now 16 dropped out. This helped to discourage negative play, and a more attacking style of football has made the Copa Libertadores much more entertaining.

Olimpia won the cup for the second time in 2002, while Boca Juniors beat Santos in both legs the following year. In 2004 the underdogs triumphed as tiny Colombian side Once Caldas put Brazilian giants Santos and São Paulo to the sword on the way to the final. Waiting for them would be Boca Juniors, who had scraped through two violent semi-final clashes with local rivals River Plate. The Colombians defended

well in Buenos Aires to come away with a draw, but the River Plate players lost their nerve in the return leg, missing four penalties in a row in the shoot-out to allow Once Caldas to lift the Copa Libertadores trophy for the first time.

Due to a change to the rules the 2005 final was the first contested between teams from the same country. It was also the first time that the 'away goals' rule could be employed to decide games, although not for the final when penalties would be used at the end of the second leg. After a 1-1 draw with Atlético Paranaense in the first leg of the 2005 competition, São Paulo won the cup with a 4-0 home win in the return, with Atlético blowing their chance to score from the penalty spot when only one goal down. São Paulo reached the final in 2006 but lost to Internacional in an all-Brazilian encounter.

The 2008 final finished 5-5 on aggregate, but despite losing the second leg 3-1 in front of a crowd of 86,000 at the Maracanã, LDU Quito of Ecuador won the penalty shoot-out thanks to keeper José Francisco Cevallos, who stopped three of Fluminense's four spot-kicks.

Ahead of the 2009 final, Estudiantes captain Juan Sebastián Verón announced, 'I would swap all my medals... just to win this trophy', and he put in a Man Of The Match performance to ensure his side beat Brazil's Cruzeiro 2–1 in the second leg. The victory was a special achievement for him, as his father Juan Ramón had been the outstanding player of the Estudiantes side that won the club's three previous titles in the late Sixties.

In 2010 Internacional of Brazil beat Mexican side Guadalajara and received the trophy from Pelé, but the conclusion to the second leg had already been marred by a brawl between rival players after Internacional fans had invaded the pitch at the final whistle.

The competition has now become more popular than ever. Despite its many problems in the past, the ever-improving Copa Libertadores will to keep evolving, and is now established as one of the great international club competitions.

THE WINNERS OF THE COPA LIBERTADORES

1960: PEÑAROL
1ST LEG June 12
Peñarol **1-0** Olimpia
(Uruguay)   (Paraguay)
2ND LEG June 19
Olimpia **1-1** Peñarol
Peñarol won on points aggregate

1961: PEÑAROL
1ST LEG June 4
Peñarol **1-0** Palmeiras
(Uruguay)   (Brazil)
2ND LEG June 11
Palmeiras **1-1** Peñarol
Peñarol won on points aggregate

1962: SANTOS
1ST LEG July 28
Peñarol **1-2** Santos
(Uruguay)   (Brazil)
2ND LEG August 2
Santos **2-3** Peñarol
PLAY-OFF August 30
Santos **3-0** Peñarol

1963: SANTOS
1ST LEG September 3
Santos **3-2** Boca Juniors
(Brazil)   (Argentina)
2ND LEG September 11
Boca Juniors **1-2** Santos
Santos won on points aggregate

1964: INDEPENDIENTE
1ST LEG August 6
Nacional **0-0** Independiente
(Uruguay)   (Argentina)
2ND LEG August 12
Independiente **1-0** Nacional
Independiente won on points aggregate

1965: INDEPENDIENTE
1ST LEG April 9
Independiente **1-0** Peñarol
(Argentina)   (Uruguay)
2ND LEG April 12
Peñarol **3-1** Independiente
PLAY-OFF April 15
Independiente **4-1** Peñarol

1966: PEÑAROL
1ST LEG May 12
Peñarol **2-0** River Plate
(Uruguay)   (Argentina)
2ND LEG May 18
River Plate **3-2** Peñarol
PLAY-OFF May 20
Peñarol **4-2** River Plate
(aet)

1967: RACING CLUB
1ST LEG August 15
Racing Club **0-0** Nacional
(Argentina)   (Uruguay)
2ND LEG August 25
Nacional **0-0** Racing Club
(aet)
PLAY-OFF August 29
Racing Club **2-1** Nacional

1968: ESTUDIANTES DE LA PLATA
1ST LEG May 2
Estudiantes **2-1** Palmeiras
de La Plata
(Argentina)   (Brazil)
2ND LEG May 7
Palmeiras **3-1** Estudiantes
de La Plata
PLAY-OFF May 15
Estudiantes **2-0** Palmeiras
de La Plata

1969: ESTUDIANTES DE LA PLATA
1ST LEG May 15
Nacional **0-1** Estudiantes
de La Plata
(Uruguay)   (Argentina)
2ND LEG May 22
Estudiantes **2-0** Nacional
de La Plata
Estudiantes de La Plata won on points aggregate

1970: ESTUDIANTES DE LA PLATA
1ST LEG May 21
Estudiantes **1-0** Peñarol
de La Plata
(Argentina)   (Uruguay)
2ND LEG May 27
Peñarol **0-0** Estudiantes
de La Plata
Estudiantes de La Plata on points aggregate

1971: NACIONAL
1ST LEG May 26
Estudiantes **1-0** Nacional
de La Plata
(Argentina)   (Uruguay)
2ND LEG June 2
Nacional **1-0** Estudiantes
de La Plata
PLAY-OFF June 9
Nacional **2-0** Estudiantes
de La Plata

1972: INDEPENDIENTE
1ST LEG May 17
Universitario **0-0** Independiente
de Deportes
(Peru)   (Argentina)
2ND LEG May 24
Independiente **2-1** Universitario
de Deportes
Independiente won on points aggregate

1973: INDEPENDIENTE
1ST LEG May 22
Independiente **1-1** Colo Colo
(Argentina)   (Chile)
2ND LEG May 29
Colo Colo **0-0** Independiente
PLAY-OFF June 6
Independiente **2-1** Colo Colo
(aet)

1974: INDEPENDIENTE
1ST LEG October 12
São Paulo **2-1** Independiente
(Brazil)   (Argentina)
2ND LEG October 16
Independiente **2-0** São Paulo
PLAY-OFF October 19
Independiente **1-0** São Paulo

1975: INDEPENDIENTE
1ST LEG June 18
Unión Española **1-0** Independiente
(Chile)   (Argentina)
2ND LEG June 25
Independiente **3-1** Unión Española
PLAY-OFF June 29
Independiente **2-0** Unión Española

1976: CRUZEIRO
1ST LEG July 21
Cruzeiro **4-1** River Plate
(Brazil)   (Argentina)
2ND LEG July 28
River Plate **2-1** Cruzeiro
PLAY-OFF July 30
Cruzeiro **3-2** River Plate

1977: BOCA JUNIORS
1ST LEG September 6
Boca Juniors **1-0** Cruzeiro
(Argentina)   (Brazil)
2ND LEG September 11
Cruzeiro **1-0** Boca Juniors
PLAY-OFF September 14
Boca Juniors **0-0** Cruzeiro
(aet)
Boca Juniors won 5-4 on penalties

1978: BOCA JUNIORS
1ST LEG November 23
Deportivo Cali **0-0** Boca Juniors
(Colombia)   (Argentina)
2ND LEG November 28
Boca Juniors **4-0** Deportivo Cali
Boco Juniors won on points aggregate

1979: OLIMPIA
1ST LEG July 22
Olimpia **2-0** Boca Juniors
(Paraguay)   (Argentina)
2ND LEG July 27
Boca Juniors **0-0** Olimpia
Olimpia won on points aggregate

1980: NACIONAL
1ST LEG July 30
Internacional **0-0** Nacional
Porto Alegre
(Brazil)   (Uruguay)
2ND LEG August 6
Nacional **1-0** Internacional
Porto Alegre
Nacional won on points aggregate

1981: FLAMENGO
1ST LEG November 13
Flamengo **2-1** Cobreloa
(Brazil)   (Chile)
2ND LEG November 20
Cobreloa **1-0** Flamengo
PLAY-OFF November 23
Flamengo **2-0** Cobreloa

1982: PEÑAROL
1ST LEG November 26
Peñarol **0-0** Cobreloa
(Uruguay)   (Chile)
2ND LEG November 30
Cobreloa **0-1** Peñarol
Peñarol won on points aggregate

1983: GRÊMIO
1ST LEG July 22
Penarol **1-1** Grêmio
(Uruguay)   (Brazil)
2ND LEG July 28
Grêmio **2-1** Peñarol
Grêmio won on points aggregate

1984: INDEPENDIENTE
1ST LEG July 24
Grêmio **0-1** Independiente
(Brazil)   (Argentina)
2ND LEG July 27
Independiente **0-0** Grêmio
Independiente won on points aggregate

1985: ARGENTINOS JUNIORS
1ST LEG October 17
Argentinos **1-0** América Cali
Juniors
(Argentina)   (Colombia)
2ND LEG October 22
América Cali **1-0** Argentinos
Juniors
PLAY-OFF October 24
Argentinos **1-1** América Cali (aet)
Juniors
(aet)
Argentinos Juniors won 5-4 penalties

1986: RIVER PLATE
1ST LEG October 22
América Cali **1-2** River Plate
(Colombia)   (Argentina)
2ND LEG October 29
River Plate **1-0** América Cali
River Plate won on points aggregate

1987: PEÑAROL
1ST LEG October 21
América Cali **2-0** Peñarol
(Colombia)   (Uruguay)
2ND LEG October 28
Peñarol **2-1** América Cali
PLAY-OFF October 31
Peñarol **1-0** América Cali
(aet)

1988: NACIONAL
1ST LEG June 2
Newell's Old Boys **1-0** Nacional
(Argentina)   (Uruguay)
2ND LEG October 26
Nacional **3-0** Newell's Old Boys
(aet)
Nacional won 3-1 on goal aggregate

1989: ATLÉTICO NACIONAL
1ST LEG May 24
Olimpia **2-0** Atlético Nacional
(Paraguay)   (Colombia)
2ND LEG May 31
Atlético Nacional **2-0** Olimpia
(aet)
Atlético Nacional won 5-4 on penalties

1990: OLIMPIA
1ST LEG Oct 3
Olimpia **2-0** Barcelona
(Paraguay)   (Ecuador)
2ND LEG October 10
Barcelona **1-1** Olimpia
Olimpia won on points aggregate

1991: COLO COLO
1ST LEG May 29
Olimpia **0-0** Colo Colo
(Paraguay)   (Chile)
2ND LEG June 5
Colo Colo **3-0** Olimpia
Colo Colo won on points aggregate

1992: SÃO PAULO
1ST LEG June 10
Newell's Old Boys **1-0** São Paulo
(Argentina)   (Brazil)
2ND LEG June 17
São Paulo **1-0** Newell's Old Boys
(aet)
São Paulo won 3-2 on penalties

1993: SÃO PAULO
1ST LEG May 19
São Paulo **5-1** Universidad
Católica
(Brazil)   (Chile)
2ND LEG May 26
Universidad **2-0** São Paulo
Católica
São Paulo won 5-3 on goal aggregate

1994: VÉLEZ SARSFIELD
1ST LEG August 24
Vélez Sarsfield **1-0** São Paulo
(Argentina)   (Brazil)
2ND LEG August 31
São Paulo **1-0** Vélez Sarsfield
(aet)
Vélez Sarsfield won 5-3 on penalties

1995: GRÊMIO
1ST LEG August 24
Grêmio **3-1** Atlético Nacional
(Brazil)   (Colombia)
2ND LEG August 30
Atlético Nacional **1-1** Grêmio
Grêmio won on points aggregate

1996: RIVER PLATE
1ST LEG June 19
América Cali **1-0** River Plate
(Colombia)   (Argentina)
2ND LEG June 26
River Plate **2-0** América Cali
River Plate won 2-1 on goal aggregate

1997: CRUZEIRO
1ST LEG August 6
Sporting Cristal **0-0** Cruzeiro
(Peru)   (Brazil)
2ND LEG August 13
Cruzeiro **1-0** Sporting Cristal
Cruzeiro won on points aggregate

1998: VASCO DA GAMA
1ST LEG August 12
Vasco da Gama **2-0** Barcelona
(Brazil)   (Ecuador)
2ND LEG August 26
Barcelona **1-2** Vasco da Gama
Vasco da Gama won on points aggregate

1999: PALMEIRAS
1ST LEG June 2
Deportivo Cali **1-0** Palmeiras
(Colombia)   (Brazil)
2ND LEG June 16
Palmeiras **2-1** Deportivo Cali
(aet)
Palmeiras won 4-3 on penalties

2000: BOCA JUNIORS
1ST LEG June 14
Boca Juniors **2-2** Palmeiras
(Argentina)   (Brazil)
2ND LEG June 21
Palmeiras **0-0** Boca Juniors
Boca Juniors won 4-2 on penalties

2001: BOCA JUNIORS
1ST LEG June 20
Cruz Azul **0-1** Boca Juniors
(Mexico)   (Argentina)
2ND LEG June 28
Boca Juniors **0-1** Cruz Azul
(aet)
Boca Juniors won 3-1 on penalties

2002: OLIMPIA
1ST LEG July 24
Olimpia **0-1** São Caetano
(Paraguay)   (Brazil)
2ND LEG July 31
São Caetano **1-2** Olimpia
(aet)
Olimpia won 4-2 on penalties

2003: BOCA JUNIORS
1ST LEG June 25
Boca Juniors **2-0** Santos
(Argentina)   (Brazil)
2ND LEG July 2
Santos **1-3** Boca Juniors
Boca Juniors won on points aggregate

2004: ONCE CALDAS
1ST LEG June 23
Once Caldas **0-0** Boca Juniors
(Colombia)   (Argentina)
2ND LEG June 30
Boca Juniors **1-1** Once Caldas
Once Caldas won 2-0 on penalties

2005: SÃO PAULO
1ST LEG July 6
Atlético **1-1** São Paulo
Paranaense
(Brazil)   (Brazil)
2ND LEG July 14
São Paulo **4-0** Atlético
Paranaense
São Paulo won on points aggregate

2006: INTERNACIONAL
1ST LEG August 9
São Paulo **1-2** Internacional
(Brazil)   (Brazil)
2ND LEG August 16
Internacional **2-2** São Paulo
Internacional won on points aggregate

2007: BOCA JUNIORS
1ST LEG June 13
Boca Juniors **3-0** Grêmio
(Argentina)   (Brazil)
2ND LEG June 20
Grêmio **0-2** Boca Juniors
Boca Juniors won on points aggregate

2008: LDU QUITO
1ST LEG June 25
LDU Quito **4-2** Fluminense
(Ecuador)   (Brazil)
2ND LEG July 2
Fluminense **3-1** LDU Quito
LDU Quito won 3-1 on penalties

2009: ESTUDIANTES DE LA PLATA
1ST LEG July 8
Estudiantes **0-0** Cruzeiro
de La Plata
(Argentina)   (Brazil)
2ND LEG July 15
Cruzeiro **1-2** Estudiantes
de La Plata
Estudiantes de La Plata won 2-1 on points aggregate

2010: INTERNACIONAL
1ST LEG: August 11
Guadalajara **1-2** Internacional
(Mexico)   (Brazil)
2ND LEG: August 18
Internacional **3-2** Guadalajara
Internacional won on points aggregate

INTERCONTINENTAL CUP & FIFA CLUB WORLD CUP

Above from left to right: Hernan Bermudez of Boca Juniors raises the cup after victory over Real Madrid in the 2000 World Club Cup; Ajax, winners in 1995; Bayern Munich in 2001.

Opposite clockwise from top left: Barcelona win the 2009 Club World Cup; Corinthians celebrate victory in the World Club Championship in 2000; 2007 champions AC Milan; Nacional of Uruguay after winning the 1980 world title.

For many years the idea of a world title for club sides was widely regarded as an annual sideshow by all but the holders and their fans, although since the competition was relaunched by FIFA in 2006 as the FIFA Club World Cup, it has finally started to grow in importance in the football calendar.

The original competition was an annual fixture between the champions of Europe and South America, pitting the winners of the European Cup against the winners of the Copa Libertadores. The Intercontinental Cup, or the World Club Cup as it was commonly known, was a logical progression from the European Cup for UEFA general secretary Henri Delaunay, although it took several more years to get it off the ground, finally beginning in 1960. However, the early years of the competition were marred by violent encounters and frequent withdrawals that often highlighted the cultural differences between the two competing continents.

Played over two legs, home and away, the inaugural trophy was won by Real Madrid who had enjoyed an unbroken run of success in the European Cup since it commenced five years earlier. Just two months after the club's 7-3 European Cup final victory over Eintracht Frankfurt, Madrid travelled to Montevideo to face Peñarol. The encounter, a 0-0 draw, was played in monsoon conditions, but Real won 5-1 in the second leg with Puskás scoring twice.

Peñarol returned the following year and this time struck the first blow for South America, beating Portugal's Benfica in a play-off, as aggregate goals did not count at the time.

Eusébio made his competition debut in the deciding match after being flown in especially, scoring from distance in a 2-1 defeat.

The cup was to reside in South America for three years with Pelé's awesome Santos side winning it twice in succession. However, the contest against AC Milan in 1963 began the trend towards foul play, with one player from each side sent-off in the bad-tempered play-off game. The cup did eventually arrive in the city of Milan the following year when the ultra-defensive Inter side won the first of two consecutive finals, facing Argentinian team Independiente in both 1964 and 1965. Inter conceded only one goal in the five dour games that it took to win both finals.

The competition's descent into bad feeling plumbed new depths as the decade came to an end. In 1966 the Spanish press had rubbished the quality of the Uruguayan pitch, but it was the introduction of no-nonsense British teams that led to the descent into anarchy.

In 1967 Celtic's 'Lisbon Lions' had become the first British side to lift the European Cup and five months later they faced Argentina's Racing Club in a series of matches memorable only for the violence of the encounters. Anti-English feeling in Argentina was still running high after the 1966 World Cup encounter, which had provoked England manager Alf Ramsey to describe the Argentine team as 'animals', and the Scots took the brunt of this sentiment.

Celtic won a bad-tempered first leg 1-0, but in the return tie at the Avellaneda Stadium goalkeeper Ronnie Simpson was struck by a

brick before the kick-off and John Fallon had to take his place. The deciding game, staged in Montevideo, degenerated into war as Celtic had four players sent-off and Racing two. By the final whistle the 1-0 scoreline in the South Americans' favour was of little consequence. 'We should have stuck to our guns and refused to play a third match,' lamented Celtic chairman Bob Kelly after the event.

If at all possible the spirit of competition worsened still further the following year when Manchester United met Estudiantes. Upon landing in Buenos Aires for the first leg, the English team were greeted with a polo match in their honour, but when their opponents boycotted the official reception the tone was set. The game descended into hostility, with Nobby Stiles, who was described in the programme as 'brutal, badly intentioned and a bad sportsman', the target for ill treatment. The aggression of Estudiantes was led by Carlos Bilardo, who was later to become Argentina's national team coach, lifting the World Cup in 1986.

Kicked and punched regularly, Stiles was eventually dismissed, not for retaliating but for gesturing at a linesman over an offside call. George Best later recalled objects raining down on him every time he got the ball and decided he was better off not calling for it. In the equally bad-tempered return leg at Old Trafford he was dismissed for thumping his tormentor Medina while the referee was in the process of booking him. Matt Busby later declared: 'Holding the ball out there put you in danger.'

Paddy Crerand's conclusion that 'the whole

Above: Celtic's John Hughes in action against Racing Club in the 1967 final.

Opposite top: Juan Veron scores against Manchester United as Estudiantes de La Plata win the 1968 World Club Cup.

Opposite bottom: Wayne Rooney after scoring for Manchester United in the 2008 final.

Below: Waldemar Victorino of Nacional scores against Nottingham Forest in the 1980 final, actually played in 1981.

thing was a total waste of time' began to take seed with many European sides. The travelling was demanding, especially mid-season, and clubs were not willing to risk injury. As a result the Seventies were marked by a succession of withdrawals. Ajax declined to take part in 1971 and 1973 and were replaced by defeated finalists Panathinaikos and Juventus, both losing out to South American opposition.

In 1975 Bayern Munich's decision to opt out led to the cancellation of the match, but after retaining the European Cup the following season the Germans were rewarded with the title 'world champions' after beating Brazilians Cruzeiro. However, two years later the event was cancelled again when Liverpool declined to travel. Nottingham Forest followed suit in 1979 and were replaced by Swedes Malmö, who lost out to Olimpia of Paraguay.

The competition was clearly doomed unless action was taken. The solution arrived in 1980 when Japanese vehicle manufacturers Toyota offered to sponsor the trophy if it was held in Tokyo. The 1980 competition was staged on February 11, 1981, when 62,000 fans packed into Tokyo's National Stadium to witness the first Toyota Cup between Nacional of Uruguay and Brian Clough's Nottingham Forest. The

Uruguayans won the tie 1-0 in a tight and defensive encounter that saw them shut up shop after Waldemar Victorino scored the only goal in the tenth minute.

With English clubs dominating European football they contested the trophy for the next two seasons, but both Liverpool and Aston Villa lost out, to Flamengo and Peñarol respectively. In fact, South American sides had won the trophy on seven consecutive occasions by the time a Michel Platini-inspired Juventus ended the streak with a penalty shoot-out victory over Argentinos Juniors in 1985.

The competition's farcical side was again demonstrated in 1997 when Cruzeiro of Brazil signed several players on loan, including Bebeto, for the encounter with Borussia Dortmund. However, it did not help them to win.

In 1999 Manchester United added to an impressive 'treble' when Roy Keane volleyed home the only goal against Brazilians Palmeiras, but the impact of the victory was undermined by the knowledge that the trophy was to be superseded by the World Club Championship just a few weeks later.

After ten years in which the competition had degenerated into a pleasant sideshow, FIFA decided to flex its muscles over rivals UEFA and launch a new competition to be decided by a mini-tournament, something not greeted with much warmth by European leagues already suffering from fixture congestion.

The competition was staged in Brazil and Manchester United and Real Madrid were selected to represent Europe against sides from South America, Oceania, Africa and Central America, but in England there was controversy over the withdrawal of the holders from the FA Cup to take part in the tournament. The club had even been put under pressure to participate by a government wanting to secure the 2006 World Cup. In the end the European teams failed to progress and the final was contested between Brazilian sides Corinthians and Vasco Da Gama,

with Corinthians winning in a penalty shoot-out and pocketing a purse of $6 million.

Having rejigged the template once, FIFA attempted to expand the competition to 12 teams the following year, adding Japan's Jubilo Iwata as compensation for the curtailment of the Toyota Cup. The 2001 tournament was scheduled to be played in Spain, but it had to be cancelled due to the bankruptcy of ISMM-ISL, FIFA's former marketing partner. All the teams and the Spanish government were compensated.

In the absence of FIFA's new championship, the Intercontinental Cup continued in its usual format in Tokyo in 2000, still under the auspices of UEFA and CONMEBOL. However, in 2004 Porto became the last winner of the competition in that guise, beating Once Caldas of Colombia in a penalty shoot-out that needed 18 spot-kicks to settle the tie in favour of the Portuguese team.

The following year it was decided to merge the competition with FIFA's World Club Championship, although FIFA does not currently recognise the new competition as a continuation of the Intercontinental Cup. This merger resulted in a six-team tournament between the winners of the Copa Libertadores (São Paulo), the CONCACAF Champions Cup (Saprissa), and the Champions Leagues of Europe (Liverpool), Asia (Al Ittihad), Africa (Al-Ahly) and Oceania (Sydney). Against the run of play, São Paulo beat Liverpool 1-0 in Yokohama to win the cup.

The following year the competition was renamed the FIFA Club World Cup and it has been held annually ever since, with the occasional change of format and location. For the 2007 competition, in order to increase home interest in the tournament an opening play-off match was introduced between the OFC champions and the champions of the host nation, with the winner gaining a place in the tournament proper.

Filippo Inzaghi scored twice as AC Milan beat Boca Juniors 4-2 to win the competition in 2007 in Yokohama, while a late goal from Wayne Rooney was enough to secure the title for Manchester United in 2008. Having dominated the first half of the match, ten-man United survived the sending-off of Nemanja Vidic soon after the interval to beat LDU Quito of Ecuador.

The 2009 competition was staged in Abu Dhabi, with 2006 runners-up Barcelona pulling off a magnificent comeback to beat Estudiantes. Having trailed since the 39th minute, Barcelona equalised through Pedro with just a minute of the game remaining, and after dominating the latter stages of the contest, the Spanish club eventually took the lead when Lionel Messi scored deep in extra-time.

After 50 years in the making, and various names and formats, the idea of a world championship for club sides finally seems to be taking hold, but whether it can ever rate as highly as FIFA's competition for international teams remains to be seen.

WINNERS OF THE WORLD CLUB CUP (INTERCONTINENTAL CUP/TOYOTA CUP)

INTERCONTINENTAL CUP

1960: REAL MADRID
1ST LEG July 3
Peñarol **0-0** Real Madrid
(Uruguay)   (Spain)
2ND LEG September 4
Real Madrid **5-1** Peñarol
Real Madrid won 5-1 aggregate

1961: PEÑAROL
1ST LEG September 4
Benfica **1-0** Peñarol
(Portugal)   (Uruguay)
2ND LEG September 17
Peñarol **5-0** Benfica
PLAY-OFF September 19
Peñarol **2-1** Benfica

1962: SANTOS
1ST LEG September 19
Santos **3-2** Benfica
(Brazil)   (Portugal)
2ND LEG October 11
Benfica **2-5** Santos
Santos won 8-4 on aggregate

1963: SANTOS
1ST LEG October 16
AC Milan **4-2** Santos
(Italy)   (Brazil)
2ND LEG November 14
Santos **4-2** AC Milan
PLAY-OFF November 16
Santos **1-0** AC Milan

1964: INTER MILAN
1ST LEG September 9
Independiente **1-0** Inter Milan
(Argentina)   (Italy)
2ND LEG September 23
Inter Milan **2-0** Independiente
PLAY-OFF September 26
Inter Milan **1-0** Independiente
(aet)

1965: INTER MILAN
1ST LEG September 8
Inter Milan **3-0** Independiente
(Italy)   (Argentina)
2ND LEG September 15
Independiente **0-0** Inter Milan
Inter Milan won 3-0 on aggregate

1966: PEÑAROL
1ST LEG October 12
Peñarol **2-0** Real Madrid
(Uruguay)   (Spain)
2ND LEG October 26
Real Madrid **0-2** Peñarol
Peñarol won 4-0 on aggregate

1967: RACING CLUB
1ST LEG October 18
Celtic **1-0** Racing Club
(Scotland)   (Argentina)
2ND LEG November 1
Racing Club **2-1** Celtic
PLAY-OFF November 4
Racing Club **1-0** Celtic

1968: ESTUDIANTES DE LA PLATA
1ST LEG September 25
Estudiantes **1-0** Manchester
de la Plata   United
(Argentina)   (England)
2ND LEG October 16
Manchester **1-1** Estudiantes
United   de la Plata
Estudiantes de la Plata won 2-1 on aggregate

1969: AC MILAN
1ST LEG September 8
AC Milan **3-0** Estudiantes
     de la Plata
(Italy)   (Argentina)
2ND LEG October 22
Estudiantes **2-1** AC Milan
de la Plata
AC Milan won 4-2 on aggregate

1970: FEYENOORD
1ST LEG August 26
Estudiantes **2-2** Feyenoord
de la Plata
(Argentina)   (Holland)
2ND LEG September 9
Feyenoord **1-0** Estudiantes
     de la Plata
Feyenoord won 3-2 on aggregate

1971: NACIONAL MONTEVIDEO
1ST LEG December 15
Panathinaikos **1-1** Nacional
     Montevideo
(Greece)   (Uruguay)
2ND LEG December 29
Nacional **2-1** Panathinaikos
Montevideo
Nacional Montevideo won 3-2 on aggregate

1972: AJAX
1ST LEG September 6
Independiente **1-1** Ajax
(Argentina)   (Holland)
2ND LEG September 28
Ajax **3-0** Independiente
Ajax won 4-1 on aggregate

1973: INDEPENDIENTE
OLYMPIC STADIUM, ROME November 28
Independiente **1-0** Juventus
(Argentina)   (Italy)

1974: ATLÉTICO MADRID
1ST LEG March 12, 1975
Independiente **1-0** Atlético Madrid
(Argentina)   (Spain)
2ND LEG April 10, 1975
Atlético Madrid **2-0** Independiente
Atlético Madrid won 2-1 on aggregate

1975
Bayern Munich **v** Independiente
(West Germany)   (Argentina)
Not contested

1976: BAYERN MUNICH
1ST LEG November 23
Bayern Munich **2-0** Cruzeiro
(West Germany)   (Brazil)
2ND LEG December 21
Cruzeiro **0-0** Bayern Munich
Bayern Munich won 2-0 on aggregate

1977: BOCA JUNIORS
1ST LEG March 21, 1978
Boca Juniors **2-2** Borussia
     Mönchengladbach
(Argentina)   (West Germany)
2ND LEG August 1, 1978
Borussia **0-3** Boca Juniors
Mönchengladbach
Boca Juniors won 5-2 on aggregate

1978
Liverpool **v** Boca Juniors
(England)   (Argentina)
Not contested

1979: OLIMPIA
1ST LEG November 18, 1979
Malmö **0-1** Olimpia
(Sweden)   (Paraguay)
2ND LEG March 2, 1980
Olimpia **2-1** Malmö
Olimpia won 3-1 on aggregate

TOYOTA CUP

1980: NACIONAL
NATIONAL STADIUM, TOKYO Feb 11, 1981
Nacional **1-0** Nottingham
     Forest
(Uruguay)   (England)

1981: FLAMENGO
NATIONAL STADIUM, TOKYO December 13
Flamengo **3-0** Liverpool
(Brazil)   (England)

1982: PEÑAROL
NATIONAL STADIUM, TOKYO December 12
Peñarol **2-0** Aston Villa
(Uruguay)   (England)

1983: GRÊMIO
NATIONAL STADIUM, TOKYO December 11
Grêmio **2-1** Hamburg
(Brazil)   (West Germany)

1984: INDEPENDIENTE
NATIONAL STADIUM, TOKYO December 9
Independiente **1-0** Liverpool
(Argentina)   (England)

1985: JUVENTUS
NATIONAL STADIUM, TOKYO December 8
Juventus **2-2** Argentinos
     Juniors (aet)
(Italy)   (Argentina)
Juventus won 4-2 on penalties

1986: RIVER PLATE
NATIONAL STADIUM, TOKYO December 14
River Plate **1-0** Steaua
     Bucharest
(Argentina)   (Romania)

1987: PORTO
NATIONAL STADIUM, TOKYO December 13
Porto **2-1** Peñarol (aet)
(Portugal)   (Uruguay)

1988: NACIONAL
NATIONAL STADIUM, TOKYO December 11
Nacional **2-2** PSV Eindhoven
     (aet)
(Uruguay)   (Holland)
Nacional won 7-6 on penalties

1989: AC MILAN
NATIONAL STADIUM, TOKYO December 17
AC Milan **1-0** Atlético Nacional
     (aet)
(Italy)   (Columbia)

1990: AC MILAN
NATIONAL STADIUM, TOKYO December 9
AC Milan **3-0** Olimpia
(Italy)   (Paraguay)

1991: RED STAR BELGRADE
NATIONAL STADIUM, TOKYO December 8
Red Star Belgrade **3-0** Colo Colo
(Yugoslavia)   (Chile)

1992: SÃO PAULO
NATIONAL STADIUM, TOKYO December 13
São Paulo **2-1** Barcelona
(Brazil)   (Spain)

1993: SÃO PAULO
NATIONAL STADIUM, TOKYO December 12
São Paulo **3-2** Milan
(Brazil)   (Italy)

1994: VÉLEZ SARSFIELD
NATIONAL STADIUM, TOKYO December 1
Vélez Sarsfield **2-0** AC Milan
(Argentina)   (Italy)

1995: AJAX
NATIONAL STADIUM, TOKYO November 28
Ajax **0-0** Grêmio (aet)
(Holland)   (Brazil)
Ajax won 4-3 on penalties

1996: JUVENTUS
NATIONAL STADIUM, TOKYO November 26
Juventus **1-0** River Plate
(Italy)   (Argentina)

1997: BORUSSIA DORTMUND
NATIONAL STADIUM, TOKYO December 2
Borussia **2-0** Cruzeiro
Dortmund
(Germany)   (Brazil)

1998: REAL MADRID
NATIONAL STADIUM, TOKYO December 1
Real Madrid **2-1** Vasco da Gama
(Spain)   (Brazil)

1999: MANCHESTER UNITED
NATIONAL STADIUM, TOKYO November 30
Manchester **1-0** Palmeiras
United
(England)   (Brazil)

2000: BOCA JUNIORS
NATIONAL STADIUM, TOKYO November 28
Boca Juniors **2-1** Real Madrid
(Argentina)   (Spain)

2001: BAYERN MUNICH
NATIONAL STADIUM, TOKYO November 27
Bayern Munich **1-0** Boca Juniors (aet)
(Germany)   (Argentina)

2002: REAL MADRID
YOKOHAMA STADIUM December 3
Real Madrid **2-0** Olimpia
(Spain)   (Paraguay)

2003: BOCA JUNIORS
YOKOHAMA STADIUM December 14
Boca Juniors **1-1** AC Milan (aet)
(Argentina)   (Italy)
Boca Juniors won 3-1 on penalties

2004: PORTO
YOKOHAMA STADIUM December 12
Porto **0-0** Once Caldas (aet)
(Portugal)   (Colombia)
Porto won 8-7 on penalties

FIFA WORLD CLUB CHAMPIONSHIP

2000: CORINTHIANS
MARACANÃ, RIO DE JANEIRO January 14
Corinthians **0-0** Vasco da Gama
     (aet)
(Brazil)   (Brazil)
Corinthians won 4-3 on penalties

2005: SÃO PAULO
YOKOHAMA STADIUM December 18
São Paulo **1-0** Liverpool
(Brazil)   (England)

FIFA CLUB WORLD CUP

2006: INTERNACIONAL
YOKOHAMA STADIUM December 17
Internacional **1-0** Barcelona
(Brazil)   (Spain)

2007: AC MILAN
YOKOHAMA STADIUM December 16
AC Milan **4-2** Boca Juniors
(Italy)   (Argentina)

2008: MANCHESTER UNITED
YOKOHAMA STADIUM December 21
Manchester **1-0** LDU Quito
United
(England)   (Ecuador)

2009: BARCELONA
SHEIKH ZAYED STADIUM, ABU DHABI
December 19
Barcelona **2-1** Estudiantes
     (aet)
(Spain)   (Argentina)

OTHER INTERNATIONAL CLUB COMPETITIONS

EUROPEAN SUPER CUP

The Super Cup was originally conceived by UEFA as a celebration match between the winners of the European Cup and the Cup Winners' Cup. It is currently contested between the winners of the Champions League and the Europa League. AC Milan have been the competition's most successful club.

AFC CHAMPIONS LEAGUE

In 2003 the AFC launched the Asian Champions League after amalgamating the Asian Champions Cup and the Asian Cup Winners' Cup, also making the Asian Super Cup redundant in the process. The tournament is currently contested by the top 32 clubs from the ten leading Asian leagues, plus additional clubs who qualify through a play-off system or by winning other AFC competitions. The teams are divided into eight regional groups of four who play each other home and away, with the winners and runners-up progressing through to the knockout stages. The competition is decided by a single game, although two-legged finals were the norm between 2003 and 2008.

Al Ain of the United Arab Emirates were the inaugural winners of the revamped tournament in 2003, while Al Ittihad of Saudi Arabia won successive competitions in 2004 and 2005. Subsequent winners have included Jeonbuk Hyundai Motors and Pohang Steelers of South Korea and Urawa Red Diamonds and Gamba Osaka of Japan.

Above from left to right: Pohang Steelers lift the AFC Champions League trophy in 2009; Etoile Du Sahel celebrate victory in the 2007 African Champions League Final; Atlético Madrid win the European Super Cup in 2010.

Before the relaunch of the competition there had been a fledgling Asian Champions Club Cup between 1967 and 1971, dominated by the Israelis. Maccabi Tel Aviv won it twice, in 1968 and 1971, while Hapoel Tel Aviv won the inaugural cup and lost the 1970 final to Taj Club of Iran. The competition was revived in the mid-Eighties with increasing success and it was dominated by the South Koreans and the Japanese. Between 1996 and 2002 Korean clubs won the event five times, with Suwon Samsung Bluewings and Pohang Steelers lifting the trophy twice each, and on two occasions the cup climaxed with an all-Korean final, in 1997 and 2002.

AFC CUP

The AFC Cup was launched in 2004 and is contested by representatives of the next 14 developing countries that are not represented in the Asian Champions League. Six nations did not take part or withdrew teams from the first competition but the prize is worthwhile as success in this tournament earns elevation to the AFC Champions League the following season (only if a club's league is deemed up Champions League criteria).

The competition kicks off with eight groups of four teams, with the group winners and runners-up qualifying for the knockout stages. The competition is decided by a single game, although two-legged finals were used between 2004 and 2008.

The first final in 2004 was an all-Syrian affair between Al Jaish and Al Wahda. Al Jaish won on the away goals rule after a 3-3 aggregate draw, despite both matches being played in the same stadium in Damascus. Al Jaish became the first Syrian side to win a major Asian trophy and were elevated to the Champions League the following season. Al-Faisaly of Jordan lifted the cup in both 2005 and 2006, while subsequent competitions have been won by Shabab Al-Ordon of Jordan in 2007, Al-Muharraq from Bahrain who beat Safa of Lebanon 10-5 on aggregate in 2008, and Al-Kuwait in 2009.

AFC PRESIDENT'S CUP

The Asian nations not deemed 'mature' enough for the Champions League or 'developing' for the AFC Cup were allowed to enter the inaugural AFC President's Cup in May 2005. However, nine of the 17 countries declined to take part, leaving the national champions of Tajikistan, Nepal, Taiwan, Bhutan, Kyrgyzstan, Sri Lanka, Pakistan and Cambodia to contest the competition. Other nations that could enter a team but have yet to do so are Brunei, East Timor, Laos, Philippines, Guam, Macau, Mongolia, North Korea, Palestine and Afghanistan.

The knockout stages are played as a mini tournament in a host country and it has grown from the eight representatives for the first competition to the 12 clubs that will contest the cup from 2011. Teams compete in three groups with the winners and the best of the second-placed teams reaching the semi-finals.

AFRICAN CHAMPIONS LEAGUE

The African Champions League succeeded the African Champions Cup in 1997. The two cups have delivered the most competitive and open of the major continental tournaments, having produced 25 different winners from 12 different nations over the years.

The African Champions' Cup was born in the 1964-5 season when an international club competition on the continent first became feasible. Many nations had become independent from their former colonial rulers and formed their own leagues. With the exception of the first tournament the competition was based on the format of Europe's established club competitions. Ties were to be played home and away, including the final. Zaïre's TP Englebert were a leading force early on, appearing in four successive finals between 1967 and 1970, winning the first two of these.

Guinea's Hafia Conakry were the team to beat in the Seventies as they reached the final on five occasions, winning in 1972, 1975 and 1977. Hafia's presence confirmed the early dominance of west and central Africa but this was because the north of the continent showed little interest until the 1980s, when the clubs of Algeria, Egypt, Morocco and Tunisia finally started to come to the fore. Egyptian clubs have since been the most successful in the competition's history, winning 12 times and reaching the final on 17 occasions in total, with Al-Ahly winning six titles and Zamalek lifting the cup five times.

The Champions League format replaced the traditional knockout style of competition in 1997. The cup currently kicks off in March and initially goes through a preliminary round, plus first and second round knockout stage until the eight remaining teams play home and away in two league groups of four. The top two sides from each group contest the two-legged semi-finals and the winners play a two-legged final.

CAF CONFEDERATION CUP

The CAF Confederation Cup replaced the African Cup Winners' Cup and the CAF Cup in 2004 and is a result of allowing more than one team from a country to take part in the African Champions League. It is contested by

the national cup winners and highly placed league teams. As with the European Champions League, clubs knocked out of the early stages of the African Champions League have a second attempt at international club glory in the Confederation Cup.

After the preliminary, first and second rounds, there is an intermediate round where the unlucky teams knocked out from the second round of the Champions League join the remaining eight teams in the Confederation Cup. From this intermediate round the eight winners form two groups of four and the group winners qualify for the two-legged final.

In the first final in 2004 Hearts Of Oak beat Asante Kotoko on penalties in an all-Ghanaian contest. In 2005 it was Morocco's FAR Rabat who were successful, beating Nigeria's Dolphins 3-1 on aggregate. Tunisian clubs enjoyed a hat-trick of wins, with Étoile Sportive Du Sahel's triumph in 2006 followed by back-to-back titles for Club Sportif Sfaxien, with the two teams facing each other in the final of 2008. Stade Malien of Mali won the competition in 2009.

THE CAF SUPER CUP

The CAF Super Cup is an annual match played between the winners of the CAF Champions League and the CAF Confederation Cup. It was first contested in 1993, with Egyptian sides Al-Ahly and Zamalek enjoying the most success in the competition.

CONCACAF CHAMPIONS LEAGUE

The CONCACAF Champions League was launched in the 2008-9 season, replacing the CONCACAF Champions Cup, which had first started in 1962 and was initially contested by the clubs of Central America. In the late 1990s clubs from USA's Major League Soccer also joined the fray. The competition has experimented with tournament and league formats and has settled on a mixture of the two.

The newly expanded Champions League currently starts off with 24 teams, which are reduced in a preliminary round to 16 and drawn into four groups of four teams. After the group stage, the competition is contested home and away on a knockout basis until being settled by a two-legged final.

Mexican teams have tended to dominate the competition since its inception in 1962, with Pachuca recording the country's 27th win in 2010. Compatriots Cruz Azul and América have been the most successful clubs in the competition's history with five wins each.

COPA SUDAMERICANA

An annual international club competition organised by CONMEBOL, it has been contested on a knockout basis in South America since 2002. Participation is by invitation

and from 2004 to 2008, clubs from Central America and North America were also asked to compete. Each national federation decides the qualification criteria for their allotted places in the competition. It was first played in 2002, replacing the Copa CONMEBOL, the Copa Mercosur and the Copa Merconorte, which in turn had displaced the Supercopa in 1997. It is effectively South America's second most important club competition after the Copa Libertadores. Argentinian clubs have lifted the cup the most, with San Lorenzo winning the inaugural title in 2002.

Above: Despite losing the second leg of the final 3-0, LDU Quito enjoy the moment after winning the Copa Sudamericana in 2009.

RECOPA SUDAMERICANA

The winners of the Copa Sudamericana and the Copa Libertadores face each other the following year in the Recopa Sudamericana. The trophy has been contested in South America on an annual basis since 1989, with Argentinian clubs enjoying the most success.

OCEANIA CHAMPIONS LEAGUE

The OFC Champions League has been contested in the Oceania region since 2007, when it was introduced as a replacement for the Oceania Club Championship. The original competition had been running on an ad hoc basis since 1987, with Australian clubs winning each edition until the country's football federation joined the Asian Football Confederation in 2006. Clubs from New Zealand subsequently dominated the rebranded competition until PRK Hekari United of Papua New Guinea lifted the cup in 2010.

Left: Atlante lift the CONCACAF Champions League trophy after winning in 2009.

GREAT CLUBS OF THE WORLD

AJAX

AMSTERDAM, HOLLAND
Stadium: Amsterdam Arena
(51,700)

Founded: 1900 **Honours:** World Club Cup 1972, 1995; European Cup/Champions League 1971, 1972, 1973, 1995; European Cup Winners' Cup 1987; UEFA Cup 1992; European Super Cup 1972, 1973, 1995; League 29; Cup 18

The name Ajax is synonymous with the term 'Total Football'. This was a concept of play that saw footballers of supreme technical ability able to interchange positions during a game in a way that had never been seen on the European stage. Not only was it magnificent to watch, it was also highly successful. At the height of the team's powers in the early Seventies, Ajax not only lifted the European Cup on three successive occasions (beating Panathinaikos in 1971, followed by victories over Inter Milan and Juventus) but they also enjoyed back-to-back European Super Cup wins and a World Club Cup triumph.

This Ajax side had talent in abundance, with the likes of Johan Neeskens, Arie Haan and Ruud Krol, but the star of the side was Johan Cruyff. These were all products of the revered Ajax youth system, which has also unearthed such players as Frank Rijkaard, Marco Van Basten, Dennis Bergkamp, Patrick Kluivert, Edwin Van Der Sar and Klaas-Jan Huntelaar.

The relaxation of rules governing overseas signings saw Ajax lose many of their young stars. With the club fielding a more international line-up, it was fitting that their last major success on the European stage, a Champions League final victory over Milan in 1995, saw Louis Van Gaal's side fielding the backbone of the Dutch national team – Van Der Sar, Reiziger, the De Boer brothers, Blind, Davids, Seedorf and Overmars. The win was also sealed by a goal from Patrick Kluivert. Ajax's subsequent successes have been domestic, including the league title in 2004, the second under coach Ronald Koeman, and Dutch Cup wins in 2006, 2007 and 2010.

AL-AHLY

CAIRO, EGYPT
Stadium: Cairo Stadium
(74,100)

Founded: 1907 **Honours:** African Champions League 1982, 1987, 2001, 2005, 2006, 2008; African Cup Winners' Cup 1984, 1985, 1986, 1993; CAF Super Cup 2002, 2006, 2007, 2009; League 35; Cup 35

One of the most successful football clubs on the African continent, Al-Ahly was formed by students in 1907 but began its rise to prominence in the 1920s with the country's greatest striker Mahmoud Mokhtar El-Tetsh spearheading the side. After the launch of the Egyptian league in 1948 Al-Ahly dominated the competition, winning the title nine times in a row.

In 1982 the club experienced success on the international stage for the first time, winning the African Cup Of Champions Clubs after beating Asante Kotoko of Ghana 4-1. The club's star player was striker Mahmoud El-Khatib, who became the first Egyptian to be voted African Player Of The Year in 1983 and he was still in the team when Al-Ahly lifted the trophy again in 1987. After the competition became the African Champions League they have since become the most successful club in the history of the cup. They have won it on a further four occasions since 2001, finishing runners-up once more, all under the guidance of Portuguese coach Manuel Jose. Only bitter local rivals Zamalek have come close to winning the trophy as many times.

Nicknamed the 'Red Devils', the club's big name coaches have included Nandor Hidegkuti and Don Revie. The club formerly played home games at the Mokhtar El-Tetsh Stadium, but currently share the Cairo International Stadium with Zamalek to satisfy the demand of their huge fanbase. In 2000 the Confederation Of African Football named Al-Ahly as the African Club Of The Century and in 2006 they finished third in the FIFA Club World Cup.

ANDERLECHT

BRUSSELS, BELGIUM
Stadium: Constant Vanden Stock (28,063)

Founded: 1908 **Honours:** European Cup Winners' Cup 1976, 1978; UEFA Cup 1983; European Super Cup 1976, 1978; League 30; Cup 9

RSC Anderlecht is Belgium's most successful club. Formed in Brussels on May 27, 1908, it was not until 1947 that the team won a first league title. However, a further 29 league championships, a national record by some margin, illustrates the Mauves' willingness to make up for lost time and the level of their domestic dominance.

Success on the European stage came in the late Seventies, a golden period when the club reached three consecutive Cup Winners' Cup finals. In 1976 the team got the better of West Ham, winning 4-2 to claim a first European title. The following campaign they were runners-up to Hamburg but a year later they again lifted the cup, beating FK Austria 4-0.

As a consequence of the victories, Anderlecht faced the European champions in the Super Cup, beating Bayern Munich on aggregate in 1976 and Liverpool in 1978. The club added the UEFA Cup to their honours list in 1983 with a 2-1 aggregate victory over Benfica. The following season saw another UEFA Cup final, but this time it ended with defeat to Tottenham after a penalty shoot-out.

The second half of the following decade saw a decline in the club's fortunes, with numerous managerial changes but with league title wins in 2000, 2001, 2004, 2006, 2007 and 2010, Anderlecht remain a dominant force in the Belgian game. This revival has not been matched by success on the continental stage and while the club makes regular appearances in the Champions League, there has been no success. In the 2004-5 season the team even lost all six group games, conceding 17 goals.

Above: Al-Ahly celebrate winning the African Super Cup in 2009.

ARSENAL

LONDON, ENGLAND
Stadium: Emirates Stadium
(60,361)

Founded: 1886 **Honours:** European Cup Winners' Cup 1994; Fairs Cup 1970; League 13; Cup 10; League Cup 2

The club was formed as Dial Square by workers at the Woolwich armaments factory in south London, before turning professional in 1891 as Woolwich Arsenal. The club gained election to Division Two in 1893 and promotion followed 11 years later. Relegation in 1913 was tempered by the club's move to Highbury, when they dropped the 'Woolwich' prefix. The move was the work of chairman Sir Henry Norris, who saw great potential in the north London catchment area.

Despite finishing in fifth place in Division Two in 1915, promotion to the top division was engineered by Norris in somewhat strange circumstances when the league resumed after World War I, and his appointment of manager Herbert Chapman in 1925 transformed the club into one of the greatest in world football.

Not only did Arsenal get white sleeves and their own tube station after Chapman rebuilt the team, they also won five championships in the 1930s and two FA Cups. Chapman died before he could see all of these achievements and after the Second World War the club did not offer the same threat. Although the team went on to win the title in 1948, 1953 and the league and cup 'double' of 1971, it was not until the appointment of George Graham in 1986 that Arsenal emerged as a consistent force.

Opposite clockwise from top: Ajax celebrating victory in the 1995 Champions League Final; Johan Cruyff in 1972; Michael Laudrup raising the Dutch Cup after beating PSV 5-0 in 1998.

Above: The Arsenal players celebrate with the Cup Winners' Cup after beating Parma in 1994.

Above right: Aston Villa's Johnny Dixon lifts the FA Cup after victory over Manchester United in 1957.

Graham's disciplinarian style, shrewd buying and faith in the club's youth system yielded the championship within three years. As the team matured, Arsenal won the title again in 1991, the League Cup and FA Cup 'double' in 1993, and enjoyed success in the European Cup Winners' Cup against Parma a year later.

Under George Graham Arsenal's one-dimensional play won few friends but the appointment of Arsene Wenger in 1996 changed the club's image emphatically. The Frenchman championed a stylish approach on the pitch and a forward-thinking attitude to preparation off it. His team won the 'double' in 1998 and 2002, the Premiership in 2004 without losing a game, and the FA Cup in 2003 and 2005. After stuttering form in the Champions League, he took the club to its first European Cup final in 2006 but suffered defeat at the hands of Barcelona in Paris.

At the start of the 2006-7 season, the club left historic Highbury and relocated to the nearby Emirates Stadium, its new 60,000 seater home.

ASTON VILLA

BIRMINGHAM, ENGLAND
Stadium: Villa Park
(42,783)

Founded: 1874 **Honours:** European Cup 1982; European Super Cup 1982; League 7; Cup 7; League Cup 5

A founding member of the Football League, Aston Villa is one of the oldest clubs in the world. While five of its seven league titles and three of its six FA Cups were won by 1900, between the turn of the century and the club's first relegation in 1936, Villa remained a powerful force in the English game: champions in 1910, runners-up on seven occasions, and FA Cup winners three times. Although return to the top flight was swift, the club was never the same force again, sinking as far as the Third Division in 1970.

There were occasional high points in this period. Villa beat Manchester United's 'Busby Babes' in controversial circumstances in the

1957 FA Cup Final, with United playing with ten men after keeper Ray Wood was left unconscious following a collision. There was also success in the inaugural League Cup in 1961 after defeating Rotherham over two legs.

League Cup finalists again as a Third Division team ten years later, promotion under Vic Crowe in 1972 proved the impetus the club needed, and with Ron Saunders at the helm from 1974 the revival continued. He took Villa back to the top flight the following year and won the league title in 1981. However, midway through the next season Saunders resigned after a contract dispute, leaving his assistant Tony Barton to take over the team just three months before Villa's greatest ever night, when Peter Withe's single goal beat Bayern Munich in Rotterdam to win the 1982 European Cup Final.

Relegation came again in the late 1980s but Graham Taylor soon reversed the fortunes of the club. His team finished runners-up in the title race in 1990, and the feat was repeated in 1993 under Ron Atkinson. League Cup final victories in 1994 and 1996, an FA Cup final appearance in 2000, and another League Cup final in 2010 have at least given the club's fans a case for arguing that Villa remain a strong force in the game, while after the appointment of Martin O'Neill as coach in 2006, the club very nearly closed the gap on the big four clubs that have dominated English football.

ATHLETIC BILBAO

BILBAO, SPAIN
Stadium: San Mamés
(39,750)

Founded: 1898 **Honours:** League 8; Cup 23

Among the oldest clubs in Spain, along with Real Madrid and Barcelona, Athletic Club of Bilbao shares the honour of having never been relegated from Spain's top flight. This Basque club's English name originally stems from the British influence in the region, and from local suspicion of anything Spanish. Engineers from Great Britain brought football to the quarry

workers of this area of northern Spain in the late 1800s and the club still attempts to adhere to its selection policy of 'la cantera' or 'the quarry': only picking players of Basque origin. The most famous was Rafael Moreno Aranzadi, or 'Pichichi', and the top goalscorer in La Liga each season still wins a trophy named after him.

In the early years of the club's history Athletic Bilbao often employed English coaches. The most successful was Freddy Pentland, who won two league championships and five cups in the 1920s and 1930s after revolutionising the way the team played.

Despite the club's lack of impact on the European stage over the years, at home Bilbao are still second only to Barcelona as winners of the Spanish Cup. However, the club lists one more triumph than most official sources, as it chooses to include a 1902 victory by Club Bizcaya, a team made up of players from Athletic Club and Bilbao FC (a year later the two clubs merged as Athletic Club).

Although Bilbao's greatest years were largely over by the end of the 1950s, the club enjoyed a renaissance under Javier Clemente in the Eighties. His fearsome team won the league in 1983 and the league, Spanish Cup and Super Cup 'treble' in 1984, boasting players such as Andoni Zubizarreta and notorious defender Andoni Goikoetxea, 'The Butcher Of Bilbao'. During this period Clemente waged a war of words with Barcelona coach César Luis Menotti, which culminated in a brawl between the two teams at the end of the 1984 Spanish Cup Final.

The club has won no honours since, although under Luis Fernández it finished second in La Liga in 1996 and qualified for the Champions League. Fernández benefited from the adoption of a more flexible approach to 'la cantera', which has allowed for non Basque players to represent the club as long as their talent was initially developed in the region.

Athletic Bilbao's home ground, nicknamed 'La Catedral', is due to be replaced in 2014 by a new 53,000 capacity venue built adjacent to the current stadium.

ATLÉTICO MADRID

MADRID, SPAIN
Stadium: Vicente Calderón
(54,851)

Founded: 1903 **Honours:** World Club Cup 1974; Europa League: 2010; European Cup Winners' Cup 1962; European Super Cup 2010; League 9; Cup 9

The club is nicknamed 'Los Colchoneros', or 'The Mattressmakers', due to the resemblance of the team's famous red and white striped shirts to old fashioned mattresses. Originally formed in 1903 by three Basque students based in Madrid, although performances were poor in the early years, it was after the country's Civil War and a 1939 merger with the Spanish air force side Atlético Aviacion that success was finally achieved. Although a large part of the club's history has been spent in the shadow of neighbours Real Madrid, it has regularly won Spanish domestic competitions.

An impact has also been made on the international stage. In 1959 the team reached the semi-finals of the European Cup but they were beaten to a place in the final by city rivals Real Madrid. However, Atlético did manage to lift the European Cup Winners' Cup with a replay victory over Fiorentina in 1962. After finishing as runners-up to Bayern Munich in the 1974 European Cup, the team went on to beat Independiente over two legs to win the World Club Cup, following the refusal of Bayern to take part in the competition.

After a decade of little success, the club was taken over by the flamboyant Jesus Gil in 1987, and his erratic and often dubious financial behaviour defined Atlético in the years that followed. Under his presidency the club managed to hire and fire 37 coaches in 16 years, including César Luis Menotti, Ron Atkinson, Javier Clemente and Arrigo Sacchi. However, his unique approach was vindicated in 1996 when Atlético won the Spanish league and cup 'double' under Radomir Antic, and for just a short while they crept out of the shadow of Real Madrid.

After the suspension of Jesus Gil and an investigation of the board in December 1999, Atlético struggled for direction. In addition to losing to Espanyol in the final of the Spanish Cup in 2000, the club also suffered relegation and spent two years out of the top flight before promotion back the Primera Liga in 2002.

Largely a mid-table side ever since, successive fourth place finishes in the league in 2008 and 2009 opened up Champions League football once again and in 2010 the club celebrated its first European success in 48 years, beating Fulham to win the Europa League and Inter Milan to lift the UEFA Super Cup.

ATLÉTICO NACIONAL

MEDELLIN, COLOMBIA
Stadium: Atanasio Girardot (52,872)

Founded: 1936 **Honours:** Copa Libertadores 1989; Copa Interamericana 1989; Copa Merconorte 1998, 2000; League 10

Atlético Nacional's first league title in 1954 coincided with the Colombian FA rejoining FIFA after a four-year dispute over transfer payments. The club has subsequently added a further ten league titles to its honours list. However, it enjoyed its greatest moment of success on the continental stage, becoming the first Colombian team to win the Copa Libertadores in 1989. Future national team coach Francisco Maturana led Nacional to the trophy with a win over Olimpia of Paraguay. This was followed by a 1-0

defeat to Milan in Tokyo in the final of the World Club Cup. This success came in a period when the team played with an entertaining style and for a while the club adopted a policy of fielding only Colombian players, preferably those from Medellin itself. The stars of this era, such as René Higuita, Faustino Asprilla, Andrés Escobar and Luis Fernando Herrera, formed the backbone of the Colombian national team.

The club's home city of Medellin is at the centre of the country's illegal drug industry. Indeed, Pablo Escobar, the leader of the biggest drug cartel, was a lifelong Nacional fan, and at his funeral in 1993 the club flag was controversially draped over his coffin.

After 2002 Colombian football switched back to a split season, with the 'Apertura' (opening) and the 'Clausura', or 'Finalización' (closing), resulting in two league champions each year, one for each campaign. Both competitions are settled by a play-off final and since the introduction of this format, Nacional have won the Apertura in 2005 and lifted both titles in 2007.

AUSTRIA VIENNA

VIENNA, AUSTRIA
Stadium: Franz Horr Stadion (13,000)

Founded: 1911 **Honours:** League 23; Cup 27

Founded in the Austrian capital on March 12, 1911, by members of the Vienna Cricket and Football Club, the team initially played under

the name SV Amateur Vienna, winning a first league title in 1924. However, with the onset of a professional league the name was changed to FK Austria two years later.

The early 1930s were the club's most famous years and corresponded with the Austrian national team's domination of European football. The so-called Austrian 'Wunderteam' contained many players from FK Austria, including the legendary Matthias Sindelar. Club success came not only in the form of domestic league titles but also with victories in the Mitropa Cup. FK Austria claimed this prestigious central European trophy in both 1933 and 1936, beating Inter Milan and Sparta Prague respectively.

In 1977 a new sponsor changed the name to the rather unwieldy FK Austria Memphis, and the club subsequently enjoyed a run of seven league titles in the following nine seasons, plus an appearance in the 1978 European Cup Winners' Cup Final, which led to a heavy 4-0 defeat at the hands of Anderlecht. The following year they were knocked out of the European Cup by Malmö at the semi-final stage.

In more recent times the club has failed to live up to the Violets' glorious past. After changing ownership in 1999, the club became known as FK Austria Memphis Magna and received a significant increase in its budget to buy players. It may have won the league and cup 'double' in both 2003 and 2006, and the Austrian Cup again in 2007 and 2009, but it has been a poor return on a quite significant investment. The club finally returned to its traditional name, FK Austria Vienna, in July 2008.

Below: Nacional coach Santiago Escobar celebrates with his team after winning the Colombian championship in 2002.

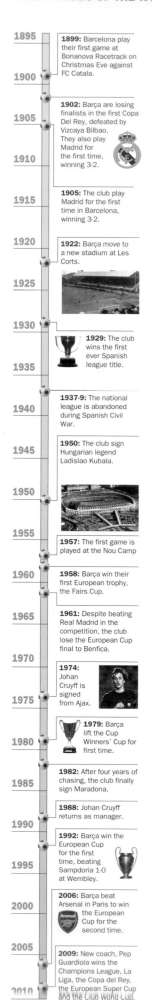

BARCELONA

BARCELONA, SPAIN
Stadium: Camp Nou
(98,772)

Founded: 1999 **Honours:** World Club Cup 2009; European Cup/Champions League 1992, 2006, 2009; European Cup Winners' Cup 1979, 1982, 1989, 1997; Fairs Cup 1958, 1960, 1966; European Super Cup 1992, 1997, 2009; League 20; Cup 25

One of the biggest and best-supported clubs in world football, FC Barcelona did not win the European Cup for the first time until 1992, and despite renewed success in the Champions League in the first decade of the 21st century, the club's achievements will always be judged by the yardstick set by bitter rivals Real Madrid, who dominated the competition for much of its first ten years. It is this rivalry that underpins the story of football in Spain.

With a club history mired in the politics of mid-20th century Spain, for many years Barcelona became a symbol of Catalan defiance in a country oppressed by General Franco's centralist government in Madrid. Yet for a club synonymous with the spirit of the region of Catalonia, ironically its roots were originally in the expatriate communities of the city.

In October 1899 Swiss football enthusiast Joan Gamper placed an advert in the local sports newspaper *Los Deportes* and recruited a team largely drawn from the various English businesses of the city, with the club's famous strip inspired by the old school colours of one of the English players, Arthur Witty. Fielding a team comprised largely of foreigners, FC Barcelona played its first game on Christmas Eve 1899, with Arthur Witty scoring to seal the 3-1 win over local side FC Catala 3-1.

Swift progress was made in the early years of the century, with Barcelona reaching the first final of the Spanish Cup (the Copa Del Rey) in 1902, although by the time the club finally won the competition in 1910, Madrid had already lifted the trophy four times. When the first Spanish national league came into being in the 1928-9 season, Barcelona beat Real Madrid to the title by just two points, and since then the club has never been relegated, a feat matched only by Real and Athletic Bilbao.

Although Barça continued to win domestic honours for the next 20 years, it was really in the period from 1948 to 1960 that the club built a team of substance and a stadium to house it, opening the Nou Camp in 1957. Barcelona's greatest period of achievement was under the management of Argentinian Helenio Herrera, who arrived at the club in 1958, shortly after their first European triumph in the Fairs Cup. During his two-year spell at Barça, Herrera shook the club at its roots. He placed his faith in young Catalan players nurtured through the youth team and his 'lucky foreigners', Hungarians Sandor

Kocsis and Zoltan Czibor. In Herrera's first season in charge, Barça eclipsed the Real Madrid of Di Stéfano and Puskás to take the league title with a then record haul of points.

Victory over Birmingham City in the 1960 Fairs Cup was followed by another league title, but no amount of success could ease the pain caused by the end of that season's European Cup campaign, when despite recording significant aggregate victories over CDNA Sofia (8-4), Milan (7-1) and Wolves (9-2), semi-final humiliation by Real Madrid was deemed disastrous. Before the clash Herrera had fallen out with his star Ladislao Kubala over bonus payments. Zoltan Czibor backed his fellow Hungarian and both were dropped. Barcelona lost each leg 3-1 and Herrera took the blame and was forced to resign.

The following season Barça dumped Real out of the European Cup in the first round but finished runners-up following a 3-2 defeat by Benfica in the final. In La Liga it was the onset of a decade of dominance by Madrid, who won eight of the remaining nine titles during the Sixties (Atlético Madrid interrupted this run in 1966). Triumphs in the Copa Del Rey in 1963 and 1968 were scant consolation, and although Barcelona won the Fairs Cup in 1966, the club would not clinch the league title again until 1974. In the mid-Sixties Spain had barred imported players but the ban was lifted in 1973 in time for the club to spend a world record fee

of £922,000 on Johan Cruyff, who took the club from the relegation zone to the title for the first time in 14 years. The season also included a 5-0 away thrashing of Real Madrid.

Although further success in La Liga would evade the club until Terry Venables won the title in 1985, it was Cruyff who would again prove the biggest saviour, returning as coach to deliver the club's first triumph in the European Cup. A single Ronald Koeman goal at Wembley in the 1992 final was enough to beat Sampdoria to the prize. However, a 4-0 defeat to Milan in the final two years later did little to endear Cruyff to the board, and despite having taken the club to four league titles in a row, failure to win a trophy in 1995 and 1996 led to his acrimonious departure.

Dutchman Louis Van Gaal brought back-to-back titles to the Nou Camp in 1998 and 1999, but by filling the side with so many of his countrymen – Kluivert, Reiziger, Cocu, Overmars and the De Boers – he proved unpopular and was forced to resign. A second spell for Van Gaal just a year later was unsuccessful and he was replaced midway through his second season, but under Radomir Antic the club finished sixth in La Liga in 2003, their worst position since 1942.

Under enthusiastic young president Joan Laporta and coach Frank Rijkaard the club started to dominate Spanish football once again. With players of the calibre of Larsson, Ronaldinho, and Eto'o, Barcelona won back-to-back titles, and triumphed in the 2006 Champions League Final, beating ten-man Arsenal 2-1 in Paris.

After the departure of Rijkaard in 2008, former player and B team coach Pep Guardiola was promoted to top job at just 37 years of age. In his first season he won the league, the Spanish Cup and beat Manchester United to the Champions League. Before the end of the year he had completed an amazing 'sextuple' by adding the Spanish Super Cup, the European Super Cup and the FIFA Club World Cup to the haul, reasserting Barcelona's reputation in the game.

Above: After winning the 1992 European Cup in their away strip, Barcelona changed into their famous 'blaugrana' shirts to collect the trophy. Opposite from top left: Puyol lifts the league trophy, 2005; Ronaldinho and Belletti with the Spanish Super Cup, 2006; Lineker holds the Cup Winners' Cup, 1989; Messi and Iniesta with the Champions League trophy, 2009.

The Nou Camp: one of the great venues of world football.

Above: Franck Ribéry with the German Cup as Bayern Munich clinch the 'double' in 2010.

BAYERN MUNICH

  MUNICH, GERMANY
Stadium: Allianz Arena
(69,901)

Founded: 1900 **Honours:** World Club Cup 1976, 2001; European Cup/Champions League 1974, 1975, 1976, 2001; European Cup Winners' Cup 1967; UEFA Cup 1996; League 22; Cup 15

Bayern celebrated its centenary year in 2000 by winning the Bundesliga and DFB Cup 'double' for the third time, following it in 2001 with a seventh appearance – and fourth victory – in the European Cup final, defeating Valencia on penalties to lift the trophy for the first time since the competition had been rebranded as the Champions League.

Despite this success, the club was not even its city's representative in the initial Bundesliga campaign of 1963. That honour fell to TSV Munich 1860, as by that time Bayern had triumphed just once in the regional play-offs that previously decided the German championship, back in 1932. It was not until attack-minded Yugoslav coach Tschik Cajkovski took over in 1963 that Bayern started their climb to the top.

In the 1965 Bundesliga promotion play-offs Cajkovski included three promising youngsters in his team: Sepp Maier in goal, Gerd Müller in attack, and Franz Beckenbauer in midfield. Maier still holds Bayern's appearance record, including 422 consecutive games; Müller, 'Der Bomber', netted an astonishing 365 league goals in 427 games; and Beckenbauer, 'Der Kaiser', was one of the greatest footballers ever.

This trio helped Bayern to cup wins in 1966 and 1967, and a Cup Winners' Cup victory in 1967 against Rangers. The club completed its first league and cup 'double' in 1969 under new boss Branko Zebec. With the addition of three more world-class players, Paul Breitner, Uli Hoeness and Hans-Georg Schwarzenbeck, Bayern witnessed the dawn of a golden era.

Zebec's replacement, Udo Lattek, led the club on a four-year unbeaten home run, winning three league titles in a row and enjoying the first of three consecutive European Cup wins in 1974, with a 4-0 victory over Atlético Madrid. After his sacking during the following season, it was left to his successor Dettmar Cramer to complete the hat-trick with European Cup final victories over Leeds United in 1975 and Saint-Etienne in 1976.

Bayern's triumphs dried up as the old guard left or retired, but the club enjoyed a renaissance following the emergence of striker Karl-Heinz Rummenigge and the return of Breitner, the formidable duo dubbed 'Breitnigge'. The arrival of the influential Lothar Matthäus in 1984 prompted another trio of league wins. However, Bayern struggled in the early 1990s and 'Der Kaiser' returned as club president in 1994 to reverse the club's fortunes, also overseeing the team's UEFA Cup win in 1996 as coach.

Under Ottmar Hitzfeld, the club's most successful coach, a new generation of Bayern stalwart emerged, with players such as Oliver Kahn, Stefan Effenberg and Thomas Linke. The team put a last minute defeat by Manchester United in the 1999 Champions League Final behind them to win in 2001 against Valencia, while pocketing another string of German titles, including the league and cup 'double' in 2000 and 2003. However, after a poor season when Bayern were defeated in the quarter-final of the German Cup by second division Alemannia Aachen, Hitzfeld lost his job.

He was replaced by Felix Magath, who won the league and cup 'double' in both 2005 and 2006. In January 2007 Hitzfeld returned, and after some serious investment in the transfer market that saw the arrival of players of the calibre of Luca Toni, Miroslav Klose and Franck Ribéry, the team won the 'double' once more in 2008, but it was under Louis Van Gaal in 2010 that Bayern reached the Champions League final once again, where they lost 2-0 to Inter Milan.

In 2005 Bayern moved from the Olympic Stadium to the Allianz Arena, which it shares with TSV 1860. The two clubs initially owned the stadium jointly, but after flirting with insolvency, TSV sold its share of the ground to Bayern. For UEFA and FIFA competitions the stadium has a seated capacity of 66,000, while for Bundesliga games a small standing area, still a tradition in the German league, raises the capacity to 69,901.

BENFICA

LISBON, PORTUGAL
Stadium: Estadio da Luz (65,647)

Founded: 1904 **Honours:** European Cup 1961, 1962; League 32; Cup 27 *(including three wins when Portuguese Championship was a cup competition, 1922-38)*

Few teams in the history of the game compare to the famous Benfica side of the 1960s. Yet while the club dominated the game at home by winning the Portuguese title eight times during the course of the decade, an incredible five European Cup final appearances between 1961 and 1968 resulted in just two victories. On both occasions Benfica defeated Spanish opposition to become European champions, beating Barcelona in 1961 and Real Madrid in 1962. The latter final finished 5-3 as the great Eusébio scored twice after the interval to help eclipse the first-half Ferenc Puskás hat-trick that had given Real the advantage.

As the decade progressed Italian clubs proved not quite as charitable as the Spanish, with both AC Milan (1963) and Inter Milan (1965) foiling Benfica in the European Cup finals that followed. In 1968 it was Manchester United's turn to heap further misery on the Lisbon giants, inflicting a 4-1 defeat after extra-time at Wembley Stadium.

In 1978, in an effort to compete with the best sides in Europe, the club finally scrapped its policy of fielding only Portuguese citizens (and those from its colonies – Eusébio was born in Mozambique). The change seemed to work as once again Benfica enjoyed a high profile on the continental stage. However, the club fell at the final hurdle on each occasion, finishing as runners-up in the UEFA Cup in 1983 and in the European Cup in 1988 and 1990. The most heartbreaking result of all was a 6-5 penalty shoot-out defeat to PSV Eindhoven in 1988.

In 2003 Benfica moved from the world famous Estádio da Luz (Stadium Of Light) in order to take residence at the new Estádio da Luz, built as the showpiece stadium for the final of Euro 2004 just yards away from the original. Despite going eight years without a major trophy from the mid-1990s, Benfica managed to remain Portugal's best known club. Success in the domestic cup in 2004, with a 2-1 victory over Porto, kickstarted a mini revival, and

the following season under coach Giovanni Trapattoni the club won its first league title in 11 years, also finishing as runners-up to Vitória Setúbal in the Portuguese Cup.

Failing to capitalise on this triumph under a succession of coaches, it has only been since the arrival of Jorge Jesus in June 2009 that the team have once again taken on the look of contenders, finishing the 2009-10 league campaign as champions for the 32nd time.

BOCA JUNIORS

BUENOS AIRES, ARGENTINA
Stadium: La Bombonera (49,000)

Founded: 1905 **Honours:** World Club Cup 1977, 2000, 2003; Copa Libertadores 1977, 1978, 2000, 2001, 2003, 2007; Supercopa Sudamericana 1989; Recopa Sudamericana 1990, 2005, 2006, 2008; Copa Sudamericana 2004, 2005; League 23

Although Club Atlético Boca Juniors is often associated with former player and celebrity fan Diego Maradona, in truth the great man only played a bit part in the club's long and eventful history. Founded in 1905 by a group of Italian immigrants who had been inspired by the football coaching of Irishman Paddy McCarthy, Boca's home was in the poor docklands of Buenos Aires, the neighbourhood that gave birth to the tango. The club's humble roots have not been forgotten and Boca Juniors continue to represent the working class.

Six titles in the national amateur league

between 1919 and 1930 signalled the club's arrival as a domestic force, and in 1931 the team became the first winners of the inaugural Argentine Professional League. A decade later Boca moved to the Estadio Dr Camilo Cichero, or 'La Bombonera' (The Chocolate Box), as it became commonly known.

Despite regularly winning domestic titles, it was only with the arrival of disciplinarian coach Juan Carlos Lorenzo in 1976 that the club emerged as a force outside of Argentina. During his five-year tenure Boca won South America's club championship, the Copa Libertadores, for the first time in 1977. A year later the title was defended with 4-0 aggregate victory over Colombia's Deportivo Cali. While Boca's physical style of play under Lorenzo did not win any friends among football purists, a 5-2 aggregate victory over European Cup runners-up Borussia Mönchengladbach in the 1977 World Club Cup Final (actually played in March 1978) kept fans satisfied.

In 1980 Boca paid £1 million for Maradona, but he was sold on to Barcelona in a £3 million world record deal two seasons later. After his departure Boca's dominance waned and it was not until the club's back-to-back successes in the Copa Libertadores in 2000 and 2001, under Carlos Bianchi, that its status as a genuine intercontinental superpower was reaffirmed.

Success in the World Club Cup has helped cement this reputation, with victory over Real Madrid in 2000, and a penalty shoot-out win against Milan in 2003. The club also won the Copa Libertadores again in 2003 and 2007, beating Santos and Grêmio.

Below: The Boca Juniors players celebrate with the Copa América trophy in 2005.

Above: Borussia Dortmund with the Champions League trophy after beating Juventus in 1997.

BORUSSIA DORTMUND

DORTMUND, GERMANY
Stadium: Westfalen Stadium (80,552)

Founded: 1909 **Honours:** World Club Cup 1997; Champions League 1997; European Cup Winners' Cup 1966; League 6; Cup 2

Borussia Dortmund's success has been in two distinct eras separated by a barren period stretching for more than 30 years. The club's first taste of silverware occurred during the 1956-7 campaign when the team celebrated a first West German championship triumph, a feat that was repeated the following season.

This heralded the start of the first golden era for the club and Dortmund celebrated another championship in 1963, the last before the beginning of Germany's professional Bundesliga era the following season. This was followed by victory in the German Cup in 1965 and in the European Cup Winners' Cup a year later. The 2-1 extra-time victory over Liverpool at Hampden Park gave Dortmund a special place in the record books as the first German side to win a European trophy.

With the exception of a second German Cup in 1989, nothing but dust was added to the trophy cabinet at the Westfalen Stadium until 1995, when a Matthias Sammer-inspired Dortmund pipped Werder Bremen to the Bundesliga title. The following year the club ran out winners again but better was to come.

The 1997 Champions League Final in Munich's Olympic Stadium saw Dortmund defeat a strong Juventus side 3-1, thanks to two goals from Karl-Heinz Riedle and one from 20-year-old substitute Lars Ricken, who scored only 16 seconds after coming on the pitch. A subsequent 2-0 victory over Brazil's Cruzeiro

in the World Club Cup final later that year established Borussia's position as a force on the global football stage.

At the turn of the millennium Dortmund became the first publicly traded football club on the German stock market and soon afterwards clinched a third Bundesliga title at the end of the 2002 season. The club also lost the UEFA Cup final that season, after a 3-2 defeat to Feyenoord in Rotterdam, but that was an insignificant blow compared with the off-the-pitch problems that were besetting the club. Poor financial management forced the sale of the stadium in 2002, with the club having to lease it back. In 2006 Borussia were able to reacquire the stadium but as a consequence it was renamed Signal Iduna Park in a sponsorship deal to help reduce the debt.

Although the club reached the final of the German Cup in 2008, losing 2-1 to Bayern, it has struggled to compete in recent years. However, despite its problems, the club's average home attendance remains well over 70,000 a game, the highest in Germany.

CELTIC

GLASGOW, SCOTLAND
Stadium: Celtic Park (61,000)

Founded: 1888 **Honours:** European Cup 1967; League 42; Cup 34; League Cup 14

Celtic's crowning moment came in the 1967 European Cup Final in Lisbon, when the team beat Inter Milan 2-1 to become the first British side to win the competition. The achievement of the 'Lisbon Lions' was especially heartening as all of the players originated from within a 30-mile radius of Celtic Park. With the majority of the team still in place, and skippered again by

Billy McNeill, Celtic lost the 1970 European Cup Final to Feyenoord in Milan.

Traditionally the club was very much the team of Glasgow's Irish immigrant community. A Catholic priest originally founded Celtic as a charity but they were never charitable to opponents and the ongoing rivalry with the Protestants of Rangers started early.

Under long-serving manager Willie Maley, the club won six consecutive championships before World War I. Between the wars Maley introduced such legends as Patsy Gallagher and Jimmy McGrory, still Celtic's leading goalscorer. After World War II the club faltered until the appointment of ex-player Jock Stein in 1965. He soon moulded a great side from the likes of Tommy Gemmell, Bertie Auld and tricky winger Jimmy Johnstone, and in 1967 the team won every competition it entered, including the European Cup. Joined along the way by players of the calibre of Kenny Dalglish and Lou Macari, Celtic won a record nine league titles in a row.

In the years that followed, league glory was shared between Celtic, 'Old Firm' adversaries Rangers, and new force Aberdeen. However, the 1990s belonged to Rangers. Celtic underwent a transformation to be able to compete and new owner Fergus McCann, who had bought a club on the edge of bankruptcy, rebuilt both the team and the stadium. Following the example set by Rangers, Celtic imported foreign players, including the prolific Swedish striker Henrik Larsson. The strategy paid off as under coach Wim Jansen the club won the 1998 Premier Division championship and prevented Rangers from breaking Celtic's own record of successive league title wins.

Martin O'Neill arrived at the helm in 2000 and won the 'treble' in his first season and the 'double' in 2004. He took Celtic to their first European final in 33 years in 2003 but the team lost the UEFA Cup to Porto. O'Neill left in May 2005 to be replaced by Gordon Strachan, who clinched the 2006 league title and League Cup in his first season. He won the league and Scottish Cup 'double' the following year and another league title in 2008, but he resigned after failing to retain the title in 2009.

Right: Celtic captain Neil Lennon kisses the Scottish Cup in 2007.

CHELSEA

LONDON, ENGLAND
Stadium: Stamford Bridge
(41,841)

Founded: 1905 **Honours:** European Cup Winners'
Cup 1971, 1998; European Super Cup 1998;
League 4; FA Cup 6; League Cup 4

The history of Chelsea Football Club begins with the team's home ground, Stamford Bridge. Opened in 1877, for the best part of 30 years it was used only for athletics meetings. Then, in 1904, football enthusiast Gus Mears and his brother bought the deeds to the ground and had architect Archibald Leitch build a football stadium on it. The new arena was initially offered to Fulham FC but they declined to move from their Craven Cottage home nearby, leaving Mears little choice but to form his own club. Although based in the London borough of Fulham, the new team took its name from a neighbouring borough and on March 10, 1905, in a Fulham Road pub called The Rising Sun, Chelsea FC was born.

Elected to Division Two of the Football League on May 29, 1905, the club played its first competitive match in September of the same year (an away defeat to Stockport County) and achieved promotion to Division One in 1907. The highlight of the club's early years, though, was reaching the 1916 FA Cup Final. Chelsea lost 3-0 to Sheffield United at Old Trafford in a match that became known as 'The Khaki Final' because of the number of army uniforms that could be seen in the crowd.

It was not until the 1950s, when managed by Ted Drake, that Chelsea made an impact on English football. Drake had a no-nonsense style and was determined to reshape the club in his image. Out went Chelsea's rather fusty nickname 'The Pensioners' and in came a host of young players hungry for success, the so-called 'Drake's Ducklings'. Under this regime the club won its first league title in 1955, clinching victory in the season's penultimate game against Sheffield Wednesday.

Drake's side could not repeat the heroics in the seasons that followed and the manager finally left the club early in the 1961-2 campaign, with Chelsea briefly relegated at the end of the season. Performances improved under Tommy Docherty, with the team winning the League Cup for the first time in 1965 and reaching the final of the FA Cup in 1967, only to lose to Tottenham. Dave Sexton arrived as manager that year and with players like striker Peter Osgood and young midfield wizard Charlie Cooke, the Chelsea team were praised for the stylish football they played. There was grit in this side too, evidenced when beating Don Revie's uncompromising Leeds United after a hard-fought replay to lift the FA Cup

Above: The Chelsea players celebrate winning the Premier League title on the final day of the 2009-10 season.

in 1970. The following year the players had to roll up their sleeves again, this time to win the European Cup Winners' Cup in extra-time against the mighty Real Madrid.

The success was short-lived and Chelsea spent seven of the nine seasons between 1976 and 1984 in the Second Division, while in 1983 the club was almost relegated to Division Three. There were other problems for new owner Ken Bates, who had taken on Chelsea for the nominal sum of £1 in 1982: attendances at Stamford Bridge were poor, hooliganism was rife and the club was sinking under a mountain of debt, the result of over-ambitious ground improvements begun in the 1970s. Worst of all, Chelsea no longer owned Stamford Bridge, which had been sold to property developers in the late Seventies. It was not until 1994 that Bates was able to buy it back.

After the famine of the 1980s, the following decade proved something of a feast. Glenn Hoddle (1993-6), Ruud Gullit (1996-8) and Gianluca Vialli (1998-2000) were recruited as managers and each one took a multinational Chelsea team just a little bit further. Hoddle took them to the FA Cup final in his first season, while under Gullit the club won the trophy for the first time in 26 years. However, it was under Vialli that the trophies started flooding in. Chelsea won the FA Cup, the League Cup, the Cup Winners' Cup and the European Super Cup all in the space of two years. Success in the Cup Winners' Cup in 1998 was particularly sweet, with Gianfranco Zola hitting the winner against Stuttgart just moments after coming on as a second-half substitute.

Chelsea's success on the pitch had come at a price, as had the ambitious Chelsea Village hotel and business project built at Stamford Bridge. The club's borrowing had raged out of control and it was close to financial collapse in

2004 as huge loan repayments became due. However, a financial saviour was found in Roman Abramovich, who brought to an end the 22-year reign of Ken Bates.

The Russian oil billionaire bought the club for £60 million and bankrolled a spending spree on players unprecedented in world football at the time. Abramovich's cash injection into the team reaped dividends as Claudio Ranieri's side made the semi-finals of the Champions League for the first time and came second to Arsenal in the Premiership, the club's highest league finish for nearly half a century.

However, for Abramovich this was deemed not good enough and the amiable 'Tinkerman' Ranieri was soon replaced by José Mourinho, the methodical and outspoken Portuguese coach who had guided little-fancied Porto to Champions League success in 2004.

Mourinho's impact was immediate, with Chelsea winning the club's first league title in 50 years in 2005. The title was retained the following season in a campaign that saw the team leading the title race by 18 points with two months to play, but a late surge by Manchester United gave the campaign some belated excitement. After clinching the title playing against United, Mourinho threw his winners' medal into the Stamford Bridge crowd.

Despite league success, European glory has continued to elude Chelsea. Mourinho ultimately paid the price for this and although his successor Avram Grant led the club to its first Champions League final in 2008, defeat to Manchester United on penalties was not enough to keep him in a job. For all of Abramovich's millions, subsequent managers have failed to deliver the ultimate prize, although Carlo Ancelotti made history of a different kind when he led the club to its first league and cup 'double' in 2010.

1905

1905 The club is founded at The Rising Sun pub.

1910

1905 The first match is an away defeat to Stockport.

1915

1915 FA Cup final defeat to Sheffield United at Old Trafford.

1950

1952 Arsenal legend Ted Drake becomes manager.

1955

1955 Chelsea win the title, but are not allowed to enter the first European Cup.

1965

1965 'The Blues' beat Leicester City to win the League Cup.

1970

1970 Leeds are defeated 2-1 in a replay to win the FA Cup.

1975

1971 Beat Real Madrid after replay to win Cup Winners' Cup.

1975 Relegated to Division Two.

1980

1982 Ken Bates buys the club for £1.

1992

1993 Glenn Hoddle is appointed as player-manager.

1994

1996 Hoddle quits to take charge of England and Ruud Gullit is appointed player-manager.

1996

1997 Chelsea win the FA Cup, the first trophy for 27 years.

1998

1998 Vialli appointed player-manager and wins League Cup and Cup Winners' Cup.

2000

2000 Victory over Aston Villa in the last FA Cup at the old Wembley Stadium.

2002

2003 Bates sells club to Roman Abramovich for £60 million.

2004

2005 The club celebrates its centenary year by winning the Premiership.

2006

2006 'The Blues' retain the title.

2008

2008 Chelsea lose the Champions League final on penalties.

2010 Chelsea win the league and cup 'double' for the first time.

Above: Dynamo Kiev captain Valentin Belkevich lifts the Russian Cup in 2006.

COLO COLO

SANTIAGO, CHILE
Stadium: Estadio Monumental David Arellano (47,000)

Founded: 1925 **Honours:** Copa Libertadores 1991; Recopa Sudamericana 1992; Copa Interamericana 1991; League 29; Cup 10

Chile's most successful football club gained its exotic name from the local slang term for a wildcat. Based in the capital city, Santiago, it was one of the first South American teams to tour Europe, visiting both Spain and Portugal in 1927. Founder members of the Chilean league in 1933, Colo-Colo is the only club to have played in every season without relegation and it has won the championship more than twice the number of times achieved by its nearest rival, Universidad de Chile. It also holds the record for the most titles in the haphazardly scheduled Chilean Cup – established in 1958 but not played between 1963 and 1973, or between 2001 and 2007.

In 1973 Colo Colo reached the final of the Copa Libertadores but lost 2-1 to Independiente of Argentina in a play-off. However, under Croatian coach Mirko Jozic, a 3-0 aggregate win over Olimpia of Paraguay in 1991 meant

that Colo Colo became the first Chilean club to be crowned South American champions. The achievement was all the more impressive for a well-deserved victory over Boca Juniors in the semi-final. The resulting appearance in the World Club Cup final later the same year ended in a 3-0 defeat to Red Star Belgrade.

At the turn of the millennium Colo Colo experienced significant financial problems, but after being declared bankrupt in 2002 the club bounced back to its winning ways. The appointment of former player Claudio Borghi as coach in 2006 kickstarted a run that saw the club win both of the annual Apertura and Clausura titles for two years running. He also led the team to the final of the 2006 Copa Sudamericana and was named South American Coach Of The Year. Following his departure the club won the Clausura title in both 2008 and 2009.

CORINTHIANS

SÃO PAULO, BRAZIL
Stadium: Parque São Jorge (17,900)/ Pacaembu (40,000)

Founded: 1910 **Honours:** World Club Cup 2000; São Paulo State League 26; League 4; Cup 3

In 1910 the famed Corinthians, one of English football's pioneering teams, toured Brazil. Such was the club's influence that a group of students from the Tatuapé area of São Paulo were inspired to set up their own club, Sport Club Corinthians Paulista, adopting the English team's name in their honour. São Paulo expanded rapidly to become one of the world's biggest cities and the club grew with it, becoming one of the best supported teams in Brazil and causing its fixtures to be switched from its modest home ground, the Parque São Jorge, to the council-owned Pacaembu stadium with its much larger 40,000 capacity.

The club's fans are known as the 'Fiel' – the 'faithful' – and are also among the country's most fervent supporters, so much so that when the team was flirting with relegation during the mid-Nineties a group of them ambushed the Corinthians team bus.

Despite the club's huge popularity in Brazil, Corinthians failed to win a national title until 1990 and then had to wait until the end of the decade to repeat the feat. The team cashed in on that success by winning the first FIFA World Club Championship (now the FIFA Club World Cup) in January 2000, beating rivals Vasco De Gama on penalties in the Maracanã Stadium.

Poor management of the club's financial affairs caused Corinthians to struggle in the early years of the new millennium, but after signing a ten-year deal that gave Media Sports Investments control of the finances of the club, quality players were recruited for the team, such as Argentinians Carlos Tevez and Javier Mascherano. In December 2005, under coach

Antônio Lopes, they were crowned champions for the fourth time.

Among the famous players to have worn the Corinthians shirt in the past are Rivelino, Socrates, Dunga and Rivaldo, while Ronaldo and Roberto Carlos both joined the club to play out the tailend of their careers.

CSKA MOSCOW

MOSCOW, RUSSIA
Stadium: : CSKA Moscow Stadium (30,000)

Founded: 1911 **Honours:** UEFA Cup 2005; Soviet League 7; Russian League 3; Soviet Cup 5; Russian Cup 5

Known by several names since the formation of the club in 1911, CSKA took its current moniker – the Central Sports Club For The Army – in 1960. It is ranked among the country's best-known football clubs and has been one of the most successful in the post-Soviet era.

Although crowned champions in the final season of the Soviet League in 1991, CSKA would not win the new Russian Cup until 2002 and the Russian Premier League until 2003. However, the team's achievements in the first decade of the 21st century came close to matching the most successful period in the club's history, when they won five league and three cup titles in the years immediately after the Second World War.

In 2005 CSKA became the first Russian club to win a major European trophy, beating Sporting 3-1 on their home ground in Lisbon to lift the UEFA Cup. Despite falling behind in the first-half, goals from Vasili Berezutski, Yuri Zhirkov and Vágner Love clinched the trophy for CSKA. They were less fortunate in European Super Cup, losing 3-1 to Liverpool.

DYNAMO KIEV

KIEV, UKRAINE
Stadium: Valeri Lobanovsky Dynamo (16,873)

Founded: 1927 **Honours:** European Cup Winners' Cup 1975, 1986; European Super Cup 1975; Ukrainian League 13, Soviet League 13; Ukrainian Cup 9, Soviet Cup 8

Founder members of the Soviet Union league in 1936, Dynamo Kiev had to wait until 1961 for a first championship win. After this landmark was reached the club established itself as a major force in Soviet football and Dynamo's final total of 13 Soviet League titles, beating the 12 of rivals Spartak Moscow, will forever remain a record following the dissolution of the Soviet Union in 1991. The club's star striker of the Seventies and the Eighties, Oleg Blokhin, also remains the Soviet League's all-time top scorer with 211 goals.

In 1975, under the guidance of legendary

coach Valery Lobanovsky, Dynamo became the first team from the Soviet Union to win a European trophy, demolishing Ferencváros 3-0 in the final of the Cup Winners' Cup. Indeed, the history of the club cannot be separated from that of Lobanovsky, who again guided Dynamo to success in the same competition in 1986. His death in 2002 cast a great shadow over Ukrainian football and as a mark of respect the club's stadium was renamed after him.

Since the formation of the post-Communist Ukrainian league the club has dominated domestic football. With the aid of star talent such as Andriy Shevchenko and Sergei Rebrov, Dynamo Kiev won 13 of the 20 championships contested up until 2010, never finishing lower than second. The biggest threat to Dynamo's dominance has come from Shakhtar Donetsk, who pipped them to the 2010 title.

DYNAMO MOSCOW

MOSCOW, RUSSIA
Stadium: Dynamo (36,540)

Founded: 1923 **Honours:** Soviet League 11; Soviet Cup 6; Russian Cup 1

Dynamo Moscow will always be associated with goalkeeping legend Lev Yashin. It was during his tenure between the posts that the club experienced its most successful era. The 'Black Spider' played 326 times in the league for the club, winning the title five times, and since his departure in 1970 Dynamo have for the most part lived in the shadow of great rivals Spartak Moscow. Despite this, the club can lay claim to being the first Soviet side to reach a European final, losing 3-2 to Glasgow Rangers in the 1972 Cup Winners' Cup in Barcelona.

The club was founded in 1923 by Felix Dzerzhinsky, the leader of the Russian secret police and future head of the KGB. During the Soviet era it was affiliated with the Ministry of Internal Affairs (the Soviet Militia and the KGB). However, in purely football terms the club became internationally recognised as the first Soviet side to tour the West, playing a historic four-match tour of Britain in 1945. Helping to feed the appetite of a public starved of competitive football due to the Second World War, the Dynamo players greatly impressed with their ball skills and progressive play, beating a strong Arsenal side on the tour, demolishing Cardiff 10-1, and gaining creditable draws against Chelsea and Glasgow Rangers.

Since the formation of the post-Communist Russian league in 1991 Dynamo have largely disappointed, with only a Russian Cup victory in 1995 putting silverware in the trophy cabinet. To add insult to injury, the club's undersoil heating malfunctioned in 1998, scorching the playing surface and rendering it unplayable.

In 2005 the club broke Russian transfer

records when signing Portuguese stars Maniche and Costinha from Porto, but both players failed to settle and Maniche transferred to Chelsea within six months, leaving Dynamo to continue to struggle in the Russian league. In 2008 the club was again involved in breaking the Russian transfer record when selling Portuguese midfielder Danny to Zenit Saint Petersburg.

EINTRACHT FRANKFURT

FRANKFURT, GERMANY
Stadium: Waldstadion (52,300)

Founded: 1899 **Honours:** UEFA Cup 1980; League 1; Cup 4

Eintracht Frankfurt may have been formed more than 110 years ago, and were founder members of the Bundesliga in 1963, but to most people the club's reputation is based on just one game: the 1960 European Cup Final at Hampden Park in Glasgow. That day the Frankfurt team were on the wrong end of a 7-3 scoreline dished out by a Real Madrid side inspired by the combined genius of Ferenc Puskás and Alfredo Di Stéfano, but many football pundits still look back on the match as the finest ever played.

This is of scant consolation to Eintracht fans, as the club has perpetually struggled to escape from the shadow of the game. There have been successes, most obviously the 1980 UEFA Cup Final victory over Borussia Mönchengladbach, while in the early Nineties the club underwent a brief renaissance when inspired by such world-class stars as German midfielder Andy Möller and Ghanaian striker Tony Yeboah, making a series of impressive tilts at the league title. However, in recent years the club has bounced between the top two divisions, and has been beset by crippling financial problems.

Mismanagement meant that expulsion to the amateur leagues in 2002 was a very real threat until the club managed to retain its status after an appeal. Eintracht's only success in recent years has been reaching the German Cup final in 2006, and although losing 1-0 to Bayern, it was enough to guarantee a rare place in the UEFA Cup for the following season.

ESTUDIANTES DE LA PLATA

LA PLATA, ARGENTINA
Stadium: Jorge Luis Hirschi Stadium (23,000)

Founded: 1905 **Honours:** World Club Cup 1968; Copa Libertadores 1968, 1969, 1970, 2009; Copa Interamericana 1969; League 4

Formed as Club Atlético Estudiantes in 1905, the current name was adopted some 30 years later. While Estudiantes De La Plata may not be among the giants of Argentinian football, there

have been times when the club has punched above its weight on the world stage. Under Osvaldo Zubeldía, who became Estudiantes coach in 1965, the side was transformed from relegation fodder into world champions. Adding a few judicious buys to the homegrown talent developed through the club's youth team ('the killer juveniles'), Zubeldía built one of the most successful side's in Argentinian club football.

With future World Cup-winning coach Carlos Bilardo and Juan Ramón Verón in the side, Estudiantes won the Copa Libertadores three years in a row between 1968 and 1970. They beat European champions Manchester United in 1968 to win the World Club Cup and a year later defeated CONCACAF champions Toluca of Mexico over three legs to win the first Inter-American Cup. They were also runners-up in the World Club Cup in 1969 (to AC Milan) and 1970 (to Feyenoord).

This success was not without controversy. Nicknamed Los Pincharratas ('The Rat Stabbers'), the so-called 'pincharrata school' of football that the club adopted under Zubeldía was regarded as very un-Argentinian in its approach to the game, favouring European-style tactics and discipline over South American technique and flair.

Estudiantes won the league championship twice in the 1980s, first under Carlos Bilardo and then coached by Eduardo Luján Manera, both former stars of Zubeldía era. In 2009 the club experienced another renaissance under coach Alejandro Sabella, winning the Copa Libertadores with a side starring Juan Sebastián Verón, son of Juan Ramón Verón. The same year the club reached the final of the FIFA Club World Cup in Abu Dhabi, losing to Barcelona in extra-time.

Below: Boselli of Estudiantes celebrates during the 2009 FIFA Club World Cup semi-final against Pohang Steelers.

garnered not just from the favellas of Rio itself, but from districts throughout the country. Ironically, the club was formed when disaffected members of Fluminense joined the Flamengo Rowing Club in 1911 to create a football team (the club itself regard the 1895 formation of the rowing club as its foundation date).

Despite enormous popularity within Brazil, it was not until the early 1980s that the club established a reputation as a force to be reckoned with on the world stage. Under the influence of Zico, one of the club's greatest players, Flamengo finally lifted the Copa Libertadores in 1981 by beating Cobreloa of Chile in an ill-tempered game. In doing so 'Fla' fielded what is still regarded as one of the strongest ever Brazilian sides. Later in the same year the team produced another great performance in Tokyo, with Zico putting in a Man Of The Match performance to defeat a strong Liverpool side 3-0 in the World Club Cup final.

The club's home is the Gávea Stadium but all of the team's games are played at the much bigger Maracanã. Financial problems have meant the club has struggled to challenge for honours in recent times, although on the final day of the 2009 season Flamengo won a first league title in 17 years.

FLUMINENSE

RIO DE JANEIRO, BRAZIL
Stadium: Laranjeiras (8,000)
Maracana (90,000

Founded: 1902 **Honours:** Rio State League 30; League 1

Fluminense may have been founded in 1902 by the wealthy expatriate British community, but those privileged origins continue to define the club. 'Flu' are still regarded as the club of Rio's elite middle classes, in direct contrast to the 'everyman' appeal of bitter rivals Flamengo.

The club was a founding member of the Rio de Janeiro Amateur League and trophies came early, with four successive titles spanning 1906 to 1909. Further domestic trophies were captured, including five consecutive Rio State League titles between 1936 and 1941, but since the national championship was first staged in 1971, Fluminense has only won the Brazilian league once, in 1984. It also suffered successive relegations in the 1990s, at one point settling in the third tier of the Brazilian league.

For all of Fluminense's popularity in Brazil, the club has never reached the final of the Copa Libertadores. However, it did win the Copa Rio in 1952, a prototype world club championship that featured teams such as Juventus, Peñarol, Austria Vienna, Sporting Lisbon and Racing Club. Despite flirting with relegation again in 2009, 'Flu' did reach the final of the Copa Sudamericana, losing 5-4 on aggregate to LDU Quito of Ecuador after losing the away leg 5-1.

Above: Feyenoord players take the trophy to their fans at the San Siro after beating Celtic in the 1970 European Cup Final.

FEYENOORD

ROTTERDAM, HOLLAND
Stadium: Feyenoord Stadium (51,177)

Founded: 1908 **Honours:** World Club Cup 1970; European Cup 1970; UEFA Cup 1974, 2002; League 14; Cup 11

Feyenoord became the first Dutch side to land a continental trophy when the club won the European Cup in 1970. Amsterdam-based rivals Ajax had missed out in the final the previous year to Milan, but the Rotterdam side's 2-1 victory over Celtic at the San Siro in Milan began a four-year monopoly of Europe's top prize for Dutch clubs. Sadly for Feyenoord, the team's defence of the trophy ended in the ignominy of going out to Romanian minnows UTA Arad and the club's 1970 victory proved to be just the forerunner to an Ajax hat-trick of successes.

More European glory followed in 1974 with victory over Tottenham in the UEFA Cup final, but the Eighties and Nineties saw the club eclipsed by both Ajax and PSV in the league. Domestic cup triumph proved to be Feyenoord's biggest area of success, but problems off the pitch dogged the club as financial difficulties and a disturbing hooligan problem mirrored the decline in fortunes on the field.

Leo Beenhakker took Feyenoord to the league title in 1999, and under Bert Van Marwijk the club beat Borussia Dortmund 3-2 to win the 2002 UEFA Cup Final in front of a partisan crowd at home stadium De Kuip, but subsequent managers have failed to match this achievement, including Ruud Gullit in his one season at the club. Van Marwijk returned to help Feyenoord win the 2008 Dutch Cup but fans have had little else to cheer in recent times, losing the same cup in 2010 to Ajax under coach Mario Been.

While struggling to make an impact on the pitch, the club has announced its intention to build a new 100,000 capacity stadium.

FLAMENGO

RIO DE JANEIRO, BRAZIL
Stadium: Gavea (8,000)
Maracanã (90,000)

Founded: 1911 **Honours:** World Club Cup 1981; Copa Libertadores 1981; Mercosur Cup 1999; Rio State League 31; League 6; Cup 2

Football in Rio still reflects the divisions of race and class in the city, and while rivals Fluminense are seen to represent the middle class, Clube de Regatas Flamengo has always been the club of the people. This appeal makes Flamengo by far the most popular team in Brazil, with its support

Some of the greats of Brazilian football have represented Fluminense over the years. The magical Didi played for the club in the early 1950s, pulling the strings in midfield as much as he did for Brazil's World Cup winning sides of 1958 and 1962. Carlos Alberto, Brazil's 1970 World Cup winning captain, and Rivelino also rank among the legends of the club.

GALATASARAY

ISTANBUL, TURKEY
Stadium: Türk Telekom Arena (56,147)

Founded: 1905 **Honours:** UEFA Cup 2000; European Super Cup 2000; League 17; Turkish Cup 14

Turkey's most successful football club, Galatasaray has had a long and distinguished history. Founded by Ali Sami Yen and a group of friends from the Galatasaray Lisesi school, the club's stated aim was 'to play together like Englishmen, to have a colour and a name, and to beat the non-Turkish teams'.

Winners of the Istanbul league 15 times before the establishment of a national Turkish league in 1959, it took four seasons for the club to win the national championship, having been eclipsed in preceding campaigns by Istanbul rivals Fenerbahçe (twice) and Besiktas. The following year the team won the first Turkish Cup final, beating Fenerbahçe over two legs. They went on to retain the trophy in each of the next three campaigns.

The club's greatest triumph came in 2000 with a penalty shoot-out victory over Arsenal in the UEFA Cup final, having already won the domestic league title. A few months later the team beat Real Madrid to win the European Super Cup with a 'golden goal' from Mario Jardel. Coach Fatih Terim was already a club legend, having made 327 appearances as a player, but UEFA Cup success raised him above other Galatasaray greats such as Metin Oktay, Turgay Seren, Gheorghe Hagi and 1988 European Golden Boot winner Tanju Çolak.

The intimidating atmosphere created by supporters led to the Ali Sami Yen Stadium being dubbed 'Hell', but it remains to be seen whether fans can recreate this in the club's new purpose built Türk Telekom Arena.

HAMBURG SV

HAMBURG, GERMANY
Stadium: Volksparkstadion (57,274)

Founded: 1887 **Honours:** European Cup 1983; European Cup Winners' Cup 1977; League 6; Cup 3

On paper Hamburg can lay claim to being the oldest football club in Germany. Having been formed in 1887 as SC Germania, initially as an athletics club before taking up football in 1891, the club merged with Hamburg FC and FC Falke in June 1919 to create Hamburg SV. The red and white strip was picked as a compromise that was suitable for all parties.

Although national champions twice in the 1920s when the title was decided in a play-off format between the winners of the various regional leagues, Hamburg would not win the title again until clinching the West German championship in 1960, under the leadership of legendary centre-forward Uwe Seeler. This

Hamburg side took Barcleona close in the semi-finals of the 1961 European Cup, losing in a play-off, and seven years later finished as runners-up to AC Milan in the Cup Winners' Cup. By the time of Seeler's retirement in 1972, the club had yet to taste European glory. That changed in 1977 with a 2-0 Cup Winners' Cup victory over Anderlecht, with late goals from Georg Volkert and Felix Magath.

The team was spearheaded by Kevin Keegan in the late Seventies and his performances saw him voted European Player Of The Year for both 1978 and 1979. With him in the side Hamburg clinched a first Bundesliga title in 1979, ushering in a truly golden period. However, the magic of Keegan could not help Hamburg avoid a 1-0 defeat to Nottingham Forest in the 1980 European Cup Final. Without him the team went on to win the Bundesliga in 1982 and 1983, also finishing runners-up four times in the decade.

In 1983 Felix Magath was the Hamburg hero once again as he scored the only goal of the European Cup final against a Juventus team that could boast Michel Platini, Dino Zoff, Gentile, Claudio Tardelli and Paolo Rossi. However, since the Eighties Hamburg fans have not had much to cheer about, with the side too often settling for mid-table mediocrity.

In August 2004 the team was knocked out of the German Cup 4-2 by regional league side Paderborn in one of the most infamous games in recent football history. It was discovered that referee Robert Hoyzer had accepted money from a Croatian gambling syndicate to 'fix' the match and the resulting scandal sent shockwaves through German football.

In recent years silverware has been sparse for this once great club, with just a German League Cup triumph in 2003 and Intertoto Cup victories in 2005 and 2007 to boast about in the 21st century.

Above: Hamburg's Horst Hrubesch after the 1983 European Cup Final.

Left: Galatasaray celebrate beating Arsenal on penalties in the 2000 UEFA Cup Final.

Above: Sergio Aguero in the red shirt of Independiente in action against River Plate in 2006.

INDEPENDIENTE

BUENOS AIRES, ARGENTINA
Stadium: Libertadores de América (44,000)

Founded: 1905 **Honours:** World Club Cup 1973, 1984; Copa Libertadores 1964, 1965, 1972, 1973, 1974, 1975, 1984; Copa Interamericana 1973, 1974, 1975; Recopa Sudamericana 1995; Supercopa Sudamericana 1994, 1995; League 14

Formed in the Avellaneda suburb of Buenos Aires, Club Atlético Independiente was founded by employees of the City Of London department store. The club may not possess the global glamour of higher-profile city rivals River Plate or Boca Juniors, but it can boast far greater success in the Copa Libertadores. Indeed, Independiente became the first Argentine side to claim the trophy in 1964, getting the better of Uruguay's Nacional. A record-breaking seven Copa Libertadores titles, including an unlikely to be equalled run of four successive triumphs from 1972 to 1975, has earned the club the deserved nickname, 'The King of Cups'.

The run of silverware did not end there as two World Club Cups have also competed for space in the club's crowded trophy cabinet. The first of these wins was by a single goal against Juventus in Rome in 1973, followed 11 years later by victory over Liverpool in Tokyo, with José Alberto Percudani scoring the game's only goal.

Since the glory days Independiente's fortunes have declined, with mounting debts, poor management and declining crowds forcing the club to offload its top players. The sale of Sergio Agüero to Atlético Madrid in 2006 for a rumoured £15 million proved absolutely vital to the club's survival, and with a newly reconstructed home stadium the club appear to be moving in the right direction.

INTER MILAN

MILAN, ITALY
Stadium: Giuseppe Meazza (80,074)

Founded: 1908 **Honours:** World Club Cup 1964, 1965; European Cup/Champions League 1964, 1965, 2010; UEFA Cup 1991, 1994, 1998; League 18* *(including 2006 title stripped from Juventus)*; Cup 6

Giovanni Paramithiotti founded Football Club Internazionale Milano on March 9, 1908, after he and a group of his supporters broke away from AC Milan following a major policy disagreement with the club's owners. Although the club would become widely known by its abbreviated title Inter Milan, the name Internazionale was chosen because the club was to be open to players of all nationalities, unlike AC Milan who only allowed Italians to join. To underline the commitment to internationalism, the club's first captain came from Switzerland. The rivalry between Milan's two teams remains one of the fiercest in world football more than a century after the split.

The club won its first Italian championship in 1910 and picked up another in 1920. It was among the founders of Serie A in 1929 and after the demotion of Juventus in 2006, Inter became the only Italian side never to have been relegated. Along the way the club has been able to boast many world-class players, including Brazilians such as Ronaldo and Jair, Germans Jürgen Klinsmann, Andreas Brehme and Lothar Matthäus, Portugal's Luis Figo, and from Italy, goal-scoring defender Giacinto Facchetti, who became club chairman in 2004, and Giuseppe Meazza, the prodigious striker after whom the San Siro stadium is formally named – a stadium that the club share with city rivals AC Milan.

When the Fascists came to power under Benito Mussolini, Internazionale was forced to take on a less cosmopolitan name: in 1929 the club became Ambrosiana, after the patron saint of the city. The name switch did not do Inter any harm on the pitch as the team won Serie A titles in 1930, 1938 and 1940, as well as the Coppa Italia in 1939. They were also successful in the Mitropa Cup, a prototype of today's European Cup, making the semi-finals twice (1930 and 1936) and the final once (1933).

After the Second World War and the defeat of fascism, Inter reverted to the club's original name. Appointing Alfredo Foni as coach, back-to-back titles were celebrated in 1953 and 1954. However, it was not until the 1960s, under Helenio Herrera, that the club was able to enjoy domestic and international success at the same time. Serie A winners in 1963, Inter were crowned European champions for the first time the following season, comfortably beating Real Madrid 3-1 in the final in Vienna, with two goals from striker Sandro Mazzola. They then beat

Independiente of Argentina in the same year's World Club Cup, before pulling off an even more impressive trophy haul in 1965.

Having already been crowned Italian title winners and eliminating Liverpool in the semi-finals of the European Cup, Inter retained the trophy with a 1-0 defeat of Benfica in Milan, before beating Independiente 3-0 over two legs to keep hold of the world title. Inter retained the league championship the following season and made it to the final of the European Cup in 1967, only to lose to Celtic 2-1 after initially taking the lead through a Mazzola penalty.

A title win in 1971 and a European Cup final appearance the following season, losing 2-0 to Ajax, could not disguise the fact that without the massively influential coach Herrera, who had joined Roma, Inter's time as one of the world's biggest clubs had come to an end.

The remainder of the Seventies and Eighties were hardly unkind, as the club won the Serie A title in 1980 and 1989, and the Coppa Italia in 1978 and 1982, but it was not until the Nineties that the 'Nerazzurri' once again made significant waves in Europe. In 1991 Inter won the UEFA Cup for the first time, beating AS Roma, and repeated the feat three years later with a 2-0 aggregate victory over Austria Salzburg.

Another UEFA Cup final appearance followed in 1997, but having battled to a draw with German side Schalke over two legs, the Italians lost 4-1 on penalties in Milan. The team returned to put matters right in 1998, and in the club's fourth UEFA Cup final appearance in eight years they beat Lazio 3-0 in a one-off final.

In a concerted attempt to re-establish Inter as a force in both the Italian league and the much-coveted Champions League, the club appointed Hector Cúper as coach in 2001. The Argentinian had taken his previous side, Valencia, to successive European Cup finals, and it did not take long for him to make an impact at Inter. The team were involved in the fight for the 2001-2 league title right up until the last day of the season, but Inter eventually finished third behind Juventus and Roma, with just two points separating the top three.

Roberto Mancini took over as coach in 2004 and in his first two seasons Inter won the Italian Cup twice. In 2006 they finished the title race third behind Juventus and Milan, but after Juventus were relegated and stripped of the title for attempting to influence the appointment of referees, and Milan were deducted 30 points, the title was retrospectively awarded to Inter, the club's 14th championship win.

Capitalising on this shake up in Italian football, Inter retained the title for the next three seasons. Two of those campaigns ended in the league and cup 'double', while the 2009 championship was the first won under José Mourinho. He achieved the 'treble' in 2010 when he added the Champions League to the club's trophy haul with a 2-0 defeat of Bayern Munich. It was Inter's first European Cup win in 45 years.

JUVENTUS

TURIN, ITALY
Stadium: Juventus Arena
(40,200)

Founded: 1897 **Honours:** World Club Cup
1985, 1996; European Cup/Champions
League 1985, 1996; Cup Winners' Cup
1984; UEFA Cup 1977, 1990, 1993;
European Super Cup 1984, 1996; League
27* (stripped of 2005 & 2006 titles); Cup 9

Famously founded on a Turin park bench by a
group of students in November 1897, Juventus
has become the most successful Italian club
of all time. With a history crammed with
triumphant moments, it has been able to field
teams that have included some of the world's
most celebrated players, including Omar Sivori,
Michel Platini, Paolo Rossi, Zinédine Zidane,
Dino Zoff and Giampiero Boniperti, whose
name is still revered in Turin more than 60
years after he first made his mark in the team.
Indeed, his scoring record for the club was only
broken on January 10, 2006, when Alessandro
Del Piero scored three times in a match against
Fiorentina to pass Boniperti's record of 182.

Originally playing in pink shirts, Juventus
adopted the club's now famous black-and-
white stripes in 1903 after a club official visited
England and liked Notts County's shirts so
much that he took a bundle back with him.

It was not until the 1930s that Juventus
truly emerged as a superpower in the Italian
league. The club won five consecutive league
titles between 1931 and 1935, a feat that was not
equalled by another club until 2010. The first
four were secured under coach Carlo Carcano,
with players such as keeper Gianpiero Combi,
centre-half Luis Monti, winger Raimondo Orsi
and striker Giovanni Ferrari all going on to help
Italy win the 1934 World Cup. Orsi even scored
the equaliser in the final.

During this period Juventus also reached
the semi-final of the Mitropa Cup on four
consecutive occasions without ever making the
final, and on one occasion the team was actually
disqualified after a brutal semi-final against
Slavia Pague, who were also banned.

Intermittent success in the league and cup
continued throughout the Fifties and Sixties,
with back-to-back cups in 1959 and 1960 and
league titles in 1960 and 1961, but it was not
until the Seventies that the club translated
domestic success into European progress.
Reaching the final of the Fairs Cup in 1971, after
three drawn games with Leeds (one a replay of
the abandoned first leg), Juventus eventually lost
on the away goals rule.

In 1977 the club benefited from the same rule,
winning the UEFA Cup after a 2-2 aggregate
draw with Athletic Bilbao, although they came
close to throwing the tie away having led 2-0
on aggregate before being pegged back by the

Above: Juventus captain Gaetano Scirea greets Liverpool's Phil Neal before the 1985 European Cup final. Opposite top:
Torricelli, Padovano and Del Piero with the European Cup in 1996. Opposite bottom left to right: Vialli, Baggio and Zidane.

determined Spaniards. The Cup Winners' Cup
was added to the trophy cabinet in 1984 with a
2-1 victory over Porto.

The European Cup continued to elude the
club and a 1-0 defeat to Ajax in the 1973 final was
followed ten years later by defeat to Hamburg
by the same scoreline. The team were finally
crowned European champions for the first time
in the Heysel Stadium in 1985, when a team
featuring Italy's 1982 World Cup hero Paolo
Rossi defeated Liverpool 1-0. Sadly this moment
was overshadowed by the deaths of 39 Italian
fans during pre-match violence.

The Nineties promised a great deal for
Juventus. Massive sums of money were spent
on securing the services of Roberto Baggio from
Fiorentina and Gianluca Vialli from Sampdoria,
and the club won the UEFA Cup twice, in 1990
and 1993. However, it was only when Marcello
Lippi joined as coach from Napoli in 1994 that
the Juventus success story moved up a gear.

The 'Old Lady', as the club is nicknamed,
claimed its first league title in nine years in
1995 (as part of a 'double' with the Coppa
Italia) and won back-to-back championships in
1997 and 1998. Even more impressively Lippi's
side had beaten Ajax on penalties to clinch
the Champions League in 1996, following it
with a crushing 9-2 aggregate win over Paris
Saint-Germain in the same year's European
Super Cup. 'Juve' also reached the final of the
European Cup in 1997 and 1998, but despite
starting the games as favourites they lost on
both occasions – 3-1 to Borussia Dortmund and
1-0 to Real Madrid.

Lippi left for Inter Milan in 1999 after a
final trophy-free campaign but returned after
only a year at the San Siro. He won the Serie
A title in dramatic fashion in his first season
back, pipping Lazio and Inter to the title on
the final day of the season. After winning the
title again in 2003 the club was within reach

of the Champions League trophy once again,
having made it to the final after dispensing with
Barcelona and Real Madrid. However, after a
scoreless match at Old Trafford, Italian rivals
Milan won on penalties after five of the first
seven spot-kicks had been missed.

The following season proved disappointing
and Marcello Lippi quit to take on the national
team. Juventus announced Roma coach Fabio
Capello as his replacement and the new boss
guided the team to consecutive Serie A titles in
2005 and 2006. However, after it was revealed
that Juventus had been involved in the biggest
match-fixing scandal in Italian football history,
the club was stripped of both titles and relegated
to Serie B. At the centre of the allegations was
Juventus general manager Luciano Moggi,
who was accused of influencing the selection
of referees.

At the beginning of the club's first ever season
in the second tier of Italian football, Juventus
started the campaign with a points deduction
(reduced from 30 points to 17 points, and finally
to nine points after an appeal). Many big name
stars left the club, such as Fabio Cannavaro,
Patrick Vieira and Zlatan Ibrahimovic, but
others remained loyal and with the help of
Gianluigi Buffon, Alessandro Del Piero, Pavel
Nedved and David Trezeguet, the club bounced
back to Serie A at the first attempt.

After sharing a ground with Torino for
many years, the club demolished the hugely
unpopular Stadio Delle Alpi just 19 years after
it was built and in 2011 will move into a new
40,000-capacity stadium, provisionally known
as the Juventus Arena. In the meantime the
club has returned to the Stadio Comunale, the
ground it called home between 1933 and 1990
and the scene of 18 of its league title wins.
Completely redeveloped for the 2006 Winter
Olympics and rechristened Stadio Olimpico, it
is also now Torino's home stadium.

1895

1897: Students from
Turin's Liceo D'Azeglio
form a sports club. The
team play in pink shirts.

1900

1903: Juve
adopt the
famous
black and white shirt,
inspired by the strip of
Notts County.

1905

1905: Juventus beat
more experienced
teams from Genoa and
Milan to win
their first
Italian title.

1910

1915

1923: Edoardo Agnelli,
son of Fiat's founder, is
elected club president.
The club moves to a new
stadium.

1920

1926: Juventus win their
second title.

1925

1931: Juve win the title
for five years in a row,
from 1931 to 1935.

1930

1933: Juve move home
again. A stadium is built
for the World University
Games and the team
plays here until 1990.

1935

1940

1945

1947: Giovanni Agnelli
becomes president of
Juventus.

1950

1955: Umberto
Agnelli takes over the
presidency from his
older brother Giovanni.

1955

1957: John
Charles is
bought for
£70,000 from
Leeds United.

1960

1961: Juve
become the
first Italian club
entitled to wear the star
after winning ten titles.

1965

1972 to 1986: Juve
win nine titles and
many major European
and intercontinental
trophies.

1970

1975

1985: Juventus
defeat Liverpool
to win the
European Cup,
but it is a game
remembered for the
deaths on the terraces
of the Heysel Stadium.

1980

1985

1990: Juve win
the UEFA Cup
and Italian Cup.
They reluctantly
move to the
Stadio Delle Alpi.

1990

1996: Juve
beat Ajax on
penalties to win
the Champions
League.

1995

2000

2006: The club win
Serie A but are stripped
of the title and relegated
for involvement in a
match-fixing scandal.

2005

2007: After one season
in Serie B, Juve bounce
back as champions.

2010

KASHIMA ANTLERS

KASHIMA, JAPAN
Stadium: Kashima Soccer
Stadium (40,728)

Founded: 1947 **Honours:** League 7; League Cup 3;
Emperor's Cup 3

The most successful Japanese football club since the creation of the country's professional J.League in 1992, Kashima Antlers first formed in 1947 as the factory team of Sumitomo Metals in Osaka, relocating to Kashima in 1975. The club achieved little success until it was transformed into Kashima Antlers in 1991. The 'Antlers' name and logo was derived from a literal translation of the city name, Kashima, which means 'deer island'.

Beginning J.League life by winning the first ever stage of the two-stage title race, the club ultimately finished second that season and had to wait until 1996 for a first full title. In the following five years the club overtook more traditional sides like Verdy Kawasaki to become Japan's strongest team, winning an unprecedented 'treble' (league, Emperor's Cup and League Cup) in 2000. This dominance was built on the presence of Brazilian imports, such as Jorginho, Alcindo and the legendary Zico, who joined for the first J.League season and eventually became the club's general manager. Zico retired before the Antlers won a first title but he is so revered at the club that he has had two statues dedicated to him.

After several seasons without a trophy, the club continued its tradition of appointing Brazilian coaches when Oswaldo de Oliveira joined in 2007. In his first season Kashima became only the second team to win a second league and cup 'double' and by 2009 he had taken the club to a trio of league titles.

Although based in a modest-sized town, Kashima Antlers attract an average 17,000 fans per game and are one of only five clubs to have played in the J.League since its inception.

LAZIO

ROME, ITALY
Stadium: Olimpico
(72,698)

Founded: 1900 **Honours:** European Cup Winners'
Cup 1999; European Super Cup 1999; League 2;
Cup 5

Until the arrival of Sven-Göran Eriksson as coach at the start of the 1997-8 season, it is safe to say that SS Lazio had been one of Italian football's great underachieving football clubs. Founded on January 9, 1900, by Luigi Bigiarelli and eight friends, the club had endured decades waiting in the wings while Juventus and AC Milan paraded centre stage. However, Lazio's sparse trophy

cabinet – containing an Italian Cup (1958) and a single league title (1974) – was soon filled to bursting as the Rome side took seven trophies in three heady seasons of achievement.

With a team that included Marcelo Salas, Juan Sebástian Verón and Christian Vieri, Eriksson won two Italian Cups, two domestic Super Cups (played between the Italian league champions and cup winners), the UEFA Super Cup and the last ever European Cup Winners' Cup. He also steered Lazio to a second league title in 2000, before leaving the club the following season.

In 2002 a financial scandal forced owner Sergio Cragnotti to quit the club, leaving Lazio in the hands of financial caretakers until it was sold in 2004. Despite this the club managed to win the Italian Cup in 2004 but it had to lower overheads by losing many veteran players. After being caught up in Italy's match-fixing scandal in 2006 Lazio received a points deduction, but after the punishment was reduced on appeal it did not prevent a top three finish and qualification for the Champions League. However, subsequently the club has struggled in Serie A, enjoying only an Italian Cup win after beating Sampdoria on penalties in 2009.

LEEDS UNITED

LEEDS, ENGLAND
Stadium: Elland Road
(39,460)

Founded: 1919 **Honours:** Fairs Cup 1968, 1971;
League 3; Cup 1; League Cup 1

Following allegations of illegal payments to players, Second Division Leeds City were wound-up in October 1919. Leeds United were formed the following month but with Port Vale having taken over City's fixtures, the new United began in the Midland League before entering the Second Division after turning pro in 1920.

In the 1930s, in Edwards, Hart and Copping, Leeds United boasted one of the great half-back lines in English football, while in 1957 the club made headlines by selling John Charles to Juventus for a British record of £67,000.

However, for much of the clubs first 40 years Leeds merely bounced between the top two divisions. It was not until the mid-Sixties that the team really became a force in English football, mainly as a result of the appointment in 1961 of Don Revie as player-manager.

Although relegated in 1960, over the next five years Revie would transform the club, changing the team colours from blue and gold to all-white (inspired by the European triumphs of Real Madrid), and rebuilding the team around a talented group of young players that included Jack Charlton, Billy Bremner, Peter Lorimer, Norman Hunter, Paul Reaney, Paul Madeley, Eddie Gray and Johnny Giles.

Promoted to Division One as champions in 1964, in the first year back in the top flight Revie's team narrowly lost the title on goal average to Manchester United and the FA Cup final to Liverpool, helping to establish a reputation that would haunt the club for the next decade. In the next ten years they would be known as the greatest runners-up in English football: five times they would finish second in the league, three times in the FA Cup, and once each in all three European competitions.

That's not to say that success eluded this team. In 1968 victory over Arsenal delivered the League Cup, while the Fairs Cup followed with a 1-0 aggregate win over Ferencváros. The following year saw the club's first league title, and in 1971 they beat Juventus to lift the Fairs Cup again. In 1972 a single Allan Clarke goal beat Arsenal to win the centenary FA Cup, and in 1974, at the end of the Revie era, they won a second league championship.

Following this success, Revie left to take charge of the national team. Brian Clough was the nominated successor but his tenure lasted days rather than months, leaving Jimmy Armfield to complete the season and take the team to the 1975 European Cup Final. The match proved pivotal in the history of Leeds United – not only did they lose 2-0 to an understrength Bayern Munich, but after a riot by fans, the club was banned from all European competition for the next five years.

Leeds were relegated in 1982, their glory days seemingly behind them. Managed in turn by former legends Allan Clarke, Eddie Gray and Billy Bremner, United looked outside to Howard Wilkinson in 1988. Achieving promotion in 1990, he took Leeds back to the very top of the English game two years later when, inspired by the mercurial Eric Cantona, the club clinched the final Football League title before the onset of the Premier League.

Building on that revival under David O'Leary, Leeds reached the semi-finals of the Champions League in 2001. However, in attempting to reach those heady heights the club financially overstretched itself. It is still paying the price for this ambition today after financial administration and relegation to the third tier of English football.

Right: Lazio's were the winners
of the last ever European Cup
Winners' Cup in 1999.

LIVERPOOL

LIVERPOOL, ENGLAND
Stadium: Anfield
(45,276)

Founded: 1892 **Honours:** European Cup/
Champions League 1977, 1978, 1981,
1984, 2005; UEFA Cup 1973, 1976, 2001;
European Super Cup 1977, 2001, 2005;
League 18; Cup 7; League Cup 7

Liverpool FC has had a long and successful history but it has city neighbours and great rivals Everton to thank for its existence. Then resident at Anfield, Everton became embroiled in an argument with the stadium's owner, John Houlding, over rent payments, and left to set up a new home at Goodison Park. In possession of a football ground but no team to play in it, Houlding formed Liverpool FC on March 15, 1892, and soon saw the club rise from the local Lancashire League to Division Two, and then gain promotion to the top-flight in 1894.

The first of 18 league titles came in 1901, with four more arriving over the course of the next 50 years. However, Liverpool returned to the Second Division in 1954 and it was not until the arrival of charismatic Scottish manager, Bill Shankly, in December 1959, that the foundations were laid for the success enjoyed by the club in the Seventies and Eighties.

Shankly's approach combined great tactical acumen with infectious enthusiasm, and his ability to instil self-belief in his players was second to none. Liverpool finally returned to Division One in 1962 and claimed a sixth championship two years later, but Shankly was only just getting started. Two more league titles (1966 and 1973) and two FA Cups (1965 and 1974) followed, before his retirement in 1974. However, the most significant of all of his achievements was the club's first European trophy, when Liverpool beat Borussia Mönchengladbach 3-2 over two legs to lift the UEFA Cup in 1973.

Shankly's successor was Bob Paisley, a quietly spoken Geordie, who had been first-team coach and a vital member of the legendary

Above: The legendary Liverpool manager, Bill Shankly.

Above: Liverpool's champions of Europe in 1978: Case, Neal, Clemence, Kennedy, Hughes, Souness and Dalglish.

Anfield 'boot room'. Paisley's achievements at Liverpool have never been matched. In nine extraordinary years he took 'The Reds' to six league titles, three League Cups, one UEFA Cup and three European Cups, the first of which came in 1977 with a 3-1 win against Borussia Mönchengladbach. Liverpool retained the trophy in 1978 with a 1-0 win over Club Brugge and lifted it again in 1981, beating Real Madrid 1-0.

When Paisley stepped down as manager in 1983 he was replaced by another member of the Anfield backroom staff, Joe Fagan. Any notions that the Liverpool success story was about to come to a halt were dispatched in his first season, as Liverpool claimed an impressive 'treble': league title, League Cup and European Cup, won on penalties against AS Roma.

Liverpool reached the European Cup final the following year but lost 1-0 to Juventus in the Heysel Stadium in Brussels. The game itself was overshadowed by the terrible events that occurred as supporters of the two sides rioted. Thirty-nine Italian fans lost their lives when a wall collapsed, leading to a ban that kept English clubs, including Liverpool, out of European competition for the next five years.

Fagan's reign at Anfield was surprisingly short and when he stepped down at the end of the 1984-5 season he was replaced by Kenny Dalglish, the first player-manager in the club's history. The Scottish international guided 'The Reds' to a league and FA Cup 'double' in his first season in charge and further league titles in 1988 and 1990. Dalglish's side also won the FA Cup in 1989 but their triumph was

tinged with tragedy: on April 15 of that year 96 Liverpool fans were crushed to death at Sheffield Wednesday's Hillsborough ground before kick-off in an FA Cup semi-final tie between 'The Reds' and Nottingham Forest.

Dalglish quit suddenly at the end of the 1991 season to be replaced by Graeme Souness. In his three seasons in charge, Souness won the FA Cup (1992) but Liverpool's primacy in the league started to slip. He was replaced in 1994 by veteran Anfield coach Roy Evans, an appointment that suggested Liverpool were trying to recapture the old 'boot room' philosophy of promoting from within. When Evans failed to bring back the glory days, Gerard Houllier was brought in to work alongside him, eventually taking over the role.

Houllier returned the club to winning ways, with triumphs in the FA Cup, League Cup, UEFA Cup and European Super Cup in 2001, and the League Cup again in 2003, but a 19th league title and success in the Champions League continued to elude Liverpool, and at the end of the 2003-4 season he became the first manager in the club's history to be sacked.

It was his replacement Rafael Benítez who finally delivered what this great club wanted. At the end of his first rather lacklustre season, Liverpool reached the 2005 Champions League final, and despite going 3-0 down before half-time, a comeback inspired by captain Steven Gerrard saw 'The Reds' push the game to extra-time and a penalty shoot-out brought the club its fifth European Cup. He was unable to repeat the trick two years later as Milan gained revenge, beating Liverpool 2-1 in the final.

1890

1892: The club is founded on March 15. The team win their first game 7-1, a friendly against Rotherham.

1900

1901: Liverpool clinch the league title for the first time.

1910

1906: The famous Spion Kop is built at Anfield.

1945

1947: The club win a fifth league title, 24 years after the previous one.

1950

1954: After finishing 22nd in the league, 'The Reds' are relegated to Division Two.

1955

1959: Bill Shankly is appointed manager.

1960

1965: Leeds are defeated in the FA Cup Final, one of many trophies won in a golden era under Shankly.

1965

1973: Kevin Keegan scores two goals to win the UEFA Cup.

1970

1974: Bill Shankly retires and is replaced by first-team coach Bob Paisley.

1975

1977: Liverpool win the European Cup for the first time.

1980

1981: Alan Kennedy's goal is enough to defeat Real Madrid and win the European Cup again.

1984: New manager Joe Fagan wins a league title, a European Cup and a League Cup in his first season.

1985

1986: Kenny Dalglish is appointed player-manager and guides the club to the 'double'.

1990

1989: During an FA Cup semi-final 96 Liverpool fans die.

1995

2001: Victory in the League Cup, the FA Cup and the UEFA Cup.

2000

2004: Rafael Benítez joins as manager.

2005

2005: 'The Reds' win the Champions League on penalties.

THE CHAMPIONS CUP WITH FIVE WINS, LIVERPOOL HAVE THE BEST RECORD OF ANY ENGLISH CLUB IN THE EUROPEAN CUP.

1977	
Liverpool	3
B. Mönchengladbach	1
Olympic Stadium, Rome	

1978	
Liverpool	1
Club Brugge	0
Wembley Stadium, London	

1981	
Liverpool	1
Real Madrid	0
Parc Des Princes, Paris	

1984	
Liverpool	1
Roma	1
Liverpool won 4-2 on penalties	
Olympic Stadium, Rome	

2005	
Liverpool	3
AC Milan	3
Liverpool won 3-2 on penalties	
Atatürk Stadium, Istanbul	

1875

1880

1878: Workers from the Lancashire and Yorkshire railway form Newton Heath. The team play in gold and green halved shirts.

1900

1902: The club's name is changed to Manchester United.

1905

1908: Inspired by ex Manchester City star Billy Meredith, United win the title.

1910

1909: United beat Bristol City 1-0 in their first FA Cup final.

1915

1910: United move to a new ground in Warwick Road, Old Trafford, losing the first game to Liverpool.

1920

1925

1927: United's club colours are switched to red and white.

1930

1935

1941: Old Trafford is destroyed by enemy planes. Manchester City allow United to use Maine Road.

1940

1945

1945: Matt Busby is taken on as manager.

1950

1957: The 'Busby Babes' win the league and look set to conquer Europe.

1955

1958: The Munich air disaster kills eight members of the United team, including Duncan Edwards.

1960

1963: Young Irishman George Best makes his debut.

1965

1968: United become the first English side to win the European Cup, defeating Benfica at Wembley.

1970

1975

1977: Tommy Docherty's side beats Liverpool to win the FA Cup.

1980

1986: Alex Ferguson is appointed manager.

1985

1990

1993: United win the club's first title in 26 years.

1995

1999: A late comeback sees United beat Bayern to win the European Cup 2-1.

2000

2005: Malcolm Glazer buys the club in an £800 million hostile takeover.

2005

2008: United win the Champions League on penalties.

2010

MANCHESTER UNITED

MANCHESTER, ENGLAND
Stadium: Old Trafford
(75,957)

Founded: 1878 **Honours:** World Club Cup 1999, 2008; European Cup/Champions League 1968, 1999, 2008; Cup Winners' Cup 1991; European Super Cup 1991; League 18; Cup 11; League Cup 4

The story of Manchester United is a rags-to-riches tale. Now a worldwide commercial giant, the club has come a long way from its humble beginnings. Formed as Newton Heath by employees of the Lancashire and Yorkshire Railway Company, the club had severe financial problems and was saved from bankruptcy in 1902 by a local brewery owner. The club took on the name Manchester United and a period of success followed almost immediately, with a first league championship in 1908, followed 12 months later with victory in the FA Cup final.

To cope with growing attendances the club left its Bank Street home and moved to Old Trafford in 1910, losing the first game at the new ground 4-3 to Liverpool. The 1920s and 1930s saw United bounce between the top two divisions, and in 1934 relegation to Division Three was only avoided on the final day of the season. Financial difficulties again struck the club as attendances fell and during the Second World War the main stand at Old Trafford was destroyed during a German bombing raid. However, United's fortunes were to change forever when the club appointed Matt Busby as manager in February 1945.

Claiming his first trophy with the 1948 FA Cup victory over Blackpool, Busby made the club a force in English football once again, giving youth its chance by promoting players like Jackie Blanchflower and Roger Byrne to the first team. His policy paid dividends in 1952 when United finally won the league.

Rising star Duncan Edwards was thrown into

OLD TRAFFORD

Constructed in 1909, Old Trafford was rebuilt after World War II bomb damage. In the 1970s it became the first English stadium to erect perimeter fencing. With the rebuilding of the Stretford End in 1994, it became a perfect bowl. Known as 'The Theatre Of Dreams', the stadium features a memorial clock outside, commemorating the Munich air disaster.

Above: Bobby Charlton, Shay Brennan and Alex Stepney celebrate with the European Cup in 1968. Opposite clockwise from top left: George Best takes on Norman Hunter of Leeds in 1970; Cristiano Ronaldo kisses the Premier League trophy in 2009; the United team after winning the 1963 FA Cup final; the class of 1999 win the Champions League.

the first-team as a 16-year-old and further league titles followed in 1956 and 1957. However, the club was rocked by tragedy the following year when a plane carrying the team back from a European match against Red Star Belgrade crashed after refuelling in Munich, killing 22 people, including seven players. Fifteen days later Edwards also died, failing to recover from his injuries.

United still managed to reach the FA Cup final that year but Busby had to rebuild another great side for the next decade and he did so with the likes of Nobby Stiles, Denis Law, Brian Kidd and George Best combining brilliantly with players such as Bobby Charlton, a survivor of the Munich crash.

The title was won again in 1965 and 1967 and this time United made an impact on European football. Extra-time goals at Wembley from Best, Charlton and Kidd gave United a 4-1 victory over Benfica to lift the 1968 European Cup, a remarkable achievement just ten years after the Munich air crash. Busby was knighted but he bowed out at the top, retiring in 1969, and United found him a difficult man to replace.

Briefly out of the top flight in the mid-Seventies, United fans were becoming starved of the kind of success that they had become accustomed to, despite FA Cup victories in 1977, 1983 and 1985. Alex Ferguson was appointed manager in November 1986 and gradually the balance of football power in England began to shift from Merseyside to Manchester.

The Nineties began with Ferguson guiding the club to success in the FA Cup, the European Cup Winners' Cup and the League Cup in three consecutive seasons, but the championship still eluded the club. The wait, having now stretched

to 25 years, looked certain to come to an end in 1992, but United somehow contrived to hand the title to Leeds. The Yorkshire club repaid the favour by selling Eric Cantona to Old Trafford and he provided the missing link for Ferguson's side. Inspired by the Frenchman, United won the title in 1993 and 1994 and were crowned champions five times in the Nineties.

Cantona retired in 1997 at the age of 30, but by now Ferguson, like Busby, had built his side around the products of the club's youth system, with players like Ryan Giggs, David Beckham, Paul Scholes and the Neville brothers. The crowning year came in 1999, when United's all-conquering side added the European Cup and World Club Cup to their domestic 'double'.

Not only was the manner of the European Cup victory amazing (substitutes Sheringham and Solskjaer each scored in injury-time to beat Bayern Munich 2-1), it enabled Ferguson to emulate the achievement of Busby. Ferguson too was knighted as the league domination continued in 2000 and 2001, although he reneged on his promise to retire, bringing the title back again in 2003.

For a time United struggled to keep pace with the huge financial clout of Chelsea, while fans had to come to terms with the hostile £800 million takeover of United in 2005 by American businessman Malcolm Glazer, a bid financed largely by heaping debt on the club. However, under Ferguson's canny stewardship United beat Chelsea on penalties to win the 2008 Champions League in Moscow, and although beaten by Barcelona in the following year's final, a hat-trick of league titles between 2007 and 2009 reaffirmed the club's dominance of domestic football.

MARSEILLE

MARSEILLE, FRANCE
Stadium: Vélodrome
(60,031)

Founded: 1898 **Honours:** Champions League 1993; League 9* *(stripped of 1993 title)*; Cup 10

The most internationally recognised club in France, Olympique Marseille have made a sizeable impact on the history of the French game. Winning a first league title in 1937, the club added a second in 1948 during the early days of professional football and they enjoyed huge popular support in their native south of France. Further success was difficult to come by, but in another period of glory in the early Seventies the team won back-to-back titles in 1971 and 1972, with Yugoslav striker Josip Skoblar setting a league record of 44 goals in a season in the 1970-1 campaign.

Known as 'l'OM', the club failed to build on these triumphs but returned to prominence in glorious fashion in 1986 when businessman Bernard Tapie became chairman, triggering Marseille's most successful and controversial spell. He spent lavishly on star players such as Jean-Pierre Papin, Chris Waddle and Enzo Francescoli, and guided the club to four consecutive league titles from 1989 to 1992. Tapie established Marseille as a force to be reckoned with at home and abroad. Papin was the league's top scorer five seasons in a row, Waddle became a cult hero, and others, such as Brazilian Carlos Mozer and Ghanaian midfielder Abedi Pele, added class to the side.

The club reached the European Cup semi-finals in 1990, losing to a controversial Benfica goal, and the final in 1991, defeated on penalties by Red Star Belgrade. However, in 1993 this magical team lifted the trophy after beating Milan, thanks to a headed goal from Basile Boli.

Joy turned to agony when the club was found guilty of fixing a league match with Valenciennes. Tapie was forced out and the club faced financial ruin after being punished with relegation and stripped of the 1993 league title. The long comeback started with promotion in 1996 and the team battled to the UEFA Cup final in 1999, before losing 3-0 to Parma. Inspired by Didier Drogba, they reached the final again in 2004, losing this time to Valencia, and the following year they lifted the little regarded Intertoto Cup.

While success in the league has been harder to come by, the club finished as runners-up in 2007 and 2009, and finally celebrated winning the championship once again in 2010 when coached by Didier Deschamps.

MILAN

MILAN, ITALY
Stadium: Giuseppe Meazza
(80,074)

Founded: 1899 **Honours:** World Club Cup 1969, 1989, 1990, 2007; European Cup/Champions League 1963, 1969, 1989, 1990, 1994, 2003, 2007; Cup Winners' Cup 1968, 1973; European Super Cup 1989, 1990, 1994, 2003, 2007; League 17; Cup 5

AC Milan was founded by Englishman Albert Edwards as the Milan Cricket And Football Club on December 16, 1899, and over the last century it has become one of the world's richest clubs: first bankrolled by tyre magnate Piero Pirelli, but in more recent times by Silvio Berlusconi, Italy's Prime Minister and one of his country's richest men.

Ranked among the most successful club's in world football, Milan has won the Champions League, and its predecessor the European Cup, seven times. It is a record only bettered by Spanish giants Real Madrid.

The club won the Italian championship in 1901, 1906 and 1907, and finished third in 1929-30 when the competition was played in a league format for the first time. However, it was not until the 1950s that the club found its feet, winning four league titles in nine years. This success initially stemmed from the purchase of Gunnar Gren, Nils Liedholm and Gunnar Nordahl, the stars of Sweden's Olympic gold medal-winning team of 1948. Nordahl went on to score 210 goals in 257 games for the club, while Liedholm later had two stints as club coach in late Seventies and mid Eighties.

Milan's first serious foray into European competition saw the club reach the semi-finals of the first European Cup in 1956. They lost to Real Madrid 5-4 on aggregate on that occasion and were beaten again by Real in the 1958 final, 3-2 after extra-time. Starting the 1960s in impressive form, the club notched its fifth Serie A title in 1962 and beat Benfica to lift the European Cup for the first time the following year at Wembley, winning 2-1 despite falling behind to a Eusébio goal.

In 1965 Milan claimed another European title after beating Hamburg 2-0 in the final of the Cup Winners' Cup. A second European Cup followed in 1969, when Milan put out holders Manchester United in the semi-finals, before thumping Ajax 4-1 in the final thanks to a Pierino Prati hat-trick. In the same year the club clinched its first World Club Cup title, overcoming the inexcusably violent behaviour of Estudiantes de La Plata in the second leg to win 4-2 on aggregate.

Milan started the Seventies brightly with appearances in two consecutive Cup Winners' Cup finals. In 1973 a 1-0 victory over

Below: Marseille's Franck Sauzée enjoys the moment after winning the European Cup in 1993.

Leeds secured the trophy, but a 2-0 defeat to Magdeburg ended Milan's fine run in Europe for a while. The club had to be content with domestic honours as the Seventies progressed, winning the Coppa Italia three times between 1972 and 1977, and the Italian title in 1979, but dark days were just around the corner. In 1980 a betting scandal broke, implicating Milan's goalkeeper, Enrico Albertosi, and president, Felice Colombo. The club was relegated to Serie B as punishment and nearly went out of business altogether, before Berlusconi stepped in to save it from bankruptcy in 1986.

Much rejuvenated by Berlusconi's millions and the inspired management of Arrigo Sacchi, the club dominated European football in the late Eighties and early Nineties. A 4-0 victory over Steaua Bucharest won the 1989 European Cup Final, with Dutch superstars Ruud Gullit and Marco Van Basten each scoring twice.

THE SAN SIRO

The home of both AC Milan and Inter Milan, the Stadio Giuseppe Meazza is still largely known as the San Siro, the original name it took from the district in which it is located. Built in 1926, a £50 million overhaul for the 1990 World Cup included the addition of a third tier built on impressive cylindrical towers at the corners of the stadium.

Milan retained the trophy the following year, with a single Frank Rijkaard goal delivering victory over Benfica. Defeat in the 1993 final to Marseille was a momentary blip and the club triumphed once again the following year with a solid 4-0 demolition of Barcelona. A further European Cup final appearance came in 1995, when future Milan striker Patrick Kluivert scored a late winner for Ajax.

Milan proved equally impressive domestically, winning the club's first league title for nine seasons in 1988 and three more consecutively between 1992 and 1994. The trio of titles coincided with an extraordinary 58-match unbeaten streak between 1991 and 1993. A fifth title in nine years came in 1996, with George Weah providing the firepower up front, and three years later the team won their final seven games to pip Lazio to the title by just a point.

The club also won the championship in 2004, but the first decade of new millennium brought more success in the Champions League, with Andriy Shevchenko scoring the winning spot-kick in 2003 to beat Juventus on penalties at Old Trafford. Two years later the team reached the final again but after leading Liverpool 3-0 at half-time, Milan somehow managed to surrender the lead to a Steven Gerrard-inspired comeback, with Shevchenko failing to convert the penalty that handed the trophy to Liverpool.

Despite a lack of domestic success in recent years following the club's involvement in the 2006 Italian match-fixing scandal, Milan again faced Liverpool in the 2007 Champions League Final, winning 2-1 thanks to goals from Filippo Inzaghi. Before the end of the year he would score again in the 3-1 defeat of Sevilla in the UEFA Super Cup and twice more in Milan's 4-2 victory over Boca Juniors in the final of the FIFA Club World Cup.

Top left: Ruud Gullit lifts the European Cup in 1989. Top right: the Milan team after the 2003 Champions League Final. Above: Cesare Maldini holds up the European Cup in 1963.

MILLONARIOS

BOGOTA, COLOMBIA
Stadium: Nemesio Camacho
(44,000)

Founded: 1938 **Honours:** Copa Merconorte 2001;
League 13; Cup 2

Club Deportivo Los Millonarios is one of the most successful football clubs in Colombia but this dominance at home has never translated into silverware on the continental stage, with Millonarios enjoying a particularly poor record in the Copa Libertadores (the South American club championship) for a club of its size and stature.

The bulk of the club's major triumphs were achieved in the Fifties, in an era known as 'El Dorado'. Millonarios were at the centre of a worldwide transfer controversy and along with Independiente Santa Fe, 'Los Albiazules' refused to pay transfer fees to overseas club, resulting in the formation of a rebel league. This coincided with a strike in Argentine football and star players were lured to Colombia by the massive signing-on fees and wages on offer, allowing Millonarios to sign the most famous player in the club's history, Alfredo Di Stéfano.

With Di Stéfano playing alongside fellow Argentines, Nestor Rossi and Adolfo Perderna, the team won four league titles in five years, earning the nickname the 'Blue Ballet' for their artistry on the pitch. Di Stéfano scored a remarkable 267 goals in 292 games before swapping Colombia for further fame and fortune in Europe with Real Madrid.

The club has not been without its share of problems. In the past it was dogged by a close association with the Medellin drug cartel, while the club's perilous finances have hindered performances in more recent years, leading to the cancellation of plans to move to a new stadium in 2005. However, a fine run in the Copa Sudamericana in 2007 saw the team reach the semi-finals before losing 5-2 on aggregate to Mexican club América.

NACIONAL

MONTEVIDEO, URUGUAY
Stadium: Parque Central
(22,000)

Founded: 1899 **Honours:** World Club Cup 1971, 1980, 1988; Copa Libertadores 1971, 1980, 1988; Recopa Sudamericana 1989; Copa Interamericana 1971, 1988; League 42

Fans of Nacional proudly lay claim to being the first South American club formed by its citizens rather than the expatriate community, coming into being as the result of a merger between Uruguay Athletic Club and Montevideo Football Club. The impact was almost immediate and in 1903 the entire Nacional team was selected to play for Uruguay in an international against Argentina – they won 3-2 and the date continues to be part of the club's annual celebrations.

Along with city rivals Peñarol, Nacional has remained a controlling force in Uruguayan football ever since, and there have only been ten occasions since the league turned professional in 1932 when a club other than Nacional or Peñarol has been crowned champions.

The club's triumphs have not been confined to home soil and a trio of victories in the Copa Libertadores is matched by the same number of successes in the World Club Cup. The most eye-catching was a 1-0 victory against European champions Nottingham Forest to win the 1980 match (actually played the following year), when the trophy was contested in Tokyo for the first time and rebranded the Toyota Cup.

Famous footballers to play in Nacional's colours include José Andrade and Hèctor Scarone, two of the stars of Uruguay's World Cup triumph in 1930.

NOTTINGHAM FOREST

NOTTINGHAM, ENGLAND
Stadium: City Ground
(30,576)

Founded: 1865 **Honours:** European Cup 1979, 1980; European Super Cup 1979; League 1; Cup 2; League Cup 4

Before Brian Clough took charge of Second Division Nottingham Forest in 1975 the club had never won the league and had won the FA Cup just twice, in 1898 and 1959. Five years later they had become champions of Europe twice over.

Promoted to the top flight of English football in 1977, Forest clinched the title the following season and to consolidate the club's bid for European glory Clough signed Trevor Francis from Birmingham City, making him English football's first million-pound player. In his first European game Francis scored the goal that brought victory against Malmö in the 1979 European Cup Final, helping Forest to become only the third club in the competition's history to lift the trophy at the first attempt. One year later they repeated the feat, winning the trophy in the Bernabéu Stadium in Madrid after beating a Hamburg side boasting European Footballer Of The Year Kevin Keegan.

Under Clough's stewardship Forest featured in six League Cup finals in 12 years, running out winners four times. The club's one appearance in the FA Cup final in this period resulted in defeat to Tottenham Hotspur in 1991, and two years later Forest were relegated in Clough's last game before retirement.

Powered by the goals of striker Stan Collymore the club secured promotion to the top flight under Frank Clark in 1994, and returned again as Division One champions in 1998, but although relegation to the third tier of English football in 2005 signalled that this once great club's glory days may be over, a good run in the 2009-10 season took Forest to play-offs with the Premier League tantalisingly in sight.

PACHUCA

PACHUCA, MEXICO
Stadium: Estadio Miguel
Hidalgo (30,000)

Founded: 1901 **Honours:** CONCACAF Champions Cup: 2002, 2007, 2008, 2010; North American SuperLiga 2007; Copa Sudamericana 2006; League 5

Although Club De Fútbol Pachuca was a founding member of Mexico's amateur Primera División in 1907 and is the oldest professional football club in the country, most of its successes have come in the 21st century, a period when it has been one of the strongest contenders in the domestic game. Since finally re-establishing a

Below: Nacional's Victor Espárrago parades with the trophy after winning the 1980 World Club Cup in Tokyo. The match was actually played in February 1981.

that helped to defeat Deportivo Cali of Colombia in the Copa Libertadores final.

The club was founded after Italian sides Torino and Pro Vercelli visited Brazil in 1914, and a group of Italians who lived in São Paulo decided to create an Italian club, Palestra Itália. That visit inspired one of the fiercest local derbies in the world, as the creators of the club were former members of Corinthians. From that moment they were branded 'the betrayers'.

After Palestra split from Corinthians, the first São Paulo derby was played on May 6, 1917, and the intensity and passion of the clash has remained ever since, even surviving Palestra's change of name to Palmeiras in 1942. Derbies between the two teams often have to be played in São Paulo's Morumbi Stadium, which has a capacity of 80,000.

Palmeiras last won the Brazilian league title in 1994 but suffered relegation to the Second Division in 2002, two years after the departure of Scolari. They bounced back as champions at the first attempt. With one eye on the 2014 World Cup, the club is currently transforming the Palestra Itália Stadium and when finished it will have a capacity of 45,000.

PARIS SAINT-GERMAIN

PARIS, FRANCE
Stadium: Parc des Princes (48,712)

Founded: 1970 **Honours:** European Cup Winners' Cup 1996; League 2; Cup 8

Paris Saint-Germain formed in 1970 after the demise of some of the capital's major clubs. Founded out of a merger between a group of financial investors, under the name of FC Paris, and Stade Saint-Germain, the club was a result of the huge desire to see top class football in Paris once more. PSG played its first campaign in France's second division before being promoted at the first attempt.

The following season the club finished 16th but was forced to split in two, under pressure from a city council wanting a more Parisian club without reference to nearby Saint-Germain in the name. As a result Paris FC continued in the top division with all of the professional players and the backing of the Paris city council, whereas PSG began in the third tier of French football as an amateur side. However, in 1974 PSG gained promotion back to the top flight, ironically in the same season that Paris FC were relegated.

PSG developed into a strong force in French football and the club has since won the title twice, in 1986 and 1994, and the Coupe de France seven times, most recently in 2006. There has also been success in Europe, with the team reaching European semi-finals in five consecutive seasons between 1993 and 1997, culminating in victory over Rapid Vienna in the Cup Winners' Cup Final in 1996.

place in Mexico's top flight in 1998, the club has been crowned national champions five times, been runners-up twice and has won the CONCACAF Champions Cup on four occasions.

This run of success was started under coach Javier Aguirre with a victory over Cruz Azul in the 1999 winter league championship play-off, thanks to a 'golden goal' scored by Argentinian striker Alejandro Glaria. After Aguirre quit to take over the national team in 2001 the success continued under a succession of coaches with the club winning the CONCACAF Champions Cup for the first time in 2002 after victory over Monarcas Morelia.

In 2006 Pachuca beat Colo Colo of Chile to win the Copa Sudamericana, becoming the first central American team to win a South American title. The following year they won their second Champions Cup with a defeat of Guadalajara on penalties in the second leg of the final. As a consequence they represented the confederation at that year's Club World Cup but were knocked out in their first game by Étoile du Sahel.

In 2008 they retained the Champions Cup,

needing an injury time goal from Edgar Benítez to win it again in 2010 after the competition was rebranded the Champions League.

PALMEIRAS

SÃO PAULO, BRAZIL
Stadium: Palestra Itália (27,000)

Founded: 1914 **Honours:** Copa Libertadores: 1999; Copa Mercosur 1998; São Paulo State League 22; League 4; Cup 1

For all the great players to have come through the ranks at Palmeiras – Oberdan, Ademir da Guia, Djalma Santos, Vavá, Edmundo – perhaps the most recognisable name linked with the club would be future World Cup winning coach Luiz Felipe Scolari, who guided the team to victory in the Copa Mercosur (1998) and the Copa Libertadores (1999). The stars of that side included Zinho and Roque Júnior, both of whom took spot-kicks (Zinho missing and Roque Júnior scoring) in the penalty shoot-out

Above: Pohang Steelers lift the AFC Champions League trophy after beating Al-Ittihad in 2009.

The club has had two players on its books who have gone on to win major individual accolades: George Weah was voted the European and World Footballer Of The Year in 1995, while Ronaldinho left PSG in 2003 and became World Footballer Of The Year in 2004 and 2005.

The club was bought in 1994 by media company Canal+ and sold again in April 2006 to a consortium of US firms for £34 million. Since then very little silverware has made it to the PSG trophy cabinet, with fans having only the 2008 League Cup victory over Lens and the 2010 French Cup defeat of Monaco to cheer.

PEÑAROL

MONTEVIDEO, URUGUAY
Stadium: Centenario (65,235)

Founded: 1891 **Honours:** World Club Cup 1961, 1966, 1982; Copa Libertadores 1960, 1961, 1966, 1982, 1987; League 48

Club Atlético Peñarol was originally formed in 1891 by the large British expatriate community in Montevideo under the rather cumbersome name of Central Uruguayan Railways District Club. Inaugural winners of the league in 1900, as British influence waned the football team changed its name to the more acceptable Peñarol in December 1913, after the poor, rural area of the city from where it emerged.

To this day the club's support is associated with the working class element of the nation's capital. Along with bitter rivals Nacional, the two clubs have dominated Uruguayan football. However, Peñarol have also been fantastic ambassadors for the Uruguayan game outside of its borders. After winning the first ever Copa Libertadores final in 1960 against Olimpia of Paraguay, the club successfully defended the crown a year later against Brazil's Palmeiras. Three more Copa Libertadores titles have been won, the last being a play-off victory against América de Cali of Colombia in 1987.

Peñarol's pedigree on the international stage was further enhanced when it became the first team to win the World Club Cup three times. This feat was achieved with victory over a Eusébio-inspired Benfica in 1961, a 4-0 aggregate win over Real Madrid in 1966, and a 2-0 victory against Aston Villa in 1982.

In 1997 Peñarol celebrated winning five league titles in a row – the 'quinquenio' – for the second time. Having won the title in 2003, Peñarol had to wait seven years before winning again, beating Nacional in the 2009-10 league title play-off to end the campaign as champions.

POHANG STEELERS

POHANG, SOUTH KOREA
Stadium: Steelyard Stadium (25,000)

Founded: 1973 **Honours:** AFC Champions League 1997, 1998, 2009; League 4; Cup 2

Despite only forming in 1973, Pohang Steelers have become the most successful team in Asia, winning the AFC Champions League on a record three occasions. Originally called POSCO, after the Pohang Iron and Steel Company that owned and created it, the club did not change its name to the Pohang Steelers until 1997, by which time it had also been known as POSCO Dolphins, POSCO Atoms and Pohang Atoms.

The club won its first South Korean league title in 1986, when known as Pohang Atoms, and they clinched the championship twice more in 1988 and 1992 when coached by Lee Hoi-Taek, a star at the club in its earliest days and a future coach of the South Korean national team.

A year after becoming the Pohang Steelers, and coached by another former player, Park Seong-Hwa, the club reached its first continental final. With a side that included Hong Myung-Bo, the Steelers beat reigning champions Cheonan Ilhwa Chunma to lift the Asian Club Championship (now the AFC Champions League) in Kuala Lumpur, with a penalty deep in extra-time to thank for their victory. A year later they retained the trophy after a penalty shoot-out victory over Chinese champions Dalian Wanda in Hong Kong.

After Park Seong-Hwa left to take on the South Korean Under-20 team in 2000, the club went into relative decline for several years, a slide that was finally arrested by the appointment in 2005 of their first foreign-born coach, Brazilian Sergio Farias. Introducing a stylish, attacking brand of football to the Steelyard, Farias helped the club to their fourth K-League title in 2007 and two years later, after defeating Al-Ittihad 2–1 to win the AFC Champions League, they beat Atlante of Mexico on penalties to finish third in the FIFA Club World Cup.

PORTO

PORTO, PORTUGAL
Stadium: Estádio do Dragão (50,399)

Founded: 1893 **Honours:** World Club Cup 1987, 2004; European Cup/Champions League 1987, 2004; UEFA Cup 2003; European Super Cup 1987; League 24; Cup 19* *(including four wins when Portuguese Championship was a cup competition, 1922-38)*

It was in the late 1970s that Porto really came of age and began to threaten the Lisbon monopoly of Sporting and Benfica. That the club succeeded in shifting the balance of power owes much to the presidency of Pinto da Costa and, in the early years of this period, the management of Jose Maria Pedroto, who led the club to its first league title in 19 years in 1978.

Retaining the title the following year, in the seasons that followed Porto assumed almost total dominance of the league. Despite a rotation of managers and high profile players, the team went on to win 17 league championships and ten Portuguese Cups in the following 30 years, all achieved under the presidency of Pinto da Costa.

The club's greatest moment came in 1987. While it may have been a season when the club enjoyed no domestic success, Porto did complete a memorable international 'treble', winning the European Cup, the European Super Cup and the World Club Cup. The European Cup came at the expense of Bayern Munich in Vienna, with late goals from Rabah Madjer and Juary clinching a 2-1 victory. It made up for the disappointment experienced three years earlier, when losing the final of the Cup Winners' Cup to Juventus.

Porto won eight of the ten league titles in the

1990s, and in 2003 the club further asserted its dominance by adding the UEFA Cup to a domestic league and cup 'double'. This proved to be just the start as the following season, still led by coach José Mourinho, Porto won the Champions League with a victory over Sevilla. The departure of Mourinho did not stop the team from lifting the World Club Cup later the same year, after an epic 8-7 penalty shoot-out victory over Once Caldas of Colombia.

When Porto won the league in 2009, it was the club's fourth consecutive title, two of them as 'doubles'. A third place finish in 2010 ended this fine run but a victory in the Portuguese Cup gave fans something to cheer about.

PSV EINDHOVEN

EINDHOVEN, HOLLAND
Stadium: Philips Stadion
(35,000)

Founded: 1913 **Honours:** European Cup 1988; UEFA Cup 1978; League 21; Cup 8

Funded by electronics giants Philips, PSV first won the championship in 1929, just 15 years after joining the league, and the club has since overtaken Feyenoord to offer the greatest challenge to Ajax's dominance of Dutch football. Some of the top players of recent times have played for PSV. Ronald Koeman, Ruud Gullit and Ruud Van Nistelrooy all had spells in Eindhoven, while Brazilian stars Romario and Ronaldo each preceded their Barcelona careers with spells at the Philips Stadium.

The late Eighties and early Nineties saw PSV as a major force in world football. Coached by Guus Hiddink and captained by Eric Gerets, the club beat Benfica in a penalty shoot-out to win the 1988 European Cup Final. On the domestic front the club were almost unstoppable, with six league titles in seven seasons between 1986 and 1992. The final two came under Bobby Robson, who joined PSV for two seasons straight after leading England to the semi-finals of the 1990 World Cup.

The new millennium began with PSV back in dominant form in Holland, with former player Eric Gerets coaching the club to the league title in 2000 and 2001. In his second spell in charge, Guus Hiddink brought the trophy back in 2003, 2005 and 2006. He also won the Dutch Cup in 2005 and reached the final again in 2006, losing 2-1 to Ajax. However, with star players often lured to other European leagues, the club has been unable to make an impact in the Champions League. Hiddink did manage to inspire the team to the semi-finals in 2005, but elimination by AC Milan on the away goals rule was a cruel blow. Despite winning the second leg 3-1 at home, it was an injury time goal from Milan midfielder Massimo Ambrosini that ended PSV's ambitions.

Hiddink left Eindhoven to take control of the Russian national team in 2006. Without him the club won the next two league titles, the first of them under Ronald Koeman. It was only the third time in the history of Dutch football that a team had won four championships in a row.

RANGERS

GLASGOW, SCOTLAND
Stadium: Ibrox Park
(51,082)

Founded: 1873 **Honours:** European Cup Winners' Cup 1972; League 53; Cup 33; League Cup 26

Rangers are the historically Protestant half of perhaps the most passionate rivalry in all of football: the 'Old Firm' battle with Catholic club Celtic. The 'Gers' have the edge in domestic triumphs, due largely to three sustained periods of dominance. The first came in the inter-war years (1918-39) under manager Bill Struth, when Alan 'Wee Blue Devil' Morton and Bob McPhail terrorised defences. The second great Rangers team emerged after the Second World War, built around George Young in the team's 'Iron Curtain' defence, and schemer Willie Waddell.

The Rangers team of 1972 won the club its only European trophy, with skipper John Greig lifting the Cup Winners' Cup before going on to manage the club in the late Seventies, when he inherited the team from Jock Wallace who had won the 'treble' twice in his six years at Ibrox.

The third era of success arrived with the appointment of Graeme Souness as player-manager in 1986. With the lavish financial backing of the club's owner, David Murray, he brought in English players like Terry Butcher and Trevor Steven, and to the horror of the more bigoted fans, signed Mo Johnston, a Catholic and a former Celtic player. Walter Smith continued the modernisation through the 1990s, bringing Paul Gascoigne to the club and equalling Celtic's record of nine consecutive titles, a run that had started under the stewardship of Souness.

With Alex McLeish at the helm Rangers retook the title in 2003 and stopped a Celtic hat-

trick. Led once again by Walter Smith, in his second stint as manager, the club won back-to-back titles in 2009 and 2010.

Above: Rangers take the Scottish Cup to the blue half of Glasgow in 1969.

RAPID VIENNA

VIENNA, AUSTRIA
Stadium: Gerhard Hanappi
(18,500)

Founded: 1899 **Honours:** Austrian League 32; Austrian Cup 14; German League 1; German Cup 1

One of Austria's oldest clubs and one of the best teams in the earliest days of European football, Rapid Vienna has had a long and eventful history. The Viennese side captured the inaugural Austrian league championship in 1912, and reclaimed the title on 11 more occasions before World War II. After the 1938 annexation by Germany, Rapid competed in the German championship and even managed to win the German Cup in 1938 and the German league title in 1941.

The club has also been able to showcase many famous players over the years, including master goal poacher Franz 'Bimbo' Binder, who scored more than 1,000 goals in a remarkable career. Midfielder Gerhard Hanappi not only played 93 times for Austria, but as an architect he also designed the club's stadium, opened in 1977 as the Weststadion and named after him following his death just three years later. Other legends to have played for the club include Karl Rappan, Walter Zeman, Ernst Happel, Franz Hasil and the prolific marksman Hans Krankl, who won the European Golden Boot with 41 goals when playing for Rapid in 1978.

Despite success in Austrian football, the club has never won a major European trophy, coming closest when finishing runners-up in the Cup Winners' Cup in 1985 and 1996, losing to Everton and Paris Saint-Germain respectively. However, in both 1930 and 1951 Rapid won the Mitropa Cup, a central European prototype of the European Cup.

Left: PSV celebrate with the European Cup in 1988.

REAL MADRID

MADRID, SPAIN
Stadium: Santiágo Bernabéu
(80,354)

Founded: 1902 **Honours:** World Club Cup 1960, 1998, 2002; European Cup/Champions League 1956, 1957, 1958, 1959, 1960, 1966, 1998, 2000, 2002; UEFA Cup 1985, 1986; League 31; Cup 17

In the ongoing debate to decide the greatest club of all time it is hard to make a case for anyone other than Real Madrid, who have won the Spanish title on 31 occasions and the European Cup a record nine times.

Madrid Football Club was born in 1902 but did not take the regal prefix 'Real' until 1920 when King Alfonso XIII granted the title in recognition of the club's role in founding the tournament that eventually became the Copa Del Rey. Real's first chairman Julian Palacios was aided – with some irony, given the club's bitter rivalry with Barcelona – by two Catalans, the Padrós brothers, Carlos and Juan. The former went on to become club president and Spain's representative at the inaugural meeting of FIFA in 1904, a gesture symbolic of the club's status at the centre of the national game.

While Madrid's founding fathers were all Spaniards, its first player-manager was an Englishman, former Corinthians player Arthur Johnson, and it was he who also instigated the famous all-white strip. In the early years the club struggled to make its mark in Spanish football, with Athletic Bilbao and Barcelona holding sway. The most significant development at this time was the arrival at the club of the young Santiágo Bernabéu, the single most important individual in Real's history. Bernabéu joined the club as

ESTADIO SANTIAGO BERNABÉU

The home of Real Madrid, the Bernabéu was built between 1943 and 1947 to replace the Charmartín ground, which was all but destroyed in the war. Initially financed by a membership scheme, at one time the ground boasted a capacity of 125,000. Overhauled for the 1982 World Cup, it was the venue for that year's World Cup final.

Above: Alfredo Di Stefano scores in the 1960 European Cup final. Opposite clockwise from top: European Cup victory in 2002; Savio and Roberto Carlos kiss the World Club Cup trophy in 1998; Cristiano Ronaldo celebrates scoring in 2009.

a junior in 1909 and he helped erect its first purpose-built ground, the O'Donnell Stadium, going on to captain the side. He was associated with the fortunes of the club for nearly 70 years until his death in 1978.

By the 1920s the newly-titled Real Madrid had embarked on a strategy designed to install it as Spain's most prestigious club. It demonstrated its intention, as it has done on many occasions since, with a string of big-name signings, an act that accelerated the growth of professionalism in the country. However, when the first national league began in 1929, Real were runners-up to Barcelona. It took three more seasons to win the first of two back-to-back titles, but by the time the club won the league again in 1954, the capital had been destroyed by civil war, rebuilt, and Bernabéu was the club's president.

His presence at the helm ushered Real into an era of dominance. It was Bernabéu who brokered the deal for a bold new stadium in the city's richest district in 1947, eventually named after him, and it was he who financed deals to bring in a string of talented players, including Gento, Puskás, Kopa and, the biggest of all, Alfredo Di Stéfano, 'the Blond Arrow'.

It was Di Stéfano, more than any other player, who propelled Real to glory, scoring 227 league goals between 1953 and 1964. More importantly, his 49 goals in Europe established the club's name outside Spain as Real drove on to improbable heights by winning the newly created European Cup for five years in succession, an unparalleled feat. Di Stéfano scored in all five finals, crowning his efforts with a hat-trick in the 7-3 victory over Eintracht Frankfurt at Hampden Park in 1960, a game regarded as one of the finest ever.

League titles continued at regular intervals,

but while there was one more European Cup triumph in 1966 over Partizan Belgrade – making an astonishing six winners' medals for the team's outstanding winger 'Paco' Gento – Real could not maintain these high standards.

The next 29 years became known as 'The Wilderness Years' as the team strived in vain to rekindle the chemistry that had made it so unbeatable. Two successive UEFA Cup wins in the mid-Eighties would have satisfied most fans, but not those of Real. Nevertheless, that squad – which featured Emilio Butragueño, Michel and Martin Vásquez (dubbed 'the Vulture Squadron') and back-flipping Mexican goal machine Hugo Sanchez – revived memories.

The glory days returned in 1998 thanks to Predrag Mijatovic's Champions League-winning strike against Juventus. That victory began a fresh golden era as Real embarked on a huge spending spree financed by the sale of its training ground. The signing of superstars like Zinédine Zidane and Luis Figo smashed the transfer barrier and embellished a team already packed with players like Raúl and Iker Casillas.

Real has won three European Cups since the beginning of the Champions League format, the most special win coming in the club's centenary year, with a 2-1 victory over Bayer Leverkusen. Although FIFA rapidly declared Real 'The Best Club Of The 20th Century', the pressure to constantly deliver success on the biggest stage has led to a succession of coaches in recent years.

Back-to-back titles came under Fabio Capello in 2007 and Bernd Schuster in 2008, but the club has subsequently had to play second fiddle to a Barcelona revival. However, Real responded in typical fashion by smashing the world transfer record twice in 2009, paying £56 million of Kaká and £80 million for Cristiano Ronaldo.

KINGS OF EUROPE

REAL MADRID'S VICTORIES IN THE EUROPEAN CUP/CHAMPIONS LEAGUE

Year	Match	Score	Venue
1956	Real Madrid / Stade De Reims	4 / 3	Parc Des Princes, Paris
1957	Real Madrid / Fiorentina	2 / 0	Bernabéu, Madrid
1958	Real Madrid / AC Milan	3 / 2	Heysel, Brussels
1959	Real Madrid / Stade De Reims	2 / 0	Neckar, Stuttgart
1960	Real Madrid / Eintracht Frankfurt	7 / 3	Hampden Park, Glasgow
1966	Real Madrid / Partizan Belgrade	2 / 1	Heysel, Brussels
1998	Real Madrid / Juventus	1 / 0	Arena, Amsterdam
2000	Real Madrid / Valencia	3 / 0	Stade De France, Paris
2002	Real Madrid / Bayer Leverkusen	2 / 1	Hampden Park, Glasgow

Timeline:

1900

1902: Founded as Madrid Football Club, the team takes its all-white strip from English club Corinthians. Their first coach is Englishman Arthur Johnson.

1905

1910

1912: Santiago Bernabéu debuts in the first-team.

1915

1920: The club's name is changed to Real Madrid in June 1920 after King Alfonso XIII gives his official blessing to the team.

1920

1924: The opening of Chamartin Stadium is celebrated with a match between Madrid and Newcastle United.

1925

1930

1932: Real win their first Spanish title.

1935

1943 Santiago Bernabéu is appointed club president.

1940

1945

1947: A new stadium is built. It is later named after Santiago Bernabéu.

1950

1953: Argentine legend Alfredo Di Stéfano is signed by the club.

1955

1956: Real win the first European Cup with a 4-3 victory over Reims.

1960

1958: Hungarian star Ferenc Puskás signs for Madrid.

1965

1960: Real Madrid defeat Eintracht Frankfurt 7-3 to claim their fifth successive European Cup title.

1970

1971: Paco Gento winds up an 18-year career with the club in a European Cup Winners' Cup final defeat.

1975

1980

1986: The UEFA Cup is won for a second consecutive year with a victory over Köln.

1985

1990: Real win fifth consecutive Spanish title, setting scoring record of 107 goals in 38 games.

1990

1998: Named by FIFA as best club in football history, Real also beat Juventus in the Champions League final.

1995

2000

2001: One year after signing Figo for £37.5m, Real spend £45.8m on Zinédine Zidane.

2005

2009: Real pay £80m for Cristiano Ronaldo, smashing the world transfer record.

2010

Above: The sweet relief of winning a penalty shoot-out – Red Star Belgrade players celebrate after the 1991 European Cup Final.

RED STAR BELGRADE

BELGRADE, SERBIA
Stadium: Red Star
(53,000)

Founded: 1945 **Honours:** World Club Cup 1991; European Cup 1991; League 25; Cup 23

Known as Crvena Zvezda in Serbia (formerly Yugoslavia), it was students of the city's university who founded Red Star Belgrade in March 1945. The first football team to be created in Yugoslavia after liberation, the club won its debut league title in 1951. Historically Red Star dominated the domestic game, outstripping bitter rivals Partisan to a record number of successes in both the league and cup. However, in the years since the disintegration of Yugoslavia in 1991 the most successful team in Serbia has been Partisan.

Always associated with playing precise, technical football, and producing a constant stream of homegrown talent, the club has a strong reputation in European competition, establishing it early after reaching the semi-finals of the second European Cup in 1957 where they lost to Fiorentina. Semi-final defeat was even harder to take in 1971 when Red Star went out on the away goals rule after beating Panathinaikos 4-1 at home in the first leg.

The club reached the final of UEFA Cup in 1979 but lost 2-1 on aggregate to Borussia Mönchengladbach, despite a home crowd of 87,000 roaring on the team in the first leg.

The Red Star Stadium was the first ground in the old Eastern Bloc to host a major continental final, staging the deciding game of the 1973 European Cup. The club's greatest moment came in the same competition in 1991, when the team were crowned champions of Europe in Bari, having clinched victory thanks to a penalty shoot-out after a generally negative 0-0 draw with Marseille. A 3-0 defeat of Colo Colo to win the World Club Cup was more convincing later in the same year.

There may have been many more successes in European competition had it not been for the fact that the club has always struggled to hold on to its best players. The exit door at the Red Star Stadium, affectionately known to home fans as 'the Marakana', has seen such world-class talent as Dragan Stojkovic, Robert Prosinecki, Dejan Stankovic and Darko Pancev walk through it.

RIVER PLATE

BUENOS AIRES, ARGENTINA
Stadium: Monumental
(65,645)

Founded: 1901 **Honours:** World Club Cup 1986; Copa Libertadores 1986, 1996; Copa Interamericana 1987; Supercopa Sudamericana 1997; League 33

Founded in 1901, the club was originally formed in the poor Boca district of Buenos Aires but later migrated north to the altogether more affluent Retiro area of the city. The move led to the nickname of 'Los Millonarios', or 'the Millionaires', and it helped to establish, with erstwhile neighbours Boca Juniors, one of the fiercest rivalries in world football.

A major force in the foundation of the first Argentine professional league, River Plate has enjoyed two distinct golden eras. Between 1932 and 1957 the club was the strongest force in the domestic game, winning 12 national titles, and in the late 1940s producing the much-admired forward line of Jose Manuel Moreno, Omar Labruna and Adolfo Pedernera known to the fans as 'La Maquina', meaning 'The Machine'.

The 1960s was a lean decade for the club, but since winning the league title in 1975 River Plate has been re-established as one of the giants of the game in Argentina, winning the championship on a regular basis. In 1986, inspired by Uruguayan playmaker Enzo Francescoli and Norberto Alonso, the club finally won the Copa Libertadores, beating América De Cali. Just a month and a half later the team went on to lift the World Club Cup after getting the better of Steaua Bucharest, thanks to a goal from Antonio Alzamendi. Ten years later River once again beat América to capture a second Copa Libertadores title but this time the club was denied the World Club Cup by a single Alessandro Del Piero strike in a closely fought match with Juventus in Tokyo.

While Boca Juniors can name Maradona as the club's most famous former player, the roll call of River Plate old boys reads like a who's who of goalscoring greats. Alfredo Di Stéfano scored 27 league goals for River in 1947, topping Argentina's goalscoring charts in his first full season in the first-team, while prolific marksmen such as Omar Sivori, Luis Artime, Mario Kempes, Marcelo Salas, Hernan Crespo and, more recently, Javier Saviola have all played with distinction for the club.

In 2008 former player Diego Simeone was appointed coach and in his debut season he led the team to their first championship in four years, winning the Clausura title. However, after a poor run of results he resigned midway through the following season, leaving the club to finish last in the 2008 Apertura championship, the first time River Plate had finished bottom of the league in 107 years.

ROMA

ROME, ITALY
Stadium: Olimpico
(72,700)

Founded: 1927 **Honours:** Fairs Cup 1961;
League 3; Cup 9

AS Roma was founded in 1927 with the merger of four local clubs (Roman, Pro Patria, Alba and Fortitudo), becoming a member of Serie A for the league's inaugural season two years later. The club's record since has been one of occasional highs and ever more frequent lows.

A first Serie A title did not arrive until 1942, although the team did finish as runners-up in both 1931 and 1936. Struggling to compete in the years after the war, the club was relegated from Serie A for the first time in 1951 but bounced back as champions at the first attempt under future national team coach Giuseppe Viani. Nine years later Roma became the first Italian team to win a major European trophy, defeating Birmingham City 4-2 on aggregate in the 1961 Fairs Cup Final.

Domestic cup wins in 1964 and 1969, the latter under coach Helenio Herrera, could not disguise the fact that Roma spent much of the Sixties and Seventies in the football wilderness, but performances improved dramatically in the 1980s. The club won the Coppa Italia four times in seven seasons, added a second Serie A title in 1983 and reached the European Cup final the following season, losing 4-2 to Liverpool on penalties after a 1-1 draw. It was particularly disappointing as the match was played at the club's home stadium in Rome.

In 2001, under former AC Milan coach Fabio Capello, Roma won the Serie A title for the first time in 18 years, helped by the prolific firepower of Gabriel Batistuta, Vincenzo Montella and Francesco Totti. The following season, after a terrific three-way title race with Juventus and Inter, the championship was only lost on the last day of the campaign.

Roma finished runners-up five times in the first decade of the new millennium, and in 2008 won the Italian Cup with a 2-1 victory over Inter Milan. In 2010 Roma achieved the runners-up 'double', finishing second to Inter in both the league and cup, having taken the battle for Serie A to the last day of the season.

In 2009 the club unveiled plans to move from the Olympic Stadium, which it shares with Lazio, and build its own 55,000-capacity stadium in the western suburbs of Rome.

Left: Claudio Caniggia in full flow for River Plate in 1988.

Opposite: Pelé, the young rising star of Santos.

SANTOS

SANTOS, BRAZIL
Stadium: Vila Belmiro
(20,120)

Founded: 1912 **Honours**: World Club Cup 1962, 1963; Copa Libertadores 1962, 1963; São Paulo State League 18; League 2

There are very few clubs in the world game whose reputation is based so solely on the exploits of just one player. However, when that player is Pelé, the synonymous relationship becomes all the more understandable. The great man joined Santos as a 15-year-old in 1956, and made his final appearance in the famous all-white kit in 1974.

During his tenure at the club Santos triumphed for five consecutive seasons in the Taça Brasil, the cup competition that held sway before the start of the Brazilian league in 1971. With Pelé in the side, the club also became South American champions, achieving back-to-back Copa Libertadores wins in 1962 and 1963, and won two World Club Cup titles, with victories over Benfica and Milan. The defeat of Benfica included a 5-2 win at the Stadium Of Light in the second leg, featuring a hat-trick from Pelé. He scored twice in the home leg too.

It would be unjust to label Santos as purely a one-man team during this era, and the club provided the Brazilian national side with many other players who took part in the victorious World Cup campaigns of 1958, 1962 and 1970, including goalkeeper Gilmar, midfielder Zito and defender Clodoaldo, plus the winning captains in 1962 and 1970, Mauro and Carlos Alberto. However, it was its one truly great player who ensured that Santos were always in demand, allowing it to take to the world stage for a stream of lucrative friendly tours.

Pelé was a difficult act to follow, and with his retirement the club saw fortunes both on and off the pitch take a severe dip. Debts mounted and the lack of silverware gradually took the club away from the elite group in Brazilian football. Victory in the Rio-São Paulo Tournament in 1997 was the exception rather than the rule. Supporters seemed to lose faith and even the appointment of Pelé as the club's youth academy director in 1999 was regarded more as a promotional tool rather than an effective measure.

However, it was the club's youth policy that proved to be a turning point once again. With a team boasting the home grown talents of Alex, Diego, Elano and Robinho, against the odds Santos revived the glory days by adding the 2002 Brazilian championship to the club's list of honours and reached the final of the following year's Copa Libertadores. The club won the title again in 2004 and lifted the Copa Do Brasil and the São Paulo State title in 2010.

SÃO PAULO

SÃO PAULO, BRAZIL
Stadium: Morumbi
(80,000)

Founded: 1935 **Honours**: World Club Cup 1992, 1993, 2005; Copa Libertadores 1992, 1993, 2005; Recopa Sudamericana 1993, 1994; Supercopa Sudamericana 1993; São Paulo State League 21; League 6

The youngest of the five São Paulo-based clubs that participate in the Brazilian championship, São Paulo FC was founded in 1935, the result of a coming together of Clube Atlético Paulistino and Associação Atlética das Palmeiras. The signing of the legendary Leônidas da Silva was an important move in 1942 and with him in the side the club won five São Paulo state titles between 1943 and 1949, signalling the arrival of a new major football force in the industrial city of São Paulo.

As a result of this success, the massive 140,000 capacity Morumbi Stadium was built in 1960 (now reduced to 80,000). However, the club spent much of the decade in the shadow of crosstown rivals Santos.

Under the attack-minded guidance of the influential Brazilian coach Telê Santana, São Paulo's very own glory days were to arrive in the early 1990s, when the club fielded arguably the strongest side in the world. Two consecutive Copa Libertadores titles, with victories over Paraguay's Olimpia and Newell's Old Boys of Argentina, were followed up by back-to-back triumphs in the World Club Cup. The first saw São Paulo defeat Barcelona 2-1 with both goals from Raí, while the 1993 final witnessed victory over the much-heralded masters of Europe, AC Milan, with full-back Cafu at the centre of everything good that the team produced.

São Paulo's position as the major power in the city from which they take their name suffered a blow after Telê Santana quit in 1996, allowing Corinthians and Palmeiras to become the dominant clubs. However, São Paulo were back in the news in 1998 after selling Denilson for a then world record £22 million fee to Spanish club Real Betis.

In 2005, under former Peru coach Paulo Autuori, São Paulo became the first Brazilian club to win the Copa Libertadores three times, and later the same year they clinched the FIFA World Club Championship after beating Liverpool in Tokyo. Muricy Ramalho was appointed as coach the following year and he led the team to three consecutive league titles between 2006 and 2008 and to the final of the Copa Libertadores in 2006, when the team lost out to fellow Brazilians, Internacional.

SEVILLA

SEVILLE, SPAIN
Stadium: Ramón Sánchez Pizjuán (45,000)

Founded: 1905 **Honours**: UEFA Cup 2006, 2007; European Super Cup 2006; League 1; Cup 5

Formed by employees of the Rio Tinto mines in 1905, although Sevilla were briefly contenders either side of the Second World War, they have only really been a strong force in football in recent years. Winning the Spanish Cup in 1935 and 1939, they missed out on the league championship on the final day of the 1939-40 season when they lost the trophy to Atletico Aviation in controversial circumstances.

After clinching the runners-up spot again in 1942, they finally won the title in 1946 under coach Ramon Encinas, pipping Barcelona to the top of the table by just a point. The two contenders had met in Barcelona on the final day of the season, with Sevilla scoring early through the prolific Pato Araujo. After Barça pulled back an equaliser, Sevilla were able to hang on through five minutes of injury time to achieve the draw they needed to win the championship.

Two years later they won the Spanish Cup once again, but it would prove to be their last major trophy for 58 years as the club's revival did not begin until coach Joaquín Caparrós oversaw promotion from the second division as champions in 2001. The sale of homegrown José Antonio Reyes to Arsenal in 2004 helped balance the books and an investment was made in youth development.

With Juande Ramos taking over as coach in 2005, the club went on to enjoy a golden period, comfortably beating Middlesbrough 4-0 to win

Below: São Paulo parade the Paulista championship trophy at the Morumbi Stadium in 2005.

the UEFA Cup in 2006, retaining the trophy after a penalty shoot-out victory over Espanyol the following year. They also beat Barcelona 3-0 in 2006 to win the European Super Cup and clinched the Spanish Cup in 2007 after Frederic Kanouté's early goal gave them victory over Getafe. They won it again in 2010 after defeating Atlético Madrid.

While the club has yet to seriously challenge the dominance of Real Madrid and Barcelona in the Spanish game, the 'Sevillistas' have established a reputation as serious contenders.

SHAKHTAR DONETSK

DONETSK, UKRAINE
Stadium: Donbass Arena
(51,504)

Founded: 1936 **Honours:** UEFA Cup 2009; Ukrainian League 5; Ukrainian Cup 6; Soviet Cup 4

Although never ranking among the powerhouses of Soviet football, Shakhtar Donetsk earned a reputation as a fine cup team. However, after Ukrainian independence 'the Miners' became one of the dominating clubs in the country's domestic football, making an impact on the international stage when lifting the UEFA Cup in 2009. Formed in 1936, the club was initially called Stakhanovets before changing its name to Shakhtyor. It has been known as Shakhtar Donetsk since 1992.

It was in the early 1960s that the club first established its reputation in knockout competitions, winning the Soviet Cup in 1961 and 1962 under coach Oleg Oshenkov. Twice runners-up in the Soviet League in the 1970s, under coach Viktor Nosov, they again won the

Below: Shakhtar Donetsk pose for the press after beating Werder Bremen to the 2009 UEFA Cup.

Soviet Cup in 1980 and 1983, also winning the Soviet Super Cup in the latter year after defeating champions Dnipro Dnipropetrovsk over two legs.

After the onset of the Ukrainian league in 1992 the competition was dominated by Dynamo Kiev through its first decade, although Shakhtar finished as runners-up on six occasions before they finally lifted the trophy in 2002, the first club other than Dynamo to do so. This trophy was achieved under Italian coach Nevio Scala and 'the Miners' subsequently repeated the feat on several occasions with Romanian Mircea Lucescu at the helm. Their greatest moment came in the 2009 UEFA Cup Final, when an extra-time goal from Brazilian midfielder Jádson helped them to a 2-1 victory over Werder Bremen in Istanbul.

The club was the inspiration behind the 2001 song 'Shakhtar Donetsk' by Joe Strummer and The Mescaleros. Since August 2009 home games have been staged at the newly built Donbass Arena, which will be one of the venues for Euro 2012.

SPARTA PRAGUE

PRAGUE, CZECH REPUBLIC
Stadium: Letná
(20,854)

Founded: 1893 **Honours:** League 32; Cup 25

Despite several periods when fortunes have faltered, Sparta has always been the most successful football club in the history of the Czech game. Established as AC Kralovske Vinohrady in 1893 (the name translates as King's Vineyard), it was not until after the First

World War that the club's reputation as 'Iron Sparta' really grew, when the team competed under the name of AC Sparta.

In the inter-war years the club vied for dominance constantly with neighbours Slavia Prague and won numerous trophies in the process. A powerful force in European football, Sparta also won the Mitropa Cup – a prestigious forerunner of the European Cup – in both 1927 and 1935, beating Rapid Vienna and Ferencváros. They made their impact felt on the world stage in other ways too. Oldrich Nejedly, the club's star player during the Thirties, finished top scorer in the 1934 World Cup, playing in a Czechoslovakia team that finished the competition as runners-up. Sparta and rivals Slavia had provided all 11 Czech players for that World Cup final team.

After the Second World War the club suffered several name changes, becoming for a time Sparta Bratrstvi and Spartak Praha Sokolovo, before settling on the current moniker in 1965, but fans always called the team Sparta regardless. The Sixties proved to be one of the great periods in the club's history, with a side featuring playmaker Andrej Kvasnak, one of the stars of Czechoslovakia's run to the 1962 World Cup Final. Along with international team-mates Jiri Tichy and Vaclav Masek, Kvasnak helped form the fine Sparta team that won the 1964 Mitropa Cup and the league championship for the first time in 11 years the following season.

After the relatively dark days of the Seventies when the club was even relegated in 1975 for the first time in its history, Sparta finally returned to winning ways when celebrating a league and cup 'double' in 1984, and four more league titles followed before the end of the decade. Players like Tomas Skuhravy, who shone at the World Cup in 1990, and Ivan Hasek were followed by Martin Frydek and Petr Kouba, and the club continued to succeed despite seeing much of its talent travel abroad.

Throughout the post-Communist era – and despite some financial and managerial upheavals – Sparta has consistently dominated Czech football, and has even ruffled the feathers of bigger clubs in European competition.

SPARTAK MOSCOW

MOSCOW, RUSSIA
Stadium: Luzhniki
(78,360)

Founded: 1922 **Honours:** Soviet League 12; Russian League 9; Soviet Cup 10, Russian Cup 3

Formed as MKS in 1922 before becoming Krasnaya Presnya, in its early years the club was linked to the Moscow food producers' co-operative. However, it was not until the Spartak name was adopted in 1935 that the team began to prosper, winning its first Soviet league

title the following year. The club triumphed again twice more before the end of the decade.

Always leading lights in the Soviet Union, the Spartak team were crowned champions four more times in the 1950s and also inspired the founding of the European Cup with their friendly matches played against Wolverhampton Wanderers in 1954 and 1955.

Although league titles later became a more infrequent occurrence, Spartak completely dominated domestic football in the early years of the post-Communist era, winning nine of the first ten titles after the formation of the Russian league in 1992. The team also achieved a hat-trick of league and cup 'doubles' in this fruitful period, but after oil magnate Andrei Chervichhenko bought the club in 2000 and fell out with coach Oleg Romantsev, Spartak's grip on Russian football was loosened.

Chervichhenko sold his interest in Spartak in 2004 and the following season the team finished runners-up in the league under coach Aleksandrs Starkovs, the best finish since the previous title win in 2001. Despite regularly appearing in the Champions League and enjoying several encouraging campaigns, European silverware has remained elusive. Reaching the semi-finals of the UEFA Cup is the best the club has achieved in recent times.

SPORTING LISBON

LISBON, PORTUGAL
Stadium: José de Alvalade (50,076)

Founded: 1906 **Honours:** European Cup Winners' Cup 1964; League 18; Cup 19 (including four wins when Portuguese Championship was a cup competition, 1922-38)

Sporting Clube de Portugal has always been in the difficult position of competing for Lisbon dominance with local rivals Benfica, and although achieving a league and cup 'double' in 2002, the club has been unable to prevent the balance of power from moving 200 miles north to Porto.

In the Forties and Fifties Sporting could lay claim to having the upper hand over Benfica, winning championships in each decade. The club also made an impact in European competition, staging the first ever tie of the inaugural European Cup on September 4, 1955. The match may have concluded in a 3-3 draw with Partizan Belgrade but it was Joao Martins of Sporting who scored the first ever European Cup goal. Success in Europe came in 1964, with a 1-0 replay victory over MTK Budapest in the Cup Winners' Cup, but the club flattered to deceive over a long period of time, with only six more league titles gracing the Sporting trophy cabinet between the beginning of the Sixties and the end of the century.

Sporting's cause was not aided by the fact

that a number of top players had to be sold due to financial problems, among them Luis Figo, who left for Barcelona after helping the club to Portuguese Cup success in 1995. The departures on the field have been mirrored by the changes off it, with the likes of Bobby Robson and Carlos Queiroz paying the ultimate price for the dearth of league success, as the club spent 18 years trying to follow up the title win of 1982. Winning the championship in 2000 and 2002 at least reminded Portuguese football fans that Sporting can compete at the top of the table.

Sporting did reach the final of the UEFA Cup in 2005, staged at the club's own stadium, but despite taking the lead through Rogério, the match ended in a 3-1 defeat to CSKA Moscow.

STEAUA BUCHAREST

BUCHAREST, ROMANIA
Stadium: Ghencea (28,000)

Founded: 1947 **Honours:** European Cup 1986; European Super Cup 1986; League 23; Cup 20

Initially formed as ASA Bucharest by the Army Sports Association in 1947, the club adopted the name CSCA the following year and CCA Bucharest two years later, winning the national league three times in a row in the early Fifties. The Steaua name – the word means 'star' – was not adopted until 1961, and silverware under this name was first achieved in the Romanian Cup in the same season.

Three league titles followed in the late Sixties and mid Seventies. However, it was the Eighties that proved to be a golden decade for the club. Under coach Emerich Jenei Steaua won the

league and cup 'double' in 1985 and lifted the European Cup the following year. Disposing of Rangers and Anderlecht on the way to the final, Steaua pulled off the improbable to beat Barcelona in a penalty shoot-out, with keeper Helmuth Duckadam saving four consecutive spot-kicks. The victory was a remarkable achievement in itself but it was also the first time that a Communist country had won the European Cup.

Buoyed by this continental success, the talented Gheorghe Hagi was added to the squad a year later and the result was a hat-trick of 'doubles' from 1987 to 1989, won under Jeniei's assistant coach, Anghel Iordanescu, the club's all-time record goalscorer. This era also produced another fine run in the European Cup but the 1989 final saw Steaua defeated 4-0 by an AC Milan side inspired by Ruud Gullit and Marco Van Basten.

The period was not without controversy. In the 1988 Romanian Cup Final the Steaua team famously walked off the pitch in protest after their possible winning goal had been disallowed. The Romanian football association later awarded them both the goal and the match, and although the victory remains in the record books, after the 1989 revolution the club handed the trophy to opponents Dinamo Bucharest.

Since the dissolution of the Soviet Union, unlike most Eastern Bloc army teams Steaua initially continued as the nation's most powerful and successful team. The football club finally went its own way in 1998 and currently the only link to the army is the club's stadium. In the first decade of the new millennium Steaua won the title on just three occasions as other clubs started to challenge the team's dominance of Romanian football.

Above: Sporting's Leandro Romagnoli celebrates scoring in 2008.

TOTTENHAM HOTSPUR

LONDON, ENGLAND
Stadium: White Hart Lane (36,240)

Founded: 1882 **Honours:** UEFA Cup 1972, 1984; European Cup Winners' Cup 1963; League 2; FA Cup 8; League Cup 4

Hotspur FC was formed in 1882 by grammar school boys from the local Hotspur cricket club. Renamed Tottenham Hotspur Football And Athletic Club two years later, the team turned professional in 1895 and became the first non-league club to win the FA Cup in 1901, gaining entry to the second tier of the Football League in 1908. The club won the FA Cup again in 1921, beating Wolverhampton Wanderers at Stamford Bridge, but Spurs would not win the league title for the first time until 1951, when employing the 'push and run' tactics of manager Arthur Rowe.

Spurs did not enjoy a period of sustained success until the early Sixties. In 1961, under Bill Nicholson (manager from 1958 to 1974) and captain Danny Blanchflower, Tottenham became the first English club to complete an English league and cup 'double' since Preston North End achieved the feat in 1889. It was followed up with further FA Cup triumphs in 1962 and 1967, and European Cup Winners' Cup success in 1963.

Tottenham started the Seventies in fine fettle, winning two League Cups and appearing in the final of the UEFA Cup twice (winning against Wolverhampton Wanderers in 1972 and losing to Feyenoord in 1974). However, after a poor start to the 1974-5 season, Bill Nicholson quit. The club has since struggled to recapture its glory days, although it came close in the Eighties when a stylish team featuring the silky skills of Glenn Hoddle won back-to-back FA Cups in 1981 and 1982 and the UEFA Cup in 1984. Seven years later Spurs won the FA Cup again with a side boasting Gary Lineker and Paul Gascoigne, but this failed to provide a springboard for further triumphs.

Often seen as a cup side, in 2006 under Martin Jol Spurs finished fourth in the Premiership, the club's highest league position since 1990, but a League Cup final victory over Chelsea in 2008 brought Tottenham's only trophy of the first decade of the 21st century.

VALENCIA

VALENCIA, SPAIN
Stadium: La Mestalla (55,000)

Founded: 1919 **Honours:** Fairs Cup 1962, 1963; UEFA Cup 2004; European Cup Winners' Cup 1980; European Super Cup 1980, 2004; League 6; Cup 7

Valencia's defeats in consecutive Champions League finals – to Real Madrid in 2000 and to Bayern Munich in 2001 – were more than just a disappointment to their own fans, as neutrals everywhere admired the underdogs and their style of play. However, the club was eventually rewarded in 2002 with a first league championship in 31 years, having been coached to the previous title in 1971 by the great Alfredo Di Stéfano.

'Los Chés' – nicknamed after a local greeting, roughly translated as 'mate' – have always had a tradition for silky play. The club won three league titles in the 1940s, with goalgetting wizard Edmundo 'Mundo' Suárez twice lifting the 'Pichichi' trophy as the league's top scorer. In the early Sixties another classy

Below: Tottenham Hotspur enjoy winning the league and cup 'double' in 1961.

incarnation of the team played in the style of Real Madrid, appearing in three consecutive Fairs Cup finals, winning in 1962 after beating Barcelona and in 1963 following a defeat of Dinamo Zagreb.

The club has continued to impress in European competition. Argentinian World Cup winner Mario Kempes helped Valencia to a Cup Winners' Cup final triumph over Arsenal in 1980, although he missed his spot-kick in the penalty shoot-out, and it was under the astute guidance of Hector Cúper that the club reached the first two Champions League finals of the new millennium, with players such as Claudio López, Gaizka Mendieta and Kily González helping to retain Valencia's reputation for fiesta football.

Rafael Benítez joined as coach in 2001 and the club won the Spanish title the following year, plus a league and UEFA Cup 'double' in 2004. However, financial difficulties have made continued success harder to achieve in more recent years. The club was scheduled to move to a new 75,000 capacity stadium in the north west of the city but construction of the Nou Mestalla has been delayed until the financial situation improves.

VASCO DA GAMA

RIO DE JANEIRO, BRAZIL
Stadium: São Januario
(18,000)

Founded: 1915 **Honours:** Copa Libertadores 1998; Copa Mercosur 2000; Rio State League 22; League 4

The club of Rio De Janiero's Portuguese community, Vasco Da Gama was named after the celebrated 15th century explorer. Football in Rio had been the preserve of society's elite until Vasco broke the mould by winning the 1923 state championship with a team that included mixed-race and working class players. Outraged, Rio's leading teams launched a breakaway league and were only persuaded back with the agreement that players would have to complete a registration form, a task deemed beyond most of Brazil's illiterate poor. The literacy test was abolished in 1929 but the club will always be revered for paving the way for democracy in Brazilian football.

With the club histories of Flamengo and Fluminense inexorably entwined, Vasco are regarded as the perpetual outsiders in the battle for footballing superiority in Rio. However, the club has had its successes, the greatest of which was capturing the Copa Libertadores in 1998 with a 4-1 aggregate win over Barcelona of Ecuador. As South American champions Vasco contested the World Club Cup in Tokyo the same year but lost 2-1 to Real Madrid, and in January 2000 the club reached the final of the inaugural World Club Championship,

beating Manchester United 3-1 along the way before losing to Corinthians on penalties.

After winning the Brazilian title in 2000, Vasco remained resolutely a mid-table team until relegated for the first time in 2008, but bouncing back from the second division as champions a year later has at least given the club's fans something to cheer about.

ZENIT SAINT PETERSBURG

SAINT PETERBURG, RUSSIA
Stadium: Petrovsky Stadium
(21,570)

Founded: 1925 **Honours:** UEFA Cup 2008; European Super Cup 2008; Soviet League 1; Russian League 1; Soviet Cup 1; Russian Cup 2

In keeping with the Soviet era, the club was known as Zenit Leningrad for much of its existence, winning a first major trophy in 1944 after beating CSKA Moscow 2-1 in the final of the Soviet Cup. However, the club made little impact in the league. The team should have been relegated in 1967 after finishing bottom of table but it was deemed politically unacceptable to relegate Leningrad's leading football team during the 50th anniversary of the October Revolution. Zenit remained in the top flight, winning a first league title in 1984, and the following year the club beat Soviet Cup holders Dynamo Moscow to lift the Soviet Super Cup.

After the fragmentation of the Soviet Union, the city of Leningrad reverted to its pre-Soviet name and the club kicked off the new Russian league in 1992 as Zenit Saint Petersburg. However, they were relegated at the end of the first season, returning to the top flight for the 1997 campaign. The club reached the final of the Russian Cup in 1999 and despite trailing to Dynamo Moscow in the first-half, Zenit bounced back with three goals after the interval to lift the trophy. They also finished third in the league in 2001 and ended the following season as losing cup finalists after a 2-0 defeat to CSKA Moscow.

In December 2005 the club was taken over by Gazprom, the largest company in Russia, and huge sums of money were invested, ushering in a period of great success under experienced Dutch coach Dick Advocaat. In 2007 the club won the Russian Premier League and the following year enjoyed continental success for the first time, reaching the UEFA Cup final after pulling off a shock 5-1 aggregate defeat of Bayern Munich in the semi-finals. Facing Glasgow Rangers in the final in Manchester, Zenit won 2-0 thanks to late goals from Igor Denisov and Konstantin Zyryanov. Three months later they beat European champions Manchester United to win the European Super Cup, becoming the first Russian side to lift the trophy.

Winning the Russian Cup in 2010, the club will eventually move to a newly constructed 62,000-capacity stadium in 2011, to be built on the site of its former home, the Kirov Stadium.

Above: Zenit Saint Petersburg captain Anatoliy Tymoshchuk after beating Rangers in the 2008 UEFA Cup Final.

LEGENDS OF FOOTBALL

Above: Saudi Arabia's Sami Al-Jaber celebrates scoring against Tunisia at the 2006 World Cup.

ADEMIR

Country: Brazil
Born: November 8, 1922
Position: Centre-forward
Clubs: Recife, Vasco Da Gama, Fluminense

Ademir Marques de Menezes was a superb goalscorer who went a long way in establishing Brazil as a post-war footballing power. He was exceptionally fast, immensely skilled and he could shoot with either foot. He made his international debut in 1945 and went on to score 32 goals in 39 games for his country. His finest hour came in the 1950 World Cup when he fully deserved the Golden Boot for his total of nine goals, including four against Sweden.

Brazil's World Cup attacking trio of Ademir, Zizinho and Jair is still considered one of the country's finest strikeforces, and Ademir's presence necessitated opponents to field an extra fullback which was the seed for Brazil's famed 4-2-4 formation. A prolific scorer in the Rio State League, he was a five time league winner with Vasco Da Gama, and he won a further title at city neighbours Fluminense.

MOHAMED AL-DEAYEA

Country: Saudi Arabia
Born: August 2, 1972
Position: Goalkeeper
Clubs: Al Ta'ee, Al Hilal

Mohamed Al-Deayea is the greatest goalkeeper that Asia has ever produced. He has made more international appearances than any other player, having turned out for his country 181 times. He succeeded his elder brother Abdullah Al-Deayea, who had been part of the Asian Cup winning teams of 1984 and 1988.

His international career began against Bangladesh at the Asian Games in Beijing in 1990 and ended, through international retirement, in June 2006 at his fourth successive World Cup, although in Germany he was a non-playing squad member. His 100th appearance had been at the 1998 World Cup Finals against South Africa. By then he was team captain. He continued to play his club football for Al Hilal after his international retirement.

SAMI AL-JABER

Country: Saudi Arabia
Born: December 11, 1972
Position: Forward
Clubs: Al Hilal, Wolverhampton Wanderers

Discovered as a 15-year-old by Al Hilal, Sami Al-Jaber was Saudi Arabia's golden boy of football. Other than an eight month loan spell with Wolverhampton Wanderers in 2000, when he became the first Saudi Arabian to play in the English league, his entire club career was spent at Al Hilal, with whom he won the Saudi league title on six occasions and the Asian Club Championship twice.

He made 163 appearances for Saudi Arabia, winning the Asian Cup in 1996. Playing in four successive World Cups, he scored three times at the finals and made his last international appearance at the 2006 World Cup. At his height he was an attacking player who ran at defenders and was one of the most feared strikers in Asia. He played his final game for Al Hilal in his own testimonial, scoring in the 3-2 victory over Manchester United in 2008.

FLORIAN ALBERT

Country: Hungary
Born: September 15, 1941
Position: Centre-forward
Club: Ferencváros

Florian Albert was an elegant and gifted striker who enjoyed a long and successful career at club and international level. He was difficult to mark and had an ability to bring others into play. At the 1966 World Cup he shone as Hungary beat holders Brazil 3-1 at Goodison Park and he impressed with his guile and skill during the team's run to the quarter-finals.

Albert appeared for Hungary at the 1960 Olympics when they finished third, and he also played at the 1962 World Cup Finals in Chile. At that tournament he scored a superb solo goal against England and struck a hat-trick against Bulgaria. Tall and slender, he was different from previous Hungarian strikers but equally effective and he had shown his promise while still at school, making his international debut at 17.

Albert spent his entire club career with Ferencváros, picking up four titles. He helped the club to become the first Hungarian side to lift a continental trophy with a Fairs Cup win in 1965 and he was voted European Footballer Of The Year in 1967. He played 75 times for Hungary, scoring 31 goals. He retired in 1974.

DEMETRIO ALBERTINI

Country: Italy
Born: August 23, 1971
Position: Midfielder
Clubs: AC Milan, Padova, Atlético Madrid, Lazio, Atalanta, Barcelona

Albertini brought down the curtain on an illustrious career in December 2005 while a Barcelona player, but it is the 14 seasons between 1988 and 2002, when he played for AC Milan, for which the cultured midfielder will be most remembered. A product of the club's youth system, he made his Milan debut as a 17-year-old in 1989, and after a period on loan at Padova, he established himself as a first-team regular at the San Siro in the 1991-2 season. He went on to play nearly 300 games for the club, winning five Serie A titles (including three in a row between 1992 and 1994) and the Champions League in 1994. His association with Milan ended in 2002 following a season on loan at Atlético Madrid. Moves to Atalanta and Lazio followed before he joined Barcelona in January 2005 at the age of 33. He was capped by Italy 79 times.

IVOR ALLCHURCH

Country: Wales
Born: October 16, 1929
Position: Inside-forward
Clubs: Swansea City, Newcastle United, Cardiff City

Grace and elegance were the watchwords of Ivor Allchurch, an inside-forward who is still the second highest goalscorer in Welsh international football history – just behind Ian Rush. Tall and blond, inevitably he was known as the 'Golden Boy', but he sadly failed to gain just reward for his ample talents as he spent his entire career playing for clubs at the wrong end of the table. Only at the 1958 World Cup in Sweden did a wider audience get to appreciate his sublime skills, when he was part of a talented Welsh

team that narrowly went down Pelé's Brazil in the quarter-finals. The 251 goals that he scored in 694 league appearances attest to both the quality of his finishing and his durability, while eight of his 68 Welsh caps were gained partnering his brother Len, who also played for Swansea.

LUIGI ALLEMANDI

Country: Italy
Born: November 8, 1903
Position: Left-back
Clubs: Legnano, Juventus, Inter Milan, Roma, Venezia, Lazio

An ever-present member of Italy's triumphant 1934 World Cup winning team, including the 2-1 extra-time win over Czechoslovakia in the final. Between 1925 and 1936 he played 24 times for his country and occasionally he captained the side. However, in 1927 he was accused of having been involved in fixing the Turin derby when he had been a Juventus player, even though he had played a full and active part in the game. He was banned for life but later pardoned. He went on to captain Inter Milan to the Serie A title.

JOSÉ ALTAFINI

Country: Brazil, Italy
Born: August 27, 1938
Position: Centre-forward
Clubs: XV de Piracicaba, Palmeiras, São Paulo, AC Milan, Napoli, Juventus, Chiasso, Mendrisio

José Altafini's career spanned three decades, two international careers and a change of name. In the unique nickname tradition of his native Brazil he was known as 'Mazzola' for his resemblance to the Torino captain Valentino Mazzola, who had been killed in the Superga air crash, and at 19 years of age he represented Brazil at the 1958 World Cup. Although he arrived at the tournament as the first choice

centre-forward he would play no part in the latter stages of the competition. Despite scoring twice in the first game against Austria, and having a superb overhead kick disallowed in the quarter-final against Wales, coach Vicente Feola was concerned that 'Mazzola' had an impending transfer to Italy on his mind and dropped him in favour of Vavá for the remaining games. He would not play for Brazil again.

The re-adoption of his birth name came with a move to Milan, and four years later he represented Italy at the World Cup in Chile, making him one of only five players to have turned out for two countries at the World Cup. His last appearance for the azzurri was in the notorious 'Battle Of Santiago' against the hosts, having scored a total of five goals in six games for the Italians. His finest hour came in Milan's 1963 European Cup campaign when he scored 14 goals, including both goals in a 2-1 win over Benfica in the final.

ANTONIO ALZAMENDI

Country: Uruguay
Born: June 7, 1956
Position: Forward
Clubs: Sud America, Independiente, River Plate, Nacional, Tecos UAG, Peñarol, Logrones, Mandiyú, Rampla Juniors

Antonio Alzamendi was voted South American Player Of The Year in 1986 for his performances in helping River Plate to both the Argentinian title and the Copa Libertadores, and he rounded off his year by scoring the decisive goal in the World Club Cup in Tokyo against Steaua Bucharest. Although he won this award playing his club football in Argentina, where he was a prolific striker, he also enjoyed spells in Spain, Mexico and in his home country, Uruguay. In the international game, he featured in the 1986 and 1990 World Cups, and he helped Uruguay to win the Copa América in 1987.

AMANCIO AMARO

Country: Spain
Born: October 16, 1939
Position: Inside-right/Outside-right
Clubs: Deportivo La Coruna, Real Madrid

Amancio was one of Spain's most exciting players of the 1960s. He was groomed by Real Madrid, winning – and scoring in – the 1966 European Cup Final just two years after losing the same cup to Inter. He also helped Spain to become European champions in 1964. Often known simply as Amancio, he scored 11 goals in 42 games for his country. His brilliance was in his ability to play primarily as an inside or outside-right but with equal aplomb switch to the other flank. A leg injury in a Spanish Cup game looked to have ended his career but he recovered to feature in the resurgence of Real in the 1970s.

JOSE LEANDRO ANDRADE

Country: Uruguay
Born: November 22, 1901
Position: Right-half
Clubs: Bella Vista, Nacional, Peñarol, Atlanta, Wanderers, Argentinos Juniors

Jose Leandro Andrade was among the greatest players of the early days of football. One of the mainstays of the great Uruguayan side of the late 1920s and early 1930s, he helped his country to gain Olympic gold in Paris in 1924 and Amsterdam in 1928. His career looked as if it was to finish prematurely when injury struck in 1929, but he battled back and his experience was vital when his Uruguayan side lifted the inaugural World Cup in 1930 on home soil.

A tall and classy player, he was one of the greats of the golden generation of Uruguayan football, alongside defender Jose Nasazzi and influential striker Hector Scarone. An old fashioned wing-half, the World Cup final was his last international game. He was a guest at the final match of the 1950 World Cup and watched on as his nephew Víctor Rodríguez Andrade picked up a winners' medal.

VICTOR RODRÍGUEZ ANDRADE

Country: Uruguay
Born: February 14, 1927
Position: Left-half
Clubs: Central, Peñarol, Wanderers

Victor Rodríguez Andrade emulated the triumph of his uncle, the great Jose Leandro Andrade, by winning the World Cup with Uruguay in 1950. In fact, he even took his uncle's surname in addition to his own in honour of the great

Below: Jose Altafini, scorer of both AC Milan goals, leaves the Wembley pitch following 2-1 victory over Benfica in the 1963 European Cup Final.

Right: Italy's Roberto Baggio misses the penalty that hands the World Cup to Brazil in 1994.

Uruguayan international. The diminutive Rodríguez Andrade was a tenacious left-half who was an excellent ball winner. This was perfectly epitomised in the final game of the 1950 World Cup when he often frustrated the Brazilians in their attempts to get forward, although he later admitted to being at fault for Brazil's only goal

Four years later he played as right-half in an injury-hit Uruguay side, reaching the World Cup semi-final before losing to Hungary in one of the great games in World Cup history. He was part of the Peñarol side that never finished lower than runners-up in the national league in the 1950s.

OSVALDO ARDILES

Country: Argentina
Born: August 3, 1952
Position: Midfielder
Clubs: Huracán, Tottenham Hotspur, Paris Saint-Germain, Blackburn Rovers, Queens Park Rangers, Fort Lauderdale Strikers, Swindon Town

After making his name with Argentine club side Huracán, and despite weighing in at only ten stone and 5ft 6ins in height, Osvaldo 'Ossie' Ardiles forged a reputation as a creative midfield force in the Argentinian national team under coach César Luis Menotti. Despite impressive displays picking up a World Cup winners' medal for Argentina in 1978, many believed Ardiles would struggle with the rigours of the English Football League when he signed for Tottenham. The reality couldn't have been more different and he settled into midfield alongside the muscle of Graham Roberts and the grace of Glenn Hoddle, spraying passes around the pitch at will as Spurs picked up two FA Cups in 1981 and 1982 and a UEFA Cup in 1984.

Sadly, when Argentina invaded the Falklands in 1982 Ardiles was on World Cup duty and it was decided that he should go out on loan to Paris Saint-Germain after the conflict. On his return he enjoyed five more seasons at White Hart Lane, moving to Blackburn on loan before ending his playing career as player-coach at Swindon.

Below: Ossie Ardiles on one of his mazy runs for Tottenham Hotspur.

ROBERTO BAGGIO

Country: Italy
Born: February 18, 1967
Position: Centre-forward
Clubs: Vicenza, Fiorentina, Juventus, AC Milan, Bologna, Inter Milan, Brescia

One of eight children and born in the small town of Caldogno, Baggio first made his name as a 15-year-old winger in Italy's Serie C1 (or third division) with local club side Lanerossi Vicenza. When he was 18, Baggio was signed by Fiorentina, then in Italy's top flight, and became a regular in the first-team during the 1987-8 season.

He stayed with the Florence side for five seasons, in that time becoming one of Italian football's hottest properties and making his international debut against Holland on November 16, 1988. His last two seasons in Florence saw Baggio score 32 league goals in 62 appearances, and in the 1989-90 season, his final year with the club, Fiorentina made it to the final of the UEFA Cup, only to lose out 3-1 on aggregate to Juventus.

Astonishingly, just a week after losing to Juventus, Fiorentina sold Baggio to them for a then world record fee of £8 million. The news provoked such fury amongst fans in Florence that riot police had to be called in to quell two days of violent disturbances.

Aged 23 and a recent convert to Buddhism, Baggio made his World Cup debut for Italy in 1990. He started the tournament on the bench but, against Czechoslovakia, scored one of the best goals that the tournament had ever seen: a powerful run from the halfway line that left defenders for dead. However, Italy still only managed to finish third.

Baggio's time at Juventus was extremely successful. The Turin club won the UEFA Cup in 1993, finished runners up in 1995, and under coach Marcello Lippi, claimed the league title in 1995. Baggio himself was named European and World Footballer Of The Year in 1993, and continued to score regularly for Juventus (78 goals in 99 league appearances spread over five seasons). However, with the precociously talented Alessandro Del Piero waiting in the wings, and a wealth of strike talent elsewhere in the squad, Baggio was finding it harder to hold down a first team place. He joined AC Milan in 1995 and won the title in his first year.

By 1994, Baggio had arguably become the most famous, if not the most popular player in Italy, and it was these talismanic qualities that made him the focus of his country's World Cup campaign the same year. The Italians struggled to qualify for the second round and as the tournament wore on they seemed to rely ever more on 'the Divine Ponytail', as Baggio was nicknamed. He scored a last-minute equaliser and an extra-time penalty winner to eliminate Nigeria in the second round, before snatching the decider in the quarter-final against Spain. Another brace of goals dispatched Bulgaria in the semi-final and when it came down to penalties against Brazil in the final, even though he had been carrying an injury it seemed certain that Baggio would net from the spot to keep Italy's World Cup hopes alive. However, he scooped his penalty – Italy's fifth and last – over the bar and handed victory to Brazil.

Baggio was recalled to the national team for the 1998 World Cup Finals in France, where he was able to atone for the penalty miss of four years earlier by converting a vital spot-kick against Chile to give Italy a 2-2 draw. Baggio had signed for Bologna in 1997 and then played for Inter Milan before settling at Brescia, where he finished his career in 2004. He had not been included in the Italian squads for Euro 2000 or the World Cup two years later and he made the last of his 56 appearance for his country in April of 2004, having scored 27 goals

GORDON BANKS

Country: England
Born: December 30, 1937
Position: Goalkeeper
Clubs: Chesterfield, Leicester City, Stoke City, Cleveland Stokers, Fort Lauderdale Strikers, St Patrick's Athletic

Gordon Banks was famed for his composure, agility, consistency and all-round technique, yet never played for a major club. Born the son of a foundryman in Tinsley, Sheffield, he developed his physical strength hauling bags of coal and hod-carrying when he left school. He took up goalkeeping as an amateur and was picked up by Third Division Chesterfield at the age of 15, making his league debut against Colchester on November 29, 1958. Leicester City spotted his potential and Banks moved to Filbert Street in July 1959 for £7,000, making his Division One debut that September in a 1-1 draw with Blackpool.

Banks is today credited with developing many of the facets of modern goalkeeping. He would stay for hours after training, concentrating on technique, learning angles and inventing specialised routines designed to improve his strength and agility. However, he did not adopt gloves regularly until 1970, preferring to spit sticky saliva from chewing gum on to his hands and let it dry.

In May 1961, in his second season, Banks made his first Wembley appearance, picking up a losers' medal in the FA Cup final against 'double' winners Tottenham Hotspur. Two years later he picked up his second FA Cup runners-up medal after having a poor final against Manchester United.

Banks was called into the England squad by Walter Winterbottom for a 1962 friendly against Portugal while at Leicester, but it was Alf Ramsey who awarded him his first cap on April 6, 1963. Although the game ended in defeat to Scotland, Banks rapidly became a fixture in the England side and he was the rock of the 1966 World Cup winning team, conceding just one goal before the final against West Germany, a penalty to Eusébio. He was also voted the tournament's best goalkeeper in 1966.

His finest performance came at Mexico 70, just a day after he discovered he was to be awarded an OBE. Facing Pelé for the first time in his career, he managed to scoop the Brazilian's sharp, downward header up and over the bar in the titanic clash between the holders and the tournament favourites. It became the most replayed save of all time, but when it came to the most crucial game of the tournament Banks was unfortunately absent through illness, felled by 'Montezuma's revenge'. Peter Bonetti took his place and conceded three goals against West Germany in the quarter-final, ending England's dream of retaining the Jules Rimet Trophy in Mexico.

A year after lifting the World Cup, Stoke City expressed an interest in Banks, and Leicester, knowing they had the promising Peter Shilton in reserve, let him go for £52,000. Although he never achieved FA Cup or league honours, Banks won the League Cup with Stoke in 1972 and was also voted the Football Writers' Player Of The Year. He would undoubtedly have played at the top for much longer had a car crash that summer not cost him the sight in one eye.

He kept 35 clean sheets in 73 games for England and lost just nine times. He enjoyed a short spell in the North American Soccer League with Fort Lauderdale Strikers before returning to England in 1979 for a stint in management with Telford United.

1955
1956
1957
1958
1959
1960
1961
1962
1963
1964
1965
1966
1967
1968
1969
1970
1971
1972
1973
1974
1975
1976
1977
1978

1955: Signs professional forms with Third Division North side, Chesterfield.

1959: Transferred to Leicester City for £7,000.

1961: Losing FA Cup finalist against Bill Nicholson's 'double' winning Tottenham.

1963: He makes his international debut in a 2-1 defeat to Scotland. He is also a losing FA Cup finalist again, this time to Manchester United.

1966: A member of England's World Cup winning side, Banks didn't concede a goal in the tournament until the semi-final.

1967: Opts to join Stoke City rather than Liverpool in a £52,000 move.

1970: Pulls off wonder save against Pelé at the World Cup, but misses quarter-final defeat by West Germany due to illness.

1972: Helps Stoke win League Cup and is named Footballer Of The Year, but disaster strikes as he loses an eye in a serious car crash.

1977: Plays for Fort Lauderdale Strikers in the NASL. Despite his handicap, Banks is voted the league's most valuable goalkeeper in his first season.

259

Right: Gabriel Batistuta celebrates completing his hat-trick against Jamaica at the 1998 World Cup.

FRANCO BARESI

Country: Italy
Born: May 8, 1960
Position: Sweeper
Club: AC Milan

Born near Brescia, in the Lombardy region of Italy, Baresi enjoyed two decades of football with his only club, AC Milan. Making his professional debut in an away game against Verona on April 23, 1978, Baresi went on to establish himself as the finest sweeper in the world during Milan's glory years of the late Eighties and early Nineties.

The consummate modern defender, Baresi was nicknamed 'The Steel Man'. He was a formidable stopper but was also comfortable bringing the ball out of defence and joining in with attacking moves. He captained Milan to six league titles, two World Club Cups, as well as to European Cup glory in 1989 and 1990. Sadly, he missed his club's 4-0 demolition of Barcelona in the Champions League final of 1994 as he was suspended. He also won the European Super Cup on two occasions.

Baresi made his international debut for Italy against Romania in December 1982, although he had been a non-playing member of the squad that had won the World Cup in Spain a few months earlier. He went on to play for his country 81 times, 31 of them as captain, but he suffered heartbreak in the World Cup final of 1994 after Italy lost to Brazil in a game that saw him miss a penalty in the climactic shoot-out. When Baresi retired from the game in 1997, Milan retired his famous Number 6 shirt.

FABIEN BARTHEZ

Country: France
Born: June 28, 1971
Position: Goalkeeper
Clubs: Toulouse, Marseille, Monaco, Manchester United, Nantes

Superbly athletic and excellent at distributing the ball from the hand or with his feet, Fabien Barthez was one of the most entertaining goalkeepers in the game. The son of a top class rugby player, he won all the major honours, with domestic titles in both France and England and success in the Champions League with Marseille in 1993. He also played a leading role in helping France to win the World Cup on home soil in 1998 and the European Championship in 2000.

In 2005 Barthez was banned for six months for spitting at a referee. He fought off the challenge of Gregory Coupet to regain his position as France's first choice goalkeeper, reaching the 2006 World Cup Final, but he failed to stop any of Italy's spot-kicks in the deciding shoot-out. Although he harboured ambitions to continue his international career, it proved to be his last appearance for France. After a brief spell with Nantes ended acrimoniously in 2007, he had to come to terms with the fact that his career was over.

CLIFF BASTIN

Country: England
Born: March 14, 1912
Position: Left-winger
Clubs: Exeter City, Arsenal

'Boy Bastin' started his career with hometown club Exeter but joined Arsenal as a raw 17-year-old in 1929. He was not just an impressive left-winger, but also a talented inside-forward, the position he preferred. He helped 'The Gunners' to their first trophy, the FA Cup, in his debut season, and four goals on the way to the final against Huddersfield set the tone for his career.

An incredible turn of pace and uncanny dribbling ability made Bastin the pivotal figure in an Arsenal team that yielded five league titles and two FA Cups in the 1930s, while he became a mainstay of the England squad from the age of 19. A cartilage operation in 1934 shortened his career, but his tally of 178 goals in 396 games remained an Arsenal record until Ian Wright passed the barrier in 1997.

GABRIEL BATISTUTA

Country: Argentina
Born: February 1, 1969
Position: Forward
Clubs: Newell's Old Boys, River Plate, Boca Juniors, Fiorentina, Roma, Inter Milan, Al Arabi

Born in Avellaneda, north of Buenos Aires, Gabriel Batistuta idolised Mario Kempes but outstripped his hero to become Argentina's all-time top scorer with 56 goals in 78 appearances. His exploits in front of goal earned him the nickname 'BatiGol' and he starred in three successive World Cups, in 1994, 1998 and 2002.

He made his league debut for Newell's Old Boys in 1988 and built his reputation with Boca Juniors in the championship-winning season of 1991, before moving to Fiorentina. There he became a club legend and was Serie A's top scorer in 1994-5 before switching to Roma and finally winning the Scudetto in 2001.

Retiring from international football after Argentina's early exit from the 2002 World Cup, he joined Inter Milan on loan, and then played for Qatar side Al Arabi before retiring in March 2005 after a series of injuries. In 2004 he was named in FIFA's centenary list of the 125 Greatest Living Footballers.

VLADIMIR BEARA

Country: Yugoslavia
Born: November 2, 1928
Position: Goalkeeper
Clubs: Hajduk Split, Red Star Belgrade, Alemania Aachen, Victoria Cologne

The 'Great Vladimir' was the outstanding Yugoslav goalkeeper during the 1950s, when he played at the 1950, 1954 and 1958 World Cup tournaments, as well as earning a silver medal at the 1952 Olympics. He represented his country

Below: AC Milan's Franco Baresi lifts the European Cup at the Nou Camp in 1989.

on 60 occasions. With Hajduk Split he won the Yugoslav league title three times between 1950 and 1955. A surprise move to Red Star gave him four more titles by 1960 and successive Yugoslav Cup triumphs in 1958 and 1959 .

BEBETO

Country: Brazil
Born: February 16, 1964
Position: Centre-forward
Clubs: Vitória, Flamengo, Vasco Da Gama, Deportivo De La Coruna, Sevilla, Flamengo, Cruzeiro, Botafogo, Toros Neza, Kashima Antlers, Al-Ittihad

The fresh-faced striker was best known outside of Brazil for his 'cradling the baby' celebration during the 1994 World Cup, but it was his unfailing ability to find the back of the net that established his pedigree. He rarely won headlines when partnering Romario, though his 39 goals in 75 internationals leaves him fifth on Brazil's all-time scoring list. In 1989 he was controversially transferred from Flamengo, where he was a fans' favourite, to rivals Vasco Da Gama. A move to Europe followed, where he won the Spanish Cup with Deportivo De La Coruna. He picked up a World Cup winners' medal in 1994 and was a losing finalist in 1998. He continued to play around the world until retirement in 2002.

FRANZ BECKENBAUER

Country: West Germany
Born: September 11, 1945
Position: Midfielder/Sweeper
Clubs: Bayern Munich, New York Cosmos, Hamburg

What Franz Beckenbauer touched, both as player and manager, invariably turned to gold, and he was a winner at club and international level. Beckenbauer picked up his nickname – 'Der Kaiser' – for his imperious style. As a footballer he was utterly in control, a chess player who read the game in his head, but he was also blessed with an excellent touch, a good change of pace and flawless distribution.

Beckenbauer joined Bayern as a junior in 1959, making his debut at 18 years of age playing on the left of midfield, but he gradually moved inside. The team were promoted to the top division of the Bundesliga in 1965, finishing third in their first season behind city rivals TSV 1860 Munich. In the following two seasons Bayern won the German Cup twice, then a European Cup Winners' Cup in 1967.

His classy performances led to a rapid call-up to the West German squad and he made his international debut in a 2-1 victory over Sweden on September 26, 1965. At the 1966 World Cup he established himself at the heart of the German side, scoring four goals, including the winner in the semi-final with Russia, but he was unable to

stop England from lifting the trophy in the final.

Four years later in Mexico he had a measure of revenge in the quarter-final. With England leading by two goals, he scored to keep the Germans in touch and minutes later, after manager Alf Ramsey withdrew Bobby Charlton from the game, Beckenbauer was freed up to inspire a comeback. The Germans lost the semi-final with Italy and Beckenbauer finished the game with a dislocated shoulder, playing on with his arm strapped across his chest.

A year later he took over as captain of the national team and led them to a European Championship final win over the Soviet Union in 1972, having redefined the sweeper's role by gliding out of defence with mazy runs to set up devastating counter attacks. Two years later he experienced his crowning moment as a player, captaining the national side to World Cup victory on home soil in a game that saw Holland threaten to overrun the Germans. Beckenbauer remained unfazed and when the Dutch flagged he marshalled his forces and pushed his side to victory. He retired from international football in 1977 with 103 caps.

In club football he helped Bayern Munich to dominate in the mid-Seventies, leading them to an impressive hat-trick of European Cups between 1974 and 1976. He finished his Bayern career with three league titles and four German Cups, twice being voted European Footballer Of The Year, in 1972 and 1976. He played for three years with New York Cosmos, winning the NASL Soccer Bowl three times before returning to West Germany with Hamburg. After one final season with the Cosmos he retired.

His cerebral style and ability to lift others made him a natural for management and without experience of coaching a club side he took over his country in 1984, pushing his players to two World Cup finals. The team's triumph at Italia 90 made him the first person to both captain and coach a World Cup winning side. After a spell with Marseille he returned to Bayern as manager in 1994, winning the Bundesliga in his first season before becoming club president, and then vice president of the German Football Federation. He was president of the German World Cup 2006 Organising Committee.

IGOR BELANOV

Country: Soviet Union
Born: September 25, 1960
Position: Forward
Clubs: SKA Odessa, Chernomerets, Dynamo Kiev, Borussia Mönchengladbach, Eintracht Braunschweig, Metalurh Mariupol

Igor Belanov was voted European Footballer Of The Year in 1986 after a sensational period when he topped the scoring charts in Dynamo Kiev's title winning season. He also won the European Cup Winners' Cup and just three weeks before the Mexico World Cup, found himself catapulted into the Soviet squad along with 11 Kiev team-mates, thanks to new Soviet coach and former Kiev manager Valery Lobanovsky. He scored a hat-trick against Belgium in the second round but the Soviets lost 4-3. After 1986 he was plagued by injuries, although he did earn a move to West Germany. He played in the 1988 European Championship Final, missing a penalty in the 2-0 defeat by Holland.

Above: 'Der Kaiser', Franz Beckenbauer slides in on England's Colin Bell during the 1970 World Cup quarter-final.

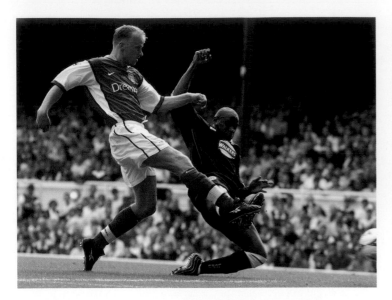

Above: Dennis Bergkamp in full flight for Arsenal.

MIODRAG BELODEDICI

Country: Romania
Born: May 20, 1964
Position: Sweeper
Clubs: Steaua Bucharest, Real Star Belgrade, Valencia, Real Valladolid, Villarreal, Atlante

Miodrag Belodedici was the first player to win the European Cup with two different clubs, Steaua Bucharest in 1986 and Red Star Belgrade in 1991. On both occasions the final was decided by penalties, with Steaua beating Barcelona 2-0 and Red Star defeating Marseille 5-3 after goalless draws. He was born in Serbia but raised in Romania and played for them 20 times between 1984 and 1988, when to escape the Ceausescu regime he sought asylum in Yugoslavia. In his absence he was convicted of treason and sentenced to ten years in prison, declining to play for Romania again until 1992, after the collapse of the Ceausescu regime. He went on to feature at the 1994 World Cup and Euro 2000.

FERENC BENE

Country: Hungary
Born: December 17, 1944
Position: Centre-forward
Clubs: Ujpest Dozsa, Volan SC, Sepsi 78, Soroksari, Kecskemeti

An iconic figure in his homeland, Ferenc Bene is best remembered for his 12 goals – including six against Morocco – at the 1964 Olympic Games, which helped Hungary to the gold medal. He joined Újpest as a teenager before inspiring the club to eight championship victories and three cup successes. Five times the Hungarian league's top marksman, he was forced to play on the right wing for his country, due to the presence of Florian Albert, but he still managed 36 goals in 76 games for Hungary, the highlight being a tremendous individual effort in a shock 3-1 victory over Brazil at Goodison Park during the 1966 World Cup Finals.

Opposite: A legend in his own lifetime and an icon of his age, George Best was dubbed 'the fifth Beatle'.

DENNIS BERGKAMP

Country: Holland
Born: May 10, 1969
Position: Centre-forward
Clubs: Ajax, Inter Milan, Arsenal

Dennis Bergkamp is one of the most famous products of the Ajax youth system. Having made his debut against Roda JC in 1986, he went on to become the pivotal figure in a side that won the Dutch title, the UEFA Cup and the Cup Winners' Cup. He was the Dutch league's top scorer between 1991 and 1993, and his 103 goals in 185 games made him a most wanted striker.

He joined Inter Milan in a £12 million deal in 1993 but despite another UEFA Cup success his 11 goal tally in two seasons was regarded as a failure. A £7.5 million transfer to Arsenal in the summer of 1995 shocked the football world but it proved to be a shrewd move. Bergkamp soon began to weave his magic as both provider and scorer following Arsene Wenger's arrival.

Bergkamp played an instrumental part in Arsenal's league and cup 'double' of 1998, and he capped the season by winning the PFA and Footballer Writers' Player Of The Year awards. He also played a prominent role in the Dutch side that reached the semi-finals of the World Cup. Although many argue he failed to recapture his form in the ensuing seasons, Bergkamp helped Arsenal to secure the club's third 'double' in 2002, the second under Wenger.

Famously afraid of flying, Bergkamp drove to many of Arsenal's European away games and quit international football in 2000 rather than face the long flight to Japan for the 2002 World Cup. He retired in 2006.

GEORGE BEST

Country: Northern Ireland
Born: May 22, 1946
Position: Centre-forward
Clubs: Manchester United, Stockport County, Cork Celtic, Fulham, Los Angeles Aztecs, Fort Lauderdale Strikers, Motherwell, Hibernian, San Jose Earthquakes, Bournemouth, Brisbane Lions

The name George Best became a byword for drinking and womanising in an era when footballers broke the superstar barrier, but the image somehow overshadowed the talent of a man who was arguably the greatest player to have emerged from the British Isles.

Best was the complete all-round player. Blessed with quick feet and even quicker intelligence he would toy with defenders like a cat with a mouse. He could pass and finish but he never forgot to work for the team. For all his razzmatazz a Best goal was generally celebrated with a hand half raised, perhaps a finger pointing upwards. Gordon Banks cites a dazzling run which left him lying on his backside as the best goal ever scored against him.

Not long after that encounter the two met again in an international. As Banks prepared to kick the ball upfield, Best flipped it out of the keeper's hands and headed it into the back of the net. It was typical of Best's impudence but the referee mistakenly disallowed it.

Best arrived in Manchester from Belfast in 1961 aged just 15 years and made his Old Trafford debut two years later against West Bromwich Albion. Sharp, quick-witted and stylish, he launched the club into a new era that helped it overcome the loss of the 'Busby Babes', and teamed with Bobby Charlton and Denis Law he helped win league titles in 1965 and 1967. In his first six seasons he scored 190 goals in 290 games, but his crowning moment was winning the European Cup at Wembley in 1968 after characteristically rounding the goalkeeper to score in the 4-1 win over Benfica.

Best was named European Player Of The Year but his taste for the game was diminishing. With the retirement of the patrician Sir Matt Busby, his behaviour became increasingly rebellious. Managers came and went in an awkward period of transition at the club and when Tommy Docherty dropped Best, the Irishman responded by walking out. FIFA became involved, issuing a ban, but it was rescinded allowing Best to join Stockport County in 1975. It was to be the first stationing post in a spiralling career.

Living the life of a pop star (he was dubbed 'the fifth Beatle') Best played in the USA before returning home to join Fulham in September 1976. There he rediscovered a taste for the game, forming an entertaining partnership with another wayward genius, Rodney Marsh. Fulham's gate doubled for their first home game together and Best put them one up with barely a minute on the clock. At Fulham he also became the first player in the Football League to be shown a red card after the introduction of the new card system. The great tragedy of his career was that despite winning 37 caps for Northern Ireland he was never able to perform on the world stage.

Best succumbed to alcoholism and received a liver transplant in July 2002, but on November 25, 2005, aged 59, he died after suffering multiple organ failure. He was buried alongside his mother, with an estimated crowd of 100,000 lining the streets of Belfast in the pouring rain, to say a final farewell to the 'Belfast Boy'.

JOSEF 'PEPI' BICAN

Country: Austria, Czechoslovakia
Born: September 25, 1913
Position: Centre-forward
Clubs: Hertha Vienna, Rapid Vienna, Admira, Slavia Prague, Vitkovice, Dynamo Prague

Josef Bican was born in Vienna to Czech parents and grew up to be a free-scoring centre-forward for both Austria and Czechoslovakia. He was elevated into Austria's 'Wunderteam' after

playing with Rapid Vienna. He played 19 times for Austria including the 1934 World Cup semi-final. Bican then moved to Prague and went on to score 14 international goals in 17 appearances for Czechoslovakia but he missed out on playing at the 1938 World Cup because of a clerical error over his citizenship.

OLIVER BIERHOFF

Country: Germany
Born: May 1, 1968
Position: Forward
Clubs: Bayer Uerdingen, Hamburg, Borussia Mönchengladbach, Casino Salzburg, Ascoli, Udinese, AC Milan, Monaco, Chievo

A prolific striker for both club and country, Oliver Bierhoff often confounded his critics. A brilliant header of the ball, he consistently added to his game and eventually reached the heights of Italy's Serie A, where he forged a reputation as a lethal finisher. Born in Karlsruhe, Bierhoff struggled to shine in the German Bundesliga before resurrecting his career in Austria with Casino Salzburg. A loan move to Italy took him to Ascoli, where he stayed for four years, three of which were spent in Serie B. He moved on to Udinese in 1995 and became top scorer in the Italian league with 27 goals in 1998, earning a transfer to AC Milan, where he won the Serie A title in 1999.

He won 70 caps for Germany, scoring 37 goals, and is best remembered for his 'golden goal' at Wembley in the final of the 1996 European Championship, the first such sudden death decider in a major tournament. He is also remembered for a six-minute hat-trick against Northern Ireland. He retired from international football after spending much of the 2002 World Cup on the bench, playing just 81 minutes. He ended his career at Chievo in May 2003.

FRANZ 'BIMBO' BINDER

Country: Austria, Germany
Born: December 1, 1911
Position: Centre-forward/Inside-left
Clubs: St Polten, Rapid Vienna

Franz 'Bimbo' Binder is credited as being the first European player to score a thousand goals in his career with clubs St Polten and Rapid Vienna, as well playing internationally for Austria (20 times) and Germany (9 times). Binder is purported to have scored 1,006 goals in 756 games before hanging up his boots in 1950, when he turned to management with Rapid Vienna. He later took charge of Austria's national team. He was certainly the greatest Austrian player of the 1930s, gaining success with Rapid both in the Austrian league and, after the Anschluss of 1938, the Greater Germany championship.

LAURENT BLANC

Country: France
Born: November 19, 1965
Position: Defender
Clubs: Montpellier, Napoli, Nimes, Saint-Etienne, Auxerre, Barcelona, Marseille, Inter Milan, Manchester United

A graceful defender, Laurent Blanc began as an attacking midfielder but converted to defence early in his career. He enjoyed a nomadic time, switching regularly from one club and league to another and winning few trophies, but made his name at international level playing for France for more than a decade. He impressed at three European Championships, particularly in 2000 when France emerged as winners, and he starred at the 1998 World Cup but missed the final through suspension. Confident on the ball and a calming influence in the team, he won 97 caps and scored 16 goals in becoming one of France's greatest players. He may have

retired from international football in September 2000, but he signed for Manchester United the following year and won the English Premier League in 2003, his final season as a player.

DANNY BLANCHFLOWER

Country: Northern Ireland
Born: February 10, 1926
Position: Half-back
Clubs: Glentoran, Barnsley, Aston Villa, Tottenham Hotspur

Having started his career at the end of World War II with Belfast side Glentoran, Robert Dennis Blanchflower signed for Barnsley for £6,000 in 1949, but his annoyance at the Yorkshire club's lack of ambition prompted a £15,000 move to Aston Villa in 1951. He made 155 appearances for Villa, but he was unhappy at a training regime that focused on physical exercise rather than ball work, and it was at Tottenham where Blanchflower emerged as one of the most astute defenders of his generation. When Arsenal pulled out of a proposed transfer in 1954, the White Hart Lane club stepped in to sign Blanchflower for £30,000 – then a record fee for a half-back.

His outspoken ways did not go down well initially, but the appointment of Bill Nicholson as manager in 1958 proved to be a defining moment in the Irishman's career. He was the manager's voice on the pitch, while his cultured yet steadfast defending became the foundation on which the club's 1961 'double' success was built. Twice voted Footballer Of The Year, he also skippered Tottenham to FA Cup success in 1962 and the European Cup Winners' Cup in 1963.

Between 1949 and 1963 he made 56 appearances for Northern Ireland, often alongside his brother Jackie. He captained his country to the quarter-finals of the World Cup in 1958. He died in December 1993.

OLEG BLOKHIN

Country: Soviet Union
Born: November 5, 1952
Position: Centre-forward
Clubs: Dynamo Kiev, Vorwärts Steyr, Aris Limassol

Oleg Blokhin was one of the quickest players to play the game, a claim that becomes all the more creditable when it is revealed that his personal trainer was Olympic sprint champion Valeri Borzov. However, he did not become the Soviet Union's most-capped player through pace alone, and after moving inside from the left-wing to centre-forward, Blokhin became a reliable and prolific goalscorer. His 39 goals in 101 international appearances is a national record and he was crowned European Footballer Of The Year in 1975 for leading Dynamo Kiev to their European Cup Winners' Cup triumph.

As a reward for his services to Soviet football Blokhin was allowed to move to Western Europe and he played out the rest of his career with Vorwärts Steyr in Austria. He later coached the Ukrainian national team and in 2002 was elected as an MP for the Ukraine parliament.

STEVE BLOOMER

Country: England
Born: January 20, 1874
Position: Centre-forward/Inside-right
Clubs: Derby County, Middlesbrough

Steve Bloomer was a Victorian football superstar. His image was used to sell products as diverse as football boots and tonics. The reason was his prolific goalscoring prowess: between 1892 and 1914 he scored a staggering 352 league goals in 598 games. He also had a phenomenal record for his country, netting 28 goals in 23 games, a record that stood until the 1950s. He helped England to six British Championships.

After retiring from the game in 1914 he took a coaching job in Germany but was interned at the beginning of World War 1.

ZBIGNIEW BONIEK

Country: Poland
Born: March 3, 1956
Position: Forward
Clubs: Widzew Lodz, Juventus, Roma

Zbigniew Boniek made his name in Poland's magnificent team that played at the 1978, 1982 and 1986 World Cups. Although he missed the crucial semi-final against Italy through suspension in 1982, he picked up a bronze medal after Poland beat France in the third place play-off game. After the tournament he was snapped-up by Juventus and featured in a star-studded team alongside Michel Platini and Paolo Rossi. With Juventus Boniek won both the European Cup Winners' Cup in 1984, scoring the winner against Porto in the final, and the European Cup in 1985. He also won a number of Italian domestic trophies with Juventus and Roma. He scored 24 goals in 80 appearances for Poland.

JEAN-MARC BOSMAN

Country: Belgium
Born: October 30, 1964
Position: Midfielder
Clubs: Standard Liege, FC Liege

The Belgian midfielder won't be remembered for his skills as a journeyman footballer, but rather the court ruling which bears his name. In December 1995 the European Court of Justice found in Bosman's favour in a case he had brought against his former club FC Liege. In 1990, Liege had prevented Bosman from joining French club Dunkirk, despite the fact his contract with them had expired and their new offer to him demanded he take a pay cut.

The 'Bosman ruling', as it quickly became known, allowed professional players within the European Union to move freely to another club at the end of their term of contract with their current team. Despite his win in court, Bosman reaped none of the rewards that the ruling should have made his. Instead he finished his playing days in the Belgian fourth division, eventually retiring from the game aged 31.

JÓZSEF BÓZSIK

Country: Hungary
Born: September 28, 1929
Position: Right-half
Club: Kispest/Honvéd

József Bózsik was a member of the 'Magical Magyars' side that inflicted a humiliating 6-3 defeat on England at Wembley in 1953. One of the goals was a stunning 30-yard effort from Bózsik. His 15-year international career began with a debut in the 9-0 thrashing of Bulgaria in August 1947 and ended with his 101st appearance in April 1962, a 1-1 draw with Uruguay in which he scored. In that period, Bózsik went to two World Cups with Hungary and made an appearance in the final against West Germany in 1954. He also won a gold medal at the Olympic Games in 1952. At club level he was a star player alongside his childhood friend Ferenc Puskás at Kispest (later Honvéd).

LIAM BRADY

Country: Republic Of Ireland
Born: February 13, 1956
Position: Midfielder
Clubs: Arsenal, Juventus, Sampdoria, Inter Milan, Ascoli, West Ham United

In an era where cultured footballers at Arsenal had become a rarity, Brady's ball skills and sweet left foot made him shine like a beacon. Given the nickname 'Chippy', for his love of fast food rather than his football ability, he made his debut in 1973 for a team in transition. As The Gunners

Below: Liam Brady on the ball for the Republic Of Ireland.

Above: West Germany's Andreas Brehme celebrates scoring in the 1990 World Cup semi-final.

continually struggled in the lower reaches of Division One, the Irish international's skilful performances were worthy of a higher stage – his swirling 25-yard effort against Tottenham in 1978 remains one of Arsenal's greatest goals.

Despite the team's inconsistencies, Arsenal did reach three successive FA Cup finals and it was following the 1980 defeat to West Ham that Brady decided to try his luck abroad. His emphatic performances against Juventus in the European Cup Winners' Cup that season (Arsenal lost the final to Valencia on penalties) made him a target for the Italian giants and it was no surprise when he moved to Turin for £600,000 that summer.

Brady's skills were custom-made for life in Serie A, and as a fundamental component of Giovanni Trapattoni's side he helped Juventus to successive Scudetto titles. Shockwaves were created when he was then sold to make way for Michel Platini, and following two seasons at Sampdoria and spells at Inter and Ascoli, he ended his career back in England. He played 89 games in three seasons for West Ham before retiring in 1990.

RAYMOND BRAINE

Country: Belgium
Born: April 28, 1907
Position: Centre-forward
Clubs: Beerschot, Sparta Prague, Vorst

One of Belgium's greatest-ever players, Braine won the Belgian championship four times with Beerschot in the 1920s. In 1931 he was suspended by the Belgian FA having violated the country's strict amateur rules. Sparta Prague,

under Englishman Harry Dick, signed Braine as a professional, where he was a huge hit to the extent that the Czech authorities tried to convince him to become a Czech citizen so he could play in the 1934 World Cup. The Belgium FA relented their suspension and he played for his native country in the 1938 tournament. Including Olympic appearances, Braine gained 54 caps over 14 years and scored 26 goals.

ANDREAS BREHME

Country: West Germany & Germany
Born: November 9, 1960
Position: Left-back
Clubs: Kaiserslautern, Bayern Munich, Inter Milan, Real Zaragoza

Andreas Brehme started and finished his career at Kaiserslautern but was most famous for winning the 1990 World Cup for West Germany, putting an end to one of the most disappointing finals of all time. West Germany were making hard work of beating an ill-disciplined Argentina side when Brehme converted an 85th minute penalty to win the game 1-0. That was a richly deserved personal triumph for Brehme, who was acknowledged as one of the world's best left-backs during the Eighties and Nineties.

Typically German in style, Brehme was all about determination, strength, endeavour and uncompromising tackling, though in the German tradition he was always willing to thunder forward too. Comfortably two-footed, he was well known for taking most penalties with his right foot and taking free kicks and corners with his left foot, believing his right foot to be more accurate while his left was harder.

He had a successful club career, notably with Inter Milan. Along with Lothar Matthäus and Jurgen Klinsmann, Brehme was one of a trio of high-profile German internationals in the Inter Milan side which won the 1989 Serie A title and 1991 UEFA Cup.

PAUL BREITNER

Country: West Germany
Born: September 5, 1951
Position: Left-back
Clubs: Bayern Munich, Real Madrid, Eintracht Braunschweig

Nicknamed 'Der Afro' for his distinctive curly hairstyle, Paul Breitner won everything there was to win in the game. A member of the all-conquering West Germany team of the 1970s, he enjoyed success in the 1972 European Championship and two years later added a World Cup winners' medal to his collection. The 1974 tournament saw left-back Breitner offering attacking flair to West Germany's play. He converted the penalty in the final against Holland that put the Germans back in

contention. The same year also saw 'Der Afro' claim the European Cup with Bayern Munich, and seal a move to Real Madrid. A falling out with the national coaching staff saw him miss the 1978 World Cup, but he returned in 1982 and again scored in the final.

BILLY BREMNER

Country: Scotland
Born: December 9, 1942
Position: Midfielder
Clubs: Leeds United, Hull City, Doncaster Rovers

Billy Bremner was Leeds United's midfield general during the club's glory years of the 1960s and 1970s and the perfect leader for Don Revie's ruthlessly single-minded side. He signed for Leeds as a 15-year-old and broke into the first team during the 1959-60 season. They were relegated that year, but returned to Division One in 1964 with a formidable team – and Bremner was the heartbeat of it.

By the time he left Leeds in September 1976 he had won the league title and the Fairs Cup twice each, plus an FA Cup, a League Cup, and he had narrowly missed out on so much more – Leeds were title runners-up five times, beaten FA Cup finalists three times, and European Cup runners-up once. The winner of 54 Scotland caps, Bremner's fiery temper was never far from the surface and his career was littered with controversial flashpoints, most famously in the 1974 Charity Shield when he squared up to Liverpool's Kevin Keegan, resulting in both players being sent-off. However, incidents like that did not detract from the fact that Bremner was a supremely talented footballer.

He later managed Leeds for a spell in the 1980s and he was hugely mourned by the club's fans when he died of a heart attack in 1997.

EMILIO BUTRAGUEÑO

Country: Spain
Born: July 22, 1963
Position: Centre-forward
Clubs: Castilla, Real Madrid, Celaya

Throughout the Eighties and Nineties defences lived in fear of 'The Vulture'. That was Butragueño's nickname and he lived up to it well. Save for a final hurrah at Mexican club Celaya, Butragueño spent his career at Real Madrid, where his avalanche of goals brought trophies galore. Graduating from Real's youth ranks and the club's second team, Castilla, Emilio established himself as a penalty box poacher, inspiring Madrid to consecutive UEFA Cups in 1985 and 1986. He is best remembered for an extraordinary four-goal display for Spain against Denmark at the 1986 World Cup. He was a Real legend by the time he left in 1995 and he also served as vice-president at the club.

KALUSHA BWALYA

Country: Zambia
Born: August 16, 1963
Position: Midfielder
Clubs: Mufulira Blackpool, Mufulira Wanderers, Cercle Brugge, PSV Eindhoven, América, Necaxa, Leon, Al Wahda, Irapuato, Vera Cruz, Correcaminos

Kalusha Bwalya, a player of exciting promise with enthralling dribbling skills and a powerful shot, was the star of Zambian football. He initially came to prominence at the African Nations Cup in 1986, but it was a sensational performance at the 1988 Olympics – his hat-trick inspiring Zambia to a shock 4-0 thrashing of Italy – that made his name. By then he had been transferred to Belgian club Cercle Brugge. Not surprisingly that year he was also voted Zambian Player Of The Year and African Player Of The Year.

CAFU

Country: Brazil
Born: June 7, 1970
Position: Right-back
Clubs: São Paulo, Juventude, Real Zaragoza, Palmeiras, Roma, AC Milan

Better known as Cafu, Marcos Evangelista de Moraes was the first person to play in the final of three World Cups and ended up a winner twice, in 1994 and 2002. He first gained success with São Paulo in the Copa Libertadores in 1992 and 1993, and went on to win the UEFA Cup with Real Zaragoza in 1995. He won the Serie A title with Roma in 2001 and AC Milan in 2004, and he played in the 2005 European Champions League Final for Milan, losing out to Liverpool on penalties.

He earned his first cap against Spain in September 1990 but was just a bit-part player in the international team through the early Nineties, only playing in the 1994 World Cup Final as a substitute for Jorginho, coming onto the pitch in the 21st minute. The final was one of three appearances he made at the tournament, all of them from the bench.

An attacking wing-back in the Brazil side that lost to France in the 1998 World Cup Final, for much of his international career he was to Brazil's right flank what Roberto Carlos was to the left. He missed only the semi-final on his way to a runners-up medal and he was appointed team captain soon afterwards. During qualification for the 2002 tournament he was stripped of the armband, only regaining it after a late injury ruled Emerson out of the World Cup squad. He led Brazil through a successful campaign and as he raised the trophy after victory in the final he shouted a message to his wife, 'Regina, I love you'.

At 36 years of age he was still captain of the misfiring Brazil team defeated by France in the quarter-finals in Germany four years later. Despite protestations that he was interested in continuing on until the 2010 World Cup, his last international game was played at the 2006

finals. Retiring in 2008, he is now regarded as Brazil's greatest ever right-back and after 143 international appearances, he is his country's most capped player.

Above: Brazil captain Cafu lifts the World Cup trophy in 2002.

ERIC CANTONA

Country: France
Born: May 24, 1966
Position: Striker
Clubs: Martigues, Auxerre, Marseille, Bordeaux, Montpellier, Nimes, Leeds United, Manchester United

Eric Cantona became a legend in English football for helping Manchester United to win a first league title for 26 years. He began his career at Auxerre and became the most expensive player in France when he joined hometown club Marseille for £2.2 million in 1988. A gifted but temperamental striker, he struggled to make an impact in France despite winning the French Cup at Montpellier, and his career came to life only when he moved to England at the age of 25.

At Leeds United he inspired the team to the league title in 1992, before controversially joining rivals Manchester United, much to the consternation of the fans at Elland Road. His skill and leadership lifted Manchester United back to the top of the English game as he claimed four more league titles, two FA Cups and the PFA Player Of The Year Award, but he was unable to inspire them to a Champions League triumph.

His biggest headlines were made when he leapt studs first into the crowd to attack a fan who had abused him from the terraces. He made just 45 appearances for his country, scoring 20 goals. He retired from the game in 1997.

ANTONIO CARBAJAL

Country: Mexico
Born: June 7, 1929
Position: Goalkeeper
Clubs: Espana, Leon

Antonio Carbajal was awarded FIFA's gold award for services to football, recognising his achievement as a player and coach. He carved out his legendary status by becoming the first player to appear in five World Cups, playing in each tournament between 1950 and 1966. He was only once on the winning side, against Czechoslovakia in 1962. In the same game he conceded the then quickest goal in World Cup history, after just 15 seconds. He gained his first and only clean sheet at the finals in his 11th and last World Cup appearance. He had made his international debut at the 1948 Olympics.

CARECA

Country: Brazil
Born: October 5, 1960
Position: Centre-forward
Clubs: Guarani, São Paulo, Napoli, Kashiwa Reysol

Adored equally in Brazil and Naples, Careca was one of the main supporting players in the Diego Maradona era that brought such unprecedented success to the Italian club. He forged his name at unfashionable Guarani, helping the club to the Brazilian championship. Careca's powerful shot and pace constantly unnerved defenders, but injury denied him a place in the 1982 World Cup. He made amends in both 1986 and 1990, scoring seven goals in nine games. He teamed up with Maradona and compatriot Alemao at Napoli in 1987 for his greatest years, winning the Italian league title and the UEFA Cup.

CARLOS ALBERTO

Country: Brazil
Born: July 17, 1944
Position: Defender
Clubs: Fluminense, Santos, Flamengo, New York Cosmos, California Surf

The career of Carlos Alberto Torres can be summed up in one sublime moment – the goal he scored in the 1970 World Cup Final

for Brazil against Italy. Charging onto a pass from Pelé 25 yards out, the right-back – and team captain – hammered the ball past hapless Italian goalkeeper Enrico Albertosi, proving the Brazilians had power to match their silky skills. His goal came four minutes from time and sealed a 4-1 victory for Brazil.

At club level, he won league titles in both Brazil (in his second spell with Fluminense) and in the USA (playing with Pelé at New York Cosmos). He moved into coaching in the early 1980s, bossing clubs in Brazil (including Flamengo and Fluminense) and Egypt (Zamalek), as well as the Azerbaijan national team.

JAN CEULEMANS

Country: Belgium
Born: February 28, 1957
Position: Centre-forward/Midfielder
Clubs: Lierse, Club Brugge

Arguably the greatest player that Belgium has produced, Jan Ceulemans had an impressive international career that spanned almost 14 years and saw him score 23 goals in 96 games for his country. For a nation of its size, Belgium overachieved on the world stage throughout the 1980s, and Ceulemans was the team's driving force. Peaking in fourth place at the Mexico World Cup of 1986, Belgium lost out in the semi-finals to the eventual winners, Argentina.

Ceulemans resisted the lure of the more wealthy leagues, and appeared happy to stay in his native country despite being courted by some of Europe's top clubs – most notably AC Milan, who were reportedly close to signing him at one point. He was the Belgian league's record signing when he moved from Lierse to Brugge in 1978 for £250,000.

JOHN CHARLES

Country: Wales
Born: December 27, 1931
Position: Centre-forward/Centre-half
Clubs: Leeds United, Juventus, Roma, Cardiff City, Hereford

Charles started his career as an apprentice with local club Swansea City aged 15 years old, before a lack of playing opportunities forced him to sign for Leeds United in 1949. It was at Elland Road that Charles made his name, making 297 league appearances before signing for Juventus for a world record transfer fee of £67,000 in 1957. He became Britain's most successful European export and in his first season in Turin he scored an incredible 29 goals. He helped Juve to three titles in five years, scoring 93 goals in 150 games. Nicknamed 'Il Buono Gigante' ('the Gentle Giant') he was later voted the best foreign player to represent the club during a fan poll in 1997.

John Charles was a strong centre-forward who was equally proficient at centre-back. It has been said that the legendary Nat Lofthouse was once asked to name the best centre-half that he had played against and he answered 'John Charles'. The same week Billy Wright was asked to name the greatest centre-forward he had faced, and he too answered 'John Charles'. He was part of the Wales side that reached the 1958 World Cup quarter-final, but injury ruled him out of the decisive game with Brazil that saw them knocked out of the competition.

After five years in Italy, in 1962 Charles returned to a Leeds side managed by Don Revie. He found it difficult to adjust and after 91 days he was back in Italy, this time with Roma. He scored on his debut against Bologna but soon returned home to Cardiff City for £20,000.

Right: John Charles scores for Wales against England at Wembley in 1954.

BOBBY CHARLTON

Country: England
Born: October 11, 1937
Position: Inside left/Outside-left/Centre-forward
Clubs: Manchester United, Preston North End

'There has never been a more popular footballer,' remarked former Manchester United manager Sir Matt Busby of Bobby Charlton. 'He was as near perfection as man and player as it is possible to be.' Certainly Charlton had his fans as part of a rejuvenated Manchester United side and an England World Cup-winning team in the 1960s (Jimmy Hill once claimed that at the peak of his powers Charlton was the most famous living Englishman), but fate so nearly cut short a wonderful career at an early age.

On February 8, 1958, Charlton was caught up in the Munich air disaster that killed eight of the 'Busby Babes' – a name given to Sir Matt Busby's Manchester United side because of their youth. Charlton was thrown 40 yards from the wreckage as the plane skidded across the runway and ploughed into the airport's perimeter fence. He escaped with a head wound but it so easily could have been worse: 23 people died in the crash, including the exciting United player Duncan Edwards.

Charlton recovered to make it to the FA Cup final just a few months later and despite the growing clamour for him to be selected for the starting line-up of England's team for the World Cup in Sweden, he was happy with his role as a non-playing squad member.

At club level, Charlton had impressed early on, scoring ten goals in his first 14 games and he became central to Busby's plans. With his quick thinking, powerful shooting and dipping, fizzing crosses, Charlton was used to devastating effect by Busby, first as an inside-forward, then as a left-winger and centre-forward, and later in central midfield. He helped United to FA Cup victory in 1963,

and two league titles in 1965 and 1967, as well as a famous European Cup victory in 1968, beating Benfica 4-1 in the final at Wembley.

He was equally explosive for England. Geoff Hurst might have stolen the headlines after his World Cup winning hat-trick in 1966, but it was Charlton who steered England to the final, kickstarting the campaign with a dazzling goal against Mexico. Running 30 yards from midfield, he blasted a drive from outside the penalty area that flew into the net, helping England to a 2-0 win. It was one of the more spectacular efforts of his 49 goals scored in an England shirt, a record that still stands. England swept aside France, Argentina, Portugal, and West Germany to become world champions in a year that Charlton was voted Footballer Of The Year, European Footballer Of The Year and Player Of The World Cup.

After a disappointing World Cup in 1970, when Charlton was controversially substituted during England's defeat to West Germany, he played out his final years at United before retiring in 1973 (on the same day as his brother, Leeds United's Jack Charlton). He turned out for Preston as player/manager the following season, but after one year in charge he decided that management was not for him.

Above: The young Manchester United star Bobby Charlton in his 1957 FA Cup final shirt. Below: Keeping a watchful eye on Brazil's Clodoaldo at the 1970 World Cup Finals.

1956: Scores twice on his debut for United and wins first league title at the end of the 1956-7 season.

1958: Survives Munich air disaster, then scores on England debut against Scotland.

1963: Manchester United win FA Cup final against Leicester.

1965: Wins his second league title with Manchester United

1966: Inspires England to World Cup victory and is voted European Footballer Of The Year.

1967: Wins the championship with United again

1968: Scores twice in United's European Cup final victory over Benfica at Wembley.

1970: Plays last game for England, substituted in 3-2 defeat by West Germany in the World Cup.

1973: Leaves Manchester United to manage Preston North End.

1984: Returns to Manchester United to take up a place on the board.

1994: Receives a knighthood from the Queen in her Birthday Honours List.

Above: Benfica's Mario Coluna talks to former Manchester United star Charlie Mitten in 1962. His team-mate Eusébio eyes the camera.

HECTOR CHUMPITAZ

Country: Peru
Born: April 12, 1944
Position: Centre-back
Clubs: Unidad Vecinal, Deportivo Municipal, Universitario, Atlas, Sporting Cristal

Hector Chumpitaz was, for much of his international career, Peru's inspirational captain and defensive rock, making 105 appearances for his country. He made his debut for Peru in 1965 and went on to appear in two World Cups, in 1970 and 1978. The latter was the most significant as the 34-year-old helped Peru through to the second phase. Three years earlier he had been a part of Peru's Copa América-winning team in Colombia.

He was nicknamed 'El Capitán de America' after captaining the continent's team against a star-studded European representative side in 1973. For almost a decade he played for Universitario in the Peruvian league and he finished his career in 1984 with Sporting Cristal.

CLODOALDO

Country: Brazil
Born: September 26, 1949
Position: Midfielder
Clubs: Santos, Tampa Bay Rowdies, Nacional

Clodoaldo played in every game of Brazil's successful 1970 World Cup campaign at the age of just 20. He scored the equaliser in the 3-1 semi-final win over Uruguay, launching their comeback for victory. A defensive midfielder, he was the baby of Mario Zagalo's team and provided a platform for the likes of Jairzinho and Rivelino to launch attacks. Despite the rock-like security he supplied, he made an uncharacteristic error that allowed Italy to equalise in the final. Injury ruled him out of the tournament four

years later and he never played at a World Cup again. At club level, Clodoaldo spent the majority of his career at Santos, making over 500 first-team appearances and winning the Paulista state championship five times between 1967 and 1978.

MARIO COLUNA

Country: Portugal
Born: August 6, 1935
Position: Centre-forward/Inside-right/Left-half
Clubs: Marques, Benfica, Lyon

Mario Esteves Coluna was a member of the great Benfica side of the 1950s and 1960s. He began as a lethal striker, but after the arrival of Eusébio he turned into a formidable midfielder. Born in Mozambique, Coluna played 57 times for Portugal and he captained the side that reached the 1966 World Cup semi-finals. His greatest achievements were with Benfica, winning 19 honours and scoring in the 1961 and 1962 European Cup Final victories over Barcelona and Real Madrid, as well as making three other European Cup final appearances in 1963, 1965 and 1968. Coluna also played in Mozambique with Marques and later became the country's Sports Minister.

GIANPIERO COMBI

Country: Italy
Born: November 20, 1902
Position: Goalkeeper
Club: Juventus

Gianpiero Combi was the first of the truly great Italian goalkeepers and he captained Italy to triumph in the 1934 World Cup Final. He had only been talked out of retirement prior to the tournament to add some experience to the squad and he actually started the World Cup as reserve keeper. The final was Combi's 47th and last appearance for his country, a career that had started dauntingly ten years earlier with a 7-1 defeat by Hungary.

He retired from club football in 1934, going out on a high with Juventus after winning a fourth successive Italian league title. Combi also won a bronze medal at the 1928 Amsterdam Olympics when Italy finished third, beating Egypt 11-3 in the third place play-off game.

RUI COSTA

Country: Portugal
Born: March 29, 1972
Position: Midfielder
Clubs: Fafe, Benfica, Fiorentina, AC Milan

On his day a brilliant playmaker, Rui Costa was a member of Portugal's 'Golden Generation' that won the 1989 Under-16 World Cup and 1991 Under-20 World Cup. His passing and

creativity saw him play for some of Europe's top clubs and two years after AC Milan paid £28 million for him in 2001 he picked up a Champions League winners' medal.

In his homeland many believed him more vital to the national side than Luis Figo. Able to score spectacular goals, injury hampered his career and inconsistency was his only weakness. He had an outstanding Euro 2000, but was disappointing at the 2002 World Cup when not fully fit. He retired from international football after defeat in the Euro 2004 final and decided to play the final two seasons of his career at Benfica, finally hanging up his boots in May 2008 and continuing at the club as Director Of Football.

ALESSANDRO COSTACURTA

Country: Italy
Born: April 24, 1966
Position: Defender
Clubs: Monza, AC Milan

If success is measured by the number of medals a player has won then this imposing Italian defender was one of the most successful footballers of recent times. In over 20 years with Milan his haul of silverware included seven Serie A titles, four European Cups (1989, 1990, 1994 and 2003) and two European Super Cups. Indeed, his career's only major disappointments both came in 1994 when suspensions ruled him out of the World Cup final and the Champions League final.

He did not make his debut for Italy until 1991 (aged 25) but went on to play 59 times. Before retiring from international football in 1998, Costacurta had played for Italy at Euro 96 and in two World Cups (1994 and 1998).

JOHAN CRUYFF

Country: Holland
Born: April 25, 1947
Position: Forward
Clubs: Ajax, Barcelona, Los Angeles Aztecs, Washington Diplomats, Levante, Ajax, Feyenoord

Hugely talented, wilful and unpredictable, Johan Cruyff symbolised the golden era of Dutch football and remains inextricably linked with the concept of 'Total Football'. Brought up just around the corner from Ajax's ground, where his mother was a cleaner, Cruyff joined the club in 1959 and made his debut on November 1964, aged 17, scoring the only Ajax goal in a 3-1 defeat to Groningen. With the arrival of Rinus Michels, the architect of 'Total Football', the club accelerated into the modern era with breathtaking style.

Lightweight but blessed with superb balance and huge stamina, Cruyff could cover acres of space and dictate the play. Ajax won five league titles in his first spell with the club but it was

three consecutive European Cup triumphs between 1971 and 1973 that helped define the legend of the 'Flying Dutchman', resulting in a hat-trick of European Footballer Of The Year awards. Scoring both of his side's goals in the 2-0 win over Inter Milan in 1972 capped one of his finest performances.

Making his first international appearance on September 7, 1966, Cruyff scored on his debut in a 2-2 draw with Hungary. He also became the first Dutchman to be dismissed in an international two months later. By the time of the 1974 World Cup he was captain and the Dutch team had gone from perennial outsiders to hot favourites. Cruyff played in a custom-made Dutch strip with two stripes on his sleeve, rather than the three stripes worn by his team-mates, insisting that as he was sponsored by a rival company he would not wear a shirt with the famous Adidas branding. He orchestrated play with teasing skills and dazzling surges, unveiling the celebrated 'Cruyff turn' to the watching millions. The shift in the balance of power was vividly demonstrated when the Dutch beat a physical Brazil 2-0 in a game notable for a sublime volley from the captain.

Losing the final to West Germany did nothing to diminish Cruyff's stature, even though he was shackled by Berti Vogts during its most crucial phase. By the summer of 1974 he had moved to Barcelona for a record fee of £922,300. The Catalan side were struggling but Cruyff scored twice on his debut and led them to their first championship since 1960.

In 1978 he refused to join the Dutch World Cup squad, although it would be 30 years before he revealed that this was a consequence of a gunpoint kidnap attempt on his family in Barcelona in 1977. Unprepared to leave his family he quit international football, having won 48 caps and scored 33 goals. He soon announced his retirement and planned to go into business. However, he returned to playing football in the North American Soccer League a year later.

He eventually rejoined Ajax in December 1981, taking them to two more championships, but his swansong came with bitter rivals Feyenoord, whom he guided to a league and cup double in 1984. In his last season, at 37, he was awarded the Golden Shoe as Dutch Player Of The Year.

Cruyff went into coaching with Ajax, in 1985 winning a European Cup Winners' Cup, but he quit three years later after another dispute. In May 1988 he took over at Barcelona, guiding the club to four consecutive league titles between 1991 and 1994. He brought them the European Cup for the first time in 1992, but four years later he was sacked after falling out with his chairman. Although often linked with managerial vacancies, he never coached again.

TEÓFILO CUBILLAS

Country: Peru
Born: March 8, 1949
Position: Midfielder
Clubs: Alianza Lima, Basel, Porto, South Florida Sun, Fort Lauderdale Strikers, Miami Sharks

Easily Peru's greatest ever player, at just 21 years old Teófilo Cubillas was the third highest goalscorer at the 1970 World Cup Finals, behind Gerd Müller and Jairzinho. He starred again in 1978 when he shot down Scotland's World Cup hopes with two goals in a surprise 3-1 win. He went on to score a hat-trick against Iran, taking his tally in the World Cup to ten, although he failed to add to this at the finals of 1982.

He was named South American Footballer Of The Year in 1972 and helped Peru to the 1975 Copa América. In contrast to his very impressive international achievements – 81 caps and 26 goals – his club career was modest, but he eventually became Peruvian Minister for Sport.

ZOLTÁN CZIBOR

Country: Hungary
Born: August 23, 1929
Position: Left-winger
Clubs: Komarom, Ferencváros, Csepel, Honvéd, Roma, Barcelona, Espanyol, Basel, Austria Vienna

Zoltán Czibor was the talented left-footer who supplied much of the ammunition for the great Hungarian forward line of Puskás and Kocsis in the 1950s. Between 1949 and 1956 he played 42 times for the 'Magical Magyars' and scored 17 goals. Having won Olympic gold in 1952, Czibor's talents helped Hungary to the World Cup final in 1954. He was outstanding in the 4-2 semi-final success over Uruguay, but the Hungarians surrendered a two-goal lead to lose the final to West Germany. At the time of the Hungarian revolution in 1956, Czibor – like Puskás and Kocsis – took advantage of a Honvéd tour to settle in Spain, where he was to win back-to-back league titles with Barcelona

ALI DAEI

Country: Iran
Born: March 21, 1969
Position: Forward
Clubs: Esteghlal Ardabil, Taxirani, Bank Tejarat, Persepolis, Al-Sadd, Arminia Bielefeld, Bayern Munich, Hertha Berlin, Al-Shabab, Persepolis, Saba Battery, Saipa

Ali Daei was one of Iran's most popular and famous players. He was the first Iranian (along with Karim Bagheri) to play professional football in Europe. In 1998, after he was dropped from the national team for criticising tactics, fans organised a poll calling for (and getting) his reinstatement. Daei made his international debut in June 1993 against Oman and went on to become one of Asia's most dangerous strikers, forming an excellent partnership with Khodadad Azizi. In 1996 he scored 22 goals for his country, including eight at the Asian Cup. He was voted the 1999 Asian Player Of The Year and became the first player to score 100 international goals.

KENNY DALGLISH

Country: Scotland
Born: March 4, 1951
Position: Centre-forward
Clubs: Celtic, Liverpool

Alan Shearer tells a story about trying to mark his then manager at Newcastle in a practice game. Dalglish kept spinning off him and racing away with the ball. 'How did you know where I was?' Shearer asked. 'I could see your shadow,' was the reply from his boss. With a football at his feet Kenny Dalglish had the instincts of a gunslinger. Possessed of quickfire reflexes, an acute awareness of opponents and team-mates, exquisite touch, and the ability to shield the ball

Above: Everton's Dixie Dean (right) is introduced to legendary Spanish keeper Zamora in 1931.

seemingly forever, Dalglish ranks among the finest players that Scotland has ever produced.

He joined Celtic as a junior in 1967 and might have gone straight to Liverpool at 15 but for a failed trial. Instead Celtic farmed him out to Cumbernauld to toughen him up. Jock Stein's Celtic were a top European side and although he made his league debut against Raith Rovers on October 4, 1969, it took time to establish himself in the first team. However, he went on to make 204 league appearances for the club, scoring 112 goals and wining four league championships and four Scottish Cups.

In August 1977 he made the move to Liverpool for a British record fee of £440,000. Signed to replace the departing Kevin Keegan, Dalglish won the European Cup in his first season. The trophies continued to come: three European Cups in total, six league titles between 1978 and 1986 (the last as player-manager), and two Footballer Of The Year awards.

Dalglish also played for Scotland at every level, making his debut as a substitute against Belgium on November 10, 1971. He was part of the 1974 Scotland World Cup squad, but despite not losing at the tournament, and holding Brazil to a draw, they crashed out on goal difference.

In Argentina four years later Dalglish opened the scoring against Holland in the superb 3-2 win, but the team were again on a plane home after the first round. No matter how Scotland performed in the World Cup, the 'Tartan Army' still idolised Dalglish just for scoring in the 1977 victory over England at Wembley.

He travelled to a third World Cup in 1982, and scored in the opening game against New Zealand, and would have appeared at a fourth tournament under Alex Ferguson but for injury. He made his last international appearance against Luxembourg in November 1986, retiring with 102 caps, having equalled Denis Law's scoring record of 30 goals.

In 1985 Dalglish succeeded Joe Fagan when he became the club's player-manager, winning the elusive league and cup 'double' in his first season in charge, and going on to win a total of three league titles as manager of Liverpool. Dalglish conducted himself impeccably through the aftermath of the Hillsborough disaster in 1989, but following on as it did from the deaths at Heysel four years earlier it was a significant added pressure and he quit the club unexpectedly in February 1991.

Eight months later he surprised everyone by

coming out of retirement to manage Blackburn Rovers, taking the dormant club into the Premier League and then to a league championship in 1995. He was unable to repeat the trick when he moved to Newcastle United in February 1997 but still took the club to a first major cup final in 20 years.

WILLIAM 'DIXIE' DEAN

Country: England

Born: 21 January, 1907

Position: Centre-forward

Clubs: Tranmere Rovers, Everton, Notts County

Things could have worked out so differently had William 'Dixie' Dean not recovered from the motorcycle accident that nearly ended his career in 1926. However, just one year on from a 36-hour coma Dean scored twice on his England debut. It was a miraculous rehabilitation.

Dean's career had started promisingly at Tranmere Rovers but it was after his £3000 transfer to Everton in 1925 that Dean earned a reputation as a quick striker with devastating aerial strength. During the 1927-8 season he scored 60 league goals, with a further 22 strikes

Above: Didier Deschamps in action for Juventus. He would lift the World Cup for France just four months later.

in other competitions as Everton went on to take the title. 'People ask me if that 60-goal record will ever be beaten,' he once said. 'I think it will, but there's only one man who will do it and that's the fella who walks on water.'

Dean continued to score regularly at both club and international level, notching a total of 399 goals for Everton and 18 international goals despite only representing England 16 times, but by the time he was transferred to Notts County in 1938 he was past his best. Sadly he passed away in 1980, but the venue was fitting: Goodison Park, while at a game between Everton and Liverpool. Dean had died in his spiritual home.

JIMMY DELANEY

Country: Scotland
Born: September 3, 1914
Position: Outside-right
Clubs: Celtic, Manchester United, Aberdeen, Falkirk, Derry City, Cork Athletic, Elgin City

Jimmy Delaney's career spanned both sides of the Second World War and he made a unique mark on the game by becoming the only player to have won the Scottish Cup, the FA Cup and the Irish Cup. He won the Scottish Cup with Celtic in 1937, beating Aberdeen 2-1 in the final. He also won two league titles with the club. He lifted the FA Cup with Manchester United in 1948 in a thrilling 4-2 win over Blackpool, and in 1954, at the age of 39 and as the Irish league's most expensive player at £1,500, he finally won

the Irish Cup playing for Derry City after two replays with Glentoran. He won 15 caps for Scotland and scored six international goals.

MARCEL DESAILLY

County: France
Born: September 7, 1968
Position: Defender
Clubs: Nantes, Marseille, AC Milan, Chelsea, Al Gharafa

A colossal player for club and country, Marcel Desailly is one of the greatest defenders in the history of the game. He started his career alongside Didier Deschamps at Nantes, moved to Marseille and won the European Cup in 1993, and scored in the final when Milan clinched the trophy the following year. Strong and powerful, he was a midfielder during five years at Milan but always played in defence for his country. He was a key figure as France won the World Cup in 1998, despite being sent-off in the final. He was also part of the team that won Euro 2000.

He became France's most capped player in April 2003 (a record since broken by Lilian Thuram) and retired from international football after Euro 2004. During his time with Chelsea, Desailly became captain and was so solid in defence that he became known as 'The Rock', winning the FA Cup and UEFA Super Cup with the club, leaving in July 2004 to finish his playing career with Al Gharafa in Qatar. He ended the 2005 season as the club's top scorer.

DIDIER DESCHAMPS

Country: France
Born: October 15, 1968
Position: Midfielder
Clubs: Nantes, Marseille, Bordeaux, Juventus, Chelsea, Valencia

A hugely successful footballer, Deschamps started out at Nantes and captained Marseille to a European Cup triumph aged just 24 in 1993 in his second spell at the club. He joined Juventus and became a key figure in the side, winning the European Cup and World Club Cup in 1996, and Italian titles in 1995, 1997 and 1998.

Deschamps captained France to World Cup victory on home soil in 1998 and led the side's triumphant European Championship campaign in 2000 before quitting international football. A prodigious worker, he read the game well and provided a platform for more creative players. He won 103 caps, retiring in 2001.

KAZIMIERZ DEYNA

Country: Poland
Born: October 23, 1947
Position: Midfielder
Clubs: Wlokniarz Starogard Gdanski, LKS Lodz, Legia Warsaw, Manchester City, San Diego Sockers

Kazimierz Deyna was the creative midfield driving force of Poland's greatest ever team during the 1970s. The Legia Warsaw player had shot to prominence at the 1972 Olympics, scoring both goals in the 2-1 victory over Hungary in the final. He went on to captain his country at two successive World Cup tournaments: in 1974 Deyna helped a free-scoring Poland to third place, and in 1978 helped them to the second round group stage. During this period he figured in the top ten of Europe's Footballer Of The Year award on three occasions. He also appeared in the film *Escape To Victory*. He died in a car crash in 1989.

Left: Polish midfielder Kaimierz Deyna wearing the colours of Manchester City.

ALFREDO DI STÉFANO

Country: Argentina, Colombia, Spain

Born: July 4, 1926

Position: Centre-forward

Clubs: River Plate, Huracán, Millonarios, Real Madrid, Espanyol

Born in Argentina of Italian parentage, Alfredo Di Stéfano was just 15 years of age when he joined the famous River Plate side of the 1940s and within a year he had made his debut in a team that included Adolfo Pedernera and Labruna, two of Argentina's greatest ever players. Unable to make an immediate impression in an attack that included such players, he was loaned to Huracán to hone his skills, and some 10 goals in 25 games saw his return following Pedernera's departure.

Back with the club, his impact was immediate and he helped River Plate to win the 1947 championship as he scored 27 goals in 30 games. His elevation to the Argentinian national team was inevitable, and his six goals helped his country retain the Copa América championship that year.

Above: Di Stéfano heads wide for Real against Barcelona at the Bernabéu in 1960. Below left: He scores the first goal in Real's 5-3 away league victory over Barcelona in 1960. Below right: Posing for Espanyol in 1964.

A players strike in 1949, the result of a poor wage structure, led to an exodus of players into the pirate 'Di Mayor' league in Colombia. As this league was outside of the jurisdiction of FIFA, no transfer fees were paid and therefore the clubs could afford to tempt players with higher wages. Alongside Pedernera, Di Stéfano joined Millonarios of Bogota, scoring 88 goals as they won four championships in five seasons. He was twice the league's top scorer.

With his place in the country's football history assured, Di Stéfano went on to represent the Colombian national team, regardless of the fact that he had already played for Argentina. However, with few fixtures arranged he made just four appearances for his adopted nation.

Di Stéfano was regarded as the best player in South America and when he was lured to join Real Madrid in 1953, the opportunity came late in his career. Santiago Bernabéu, president of

the Spanish club, orchestrated the move after the 27-year-old impressed in a friendly between Real and Millonarios. For a while the club was involved in a tug-of-war with Barcelona for his services, but he signed for Madrid for $70,000.

The next ten seasons would see him revered as one of the greatest players on the planet and he became the most popular player in Real's history. His first season delivered the Spanish title, and within three years his opening goal inspired the club to an inaugural European Cup final victory against Stade de Reims. Di Stéfano would score in each of the next four European Cup finals as Real made the trophy their own. The club's second triumph was against Fiorentina and was significant as it capped a tremendous season in which he not only topped the scoring in the competition but also in the Spanish league, where Real reigned supreme. His exploits made him a household

name and it was little surprise when he was voted European Player Of The Year.

It was the fifth European Cup success that highlighted both Di Stéfano's standing in the game and Real's dominance. Having finished the previous campaign as Spain's top scorer for the fourth consecutive season, he led the club to a 7-3 drubbing of Eintracht Frankfurt in the 1960 final. His hat-trick, allied to the four goals of Ferenc Puskás, saw Di Stéfano at his peak, and although he would reach two more finals, his star was on the wane.

He scored 23 goals for Spain in 31 games, but the greatest shame was that despite playing internationally for three countries, he never graced the World Cup. A 3-1 European Cup defeat by Inter Milan in 1964 was his last major game for Real, and although he scored 19 goals in two seasons for Espanyol, a back injury forced him to hang up his boots at 40.

1943 — **1943:** Makes his debut for River Plate at the age of 17.

1947 — **1947:** Copa América winner with Argentina. He gains six caps for his country.

1949

1951 — **1949:** During a strike in Argentina, he moves to Millonarios of Bogota to play in a pirate league. Capped three times by Colombia.

1953: Joins Real Madrid for $70,000.

1953

1955 — **1956:** Wins first of five consecutive European Cups and makes the first of 31 appearances for Spain.

1957 — **1959:** The 'Blond Arrow' is named European Footballer Of The Year for a second time.

1959

1961 — **1960:** Scores a hat-trick in Real's incredible 7-3 defeat of Eintracht Frankfurt in European Cup final.

1963 — **1963:** Kidnapped by the Venezuelan Liberation Front while on tour of the country with Real. He is released unharmed.

1965 — **1964:** Leaves Real to join Espanyol, before retiring to take up coaching.

1971 — **1971:** Guides Valencia to Spanish championship.

1981 — **1981:** He coaches River Plate to Argentine National League title.

1983 — **1983:** Returns to Real Madrid as first team coach.

2000 — **2000:** Appointed Honourary President at Real Madrid.

Above: Manchester United's Duncan Edwards takes to the field in Belgrade in 1958. On the way back from the match he died from injuries sustained in the Munich air disaster at just 21.

DIDI

Country: Brazil
Born: October 8, 1928
Position: Midfielder
Clubs: Americano, Lençoense, Madureiro, Fluminense, Botafogo, Real Madrid, Valencia, Sporting Cristal, São Paulo, Veracruz

Waldyr Pereira, more famously known as Didi, was the inspiration behind Brazil's successive World Cup triumphs of 1958 and 1962. Indeed, Brazil's free-flowing 4-2-4 system owed much to Didi's thoughtful play and extraordinary technique, something that compensated for his lack of pace. He was the first of the great free-kick specialists, scoring 12 of his 31 international goals from dead ball situations. He forged his playing reputation with Fluminense and Botofogo, but a dream move to Real Madrid did not work out. He later became coach of Peru and shocked South American football when he guided them to the 1970 World Cup.

IGOR DOBROVOLSKI

Country: Soviet Union, CIS, Russia
Born: August 27, 1967
Position: Midfielder
Clubs: Nistru Chisinau, Dinamo Moscow, CD Castellon, Servette, Genoa, Marseille, Dynamo Moscow, Atlético Madrid, Fortuna Dusseldorf, Tiligul-Tiraspol

Igor Dobrovolski was the star of the Soviet Union's 1988 Olympic gold medal winning team in Seoul. When the Soviet Union subsequently fell apart Dobrovolski, a Moldovan by birth, went on to play for CIS and Russia. However, although he refused to play for coach Pavel Sadyrin at the 1994 World Cup, he did play at Euro 96 without being at a club. He made several attempts to be a success abroad but always returned to Dynamo. In all he played 47 international matches.

DOMINGOS

Country: Brazil
Born: November 19, 1912
Position: Centre-back
Clubs: Bangu, Vasco Da Gama, Nacional, Boca Juniors, Flamengo, Corinthians

Domingos da Guia is regarded as one of the all-time great Brazilian defenders. He played at the 1938 World Cup, where he reached the semi-finals, and enjoyed a club career across South America. He started at Bangu and starred for Vasco Da Gama and Flamengo. He also played abroad and won the Uruguayan league at Nacional and the Argentine title at Boca Juniors.

Nicknamed 'The Divine Master', Domingos was a highly skilled player, introducing a refined technique at the back. He often dribbled the ball out of the penalty area, something rarely seen at the time. He made 30 appearances for Brazil and died in 2000.

TED DRAKE

Country: England
Born: August 16, 1912
Position: Centre-forward
Clubs: Southampton, Arsenal

Edward Joseph Drake is part of Arsenal folklore, having scored all seven goals in the 7-1 thrashing of Aston Villa on December 14, 1935. The Villa Park slaying showed Drake at his fearless best in a Highbury career that yielded three league championships, an FA Cup winners' medal and five England caps. Drake signed from Southampton in March 1934 and although his seven goals in ten games that season helped wrap up the title for Arsenal, he had not played enough games to secure a medal. He made up for the disappointment by netting 42 goals in 41 league appearances the following season as The Gunners retained the title and he picked up another winners' medal with the club in 1938. After retiring, Drake managed Chelsea to the First Division title in 1955.

DRAGAN DZAJIC

Country: Yugoslavia
Born: May 30, 1946
Position: Outside-left
Clubs: Red Star Belgrade, SEC Bastia

Dragan Dzajic is regarded as the greatest Yugoslav player of all time. After making his international debut at the age of 18, the Red Star Belgrade winger scored 23 goals in 85 appearances for his country. He helped Yugoslavia to the European Championship final of 1968 and the semi-finals in 1976, as well as playing at the 1974 World Cup Finals. A winger who truly mesmerised defenders with his speed and agility when carving out chances, his power also made him a direct threat to any goalkeeper. With Red Star he won five Yugoslav titles and four Yugoslav Cups between 1961 and 1975, scoring 287 goals in 590 appearances.

DUNCAN EDWARDS

Country: England
Born: October 1, 1936
Position: Midfielder
Club: Manchester United

Even today, some people still rate Duncan Edwards as the greatest player to have worn the Manchester United shirt. For someone who played only 151 matches for his club and 18 for his country before his death following the Munich air disaster at the age of 21, that appears difficult to believe, but not to those lucky fans who saw him play.

Unusually strong and quick, he played his first game for Manchester United aged 16. Comfortable anywhere on the pitch, he could play in defence, midfield or attack. His all round game, speed and power meant he was the brightest of the 'Busby Babes' who won back-to-back championships before the heart of the side was lost on an icy runway. After the crash, Edwards clung to survival for 15 days before slipping away. He would have been 29 at the 1966 World Cup and had he lived, many believe he, rather than Bobby Moore, would have been the man who lifted the World Cup.

STEFAN EFFENBERG

Country: Germany
Born: August 2, 1968
Position: Midfielder
Clubs: Borussia Mönchengladbach, Bayern Munich, Fiorentina, Wolfsburg, Al-Arabi

Stefan Effenberg has graced some of Europe's leading teams and at his peak was among Europe's top players, but he will probably be best remembered for being sent home from the 1994 World Cup after making obscene gestures to the German fans from the pitch. It was a rash act that more or less ended his international career and he only added two more German caps to his collection afterwards, bringing his overall tally up to 35.

A German Cup winner in 1995 with Mönchengladbach, he had two spells at the club, as he did with Bayern Munich, with whom he won three German league titles and the Champions League in 2001. He also had a spell with Fiorentina in the early 1990s, finishing his career in 2004 after one season with Qatari side Al-Arabi.

PREBEN ELKJAER LARSEN

Country: Denmark
Born: September 11, 1957
Position: Striker
Clubs: Vanlose, Köln, Lokeren, Verona, Vejle BK

Denmark matured as a football nation in the 1980s when they boasted three players of world class: the Laudrup brothers and Preben Elkjaer Larsen. Explosive on and off the field, Preben Elkjaer, as he was known in his home country, was the kind of player who made things happen. First capped in 1977, he starred in the 1984 European Championship and was voted third best player of the 1986 World Cup, in which he scored a hat-trick in Denmark's 6-1 rout of Uruguay. A fast and robust centre-forward with a fierce left-foot, his goals helped Hellas Verona to the Italian title in 1985. He had retired by the time of his country's greatest triumph, the 1992 European Championship.

ARSENIO ERICO

Country: Paraguay
Born: March 30, 1915
Position: Centre-forward
Clubs: Nacional, Independiente, Huracán

In 1937 the Argentine league witnessed a goalscoring sensation when Independiente's Arsenio Erico netted a record 47 goals in 34 games during the league season. It was a record that epitomised Erico as a prolific goalscorer, and on numerous occasions he managed to find the net five times in a game. He was discovered at the age of 17 when he played in a charity match for the Paraguay Red Cross in Buenos Aires. He was spotted by the directors of Independiente and immediately signed in exchange for a donation to the Red Cross. His career was blighted by injury though and he retired in 1947 while playing for Huracán.

EUSÉBIO

Country: Portugal
Born: January 25, 1942
Position: Centre-forward
Clubs: Marques, Benfica, Rhode Island Oceaneers, Boston Minutemen, Monterrey, Beira-Mar, Toronto Metros, Las Vegas Quicksilver, New Jersey Americans

Eusébio Da Silva Ferreira was born in the Portuguese colony of Mozambique in 1942 and although he excelled at basketball and athletics, he made his name as a footballer with local club Sporting Lourenço Marques, a feeder for Portuguese side Sporting Lisbon. In

1960, he was deemed ready for the Portuguese league, but having successfully arrived at Lisbon airport, en-route to Sporting's headquarters he was 'kidnapped' by rival club Benfica and hidden in an Algarve fishing village until a deal was struck in the best interests of all parties.

Benfica were prompted to take such evasive action after their coach, Bela Guttmann, heard about Eusébio in a hairdresser's salon. Having flown out to Mozambique to witness his talent at first hand, Guttmann made it his mission to sign 'The Black Panther' as soon as the opportunity presented itself.

As a fresh-faced 18-year-old, it took Eusébio a little time to adapt to his new surroundings, but within two years he had managed to secure

a place in Benfica folklore as a member of the triumphant 1962 European Cup side that beat Spanish giants and five-times winners, Real Madrid. Eusébio scored twice in the 5-3 victory and the following year he was selected to play for a Rest Of The World side against England at Wembley, as part of the Football Association's centenary celebrations.

He endeared himself to the British public in the game and the bond was further cemented three years later when he became a star of the 1966 World Cup Finals as a member of the Portuguese team. Having reached the quarter-finals, Portugal were shocked when North Korea took a 3-0 lead, but Eusébio inspired his team-mates into one of the greatest ever World Cup

Above: 'The Black Panther', Eusébio of Benfica.

Above: Paulo Falção celebrates scoring against New Zealand at the 1982 World Cup.

Right: Luis Figo lifts the Serie A trophy for Inter Milan in 2007.

comebacks. He scored four goals as Portugal won the game 5-3, and although he left the tournament in tears following semi-final defeat against England, he was the competition's top scorer with nine goals. Such was his impact, he even had a waxwork model erected in his honour at Madame Tussauds in London.

Goals were certainly Eusébio's forte and from 1964 to 1968, and again in 1970 and 1973, he was Portugal's top league scorer. He was also the continent's top scorer in 1968 and 1973, with 42 and 40 goals respectively, and in his 15 years at Benfica there were just two seasons in which he did not win a club honour.

With one European Cup winners' medal already to his name, when Benfica faced Manchester United at Wembley in 1968 he again had an opportunity to make up for the runners-up medals he had picked up in the finals of 1963 and 1965. With the scores at 1-1, he was denied a late winner by a fine save from Alex Stepney and United went on to win in extra-time. Eusébio again left Wembley in tears but the bittersweet experience of the competition was tempered by his total tally of 46 goals in the competition, for many years a record second only to Alfredo Di Stéfano.

A knee injury forced Eusébio to end his top-flight career at 32 and he saw out his playing days in the North American Soccer League. He returned to Benfica as coach in 1977, but having scored 41 goals in 64 games for Portugal, and 727 goals in 715 games in total, it is undoubtedly as a scorer of goals that he will be best remembered.

GIACINTO FACCHETTI

Country: Italy
Born: July 18, 1942
Position: Left-back
Clubs: Trevigliese, Inter Milan

Starting out as a striker at his first club Trevigliese, Giacinto Facchetti was converted into a left-back by team coach Helenio

Herrera when he joined Inter Milan in 1960. Encouraged to attack as well as taking care of his defensive duties – something unique at the time in Italian football – Facchetti netted 59 league goals in an Inter career lasting 17 years. His most celebrated goal came in 1965 in a European Cup semi-final second leg match against Liverpool, when despite being 3-1 down from the first leg at Anfield, Inter defeated the English side 3-0 in the return match, with Facchetti netting the decider. He made 94 appearances for Italy and was team captain when his country lost the 1970 World Cup Final to Brazil.

FALÇÃO

Country: Brazil
Born: October 16, 1953
Position: Midfielder
Clubs: Internacional, Roma, São Paulo

Paulo Roberto Falção was an elegant and graceful midfielder who sprang to prominence as part of the outstanding Brazilian side at the 1982 World Cup. He played alongside Zico, Socrates and Toninho Cerezo in a wonderfully creative midfield and brought his own flair and style to the team.

At club level he played for Internacional in Brazil and was their greatest-ever player. With excellent passing vision and an eye for goal – he often scored from long range – he led the side to three national titles in 1975, 1976 and 1979. He moved to Italy in 1980, and in 1983 helped Roma to their first title triumph in over 50 years. Roma reached the European Cup final the following year, where they lost to Liverpool on penalties in their own Stadio Olimpico.

Falção returned to Brazil in 1985 and played a final season at São Paulo. He later coached the Brazil team, as well as the USA and Japan.

ATTILIO FERRARIS

Country: Italy
Born: March 26, 1904
Position: Right-half/Centre-half
Clubs: Roma-Fortitudo, Roma, Lazio, Bari

Attilio Ferraris got the attention of Italy coach Vittorio Pozzo when injury to Roma's centre-half saw Ferraris switch from right-half to centre-half in an Italian league match. He displayed such unwavering commitment to the position and the Roma cause that Pozzo elevated him to the national side. Between 1926 and 1935 Ferraris played 28 times for Italy including the 1934 World Cup. Getting Ferraris to the World Cup took some work by Pozzo, as the player was a heavy smoker, owned his own bar and was incredibly unfit, but the Italian coach turned him around to great effect for Italy's first World Cup Final triumph. He died in a veteran's match at just 43 years of age.

BERNABE FERREYRA

Country: Argentina
Born: February 12, 1909
Position: Inside-forward
Clubs: Tigre, River Plate

Bernabe Ferreyra was the first legendary player of Argentinian football, although he only played four times for his country. His name was made in the domestic game, particularly with River Plate after he joined in 1932 for a world record fee of £23,000. During his debut season with the club he helped them to the championship and topped the league's scoring charts with 43 goals. No-one, it seems, could stop the player, causing one Buenos Aires newspaper to offer a gold medal to any goalkeeper who could keep a clean sheet against him. However, Ferreyra was not fêted with honours, winning the Argentine title just twice more in 1936 and 1937.

LUIS FIGO

Country: Portugal
Born: November 4, 1972
Position: Midfielder
Clubs: Sporting Lisbon, Barcelona, Real Madrid, Inter Milan

A strong, tricky winger, Luis Felipe Madeira Figo enthralled fans across Europe and at his height he was regarded as the best footballer in the world. His career began in the alleyways of Lisbon where he played for the street team Os Pastilhas, and it was here that he attracted the attention of Sporting Lisbon, signing schoolboy forms at the age of 11.

A member of the successful Portugal sides that won the 1989 Under-16 World Cup and 1991 Under-20 World Cup, he had made his full debut for Sporting Lisbon at the age of 17.

After helping the club to a Portuguese Cup win in 1995, he attracted the attention of some of the giants of European football and signed for Barcelona for £1.5 million.

Under coaches Johan Cruyff, Bobby Robson and Louis Van Gaal, Figo developed into a world-class player, mesmerising fans and defenders with his quick feet and acute football brain. He drove the team to success in the Cup Winners' Cup and the European Super Cup in 1997, two Spanish league titles in 1998 and 1999, and two Spanish Cups in 1997 and 1998.

After a three-year love affair with the Nou Camp and a hugely successful Euro 2000 (Figo helped Portugal to the semi-finals and was viewed by many as the player of the tournament), he made a controversial big-money move to arch rivals Real Madrid. The transfer caused an outrage that would never be forgiven in Barcelona, but the anger that greeted his departure (a pig's head was thrown at him during a clash between the two teams) was as much to do with his talent as it was to do with traditional rivalry.

His impact at Real Madrid was immediate and alongside team-mates Roberto Carlos and Raúl, and later Zinédine Zidane and Ronaldo, Figo helped the side to the title in 2001 and 2003, plus victory in the Champions League in 2002. He also picked up the European Player Of The Year Award in 2000 and the World Player Of The Year Award in 2001. 'We are so used to Figo playing brilliantly, that we think he's playing badly when he just plays normally,' said Real's technical director, Jorge Valdano.

After losing his place in the Real team to David Beckham, Figo moved to the Inter Milan on a free transfer in the summer of 2005. He made his last international appearance for Portugal in the third place play-off game at the 2006 World Cup, continuing to play his club football with Inter until the end of the 2008-9 season. He announced his retirement on the same day that he clinched his fourth consecutive Serie A title win with Inter.

ELIAS FIGUEROA

Country: Chile
Born: March 25, 1946
Position: Left-back
Clubs: Unón La Calera, Santiago Wanderers, Peñarol, Internacional, Palestino, Fort Lauderdale Strikers, Colo Colo

Elias Figueroa Brander is the greatest Chilean player ever, having won consecutive South American Footballer Of The Year titles in 1974, 1975 and 1976. Only Carlos Tevez has achieved the same feat. His talent was recognised early on and he was captain of Chile's Under-17 team. Born in Valpariso, Figueroa quickly established himself as a player of elegance, earning the respected nickname 'Don Elias'. At the 1974

World Cup he was voted the tournament's best defender, while at club level he won the national titles in three countries: twice in Uruguay with Peñarol in 1967 and 1968, twice in Brazil with Internacional in 1975 and 1976, and once in Chile with Palestino in 1978.

TOM FINNEY

Country: England
Born: April 5, 1922
Position: Winger
Club: Preston North End

Tom Finney started his love affair with Preston North End in the summer of 1940 when he signed as a part-time professional. Slight of build and with a quick turn of pace, he made an immediate impression by scoring on his debut in a 2-1 defeat at Liverpool that August. The Second World War interrupted his career and he was shipped off to the Middle East before

he could sign as a full professional. On his return at the start of the 1946-7 season Finney scored in a 3-2 win against Leeds United and his flourishing reputation was soon rewarded with an England call-up for a match against Northern Ireland. His debut goal in a 7-2 victory was the first of 30 he would score in 76 appearances for his country, and with 18 of them coming in his first 24 appearances he was vying with Stanley Matthews for the title of the greatest England player of his generation.

Naturally left-footed, Finney preferred playing on the right wing but often shifted flanks for England to make way for Matthews. A host of clubs tried to prise him from Preston, including Italian club Palermo, who reportedly offered him £10,000, a car, a villa and huge salary, but he stayed loyal and spent his entire career at Deepdale. He failed to win a major honour but he was twice voted England's Footballer Of The Year in 1954 and 1957, and his 187 league goals remain a club record.

JUST FONTAINE

Country: France
Born: August 18, 1933
Position: Centre-forward
Clubs: AC Marrakesh, US Marocaine Casablanca, Nice, Stade de Reims

Just Fontaine made history when he scored 13 goals at the World Cup finals in 1958, setting a record that looks unlikely to be beaten. It stands as the highest number of goals scored by one player in a single World Cup tournament, yet he was not even France's first choice centre-forward before the competition began. Only an injury to René Bliard gave him the chance to make football history in Sweden.

Fontaine was born in Morocco and won his first cap for France in 1953, scoring a hat-trick in an 8-0 defeat of Luxembourg. He was left out for nearly three years and returned to the international fold to play just four times before the World Cup in 1958. At the finals he formed a wonderful partnership with Raymond Kopa. Fontaine's assets were pace and a potent left foot, and he couldn't stop scoring.

He was a star in the French league with Nice and Stade de Reims, with whom he lost in the 1959 European Cup Final. He finished the European campaign as the competition's leading scorer in that season, with ten goals. A broken leg ended his career and he went on to briefly manage France. He won 21 caps and scored 30 goals.

Above: Just Fontaine, scorer of a record 13 goals in the 1958 World Cup, is chaired off after the third-place play-off.

ENZO FRANCESCOLI

Country: Uruguay
Born: November 12, 1961
Position: Forward/Midfielder
Clubs: Wanderers, River Plate, Racing Club Paris, Marseille, Cagliari, Torino

When a footballer of the stature of Zinédine Zidane names his first born son after his hero, you know the player receiving the tribute must have been exceptionally special. Enzo Francescoli certainly was. He graced Latin and European football for two decades in a career that yielded almost 200 club goals in the league. He was voted South American Footballer Of The Year in 1984, and again in 1995 when he had returned from Europe, winding down his career with a second spell at River Plate. Nicknamed 'El Principe' (The Prince), he combined silky movement with great attacking play from midfield, and he was as adept at creating chances as he was converting them. He was top scorer in the Argentine league in 1984, 1986 and 1994.

ARTHUR FRIEDENREICH

Country: Brazil
Born: July 18, 1892
Position: Striker
Clubs: Germania, Ypiranga, Americano, Paulistano, São Paulo, Flamengo, Santos

Few players can claim to be better than Pelé, but in sheer volume of goals scored, Arthur Friedenreich can. In a 26-year career, it is claimed 'The Tiger' scored 1,329 goals. Of German and Brazilian parentage, his significance extends far beyond the playing field. An Englishman had originally introduced football to Brazil in the late 19th century, and for the first two decades of the 20th century it remained the preserve of white people. Friedenreich helped to change that. He played for the first Brazilian national side in a friendly against Exeter City in 1914 and went on to win 17 caps, scoring eight goals, until his final international appearance in 1930.

GARRINCHA

Country: Brazil
Born: October 28, 1933
Position: Right-wing
Clubs: Pau Grande, Botafogo, Corinthians, Portuguesa Santista, Atletico Junior Barranquilla, Flamengo, Red Star Paris, Olaria

It was a miracle that Garrincha became one of Brazil's greatest players because a childhood illness had left one leg curved and the other slightly shorter. The nickname Garrincha meant 'Little Bird' or 'wren', and he was an outstanding dribbler with the ball, possessing

a wonderful swerving 'banana' shot. Garrincha was part of the Brazil side that lifted the 1958 World Cup but although he might have been overshadowed by the exciting young Pelé on that occasion, in the 1962 finals he was Brazil's inspiration. He scored twice in the quarter-final win over England and then twice again in the semi-finals against hosts Chile, fully deserving his second winners' medal. His last game for Brazil was against Hungary at the 1966 World Cup; it was the first time in his 50 international matches that Brazil had lost with Garrincha in the side. Sadly, his wild off-the-field lifestyle caught up with him in 1983, when he died aged 49.

PAUL GASCOIGNE

Country: England
Born: May 27, 1967
Position: Midfielder
Clubs: Newcastle United, Tottenham Hotspur, Lazio, Rangers, Middlesbrough, Everton, Burnley, Gansu Tianmu, Boston United

The English game has produced legends like Bobby Moore, Bobby Charlton and Stanley Matthews, but none more talented than Paul Gascoigne. At his best Gascoigne could do things with a football beyond the scope of those men. He could run with it at pace, dance through tackles, see a pass no-one else could, strike the ball with power or caress it. Yet he proved incapable of handling his talent.

Born in Gateshead, Gascoigne joined nearby Newcastle United as a boy and made his senior debut at just 17 years of age, coming on as a substitute against QPR on April 13, 1985. He went on to make 104 league and cup appearances for the club, scoring 22 goals, but he never truly won over the Geordie crowd.

He moved south to Tottenham in July 1988 for £2 million and rapidly flowered under Terry Venables in a stylish attacking side. England manager Bobby Robson gave him his international debut as a substitute against Denmark on September 14, 1988, and he forced his way into the World Cup squad for Italia 90. England rode their luck to the semi-finals, losing on penalties to Germany. As the dream of World Cup glory ebbed away, 'Gazza' lifted his shirt to wipe away the tears, creating one of the game's most iconic images.

In May 1991 Spurs agreed an £8 million move to Lazio after that season's FA Cup final against Nottingham Forest, but Gascoigne ruptured a cruciate ligament in a wild challenge on Gary Charles. Four months later he fell down outside a nightclub, smashing the same kneecap and delaying his comeback by three months. In subsequent years 27 operations would take their toll on his body.

He debuted for Lazio in a friendly with Spurs on September 23, 1992, and two months later scored his first goal in Serie A, an 87th minute

Above: Paul Gascoigne scores for Lazio from a free-kick in 1994.

headed equaliser in the Rome derby that forever endeared him to the Lazio fans.

Gascoigne's career in Italy proceeded in fits and starts as he drifted in and out of games. Then, in April 1994, a wild training tackle on Alessandro Nesta shattered his shin in two places. It was a year before he returned to the game but within a month of the season ending he joined Rangers, where he won the Scottish Player Of The Year award in 1996, two Scottish Cups, and two championship medals. Terry Venables, now England coach, brought him back for Euro 96, where he demonstrated flashes of his old brilliance, not least with a delicious goal against Scotland.

A £3.5 million move to Middlesbrough in March 1998 failed to convince critics he was anything but a shadow of the player he once was. He made his debut in the League Cup final but could not wrench the game from Chelsea's grasp. Glenn Hoddle subsequently omitted him from England's 1998 World Cup squad.

Former Rangers boss Walter Smith took him to Everton in July 2000 and the move initially worked for Gascoigne but he was also plagued by injury niggles exacerbated by years of heavy drinking. Following Smith's dismissal he headed for Burnley, a stint that lasted just four months. Attempts to find a suitable British club the following season foundered and he moved to Gansu Tianmu in the Chinese B League, marking another bizarre downward turn in the Gazza soap opera. He had a brief foray into management with Kettering Town in 2005, but he lasted just 39 days at the club.

FRANCISCO GENTO

Country: Spain
Born: October 21, 1933
Position: Left-wing
Clubs: Rayo Cantabria, Real Santander, Real Madrid

Supporters love to see wingers in full flight and none came more dazzling or decorated than outside-left Francisco 'Paco' Gento. Blessed

Opposite: The majestic Garrincha in full flight against Sweden in the 1958 World Cup Final.

with electric pace and intricate dribbling ability, he provided the ammunition for Puskás and Di Stéfano in Real's heyday. Gento joined Real from Santander in 1953 and played for the club for 17 seasons, scoring 128 league goals and winning 12 championship medals. He was capped 43 times for Spain and featured in the 1960 European Championship winning squad, but his greatest achievement was to appear in all eight of Real Madrid's European Cup finals between 1956 and 1966, picking up a winner's medal in six of them. He scored against Fiorentina in the 1957 final and hit an extra-time winner in the 1958 game against Milan.

ERIC GERETS

Country: Belgium
Born: May 18, 1954
Position: Right-back
Clubs: Standard Liège, AC Milan, MVV Maastricht, PSV Eindhoven

The Belgian defender is one of his country's most celebrated players, picking up 86 caps in an international career that stretched between 1975 and 1991. Gerets was also part of the Belgian team that reached the final of the 1980 European Championship in Italy, where they ultimately lost to a West Germany winner only two minutes from time. At club level Gerets' greatest achievement came with Dutch side PSV Eindhoven, who he captained to a penalty shoot-out victory over Benfica in the 1988 European Cup Final. As a coach, Gerets guided Lierse and Club Brugge to the Belgian title, and won back-to-back championships with PSV in 2000 and 2001.

Below: PSV captain Eric Gerets lifts the European Cup trophy after beating Benfica on penalties in 1988.

GÉRSON

Country: Brazil
Born: January 11, 1941
Position: Midfielder
Clubs: Flamengo, Botafogo, São Paolo, Fluminense

Gérson was predicted to be the successor to Didi as Brazil's midfield general at the 1966 World Cup, but he only made one appearance before his country's ageing team were eliminated early. However, four years later it was a very different story. Gérson had a superb World Cup in 1970, where he orchestrated most of Brazil's attacking moves. In the first round, against Czechoslovakia, he provided a trademark 40-yard pass from midfield for Pelé to score, and his range of distribution, together with his midfield scheming, was a consistent delight for all. In the final against Italy, Gérson was arguably the man of the match and scored Brazil's second goal in the memorable 4-1 rout. He will be forever remembered as an integral part of Mario Zagalo's Brazil 1970 side.

JOHNNY GILES

Country: Republic Of Ireland
Born: January 6, 1940
Position: Midfielder
Clubs: Manchester United, Leeds United, West Bromwich Albion, Philadelphia Fury Shamrock Rovers

When Leeds recruited Giles from Manchester United in 1963 it proved a brilliant bit of business and a crucial move in manager Don Revie's team-building plans. The Irishman became one of the key players in Revie's superb side of the Sixties and Seventies, forming a lengthy partnership in central midfield with Billy Bremner. It was Bremner who supplied the fire and Giles the coolness of passing, though he was not shy of a strong challenge himself when it was needed.

His period at Elland Road was filled with honours. Leeds won the league title in 1969 and 1974, and the FA Cup in 1972, but while Giles twice picked up Fairs Cup winners' medals, the closest he came to success in the European Cup was defeat to Bayern Munich in the 1975 final. After leaving Leeds, Giles became player-manager at West Brom and later managed the Republic Of Ireland, stepping down in 1980.

GILMAR

Country: Brazil
Born: August 22, 1930
Position: Goalkeeper
Clubs: Jabaquara São Paulo, Corinthians, Santos

Gilmar is regarded as the finest goalkeeper Brazil has ever produced. He played in goal when they became world champions for the first time in 1958 and retained the title four years later. In 1958 he let in only three goals in six matches and was equally impressive at the 1962 World Cup in Chile. Agile and brave, he proved a formidable last line of defence.

Gilmar played for Corinthians and after a decade joined Santos, where he enjoyed his greatest moments at club level, clinching the World Club Cup in 1962 and 1963. He won 94 caps and retired in 1969.

FERNANDO GOMES

Country: Portugal
Born: November 22, 1956
Position: Centre-forward
Clubs: Porto, Sporting Gijon, Sporting Lisbon

Fernando Mendes Soares Gomes twice won Europe's Golden Boot, in 1983 and 1985. Both times he was captaining Porto, his hometown club, scoring 36 and 39 league goals respectively. Both Porto, with whom he signed at the age of the 17, and Gomes were at the height of their powers, but the striker missed out on the club's greatest moment, the 1987 European Cup Final, with a broken leg. He was the Portuguese league's top scorer six times in all and won five titles and three Portuguese Cups. During a 17-year career Gomes also played 48 times for Portugal.

ALAIN GOUAMENE

Country: Ivory Coast
Born: June 15, 1966
Position: Goalkeeper
Clubs: ASEC Mimosas, Raja Casablanca, ASEC Abidjan, Toulouse, SCO Angers, FC Lorient, Deauville, Toulouse

Alain Gouamene became the first ever player to appear in seven African Nations Cup tournaments, representing Ivory Coast between 1988 and 2000. The highlight was the 1992 tournament in which Gouamene saved three penalties in the semi-final shoot-out with Cameroon, and then in the final he was the hero in an incredible penalty shoot-out, which ended 11-10 in Ivory Coast's favour. Gouamene scored from the spot himself to make it 10-9 before pulling off the trophy winning save.

JIMMY GREAVES

Country: England
Born: February 20, 1940
Position: Centre forward
Clubs: Chelsea, AC Milan, Tottenham Hotspur, West Ham United

Jimmy Greaves always knew how to make an impression, scoring on every debut he made. His guile and pace helped him to notch up 357 goals throughout his career in league football, an English record.

After working his way through the Chelsea youth ranks in the late Fifties, he was soon impressing fans in Division One with his quick feet and imaginative individualism. After four seasons at Stamford Bridge, including two as the league's top scorer, Greaves moved to Milan in 1961 in search of higher wages but found it difficult to settle and signed for Tottenham Hotspur only six months later for a then British record of £99,999. He settled at White Hart Lane, helping Spurs to two FA Cups and European glory in the Cup Winners' Cup, the first European trophy for any British club. He was also the league's top scorer four times while at the club.

An England favourite throughout his career, the disappointment of sitting out the World Cup final in 1966 took its toll (injured early in the tournament, he was fit enough to return to the starting line-up but Alf Ramsey persevered with a winning team). By the time he signed for West Ham as part of a cash plus player exchange for Martin Peters in 1969, his talents were in decline. During the latter stages of his career, and then in retirement, Greaves struggled with alcoholism and became a shadow of his former self. He later recovered and resurrected his career as a football pundit on the popular British television show *Saint And Greavsie*.

GUNNAR GREN

Country: Sweden
Born: October 31, 1920
Position: Inside-right
Clubs: Garda, IFK Gothenburg, AC Milan, Fiorentina, Genoa, Orgryte, GAIS Gothenburg, Skogens

Gunnar Gren was the inside-right of Milan's famous 'Grenoli' Swedish midfield triumvirate – alongside Gunnar Nordahl and Nils Liedholm. Gren had been spotted by the Italian club at the 1948 London Olympics, where he had captained Sweden to the gold medal, scoring twice in the 3-1 victory over Yugoslavia in the final. The lure of a professional career took him to Milan and later to Fiorentina and Genoa. When his native Sweden opened the doors to professionalism, Gren returned home and was instrumental in helping the Swedes reach the 1958 World Cup final as hosts.

GYULA GROSICS

Country: Hungary
Born: February 4, 1926
Position: Goalkeeper
Clubs: Dorog, Mateosz, Honvéd, Tatabanya

A member of the 'Magical Magyars' team of the 1950s, Grosics was Hungary's greatest ever goalkeeper. Spectacular and assured in equal measures, he was a resilient last line of defence, dominating his penalty area and directing the play. He represented his country 86 times from 1947 onwards, winning a gold medal at the 1952 Helsinki Olympics, as well as playing at the World Cups of 1954, 1958 and 1962.

Grosics was turned from hero to villain in 1954 after ending up on the losing side in the World Cup final. On his return to Hungary, he was falsely accused of spying and was kept under house arrest for 13 months and exiled from army club Honvéd, eventually being allowed to play for Second Division Tatabanya. He was recalled to the national team in August 1956, but later lived in exile after the Soviet invasion. He returned to Hungary and played in the 1958 and 1962 World Cups.

Above: Jimmy Greaves scores for Chelsea against Tottenham at Stamford Bridge in 1961.

RUUD GULLIT

Country: Holland
Born: September 1, 1962
Position: Centre-forward/Sweeper/Midfielder
Clubs: Haarlem, Feyenoord, PSV Eindhoven, AC Milan, Sampdoria, Chelsea

Ruud Gullit (born Ruud Dil) was one of the most versatile and intelligent players that the European game has produced. Comfortable in a number of positions, he was enormously successful with clubs in three different countries, as well as at international level.

He made his professional debut in 1978, aged 16, for Haarlem, who were then managed by former West Bromwich Albion player Barry Hughes. Gullit's confident appearances at sweeper for the Dutch minnows led to a debut for the national team on his 19th birthday in 1981, in a 2-1 win over Switzerland. Successful moves to Feyenoord (1982 for £300,000) and PSV Eindhoven (1985 for £400,000) followed, but when he became unhappy at PSV he was snapped up by Italian giants AC Milan in 1987 for a world record fee of £5.5 million.

The following year was truly extraordinary for Gullit, as Milan won the club's first league title for a decade and Holland became European champions for the first time. Gullit captained the Dutch side that day and scored one of their goals in the 2-0 win over the Soviet Union. To cap a fantastic year he was named European and World Player Of The Year.

Gullit's success story continued the next season as Milan thumped Steaua Bucharest 4-0 in the European Cup final, with the Dutchman recovering from a serious knee injury in time to score two of the goals. Milan retained their European crown the following season but Gullit's year was again disrupted by knee problems, causing doubts to arise about the future of his career.

Frustrated by injuries and after failing to make the side for Milan's European Cup final defeat to Marseille in 1993, Gullit joined Sampdoria on a free transfer but his form there was so good

that his former club quickly swooped to re-sign him. Around the same time he brought to an end an international career that had seen him grace just one World Cup, despite the fact that he was regarded as one of the best players on the planet.

After quitting Holland in 1992 for 'personal reasons' Gullit had a change of heart and returned to the fold. However, it proved a short-lived decision and after a spat with national team coach Dick Advocaat, he walked out on the Holland squad just three weeks before the 1994 World Cup Finals. It took Dutch fans a long time to forgive him.

After one last season with Sampdoria, Gullit finally left Italian football for good in 1995 to join Chelsea on a free transfer, taking over as player-manager after Glenn Hoddle became England manager. In 1997 Chelsea beat Middlesbrough 2-0 in the FA Cup final, but Gullit's time at Stamford Bridge turned sour following disputes with both players and the club's hierarchy. He was sacked in February 1998, only to resurface as manager of Newcastle later the same year, another relationship that ended in his dismissal.

GHEORGHE HAGI

Country: Romania
Born: February 5, 1965
Position: Midfielder
Clubs: Farul Constanta, Sportul Studentesc, Steaua Bucharest, Real Madrid, Brescia, Barcelona, Galatasaray

Known as the 'Maradona of the Carpathians', Gheorghe Hagi arrived on the world stage as the inspirational goalscoring flair behind the Steaua Bucharest team of the 1980s. After his controversial arrival in 1986 (with government approval he was all but kidnapped from his previous team, Sportul Studentesc), they won the European Super Cup, three consecutive league titles and also reached the final of the European Cup. His performances did not go unnoticed and a big money move to Real Madrid followed, but despite glimpses of his trademark magic he failed to fulfil his enormous potential in Spain and moved on to Italy to play for Brescia.

Hagi was never less than a talismanic figure for his country, inspiring them to great things over the course of three World Cups. In 1990, his Romanian side were eliminated in the second round after doing well to qualify from a tough group. The following tournament saw a series of fantastic performances at they won their group and got the better of a strong Argentina 3-2 in the second round. At the 1998 World Cup he captained an ageing side that admirably beat England before narrowly losing to Croatia in the second round. He retired from international football after Euro 2000, having made 125 appearances and scored 35 goals.

Towards the end of his playing career Hagi joined Galatasaray, where his famed creative qualities had a significant impact and he led the

Turkish side to their first ever piece of European silverware when they beat Arsenal in 2000 to lift the UEFA Cup.

KURT HAMRIN

Country: Sweden
Born: November 19, 1934
Position: Forward/Outside-right
Clubs: AIK Stockholm, Juventus, Padova, Fiorentina, AC Milan, Napoli, IFK Stockholm

Kurt 'Kurre' Hamrin was a gifted attacker who made his name in Italy, winning several European club trophies with Fiorentina (Cup Winners' Cup in 1961) and AC Milan (Cup Winners' Cup in 1968 and European Cup in 1969). He scored both goals in the 1968 final against Hamburg in Rotterdam. Hamrin was also a World Cup runner-up in 1958, scoring four times in the tournament, including one sensational semi-final goal that typified his skill as he dribbled past several West German players before netting.

HOSSAM HASSAN

Country: Egypt
Born: August 10, 1966
Position: Striker
Clubs: Al-Ahly, PAOK Salonica, Neuchatel Xamax, Al-Ain, Zamalek, El-Masry, Tersana

A member of Egypt's 2006 African Nations Cup winning squad, Hossam Hassan scored in the quarter-final against Congo DR and played his last game for his country as a substitute in the semi-final, setting an African record at the time with his 169th international appearance – not bad for a player who had first retired four years earlier after winning the African Champions League with Zamalek. He had previously lifted the cup with Al Alhy in 1987.

Making his debut for Egypt in September 1985 in a friendly against Norway, he established himself as captain of the national team and his performances earned him a move to Europe, the first of several Egyptian players to do so. He played for Egypt at the 1990 World Cup.

JOHNNY HAYNES

Country: England
Born: October 17, 1934
Position: Inside-forward
Clubs: Fulham, Durban City

For two decades Johnny Haynes was Fulham's brightest star and he is still considered to be the best player in the club's history. Renowned for his superb passing, Haynes became the first British player to earn £100 a week and repaid Fulham's faith in him by staying loyal to the club. He won 56 caps for England, scoring 18 goals, and captained the side 22 times. He also played

Below: Ruud Gullit celebrates scoring in the 1989 European Cup final.

at the 1958 and 1962 World Cups. He joined South African side Durban City in 1970 after 594 league appearances for Fulham, still a club record. He died after a car crash in Scotland in 2005. A statue of Haynes was unveiled outside Craven Cottage in 2008.

NANDOR HIDEGKUTI

Country: Hungary
Born: March 3, 1922
Position: Outside-right/Centre-forward
Clubs: Herminamezo, MTK Budapest

Nandor Hidegkuti was the first foreign player to score a hat-trick against England at Wembley in Hungary's historic 6-3 win in 1953. A star of MTK Budapest, he scored 39 international goals in 69 appearances, but it was more than his statistics that made him special, it was also the way he played. Hidegkuti was not an out-and-out striker but a deep-lying centre-forward. It was this role that contributed to Hungary's free-scoring reputation, creating space for others and opportunities for himself. Appearances at the Worlds Cups of 1954 and 1958, and an Olympic gold medal in 1952, underlined Hidegkuti's world-class reputation in the 1950s.

FERNANDO HIERRO

Country: Spain
Born: March 23, 1968
Position: Centre-back/Midfielder
Clubs: Real Valladolid, Real Madrid, Al Rayyan, Bolton Wanderers

One of Spain's most-capped players, Fernando Hierro was justifiably described by coach Fabio Capello as 'the Spanish Baresi'. Malaga-born Hierro was a tough-tackling ball-winner who broke the record for the most bookings and dismissals in the history of the Spanish league. He was also a skilful player, comfortable as a centre-back with Real Madrid or in a midfield holding role with Spain. He featured in four World Cup squads, evolving from non-playing member in 1990 to captain in 2002. He also won the European Cup three times, the Spanish league five times, as well as the Spanish Cup and World Club Cup. He retired in 2005 after a sterling season with Bolton Wanderers.

RENÉ HIGUITA

Country: Colombia
Born: August 27, 1966
Position: Goalkeeper
Clubs: Millonarios, Atlético Nacional, Real Valladolid, Veracruz, Independiente Medellín, Real Cartagena, Atlético Junior Barranquilla

Eccentric on the pitch and troubled off it, there has never been a keeper quite like Colombia's 'El Loco'. Renowned for dribbling the ball out of his area, taking on opposition players and even getting on the scoresheet, his defining moment came at Wembley in 1995 against England: to save a lob from Jamie Redknapp, Higuita flipped in midair, his feet above his head, and flicked the ball away with the bottom of his boots. The move became known as the 'scorpion kick' and the fame it bought Higuita marked an upturn in his fortunes. His earlier mistake at the World Cup finals in 1990 had seen Colombia eliminated, and he had also spent six months in jail in 1993 for involvement in a kidnapping case.

HONG MYUNG-BO

Country: South Korea
Born: February 12, 1969
Position: Sweeper
Clubs: Posco Atoms, Pohang Steelers, Bellmare Hiratsuka, Kashiwa Reysol, Los Angeles Galaxy

Hong Myung-Bo was regarded as Asia's best sweeper, gaining his experience and leadership qualities in four successive World Cups for South Korea. His influence was apparent when captaining the team to the semi-finals in 2002, and it was Hong who inspired the win over Italy and converted the decisive penalty that knocked out Spain. He retired from international football the same year, having gained 136 caps.

He was equally successful in club football, being voted Most Valuable Player in the Korean league in 1992 and the Japanese league in 1999. In 2000 he became the first Korean to captain a Japanese club, Kashiwa Reysol, and in 2002 he signed for Los Angeles Galaxy. He hung up his boots in July 2004, just after being included by Pelé and FIFA in their list of the 125 greatest living footballers. He has subsequently joined South Korea's coaching team.

GEOFF HURST

Country: England
Born: December 8, 1941
Position: Forward
Clubs: West Ham United, Stoke City, West Bromwich Albion, Seattle Sounders, Cork Celtic

Although not England's most prolific goalscorer, Geoff Hurst will always be his nation's most celebrated for scoring the first hat-trick in a World Cup final: the three goals that secured England the Jules Rimet Trophy for the first time. The son of a pre-war centre-half, Hurst was born in Ashton-Under-Lyme but moved to Essex as a boy. He joined West Ham as a junior, making his league debut in February 1960 against Nottingham Forest.

Manager Ron Greenwood fashioned 'The Hammers' into an exciting, stylish unit and Hurst, a fierce striker of the ball and powerful in the air, became its cutting edge. He won the FA Cup in 1964 and the European Cup Winners' Cup a year later, scoring 180 goals in

410 appearances before moving to Stoke City in August 1972 and West Brom three years later.

Hurst scored 24 goals in 49 appearances for his country but was only a fringe member of the England squad in the early stages of the 1966 World Cup. He would not have played in the final but for an injury to Jimmy Greaves earlier in the tournament. Hurst seized the opportunity, and even when Greaves was declared fit before the final, Hurst held on to his place in the line-up. He became player-manager of Telford in 1976, coached with England for five years and had an unsuccessful six-month spell as manager of Chelsea. He was knighted in 1998.

Above: England's Geoff Hurst, the only player to score a hat-trick in a World Cup final.

VALENTIN IVANOV

Country: Soviet Union
Born: November 19, 1934
Position: Inside-forward/Midfielder
Club: Torpedo Moscow

Soviet football enjoyed a purple patch in the early 1960s: the national team won the inaugural European Championship in 1960, and two years later they reached the quarter-finals of the World Cup, thanks largely to Ivanov's lethal finishing. He had been on target once in the 1958 finals but in 1962 he scored four goals, finishing the tournament as joint top scorer. It was an accolade he shared with five other players, including the Brazilians Garrincha and Vavá. Scoring in the opening match against Yugoslavia, he was on target twice in the 4-4 draw with Colombia, and again against Uruguay before the Soviets bowed out 2-1 to Chile in the quarter-final. He scored 26 international goals between 1955 and 1966 and was Soviet Player Of The Year in 1960.

1959: Joins Rio club Botafogo and learns trade from his hero Garrincha.

1964: Makes international debut against Portugal.

1966: Plays in the same World Cup squad as Garrincha.

1970: Comes back from injury after breaking his leg twice. Scores seven goals and is given the nickname 'the Hurricane of the World Cup'.

1974: Sporting an 'afro' hairstyle for the World Cup finals in Germany, Jairzinho plays as centre-forward but fails to make an impression.

1975: Leaves Botafogo after a long career and joins French giants Marseille. Returns to Brazil after an altercation with a linesman.

1976: Wins the Copa Libertadores with Cruzeiro, scoring the winning goal in the victory over River Plate.

1978: Fails to make the Brazilian World Cup squad.

1979: Joins Venezuelan club Portuguesa.

1981: Retires from football.

1991: Working as a scout he is credited with discovering the teenage Ronaldo.

JAIRZINHO

Country: Brazil
Born: December 25, 1944
Position: Winger/centre-forward
Clubs: Botafogo, Marseille, Cruzeiro, Portuguesa, Noroeste, Fast Club

If Pelé was the greatest player ever to play for Brazil, then there's a long list of legends not too far behind him battling it out to be recognised as the next best. Jairzinho would be close to the top of that list, largely for his performances in the team's 1970 World Cup triumph. He had already played at the 1966 finals in England, though there was little evidence then that he would make such an impact on the tournament four years later. With Garrincha still in the side in 1966, 21-year-old Jairzinho had to make do with a role on the left wing of Brazil's attack and he was not at his best. He played in all three matches but Brazil were poor and went home after the group stages.

Four years later it was another story. Jairzinho arrived in Mexico as a member of a very different Brazil side indeed, and with Garrincha retired he was able to play in his natural position as an attacking right-winger. Blessed with a direct style, scorching pace and a fierce shot, he was simply too much for opposing defenders to handle, and by the end of the tournament he had collected a winners' medal and made history by scoring in every round of the competition.

Jairzinho started off with a double in his first match, a 4-2 defeat of Czechoslovakia, and then scored the winning goal in the victory over

Above: Jairzinho was a star of the 1970 World Cup Final against Italy, a game Brazil won 4-1. Below: Jairzinho takes on Romania, on the way to scoring a goal in every round of the 1970 World Cup tournament.

England, lauded as one of the most memorable matches of all time. The outstanding incident from the encounter was Gordon Banks's gravity-defying save from Pelé's downward header, but it is often forgotten that it was Jairzinho's run and cross that provided the chance. He continued scoring and in the semi-final he found the net again as Brazil beat Uruguay, memorably running to the by-line and dropping to his knees to cross himself in both thanks and celebration. He finally made

it a goal in every round with the third in the 4-1 win over Italy in the final, even if the ball did roll in off his chest.

Jairzinho's record was remarkable, as only two other players in World Cup history had achieved something similar, but Uruguay's Alcides Ghiggia only had to play in four games in 1950 and Just Fontaine completed the feat in the 1954 third place play-off game rather than in the final itself.

His club career was always overshadowed somewhat by his international achievements and, typically for many Brazilian players of his generation, Jairzinho rarely strayed far from his homeland. He had a short spell in France with Marseille but only enjoyed success after returning to South America with Cruzeiro, scoring the winning goal in the final of the 1976 Copa Libertadores.

Jairzinho played in the 1974 World Cup Finals, but it wasn't just the 'afro' that made him look like a different player. A dearth of quality resulted in him leading the line as centre-forward, where he had often featured for his club side, but he scored only twice as Brazil finished the tournament fourth, losing to Poland in the third place play-off. It effectively marked the end of his international career, although he would make one final appearance for Brazil against Czechoslovakia, some eight years later and aged 37.

JAIRZINHO'S RECORD-BREAKING GOALS

1ST GROUP GAME		2ND GROUP GAME	3RD GROUP GAME	QUARTER-FINAL	SEMI-FINAL	FINAL
v Czechoslovakia **61 mins:** Puts Brazil 3-1 ahead after receiving a pass in an offside position.	**v Czechoslovakia** **81 mins:** Beats four men to score the final goal, making it 4-1.	**v England** **59 mins:** Pelé lays off a Tostão cross for Jairzinho to fire home for a 1-0 win.	**v Romania** **22 mins:** The second goal in a 3-2 win, Jairzinho scores from close range.	**v Peru** **75 mins:** Jairzinho rounds the goalkeeper to score, completing a 4-2 win.	**v Uruguay** **76 mins:** Scores Brazil's second goal after starting move in his own half.	**v Italy** **71 mins:** Pelé nods on for Jairzinho to score the third in 4-1 victory.

ALEX JAMES

Country: Scotland
Born: September 14, 1901
Position: Forward
Clubs: Raith Rovers, Preston North End, Arsenal

Lanarkshire born inside-forward Alex James was the inspiration behind the great Arsenal side of the 1930s, winning four league championship medals and two FA Cups while with 'The Gunners'. The diminutive Scot was probably the most influential player of his generation and a huge favourite with football fans around the country. A natural showman, he was easily recognisable because of his trademark baggy shorts.

His showmanship often infuriated his managers, and it was this, coupled with a fiery temper, which probably contributed to the fact that James only gained eight Scotland caps throughout his career, although he was one of the 'Wembley Wizards' who crushed the mighty England 5-1 in 1928. The legendary 'Gunners' striker of the period, Cliff Bastin, along with his contemporaries in the Arsenal attack, had much to thank him for, because it was James the creator who supplied them with the ammunition they needed.

PETAR JEKOV

Country: Bulgaria
Born: October 10, 1944
Position: Centre-forward
Clubs: Beroe, CSKA Sofia

Throughout a playing career that spanned from 1962 to 1975, Jekov was an outstanding striker. He was the first Bulgarian to win the European Golden Boot after netting 36 goals for CSKA Sofia in the 1968-9 season, and his career total of 253 goals in 333 club appearances points to his lethal finishing ability. He won the Bulgarian championship four times with CSKA, scored 25 goals for his country and captained them to Olympic silver in 1968.

PAT JENNINGS

Country: Northern Ireland
Born: June 12, 1945
Position: Goalkeeper
Clubs: Watford, Tottenham Hotspur, Arsenal

If you were designing the perfect goalkeeper on a computer, the finished article would end up very much like Pat Jennings. He was tall but agile, athletic but sturdy, and famously possessed huge hands. He was great on crosses, superb in one-on-one confrontations, and he could improvise point-blank saves. He was consistent too, made few errors in his career, had excellent powers of concentration and was incredibly durable, completing over 1,000 first class games in a long and distinguished career.

He first left his Irish home for Third Division Watford in 1963, but it was after signing for Tottenham Hotspur a year later that he made his name. After two seasons vying with Bill Brown for the number one jersey, by the time of the 1967 FA Cup Final victory Jennings had long since established himself as the side's custodian. He enjoyed one of his most famous moments in the 1967 Charity Shield at Old Trafford, when a mighty kick from his own goal area bounced over the head of Manchester United keeper Alex Stepney and into the net.

After 13 years with the club Spurs mistakenly suspected his career was on the wane at 33 and sold him to bitter North London rivals Arsenal. He continued his incredible career with 'The Gunners', winning the FA Cup in 1979 before finally retiring in 1985. He had played in four FA Cup finals, and had two English Player Of The Season accolades, two World Cup campaigns and 119 caps under his belt.

JIMMY JOHNSTONE

Country: Scotland
Born: September 30, 1944
Position: Right-winger
Clubs: Celtic, San Jose, Sheffield United, Dundee, Shelbourne

'Jinky' Jimmy Johnstone will be remembered as one of Scotland's greatest players. The former ballboy at Celtic Park rose to become one of the stars of the great Celtic side of the late Sixties and early Seventies and was a key player in the team that won nine back-to-back league titles and seven Scottish cups.

Johnstone loved the big occasion and his finest season probably came in 1967, when Celtic became the first Scottish side to lift the European Cup after beating Inter Milan in the final, crowning a season in which the club had won every competition they entered.

Johnstone, who left Celtic in 1975 to play for San Jose in the North American league, could perhaps have made even more of his career, but a typically fiery redhead, he led a less than exemplary off-the-field lifestyle. Johnstone was a superb dribbler, an accurate crosser of the ball, and an expert finisher, but like many inspirational players, consistency was his problem and he tended to have his fair share of off games. He died in 2006.

OLIVER KAHN

Country: Germany
Born: June 15, 1969
Position: Goalkeeper
Clubs: Karlsruher, Bayern Munich

Highly motivated and imposing, Oliver Kahn was one of the game's great goalkeepers. He

started his career at Karlsruher but was snapped up by Bayern Munich in 1994 for £1.6 million, a record fee for a goalkeeper in the Bundesliga at the time. At Bayern he won the league title eight times, the German Cup six times, plus the 1996 UEFA Cup and the 2001 Champions League, crucially saving three times in the decisive penalty shoot-out. It was a performance that saw him voted German Player Of The Year for the second successive season.

Kahn made his international debut in 1995 and was a non-playing squad member in two World Cups until he captained the side in Japan and Korea in 2002. He was instrumental in guiding the team to the final and was named Player Of The Tournament, the first time a goalkeeper had received the award. He was also voted the best keeper of the competition.

Before the 2006 World Cup Kahn struggled to hide his anger when asked to understudy Jens Lehmann, but in the moments before Germany's quarter-final penalty shoot-out with Argentina, the sight of Kahn approaching Lehman to shake his hand and wish him luck gave the tournament one of its most abiding memories. He was given his only game of the competition as the Germans beat Portugal in the third place play-off. He retired from international football after the tournament, having captained the German side on 50 occasions.

He played on for Bayern Munich for two more seasons, retiring in May 2008. He holds the record for keeping the most clean sheets in the history of the Bundesliga.

Above: Celtic's Jimmy Johnstone takes on Alex Miller of Rangers in the 'Old Firm' derby.

ROY KEANE

Country: Republic Of Ireland
Born: August 10, 1971
Position: Midfielder
Clubs: Cobh Ramblers, Nottingham Forest, Manchester United, Celtic

A strong, fiery, ball-winning midfielder, Roy Keane was one of the English Premier League's most outstanding and consistent performers. He began his career with Cobh Ramblers in his native Ireland before Brian Clough took him to Nottingham Forest as an 18-year-old. Clough gave him his debut away at Liverpool and it was not long until the combative youngster instantly won admirers with his tireless box-to-box running and his ability to score vital goals.

At the end of his first full season at Forest Keane made an appearance in the 1991 FA Cup Final, collecting a runners-up medal after the defeat by Tottenham Hotspur. A Republic Of Ireland debut against Switzerland was to follow under the guidance of manager Jack Charlton.

Signed by Manchester United for £3.75 million in 1993 (at the time it was a record fee between English clubs), Keane was seen as the natural successor to Bryan Robson. His immense presence and fearless tackling in the centre of midfield, coupled with his intelligent, accurate passing, contributed greatly to United's success, and he was made club captain after Eric Cantona's retirement. However, months later a serious knee injury saw him miss much of the 1997-8 campaign, but his return coincided with his club's historic treble-winning season.

In the second leg of the 1998-9 Champions League semi-final against Juventus Roy Keane delivered his greatest performance, hauling the team back from two goals down to win 3–2. However, a booking early in the match meant that he missed out on the final victory over Bayern Munich due to suspension.

Highly regarded by his peers and critics alike, he was voted Player Of The Year for the 1999-2000 season by both the football writers and the Professional Footballers' Association.

A brutally honest man, Keane often courted notoriety. His biting 'prawn sandwich' outburst against United's executive fans was followed by a series of stinging comments about his fellow players. Those remarks were nothing compared to his fall-out with Republic Of Ireland manager Mick McCarthy. Keane had gone to the 2002 World Cup as Republic Of Ireland captain, but the personality clash with McCarthy saw him return before the tournament had kicked-off.

As Manchester United struggled to recover their dominance Keane was critical of the team in a programme for the club's television channel. The show was pulled from the schedules and by December 2005, after 13 years at the club, he was edged out of Old Trafford, finishing his career in Scotland where he helped Celtic to the Premier Division title that season.

KEVIN KEEGAN

Country: England
Born: February 14, 1951
Position: Centre-forward
Clubs: Scunthorpe United, Liverpool, Hamburg, Southampton, Newcastle United

It seems apt that Kevin Keegan was born on Saint Valentine's Day. During his career as both player and manager, the man nicknamed 'Mighty Mouse' (because of his diminutive stature and physical power) has been one of the game's great romantics, whipping up enthusiasm amongst fans and players alike.

However, that was not how Liverpool coach Bill Shankly viewed him in 1971, when he bought the Scunthorpe United striker to Anfield for £33,000. After describing him as 'playing like a rat after a weasel', Shankly was thanked for his veiled compliment when Keegan scored a goal on his club debut in a 3-1 victory against Nottingham Forest.

The striker immediately became a crowd favourite (one popular Anfield chant of the day was 'Kevin Keegan walks on water') and he was arguably Shankly's best signing for the club. Certainly he had an impact, scoring 100 goals in 321 appearances and helping Liverpool to three league titles (1973, 1976, 1977), two UEFA Cups (1973, 1976) and the European Cup (1977) before moving to the German side Hamburg in 1977 for £500,000.

His England career was successful too, and after forcing his way into Alf Ramsey's side in 1972 he soon became an international regular, later forging an exciting partnership with Trevor Brooking in the early 1980s. 'He was the first person to admit he wasn't a naturally gifted player,' said Brooking much later, 'but he was fabulous with man markers and would run them into the ground with his determination by twisting and turning and he was a strong little feller as well. People would knock him down and he would just get up again.'

Sadly trophies would elude England during that period and Keegan missed out on the chance of international glory when Ron Greenwood's team were knocked out of the 1982 World Cup in the second group stage. Keegan had missed most of the tournament through a recurring back injury.

Despite a lack of trophies with his country, he had already made his mark with Hamburg. In 1978 he claimed the European Player Of The Year award, a feat he repeated the following year when he helped the club to the Bundesliga title. He returned to England in 1980 to play for Southampton in a £420,000 deal, having just picked up a European Cup runners' up medal.

Despite Southampton's lowly status in the top flight, Keegan sparkled. He scored 42 goals in 80 games for the club, helping 'The Saints' lead the title race for two months during the 1981-82 campaign before finally finishing

seventh. Keegan was to pick up the PFA Player Of The Year Award that year, but almost as quickly as he had arrived he moved again, this time to Newcastle United for £100,000.

Newcastle were languishing in the second tier of English football but after scoring on his debut against QPR, he helped 'The Magpies' to promotion in 1984. As soon as this happened, Keegan announced his retirement from the game and in May of that year, directly after the end of his final match, a helicopter picked him up from the centre of the pitch at St James' Park. He was looking to a life away from the game on a golf course in Spain. Little could he have imagined that he would return to football, and to Newcastle United, for two an explosive periods as manager. His other coaching jobs – in charge of Fulham, England and Manchester City – were no less eventful.

MARIO KEMPES

Country: Argentina
Born: July 15, 1954
Position: Forward
Clubs: Instituto Cordoba, Rosario Central, Valencia, River Plate, Hercules, First Vienna, St Pölten, Kremser

Mario Kempes was a prolific goalscorer for both club and country. Only Diego Maradona is held in higher esteem among the football fans of Argentina, while in Spain his lethal finishing in front of goal earned him the nickname 'El Matador', or 'The Killer'.

Kempes started his career with hometown

Opposite: Kevin Keegan kisses the FA Cup after Liverpool beat Newcastle in the 1974 final.

Below: Mario Kempes celebrates scoring against Holland in the 1978 World Cup Final.

Above: The infamous Stuttgart dive bomber Jürgen Klinsmann.

WIM KIEFT

Country: Holland
Born: November 12, 1962
Position: Centre-forward
Clubs: Ajax, Pisa, Torino, PSV Eindhoven, Bordeaux

Had Marco Van Basten not been around at a similar time, Wim Kieft would undoubtedly have figured in the Dutch national team on a far more regular basis than the 43 occasions he represented his country. Frequently those appearances came from the bench but that did not stop him from scoring some important goals. As part of the squad that won the 1988 European Championship, Kieft netted the crucial winner against the Republic Of Ireland in the group stage but he was a non-playing substitute for the final. His goalscoring talents were equally at home in the Dutch top flight and Italy's Serie A.

JÜRGEN KLINSMANN

Country: West Germany & Germany
Born: July 30, 1964
Position: Striker
Clubs: Stuttgart Kickers, VfB Stuttgart, Inter Milan, Monaco, Tottenham Hotspur, Bayern Munich, Sampdoria

Klinsmann was an athletic and charismatic striker who first played for West Germany in 1987 and made an impact with his intelligent, all-round play. His tendency to dive added a less appealing facet to his reputation but one that barely dimmed his popularity, and he was able to mock his critics with his famous diving goal celebration. He loved testing himself in different football cultures and played top-flight football in Germany, Italy, France and England.

He is best remembered for his outstanding feats at international level, most notably in 1990 when West Germany lifted the World Cup in Italy. He scored three goals on the way to the final and was voted into FIFA's all-star team for the tournament. Club success followed when Klinsmann, together with fellow countrymen Lothar Matthäus and Andreas Brehme, helped Inter Milan to lift the UEFA Cup in 1991. He won the competition again in 1996 with Bayern Munich, scoring in the final's second leg.

In 1994 he represented the newly unified Germany, scoring five more World Cup goals in a side that lost in the quarter-finals. Afterwards he earned a high profile move to Tottenham Hotspur and his performances in one glorious season at White Hart Lane made him England's Player Of The Year in 1995. The following year he spearheaded Germany to European Championship victory in England and although he did not score in the final, he was his country's leading goalscorer in the tournament.

He returned to Tottenham on loan in the

1997-8 season and his goals saved the club from relegation. His World Cup swansong in 1998 yielded another three goals at the finals. He retired afterwards having won 108 caps and scored 47 goals for his country. He relocated to the USA for a life without football, but in 2004 he was given the task of reviving the fortunes of the German national side, and despite having no previous coaching experiences he took them to the 2006 World Cup semi-finals.

SANDOR KOCSIS

Country: Hungary
Born: September 23, 1929
Position: Inside-right
Clubs: Ferencváros, Honvéd, Young Fellows Zurich, Barcelona

Sandor Kocsis was top scorer at the 1954 World Cup with 11 goals and was nicknamed 'Golden Head' for his superb ability in the air. He recorded a remarkable tally of 75 goals in 68 internationals and is regarded as one of the finest Hungarian footballers of all time. Born in Budapest, he played for Ferencváros and then Honvéd, where he formed a superb partnership with Ferenc Puskás. He also won four titles in his home country and was the top scorer in the league on three occasions.

He made his international debut in 1949 and was a member of the team that won gold at the 1952 Olympics. He made his name as part of the fabulous Hungary side that beat England 6-3 at Wembley in 1953 and the same team went into the World Cup the following year as heavy favourites to claim the trophy. However, despite his outstanding personal exploits, including two goals in the semi-final against Uruguay, Hungary lost to West Germany in the final.

Kocsis moved to Barcelona in 1958 and during his eight years with the Catalan giants he won both the Spanish league and the Spanish Cup twice each, plus the Inter-Cities Fairs Cup in 1960. He retired in 1966 and died in 1979.

RONALD KOEMAN

Country: Holland
Born: March 21, 1963
Position: Defender
Clubs: Groningen, Ajax, PSV Eindhoven, Barcelona, Feyenoord

Ronald Koeman's strike-rate belied his role as a defender. He netted almost 200 league goals in a career spanning over 500 games, earning himself a reputation as a set-piece specialist, both from the penalty spot and from free-kicks. His power and accuracy also meant that he was capable of delivering precision passes into the attacking third of the field and he was comfortable on the ball in any area of the pitch.

He began his career alongside his brother Erwin at Groningen before joining Ajax.

team Instituto Cordoba before moving to Rosario in 1974, where he twice became top scorer in the Argentine league. He made his international debut against Bolivia during the qualifying rounds of the 1974 World Cup, and he played every game at the finals, although he disappointingly failed to deliver on any of his great promise.

He went on to appear at three successive World Cup tournaments, making 18 of his 43 international appearances on the biggest stage. At the finals of 1978 he was the only European based player in César Luis Menotti's squad. By then Kempes had made his name at Valencia, where he had twice won the Pichichi Trophy, given to the top scorer in the Spanish league. He scored six goals at the 1978 World Cup, including two in the victory over Holland in the final, finishing the tournament as its top scorer.

He later moved to Austria and then to the Far East before retiring at 41. Coaching subsequently took him to obscure destinations and he became the first foreign manager in Albania when he took charge of Lushnja, but he was forced to flee during civil unrest and later coached a series of clubs in Bolivia.

However, it was with PSV Eindhoven, and then Barcelona, that Koeman was to enjoy his most successful spells, winning the European Cup with both clubs and becoming only the second player, after Belododici the year before, to win the competition with two different sides. He also had a key role to play in both finals, netting for PSV in the penalty shoot-out victory over Benfica in 1988 and then scoring Barcelona's winner against Sampdoria at Wembley in 1992.

Success for Koeman was not consigned to club football, as he was also a member of the Dutch side that won the European Championship in 1988. After ending his playing days in Holland with Feyenoord, he moved into coaching, joining the staff of the Dutch national side before moving to Barcelona as assistant. His first managerial role was with Vitesse Arnhem, but he has since held the top job at Ajax, Benfica, PSV, Valencia and AZ Alkmaar.

KALMAN KONRAD

Country: Hungary
Born: March 23, 1896
Position: Inside-forward
Clubs: MTK Budapest, FK Austria Vienna, Brooklyn Wanderers

Kalman Konrad was part of the dominant MTK Budapest side that ruled the Hungarian game from 1914 to 1925. In 1919, after scoring 88 goals in 94 games for MTK, Konrad was lured to Vienna to play for FK Austria, who went by the name Amateure at the time. In 1926 he travelled to the USA to join Brooklyn Wanderers for one successful season, before ending his career back with MTK in 1928 and becoming a respected coach. Konrad was an overtly skilful ball player, making him the grandfather of the 'Magical

Magyars'. His abilities inspired a generation of Hungarian footballers, including Alfred Schaffer and Gyorgy Orth. These players in turn inspired the players that were to become legends in their own right in the 1950s.

RAYMOND KOPA

Country: France
Born: October 13, 1931
Position: Centre-forward
Clubs: Angers, Stade de Reims, Real Madrid

Raymond Kopa became France's first winner of the European Footballer Of The Year Award in 1958 and was regarded as his country's greatest player until Michel Platini took on the mantle. He made his name as a deep-lying centre-forward at Reims and helped the side reach the first European Cup final in 1956, when they lost to Real Madrid. The Spaniards snapped him up in 1956 and he played as a right-winger when Real Madrid won the European Cup in 1957, 1958 and 1959. He was outstanding at the World Cup in Sweden in 1958, helping France reach the semi-finals. In total he scored 18 goals in 45 international appearances.

HANS KRANKL

Country: Austria
Born: February 14, 1953
Position: Centre-forward
Clubs: Austria Salzburg, Vienna AC, Rapid Vienna, Barcelona, First Vienna, Kremser

Hans Krankl was one of Austria's most successful footballers and a prolific goalscorer, racking up a staggering 321 goals in 432 Austrian league appearances, as well as 34 goals in a

69-game international career that ran from 1973 to 1985. Included in this international record was a six-goal haul in April 1977 when Austria thrashed Malta 9-0. The following season Krankl was the winner of Europe's Golden Boot with 41 goals for Rapid Vienna. He was also the Austrian league's top scorer on four occasions, and in 1979 he became the Spanish league's top scorer while playing for Barcelona, with whom he won the European Cup Winners' Cup the same year.

RUUD KROL

Country: Holland
Born: March 24, 1949
Position: Defender
Clubs: Ajax, Vancouver Whitecaps, Napoli, Cannes

Rudolf Josef Krol epitomised Holland's 'Total Football' philosophy. Described as an all-round defender he could play at fullback on either flank or in the centre of defence. Indeed, he was one of the first attacking fullbacks. He played 83 times for the Dutch, including two losing World Cup final appearances in 1974 and 1978, the second time as captain. Krol was a European Cup and European Super Cup winner in both 1972 and 1973 with the great Ajax side that featured Cruyff, Neeskens and Haan.

LADISLAV KUBALA

Country: Czechoslovakia, Hungary, Spain
Born: June 10, 1927
Position: Forward
Clubs: Ferencváros, Slovan Bratislava, Vasas, Pro Patria, Barcelona, Espanyol, FC Zurich

Ladislav Kubala is revered at Barcelona and was voted the club's greatest player above Cruyff and Maradona in a poll carried out in the club's

Left: Ruud Krol in action against West Germany's Horst Hrubesch at the 1980 European Championship.

Below: Austria's Hans Krankl at the 1982 World Cup.

1999 centenary year. Born to Slavic parents in Budapest in 1927, he began his career at Ferencváros and had just moved to Vasas when he defected in 1949, a decision that saw him banned from playing by FIFA.

A powerful, hard-running striker who was good in the air and a lethal finisher, he was approached by Real Madrid in 1950 but snatched by Barcelona who made him the club's highest paid player. He went on to win four titles and five Spanish Cups for them between 1950 and 1961. He had the distinction of playing international football for three countries, Hungary, Czechoslovakia and Spain, winning 19 caps and scoring 11 goals with the latter.

He subsequently played for Barcelona's city rivals Espanyol and after retiring he went into coaching and enjoyed two stints at Barcelona. He coached the Spanish national team for 68 games between 1969 and 1980, spending longer in the job than any other incumbent and taking them to the 1978 World Cup. He became president of the Barcelona Veterans Association in 1990. He died aged 74 on May 17, 2002 and was posthumously awarded FIFA's Order Of Merit.

ANGEL LABRUNA

Country: Argentina
Born: September 26, 1918
Position: Inside-left
Clubs: River Plate, Rampla Juniors, Platense, Rangers de Talca

At the age of 40, and nicknamed 'El Viejo' (The Old One), Angel Amadeo Labruna represented Argentina at the 1958 World Cup Finals. His two appearances in Sweden took his tally to 36 international appearances, in which he scored 17 goals and reaped two South American Championships in 1946 and 1955. Labruna also served River Plate like no other player, turning out for them in 515 league games and scoring 293 league goals over a 29-year period, finally retiring at the age of 41. He won the league championship nine times, earning a feared reputation as part of the club's famed 'Maquina' forward line.

HENRIK LARSSON

Country: Sweden
Born: September 20, 1971
Position: Forward
Clubs: Hogaborg, Helsingborgs, Feyenoord, Celtic, Barcelona, Manchester United

Tricky, fast and good in the air, Henrik Larsson had the full repertoire of skills required of a world-class striker and he won league titles in Scotland, England and Spain. He also picked up a Champions League winners' medal with Barcelona in 2006 and won the European Golden Boot in 2001 when playing for Celtic.

He joined Celtic in 1997 after a dispute with Feyenoord and in an amazing spell of form he was the league's top goalscorer in five of his seven seasons at the club, hitting 242 goals in 315 games. He was twice voted Scotland's Player Of The Year, in 1998 and 2001 by both the football writers and by the players' association, and he won a host of domestic honours, including four Scottish Premier Division titles, the Scottish Cup twice and the Scottish League Cup four times. In 2006 he was also awarded an MBE for his services to Scottish football.

Success followed him to Barcelona where he won the league title twice in his two seasons at the Nou Camp, and he also won the European Champions League in 2006 after victory over Arsenal. The Champions League final was his last appearance for the club as he fulfilled a longstanding desire to return to his home town club of Helsingborgs. In the winter break of his first season back in Sweden he went on a three-month loan to Manchester United, scoring on his debut in the FA Cup and picking up a Premier League winners' medal. He played on for Helsingborgs until his retirement in 2009.

With Sweden's national side he played in three World Cups: in 1994 (when Sweden reached the semi-final), 2002 and 2006. He is his country's third highest goalscorer at international level and in 2003 the Swedish football association voted him 'the greatest Swedish player of the last 50 years'.

GRZEGORZ LATO

Country: Poland
Born: April 8, 1950
Position: Winger
Clubs: Stal Mielec, KSC Lokeren, Atlante

One of Poland's leading goalscorers, in an international career spanning 13 years Grzegorz Lato made 95 appearances for his country and scored 42 goals. He starred in three consecutive World Cups and was the tournament's top goalscorer in 1974, helping Poland to an unlikely third place finish. The team was blessed with attacking talent such as Robert Gadocha and Kazimierz Deyna, but it was Lato who had the biggest impact, netting seven of his team's 14 goals from his position on the right wing. In 1982 his international swansong brought him closest to success when the Poles finished third at the World Cup in Spain. The following year he won the CONCACAF Champions Cup with Mexican side Atlante and retired from international football.

BRIAN LAUDRUP

Country: Denmark
Born: February 22, 1969
Position: Forward/Midfielder
Clubs: Brondby, Bayer Uerdingen, Bayern Munich, Fiorentina, AC Milan, Rangers, Chelsea, Copenhagen, Ajax

A skilful dribbler and crowd entertainer, Brian Laudrup is the brother of Michael Laudrup. Starting his career at Brondby in 1986, the forward moved to Germany in 1989, first with Bayer Uerdingen and later with Bayern Munich, before making the glamorous move to Italian side Fiorentina after winning the 1992 European Championship with Denmark.

Following Fiorentina's relegation Laudrup had an unhappy loan stint at Milan and he played only nine games before finally leaving to become a crowd favourite at Glasgow Rangers in 1994.

After four seasons and 44 league goals he left Scotland for Chelsea (on a free 'Bosman' deal), before controversially returning home to FC Copenhagen after a bout of homesickness. He retired in 2000 after a recurring Achilles heel problem hampered his performances.

MICHAEL LAUDRUP

Country: Denmark
Born: June 15, 1964
Position: Midfielder/Forward
Clubs: KB, Brondby, Juventus, Lazio, Barcelona, Real Madrid, Vissel Kobe, Ajax

Laudrup was the most elegant cog in the Danish side that electrified world football in the mid-1980s. Supremely gifted, he even scored on his international debut and won the European Cup while with Barcelona in 1992. He celebrated league titles in three countries, winning the Spanish title with both Barcelona and Real Madrid and picked up a winners' medal in the competition for five consecutive seasons. Highly technical and unselfish, he shone in both midfield and attack. Laudrup played in the 1986 and 1998 World Cups before retiring with 37 goals in 104 games, but he missed Denmark's European Championship success in 1992 after falling out with the coach. In 2005 he coached Brondby to the league and cup 'double'.

Below: Michael Laudrup on the ball for Ajax in 1997.

LUCIEN LAURENT

Country: France
Born: December 10, 1907
Position: Midfielder/Left-wing
Clubs: CA Paris, Sochaux, Club Français, Mulhouse, Rennes, RC Strasbourg, Toulouse

Lucien Laurent scored the first ever World Cup goal with a 19th minute volley, putting France on the way to a 4-1 victory over Mexico. He was injured in the next game against Argentina and did not appear in the World Cup again. The short but tenacious Laurent only played made ten appearances for France between 1930 and 1935. Cruelly injury ruled him out of the 1934 tournament, but in honour of his achievement he was a guest at the 1998 World Cup Final, witnessing France lift the trophy for the first time. He died at the age of 97 in April 2005.

DENIS LAW

Born: February 24, 1940
Country: Scotland
Position: Forward
Clubs: Huddersfield Town, Manchester City, Torino, Manchester United

Nicknamed 'The King' at Old Trafford, Denis Law was one of the most popular players to have worn a Manchester United shirt during his reign in the Sixties, with his trademark over-sized shirt and his one-armed goal celebrations. Starting his career at Huddersfield, he made his professional debut in 1956, aged 16. By 18 he was wearing the Scotland jersey and a move to Manchester City followed in 1960. He smashed the British transfer record with a £100,000 move to Torino in 1961, where despite a car crash he still scored ten goals in 27 games in Italy.

In August 1962 Manchester United paid a British record fee for his services and his impact was immediate. He scored twice on his debut and went on to win a European Player Of The Year award in 1964, as well as two league titles (1965 and 1967). He was ruled out of the club's 1968 European Cup triumph through injury.

He returned to Manchester City but he refused to celebrate when his back-heeled goal at Old Trafford defeated United on the day his former club were relegated in 1974. It was his last ever club game.

TOMMY LAWTON

Country: England
Born: October 6, 1919
Position: Forward
Clubs: Burnley, Everton, Chelsea, Notts County, Brentford, Arsenal

Lawton famously scored on his league debut for Burnley aged just 16 before being picked up by Everton, who were keen to find a replacement for the great Dixie Dean. A big, powerful, bustling centre-forward, Lawton was just as recognisable for his famous centre parting as his physique.

He first donned an England shirt at just 19 and although his best years were probably lost to the Second World War, he was still able to boast an impressive scoring record, including 22 goals in 23 internationals. His England record was helped by the regular supply he received from the likes of Tom Finney and Stanley Matthews.

After the war he signed for Chelsea and although he scored 26 goals in 34 league games in the 1946-7 season, he left the club after a dispute with Chelsea manager Billy Birrell. He was at the peak of his game but he shocked English football by moving to Third Division Notts County for a British record transfer fee of £20,000. He later enjoyed a spell as player-manager of Second Division Brentford before finishing his career in the top flight with Arsenal.

LEÔNIDAS

Country: Brazil
Born: November 11, 1910
Position: Centre-forward
Clubs: São Cristóvão, Sirio Libanes, Bonsucesso, Peñarol, Vasco Da Gama, Botafogo, Flamengo, São Paulo

Renowned for his overhead kick Leônidas da Silva was dubbed the 'Black Diamond' and enjoyed his moment of fame at the 1938 World Cup when he starred in the game of the tournament. Brazil beat Poland 6-5 in the first round, with Leônidas scoring a hat-trick. The competition ended prematurely as Leônidas was rested for the semi-final against Italy, a game Brazil lost without him. Appointed captain for the third place play-off victory over Sweden, he scored twice more to take his tally to seven, making him the top scorer. Such was his fame that a chocolate bar and a brand of cigarettes were named 'Diamante Negro' after him.

NILS LIEDHOLM

Country: Sweden
Born: October 8, 1922
Position: Inside-forward/Wing-half/Sweeper
Clubs: Norrköpping, AC Milan

Liedholm was one of the most creative midfield playmakers of his generation, but his decision to move to AC Milan after winning Olympic gold as an amateur in 1948 was at the cost of his international career. Sweden would not select professionals and it was only the relaxation of this rule ten years later that allowed him to captain the national team to the 1958 World Cup Final. He served Milan for 12 years and with them he won the title in 1951, 1955, 1957 and 1959, and helped them to their first European Cup final in 1958. He played for them as a formidable sweeper later in his career.

GARY LINEKER

Country: England

Born: November 30, 1960

Position: Forward

Clubs: Leicester City, Everton, Barcelona, Tottenham Hotspur, Nagoya Grampus Eight

The son of a market trader, Gary Lineker enjoyed a glittering career as one of England's finest goalscorers. After seven seasons with his hometown club Leicester City, Lineker became a target for the country's biggest clubs and signed for Everton for £800,000 in 1985. His performances were phenomenal in his first and only season on Merseyside, but although he hit 30 league goals 'The Toffees' finished runners-up to local rivals Liverpool. When the two teams clashed again in the 1986 FA Cup Final Lineker scored early to put Everton ahead, only for 'The Reds' to triumph 3-1.

Lineker was soon back in action and in the summer he headed off to the World Cup finals in Mexico as England's number one goalscorer. It was a tournament that was to change the direction of his career. With Bobby Robson's team lurching towards a disastrous first round exit, Lineker hit a first-half hat-trick in the must-win game against Poland and his name made international headlines. Two further goals

against Paraguay, then one in the quarter-final defeat against Argentina, put the England man on six goals – enough to win the Golden Boot and earn the attention of Spanish giants Barcelona.

After the tournament Lineker swapped Goodison Park for the Nou Camp, where he spent three seasons with Barça, initially under English coach Terry Venables and then with Dutchman Johan Cruyff. Lineker was an immediate success, as he scored goals freely and pleased the critical Nou Camp fans with his pace and sharp finishing. A hat-trick against Barça's bitter rivals Real Madrid in 1987 cemented his popularity, but when Venables was replaced by Cruyff, Lineker found his status marginalised as the new coach inexplicably deployed him as a right-winger. Despite winning the European Cup Winners' Cup in 1989, a parting of the ways was inevitable. Lineker returned to English football, teaming up with Venables again at Tottenham.

He quickly showed that he had lost none of his ability. At international level he remained a permanent threat, claiming four goals in the 1990 World Cup as England reached the semi-finals, including the equaliser in the epic encounter with West Germany. For Spurs, Lineker developed a fine understanding with Paul Gascoigne and in 1991 he won his only English domestic trophy when Tottenham beat Nottingham Forest 2-1 to lift the FA Cup. Lineker

actually missed a penalty during the game, yet still ended up a winner.

The following year he accepted a lucrative offer to play for Grampus Eight in Japan, and although a toe injury limited his appearances, he proved a wonderful ambassador for a developing league. His retirement two years later opened up a second successful profession as a presenter on British television. Alongside all the goalscoring acclaim, one other major statistic stands out. Throughout his career Lineker's disciplinary record was exemplary and he was never booked.

DANNY McGRAIN

Country: Scotland

Born: May 1, 1950

Position: Right-back

Clubs: Celtic, Hamilton Academical

Despite being a childhood Rangers fan, Danny McGrain was an attacking full-back who spent a long and distinguished career at city rivals Celtic. As a schoolboy he was not recommended to Rangers because the scout who discovered him incorrectly assumed from his name that he was a catholic. He made his debut for the club in 1970 and was a member of Celtic's famous 'Quality Street Gang', which included the likes of David Hay, Lou Macari and Kenny Dalglish. He made

Above: Gary Lineker salutes the fans after his hat-trick against Poland at the 1986 World Cup.

Right: Milan's Paulo Maldini enjoys the moment after scoring against Reggina in 2005.

over 600 appearances for 'The Bhoys', and in a 20-year career with the club he won the league championship on nine occasions, although in the earliest two of these campaigns he was only a peripheral squad member.

He gained 62 caps for Scotland, but his career could have been even more impressive had he not been afflicted by a string of injuries and illnesses, which began in 1972 with a fractured skull. He also suffered a broken ankle and suffered from arthritis and diabetes.

RABAH MADJER

Country: Algeria
Born: February 15, 1958
Position: Midfielder/Forward
Clubs: Hussein Dey, Racing Club Paris, Porto, Valencia, Qatar

No-one will forget Rabah Madjer's outrageous back-heeled goal in the 1987 European Cup Final. He also set-up the winner as Porto beat Bayern Munich, and later in the year he scored the winner in the World Club Cup and was a deserving winner of the African Player Of The Year Award. Five years earlier he had been part of Algeria's 1982 World Cup victory over West Germany, scoring the first goal in a 2-1 win. He also appeared in the 1986 finals and helped Algeria to the quarter-finals of the 1980 Olympics.

SEPP MAIER

Country: West Germany
Born: February 28, 1944
Position: Goalkeeper
Club: Bayern Munich

Josef 'Sepp' Maier spent 19 seasons at Bayern Munich, including a run of 442 consecutive league games in goal for the German giants. He won the Bundesliga four times with the club and he also played in each of Bayern's

Below: Sepp Maier beats Italy's Franco Causio to the ball at the 1978 World Cup.

three European Cup successes between 1974 and 1976, keeping clean sheets in three of the four games involved. He first played for the club in the 1963-4 season, making his international debut in May 1966. He travelled to the World Cup that year as understudy to Hans Tilkowski, and although he didn't get a game, it was only injury that ruled Maier out when coach Helmut Schön considered selecting him for the final.

By the 1970 World Cup tournament he was established as his country's first choice keeper, playing in every game at the finals bar the third place play-off. Although West Germany only reached the semi-finals in Mexico, greater success was just around the corner for 'Die Katze'. Under coach Helmut Schön and captained by Franz Beckenbauer, the West Germans were crowned European champions in 1972 and world champions two years later, with Maier memorably stopping a formidable Neeskens volley as his side beat Holland 2-1 in the World Cup final.

Named German Player Of The Year three times in the 1970s, a car accident in 1979 ended his career at the age of just 35. Following his retirement, Maier returned to his first sporting love, setting up a tennis school. He later joined the coaching staff of the German national team.

PAOLO MALDINI

Country: Italy
Born: June 26, 1968
Position: Left-back/Sweeper
Club: AC Milan

Paolo Maldini was one of the finest defenders to grace the world stage. An unflappable, cultured and resilient presence at left-back for Milan, he was equally proficient when deployed at sweeper or centre-half. Famed for his ability to bring the ball out of defence, he was also more than capable of helping out in attack when needed.

He began his long and exclusive association with his local club AC Milan when only a boy.

Making his debut for the first team as a 16-year-old substitute against Udinese in January 1985, Maldini was following in the footsteps of his father, Cesare, who had won the European Cup with Milan in 1963.

In 24 years of first team football at the San Siro he helped the club to a vast collection of silverware, including seven Italian league titles and five European Super Cups. He won the European Cup on five occasions, including the 1994 Champions League final that saw Milan thrash Barcelona 4-0, with Maldini deputising at sweeper for the suspended Franco Baresi. He celebrated three world titles with the club, winning the Intercontinental Cup in both 1989 and 1990 and the FIFA Club World Cup in 2007. He was also a member of the sides that lost the Champions League finals of 1993 and 1995, to Marseille and Ajax respectively.

Maldini made his international debut against Yugoslavia as a 19-year-old in March 1988. However, he failed replicate his club success on the international arena: Italy came third in the World Cup in 1990 and reached the final in 1994, before losing to Brazil on penalties. The Italian captain was unlucky again at the 2000 European Championship. Despite missing a penalty in the semi-final shoot-out against Holland, he found himself in the final and seconds away from lifting the Henri Delaunay Trophy, but Italy's slender 1-0 lead over France was obliterated in the game's final minute and the French went on to win the match with a 'golden goal' in extra-time.

Maldini announced his retirement from international football after Italy's exit from the 2002 World Cup, quitting with a record-breaking 126 caps for his country. He continued to play for Milan, winning the Champions League in 2007, before finally retiring in 2009, having played over 900 games in all competitions for the club. It was announced that his famous number three shirt would be retired, unless one of his sons ever made a first team appearances for the club in the future.

DIEGO MARADONA

Country: Argentina
Born: October 30, 1960
Position: Forward/Midfielder
Clubs: Argentinos Juniors, Boca Juniors, Barcelona, Napoli, Sevilla, Newell's Old Boys

As well as being one of the greatest players to grace the world game, Maradona is also one of the most controversial. Indeed, there are times when his career history reads more like a rap sheet than the biography of one of the world's greatest sportsmen. However, his various bans, drug problems and occasionally perverse behaviour (he once shot at journalists with an air rifle) should not detract from Maradona's formidable achievements in a game he bestrode like a colossus throughout the 1980s.

Born to working class parents in a Buenos Aires suburb, Maradona and football were inseparable from an early age. After playing for a couple of local boys clubs, one of whom he inspired to go 136 matches unbeaten, he joined first division Argentinos Juniors, making his debut as a raw but undoubtedly talented 15-year-old on October 20, 1976.

Barely four months later Maradona was making another debut, this time as a fully-fledged Argentinian international, coming on as a substitute in a friendly against Hungary. Although he was angry at missing out on a place in the final squad for the 1978 World Cup after being selected for the provisional squad of 25, Maradona was a vital part of the Argentina side that won the World Youth Championship in 1979 in Japan.

After scoring 116 goals in 166 appearances for Argentinos Juniors, Maradona was transferred to Boca Juniors for £1 million in 1981. He stayed only one season before Barcelona snapped him up for a world record £3 million fee. Although again prodigious in front of goal, netting 38 times in 58 games, his two-year stay in Spain was undermined by injury. Far more successful was his transfer to Napoli for £5 million in 1984, another world record fee. He led them to a first league title in

1987 and again in 1990, and helped them to a UEFA Cup win in 1989.

Maradona's first World Cup finals in 1982 ended badly for the Argentinians as they failed to make it beyond the second round, while Maradona himself was sent-off against Brazil. It was a very different story in Mexico at the 1986 tournament, as Maradona lifted the World Cup as captain. However, he had lived up to his reputation as the world's best but most controversial player. His schizophrenic nature

was perfectly illustrated by his performance in the quarter-final against England, where he scored both goals in a 2-1 win. The first he pushed past goalkeeper Shilton with his fist ('a little of the hand of God, a little of the head of Maradona' is how he impishly described it at the time) but the second saw Maradona weave the ball around an army of defenders from the halfway line before stroking it into the net.

The 1986 finals proved to be the high point of his career, although he inspired a below par team to another World Cup final in 1990. The following year he was banned from the game for 15 months after testing positive for cocaine, and then arrested in Argentina for possession of the drug. His World Cup swan song came in 1994 and ended in ignominy when he was sent home for failing a drugs test. The curtain finally fell on Maradona's incredible playing career on October 29, 1997, when he turned out for Boca Juniors against rivals River Plate.

In a bizarre twist, despite little coaching experience and after years of well documented personal problems, Maradona was appointed Argentina's national coach in 2008 and after a troublesome qualifying campaign, he led the team to the 2010 World Cup.

Top: The young Diego Maradona of Boca Juniors in 1981. Above left: Argentina's captain with the World Cup in 1986. Above right: In action for Napoli against AC Milan's Franco Baresi in 1991.

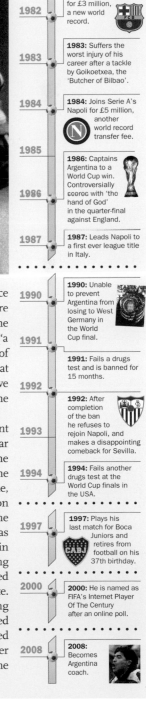

1976: Maradona makes his debut for Argentinos Juniors as a 15-year-old.

1977: He debuts for Argentina as a sub in a 5-1 friendly victory over Hungary.

1978: He makes the provisional squad of 25 players for the World Cup but is cut from the final 22.

1979: Member of Argentina's World Youth Cup winning side in Japan.

1982: Just prior to the World Cup in Spain he is bought by Barcelona for £3 million, a new world record.

1983: Suffers the worst injury of his career after a tackle by Goikoetxea, the 'Butcher of Bilbao'.

1984: Joins Serie A's Napoli for £5 million, another world record transfer fee.

1986: Captains Argentina to a World Cup win. Controversially scores with 'the hand of God' in the quarter-final against England.

1987: Leads Napoli to a first ever league title in Italy.

1990: Unable to prevent Argentina from losing to West Germany in the World Cup final.

1991: Fails a drugs test and is banned for 15 months.

1992: After completion of the ban he refuses to rejoin Napoli, and makes a disappointing comeback for Sevilla.

1994: Fails another drugs test at the World Cup finals in the USA.

1997: Plays his last match for Boca Juniors and retires from football on his 37th birthday.

2000: He is named as FIFA's Internet Player Of The Century after an online poll.

2008: Becomes Argentina coach.

SILVIO MARZOLINI

Country: Argentina
Born: October 4, 1940
Position: Left-back
Clubs: Ferro Carril Oeste, Boca Juniors

Silvio Marzolini is a Boca Juniors legend and was part of the team that dominated the Argentine league in the mid-Sixties, winning three championships. One of the first of a new breed of fullbacks to make a mark in the modern game, his dynamic, all-round style of play still gets him selected in many people's all-time XIs. He appeared in two World Cups for his country, in 1962 and 1966, and played in the infamous quarter-final against England at Wembley. After retirement he went on to manage Boca Juniors, and even took them to a league title in 1981.

JOSEF MASOPUST

Country: Czechoslovakia
Born: February 9, 1931
Position: Midfielder
Clubs: SK Most, Teplice, Dukla Prague, Molenbeek

Below: Lothar Matthäus in action for Germany against Bulgaria at the 1994 World Cup.

Known as the 'Czech Cavalier', Josef Masopust was named Czechoslovakian Player Of The Century. Born in Most, he began his career

in 1950 playing up front but was switched to midfield where his stamina and vision disguised his lack of pace. He joined Dukla Prague in 1952 and went on to win eight championships and three cups with them, making 386 appearances.

At international level Masopust won 63 caps and scored ten goals. He was an ever-present member of the 1958 World Cup side and reached the semi-final of the 1960 European Championship. The high point of his career was picking up a runners-up medal at the 1962 World Cup after scoring the 15th minute goal that gave them the lead in the final over Brazil. His performance and his legendary sportsmanship saw him named 1962 European Footballer Of The Year. He remained the only Czech player to win the coveted award until Pavel Nedved in 2003.

Such were his talents that offers flooded in from clubs in Italy and West Germany, but the communist regime did not allow him to leave until 1969, when aged 38 he moved to Molenbeek in the Belgian second division. He helped them into the top flight and he later moved into coaching, becoming assistant manager of the national side in 1984.

LOTHAR MATTHÄUS

Country: West Germany & Germany
Born: March 21, 1961
Position: Midfielder
Clubs: Borussia Mönchengladbach, Bayern Munich, Inter Milan, New York MetroStars

Lothar Matthäus is Germany's most capped star, but even at the height of his career he was never among the country's most popular players. A powerful but arrogant and often outspoken midfielder, Matthäus made his debut for Mönchengladbach in 1979, before moving to Bayern Munich in 1984. He won seven championships in two spells there, broken by a move to Inter Milan in 1988 where he won the Scudetto as captain in 1989. He also won the UEFA Cup with Inter, scoring the first goal in the home leg of the 2-1 aggregate win over Roma in 1991.

Matthäus made his international debut at 19 as a substitute in a 3-2 win over Holland in the 1980 European Championship, although he did not feature in Germany's winning side in the final. He made his first World Cup appearance in 1982, but his two games as a substitute again did not include the final, which Germany lost to Italy. He went on to establish himself as a fixture in the side, gaining 150 caps. He also appeared at five World Cups and he holds the record for the most appearances at the tournament, having played 25 games at the finals.

After finishing a World Cup runner-up in 1986, Matthäus lifted the trophy as captain four years later in Italy, and he was named

European Footballer Of The Year. He extended his playing career to 39 years of age by moving to sweeper and finishing with the New York MetroStars. As a coach he has since had spells with Rapid Vienna, Partizan Belgrade, Maccabi Netanya and the Hungarian national team. He caused a scandal by resigning his life membership of Bayern Munich and threatening to sue the club over the gate money from his testimonial game.

STANLEY MATTHEWS

Country: England
Born: February 1, 1915
Position: Winger
Clubs: Stoke City, Blackpool

Regarded as 'The Wizard Of The Dribble', Stanley Matthews made his league debut for hometown club Stoke City just six weeks after his 17th birthday. The son of a featherweight boxer, his appearance was slight against his more burly opponents, but it was his lightning burst of pace, balance and timing that few defenders could live with. Within two seasons Matthews had already made his England debut, and as the most exciting young player to emerge in the First Division at the time, it was reported that his presence regularly put 10,000 extra fans on the gate wherever Stoke played.

In 1938 Matthews fell out with manager Bob McGrory and asked to be put on the transfer list, but such was the furore in the local area that business managers claimed that production was being affected by the ongoing saga. Following a massive protest meeting, Matthews decided to stay, but following the war hostilities with McGrory resumed and in 1947 he was sold to Blackpool for £11,500, aged 32.

Despite his veteran status, Matthews reached new heights as he helped Blackpool to three FA Cup finals in six years. Defeats against Manchester United in 1948 and Newcastle United in 1951 led many to believe that an FA Cup hoodoo had a hold, and with 20 minutes remaining of the 1953 final against Bolton, that appeared to ring true for the 38-year-old. With Blackpool having fallen 3-1 behind, Matthews suddenly sprang into action, and having set up Stan Mortensen for his second goal of the game, he took a hold of the match and ran his opposing number, Ralph Banks, ragged. With just three minutes on the clock, he skipped past his marker yet again to give Mortensen his hat-trick, and deep into stoppage time he reached the by-line one last time to set up South African winger Bill Perry to snatch a dramatic winner. Despite Mortensen's heroics and Perry's goal, the game became known as 'The Matthews Final'.

In 1961 Matthews decided to end his career back at Stoke, and having paid £3,500 for his services the club recouped their money by

Above: The 'Wizard Of The Dribble'. Stanley Matthews in a rare stationary pose for Stoke.

regularly putting an extra 26,000 on their gate at the Victoria Ground. Matthews acted as a catalyst as 'The Potters' marched to the 1962-3 Second Division championship and incredibly, at the age of 48, he played 35 of the club's 42 league games. Two years later, he finally bowed out of top-flight football, aged 50 years and five days.

Although he won few honours in his career, Matthews was a truly unique phenomenon, and as a result of his exemplary disciplinary record on the pitch, he was also regarded as a true gentleman. He received the Footballer Of The Year trophy twice, in 1948 and 1963, and was knighted in 1965.

He played for England between 1934 and 1957, and although scoring on his first outing for his country, he found himself in and out of the team. In all, he played only 54 of 119 full internationals during that period, a statistic that consistently outraged fans.

SANDRO MAZZOLA

Country: Italy
Born: November 8, 1942
Position: Forward
Club: Inter Milan

Sandro Mazzola followed in the footsteps of his father Valentino to become an Italian football legend. Though Torino star Valentino died in the Superga plane crash when Sandro was just seven, a passion for the game had already been instilled in Mazzola junior. Inter Milan was to be his sole club, and he made more than 400 top flight appearances for the Nerazzurri, winning consecutive European and World Club Cups (1964 and 1965) and finishing the later season as the league's top scorer. Although not as effective at international level, he did still make 70 appearances for his country and was in the side that won the 1968 European Championship.

VALENTINO MAZZOLA

Country: Italy
Born: January 26, 1919
Position: Inside-left
Clubs: Venezia, Torino

Mazzola formed one half of a formidable strike partnership with Ezio Loik, with whom he combined superbly, initially at Venezia and then, from 1942 onwards, with Torino who bought both players together. The move was a shrewd one because Mazzola went on to lead

Right: 'The Welsh Wizard' Billy Meredith, a legend from the early days of football.

the dominant Torino side to five league titles between 1943 and 1949. Tragically he was killed in his prime in 1949 in the Superga air crash, alongside 17 of his team-mates. With the interruption of the war he had won only 12 caps, but had he lived Mazzola would surely have gone on to achieve greater international recognition in the following year's World Cup finals.

PATRICK MBOMA

Country: Cameroon
Born: November 15, 1970
Position: Forward
Clubs: Chateauroux, Paris Saint-Germain, Metz, Gamba Osaka, Cagliari, Parma, Sunderland, Al-Ittihad, Tokyo Verdy, Vissel Kobe

Patrick Mboma turned down the chance to play for Cameroon at the 1994 World Cup because, although born in Douala, he had been raised in France. Two years later he succumbed to Cameroon's overtures and he went on to win the African Nations Cup in 2000 and 2002, the Olympic Games in 2000, and play in two World Cups. He was also voted African Player Of The Year for 2000. He was initially overlooked for France 98 but was drafted into the squad as a replacement for the injured Marc-Vivien Foe.

He played for clubs in France, England and Italy, while in Japan he was known as the 'Black Panther Of Osaka' when he was the league's top scorer in 1997. He played three times at the 2002 World Cup and retired from international football in 2004. After quitting Tokyo Verdy because of differences with coach Ossie Ardiles, he ended his club career in May 2005 with J.League side Vissel Kobe.

GIUSEPPE MEAZZA

Country: Italy
Born: August 23, 1910
Position: Inside-forward
Clubs: Inter Milan, AC Milan, Juventus, Varese, Atalanta

The man after whom the San Siro stadium in Milan is now formally named was considered the complete forward player in his day; a perfect predator in front of goal, but skilled enough to create chances for others as well as himself. He made his debut for Inter in 1927 at the age of 17 and remained with the club for the next 12 seasons. In that time he was Serie A's top scorer on three occasions, hitting 33 goals in the 1929-30 season, including six in a 10-2 win against Venezia. Having scored 241 goals for Inter in 344 games, Meazza succumbed to a leg injury and missed the whole of the 1939-40 season before joining Inter Milan's arch-rivals AC Milan the following year. Further moves to Juventus and Atalanta followed but Meazza returned to Inter for the 1946-7 season as player-coach to help them battle against relegation.

His time on the international stage proved equally impressive. Playing his first 15 games for Italy as a centre-forward, he scored twice on his debut against Switzerland in 1930 and hit a hat-trick in a 5-0 win over Hungary later that year. However, Vittorio Pozzo soon switched Meazza to inside-right to accommodate centre-forward Angelo Schiavio and in that position he went on to win the World Cup in both 1934 and 1938, one of only two team members to achieve the feat. He died in 1979 aged 68.

BILLY MEREDITH

Country: Wales
Born: July 24, 1874
Position: Outside-right/Winger
Clubs: Chirk, Wrexham, Northwich Victoria, Manchester City, Manchester United

Billy Meredith was the 'Welsh Wizard', a goalscoring winger who played for both of the Manchester clubs in his career, making his debut for Manchester City in 1894. He played for his country until his mid 40s and in club football until he was 50, winning both major honours in England, as well as the Welsh Cup with Chirk. He also helped Wales to a first Home International Championship.

A driving force behind the Players' Union, he suffered the ignominy of suspension following a match-fixing scandal, but he returned as a match-winner, whether it was beating players on his way to the byline to deliver the perfect cross or finding the net himself. He died in 1958 and after years lying in an unmarked grave, the Professional Footballers' Association, the Welsh FA and both Manchester clubs agreed to pay for a new headstone to honour him.

ROGER MILLA

Country: Cameroon
Born: May 20, 1952
Position: Forward
Clubs: Eclair de Douala, Léopard de Douala, Valenciennes, Monaco, Bastia, Saint-Etienne, Montpellier, JS Saint-Pierroise

Dancing the Makossa around a corner flag, Albert Roger Milla gave the World Cup one of its most memorable goal celebrations in 1990. A natural striker who played in France for 12 years, he scored on his international debut in 1978 and was part of the Cameroon squad that returned unbeaten from the 1982 World Cup. At 38 he was playing on Reunion Island when the Cameroon president begged him to come back for Italia 90. Milla became a talisman with four goals from the bench as his team reached the quarter-finals. At 42 he was back at USA 94, with a goal against Russia, making him the oldest World Cup goalscorer ever.

LUÍS MONTI

Country: Argentina, Italy
Born: May 15, 1901
Position: Central defender
Clubs: Huracán, Boca Juniors, San Lorenzo, Juventus

Luís Monti tasted both victory and defeat in World Cup finals, but for different nations. He was on the losing side with Argentina in 1930, going down to hosts Uruguay, but four years later he helped Italy beat Czechoslovakia. A tough, uncompromising and sometimes ruthless defender, at club level Monti won league titles with both Huracán and San Lorenzo in Argentina, and four consecutive Serie A titles in Italy with Juventus.

Below: Roger Milla takes on England in the 1990 World Cup quarter-final.

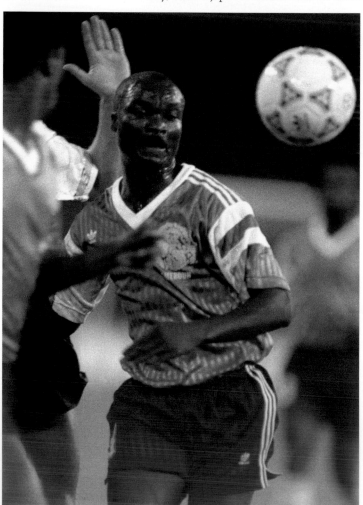

BOBBY MOORE

Country: England
Born: April 12, 1941
Position: Central defender
Clubs: West Ham United, Fulham, San Antonio Thunder, Herning FC, Seattle Sounders

In the pantheon of English sporting heroes no footballer ranks above Bobby Moore, the only England captain to lift the World Cup. His name remains synonymous with honour, dignity and sportsmanship and for what he lacked in pace he made up for with an unrivalled reading of the game, which made him incredibly hard to beat. He was a truly world-class defender.

Bobby Moore was born in Barking, East London, and joined West Ham as a schoolboy, turning professional at 17. He rose rapidly to the first-team, playing flawlessly in a 3-2 win over Manchester United on his debut on September 8, 1958. He did not establish himself fully until 1960, but thereafter became a fixture in the side. In 1964 he captained the team to an FA Cup final win over Preston and was voted Footballer Of The Year. The following season he was back at Wembley to guide West Ham to victory over TSV 1860 Munich in the European Cup Winners' Cup.

Moore won his first England cap against Peru en route to the 1962 World Cup Finals in Chile, when deputising for the injured Bobby Robson, and he played in all four of England's games at the tournament. At 22 he became the country's youngest ever captain when he led the team against Czechoslovakia on May 20, 1963.

Just three years later his crowning moment arrived when he lifted the World Cup at Wembley following the historic 4-2 win over West Germany in the final. The famous fourth goal was the result of Moore measuring a long pass to striker Geoff Hurst rather than listening to the entreaties of his partner Jack Charlton to put the ball over the stand.

Moore's finest game was not Wembley 66, but Mexico 70. However, before that summer's World Cup tournament had even kicked-off he was falsely accused of the theft of a bracelet from a jeweller in Bogota, Colombia. Moore was held under house arrest but remained calm, destroyed the false testimony of the main witness and rejoined the squad five days before England's first game. Soon afterwards he played the best game of his life against Brazil in the heat of Guadalajara, thwarting the tide of yellow shirts that flooded towards him. When the final whistle blew, signifying a narrow 1-0 defeat, Pelé stepped past everyone, including Alan Mullery who had marked him through the game, to swap shirts with Moore. The moment became an iconic football image.

He would win 108 caps for England, 90 of them as captain, but his international career was virtually ended by England's failure to qualify for the 1974 World Cup Finals. At fault for the away defeat to Poland, he was not selected for the return leg at Wembley in October 1973, and the following month he made his last England appearance against Italy.

After 544 league games for West Ham he moved across London to Fulham in March 1974 and enjoyed a last Wembley appearance in the FA Cup final the following year, ironically against his old club but this time he collected a runners-up medal. Thereafter his career tailed off as he joined Seattle Sounders, Herning in Denmark and San Antonio Thunder in Texas. Bizarrely he won three caps for Team America, playing alongside Pelé and finishing his international career against England.

He struggled to succeed in management, first at non-league Oxford City in 1979, then in Hong Kong and finally at Southend in 1984. By the late Eighties he had fallen out of the game and was working as a radio summariser when he was diagnosed with bowel cancer. He died on February 24, 1993. In June 2000 West Ham purchased his World Cup memorabilia for their club museum, having named a stand after him six years earlier.

Top: Bobby Moore enjoys World Cup success in 1966. **Left:** The rising star in 1958. **Above:** Held aloft by West Ham after winning the Cup Winners' Cup in 1965.

1958: Turns professional for West Ham aged 17.

1962: Wins first England cap in World Cup warm-up match against Peru in Lima.

1963: Plays for England against a Rest Of The World XI at Wembley.

1964: He captains West Ham to FA Cup final victory against Preston and is voted Player Of The Year.

1965: Wins European Cup Winners' Cup at Wembley.

1966: Lifts World Cup trophy as England captain after victory over West Germany.

1967: He is awarded OBE for services to football.

1970: Falsely accused of stealing bracelet in Bogota in run up to World Cup finals. Arrested and arrives in Mexico late.

1973: Plays 108th and final game for England in friendly against Italy at Wembley.

1974: He leaves West Ham after 16 years and signs for Fulham.

1975: Takes Fulham to FA Cup final but loses 2-0 to West Ham.

1976: Plays summer football with San Antonio Thunder and turns out alongside Pelé in a Team America XI against England.

1977: His final match for Fulham is the 1000th of his career.

1979: Takes over as manager of non-league Oxford City.

1984: Becomes manager of Southend.

1993: Dies February 24, seven days after attending his final England game, against San Marino.

JOSÉ MANUEL MORENO

Country: Argentina
Born: August 3, 1916
Position: Inside-forward
Clubs: River Plate, España, Universidad Catolica, Boca Juniors, Defensor, Ferrocarril Oeste, Independiente Medellin

One of Argentina's greatest players, Moreno was a winner of five league titles with River Plate, where he spent most of his career. The first of his medals came in 1936 when he broke into the side as a raw but talented 20-year-old. He was part of the club's legendary 'Máquina' attack in the 1940s, along with Munoz, Pedernera, Labruna and Loustau. He played for two years with the Mexican club España before returning to River Plate for a second spell and he spent the later years of his career playing club football in Chile, Uruguay and Columbia. He scored 19 goals in 34 games for his country.

GERD MÜLLER

Country: West Germany
Born: November 3, 1945
Position: Forward
Clubs: TSV Nordingen, Bayern Munich, Fort Lauderdale Strikers

For 36 years Gerd Müller held a special place in World Cup history as the competition's record goalscorer, and although Ronaldo finally surpassed his 14-goal tally in 2006, Müller remains a significant part of the folklore of the finals. He is still his country's most prolific marksman and he also struck the winning goal in the 1974 World Cup Final.

The early 1970s were a golden period for West German football, forged on the athleticism and unquenchable spirit that Müller typified. The ultimate poacher, he created little outside the box but his stocky build and deceptive pace made him a nightmare for defenders to handle. Besides reaching the World Cup semi-final of 1970 and winning in 1974, the West Germans also won the European Championship in 1972 and Müller scored twice in that final.

His international success was repeated at club level with the Bayern Munich side that dominated European football in the mid Seventies. With them he won the European Cup in 1974, 1975 and 1976. That he enjoyed such a glittering career is even more remarkable given his background. He grew up in a small village with no football ground, but he trained hard to make the most of his ability. Never giving less than 100 per cent, he acquired a fearsome reputation as the ultimate predator in the penalty area, earning the nickname 'Der Bomber'.

Müller had made his international debut in 1966, shortly after West Germany had lost the World Cup final to England. When the 1970 tournament arrived he was already known as one of the great strikers in world football, but despite the pressure Müller delivered in spectacular style, hitting ten goals in six games. He recorded hat-tricks against Bulgaria and Peru and the winner against Morocco. He also scored the deciding goal in a quarter-final that saw West Germany come from 2-0 down to beat defending champions England. In the semi-final Müller scored twice more but West Germany bowed out of the competition 4-3 against Italy. He ended the tournament as its top scorer.

Four years later he was less prolific but he was to prove equally lethal when it mattered most as the West Germans forged their way to a final on home soil against the more fluent Dutch. Despite going a goal down, the hosts persevered and it was Müller who scored the winning goal just before half-time. Turning on a loose ball in the box, he feinted to shoot through keeper Jan Jongbloed and the incoming Ruud Krol at the near post, before snapping the ball across the goal towards the unguarded far side of the net. The moment could not have been sweeter: not only had he achieved the greatest dream in world football but he had done so in the Olympic Stadium, where he had scored so many of his goals for Bayern Munich.

Müller retired from the international game after the 1974 final and considered quitting altogether, but instead he decided to continue with Bayern. He had won his first European honour with the club in 1967, the European Cup Winners' Cup, and in a fruitful autumn to his career he achieved his three European Cup triumphs before leaving Bayern in 1979 to wind down his playing days in the USA with Fort Lauderdale Strikers.

Named European Footballer Of The Year in 1970, Müller was also a two-time winner of the European Golden Boot in 1970 and 1972.

MIGUEL MUÑOZ

Country: Spain
Born: January 19, 1922
Position: Inside-right/Centre-half/Right-half
Clubs: Logrones, Racing Santander, Celta Vigo, Real Madrid

Miguel Muñoz was the scorer of Real Madrid's first ever goal in European Cup, against Swiss side Servette in 1955. He was also the first captain to lift the coveted trophy after the club's triumph over Reims in the inaugural final. The heart of that great team, Madrid-born Muñoz led Real to a successful defence in the Bernabéu a year later, with a 2-0 victory over Fiorentina.

He made his international debut against Switzerland in 1948, the same year he joined Real from Celta Vigo. However, he won just seven caps, most of which came at right-half. He retired as a player in 1958 after ten years with Madrid, and just two years later he became the

first man to win the trophy as both a player and a coach following Real's mesmerising 7-3 win over Eintracht Frankfurt.

Above: Japan's Hidetoshi Nakata in international action in 2003.

HIDETOSHI NAKATA

Country: Japan
Born: January 22, 1977
Position: Midfielder
Clubs: Bellmare Hiratsuka, Perugia, Roma, Parma, Bologna, Fiorentina, Bolton Wanderers

Quite simply the greatest footballers that Japan has ever produced, he was voted Asia's Player Of The Year in 1997 and 1998. Individualistic, skilful and with an iron will, throughout his career playmaker Nakata managed to show that players from the fledgling J.League could hold their own in Europe. Nakata carried the weight of his country on his shoulders, with massive media and public interest in his every move. He impressed at the 2002 World Cup but despite helping Roma to their first league title in 18 years, his career at club level was always frustrated. An £18 million move to Parma saw Nakata win the Italian Cup in 2002 but he was loaned to Bologna and finally sold to Fiorentina in July 2004. After just one season he was loaned to English Premiership side Bolton Wanderers. He played in his third World Cup at Germany 2006 and announced his retirement from the game shortly afterwards, aged just 29.

Opposite: The prolific Gerd Müller takes on Yugoslavia at the 1974 World Cup.

JOSE NASAZZI

Country: Uruguay
Born: May 24, 1901
Position: Right-back
Clubs: Lito, Roland Moor, Nacional, Bella Vista

Right-back Jose Nasazzi was not only one of Uruguay's most famous players, but he was one of the great captains in the history of the game. His leadership qualities and organisational skills earned him the nickname 'The Marshall'. As Uruguay skipper Nasazzi took the team to Olympic gold in 1924 and 1928, as well winning the Copa América three times in the 1920s. However, Nasazzi etched himself into football history when he became the first captain to win the World Cup after his country's 4-2 triumph over Argentina in the 1930 final. This was no mean feat as Nasazzi was captaining a side competing without a coach, with the players making all the tactical decisions. When asked to coach the national team in 1945, he did so for just one South American Championship. He did not believe in coaches.

PAVEL NEDVED

Country: Czech Republic
Born: August 30, 1972
Position: Midfielder
Clubs: Dukla Prague, Sparta Prague, Lazio, Juventus

Below: One of the greatest midfielders of the 1970s, Johan Neeskens gets stuck into some Total Football.

Dubbed the 'Czech Cannon' for his powerful but cultured left-foot, Pavel Nedved was the most talented and charismatic Czech footballer since Josef Masopust, a tireless runner either capable of leading the line or acting as playmaker. He represented two of Prague's major club sides, winning three league championships with Sparta, and he became an automatic choice for the national side, starring in the final of the 1996 European Championship.

He joined Lazio after the tournament, clinching the winning goal in the last ever European Cup Winners' Cup final in 1999. He also won the Italian league and cup 'double' in 2000, but a year later Juventus secured his services for £26 million as a replacement for Zinédine Zidane and he was an integral part of the club's revival in the early years of the decade. In 2003 he picked up the Ballon d'Or after being voted European Football Of The Year and he also won the Italian league championship four times in his first five seasons at the Stadio Delle Alpi, although the club was stripped of the 2005 and 2006 titles and relegated after involvement in the Serie A match-fixing scandal.

Voted Czech Player Of The Year on six occasions, Nedved had initially announced his international retirement three months after captaining the Czech Republic to the semi-finals of Euro 2004, but he was tempted back to the international side and played in the 2006 World Cup. The following season he was one of the stars who choose to stay with Juventus for the club's only season in Serie B, and he continued with the team until his retirement in May 2009, playing his last game against his former club Lazio and being applauded off the pitch by both sets of fans.

JOHAN NEESKENS

Country: Holland
Born: September 15, 1951
Position: Midfielder
Clubs: Ajax, Barcelona, New York Cosmos, Fort Lauderdale Strikers, Groningen, Baar, Zug

A feisty playmaker blessed with terrific pace, although he often lived in the shadows of Johan Cruyff, Neeskens was regarded as one of the greatest midfielders of the 1970s and was an integral part of the talented Dutch side that reached the final at both the 1974 and 1978 World Cups. In the second minute of the 1974 title decider with West Germany he scored the fastest goal in a World Cup final, converting what was also the first World Cup final penalty.

His terrific pace, skill and control was also a key feature of the Ajax side that swept all before them, both domestically and in the European Cup. He followed his Ajax team-mate Johan Cruyff to Barcelona after the 1974 final before moving to play in the NASL in America five years later. He eventually returned home to play for Groningen and later saw out his career as a player-coach in Switzerland.

IGOR NETTO

Country: Soviet Union
Born: January 9, 1930
Position: Left-half
Club: Spartak Moscow

Netto will be remembered by his countrymen as the man who led the Soviet Union to success at the Olympic Games in 1956 in Australia, and then four years later, to glory at the European Championship in France. All this during an international career that saw him gain 54 caps and score four goals. Sadly for Netto, injury kept him out of all but one game of the 1958 World Cup but he was an ever present member of the team in 1962, when the Soviets got as far as the quarter-finals before losing to Chile. A strong tackler, Netto moved into central defence when he had lost a little of his pace later in his career. A one-club man, he made more than 350 appearances for Spartak Moscow, winning five league titles in that time.

GUNTER NETZER

Country: West Germany
Born: September 14, 1944
Position: Midfielder
Clubs: Borussia Mönchengladbach, Real Madrid, Grasshopper Zurich

A flamboyant, long-haired playmaker, Netzer was the star of West Germany's European Championship winning side of 1972. He played a crucial hand in his country's advance to the final with a match-winning performance against England in the quarter-finals at Wembley, and he was equally inspirational in the 3-0 defeat of the Soviet Union in the final. Known for his long, accurate passing and ability to inspire others, Netzer usually operated just behind the strikers. He made 37 appearances before losing his place in the national team in 1974 and making just one brief appearance at that year's World Cup. After hanging up his boots, he went on to become a football summariser on television and a successful businessman.

THOMAS NKONO

Country: Cameroon
Born: July 19, 1955
Position: Goalkeeper
Clubs: Douala, Canon Yaoundé, Espanyol, Sabadell, L'Hospitalet, Club Bolivar

Thomas Nkono was twice voted African Footballer Of The Year, in 1979 and 1982. On the second occasion it was for his magnificent performances at the 1982 World Cup. Dubbed the 'Black Spider' he conceded just one goal in three unbeaten games. He had not intended to become a goalkeeper and initially he was a winger with Douala until he went between the

posts when the regular goalkeeper failed to turn up. His performances at the 1982 World Cup led to a move to Europe with Espanyol, with whom he reached the 1988 UEFA Cup Final. During the 2002 African Nations Cup in Mali, while working as goalkeeping coach to Cameroon, he was arrested for 'witchcraft'.

GUNNAR NORDAHL

Country: Sweden
Born: October 19, 1921
Position: Forward
Clubs: Hörnefors, Degerfors, Norrköpping, AC Milan, Roma, Karlstad

Former fireman Gunnar Nordahl set a blazing goal trail wherever he went. He was prolific for both Hörnefors and Degerfors, before moving to Norrköpping and scoring 93 goals in 95 appearances, including seven in one game. He led the charge for Sweden's gold medal success at the 1948 London Olympics and after turning professional with Milan he played alongside fellow Swedes Gren and Liedholm. He topped the Serie A scoring charts five times and is still the club's leading goalscorer. He racked up 43 international goals in 33 games, and picked up a runners-up medal at the 1958 World Cup Final.

ERNST OCWIRK

Country: Austria
Born: March 10, 1926
Position: Centre-half/Midfielder
Clubs: Floridsdorfer, FK Austria Vienna, Sampdoria

Ernst Ocwirk was the last of a dying breed of attacking centre-halves, and while the rest of Europe went for a stopper, FK Austria Vienna (and the Austrian national side) exploited his skill and intuition. FK won the Austrian league title five times with him the side, during his two stints at the club. Nicknamed 'Clockwork'

by the English for his ability to create and dictate matches, Ocwirk helped make Austria one of the strongest teams in Europe, playing 62 times for his country. Between his stints at FK, he also had a five-year spell in Italy with Sampdoria, where he was remodelled as a midfielder.

MORTEN OLSEN

Country: Denmark
Born: August 14, 1949
Position: Defender/Forward/Midfielder
Clubs: B1901 Nykobing, Cercle Brugge, Racing White Bruxelles, Anderlecht, Köln

Morten Olsen's 18-year playing career saw him play in every outfield position, but he will be remembered as a gifted sweeper in the thrilling Denmark side of the 1980s. The role had come to him care of his Anderlecht coach, Tomislav Ivic, after Olsen had recovered from injury. To extend his playing career Ivic cast him as libero and this was embraced by Danish national coach Sepp Piontek. Olsen was instrumental in Denmark's exciting performances at the 1984 European Championship and the 1986 World Cup. He later became a coach and in his first season he won the Danish league with Brondby. He became coach of the national team in 2000.

WOLFGANG OVERATH

Country: West Germany
Born: September 29, 1943
Position: Midfielder
Clubs: SV Siegburg 04, Köln

When Wolfgang Overath helped West Germany to World Cup success on home soil in 1974, not only did he bring his international career to a fitting end, but he also completed a remarkable 'treble'. Having been a beaten finalist in the 1966 final, he scored the winner in the third place play-off in 1970, so he can claim to be the only player to have finished first, second and

third in the World Cup (Beckenbauer was in all three teams, but he did not play in the third place play-off match in 1970). Overath won the Bundesliga in his first season with Köln and, almost 800 games later he bowed out of football after helping them to the German Cup in 1977.

MARC OVERMARS

Country: Holland
Born: March 29, 1973
Position: Winger
Clubs: Go Ahead Eagles, Willem II, Ajax, Arsenal, Barcelona

The career of Marc Overmars really took off when he joined Ajax in 1992 and became a member of the side that won three Dutch titles and the Champions League final in 1995. The following season he was already eyeing a move abroad when he suffered a cruciate ligament injury and was sidelined for 12 months. Once recovered, he joined Arsenal and in his first season proved an influential team member as the club won the league and FA Cup 'double'.

A £25 million move to Barcelona in 2000 made him the most expensive Dutch player ever. He featured in Holland's Euro 2004 side as a regular substitute, but he retired soon after, having had persistent problems with an injured knee. Four years later he came out of retirement to play for his first club, Go Ahead Eagles, in the second tier of Dutch football.

Left: Wolfgang Overath shoots for West Germany against Poland at the 1974 World Cup.

Below: Marc Overmars lifts the FA Cup for Arsenal after scoring in the final against Newcastle United in 1998.

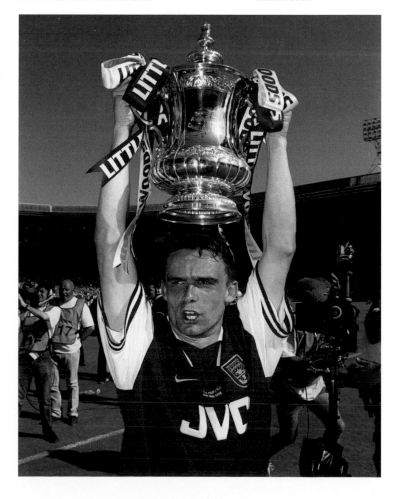

Above: Jean-Pierre Papin beats England's Des Walker at Wembley Stadium in 1992.

JEAN-PIERRE PAPIN

Country: France
Born: November 5, 1963
Position: Forward
Clubs: INF Vichy, Valenciennes, Club Brugge, Marseille, AC Milan, Bayern Munich, Bordeaux, Guingamp, JS Saint-Pierroise, US Cap-Ferret

Jean-Pierre Papin won the European Footballer Of The Year award in 1991 and was one of the most prolific goalscorers of his era. A stocky striker with a powerful shot on either foot, he starred at the 1986 World Cup for France and finished top scorer in the French league for Marseille in five consecutive seasons. Papin found the net from every angle and became synonymous with Marseille's success across Europe. He flourished at international level too, helping France qualify for the 1992 European Championship with nine goals in eight matches.

He struggled to make an impact after moving to Italy to play for AC Milan and injuries marred his spell at Bayern Munich. Yet he won four French titles with Marseille, two Italian titles with Milan, and one UEFA Cup with Bayern in 1996, joining defeated opponents Bordeaux the following year. He scored an impressive 30 goals in 54 appearances for France.

DANIEL PASSARELLA

Country: Argentina
Born: May 25, 1953
Position: Defender
Clubs: Sarmiento, River Plate, Fiorentina, Inter Milan

Right: Fans lift Argentina captain Daniel Passarella as he holds aloft the World Cup in 1978.

Passarella was an instinctive sweeper who exuded calm and he captained Argentina to World Cup glory in 1978, aged only 25. His leadership in the face of huge expectations earned him the nickname 'El Gran Capitan'. Passarella was an unusually skilful defender who contributed enormously in attack, scoring 22 goals in 70 internationals. He was particularly dangerous at set pieces and scored three goals in 12 World Cup games in 1978 and 1982. Passarella was selected for the 1986 finals but withdrew through injury. He achieved notoriety as Argentina's national coach in the mid-Nineties, banning players with long hair, or who wore earrings.

BERT PATENAUDE

Country: USA
Born: November 4, 1909
Position: Centre-forward
Clubs: Philadelphia Field Club, J&P Coats, Fall River Marksmen, Newark Americans, New York Yankees, New York Giants, Philadelphia German-Americans, St Louis' Central Breweries

Bertram Patenaude scored the first hat-trick in World Cup history with his goals against Paraguay at the 1930 tournament. However, for many years Patenaude had been credited with just two goals in the game. The official report by team manager Wilfred Cummings, written at the end of the tournament, duly credits Patenaude with all three goals, and this document, coupled with some contemporary news reports and the testimonies of several squad members years later, indicate that Patenaude should be attributed with the first World Cup hat-trick. In total he only played four times for his country but did score six goals, four of them at the World Cup.

ADOLFO PEDERNERA

Country: Argentina
Born: November 15, 1918
Position: Forward
Clubs: River Plate, Atlanta, Huracán, Millonarios

Pedernera provided the cutting edge for the devastating River Plate 'Máquina' forward line in the 1930s and 1940s. Nicknamed 'the Maestro', he is credited with evolving the deep-lying centre-forward role to great success. He won the Argentine league championship with River Plate five times between 1936 and 1945 and he played 21 times for his country.

In 1948, during the Argentine players strike, he moved to Colombia to play for Millonarios of Bogota. He attracted a huge crowd when he was presented to the fans for the first time, taking $18,000 on the gate, several times what the club would usually get for a game, let alone a player presentation. Pedernera's move began an exodus of top South American talent to Colombia, beginning a golden age for the league called 'El Dorado'. Pedernera himself helped this process, even recruiting his replacement at River Plate, Alfredo Di Stéfano.

PELÉ

Country: Brazil
Born: October 23, 1940
Position: Forward
Clubs: Santos, New York Cosmos

Edson Arantes do Nascimento, or Pelé as he is more commonly known, began kicking a ball around the yard of his Três Corações home at the age of two and had the perfect role model in his father, Dondinho, who was a striker who played at one point for Fluminese. After turning out for amateur teams, including Baquinho and Sete Setembro, Pelé was discovered by the former Brazilian international Waldemar de Brito, who recognized the 11-year-old's potential and invited him to join him at Clube Atlético Bauru.

Within four years, de Brito had seen enough and took his protégé to top São Paulo outfit Santos for a trial, telling the club at the time: 'This boy will be the greatest soccer player in the world'. Pelé went on to score on his debut that September, and although appearances were limited in his opening campaign, he netted 41 league goals the following year.

National coach Sylvio Pirilo gave Pelé his Brazil debut on July 7, 1957, and the 16-year-old scored in a 2-1 defeat to Argentina, becoming the youngest player to score an international goal. His appearances in a gold shirt made Pelé a worldwide phenomenon and the early signs of his greatness were seen at the 1958 World Cup Finals in Sweden.

Initially not selected in the starting line-up, Pelé made his bow in Brazil's final group game against the Soviet Union as a result of an approach made by his team-mates to coach Vicente Feola. He went on to score in the quarter-final against Wales – at 17 years and 239 days old it made him the youngest ever World Cup goalscorer, a record that still stands. His pace, trickery and eye for goal ensured he remained in the side and a semi-final hat-trick in a 5-2 defeat of France, and two more goals in the final against Sweden, made sure he was not out of the headlines.

Although Brazil successfully defended the world title four years later in Chile, a pulled muscle prematurely ended Pelé's tournament, and the 1966 campaign would also end in tears and frustration. The greatest player in the world became a marked man in England and was brutally fouled against Bulgaria and Portugal as Brazil crashed out at the first stage. 'I don't want to end my life as an invalid,' moaned Pelé, as he threatened to boycott the next World Cup.

Pelé's frustrations eased though, and his performances at the 1970 tournament proved to be the pinnacle of an illustrious career. He was again the focal point of a Brazil team that is still regarded as the greatest ever. A free-flowing brand of football swept all challengers aside and the team's 4-1 final victory against Italy emphasised their dominance. Pelé scored in that game, taking his tally to four and his overall World Cup total to 12 in 14 matches. He would eventually end his international career with 77 goals in 92 appearances and he is still his country's top scorer.

Pelé left Santos in 1974, having scored over a thousand goals for the club. He finished his career in the North American Soccer League with the New York Cosmos, playing the final game in a friendly against Santos on October 1, 1977. He played one half for each club and after the game he was carried around the pitch by his Cosmos team-mates.

Above: Pelé, during his 18-year career with Santos. Below left: Queen Elizabeth presents a trophy to Pelé at the Maracanã. Below right: Taking the beautiful game to the world at Mexico 70.

1950: Begins playing for local team Bauru, under former World Cup star Waldemar de Brito.

1956: Joins Santos and scores as a 15-year-old on his debut against Corinthians.

1957: Scores on his international debut for Brazil against Argentina.

1958: At 17 he becomes the youngest ever World Cup winner. He also scores twice in the final in a 5-2 victory over Sweden.

1962: Misses most of the World Cup through injury but helps Santos to win the World Club Cup.

1966: The world's best player is fouled out of the World Cup by brutal opposition tactics.

1969: Scores his 1000th career goal, a penalty against Vasco da Gama.

1970: The star of the Mexico World Cup finals, he inspires Brazil to lift the Jules Rimet Trophy for the third time.

1971: Makes his final appearance for Brazil, against Yugoslavia in Rio de Janeiro. He does not score.

1974: Plays his final game for Santos against Ponte Preta.

1975: Comes out of retirement to appear for New York Cosmos in the USA.

1977: Retires after helping Cosmos win the North American Soccer League title.

1994: Appointed as Brazil's Minister for Sport.

Above: Abedi Pele of Marseille shields the ball from AC Milan's Paolo Maldini.

ABEDI PELE

Country: Ghana
Born: November 5, 1962
Position: Winger/Midfielder
Clubs: Real Tamale United, Al Sadd, FC Zurich, Dragons de l'Ouéme, Chamois Niortais, Mulhouse, Real Tamale United, Marseille, Lille, Lyon, Torino, 1860 Munich, Al-Ain

At the age of 17 Abedi Ayew Pele won the 1982 African Nations Cup with Ghana. Although not yet an automatic choice for the team, the precocious teenager proved to be a sensation. A European club career beckoned and his greatest success was achieved with Marseille, winning the 1993 European Cup after beating the mighty AC Milan 1-0, just two years after losing the final on penalties to Red Star Belgrade. He was given an influential free role in a talented team that included Barthez, Desailly, Deschamps, Boksic and Völler and he excelled. In 1991 he was voted African Player Of The Year for his outstanding performances in Europe.

SILVIO PIOLA

Country: Italy
Born: September 29, 1913
Position: Centre-forward
Clubs: Pro Vercelli, Lazio, Torino, Juventus, Novara

Right: Real Madrid's Pirri greets Celtic's Danny McGrain before the 1980 European Cup quarter-final.

Ranking as one of the greatest goalscorers of his era, Silvio Piola was a tall and imposing centre-forward recognised for his strength on the ball and his power in the air, all factors that made him hard to play against. He scored five goals at the 1938 World Cup, including two in the final as Italy triumphed. He made his international debut in March 1935, scoring twice in a 2-0 defeat of Austria but soon coach Vittorio Pozzo was playing him alongside inside-right Giuseppe Meazza, and together they made the most formidable attacking duo at the 1938 tournament, with Piola as much a creator as a goalscorer. At club level he started at Pro Vercelli and although he challenged for the title with Lazio and Juventus, the runners-up spot was the best he managed. He continued playing after the war but he will always be best remembered for his achievements at the 1938 World Cup.

PIRRI

Country: Spain
Born: March 11, 1945
Position: Midfielder/Defender
Clubs: Ccuta, Grenada, Real Madrid, Puebla

Few players have ever served one club as loyally as Pirri did at Real Madrid. For three decades he was at the heart of the club, firstly as a player and then in a variety of positions, including sports director. He made his debut for the Madrid giants as a striker in 1964 but over the years moved back first into midfield and then defence, playing until 1979, after which he became the club doctor and later a scout. Real name José Martínez, Pirri's achievements with Madrid were numerous, including ten Spanish championships, four domestic cups and the European Cup. He also played 41 times for Spain between 1966 and 1978.

FRANTISEK PLÁNICKA

Country: Czechoslovakia
Born: June 2, 1904
Position: Goalkeeper
Club: Slovan Prague, Bubenec, Slavia Prague

Frantisek Plánicka was one of Czechoslovakia's most successful players and was a part of Slavia Prague's unstoppable side of the 1920s and 1930s. He not only won eight league titles, but in 1938 Slavia lifted the 1938 Mitropa Cup. He was an automatic choice for the national team between 1925 and 1938, captaining them in the World Cups of 1934 and 1938. In the 1934 competition his magnificent, agile performances helped the Czechoslovakians to the runners-up spot, while in the 1938 quarter-final clash with Brazil, Plánicka played much of the game with a broken arm. In total he made 73 appearances for his country in a 12-year international career.

MICHEL PLATINI

Country: France
Born: June 21, 1955
Position: Midfielder
Clubs: Nancy, Saint-Etienne, Juventus

Michel Platini is regarded as one of the greatest players of all time. With his remarkable technique, superb passing and sublime free-kicks, he was the world's best player during the first half of the 1980s. His astonishing goalscoring record from midfield made him a match-winner at the highest level and his ability to shine on the biggest occasions set him apart from his peers.

Platini excelled for France throughout an 11-year international career and he won a string of club honours at Juventus, impressing football followers across the world. He started his career at Nancy, who took a chance on him after others famously turned him down because of his frail physique. He showed elegant, natural skills and worked hard on his technique on the training field. At the relatively small club he was able to develop after making his league debut at 17 and emerged as a bright French talent, making his international debut against Czechoslovakia on March 27, 1976.

He made three appearances at the 1978 World Cup Finals, hinting at things to come with his goal against Argentina, and after the tournament

he moved to Saint-Etienne. However, the club's golden era was over and despite brilliant individual performances, Platini returned to the international spotlight only in 1982. That year he helped the French to the semi-finals of the World Cup, where they lost on penalties to West Germany following a thrilling 3-3 draw. Platini was the leader of their gifted generation, showing the vision and goalscoring ability that was his trademark.

At 27 he was coming to the peak of his powers and he moved to Juventus. It was in Serie A that he truly developed into the world's greatest player, helping the squad win the Italian title in 1984 and 1986, the Italian Cup in 1983, the European Cup Winners' Cup and the European Super Cup in 1984, and the European Cup and the World Club Cup in 1985. Platini's range of skill proved unrivalled in the world's toughest league. More remarkable still was his record as a marksman. Three times he finished as the highest goalscorer in the Italian league, thanks largely to his ability with free-kicks and penalties.

In the midst of this club success Platini also tasted victory with the national side, inspiring the team to win the European Championship in 1984 with a series of astonishing displays. He struck nine goals in five matches, including two hat-tricks and the winner in the semi-final. He also hit the opener in the 2-0 win over Spain in the final, completing a remarkable run.

He was voted European Footballer Of The Year in 1983, 1984 and 1985, becoming only the second player to win the award three times (Johan Cruyff was the first). He appeared at the 1986 World Cup as France again reached the semi-final, but retired aged 31 in May 1987. He won 72 caps for his country and scored 41 goals, becoming France's all-time highest goalscorer until Thierry Henry broke the record in 2007.

DAVID PLATT

Country: England
Born: June 10, 1966
Position: Midfielder
Clubs: Manchester United, Crewe Alexandra, Aston Villa, Bari, Juventus, Sampdoria, Arsenal

David Platt had a modest start to his professional career and was released by Manchester United in 1985, moving to Crewe and then Aston Villa. However, he made his name during the 1990 World Cup, where one goal effectively changed his life. His fantastic volley against Belgium gave England victory in the final minute of extra-time and sent his team into the quarter-finals.

The goal established Platt's place in the starting line-up and after England finished third in the tournament he returned home as a player in demand. After one more season with Aston Villa he carved out a fine career in Italian football, initially with Bari, who bought him for a British record transfer fee of £5.5 million. He signed for Juventus in 1992 but did not hold down a regular first-team place. He was with the club when they won the UEFA Cup in 1993, but he did not feature in either leg of the final. He signed for Sampdoria the following season and won the Italian Cup.

At the same time his international career boomed. He was one of England's key players during the Nineties, playing in the 1992 and 1996 European Championships, eventually winning a total of 62 caps and scoring 27 goals. He was also captain on several occasions.

Platt's Italian adventure ended in 1995 when he signed for Arsenal, and although he was troubled by knee problems, he won the league and FA Cup 'double' in 1998 with 'The Gunners' before moving into coaching.

Above: One of world football's true greats, Michel Platini on the ball for France in 1986.

Above: Hardly the classic build for a footballer, Ferenc Puskás was a Hungarian football legend.

ERNEST POL

Country: Poland
Born: November 3, 1932
Position: Centre-forward
Clubs: Legia Warsaw, Gornik Zabrze

Ernest Pol was one of Poland's greatest ever strikers, having led the line in 42 internationals and scoring 30 goals. His 16-year international career spanned the 1950s and 1960s. In October 1956 he scored four times in a 5-3 friendly win over Norway and four years later at the Olympics in Rome he scored five goals in the 6-1 thrashing of Tunisia. He scored two other international hat-tricks against Finland and Denmark. He won the Polish title twice with army side Legia and five times with Gornik Zabrze. He scored 186 league goals as Gornik dominated Polish football during this period, but the political situation of the day meant that he was never able to play for any of the big European clubs.

TONI POLSTER

Country: Austria
Born: March 10, 1964
Position: Forward
Clubs: Austria Vienna, Torino, Sevilla, Logrones, Rayo Vallecano, Köln, Borussia Mönchengladbach, SV Austria Salzburg

Toni Polster remains the biggest name in Austrian football. Such was his importance to the national side that he was still considered one of their key players at the age of 34 during France 98. He made his final appearance for his country against Iran two years later, bringing down the curtain on a career spanning 95 internationals. He is currently Austria's second most-capped player of all time behind Andreas Herzog.

In a side that was only able to qualify for the 1990 and 1998 World Cups during Polster's career, his haul of 44 international goals made him a feared opponent.

FERENC PUSKÁS

Country: Hungary, Spain
Born: April 2, 1927
Position: Forward
Clubs: Kispest, Honvéd, Real Madrid

Football can have few more unlikely stars than Ferenc Puskás, the short, barrel-chested Hungarian goal machine who became known as the 'Galloping Major'. Puskás possessed one of the most powerful and accurate left feet in the history of the game and his goalscoring record was phenomenal: 84 goals in 85 matches for Hungary and 35 goals in 39 European matches for Real Madrid from 1961 to 1965.

As a small child Puskás was entranced by the roar of the Kispest crowd, audible from his kitchen window in Budapest. The smallest kid on the block, he became inseparable from the five-year-old next door, József Bózsik. Their fathers worked together in a slaughterhouse and when Bózsik was picked up by Kispest, his friend went with him. Together they forged one of the most dynamic strike partnerships in the history of the game. Kispest was later renamed Honvéd after 1949 and turned into the army side, which is how Puskás gained his nickname.

He scored on his international debut against Austria on August 20, 1945, and in the epochal 6-3 victory at Wembley in 1953 he underlined the gulf between the 'Magical Magyars' and England with a memorable drag back and shot past goalkeeper Gil Merrick. A year later he captained the side at the 1954 World Cup and came back from an injury in the second match to play in the final. Though clearly unfit he opened the scoring after six minutes and had a late equaliser disallowed.

In a time of hardship he became chief smuggler among the Hungarian players, returning from away fixtures loaded with razor blades or machine parts, twice having to talk himself out of trouble with the secret police.

Puskás won five Hungarian league titles with Honvéd but his life took a dramatic turn in 1956 when the Soviet Union invaded his country to quell the nationalist uprising. Honvéd were touring Europe at the time, and along with Sandor Kocsis and several other players, Puskás refused to return and was banned by UEFA from playing football for anyone else.

Real Madrid arranged for the ban to be rescinded and he made his debut for them in 1958, aged 30, rapidly forging a devastating partnership with Argentine Alfredo Di Stéfano and together they helped the club to six league titles. Although not as prolific as in his heyday, Puskás scored a staggering 241 goals in 262 appearances for Real, explaining his Spanish nickname 'Cañoncito Pum' (the Little Cannon).

In 1960, against Eintracht Frankfurt, Puskás became the first player to score a hat-trick in a European Cup final. Di Stéfano became the second in the same game, while Puskás finished with a fourth from the penalty spot. He was the competition's top scorer in three campaigns, scoring another hat-trick when losing to Benfica in the final of 1962, aged 35.

Puskás picked up four caps as a naturalised Spaniard, three of which were at the 1962 World Cup, before retiring four years later. He moved to Athens to coach Panathinaikos, taking the club to the European Cup final in 1971, before finally resettling in Budapest. In 1993 he became caretaker manager of the national side but failed to guide Hungary to the 1994 World Cup. This did not deter the Hungarian government from marking his 75th birthday in 2002 by renaming the Népstadion in his honour. As he had helped build the stadium as a youth, it was a fitting tribute to a genuine football legend. He died in November 2006.

HELMUT RAHN

Country: West Germany
Born: August 16, 1929
Position: Outside-right
Clubs: Rot-Weiss Essen, Köln, Enschede, Meidericher

An outside-right with a thunderous shot, Helmut Rahn will be best remembered for the part he played in an unfancied West German side's World Cup success in 1954. Rahn scored twice in the final against the red-hot favourites Hungary, netting the equaliser and then the late winner. Yet Rahn came close to missing the finals, as he was on the verge of signing for Nacional of Uruguay while on a tour with club side Rot-Weiss Essen when West German coach Sepp Herberger summoned him home to join the squad. Rahn also made an impact at the 1958 World Cup Finals when his six-goal tally tied him with Pelé as the tournament's second highest scorer behind Just Fontaine.

THOMAS RAVELLI

Country: Sweden
Born: August 13, 1959
Position: Goalkeeper
Clubs: Osters Vaxjo, IFK Gothenburg, Tampa Bay Mutiny

The adage that you have to be a bit mad to be a goalkeeper was never more appropriate than when applied to Ravelli. Known as the clown prince of Swedish football for his humourous approach to the game, he was a magnificent, agile keeper who helped his country to the semi-finals of the 1994 World Cup in America. Ravelli made an incredible 143 appearances for his country between 1981 and 1997, a period in which Swedish football grew in stature. The commanding six-footer also featured at the 1990 World Cup and for a while he was the international game's most capped player.

ROB RENSENBRINK

Country: Holland
Born: July 3, 1947
Position: Left-winger
Clubs: DWS Amsterdam, Club Brugge, Anderlecht, Portland Timbers, Toulouse

The outstanding Dutch winger spent much of his career in Belgium with Anderlecht, helping the club to two European Cup Winners' Cup victories, scoring in both finals. On the international scene he was a leading figure in the exciting Dutch team of the Seventies. He played in the World Cup final twice, in 1974 and 1978, and although he was never a winner he does hold the honour of scoring the 1000th goal in the competition's history, which came with a penalty against Scotland in 1978. He ended his playing career with brief spells in both America and France.

FRANK RIJKAARD

Country: Holland
Born: September 30, 1962
Position: Midfielder/Central defender
Clubs: Ajax, Sporting Lisbon, Real Zaragoza, AC Milan

Hugely versatile, Frank Rijkaard made his Ajax debut in 1979 under Johan Cruyff but left the club for brief spells in Portugal and Spain after the two men fell out. He ended up in Italy where he was an integral part of the all-conquering Milan team of the late Eighties and early Nineties, alongside fellow Dutchmen Ruud Gullit and Marco Van Basten. Milan won two

European Cups, two league titles and two World Club Cups with Rijkaard in the team, and his return to Ajax earned him a further Champions League winners' medal in 1995.

Having made his international debut at just 19 years of age he went on to play an important role in the exciting Dutch side that won the 1988 European Championship, and he also earned himself a controversial exit from the 1990 World Cup. Rijkaard became national team coach in 1998 but resigned after his promising Dutch tournament favourites were eliminated from Euro 2000 on penalties by Italy at the semi-final stage. Subsequently he guided Barcelona to the Champions League title in 2006.

LUIGI RIVA

Country: Italy
Born: November 7, 1944
Position: Left-wing/Forward
Clubs: Legnano, Cagliari

Originally a left-winger, Gigi Riva's pace saw him develop into a prolific and popular striker for Italy and Cagliari. He helped the unfashionable Sardinian side to Serie A in 1964 and to the Scudetto in 1970, scoring 21 goals in 28 games that season. He was also Italy's top marksman at the 1970 World Cup and scored in extra-time during the semi-final victory over West Germany. Riva twice broke his leg while playing for the national team, the second time soon after the 1970 finals. He stayed loyal to Cagliari and turned down a big money move to Juventus, but after a poor World Cup in 1974 he lost his place in the national side. He retired in 1976 and remains Italy's leading scorer with 35 goals.

Below: Frank Rijkaard, an integral part of AC Milan's all conquering team of the late Eighties and early Nineties.

ROBERTO RIVELINO

Country: Brazil
Born: January 1, 1946
Position: Midfielder/Left-winger
Clubs: Corinthians, Fluminese, El Hilal

The arrival of Mario Zagalo as Brazil coach in the lead up to the 1970 World Cup finals proved to be a watershed in the career of Roberto Rivelino. Under former coach João Saldanha, the Corinthians midfielder had to be content with fleeting appearances, but as the tournament got underway it became evident that the greatest exponent of the 'banana shot' free-kick was ready to unleash his talents on a worldwide audience.

An inside-left by preference, Zagalo converted Rivelino into a deep-lying left winger where he combined in perfect harmony with Pelé, Gérson, Tostão and Jairzinho to form the most potent attacking force that Brazil had ever had. His best moment came against Czechoslovakia, when a swerving long-range free-kick inspired the team to victory. Scoring three goals en route to the final, Rivelino collected a winners' medal in 1970. He would play at two further World Cups, captaining the team in 1978, but he was unable to make the same impact. He represented his country a total of 92 times and scored 26 goals.

GIANNI RIVERA

Country: Italy
Born: August 18, 1943
Position: Inside-forward
Clubs: US Alessandria, AC Milan

Gianni Rivera was an Italian hero who made his Serie A debut for his local team aged 15, transferring to Milan just a year later. Staying at the San Siro throughout his long and successful career, he played at four consecutive World Cups and helped Milan to become Italian champions in 1962 and European Cup winners in 1963. His superb passes twice put José Altafini through the Benfica defence to score the goals that made Milan champions of Europe. Slender and graceful, he was a technically superb player with tremendous passing skills and a powerful shot, particularly from distance.

He was the dominating figure when Milan became Italian champions again in 1968 and followed this triumph by winning the European Cup and the World Club Cup the following year. He landed the European Footballer Of The Year award in 1969 and by the time he wound up his club career with a third title in 1979 he had also won the Italian Cup four times.

Rivera featured in Italy's winning side at the 1968 European Championship, but he had to battle for his place in the team with great rival Sandro Mazzola. Indeed, he was left on the bench for the 1970 World Cup Final against Brazil, getting on the pitch for just the last six minutes. He won 60 caps and scored 14 goals.

BRYAN ROBSON

Country: England
Born: January 11, 1957
Position: Midfielder
Clubs: West Bromwich Albion, Manchester United, Middlesbrough

Robson earned the nickname 'Captain Marvel' for his unflinching and inspiring midfield performances in what was an undistinguished era for club and country. For a decade he was consistently the most outstanding player to wear the colours of England and Manchester United. Signed by United for a British record fee of £1.5 million, Robson's battling, defensive qualities, combined with regular goals, made him a natural leader. He managed 26 strikes for England, including a 27-second effort against France at the 1982 World Cup, and a total of 97 for Manchester United.

He led United to three FA Cup triumphs but at the time of Liverpool's great dominance he looked destined to become one of the greatest players never to win the title. However, Manchester United finally achieved back-to-back Premiership wins in 1993 and 1994, in the autumn of Robson's career. He then joined Middlesbrough as player-manager. Capped 90 times by England, 65 as captain, Robson paid the price for his fearlessness by suffering regular injuries, most significantly at the 1986 and 1990 World Cups.

ROMARIO

Country: Brazil
Born: January 29, 1966
Position: Forward
Clubs: Olario, Vasco Da Gama, PSV Eindhoven, Barcelona, Flamengo, Valencia, Fluminese, Al Sadd, Miami, Adelaide United, América

Frustrating to coaches, adored by fans and feared by defenders, at his peak in the early Nineties, Romario was arguably the greatest striker on the planet and a worthy heir to the tradition of great Brazilian attackers. In 1994, the year Brazil won the World Cup, he was at his deadliest. He scored five goals at the tournament and although he failed to get on the scoresheet in the final itself, a drab 0-0 draw with Italy, at least he was among the successful penalty takers. He was named World Footballer Of The Year soon after.

A year before the World Cup, Romario had joined Barcelona for £3 million. It was a move that brought the Spanish championship but by now he was attracting as much coverage for his playboy lifestyle as for his feats on the pitch. In 1996 he returned to Brazil to join Flamengo, only to be sacked three years later. By then injury had denied him a place alongside Ronaldo at the 1998 World Cup and he was not selected by Luiz Felipe Scolari for the 2002 squad, despite huge public outcry. With his international

Above: Italy's star of the 1982 World Cup, Paolo Rossi outpaces Junior of Brazil.

career in decline he remained in demand at club level, hopping around the world to play for whichever coaches could most tolerate his indulgences. Despite his intention to retire, Romario continued to play for Brazil until 2005 and remained active at club level for many years.

JULIO CESAR ROMERO

Country: Paraguay
Born: August 28, 1960
Position: Forward
Clubs: Sportivo Luquero, New York Cosmos, Fluminese, Barcelona, Puebla, Olimpia, La Serena, Club Cerro Corá

The 1985 South American Footballer Of The Year, Romero was the star of the Paraguay side that reached the second round of the 1986 World Cup. Alongside strike partner Cabanas, he spearheaded his team to a win over Iraq and creditable draws with hosts Mexico and Belgium, finishing second in their group before losing to England. Nicknamed 'Romerito', he lit up the Brazilian league as one of the leading lights of the Fluminese team of the mid-1980s, winning the title in 1984. He was twice a champion in the North American Soccer League with New York Cosmos, in 1980 and 1982.

PAOLO ROSSI

Country: Italy
Born: September 23, 1956
Position: Centre-forward
Clubs: Juventus, Como, Vicenza, Perugia, AC Milan, Verona

Although Rossi retired young, at the age of 29, he packed a great deal of incident into a short and controversial career. A problematic knee injury saw Juventus release him in 1975 but he recovered, prospered and eventually joined Perugia for £3.5 million. Despite being banned for two years in the early 1980s following his alleged involvement in a match-fixing scandal,

Opposite: Roberto Rivelino of Brazil is tackled by an Italian defender in the 1970 World Cup final.

Rossi received a surprise late call up to the Italian squad for the 1982 World Cup Finals in Spain. It was there that his ailing reputation enjoyed an extraordinary resurrection.

He looked off the pace in the early stages of the competition but he had the perseverance of coach Enzo Bearzot to thank for his continued selection, and he repaid that loyalty in full when he scored six goals in the last three games, including a hat-trick against Brazil and the opening goal of the final against West Germany. Italy ended the tournament as champions and Rossi was named European Player Of The Year.

KARL-HEINZ RUMMENIGGE

Country: West Germany
Born: September 25, 1955
Position: Forward
Clubs: Bayern Munich, Inter Milan, Servette

For several years Rummenigge was the leading player in German football. A prolific striker, he was twice a European Cup winner and starred for Bayern Munich in the 1976 victory over Saint-Etienne. He reached his peak four years later, helping the Germans to win the European Championship. Twice European Footballer Of The Year (1980 and 1981), he scored 45 goals in 95 games for his country but did not have the best of luck: he was captain when the Germans lost the 1982 World Cup to Italy, and again four years later in defeat to Argentina.

IAN RUSH

Country: Wales
Born: October 20, 1961
Position: Striker
Clubs: Chester City, Liverpool, Juventus, Leeds United, Newcastle United, Sheffield United, Wrexham, Sydney Olympic

Below: Karl-Heinz Rummenigge scores against Algeria at the 1982 World Cup.

Ian Rush was one of the greatest goalscorers of his, or any other era. Signed by Bob Paisley

from Chester City for £300,000, he became a Liverpool stalwart for 16 years, barring a short spell in Italy with Juventus, where he failed to settle. As a result Ian Rush now stands as Liverpool's highest goalscorer of all time, with an impressive 346 goals to his name (he is the club's second highest scorer in the league with 229, just behind the record set by Roger Hunt).

Rush can also claim to be one of the most highly-decorated players in English football as his career peaked in conjunction with the greatest period in Liverpool's history, when league titles, FA Cups and European Cups flowed. Aside from his Italian sojourn, which was not quite as disastrous as has been made out, Rush's other great career disappointment was failing to grace the finals of any major international championship, but he was still capped 73 times by Wales, scoring 28 goals.

HUGO SANCHEZ

Country: Mexico
Born: June 11, 1958
Position: Forward
Clubs: UNAM, San Diego Sockers, Atlético Madrid, Real Madrid, América, Rayo Vallecano, Atlante, Linz, Dallas Burn, Celaya

Human jack-in-the-box Hugo Sanchez is probably the greatest-ever player to emerge from Central America. The livewire Mexican, whose trademark was an acrobatic somersault celebration after each goal (taught to him by his Olympic gymnast sister), was the top goalscorer in Spanish league football for an incredible five consecutive seasons. He totted up 234 goals, mainly for Madrid's senior clubs, and his partnership with Emilio Butragueño at the Bernabéu remains the stuff of legend – as does his propensity for the bicycle kick. His international career lasted from 1977 to 1998, and he captained his country during several World Cup tournaments, scoring for Mexico 29 times in 58 appearances.

LEONEL SANCHEZ

Country: Chile
Born: April 25, 1936
Position: Left-winger
Club: Universidad de Chile, Colo Colo, Palestino, Ferrobadminton

Leonel Sanchez was the star player of the Chilean team that finished third as hosts in the 1962 World Cup. Raiding from the left-wing in typically direct fashion, Sanchez ended the tournament as the Golden Boot winner with four goals, a distinction he shared with five other players. He is also remembered for his part in the infamous 'Battle Of Santiago' between Chile and Italy at the same finals. After being repeatedly kicked by Mario David he knocked the Italian defender to the floor with a left hook.

The son of a boxer, he also broke the nose of Humberto Maschio, but he escaped discipline for both fouls. He also played at the 1966 finals.

JOSÉ SANTAMARIA

Country: Uruguay, Spain
Born: July 31, 1929
Position: Centre-half
Clubs: Nacional, Real Madrid

The hard-as-nails Uruguayan centre-back was the defensive lynchpin of the all-conquering Nacional de Montevideo and Real Madrid teams of the 1950s and 1960s. With Nacional he won five Uruguayan championship titles in the Fifties, breaking into the national team. The move to Europe brought glory with Real Madrid. Playing behind the attacking talents of Puskás, Di Stéfano and Gento he won a hat-trick of European Cups and six Spanish league titles. Santamaria is also one of five players to have represented two countries at the finals of the World Cup. In 1954 he was among of the stars of the tournament while playing in the centre of defence for Uruguay. However, in 1962 he was to be found in Spanish colours and he collected 17 caps for his adopted country. He later went on to become manager of a disappointing Spain side during the 1982 World Cup Finals.

DJALMA SANTOS

Country: Brazil
Born: February 27, 1929
Position: Right-back
Clubs: Portuguesa, Palmeiras, Atlético Paranaenese

Twice a World Cup winner, Santos was aged 37 when he played in his fourth tournament in 1966. However, it was not to be a happy competition for the outstanding fullback and he lost his place after the defeat to Hungary. At the finals four years earlier he had been at the height of his powers and he formed a terrific understanding with Garrincha. He set up the third goal as Brazil retained the world title with a victory over Czechoslovakia, while in Sweden in 1958 his sole appearance was in Brazil's final victory over the hosts.

NILTON SANTOS

Country: Brazil
Born: May 16, 1925
Position: Left-back
Club: Botafogo

Referred to as a left-back Nilton Santos loved to push forward, more like a modern wing-back. He represented his country in a 14-year spell that included two victorious World Cup campaigns in 1958 and 1962 and that saw him make 75 international appearances before he retired in

1963 at the age of 37. He made his debut for Brazil in 1949 and the following year embarked upon Brazil's ill-fated World Cup campaign but failed to make it onto the pitch. In 1954 Brazil fared slightly better, making the quarter-finals, but its was four years later in Sweden when he tasted glory as part of the Brazil side who became the first team to lift the trophy outside of their own continent. Santos earned the respect of team-mates and opponents wherever he played. At club level he represented Rio de Janeiro side Botafogo throughout his career.

GYORGY SÁROSI

Country: Hungary
Born: September 12, 1912
Position: Centre-forward/Centre-half
Club: Ferencváros

Gyorgy Sárosi was an educated man with a law degree and was duly nicknamed 'The Doctor'. Between the wars he truly was one of the best footballers in the game, enhancing the reputation of both his country and his club Ferencváros, who were five times Hungarian champions with him in the team and Mitropa Cup winners in 1937 too. Sárosi also captained Hungary to the 1938 World Cup Final. The previous year he scored seven goals against Czechoslovakia in an 8-3 win, contributing to his tally of 42 goals for his country. Later, he carved out a coaching career in Italy and Switzerland.

HECTOR SCARONE

Country: Uruguay
Born: December 28, 1898
Position: Forward/Inside-right
Clubs: Nacional, Barcelona, Inter Milan, Palermo

Hector Pedro Scarone was nicknamed 'The Magician', a player who was famed for his ability to produce extraordinary skills or astounding goals from nothing. He was a star of the inaugural World Cup as Uruguay won the trophy, having already won Olympic gold in 1924 and 1928, as well as the South American Championship in 1917, 1923, 1924 and 1926. He scored a record 31 goals in 52 appearances for Uruguay. He later became Real Madrid coach.

JUAN SCHIAFFINO

Country: Uruguay, Italy
Born: July 28, 1925
Position: Inside-forward
Clubs: Peñarol, AC Milan, Roma

Small but lethal, Schiaffino was the key striker in the Uruguay team that won the 1950 World Cup in Brazil, scoring the first goal in a 2-1 win against the hosts in the final. He played again in the 1954 finals and was his country's most dynamic performer, having shifted into a more commanding midfield role, but Uruguay fell at the semi-final stage to the might of Hungary.

This prompted Milan to pay a then world record fee of £72,000 for his services, and once there he crafted a reputation as one of the greatest imports ever to play in Serie A. Schiaffino also played for the Italian national side and could have featured at the 1958 World Cup if Northern Ireland had not ended their qualification hopes.

Above: Juan Schiaffino of Milan clears the ball in the 1958 European Cup Final at the Heysel Stadium.

SALVATORE SCHILLACI

Country: Italy
Born: December 1, 1964
Position: Centre-forward
Clubs: Messina, Juventus, Inter Milan, Jubilo Iwata

Lasting less than a year and a half after his debut against Switzerland in March 1990, 'Totò' Schillaci's international career was nothing if not short. However, his place in football history is assured thanks to the six goals that made him the top scorer at the 1990 World Cup Finals.

The Juventus striker had only gained two caps before Italia 90 but his goals proved pivotal. He claimed a crucial strike against Austria after coming off the bench to score after four minutes and he also put Italy ahead in the semi-final clash with Argentina, only to lose on penalties. In the third place play-off Roberto Baggio stood aside and let Schillaci score from the spot to win the Golden Boot. He played only eight more games for his country after the finals ended and scored just one more goal.

Opposite: Uwe Seeler trains with the West German squad before their 1954 match against England at Wembley.

IMRE SCHLOSSER

Country: Hungary
Born: October 11, 1889
Position: Inside-Left
Clubs: Ferencváros, MTK Budapest

Imre Schlosser was perhaps the first Hungarian player to gain a reputation beyond his homeland. Between 1906 and 1927 he played for Hungary 68 times and scored an incredible 59 goals, including a six-goal haul against Switzerland in 1911 and five goals against Russia in Moscow a year later. The goals flowed in the Hungarian league where he was top scorer in seven seasons between 1909 and 1917. He also won 13 league titles, seven times with Ferencváros and six with MTK, the first in 1907 and the last in 1927. After his playing career ended he became a referee.

PETER SCHMEICHEL

Country: Denmark
Born: November 18, 1963
Position: Goalkeeper
Clubs: Gladsaxe-Hero, Hvidovre, Brondby, Manchester United, Sporting Lisbon, Aston Villa, Manchester City

In the early Nineties the Danish giant was regarded as the best goalkeeper in the world, collecting numerous domestic trophies and making 129 international appearances, and even scoring once for his country too. He formed an impregnable barrier behind Denmark's European Championship winning side in 1992, but his greatest period was at Manchester United. While Eric Cantona was the enigmatic talisman up front, Schmeichel was the brick wall at the back, equally important to the winning of the club's first domestic title for more than a quarter of a century.

Athletic and domineering, he was always shouting at – and organising – his defenders, never letting them lose their concentration. Schmeichel pulled off many memorable saves through his agility and speed of thought, and his long throws and accurate kicks set up many successful attacking moves from the back. Keen not to be exposed by the advancing years, he left

Below: Manchester United's Peter Schmeichel makes a spectacular save against Tottenham Hotspur in the 1992-3 season.

United after their Champions League triumph in 1999, spending two years in Portugal before returning to the English Premiership with Aston Villa. A year later he was on the move again, playing a vital role in stabilising Kevin Keegan's Manchester City on their return to the top flight. He finally announced his retirement at the end of his first season with the club, making his farewell appearance at City's last ever game at their Maine Road ground.

KARL-HEINZ SCHNELLINGER

Country: West Germany
Born: March 31, 1939
Position: Right-half/Left-back/Sweeper
Clubs: SG Düren 99, Köln, Mantova, Roma, AC Milan, Tennis Borussia Berlin

Karl-Heinz Schnellinger represented West Germany at four World Cups, as a right-half at the 1958 finals and subsequently in 1962, 1966 and 1970 as a left-back. While on the books of Düren he had performed impressively at the 1957 UEFA Youth Tournament in Madrid but by the time he was back from his first World Cup he had signed for Köln. In 1962 he was voted German Player Of The Year, primarily as a result of his performances at the World Cup in Chile. A £72,000 move to Italy with Roma in 1963 did not initially work out, but when he joined Milan he went on to win the Italian Cup, European Cup Winners' Cup, Serie A, European Cup and World Club Cup between 1967 and 1969.

GAETANO SCIREA

Country: Italy
Born: May 25, 1953
Position: Inside-forward/Sweeper
Clubs: Atalanta, Juventus

An outstanding sweeper with both Juventus and Italy in late 1970s and early 1980s, at club level Gaetano Scirea won a series of trophies with Juventus, including the European Cup in 1985 as captain, the Cup Winners' Cup in 1984, the UEFA Cup in 1977 and the European Super Cup in 1984. At home he also won seven Serie A titles and two Italian Cups, while at international level he represented Italy 78 times, ten as captain. He was a World Cup winner in 1982.

DAVID SEAMAN

Country: England
Born: September 19, 1963
Position: Goalkeeper
Clubs: Peterborough United, Birmingham City, QPR, Arsenal, Manchester City

Shown the door by Leeds United as an apprentice, David Seaman was Arsenal's first-choice goalkeeper for 13 years, winning every

domestic honour while at Highbury, including the league and FA Cup 'double' in 1998 and 2002. He signed from QPR for £1 million and helped the team secure the 1991 league title in his debut season, conceding just 18 league goals. Within three years Seaman went on to win the FA Cup, League Cup and Cup Winners' Cup.

As an integral member of the club's fabled 'back five', Seaman's consistent performances won him international recognition and although he missed England's 1990 World Cup campaign through injury, he was firmly established as first choice by the time of the Euro 96. He was one of the finest goalkeepers in the world at the time and he kept both Scotland and Spain at bay with a number of top-class saves as England progressed to the semi-finals.

At 38 years of age Seaman remained his country's first choice keeper at the 2002 World Cup, and although his tournament was tainted by conceding from Ronaldinho's long-range free-kick against Brazil, his performances against Sweden and Argentina had justified Sven-Göran Eriksson's faith in the veteran keeper. However, his England career soon came to an end after conceding a goal straight from a corner in a European Championship qualifier against Macedonia in October 2002.

His desire to continue playing club football was demonstrated by his decision to move to Manchester City in 2003, rather than remain at Arsenal in a coaching position. Time finally caught up with 'Safe Hands' Seaman when injury forced him to retire in January 2004.

UWE SEELER

Country: West Germany
Born: November 5, 1936
Position: Centre-forward
Club: Hamburg

The son of a Hamburg player, Uwe Seeler spent his entire 18-year career with the club, scoring more than 400 league goals and becoming the country's top scorer in the inaugural Bundesliga season, 1963-4. However, while his individual achievements are many, the teams in which he featured regularly fell at the last hurdle, and it was on the international stage that he shone. He made his debut for West Germany at 17 and his career took him to four World Cups, reaching one final, two semi-finals and one quarter-final. He scored in each tournament, an achievement matched only by Pelé, and his 21 appearances created a record that not broken until 1998.

Having skippered the West German side to defeat in the 1966 World Cup Final at Wembley, Seeler dropped back into a deeper role for the 1970 tournament as he turned into creator for Gerd Müller, who was to succeed him as Germany's most prolific striker. Seeler scored 43 goals in 72 appearances for West Germany and was voted German Player Of The Year on three occasions, in 1960, 1964 and 1970.

ALAN SHEARER

Born: August 13, 1970

Country: England

Position: Centre-forward

Clubs: Southampton, Blackburn Rovers, Newcastle United

It's a shame Newcastle United did not recognise the talents of a young schoolboy by the name of Alan Shearer when he failed his trial at the club. It certainly would have saved them the world record fee of £15 million that they paid to Blackburn Rovers for the highly sought-after England captain. Nevertheless, in his ten years leading the line at St James' Park, Shearer became a Geordie hero and in January 2006 he beat Jackie Milburn's club scoring record of 200 goals that had stood for 49 years.

After failing his Newcastle trials he was signed on schoolboy forms by Southampton, progressing through the ranks. After two substitute appearances he made an impressive full debut in 1988, scoring a hat-trick against Arsenal to become the youngest player ever to do so in the English top division. It was just an injury that prevented Shearer making the journey to Sweden for the 1992 European Championship, and during that summer Blackburn paid a record £3.6 million for him.

After a serious injury in his first season, the sizeable transfer fee was repaid as he went on to score more than 30 goals in each of the three subsequent campaigns. In 1995 Shearer helped manager Kenny Dalglish take Blackburn to the club's first league title in 81 years, pipping Manchester United to the trophy.

In 1996 Shearer had his most successful spell for England. Forming a devastating partnership with Spurs striker Teddy Sheringham, they helped the team win through to the European Championship semi-finals. Shearer notched up an impressive five goals, including a brace in the 4-1 demolition of Holland, and became the tournament's top scorer.

The disappointment of losing to Germany on penalties in the semi-final was soon washed away as Alan Shearer announced he would be returning to St James' Park on August 6 of that year. Manager Kevin Keegan was aware that the cost of Shearer's services would place a strain on the club's finances but that was quickly forgotten as the England hitman forged a prolific partnership with Les Ferdinand in attack, complementing the guile and vision of Ginola and Beardsley in midfield.

Sadly the team failed to win trophies under a succession of managers, including Kenny Dalglish, Ruud Gullit, Bobby Robson and Graeme Souness. Alan Shearer retired from international football after Euro 2000 and played on with Newcastle, but just a few games short of his planned retirement at the end of the 2005-6 season, injury brought the curtain down on a fantastic playing career.

PETER SHILTON

Country: England
Born: September 18, 1949
Position: Goalkeeper
Clubs: Leicester City, Stoke City, Nottingham Forest, Southampton, Derby County, Plymouth Argyle, Wimbledon, Bolton Wanderers, Coventry City, West Ham United, Leyton Orient

Peter Shilton is England's most capped player with 125 international appearances, yet his final tally could have been so much higher. For years he vied with Ray Clemence for the goalkeeper's jersey and it was not until his early 30s that Shilton clearly emerged as England's regular shot-stopper. However, he enjoyed an extraordinarily long career – he played for England until the age of 40 and in club football up until he was 48.

He succeeded Gordon Banks at Leicester City when he was just 16 years of age, but although towards the end of his career he became increasingly nomadic, at club level his name is forever associated with Nottingham Forest, who enjoyed a fairytale story of success in the late 1970s. Under Brian Clough the club won the league championship in 1978 at the first attempt after promotion to the top flight and went on to win back-to-back European Cups in 1979 and 1980.

When Ron Greenwood selected Shilton as his first choice keeper for the 1982 World Cup it signalled the end of the Shilton-Clemence rivalry. For the next eight years and three eventful World Cups he would be a regular fixture in the England goal. He kept ten clean sheets in 17 World Cup matches, at one point holding the record for minutes played without conceding a goal, but he is most remembered for the two goals that Diego Maradona put past him in 1986: the first to a handball, the second to one of the greatest goals ever.

He quit the international game after helping England to fourth place at the World Cup in Italy in 1990 but he carried on playing club football down the divisions for the following seven years, ending his career at Leyton Orient after his 1005th league game.

DIEGO SIMEONE

Country: Argentina
Born: April 28, 1970
Position: Midfielder
Clubs: Velez Sarsfield, Pisa, Sevilla, Atlético Madrid, Inter Milan, Lazio, Racing Club

Best remembered on the international stage for his role in the sending-off of England's David Beckham at the 1998 World Cup Finals, there was far more to the tough-tackling midfielder than that one moment of controversy. Diego Simeone made his international debut against Australia as far back as 1988 and became the first Argentine player to win 100 caps for his country, a feat not even achieved by the great Diego Maradona. He was also part of his country's silver medal winning team at the 1996 Olympics. He made his last international appearance in Argentina's defeat to England at the 2002 World Cup.

In club football, he was a part of the Atlético Madrid side that won the Spanish league in 1996 and he scored the winner for Lazio in the final of the 2000 Italian Cup, helping the club to a first league and cup 'double'. After a second spell with Atlético, he returned to Buenos Aires to end his playing career with Racing Club, the team he supported as a child. On retiring in February 2006 he moved into coaching.

ALLAN SIMONSEN

Country: Denmark
Born: December 15, 1952
Position: Forward
Clubs: Vejle, Borussia Mönchengladbach, Barcelona, Charlton Athletic

Simonsen was the man for the big occasion, scoring in the finals of all three major European club competitions. He was on target twice for Borussia Mönchengladbach in the 1975 UEFA Cup Final and once in the 2-1 aggregate defeat of Red Star Belgrade in the 1979 UEFA Cup Final, a season which saw him finish as the competition's top scorer with nine goals. He also netted in the 1977 European Cup Final defeat against Liverpool and for Barcelona in the 1982 European Cup Winners' Cup Final with Standard Liege, which the Spanish giants won 2-1. In 1977 he celebrated his third consecutive Bundesliga title along with the accolade of being named European Footballer Of The Year.

MATTHIAS SINDELAR

Country: Austria
Born: February 10, 1903
Position: Forward
Clubs: Hertha Vienna, FK Austria Vienna

A certain amount of mystery still surrounds the death of Matthias Sindelar, a slight man who was known on the football field as 'The Man of Paper'. Some sources have claimed that he was murdered for his anti-fascist beliefs at the time of the Anschluss, and others that he committed suicide rather than live in Nazi-run Austria. That he died of carbon monoxide poisoning remains the only certainty.

Sindelar was the star of Austria's talented 'Wunderteam' of the Thirties, falling to the hosts in the semi-finals of the 1934 World Cup in Italy. A knee injury almost ended his career before it began and following surgery he was always easy to spot due to what became a trademark bandage on his right knee.

OMAR SIVORI

Country: Argentina, Italy
Born: October 2, 1935
Position: Inside-left
Clubs: River Plate, Juventus, Napoli

Enrique Omar Sivori had a remarkable career, playing international football for both Argentina, the country of his birth, and Italy. Sivori started at River Plate and established himself as an extremely gifted inside-left, playing 19 times for Argentina before Italian side Juventus paid a world record £91,000 for him in 1957. Defecting to Turin cost Sivori his place in the national team but his club career took off spectacularly.

With Juventus he struck up a fabulous understanding with Welshman John Charles, and inspired the Bianconeri to a trio of league championships in 1958, 1960 and 1961. His personal contribution to these triumphs was significant. In the 1960 championship, he was the league's leading scorer with 27 goals from 31 games, and in 1961 he was named as the European Footballer Of The Year. The following year he represented his adopted country at the 1962 World Cup, playing three times in Chile.

Sivori's glorious reign at Juventus ended in 1965, but to this day he is fondly remembered as one of club's legends. He joined Napoli and played until a knee injury forced retirement in 1968. He later moved into coaching and was appointed as manager of Argentina in 1972.

Opposite: One of England's greatest goalscorers, Alan Shearer celebrates scoring against Luxembourg in 1999.

Below: A player for the big occasion, Barcelona's Allan Simonsen.

Above: Bulgarian legend Hristo Stoichkov of Barcelona in 1997.

JOSIP SKOBLAR

Country: Yugoslavia
Born: March 12, 1941
Position: Outside-left
Clubs: Zadar, OFK Belgrade, Hanover, Marseille

Josip Skoblar became a legend at Marseille for his goalscoring exploits. Capable of playing on both wings or as a centre-forward, he struck 44 times in the 1970-1 season to win the European Golden Boot and help the club win the league. He topped the domestic scoring charts again the following year as 'l'OM' won the 'double' and he was the league's top scorer in 1973 for a third successive season.

He represented Yugoslavia at the 1962 World Cup when the team reached the semi-finals, but in total he made only 32 appearances for his country because of a rule that prevented players based abroad turning out for the national team. He will be best remembered for his exploits at club level, particularly in France where he became known as 'Monsieur Goal'.

SOCRATES

Country: Brazil
Born: February 19, 1954
Position: Midfielder
Clubs: Botafogo, Corinthians, Fiorentina, Flamengo, Santos

An unlikely footballer, Socrates emanated from an educated middle-class background and played as an amateur for Botafogo while studying for a medical degree. After qualifying as a doctor he put his stethoscope in storage and signed pro forms for São Paulo side Corinthians in 1977.

A tall, lean and elegant midfielder, he captained his country with great distinction but limited success in the 1982 and 1986 World Cups. At the 1982 finals he scored a wondergoal against the Soviet Union, yet he was unable to prevent his side being eliminated by eventual winners Italy. A similar pattern occurred four years later when his mercurial performances were eclipsed by the pain of defeat in the quarter-final. His brother, Raí, was a member of Brazil's 1994 World Cup winning squad.

GUILLERMO STÁBILE

Country: Argentina, France
Born: January 17, 1905
Position: Forward
Clubs: Huracán, Genoa, Napoli, Red Star Paris

For many years Stábile had his name in the history books as the first player to score a World Cup hat-trick, until in 2006 FIFA finally accepted the USA's claim on behalf of Bert Patenaude. Stábile's hat-trick came in the 1930 tournament when he helped Argentina to a 6-3 defeat of Mexico. He began the tournament as a reserve but his three goals earned him a regular place in the starting line-up. He proved he was no one-hit wonder by finishing the competition as leading scorer with eight goals. He scored and hit the woodwork in the final but ended up on the losing side. It would prove to be his last game for Argentina. Stábile, whose game was based on blistering pace, went on to play his club football in Europe, in both Italy and France.

FRANK STAPLETON

Country: Republic Of Ireland
Born: July 10, 1956
Position: Forward
Clubs: Arsenal, Manchester United, Ajax, Anderlecht, Derby County, Le Havre, Blackburn Rovers, Huddersfield Town, Bradford City, Brighton & Hove Albion

Stapleton was the Republic Of Ireland's all-time leading scorer, with 20 goals in 71 internationals until surpassed by both Niall Quinn and Robbie Keane. Stapleton was also a prolific scorer at club level, leading the line admirably in a 17-year career for many outstanding sides. Strong and powerful in the air, he was a model professional who worked hard on his game after joining Arsenal as an apprentice in 1973. Signed by Manchester United for £900,000 in 1981, Stapleton became the first player to score for different teams in the FA Cup final. After leaving United in 1987 he failed to make an impact at Ajax and returned to England to finish a career that included appearances in five FA Cup finals.

HRISTO STOICHKOV

Country: Bulgaria
Born: February 8, 1966
Position: Midfielder/Striker
Clubs: Hebros, CSKA Sofia, Barcelona, Parma, Al-Nassr, CSKA Sofia, Kashiwa Reysol, Chicago Fire, DC United

Stoichkov came to prominence as an integral figure in the CSKA side that reached the semi-final of the Cup Winners' Cup in 1989. He also won the European Golden Boot the following year, prompting Barcelona coach Johan Cruyff to splash out £3 million for his services. It proved to be an inspirational signing as Barça went on to win the European Cup for the first time in 1992. He also helped fire the club to five Spanish league titles between 1991 and 1997.

In the mid-Nineties Stoichkov was ranked among the greatest footballers on the planet and at the 1994 World Cup he inspired Bulgaria to third place, winning the Golden Boot in the process. A temperamental player, his clash of personalities with Johan Cruyff led to a brief spell with Parma in 1995, but he returned to the Barça side under Louis Van Gaal before his playing career petered out with spells in the Middle East, Japan and the USA. He took over as coach of the Bulgarian national team in 2004, but failed to take them to the 2006 World Cup.

LUIS SUAREZ

Country: Spain
Born: May 2, 1935
Position: Inside-forward
Clubs: Barcelona, Inter Milan, Sampdoria

Luis Suarez Miramontes was one of the most gifted inside-forwards of his generation. Despite a fiery nature he was voted European Footballer Of The Year in 1960, which led Inter Milan to break the world transfer record to sign him the following year. He became Inter's midfield general and was influential in the European Cup winning teams of 1964 and 1965. He was already a fully established international by the late 1950s but his moment of glory came when Spain won the 1964 European Championship. His Inter career came to an abrupt end when the club sold him to Sampdoria while he was on holiday in Spain. He was recalled to the injury-ravaged national team in 1972 at the age of 37

HAKAN SÜKÜR

Country: Turkey
Born: September 1, 1971
Position: Forward
Clubs: Sakaryaspor, Bursaspor, Galatasaray, Torino, Inter Milan, Parma, Blackburn Rovers

Known as the 'Bull of the Bosphorus', Hakan Sükür is Turkey's greatest striker and a legend with Galatasaray supporters, having scored well over 200 league goals during his three spells with the club, winning eight championships plus the 2000 UEFA Cup. However, Sükür struggled to make an impact abroad. He could not settle at Torino in the 1995-6 season and returned to Galatasaray, moving on to Inter Milan for £4.9 million in 2000, and then to Parma

in January 2002 after failing to hold down a regular first-team place at the San Siro. He signed for Blackburn Rovers later the same year but broke his leg before he could make his debut, returning once again to Galatasaray having scored just twice in nine league games for the English side.

Turkey's top international scorer, he was outstanding at Euro 2000 but he laboured at the 2002 World Cup Finals and hit the net just once, in the third place play-off. He capitalised on a South Korean blunder to score and his goal is still the fastest in World Cup history, timed at 10.8 seconds.

Such is his fame in Turkey that his wedding in 2002 was televised. He made his 100th appearance for his country in a World Cup qualifier in September 2005, becoming only the third Turkish player to pass this milestone.

Left: Scorer of the fastest goal in World Cup history, Turkey's Hakan Sukur at the World Cup in 2002.

JEAN TIGANA

Country: France
Born: June 23, 1955
Position: Midfielder
Clubs: Toulon, Lyon, Bordeaux, Marseille

Jean Tigana became a star in the 1980s when a glorious French team ruled Europe and shone as one of the greatest teams on earth, despite never managing to win the ultimate trophy, the World Cup. His tireless performances for 'Les Bleus' made him hugely admired the world over, most notably at the World Cup finals in 1982 and 1986, and at the European Championship that France won on home soil in 1984.

Born in Mali, Tigana moved to France aged just three years old. Starting his professional career at Toulon, having been spotted playing part-time while working in a spaghetti factory and as a postman, he went on to make his name at Lyon before joining Bordeaux for £2 million in 1980. He played successfully there under the coaching of Aimé Jacquet, winning the French league championship in 1984, 1985 and 1987, and the French Cup in 1986 and 1987.

Tigana made his international debut in 1980 and became a fixture in the line-up alongside fellow midfielders Michel Platini, Alain Giresse and Luis Fernández. Slight and wiry, he was a prodigious worker and a great reader of the game. His most famous moment came during the 1984 European Championship when he ran half the length of the pitch deep in extra-time and crossed for Platini to score the winning goal in the 3-2 semi-final victory over Portugal. He won 52 caps for France and scored one goal.

Tigana finished his career at Marseille, adding league titles in 1990 and 1991, before moving into coaching. His Lyon side finished runners-up in the league in his second season and he replaced Arsene Wenger at Monaco in 1995. He enjoyed a spell with Fulham and won the Turkish Cup with Besiktas in 2007.

JAN TOMASZEWSKI

Country: Poland
Born: January 9, 1948
Position: Goalkeeper
Clubs: Slask Wrocław Legia Warsaw, LKS Lodz, Beerschot, Hercules

Brian Clough dubbed him 'a clown' in 1973 but after the Polish keeper produced a memorable performance that kept England from the World Cup, no-one was laughing. Tomaszewski made his international debut in 1971 and his fifth game was a home victory over England in a World Cup qualifier. The Poles were not expected to survive the return leg at Wembley but held out for a crucial 1-1 draw, with Tomaszewski pulling off a string of improbable saves.

At the 1974 World Cup Finals he conceded just five goals in seven games on the way to third place and he also became the first player to save two penalties in the same tournament. For his outstanding performances he was voted the best goalkeeper of the tournament.

Two years later he won a silver medal at the 1976 Olympics and returned for the 1978 World Cup, although he was dropped midway through the tournament. In total he made 63 appearances for Poland. The Communist regime finally let him move abroad to play in Belgium in 1978 and he subsequently moved to Spain. He retired in 1984.

TOSTÃO

Country: Brazil
Born: January 25, 1947
Position: Forward
Clubs: Cruzeiro, Vasco Da Gama

Tostão played in two successive World Cup tournaments for Brazil – in 1966 and 1970 – but in between faced the biggest challenge of his career when he battled against a serious eye

injury. The striker needed surgery to repair a detached retina after being hit in the face with a ball and though the problem eventually took its toll, he recovered to win the 1970 World Cup.

He played in all six matches at the finals in a fearsome forward line that also included Pelé, Jairzinho and Rivelino. Always at his best with his back to goal and feeding others with his deft touches and intelligent play, he was capable of powerful shooting himself, and although he did not score in the final, he will be remembered for his two goals against Peru in the quarter-finals His eye injury eventually forced him into early retirement and he went on to become a doctor.

Below: A member of France's magical midfield, Jean Tigana in 1986.

Right: Carlos Valderrama on the ball for Colombia against England at France 98.

CARLOS VALDERRAMA

Country: Colombia
Born: September 2, 1961
Position: Midfielder
Clubs: Unión Magdalena, Millonarios, Deportivo Cali, Montpellier, Real Valladolid, Independiente Medellin, Atlético Junior Barranquilla, Tampa Bay Mutiny, Miami Fusion, Colorado Rapids

Carlos Valderrama's crazy hair overshadowed a special football talent. An elegant player, during the Nineties Valderrama orchestrated Colombia's play from midfield with an unhurried air and he is rightly recognised as the country's best player. Nicknamed 'El Pibe' (The Kid), he made his first international appearance in a 3-0 defeat to Paraguay in October 1985 and it was not long before he was captaining the side. Twice South American Footballer Of The Year, he played in three World Cups between 1990 and 1998 and became the first Colombian to pass the 100-cap mark, eventually finishing with 111 international appearances and 11 goals.

Although he won the French Cup with Montpellier in 1990 and the league title twice in Colombia with Atlético Junior, Valderrama did not always deliver his talent consistently. For all his brilliance, aside from his stint in the USA he failed to shine outside of his native country at club level, and when great things were expected of Colombia at the 1994 World Cup (they had beaten Argentina 5-0 in Buenos Aires during qualification), the team were unable to get past the first round. He played his last international in 1998 and retired in 2004.

MARCO VAN BASTEN

Country: Holland
Born: October 31, 1964
Position: Centre-forward
Clubs: Ajax, AC Milan

Some goals are so stunning they will never be forgotten. Marco Van Basten scored such a goal during the 1988 European Championship final against the Soviet Union. Arnold Muhren hoisted a high ball towards the penalty area, Van Basten met the ball as it dropped, and from a tight angle sent a volley screaming into the net. It clinched the trophy for the Dutch and set the seal on a tournament of great personal success for the striker. Van Basten had earlier destroyed England with a hat-trick in the group stage and beaten Germany with a semi-final winner.

After a series of astounding performances for Ajax, where he once scored 37 league goals in a season, he joined Milan in 1987. He helped the club to the title in 1988, 1992 and 1993, and to European Cup wins in 1989 (when he scored twice in the final) and 1990. However, an ankle injury in the 1993 final against Marseille forced his retirement before the age of 30. He later coached the Dutch to the 2006 World Cup.

Opposite: Vavá celebrates scoring Brazil's third goal in the 1962 World Cup final.

WIM VAN HANEGEM

Country: Holland
Born: February 20, 1944
Position: Midfielder
Clubs: Velox, Xerxes/DHC, Feyenoord, AZ 67, Chicago Sting, FC Utrecht, Feyenoord.

Wim Van Hanegem was a gifted left-footed midfielder who made his name with European Cup winning Feyenoord and the stylish Dutch side of the 1974 World Cup, where some critics regarded him as the side's best player. Perceived as arrogant, Van Hanegem commanded the midfield with a vision, power and precision that made his lack of pace seem like an asset. He played 52 times for Holland but pulled out on the 1978 World Cup on the eve of the tournament after a dispute.

PAUL VAN HIMST

Country: Belgium
Born: October 2, 1943
Position: Forward
Clubs: Anderlecht, Molenbeek, Eendracht Aalst

Paul Van Himst is arguably the most decorated player in Belgian history. Four times the Belgian Player Of The Year, he made 81 appearances for the national side, scoring 30 goals. A product of the Anderlecht youth team, Van Himst made his club debut at the age of 16 and just a year later he was drafted into the national side. A technically outstanding and elegant player, he was so highly regarded that he was once dubbed 'the White Pelé'. He won the Belgian title eight times with Anderlecht and later led them to UEFA Cup success in 1983 as coach.

OBDULIO VARELA

Country: Uruguay
Born: September 20, 1917
Position: Centre-half
Clubs: Montevideo Wanderers, Peñarol

A gifted attacking centre-half, Varela was the inspiration behind Uruguay's 1950 World Cup triumph. In the deciding match against hosts Brazil, as captain he magnificently held his defence firm against relentless Brazilian attacks. After the break he drove his team forward and helped them turn a single goal deficit into a shock 2-1 win to lift the Jules Rimet Trophy.

Varela was captain again for his swansong four years later when Uruguay finished third in Switzerland, but he was injured shortly after scoring in the quarter-final victory against England and missed the semi-final defeat to Hungary. He won his first international honour aged 24 in Uruguay's triumphant 1942 Copa América team. He was subsequently signed by Peñarol, with whom he won six league titles.

VELIBOR VASOVIC

Country: Yugoslavia
Born: October 3, 1939
Position: Left-Half
Clubs: Partizan Belgrade, Red Star Belgrade, Ajax

Velibor Vasovic captained Ajax to European Cup success in 1971, beating Panathinaikos 2-0 in the final at Wembley. It was third time lucky for the lively Yugoslav left-half, as he had featured in the losing side for Partizan in the 1966 final and for Ajax in 1969. He won five successive Yugoslav championships with two different clubs (Partizan 1961, 1962, 1963, 1965; Red Star 1964) and followed this up with three Dutch league titles and three Dutch Cups. He also made 32 appearances for Yugoslavia before retiring after the European Cup victory of 1971.

VAVÁ

Country: Brazil
Born: November 12, 1934
Position: Forward
Clubs: Recife, Vasco Da Gama, Atlético Madrid, Palmeiras, América, Elche, Toros Neza, San Diego Toros, Portuguesa

Real name Edvaldo Izidio Neto, Vavá was not certain to play at the 1958 World Cup but was brought into the team to partner Mazzola for the second game against England. Holding his place alongside World Cup debutants Pelé, Garrincha and Zito in a refreshed line-up for the pivotal clash with the Soviet Union, he scored twice as the Brazilians really came alive. Indeed, the game's opening moments, culminating in Vavá's first goal, are considered to be the best three minutes of Brazilian football ever played.

Above: Fritz Walter scores from the spot as the West Germans beat Austria 6-1 in the 1954 World Cup semi-final. Behind him Helmut Rahn takes a rest.

A bustling centre-forward, he was curiously under-used by his country. He only played 20 full internationals spread over a decade, scoring 15 goals, but he was the ultimate big stage player. He scored two of Brazil's five goals in the 1958 World Cup Final victory over Sweden, and another in the 3-1 win over Czechoslovakia in the 1962 final, making him the first of four players to have scored in more than one World Cup final. After his success at the 1958 tournament he had a spell in Europe with Atlético Madrid, where he scored eight times on the club's run to the European Cup semi-final. However, he returned to Brazil in 1961 due to homesickness.

GIANLUCA VIALLI

Country: Italy
Born: July 9, 1964
Position: Forward
Clubs: Cremonese, Sampdoria, Juventus, Chelsea

Vialli started his career with hometown club Cremonese before joining Sampdoria in 1984. His eight seasons with the Genoa-based side coincided with the most successful period in the club's history. Sampdoria won three Italian Cups, the 1990 Cup Winners' Cup and enjoyed a first league title in 1991, with Vialli scoring 19 goals in 26 games. He signed for Juventus for £12 million in 1992 and his success story continued, captaining the side to European Cup glory against Ajax in 1996. He joined Chelsea the same year, winning both the League Cup and European Cup Winners' Cup in 1998 as player-coach and the FA Cup in 2000 as coach.

IVO VIKTOR

Country: Czechoslovakia
Born: May 21, 1942
Position: Goalkeeper
Clubs: RH Brno, Spartak Brno, Dukla Prague

Ivo Viktor will always be remembered for his magnificent performances for Czechoslovakia on the way to winning the 1976 European Championship, an achievement that helped him to third place in the European Player Of The Year Award, behind Franz Beckenbauer and Rob Rensenbrink. He was outstanding in the two-legged quarter-final clash with the Soviet Union, and in both the semi-final against Holland and the final against West Germany, where he made the decisive save in a 5-4 penalty shoot-out win. That year he was also voted the Czech Player Of The Year for the fifth time. Never booked in his career, he played 63 times for his country after making his debut in a 2-1 defeat to Brazil at the Maracanã Stadium in 1966.

RUDI VÖLLER

Country: West Germany & Germany
Born: March 13, 1960
Position: Forward
Clubs: Kickers Offenbach, 1860 Munich, Werder Bremen, Roma, Marseille, Bayer Leverkusen

A textbook goalmouth poacher, Rudi Völler was rarely spectacular but was always deadly. With 47 international goals to his name only the legendary Gerd Müller has scored more for Germany, but Völler is still remembered as much for his bubble perm and the spittle that Frank Rijkaard deposited in it at Italia 90.

He began his career in 1977 with Kickers Offenbach but it was at Werder Bremen that he established his reputation as a top predator, voted German Footballer Of The Year in 1982. He joined Roma in 1987 and reached a UEFA Cup final in 1991 before losing to Inter Milan. He signed for Marseille the following year and won the European Cup in 1993.

Having made his international debut in 1982, he scored the equaliser that took the 1986 World Cup Final with Argentina to extra-time, only to pick up a runners-up medal. However, four years later he was a World Cup winner when West Germany had their revenge in a scrappy final. Despite his lack of managerial experience he was appointed national manager in 2000 and surprised doubters by taking the team to the 2002 World Cup Final.

FRITZ WALTER

Country: West Germany
Born: October 31, 1920
Position: Midfielder/Forward
Club: Kaiserslautern

In his day Fritz Walter was the biggest star of German football. The captain of the 1954 World Cup winning team, his skill and creativity as a goalscoring midfielder was unrivalled in the immediate post-war era, and only Franz Beckenbauer could make a claim to outrank him in the list of German football legends, although Walter is held in far more affection.

Walter made his debut for hometown club

Kaiserslautern in 1937, and won the German championship twice with the club, in 1951 and 1953. However, it was on the world stage that he achieved his biggest success. He debuted for Germany in 1940, scoring a hat-trick against Romania, but his career was interrupted by the war. He returned in 1948 alongside his brother Ottmar, and at the age of 33 he was made captain of the West German team for the 1954 World Cup by national team coach Sepp Herberger. The team came back from a disastrous start in the final to beat Hungary, making Fritz and Ottmar the first siblings to win the World Cup. Fritz had scored three goals in the tournament, and his brother two.

He was a member of the West German team at the 1958 World Cup in Sweden, although not as captain. This time he lost in the semi-final and he retired the following year, but he could have gone to Chile for the finals of 1962 had he listened to Herberger's entreaties.

In his last days it had been his dream to see World Cup football played in Kaiserslautern, but his death in 2002 meant that would never happen. Four years later, on the anniversary of his death, when Italy lined up to face the USA at the 2006 finals, the Fritz Walter Stadium in Kaiserslautern fell silent to honour his memory.

GEORGE WEAH

Country: Liberia
Born: October 1, 1966
Position: Centre-forward
Clubs: Young Survivors, Bongrange, Mighty Barolle, Invincible Eleven, Africa Sports, Tonnerre Yaoundé, Monaco, Paris Saint-Germain, AC Milan, Chelsea, Manchester City, Marseille

Although born in Liberia, Weah holds French citizenship and played for many different clubs in five different countries. He helped Monaco win the French league title in 1991 and repeated the trick with Paris Saint-Germain in 1995. The striker's most successful period came in Italy

with Milan, who he joined for £3.5 million in 1995, his goals firing the club to the Serie A title in both 1996 and 1999. The former African, European and World Footballer Of The Year, Weah was also part of the Chelsea team that won the FA Cup in 2000.

Weah was also very well known for his charity work. He acted as a goodwill ambassador for UNICEF and also provided substantial financial support to the Liberian national team. He stood for the Presidency of Liberia in 2005 but his bid failed at the polls.

ERNEST WILIMOWSKI

Country: Poland, Germany
Born: June 23, 1916
Position: Inside-Left
Clubs: Katowice, Ruch, PSV Chemnitz, 1860 Munich, Chemnitz West, Hameln, Detmold, Augsburg, Offenburg, Singen, Kaiserslautern

No player in World Cup history has a better goals-per-game ratio than Ernest Wilimowski. Proving himself to be one of the most dangerous young forwards in Europe at the time, the 21-year-old scored four times in Poland's only match of the 1938 finals, but the feat was eclipsed by the result, a 6-5 defeat to Brazil. His World Cup record of four goals in a game was often equalled but not beaten until 1994, when Russia's Oleg Salenko scored five against Cameroon.

A prolific goalscorer, he netted 21 goals in 22

appearances for Poland. Invasion by Germany saw Wilimoski become a German citizen and during the war he scored 13 goals in eight games for Germany. In the Polish league he scored 112 goals in 86 games, including a ten-goal haul in Ruch's 12-1 thrashing of Union-Touring Lodz.

BILLY WRIGHT

Country: England
Born: February 6, 1924
Position: Centre-half
Club: Wolverhampton Wanderers

One of the most celebrated footballers of his day, Billy Wright joined the Wolverhampton Wanderers ground staff as a boy in 1938 and stayed at Molineux in a one-club career that spanned 15 seasons and 490 league appearances. During his tenure at the club he led them to FA Cup success in 1949, and three league titles in the 1950s. He was hardly the tallest centre-half in the world but he still managed to command the game both in the air and on the ground.

Wright's popularity was not confined to the Black Country either, and as an automatic pick for the national team, he was captain of his country for 90 of the 105 games he played, leading England in three World Cup campaigns: 1950, 1954 and 1958. Away from the pitch he became one half of a celebrity couple after his marriage to one of the Beverley Sisters. He died in North London on September 3, 1994.

Above: England captain
Billy Wright with Wolves
in the 1949-50 season.

Left: Liberia's George Weah in
action against Nigeria at the
2002 African Nations Cup in
his last international match.

Above: Yashin stops a shot from Bobby Smith in an England v Rest Of The World XI match in 1963. Below: Soviet hero Yashin playing England again, this time for his country in 1958.

LEV YASHIN

Country: Soviet Union
Born: October 22, 1929
Position: Goalkeeper
Club: Dynamo Moscow

Goalkeeping legends do not come much larger or more imposing than Lev Yashin. Dressed all in black, possessed of huge hands with, according to Gordon Banks, 'fingers the size of bananas', his nickname the 'Black Spider' was not hard to fathom.

At the age of 13, Lev Ivanovich Yashin went to work in the same Moscow tool factory as his father. After playing in goal for the factory football team he was spotted by Dynamo Moscow, eventually making his debut for the club in 1950. Chances to gain a foothold in the first team proved limited and after three seasons biding his time in the reserves, he was on the verge of taking up a career as keeper for the club's ice hockey team, with whom he had won the Soviet Cup in 1953, when an injury to the first choice keeper Aleksei 'Tiger' Khomich opened a door to the football team. He went on to play for the club until 1970, winning five league championships and three Soviet Cups.

Yashin is seen as the greatest goalkeeper in the history of the game and the first of the modern era. Extremely vocal, he kept his defence constantly on its toes and was one of the earliest keepers to venture out of his area to kick the ball away. His huge throws helped launch rapid counterattacks and he was also a penalty specialist, saving 150 in his career.

Yashin made his debut for the Soviet Union on September 8, 1954, in a 7-0 win over Sweden. In 1956 he won a gold medal with the Soviet team at the Melbourne Olympics, marking the beginning of a golden era for Soviet football. Yashin proved instrumental in securing the Soviet Union its only major trophy of the modern era, making a string of crucial saves to deny Yugoslavia in the inaugural European Nations Cup final in 1960. Four years later he was still between the posts when the Soviets were runners-up.

Yashin was also a key member of the Soviet Union team that reached the quarter-finals of the World Cups of 1958 and 1962, when they were eliminated by the hosts on both occasions. He was blamed for both of the goals against Chile in 1962, yet he was still voted the European Footballer Of The Year in 1963, the only time the award has gone to a goalkeeper.

In 1966 he was back at the World Cup in England as the Soviet team recorded its best performance in the tournament, reaching the semi-finals and losing narrowly to West Germany with ten men. He was named in the squad for the 1970 World Cup in Mexico but he did not feature during the competition. In total he won 78 caps.

By the time of his retirement Yashin was regarded as a Soviet national hero to rank alongside cosmonaut Yuri Gagarin. He received the Order Of Lenin and Honoured Master Of Soviet Sport, and in 1971 some 120,000 spectators turned up for his final testimonial game between Dynamo Moscow and a Rest Of The World XI.

Sadly he suffered pain from a knee injury in his later years and had a leg amputated in 1986. He died on March 20, 1990, following complications from surgery. To celebrate his achievements, between 1994 and 2006 the best goalkeeper at each World Cup was given the Lev Yashin Award. Its recipients were Michel Preud'Homme of Belgium, France's Fabien Barthez, Germany's Oliver Kahn and Italy's Gianluigi Buffon.

MARIO ZAGALO

Country: Brazil
Born: August 9, 1931
Position: Left-winger
Clubs: América, Botafogo

Mario Zagalo's name is synonymous with the World Cup and he is the most successful individual in the history of the tournament, having won it four times with Brazil in various roles: twice as a player in 1958 and 1962, once as a coach in 1970, and once as an assistant coach in 1994. He was also in charge of the team when the Brazilians were runners-up in 1998, which gives him an unrivalled World Cup record.

An intelligent outside-left renowned for his high work rate, it was this industry on the pitch that earned him the nickname the 'Little Ant'. He was an ever present member of the team's campaign in 1958, and he struck gold again in 1962, having dropped back to midfield and assuming a harder working role. On both occasions he only secured his place after injury to other players in the run up to the tournament.

Ultimately it was his versatility that converted Brazil from the 4-2-4 formation to their trademark 4-3-3 playing style.

IVAN ZAMORANO

Country: Chile
Born: January 18, 1967
Position: Forward
Clubs: Cobresal, Cobreandino, St Gallen, Sevilla, Real Madrid, Inter Milan, América, Colo Colo

Ivan Luis Zamorano Zamora was one of the greatest footballers to have played for Chile, scoring 34 goals in 69 international appearances for his country, including reaching the second round of the 1998 World Cup Finals. At the 2000 Olympics he was in Chile's bronze medal winning team, brought in at the last minute to replace the injured Marcelo Salas as one of the three overaged players permissible in the largely youth competition. He scored both goals in the team's 2-0 win over the USA in the bronze medal match. He had a successful career in Europe, winning La Liga with Real Madrid in 1995 and finishing the season as the league's top scorer with 27 goals.

RICARDO ZAMORA

Country: Spain
Born: January 21, 1901
Position: Goalkeeper
Clubs: Espanyol, Barcelona, Real Madrid, Nice

Zamora was the first hero of Spanish football, playing 46 games for Spain between the wars, a record that lasted for 38 years. He also became the first keeper to save a World Cup penalty, against Brazil in 1934. Although he started his career with Espanyol, he had a short stint with Barcelona before returning to the city's other club for most of the Twenties.

Completing a record-breaking transfer to Real Madrid in 1930, he won two league titles and two Spanish Cups at Real, having already lifted the cup twice with Barcelona and once with Espanyol. He retired in 1936 after moving to France at the start of the Spanish Civil War. He enjoyed a coaching career with Atlético Madrid, Celta Vigo, Espanyol and, briefly, the Spanish national side. Fittingly it was in his home city of Barcelona that Zamora died at the age of 77.

ZICO

Country: Brazil
Born: March 3, 1953
Position: Midfielder
Clubs: Flamengo, Udinese, Flamengo, Kashima Antlers

Zico represented Brazil at three consecutive World Cups from 1978, and was at his best in Spain in 1982, when he was the outstanding player of the tournament. Among the game's greatest ever dead-ball strikers, he scored with one of his speciality free-kicks on his debut against Uruguay in February 1977. He went on to add a further 51 goals to this total in 72 games, making him fourth behind Pelé, Ronaldo and Romario in Brazil's all-time goalscoring list.

A wiry, dynamic yet tricky playmaker, he was just as adept at setting up his centre-forward as he was at finding the goal for himself. At club level he inspired Flamengo to victory in the Copa Libertadores in 1981 and was almost single-handedly responsible for the subsequent undoing of Liverpool in the World Club Cup. After the 1982 World Cup he moved to Italy to play for Udinese and was voted World Footballer Of The Year. He added this to his three South American Player Of The Year Awards.

After a spell as Brazil's Minister of Sport, he joined Kashima Antlers at the start of the J.League in 1993. Such was his impact that he was appointed coach in 1999 and a statue was erected in his honour outside Kashima Stadium. He was appointed Japan coach in 2002 and led the team to the 2006 finals.

Above: Zico celebrates opening the scoring against New Zealand at the 1982 World Cup.

Left: Inter Milan's Ivan Zamarano scores against Lazio in the 1998 UEFA Cup Final.

ZINÉDINE ZIDANE

Country: France
Born: June 23, 1972
Position: Midfielder
Clubs: Cannes, Bordeux, Juventus, Real Madrid

It is impossible to overstate the talent that Zinédine Zidane possessed. At the height of his powers the Marseille-born midfielder was quite rightly mentioned in the same breath as Puskás, Pelé, Cruyff and Maradona, and in the modern game he was just untouchable. His awareness on the ball, his sublime skill, peerless touch, and his unmatched big-game mentality marked him out as a genuine footballing superstar.

The world first took note of Zidane in 1996 when, as the master of Bordeaux's midfield, his incisive passing and instinctive skill inspired the French side to the UEFA Cup final. Bayern Munich scuppered their hopes of glory but for Zidane it marked the entrance to football's hall of fame. The same summer he was bought by Juventus and helped the club to the Serie A title. Appearances in consecutive Champions League finals underlined his exceptional talent, but at France 98 he bettered that, inspiring his country to World Cup triumph. Despite blotting his copy book early in the tournament with an ugly stamping incident, 'Zizou' ran rings around the world's best players and scored the two goals that killed off Brazil in the final.

Later in 1998 FIFA announced Zidane as their World Player Of The Year. The honour was repeated in 2000, but an even greater compliment was soon bestowed upon him. In the summer of 2001 he became the world's most expensive player after Real Madrid lured him from Juventus for a £46 million transfer fee, a record that stood for eight years.

The unassuming playmaker continued to demonstrate his genius, and although injury prevented him from rescuing France's 2002 World Cup campaign from disaster, the volley he scored against Bayer Leverkusen to win the Champions League earlier the same year was a perpetual reminder of the sheer class of the man. He retired from international football after the 2004 European Championship, but in August 2005 he was encouraged to make a comeback after France struggled with World Cup qualification.

Following an injury-plagued season at Real Madrid, he announced that he would retire after the 2006 World Cup, but it was to be a sad end to an illustrious career. In the World Cup final against Italy he converted a seventh minute penalty and by half-time the world's press had voted him the tournament's best player. However, after the game went into extra-time he was sent-off for violent conduct, having been goaded into head-butting Italian defender Marco Materazzi in the chest. Minutes after the world saw the last of Zidane, France lost the World Cup on penalties.

DINO ZOFF

Country: Italy
Born: February 28, 1942
Position: Goalkeeper
Clubs: Udinese, Mantova, Napoli, Juventus

One of the finest and most consistent keepers of all-time, Zoff's career was packed with honours. He captained Italy to World Cup glory in Spain in 1982, held the Italian appearance record (112, with 59 as captain) until surpassed by Paolo Maldini and Fabio Cannavaro, and between October 1973 and August 1974 he went 1,142 minutes without conceding a goal, setting an international record.

Initially rejected as a 14-year-old by Inter Milan and Juventus for being too small, he first signed professional forms with Udinese in 1961, but on his debut he was beaten five times by Fiorentina and the club were soon relegated. A more successful spell at Mantova followed, but it was at Napoli that Zoff's career truly took off, leading to an international call-up.

He made his debut for Italy in a European Championship quarter-final match against Bulgaria in April 1968, and he retained his place as the Italians went on to win the competition. At the 1970 World Cup he missed the chance of playing in another final as Albertosi was selected at first choice keeper. Zoff then joined Juventus in 1972, and went on to win six titles, two Italian Cups and a UEFA Cup in 11 years at the club. His only major career disappointment was that he never won the European Cup, despite reaching the final twice.

He retired from playing as a 41-year-old in 1983, going on to coach Italy's Olympic team, Juventus and Lazio. He took the Italian senior team to the final of the European Championship in 2000, but despite leading until the last minute of the game, they were beaten by France in extra-time, provoking his immediate resignation.

GIANFRANCO ZOLA

Country: Italy
Born: July 5, 1966
Position: Inside-forward
Clubs: Nuorese, Torres, Napoli, Parma, Chelsea, Cagliari

Learning his trade as Diego Maradona's understudy at Napoli in the early Nineties, Sardinian-born Gianfranco Zola soon became known as a creative but hard-working attacker with a speciality in long-range free-kicks. He joined Parma in 1993, and helped them lift the Super Cup in 1994 and beat Juventus over two legs to win the UEFA Cup in 1995. Following his countrymen Gianluca Vialli and Roberto Di Matteo to Chelsea in December 1996 for £4.5 million proved to be a great move for Zola. He came off the bench to score the winner in the final of the Cup Winners' Cup against Stuttgart

in 1998, and in 2003 fans voted him the club's best ever player.

His international career has been one of few highlights. He is probably best remembered for missing the penalty at Euro 96 that effectively eliminated Italy from the tournament. He was also sent-off in a World Cup game against Nigeria in 1994, minutes after coming on as a substitute. However, neither incident should overshadow his superb winner in a World Cup qualifier against England at Wembley in 1997.

In July 2003 he decided to return home to Sardinia to fulfil a promise to end his career with his local team, Serie B side Cagliari. In his first year he helped them to promotion to Serie A, and the following season ensured that the club reached the semi-final of the Italian cup and secured a mid-table finish in the league before retiring just days shy of his 39th birthday in June 2005. The previous year he had been awarded an OBE for services to British football.

ANDONI ZUBIZARRETA

Country: Spain
Born: October 23, 1961
Position: Goalkeeper
Clubs: Alaves, Athletic Bilbao, Barcelona, Valencia

In January 1985 Andoni Zubizarreta made his international debut for Spain against Finland. Some 13 years later he played his 126th game for his country, capping an incredible career that included appearances in four World Cup tournaments – in 1986, 1990, 1994 and 1998. He started out with Athletic Bilbao, winning two Spanish titles, before switching to Barcelona and enjoying the most successful spell of his club career. As well as further domestic honours, he triumphed in Europe with Barcelona, winning the Cup Winners' Cup in 1989 and the European Cup in 1992, both times against Sampdoria.

Zubizarreta left the Nou Camp in 1994 to join Valencia but continued to defy the years with top-level performances. He bowed out of international football after captaining Spain at the 1998 World Cup at the age of 37.

Above: Gianfranco Zola in action for Chelsea in 2002.

Opposite: Zinédine Zidane scores the penalty that puts France into the 2006 World Cup Final.

GREAT PLAYERS OF TODAY

Above: Michael Ballack enjoys the moment after scoring from the spot for Bayer Leverkusen.

EMMANUEL ADEBAYOR

Country: Togo
Born: February 26, 1984
Position: Striker
Clubs: Sporting Club de Lomé, Metz, Monaco, Arsenal, Manchester City

An imposing striker of great power and strength, Emmanuel Adebayor began his career in Togo with Sporting Club de Lome before playing for Metz and Monaco in France. However, it was after a £3 million move to Arsenal in January 2006 that he really made his name, although his career at the Emirates was one of highs and lows. He was red carded in Arsenal's 2007 League Cup Final defeat to Chelsea but finished the following season as the joint second-highest scorer in the Premier League with 24 goals.

He was voted African Player Of The Year in 2008 and after being linked with many of the top clubs in Europe, he made an acrimonious £25 million move to Manchester City in July 2009. Eligible to play for Nigeria, he opted to play for the country of his birth but retired prematurely from international football after the Togo team bus was attacked by gunmen en route to the African Nations Cup in 2010, an incident that saw three passengers killed.

PABLO AIMAR

Country: Argentina
Born: November 3, 1979
Position: Midfielder
Clubs: River Plate, Valencia, Real Zaragoza, Benfica

The son of footballer Ricardo Aimar of Newell's Old Boys, Pablo Cesar Aimar made his name as a playmaker at River Plate, where at 10 he inherited the famed number 10 shirt of the great Uruguayan Enzo Francescoli. Dubbed 'The Little Clown', Aimar was a part of Argentina's triumphant 1997 World Youth Cup team. He made his international debut against Mexico in June 1999 and was signed the following year by Valencia coach Hector Cúper for £13.6 million. He went on to win the Spanish league twice, played in the Champions League final in his first season, and then lifted the UEFA Cup in 2004. He was described by Diego Maradona as, 'the only current footballer I'd pay to watch'.

Aimar played in Argentina's ill-fated 2002 World Cup campaign, while four years later an attack of acute meningitis threatened his participation at the 2006 finals but he recovered in time to feature in the squad, making three appearances from the bench. After two seasons with Zaragoza, he signed for Benfica in 2008, winning the Portuguese league title in 2010.

ANDREI ARSHAVIN

Country: Russia
Born: May 29, 1981
Position: Midfielder
Clubs: Zenit Saint Petersburg, Arsenal

Andrei Arshavin made his debut for Zenit Saint Petersburg in 2000 and after playing in a variety of midfield positions, he finally settled down as a second striker and impressed with his imaginative playmaking skills. He was voted Russian Footballer of the Year in 2006 and the following year he helped the club to the Russian league title, adding a UEFA Cup winners' medal to his collection in 2008 after being voted Man Of The Match as Zenit beat Rangers in the final. He was courted by Tottenham Hotspur and Barcelona but after a protracted bidding process, he signed for Arsenal in January 2009.

Making his international debut in 2002, Arshavin was overlooked for Russia's Euro 2004 squad but four years later, despite a suspension that would rule him out of the first two games, he kickstarted Russia's run to the semi-finals of the European Championship.

MICHAEL BALLACK

Country: Germany
Born: September 26, 1976
Position: Midfielder
Clubs: Chemnitz, Kaiserslautern, Bayer Leverkusen, Bayern Munich, Chelsea

One of the great players of the modern era, in his native Germany Michael Ballack is revered as a skilful goalscoring midfielder for both club and country. He began his career with local club Chemnitz, making his professional debut in 1995 before signing for Kaiserslautern two years later and winning the German league title in his first campaign.

He spent three seasons at Bayer Leverkusen, steering the club to the Champions League final in 2002, where they lost 2-1 to a star-packed Real Madrid side. He subsequently turned down the overtures of Real to join Bayern Munich, helping the club to three league and cup 'doubles': the first in 2003, when he scored twice in the first ten minutes of the cup final, then as captain in 2005, and once again in 2006. He has been voted Germany's Player Of The Year on three occasions.

Chelsea Michael Ballack on a free transfer in May 2006. At the end of his first season injury ruled him out of the FA Cup final but he went on to play on the winning side in the finals of 2009 and 2010. By that time he had already picked up his second Champions League runners-up medal after scoring the first of Chelsea's spot-kicks in the penalty shoot-out defeat to Manchester United in the 2008 final in Moscow. He signed for Bayer Leverkusen on a free-transfer shortly after winning the Premier League in 2010.

At international level he is one of his country's most capped players. Having made his debut as a substitute against Scotland in 1999, at the 2002 World Cup he scored the only goal of the semi-final against South Korea but by that time he already knew that he would be suspended for the final, having been booked minutes earlier. He was the captain of the team that reached the semi-finals four years later and he also led Germany to the final of Euro 2008 before losing to Spain. He missed the 2010 World Cup following an ankle injury picked up in the FA Cup final just weeks earlier.

Michael Ballack has worn his favoured number 13 shirt for the much of his career, only carrying a different number while playing for Kaiserslautern.

DAVID BECKHAM

Country: England
Born: May 2, 1975
Position: Right midfielder
Clubs: Manchester United, Preston North End, Real Madrid, LA Galaxy, AC Milan

On the opening day of the 1996-7 season David Beckham chipped the opposition keeper from the halfway line, beginning his inexorable rise to football superstardom. The London-born Manchester United trainee's subsequent marriage to Spice Girl Victoria Adams did little to take the media spotlight off him. His assured performances and long-range goals helped United to the Premier League title that season and earned him a place in Glenn Hoddle's England team.

Despite rattling in a trademark free-kick against Colombia in the World Cup group stages, France 98 was a personal disaster for

Beckham, who was sent-off against Argentina for a petulant kick at Diego Simeone in his country's narrow second round defeat. As a result, the Manchester United number 7 was made into a national pariah and booed by opposing fans whenever he played for his club the following season.

A testament to his strength of character, the barracking failed to have a detrimental effect on his football. Beckham played a vital role in United's 1999 'treble' winning team (Premier League, FA Cup and Champions League) and his efforts also earned him second place behind Rivaldo in the voting for both the World and European Player Of The Year Awards.

His main attributes have always been his fantastic range of passing and crossing, coupled with a world-class ability at taking free-kicks, a skill honed during hours of overtime on the Manchester United training pitch. However, his game is also based on tireless running, a steely determination and a ferocious will to win.

Caretaker England manager Peter Taylor rewarded his accomplishments with the England captaincy for a friendly against Italy in November 2000 and 'Becks' was to retain the armband with the appointment of Sven-Göran Eriksson. The winning goal in the 2002 World Cup qualifier against Finland at Anfield signalled the start of David Beckham's rehabilitation from scapegoat to national hero, the culmination of which was a remarkable individual performance against Greece at Old Trafford, when he scored the last-ditch free-kick equaliser that took England to the World Cup in Japan. It also landed him the BBC's coveted Sports Personality Of The Year Award.

A broken metatarsal suffered in a game against Deportivo La Coruña threatened Beckham's participation at the World Cup and his lack of fitness hampered much of his play. However, he was still able to gain a degree of revenge when he slotted home the winning penalty against Argentina. Much speculation about a move to Real Madrid surrounded Beckham at the end of the 2003 season but he still managed to pick up a sixth league winners' medal with United before moving to the Spanish giants.

He scored within three minutes of the kick-off in his league debut for the club and although popular in Spain, his time at the Bernabéu coincided with a barren spell for Real, which was not rectified until Fabio Capello took the team to the league championship in 2007. Initially out of favour with newly arrived head coach, Beckham fought his way back into the team that season to play his part in the league title win, but he had already announced his intention to transfer to LA Galaxy.

Beckham captained a disappointing England side at Germany 2006, where he became the first Englishman to score at three World Cups. He led the side to the quarter-finals but, after he had left the pitch through injury, England

lost on penalties to Portugal. He resigned the captaincy immediately afterwards, having worn the armband on 58 occasions.

Initially dropped by new England manager Steve McClaren, Beckham fought his way back into international contention and became a vital squad member during Fabio Capello's reign as England coach, captaining the team on one further occasion and becoming his country's most capped outfield player. To help extend his England career Beckham twice spent the American closed season on loan to AC Milan but after rupturing his Achilles tendon playing for the Italian club in March 2010, his dream of playing at a fourth World Cup was at an end.

GIANLUIGI BUFFON

Country: Italy
Born: January 28, 1978
Position: Goalkeeper
Clubs: Parma, Juventus

One of the greatest goalkeepers of all time, Gianluigi Buffon deservedly won the Lev Yashin Award for the best keeper at the 2006 World Cup, coming nearly nine years after he made his international debut as a substitute for Gianluca Pagliuca in a World Cup play-off against Russia. He was a non-playing member of the squad at the resulting finals in France

and he had earlier helped Italy win the 1996 European Under-21 Championship.

In July 2001 Juventus made him the world's most expensive keeper when they signed him for a staggering £32.6 million from Parma, with whom he had won the UEFA Cup in 1999. He went on to win Serie A four times between 2002 and 2006 with Juventus, although the club was later stripped of the last two of these titles as punishment for their attempts to influence the appointment of referees. While many of the club's stars choose to leave when the punishment was extended to relegation, Buffon played on with Juventus and helped them return to Serie A at the first attempt.

In 2002 had was a part of the Italy team that suffered a shock World Cup exit at the hands of South Korea, conceding a 'golden goal' to Ahn Jung-Hwan in the 116th minute. However, he played in all seven matches as the Italians won the 2006 World Cup and he was only beaten twice in the tournament, by an own goal against the USA and a penalty in the final. So impressive were his performances that he was voted runner-up in the 2006 European Player Of The Year Award.

Having made over 100 appearances for his country, Buffon started the 2010 World Cup as Italy's first choice keeper but he was replaced through injury at half-time of their first game and he did not play again at the finals.

Below: David Beckham on the ball for LA Galaxy against Columbus Crew in 2010.

FABIO CANNAVARO

Country: Italy
Born: September 13, 1973
Position: Defender
Clubs: Napoli, Parma, Inter Milan, Juventus, Real Madrid, Al-Ahli Dubai

Fabio Cannavaro captained Italy to World Cup glory in 2006, winning his 100th cap against France in the final. He is a cultured centre-back who makes up for what he lacks in height with an uncanny ability to read a game and intercept attacks. Born in Naples, he turned professional with hometown side Napoli, making his senior debut aged 20. He quit for Parma in 1995 and during his seven seasons at the club he established himself as one of the world's best defenders, winning the UEFA Cup in 1999.

He made his international debut against Northern Ireland in January 1997 and soon became a regular in the Italian team. An ever-present member of the side defeated on penalties by hosts France in the World Cup quarter-final the following year, he was one of the few Italians to come out of the tournament with an enhanced reputation. Four years later he was the glue that held Italy's defence together at the 2002 finals and, tellingly, he was absent through suspension when the team were eliminated by South Korea.

A big money move to Inter Milan came in 2002 but it was not until he joined Juventus, and was reunited with former Parma team-mates Lilian Thuram and Gianluigi Buffon, that he finally won Serie A. However, the 2005 and 2006 titles were stripped from the club after their involvement in a match-fixing scandal, and after Juventus were relegated as a punishment he followed coach Fabio Capello to Real Madrid, winning the Spanish league title twice. He returned to Juventus for one final season in 2009 before moving to the United Arab Emirates to play for Al-Ahli.

He captained Italy through a disastrous 2010 World Cup campaign before announcing his decision to retire from international football. He is Italy's most-capped player and in 2006 he became the first defender to be voted FIFA World Player Of The Year.

RICARDO CARVALHO

Country: Portugal
Born: May 18, 1978
Position: Centre-back
Clubs: Porto, Leca, Vitória de Setúbal, Alverca, Chelsea, Real Madrid

A dependable defender who has enjoyed success at the highest levels of club football, Ricardo Carvalho began his professional career at Porto, although it was while on loan to second division Leca that he made his debut. After further loans spells with Vitória de Setúbal and Alverca, it was when coach José Mourinho joined Porto that his career really took off. In the next two seasons he was at the heart of the team that won two league titles, the Portuguese Cup, the 2003 UEFA Cup and the 2004 Champions League. He was also voted UEFA's Club Defender Of The Year for the 2003-4 season.

Following Mourinho to Chelsea in 2004, he was three times a Premier League winner at Stamford Bridge but he was less lucky in the FA Cup, missing Chelsea's 2007 and 2010 victories through injury. He also missed out on the 2009 final after falling out of favour with Guus Hiddink during the Dutch coach's brief tenure at the club. However, he did pick up a runners-up medal after defeat to Manchester United in the 2008 Champions League Final. He was reunited with José Mourinho in the summer of 2010 after signing for Real Madrid.

Making his international debut for Portugal in 2003, he was named in the Euro 2004 Team Of The Tournament despite finishing on the losing side in the final. Two years later it was his clumsy challenge on French striker Thierry Henry that gave away the penalty that knocked Portugal out of the World Cup semi-final, but he was again selected for the Team of the Tournament.

IKER CASILLAS

Country: Spain
Born: May 20, 1981
Position: Goalkeeper
Club: Real Madrid

A product of the Real Madrid youth system, Iker Casillas first gained recognition outside of his hometown when, aged just 18, he performed heroics as Real Madrid defeated Valencia in the 2000 Champions League Final. However, he failed to live up to his newfound fame and was eventually replaced in the Real goal by César Sánchez. A little older and wiser Casillas had another chance to shine when he came on as a second-half substitute in the 2002 Champions League Final against Bayer Leverkusen, and having helped preserve a slender 2-1 lead with a number of fine saves, he reclaimed the jersey on a permanent basis.

An agile and spectacular shot-stopper, Casillas made his international debut in June 2000 but remained on the bench for that month's European Championship. Two years later, after the withdrawal of Santiago Cañizares through injury, Casillas arrived at the 2002 World Cup as first choice keeper and he saved two penalties in the second round game against the Republic Of Ireland, earning the nickname 'Saint Iker'. He captained the national team twice at the 2006 World Cup in Raúl's absence and he was given the armband permanently for the 2008 European Championship. He saved two penalties in the quarter-final shoot-out against Italy before leading the team to victory over Germany in the final.

At the World Cup two years later he was accused of being distracted by his TV reporter girlfriend Sara Carbonero, who was behind the goal as Spain kicked off the campaign with a shock 1-0 defeat to Switzerland but he went on to concede just once more as Spain won the competition for the first time. Casillas lifted the trophy as captain and was voted the tournament's best keeper. Only Andoni Zubizarreta has made more appearances for Spain but it is surely just a matter of time until Casillas breaks that record.

PETR CECH

Country: Czech Republic
Born: May 20, 1982
Position: Goalkeeper
Clubs: Blsany, Sparta Prague, Rennes, Chelsea

Regarded as one of the best goalkeepers in the world, Petr Cech made his name as a member of the Czech Republic side that won the Under-21 European Championship in 2002, earning praise for his performance in the penalty shoot-out that settled the final. After establishing himself as first choice keeper for his country's senior team, he helped them to the semi-finals of the European Championship in 2004 and to a place at the World Cup in 2006. However, an uncharacteristic blunder at Euro 2008, when Cech conceded a goal after allowing a cross to slip through his hands, helped Turkey overturn a 2-0 deficit and knock the Czech Republic out of the competition.

At club level, he joined Sparta Prague in 2001 and set a national record of 855 minutes without conceding a goal. A move to French side Rennes followed in 2002 but it was after his £9 million move to Chelsea in the summer of 2004 that his career really took off. A supreme shot-stopper and commanding in

Below: Ricardo Carvalho in action for Portugal against North Korea at the 2010 World Cup.

the penalty area, Cech's consistently excellent displays were vital as Chelsea won their first league title in 50 years in 2005. He also set a Premiership record of 1,025 minutes without conceding a goal in his first season with the club and he won the Premier League title again in 2006 and 2010. He has also won the FA Cup three times and was voted Czech Footballer Of The Year on four consecutive occasions between 2005 and 2008.

JOE COLE

Country: England
Born: November 8, 1981
Position: Midfielder
Clubs: West Ham, Chelsea, Liverpool

A product of West Ham's youth academy, as a 16-year-old Joe Cole was the hottest property in English football with Manchester United rumoured to be ready to break the bank to secure the services of 'the new Paul Gascoigne'. However, the player remained at Upton Park, made his senior debut at 17 and became club captain in his early twenties.

Cole's failure to live up to the early hype surrounding him did not deter Chelsea from paying £6.6 million to secure his services in 2003. After a long period where he found it difficult to hold down a regular place in the starting line-up, Cole finally came good in the 2005-6 season, operating very effectively as a left-sided winger for Chelsea. He made one substitute appearance at the 2002 World Cup, going on to become an England regular under Sven-Göran Eriksson. He featured at the 2006 World Cup, scoring one of the best goals of the tournament against Sweden but a long-term injury ahead of the finals four years later made it hard for him to regain his place in the starting line-up and he made just two substitute appearances in South Africa.

Despite picking up two Premier League winners' medals at Chelsea and lifting the FA Cup in 2007 and 2010, after the World Cup Cole was deemed surplus to requirements and was signed by Liverpool on a free transfer.

DECO

Country: Portugal
Born: August 27, 1977
Position: Midfielder
Clubs: Corinthians, Benfica, Alverca, Salgueiros, Porto, Barcelona, Chelsea, Fluminense

A gifted playmaker, Brazilian-born Deco – or Anderson Luiz de Sousa – attracts as much controversy as praise for a combative midfield style that often brings as many yellow cards as goals. Once deemed not good enough by Benfica boss Graeme Souness, he really came to prominence under José Mourinho at Porto.

The key figure in their 2003 UEFA Cup Final win, he topped that the following season with a league title and a Champions League victory, scoring in the 3-0 win over Monaco.

Never picked to play for the land of his birth, he qualified to represent Portugal and scored on his debut – against Brazil. He picked up a runners-up medal after playing in the final of Euro 2004 and signed for Barcelona shortly afterwards, spending four seasons at the Nou Camp and winning the Champions League for a second time in 2006, plus two league titles.

Two unhappy seasons followed at Chelsea, where he won the Premier League but never really established himself with a succession of managers. He featured in consecutive World Cups for Portugal, reaching the semi-final in 2006, but he called time on his international career after the 2010 finals and returned to Brazil to sign for Fluminense.

ALESSANDRO DEL PIERO

Country: Italy
Born: November 9, 1974
Position: Centre-forward/Midfielder
Clubs: Padova, Juventus

Signed from Serie B side Padova in 1993 as a 19-year-old, it was not long before the mercurial Alessandro Del Piero had forced himself into the Juventus first team, where he has since become an inspirational figure in a career that has spanned the best part of two decades. He would win seven league titles with Juventus, although the club were stripped of the last two of these in 2006. He picked up a Champions League winners' medal after Juventus beat Ajax on penalties in 1996 and he also scored as a losing finalist in 1997.

Although mostly known for his passing and creative play, it is not unusual for Del Piero to hit the net and he scored an impressive 32 goals in 47 games in all competitions during the 1997-8 season as Juventus won the league title and finished as runners-up in the Champions League. Indeed, ten of his goals had come in ten European games that season, making him the competition's leading scorer for the second time.

Del Piero never really hit the same heights for the Italian national team and his slow recovery from a knee ligament injury that kept him sidelined for nine months limited his effectiveness at the 1998 World Cup Finals. He started Euro 2000 in fine form, netting an exquisite goal against Sweden but after coming on as a second-half substitute in the final he missed two gilt-edged opportunities to score.

Coach Giovanni Trapattoni used Del Piero only sparingly at the 2002 World Cup but he still came off the bench against Mexico to score the late equaliser that helped Italy qualify for the second round. Marcello Lippi also used Del Piero mainly from the bench at the 2006 World Cup and after scoring the match-winning goal in the semi-final against Germany, he came on as an 86th minute substitute in the final and converted Italy's fourth spot-kick in their 5-3 penalty shoot-out win over France. He also featured in Italy's team at Euro 2008.

After Juventus were punished with relegation to Serie B in 2006, he stayed with the club and helped them bounce back at the first attempt. He holds the club's all-time scoring record.

Above: Alessandro Del Piero (left) celebrates scoring against Lazio with Juventus team-mate Antonio Candreva in 2010.

Right: Landon Donovan after scoring the late goal against Algeria that put USA through to the second round of the 2010 World Cup.

LANDON DONOVAN

Country: USA

Born: March 4, 1982

Position: Forward

Clubs: Bayer Leverkusen, San Jose Earthquakes, Los Angeles Galaxy, Bayern Munich, Everton

Landon Donovan is the golden boy of American football. He has represented his country at every level, first attracting attention when he was voted Player Of The Tournament at the 1999 Under-17 World Championship. This earned him a move to Germany with Bayer Leverkusen but much of his period with the club was spent back in the USA on loan with San Jose Earthquakes.

After appearing at the Olympics in 2000 and making his full international debut against Mexico a month later, Donovan went on to play at three consecutive World Cups, helping the USA to the quarter-finals in 2002. He also scored the vital last minute goal against Algeria at the 2010 finals that enabled the Americans to reach the second round. He has also enjoyed success in continental competitions, featuring in the teams that won the CONCACAF Gold Cup in 2002, 2005 and 2007. He scored the equalising penalty in the 2007 final that kickstarted a successful comeback against Mexico.

Despite his unhappy spell with Bayer Leverkusen, he has since forged a successful career in club football in his home country, winning the MLS Cup three times, twice with San Jose Earthquakes and once with LA Galaxy. He has enjoyed brief loan spells in the European leagues with Bayern Munich in 2009 and Everton in 2010 and he has been voted the Player Of The Year by the US Soccer Federation on three occasions.

DIDIER DROGBA

Country: Ivory Coast

Born: March 11, 1978

Position: Forward

Clubs: Le Mans, Guingamp, Marseille, Chelsea

A powerful and athletic striker, Didier Yves Drogba Tébily did not have the quickest journey to football superstardom. Starting his career in France, he enjoyed spells at Le Mans and Guingamp before joining Marseille in 2003 at the age of 25. He was only with the club for a season but scored 19 league goals, was named Player Of The Year in France's top flight, and collected a runners-up medal after the club lost to Valencia in the 2004 UEFA Cup Final.

Drogba joined Roman Abramovich's high-spending Chelsea for £24 million in July 2004 and despite struggling to fully justify that hefty price tag in his early seasons at Stamford Bridge, he developed as a player and saw off the frequent accusations of diving to forge a reputation as one of the world's best strikers. Winning the Premier

League title in his first two seasons at the club, he also won the trophy again in 2010, a campaign that saw him awarded the Premier League Golden Boot for a second time. He has won the FA Cup on three occasions with Chelsea, scoring in each final.

On the international stage Drogba captained Ivory Coast to the final of the African Nations Cup in 2006 but he was among those failing to convert from the spot in the deciding penalty shoot-out as they lost to Egypt. He also helped the West African nation to reach the World Cup for the first time in 2006. Four years later, after fracturing his arm on the eve of the 2010 tournament, he came close to missing out but was given permission to play with a protective cast. However, he was unable to prevent an early exit for the Ivory Coast.

Away from the pitch he has been very active in charity work to the benefit of his home country.

MICHAEL ESSIEN

Country: Ghana

Born: December 3, 1982

Position: Midfielder

Clubs: Liberty Professionals, Bastia, Lyon, Chelsea

A powerful and combative defensive midfielder, Michael Essien began his club career with Ghanaian side Liberty Professionals and first caught the eye outside of his home country with his impressive performances at the Under-17 World Cup in 1999. A defender at the time, he signed for French side Bastia in 2000 and after a couple of false starts, he moved into a central midfield role for his club and was soon doing likewise for his country. He made his

competitive debut for Ghana at the African Nations Cup in 2002.

Joining Lyon in 2003, he won the league title twice in his two seasons at the club and was voted the French league's Player Of The Year in 2005. After a protracted summer transfer saga, Chelsea signed Essien in August 2005 for a club record £24.4 million. His battling displays helped the 'The Blues' mount a fine defence of their league title in his first season and despite two subsequent FA Cup wins, injury has dogged large spells of his career at Stamford Bridge.

He helped Ghana to the 2006 World Cup, reaching the second round before losing to Brazil, a game that Essien missed through suspension. He again aided the team to reach the finals four years later but missed the tournament himself through injury. He was a member of the side that finished third at the 2008 Africans Nations Cup but was injured early in the competition two years later and played no further part as Ghana reached the final. He has featured in the top three of the African Player Of The Year Award on numerous occasions.

SAMUEL ETO'O

Country: Cameroon

Born: March 10, 1981

Position: Centre-forward

Clubs: Real Madrid, Leganés, Espanyol, Mallorca, Barcelona, Inter Milan

A three-time African Player Of The Year, Samuel Eto'o joined Real Madrid's youth academy at 15. Unable to break into a squad littered with world-class stars he spent several seasons on loan, with spells at Leganés and Espanyol before he impressed enough at Real Mallorca to earn a permanent move in 2000. While at the Son Moix he established himself as a prolific striker and in 2003 his pace and finishing helped the club to win the Copa Del Rey for the first time and he scored twice in the final.

Eto'o made his first international appearance with Cameroon in 1996, at the age of just 15, and he was the youngest player at the 1998 World Cup, making one substitute appearance. He scored in the final as Cameroon won gold at the 2000 Olympics in Sydney and he was also a winner at both the 2000 and 2002 African Nations Cups, scoring the opening goal of the 2000 final against Nigeria.

He joined Barcelona in 2004, where he soon earned his £16 million transfer fee by helping the club to the league title in his first campaign. Eto'o was the top scorer in the Spanish league the following season as Barcelona retained the championship and he picked up another winners' medal after victory over Arsenal in the 2006 Champions League Final. Eto'o played his part in the final, hitting the late equaliser that pulled Barcelona back into contention. He would collect up a second winners' medal in 2009, scoring an early goal in the final against Manchester United, and a third with Inter Milan in 2010 following his swap with Zlatan Ibrahimovic. It capped an amazing first season with Inter that had already seen Eto'o win the Italian league and cup 'double'.

CESC FABREGAS

Country: Spain
Born: May 4, 1987
Position: Midfielder
Club: Arsenal

A product of Barcelona's famed youth academy, Cesc Fabregas joined Arsenal in September 2003 as a 16-year-old and before the end of the year he had become the youngest footballer to play and score for Arsenal's first-team, both feats achieved in the League Cup. What he lacks in speed he makes up for with his excellent vision and pinpoint passing and soon he established himself as the team's midfield playmaker, going on to pick up runners-up medals in the 2005 FA Cup and the 2006 Champions League.

He first caught the eye on the international stage with his performances at the 2003 Under-17 World Championship, when he finished joint top scorer and was voted Player Of The Tournament as Spain were beaten by Brazil in the final. He earned his first full cap against the Ivory Coast in 2006, becoming the youngest player to represent the country in 70 years.

Despite making most of his appearances at Euro 2008 and the 2010 World Cup from the bench, he played in the final of both competitions as Spain were crowned European and world champions, and it was Fabregas who supplied the incisive pass to Iniesta for the winning goal in the 2010 World Cup Final.

RIO FERDINAND

Country: England
Born: November 7, 1978
Position: Defender
Clubs: West Ham, Leeds United, Manchester United

Rio Ferdinand is the trainee from Peckham who became the world's most expensive defender. Signed to West Ham United in 1995 he soon earned comparisons to local legend Bobby Moore for his composure on the ball. He made his league debut in May 1996 and his England debut against Cameroon in November 1998, demonstrating the class that would later make him such a success at the 2002 World Cup.

He joined Leeds United in November 2000 for a record fee of £18 million and helped them to the semi-final of the Champions League before Manchester United signed him for another British record fee of £30 million. He won a championship medal in his debut season at Old Trafford, the first of many honours that he would earn with the club, including captaining the team to Champions League victory against Chelsea in the 2008 final in Moscow. Earlier that season he even experienced a spell in goal for the club in an FA Cup quarter-final, donning the gloves after the first and second choice keepers were injured and sent-off in quick succession.

The most controversial moment of his career came when he was banned from football for eight months after forgetting to attend a drugs test in 2003 and as a consequence he missed the 2004 European Championship, but on returning to action he reclaimed his place for both club and country. He rehabilitated his reputation to the point that he was appointed England captain in February 2010 but after travelling to South Africa for the World Cup that summer, he had to withdraw from the squad after suffering a serious injury in training on the eve of the tournament. It was just one of many injuries that have blighted his latter career.

DIEGO FORLÁN

Country: Uruguay
Born: May 19, 1979
Position: Centre-forward
Clubs: Danubio FC, Peñarol, Independiente, Manchester United, Villarreal, Atlético Madrid

Much derided for his spell at Manchester United, it took Diego Forlán eight months and 27 games to record his first goal for the club: a Champions League penalty against Maccabi Haifa in September 2002. Signed from Independiente for £6.9 million that January, Forlán managed just 17 goals in 95 appearances and Wayne Rooney's arrival signalled the end of a difficult two-and-a-half year spell at the club.

A move to Villarreal suited the Uruguayan and he showed his worth by ending 2004-5 as the Spanish league's top scorer with 25 goals, jointly winning the European Golden Boot with Thierry Henry.

He topped the league's scoring chart again in the 2008-9 season while playing for Atlético Madrid but it was at the World Cup in 2010 that his talents were finally recognised as he was voted Player Of The Tournament. His five goals helped Uruguay to a fourth place finish and he ended the competition as the joint highest scorer, along with Thomas Müller, Wesley Sneijder and David Villa. Earlier in the year he had also helped Atlético to win the Europa League, scoring twice in the final against Fulham.

STEVEN GERRARD

Country: England
Born: May 30, 1980
Position: Midfielder
Club: Liverpool

A product of the Liverpool youth academy, Steven Gerrard is one of the most talented players in English football but he has never been tempted away from his hometown club. Making his debut for Liverpool at Anfield as a last minute substitute against Blackburn in November 1998, his robust, all-action style from the centre of midfield has seen him become the club's pivotal player in the first decade of the 21st century.

He was an integral part of the Liverpool side that won a trio of cup competitions in 2001 (UEFA Cup, League Cup and FA Cup) and he put in a captain's performance to inspire his team to come back from 3-0 down to Milan in

Below: Steven Gerrard in action for Liverpool in August 2010.

the 2005 Champions League Final. He scored Liverpool's first goal of the game and after 'The Reds' won on penalties Gerrard lifted the trophy. A similar performance earned victory in the following year's FA Cup final against West Ham, with Gerrard equalising at the death from 30 yards out. His goal took the game to extra-time and Liverpool eventually triumphed on penalties. However, he could not repeat the magic in the 2007 Champions League Final, missing a good chance to equalise shortly before Milan scored the winning goal.

A valuable member of England's national team, he has rarely been played in any of his more natural club positions for his country, finding himself utilised on the left wing by a succession of managers. He scored England's second goal from long range in the 5-1 demolition of Germany in a 2002 World Cup qualifier but missed the subsequent finals through injury. He recovered to become a permanent fixture in the England side at both Euro 2004 and the 2006 World Cup and he captained the team at the 2010 World Cup in South Africa.

RYAN GIGGS

Country: Wales
Born: November 29, 1973
Position: Winger
Club: Manchester United

As one of the original members of a generation of young players developed at Manchester United by Sir Alex Ferguson and known as 'Fergie's Fledglings', Ryan Giggs has become the most decorated player in English football history. He made his debut as a 17-year-old substitute against Everton in March 1991 and immediately

Below: Manchester United's Ryan Giggs, the most decorated player in English club football.

caught the eye with his unmatchable pace and dribbling skills. The comparisons with United legend George Best were plentiful and although he became a first-team regular the following season, making his debut for Wales and winning the PFA Young Player Of The Year Award in the process, the campaign would end in disappointment as United were pipped to the championship by rivals Leeds.

The title finally arrived at Old Trafford in 1993, signalling the start of the most illustrious period in the club's history, and Giggs has played a prominent role in all of this era's great moments. Despite constant links with a move to Serie A in his early days, he remained loyal to the club and has been repaid with a host of honours. In his first 20 seasons in the top flight he won eleven Premiership titles, four FA Cups, three League Cups, two club world titles, and most famously, the Champions League in both 1999 and 2008.

A left-winger with lightning fast pace through much of his career, he has been increasingly used as a playmaker in his later years, yet he has also scored in every season of his career, making him the only player to have hit the net in each Premier League season since the inception of the competition in 1992-3.

As a demonstration of the respect in which the British public holds him, he was voted BBC Sports Personality of the Year in 2009, while the same year his fellow professionals crowned him the PFA Player Of The Year for the first time. He was honoured with an OBE in the Queen's 2007 Birthday Honours List and in 2008 he broke Bobby Charlton's Manchester United appearance record.

AHMED HASSAN

Country: Egypt
Born: May 2, 1975
Position: Winger/Midfielder
Clubs: Aswan, Ismaily, Kocaelispor, Denizlispor, Gençlerbirliği, Besiktas, Anderlecht, Al-Ahly

One of the most capped players in international football, Ahmed Hassan has won the African Nations Cup on four occasions with Egypt. He hit the net from 25 yards in a 2-0 defeat of South Africa in the 1998 final, and despite missing a penalty in the 2006 final he was voted Player Of The Tournament after he bounced back to score Egypt's first kick in the shoot-out that decided the match. At the heart of the team's midfield in the defeat of Cameroon in 2008, he picked up his fourth winners' medal after beating Ghana in 2010, lifting the trophy as captain and pointing his finger in the air in thanks to Allah.

In club football he celebrated winning the league in Belgium with Anderlecht in 2007, and after moving to Egypt he won the championship twice with Al-Ahly and picked up a winners' medal in the 2008 African Champions League, scoring in the second leg of the final.

THIERRY HENRY

Country: France
Born: August 17, 1977
Position: Forward
Clubs: Monaco, Juventus, Arsenal, Barcelona, New York Red Bulls

At his height Thierry Henry was one of the most feared and talented strikers on the planet and during a prolific eight-year stint with Arsenal he was ranked among the most influential players in England's Premier League, topping the division's charts on four occasions and helping the club to two league titles. He was also twice on the winning side in the FA Cup final.

A highly skilled striker with a wonderful touch on the ball, he won the European Golden Boot in both 2004 and 2005 and became Arsenal's record scorer when he surpassed Ian Wright's 185-goal tally in October 2005. It was all the more impressive when considering he had played as a winger at both first club Monaco and during a disappointing spell with Juventus. However, it was when he was reunited with his former Monaco coach Arsene Wenger at Arsenal that he was transformed into a wonderfully fast and powerful striker, a decision that helped him to a host of awards. In 2003 and 2004 both the Professional Footballers' Association and the Football Writers' Association voted Henry the Premier League's Player Of The Year, and he received the FWA award for a third time in 2006. He has also been French Player Of The Year a record four times.

Although disappointed to lose the Champions League final in 2006, he stayed at Arsenal for another season before finally carrying through on his threat to leave the club when he signed for Barcelona in June 2007. While not immediately making the same kind of impact in Spain after being asked to play on the wing once again, he finished his debut season as the club's leading goalscorer in all competitions. His time at the Nou Camp saw him add to his list of honours, twice winning the Spanish league title and finally picking a Champions League winners' medal in 2009. He also played in the FIFA Club World Cup final later the same year when Barcelona beat Estudiantes to lift the trophy.

Henry made his France debut against South Africa in June 1997, going on to play for his country 123 times. His 51 international goals make him the national team's record scorer. Although an important part of France's 1998 World Cup winning squad, scoring three goals in the competition, he failed to get on the pitch in the final (he was warming up to come on as a second-half substitute when the sending-off of Marcel Desailly resulted in a tactical change). Two years later he was the main striker for the team's European Championship triumph but although playing in the 2006 World Cup Final, he was substituted in extra-time and had to look on as France were beaten 5-3 on penalties.

Henry played a significant role in helping the French to qualify for the 2010 World Cup, although it was one that caused controversy and consternation around the world. He twice used his hand to control the ball before setting up William Gallas for the winner during the qualifying play-off against the Republic Of Ireland and his actions drew heavy condemnation. Shortly after the tournament he retired from international football and signed for New York Red Bulls.

GONZALO HIGUAÍN

Country: Argentina
Born: December 10, 1987
Position: Striker
Clubs: River Plate, Real Madrid

The son of Argentine footballer Jorge Higuaín, Gonzalo was born in France where his father was playing club football and although he holds dual citizenship and was courted by France coach Raymond Domenech in 2006, he grew up in South America and eventually decided to accept the call of Argentina. Making his international debut against Peru in October 2009, by this time he had already won the Spanish league title twice with Real Madrid after moving to the Bernabéu Stadium in 2007. He was the club's leading goalscorer in the league campaigns ending in 2009 and 2010 and he started the majority of games for his country at the 2010 World Cup. Hitting three goals against South Korea at the finals, he became only the third Argentinian ever to score a World Cup hat-trick.

ZLATAN IBRAHIMOVIC

Country: Sweden
Born: October 3, 1981
Position: Centre-forward
Clubs: Malmö, Ajax, Juventus, Inter Milan, Barcelona, AC Milan

A physical yet agile striker, Zlatan Ibrahimovic has tremendous dribbling skills for a player of his height but although his suspect temperament has been known cause him problems, it has not prevented him becoming one of the world's highest paid players after a series of opportunistic transfers. The son of Bosnian and Croatian immigrants, Ibrahimovic was born in Malmö, Sweden, and began his career at his hometown club. However, it was after a move to Ajax that he began to catch the eye while helping the Dutch side to a league and cup 'double' under coach Ronald Koeman.

Ibrahimovic had an impressive Euro 2004 with Sweden, where he scored a much talked about goal that sent the Italians crashing out of the competition. Soon afterwards he made a £13 million move to Juventus, where he won consecutive league titles in his first two seasons. These were later stripped from the club in the

fall-out from the 2006 Italian match-fixing scandal but by then his goalscoring touch had already started to evade him following a move into a deeper role. He endured a poor World Cup in 2006 and jumped ship shortly before Juventus were punished with relegation to Serie B, signing for Inter Milan and winning the Serie A title in each of his three seasons with the club.

Having become one of the hottest properties in world football during his time with Inter, in July 2009 Barcelona prised Ibrahimovic away from the San Siro in a multi-million pound deal that saw him valued at more than £56 million, with Samuel Eto'o travelling in the other direction as a makeweight in the deal. Although Ibrahimovic struggled to slot into a winning Barcelona side, before the year was out he featured in the team that won the FIFA Club World Cup and he celebrated his first Spanish league title at the end of the season. However, unable to maintain a relationship with Barça coach Pep Guardiola, he transferred to AC Milan in August 2010. He has been voted Sweden's Player Of The Year on four occasions.

ANDRÉS INIESTA

Country: Spain
Born: May 11, 1984
Position: Midfielder/Winger
Club: Barcelona

An inventive and flexible midfielder equally adept at playing on the wings or in a more central role, Andrés Iniesta joined Barça from Albacete as a 12-year-old and worked his way through the ranks until given his first-team debut by Louis Van Gaal against Club Brugge in October 2002. His time at the Nou Camp has brought its rewards and the 2010 Spanish league title was his fourth win in the competition.

He was a second-half substitute as Barcelona beat Arsenal to clinch the Champions League in 2006, and while injury ruled him out of the 2009 Spanish Cup Final, he was back in action shortly afterwards to help Barcelona to glory in the Champions League once again, providing the pass from which Samuel Eto'o scored the opening goal of the final against Manchester United. Injury also caused him to miss the FIFA Club World Cup final later in the year.

Iniesta made his debut for Spain in May 2006 against Russia and played at the subsequent World Cup. He was in the team that won the 2008 European Championship and was one of the stars of the 2010 World Cup, being voted Man Of The Match in the final after scoring the goal that won the trophy for Spain. After scoring he lifted his shirt to reveal a tribute to Espanyol captain Daniel Jarque, who had died of a heart attack the previous year.

FILIPPO INZAGHI

Country: Italy
Born: August 9, 1973
Position: Centre-forward
Clubs: Piacenza, Leffe, Verona, Parma, Atalanta, Juventus, AC Milan

A lethal opportunist in the penalty area, Filippo Inzaghi is famous for his ability to play off the shoulders of the last defender, leading many critics to describe offside as 'the Inzaghi position'. After starting his career with hometown club Piacenza, he enjoyed loan spells in the lower divisions before making his Serie A debut with Parma in 1995. However, it was Inzaghi's one campaign with mid-table Atalanta in the 1996-7 season that earned him his reputation, as he netted 24 times in 33 league games and finished as Serie A's leading goalscorer.

Above: Thierry Henry (left) celebrates with his Red Bulls team-mate Seth Stammler after scoring against Tottenham.

He was immediately snapped up by Juventus and after scoring a championship winning hat-trick against Bologna at the end of his first season, he collected a Champions League runners-up medal ten days later after defeat to Real Madrid in the final.

After being edged out of the Juventus side by David Trezeguet, Inzaghi moved to AC Milan in 2001 and despite his early years at the San Siro being hampered by a persistent knee injury, he forged a strong goalscoring partnership with Andriy Shevchenko that brought its rewards, including the Serie A title in 2004 and the FIFA Club World Cup in 2007. He also won the Champions League in 2003 when Milan beat his former club Juventus in a penalty shoot-out.

Although Inzaghi was left out of the squad for the 2005 Champions League final defeat to Liverpool, he was a vital member of the team that gained revenge over 'The Reds' in the 2007 final and his two goals were enough to secure the trophy for Milan and to see him voted Man Of The Match. By the end of the 2009-10 season, along with Raúl he was the joint highest goalscorer in the history of European club competition, with 68 goals.

Inzaghi made his international debut against Brazil in June 1997 and played three matches for Italy at the 1998 World Cup Finals. He scored twice for his country at the European Championship two years later and seven times in six games during the qualification campaign for the 2002 World Cup Finals. He was a member of Italy's victorious 2006 World Cup squad but only made it on to the pitch once, early in the tournament.

KAKÁ

Country: Brazil
Born: April 22, 1982
Position: Attacking midfielder
Clubs: São Paulo, AC Milan, Real Madrid

Born Ricardo Izecson dos Santos Leite, he became known as Kaká because of his younger brother's inability to pronounce Ricardo. After demonstrating an impressive goalscoring record at club level in Brazil while still a teenager, the talented playmaker gained a big-money move to AC Milan in 2003 and helped his new side to the Serie A title and the European Super Cup in his first season. In 2005, playing in the hole behind striker Andriy Shevchenko, he provided the ammunition for the Ukrainian star and chipped in with vital goals of his own en route to second place in Serie A and a Champions League final against Liverpool.

Shevchenko's departure allowed Kaká to play in a more attacking role at times and two years later he was the star of Milan's Champions League campaign that culminated with a winners' medal. Although it was his strike partner Filippo Inzaghi who scored the goals in the final against Liverpool, Kaká topped the competition's scoring charts that season with ten goals. Before the end of the year he had also won the FIFA Club World Cup, scoring in a 4-2 victory over Boca Juniors, and he was voted both European and World Player Of The Year. Such was his stock that Real Madrid broke the world transfer record to sign him in June 2009, paying £56 million to secure his services.

He made his international debut against Bolivia in January 2002 and a few months later, as a 20-year-old, he was a member of Brazil's World Cup winning squad in 2002 but only featured as a late substitute in one group match. By the 2006 finals he was a global star and much was expected of him but he scored just once playing in a formation that became known as 'the magic square', squeezed into the team alongside Ronaldinho and behind twin strikers Ronaldo and Adriano. Long-term injuries and a lack of form were a worry in advance of the 2010 finals and while he showed flashes of his best, he also received a rather harshly awarded red card against Ivory Coast.

ROBBIE KEANE

Country: Republic Of Ireland
Born: July 8, 1980
Position: Forward
Clubs: Wolverhampton Wanderers, Coventry City, Inter Milan, Leeds United, Tottenham Hotspur, Liverpool, Celtic

Robbie Keane was just 17 years old when he made his breakthrough with Wolverhampton Wanderers. His creative skills were soon creating goalscoring opportunities both for himself and for his strike partners too. While few expected the club to be able to hold on to such a hot talent, not many would have predicted the rollercoaster ride he would take through European football, with shorts stints at Coventry City, Inter Milan and Leeds United. It was when Glenn Hoddle tempted him to sign for Tottenham Hotspur from Leeds in 2002 that he finally found a permanent home and the stability allowed him to develop into one of the most expressive players in the Premier League and a firm favourite with the fans at White Hart Lane.

A prolific goalscorer with Tottenham, he won the League Cup with the club in 2008 but shortly before the start of the following season he made a surprise move to Liverpool, the team he had supported as a child. The transfer was the cause of acrimony between the two clubs but Keane's spell at Anfield was not a success and he returned to Spurs midway through the campaign. A year later he went on loan to Celtic, where he scored 12 goals in 16 games and was voted Player Of The Year by the club's fans.

He made his debut appearance for the Republic Of Ireland against Argentina in April 1998 and he earned his 100th cap playing the same opponents in August 2010, by which time he had long since become captain of the national team. His country's leading scorer, he is most remembered for the injury-time equaliser he scored against Germany at the 2002 World Cup.

SAMI KHEDIRA

Country: Germany
Born: April 4, 1987
Position: Midfielder
Clubs: Stuttgart, Real Madrid

The son of a Tunisian father and German mother, Sami Khedira's strong and disciplined performances at the heart of Stuttgart's midfield helped him to a first international appearance in September 2009. By that time he had already won the 2007 league title in his debut Bundesliga season and captained Germany to victory in the 2009 European Under-21 Championship.

In the run up to the 2010 World Cup he was heavily tipped to replace the injured Michael Ballack, eventually playing alongside Bastian Schweinsteiger, and he was an ever present member of the team that reached the semi-finals. Indeed, it was Khedira who headed Germany's late winning goal in the third place play-off match. His performances in South Africa were enough to tempt José Mourinho to sign him for Real Madrid after the tournament.

MIROSLAV KLOSE

Country: Germany
Born: June 9, 1978
Position: Forward
Clubs: Homburg, Kaiserslautern, Werder Bremen, Bayern Munich

Miroslav Klose has proven himself to be a prolific centre-forward on every stage but in football terms he was something of a late developer, making the jump from German regional football to the World Cup in less than two years. Having worked as a carpenter he did not even make his full debut for his first professional club,

Opposite: Former World Player Of The Year, Kaká, in action for Brazil at the 2010 World Cup.

Below: Germany's Miroslav Klose, one of the most prolific strikers in the history of the World Cup.

Kaiserslautern, until he was 22, but within six months his blistering pace and lethal finishing earned him a call-up to the national team.

It could have all been so different. The son of a professional footballer, Polish-born Klose had moved to Germany with his family as a child in 1987 but although approached by Poland's national team, he declined the opportunity and held out for the call from Germany, making a dramatic match-winning international debut as a substitute against Albania in March 2001.

Klose opened his first World Cup campaign the following year with a hat-trick against Saudi Arabia, followed by goals against the Republic Of Ireland and Cameroon, but although he picked up a runners-up medal after defeat to Brazil in the final, he did not add to his tally in the knockout stages. Finishing the tournament as the second highest scorer behind Ronaldo, Klose headed all five of his goals, an unrivalled achievement at the finals.

Werder Bremen signed Klose in 2004 and in the 2005-6 season he finished top scorer in the Bundesliga. He won the Golden Boot at the 2006 World Cup with another five goals, becoming the first footballer to score five at successive World Cups, and he was voted German Footballer Of The Year. He later picked up a runners-up medal at the 2008 European Championship.

Signing for Bayern Munich in 2007, he won the German league and cup 'double' in both 2008 and 2010. In the latter campaign he was often relegated to the bench and he only appeared as a second-half substitute in the Champions League final defeat to Inter Milan. However, Klose still travelled to the 2010 World Cup as Germany's first choice striker. While lacking the pace of his youth, he was still a deadly goalmouth poacher and he scored four times en route to the semi-finals, making him the joint second highest goalscorer in the history of the competition, one goal behind Ronaldo. Unfortunately illness ruled him out of the third place play-off game and ended his hopes of beating the record.

Below: Inter Milan's Maicon (left) prepares to tackle in the 2010 Champions League Final.

PHILIPP LAHM

Country: Germany
Born: November 11, 1983
Position: Fullback
Clubs: Bayern Munich, Stuttgart

One of the best and most versatile fullbacks in the world, the naturally right-footed Philipp Lahm first grabbed the limelight for his outstanding performances as Germany's left-back at the 2006 World Cup, a position that he occupied for much of his career after being asked to switch flanks while on loan to Stuttgart in his early days. After a successful return to his preferred position at Bayern Munich for the 2009-10 season, he continued in that role for the national side and was the only German player on the field for every single minute of the 2010 World Cup campaign.

Such is coach Joachim Löw's faith in Lahm that the 26-year-old was appointed national team captain for the tournament in place of the injured Michael Ballack and he led the side to third place. He has won the German league and cup 'double' three times with Bayern and he also picked up runners-up medals for the 2008 European Championship and the 2010 Champions League.

FRANK LAMPARD

Country: England
Born: June 20, 1978
Position: Midfielder
Clubs: West Ham United, Swansea City, Chelsea

Named the world's second best player behind Ronaldinho in 2005, Frank Lampard is the complete midfielder and can boast prodigious attacking qualities. In 1995 he turned professional at West Ham, where his father Frank Lampard Snr had been both a player and assistant manager, but he was briefly loaned out to Swansea City. He captained West Ham to the final of the FA Youth Cup in 1996 and made his debut in the senior side the same year.

In May 2001, after six years at Upton Park, Lampard signed for Chelsea for £11 million, where he developed into one of the most consistent players in the Premier League. A formidable marksman from midfield, he has been Chelsea's leading goalscorer three times, including both of the Premier League title-winning seasons of 2004-5 and 2005-6. He was also named the Football Writers' Association's Player Of The Year in 2005, when he set a Premier League record of playing in 159 consecutive league matches between October 13, 2001 and November 26, 2005. He won the title again in 2010, scoring 22 league goals that season, and he has lifted the FA Cup on three occasions, hitting the winner in the 2009 final against Everton.

Lampard made his first England appearance

in October 1999 against Belgium and although he was not selected for the two tournaments that followed, he made a sizeable impact on the 2004 European Championship, scoring three times in four games as England exited in the quarter-finals.

In 2006 he took part in his first World Cup, where despite failing to score, he still made more shots at goal than any other player. He was at the centre of controversy at the finals four years later when his 20-yard shot against Germany was not given as a goal despite clearly crossing the line. As a consequence, he exited the tournament with the unenviable record of having made more World Cup shots on goal without scoring, 37, since statistics were first collected in 1966.

MAICON

Country: Brazil
Born: July 26, 1981
Position: Right-back
Clubs: Cruzeiro, Monaco, Inter Milan

A powerful right-wingback blessed with speed and strength, Maicon Douglas Sisenando is not only watertight at the back, he also has the pace to turn defence into sudden attack. He began his professional career with Cruzeiro in 2001 and won the Brazilian league during his four-year spell in the first-team. He made his international debut against Mexico at the Gold Cup in 2003 and enjoyed two seasons in France with Monaco before transferring to Inter Milan in July 2006.

It was at the San Siro that he has enjoyed his biggest highs, winning the Italian league title in each of his first four seasons at the club, along with the Italian Cup and the Champions League in 2010. A born leader, he was a member of Brazil's Copa América winning teams of 2004 and 2007, and he was one of his country's best performers at the 2010 World Cup, scoring with a blistering shot from an improbably tight angle in the group game against North Korea. FIFA later voted him into the All-Star Team Of The Tournament.

LIONEL MESSI

Country: Argentina
Born: June 24, 1987
Position: Centre-forward
Club: Barcelona

A natural dribbler with incredible acceleration and an unbeatable first touch, Lionel Messi has the kind of unrivalled control of the ball that led to him being dubbed 'the new Maradona' early in his career and helped him to be crowned both the European and World Player Of The Year in 2009 at just 22 years of age.

He started his career with hometown club Newell's Old Boys but because he was suffering from a hormone deficiency that his parents were unable to afford to treat in Argentina, the family decided to move to Barcelona. Messi had a trial with his new local club at 13 and made his league debut for the first-team against local rivals Espanyol in October 2004, given his chance at just 17 by coach Frank Rijkaard. The following May he became the youngest player to score a league goal for the club in a 2-0 defeat of Albacete after coming on as a substitute in the 88th minute. To cap an amazing debut season, he picked up the Golden Boot as Argentina won the World Youth Championship.

He has developed into the undoubted star of the Barcelona team and although he failed to recover from a thigh injury in time to feature in the Champions League final of 2006, he has played his part in the winning of four league championships while at the club. He was Barcelona's top goalscorer for the first time in 2009 and he hit the net in the finals of the Copa Del Rey, the Champions League and the FIFA Club World Cup, picking up a winners' medal in all three. He was also the top scorer in the Champions League that season with nine goals and the following year he won the European Golden Boot as the most prolific marksman on the continent.

Messi made his international debut against Hungary in August 2005 and he went on to impress at the 2006 World Cup, despite making most of his appearances from the bench. He picked up a runners-up medal in the Copa Libertadores the following year and he won a gold medal at the 2008 Olympics despite originally being barred from taking part by his club, but after personal entreaties Messi was released to compete and set-up Ángel Di María for the winning goal in the final.

Messi arrived at the 2010 World Cup ranked as the best player on the planet but like many of the biggest stars at the tournament he failed to live up to his reputation and Argentina were knocked out in the quarter-final.

DIEGO MILITO

Country: Argentina
Born: June 12, 1979
Position: Striker
Clubs: Racing Club, Genoa, Real Zaragoza, Inter Milan

A powerful centre-forward with a nose for goals, Argentinian Diego Milito may have represented his country on an infrequent basis but at club level he has been a prolific marksman wherever he has played. None of his goals have been more important than the two that clinched victory for Inter Milan in the 2010 Champions League final and he was voted Man of The Match. He also hit the winning goal in the final of the Italian Cup and he was the club's top scorer as Inter won the championship, scoring 30 goals in all competitions in his first season at the San Siro. Despite this form he made just two appearances at the 2010 World Cup, having not been selected

for the squad four years earlier. His younger brother is fellow Argentine international footballer Gabriel Milito.

THOMAS MÜLLER

Country: Germany
Born: September 13, 1989
Position: Attacking midfielder/Forward
Club: Bayern Munich

A player with speed and vision, after a year on the fringes of the Bayern Munich first-team Müller made his breakthrough following the appointment of coach Louis Van Gaal at the beginning of the 2009-10 season. Accomplished in either an attacking midfield role or out wide, Van Gaal opted to play Müller behind a lone striker and it was a decision that paid dividends, with 13 goals in 34 league games that campaign. He also played his part in Bayern's German Cup victory over Werder Bremen and picked up a runners-up medal after defeat to Inter Milan in the Champions League final.

Having only made his international debut against Argentina in March 2010, at just 20 Müller was one of the undoubted stars of the South Africa World Cup. He was voted the tournament's Best Young Player and scored five goals as Germany took third place, winning the Golden Boot on assists after tying with Wes Sneijder, David Villa and Diego Forlán. It was not a bad return considering he missed the semi-final through suspension.

ALESSANDRO NESTA

Country: Italy
Born: March 19, 1976
Position: Central defender
Clubs: Lazio, AC Milan

A product of the Lazio youth system, Nesta made his senior debut for the Rome side when he was 17. He won the first three of four consecutive Serie A Defender Of The Year awards while with Lazio but after an 18-year association with the club, which included winning the European Cup Winners' Cup in 1999, the Italian league title in 2000, and a long spell as captain, he transferred to AC Milan in August 2002 for £19 million.

In his first season at the San Siro he won both the Champions League, scoring in the deciding penalty shoot-out, and the Italian Cup. He won the Serie A title in 2004 and despite picking up a runners-up medal in the 2005 Champions League Final defeat to Liverpool, he was part of the team that gained revenge over 'The Reds' by beating them 2-1 in the 2007 final. Before the year was out he had also scored in the 4-2 defeat of Boca Juniors in the 2007 FIFA Club World Cup Final.

On the international stage he was a member of Italy's European Under-21 Championship winning team in 1996 and impressed enough to become a member of Italy's senior squad for Euro 96, although he did not make his international debut until several months later. A defensive rock with sublime ball control,

Above: Argentina's Lionel Messi takes on South Korea at the 2010 World Cup.

Above: Ji-Sung Park celebrates scoring against Greece at the 2010 World Cup.

Nesta became a regular in the national side and effectively marked Patrick Kluivert out of the game in Italy's win over Holland in the semi-final of the 2000 European Championship.

He featured at the World Cups of 1998, 2002 and 2006 but an injury sustained in the group stages of the latter tournament meant that he was not in the team that won the final and his replacement Marco Materazzi scored Italy's only goal of the game. He made just one more appearance for his country before retiring from international football and declined an opportunity to return for Euro 2008.

MICHAEL OWEN

Country: England
Born: December 14, 1979
Position: Forward
Club: Liverpool, Real Madrid, Newcastle United, Manchester United

A prolific striker, Michael Owen scored against Wimbledon on his Liverpool debut in May 1997 and showed his predatory instincts by netting 18 league goals the following season. He was rewarded with an England debut against Chile in February 1998, making him the national team's youngest player of the 20th century. He went on to make a real impact at the World Cup that summer, scoring one of the tournament's most outstanding goals against Argentina.

Owen was Liverpool's leading scorer in each of his six full seasons at Anfield and even a serious hamstring injury, sustained against Leeds United at the tail end of the 1998-9 season, did not dent a goalscoring ratio of more than one goal in every two league games. In 2001 he was voted European Footballer Of The Year after lifting both the UEFA Cup and the FA Cup with Liverpool, scoring twice in the last ten minutes

of the FA Cup final to overturn Arsenal's lead. Liverpool also won the League Cup that season but Owen remained on the bench for the final.

In August 2004, having scored 118 goals in 216 league games for Liverpool, Owen joined Real Madrid but lasted just one season in Spain. Although he was not guaranteed a first-team place he still managed to score 16 goals for the club but when new signings relegated Owen further down the pecking order, he made the surprise decision to returned to the Premier League and sign for Graeme Souness's Newcastle United in a £17 million deal. Injury ruled him out of the latter half of the 2005-6 season and although he recovered just in time to lead England's bid for the World Cup that summer, yet another injury ended his tournament in the first minute of England's final group game with Sweden.

He has struggled to regain his best form ever since and while it once looked a certainty that he would break Bobby Charlton's England scoring record, he remains stranded in fourth place in the all-time list with 40 goals to his name and without an international appearance since March 2008, when he was just 28. In an attempt to kickstart his stalling career he joined Manchester United on a free transfer in July 2009 and scored the opening goal in the 2010 League Cup Final defeat of Aston Villa. However, he left the field before half-time with an injury that ruled him out of the rest of the season.

MERSUT ÖZIL

Country: Germany
Born: October 15, 1988
Position: Attacking midfielder
Clubs: Schalke 04, Werder Bremen, Real Madrid

After coming through the youth ranks at Schalke, it was after his transfer to Werder Bremen in January 2008 that Mersut Özil's career really took off. At the end of his first full season at the club he helped Werder to the German Cup, scoring the only goal of the victory over Bayer Leverkusen in the 2009 final, and he picked up a UEFA Cup runners-up medal after defeat to Shakhtar Donetsk. Starting off at Werder in left midfield, after the departure of Diego to Juventus in May 2009 Özil was transformed into an energetic and gifted playmaker.

Just a few months after making his full international debut against Norway in February 2009, he was the star of Germany's successful campaign at the European Under-21 Championship and he was voted Man Of The Match in the 4-0 defeat of England in the final. The following year he was one of the surprise attractions of the World Cup, bringing creativity and cunning to the midfield during Germany's run to the semi-finals, and after returning from South Africa a much in demand player, he signed for Real Madrid.

JI-SUNG PARK

Country: South Korea
Born: February 25, 1981
Position: Midfielder
Clubs: Kyoto Purple Sanga, PSV Eindhoven, Manchester United

Ji-Sung Park moved to Japan in 2000 to begin his professional career in the J.League and he was the first Korean to achieve success in Japan without first starting out in South Korea's own domestic league. He made his international debut at just 18 and rose to fame with his performances at the 2002 World Cup, scoring the winning goal against Portugal that ensured his team's progress to the knockout stages and playing in all seven games on the way to a fourth place finish.

The following year Park teamed up with his former international coach Guus Hiddink at PSV Eindhoven and he began to flourish after Arjen Robben's departure in 2004. His Champions League performances, as PSV reached the 2005 semi-finals, prompted Manchester United to splash out £4 million for his services and the versatile midfielder has excelled in a host of positions since moving to Old Trafford.

Often selected by manager Alex Ferguson for the games that really matter, he has since won the Premier League title three times and the FIFA Club World Cup. He missed Manchester United's victory in the 2008 Champions League final after Owen Hargreaves was preferred, causing Ferguson to apologise much later for not even including Park in the squad for the game. Although he started the final the following year, United lost to Barcelona.

As one of the stalwarts of the South Korea team, he was ever-present at the 2006 World Cup and captained the side at the finals four years later. He has scored in every World Cup that he has played, with only two other players from the Asian continent having scored as many goals in the competition: compatriot Ahn Jung-Hwan and Sami Al-Jaber of Saudi Arabia.

GERARD PIQUÉ

Country: Spain
Born: February 2, 1987
Position: Centre-back
Clubs: Manchester United, Real Zaragoza, Barcelona

Despite coming through the youth ranks at Barcelona, at 17 years of age Gerard Piqué defected to Manchester United, where he made his debut in a cup match in October 2004. He did not make his first Premier League appearance for another 17 months and was little seen before being loaned to Real Zaragoza for the 2006-7 season. On his return he made nine appearances as United won the league title but he opted to return to Barcelona at the end of the season and his career subsequently flourished under coach Pep Guardiola.

An imposing central defender, he is a perceptive reader of the game with a good head and the ability to carry the ball forward when required. Forging an impressive central defensive partnership with Carles Puyol at both club and international level, he has won the Spanish league in each of his first two seasons back at the Nou Camp, as well as playing in Barcelona's winning sides in the 2008 Champions League Final and the 2009 Spanish Cup. Despite only making his international debut in February 2009, he was an ever-present member of the Spanish team that won the 2010 World Cup in South Africa.

ANDREA PIRLO

Country: Italy
Born: May 19, 1979
Position: Midfielder
Clubs: Brescia, Inter Milan, Reggina, AC Milan

An outstanding playmaker, an imposing ball winner and a free-kick specialist, Andrea Pirlo was one the key members of Italy's 2006 World Cup winning team, receiving FIFA's Bronze Ball after finishing in third place behind Zinédine Zidane and Fabio Cannavaro in the Player Of The Tournament voting. He was Man Of The Match in Italy's semi-final win over hosts Germany, regarded as the best game of the tournament, and again in the final itself.

Success has not come easily to Pirlo. He started his career as an attacking midfielder and made his Serie A debut for Brescia in May 1995 but it was another couple of seasons before he established himself in the team. A move to Inter Milan followed in 1998 but he was often overlooked by Marcello Lippi, later Italy's World

Cup winning coach. As a result he enjoyed loan spells with Reggina and Brescia before a move to city rivals AC Milan. It was at Pirlo's own suggestion that coach Carlo Ancelotti found him a regular place in the starting line-up as a deep-lying midfielder and by the end of that season he had established himself in the team and made his international debut against Azerbaijan.

Nicknamed 'the metronome' for the way he sets the rhythm of Milan's play, he won the Serie A title in 2004 with the club. He was also a member of the Champions League winning teams of 2003 and 2007, and he picked up a runners-up medal after failing to convert his penalty in the shoot-out that concluded the 2005 final. Injury ruled him out of all but a fleeting appearance at the 2010 World Cup, when he came on as a second-half substitute in Italy's final game of the tournament.

LUKAS PODOLSKI

Country: Germany
Born: June 4, 1985
Position: Striker/Winger
Clubs: Köln, Bayern Munich

Lukas Podolski's outstanding performances at the 2006 World Cup saw him voted FIFA Young Player Of The Tournament. The Polish-born son of a former professional footballer, he moved to Germany at the age of two and it was his adopted country that first called on him for international duty. He made his debut for Germany in the final friendly before Euro 2004 and played once in the tournament itself, but it was at the 2005 Confederations Cup that he really demonstrated his potential, scoring three times. By the time of the 2006 World Cup he was a regular in the national team, having begun to forge a strong attacking partnership with fellow Polish-born striker Miroslav Klose.

A powerful forward, he came to prominence with Köln. He scored ten goals in 19 games in his first full Bundesliga season as the club were relegated in 2004 and then netted 24 goals in 30 games as they made an immediate return to the top division. Much in demand after the 2006 World Cup, he had already agreed a deal with Bayern Munich and he went on to win the German league and cup 'double' with the club in 2008. He also finished the European Championship that summer as the competition's joint second highest scorer, picking up a runners-up medal after defeat in the final to Spain.

After the signing of Luca Toni, Podolski dropped down the pecking order at Bayern and he opted to return to Köln in 2009. By then Podolski was being reinvented as a left winger by national team coach Joachim Löw and although he struggled with the role initially, by the 2010 World Cup he looked assured in the position and contributed a great deal to Germany's third place finish at the tournament.

CARLES PUYOL

Country: Spain
Born: April 13, 1978
Position: Defender
Club: Barcelona

Recognised throughout world football for his distinctive shaggy hairstyle, Carles Puyol is the type of player the fans of Barcelona adore. A local boy, and a Catalan to boot, he has stayed at the club throughout his career. The big money imports may grab the headlines but it is club captain Puyol who helps the team bond and who has driven the side to glory. He made his first-team debut under Louis Van Gaal in 1999 against Real Madrid and he soon built a reputation as a superb fullback, gaining his international debut against Holland in November the following year.

Eventually developing into a strong and commanding centre-back, his never-say-die attitude has made him popular with fans and admired by other clubs, yet no offer has been able to tempt him away from the Nou Camp. He has won the Spanish league four times with the club and he has twice captained the team to the Champions League trophy and once to victory in the FIFA Club World Cup. He does not often score for Barcelona but one of his most important goals came in the 6-2 away defeat of Real Madrid that helped Barça to the 2009 league championship.

For all his achievements in club football, the greatest moments of his career have undoubtedly been with the Spanish national side. He was the cornerstone of the team that won the European Championship in 2008, and at the World Cup two years later he scored the only goal of the semi-final against Germany, putting Spain into the final with a powerful header. He went on to marshal the defence in the final and picked up a winners' medal after a 1-0 victory over Holland.

Above: Germany's Lukas Podolski after scoring against Australia at the 2010 World Cup.

Left: Andrea Pirlo in action for Milan in October 2009.

SERGIO RAMOS

Country: Spain
Born: March 30, 1986
Position: Defender
Clubs: Sevilla, Real Madrid

Sergio Ramos came through the youth ranks at Sevilla and made his league debut at 17 but after just two years Real Madrid paid handsomely for his services early in the 2005-6 season. A versatile and speedy defender, Ramos has impressed at the Bernabéu Stadium since switching from central defence to his now more favoured right-back position. He won the Spanish league title twice in his first three seasons at Real Madrid and after making his international debut against China at just 18 in March 2005, he was his country's first choice right-back at the World Cup the following year. It was from this position that he helped Spain win the European Championship in 2008 and the World Cup in 2010, when he was also voted into the All-Star Team Of The Tournament.

RAÚL

Country: Spain
Born: June 27, 1977
Position: Forward
Club: Real Madrid, Schalke 04

Raúl was a legend at Real Madrid from the day in 1994 that he became the youngest player to debut for the club, aged just 17 years and four months old. For 16 seasons he was the most influential player at the Bernabéu, both on the pitch and off it. It was rumoured that he was able to call the shots on his strike partners and he was always the dominant voice in Real's dressing room before a move to Schalke 04 in 2010 finally ended what was expected to be a life-long association with the club.

His career at Real certainly brought him rewards. He won the Champions league on three occasions, scoring in the defeat of Valencia in 2001 and in the 2002 final against Bayer Leverkusen. Not only has been the top scorer in the Champions League on two occasions, he has also scored more goals than any other player in the history of the competition, breaking the 41-year-old European Cup record held by Alfredo Di Stéfano in 2005. As the touchstone of the Real Madrid side he also played his part in winning six Spanish league titles and he twice finished the season as the top scorer in La Liga. The only trophy that eluded him during his years at the club was the Copa Del Rey.

He made his debut for Spain in October 1996 at the age of 19 and was a permanent fixture in the national team until being controversially dropped by Luis Aragonés ten years later. The debate over the decision was not fully silenced until Spain won the 2008 European Championship without him but he remains the nation's leading goalscorer and most-capped outfield player.

Raúl represented his country at three World Cups and two European Championships and he had the distinction of scoring both Spain's 800th and 900th international goals against Austria in 1999 and Greece in 2002. He was also ranked third in the FIFA World Player Of The Year Award in 2001.

FRANCK RIBÉRY

Country: France
Born: April 7, 1983
Position: Winger
Clubs: Boulogne, Alés, Stade Brestois, Metz, Galatasaray, Marseille, Bayern Munich

After a much travelled and troubled early career, the highlight of which was scoring in Galatasaray's 5-1 victory over rivals Fenerbahçe in the 2005 Turkish Cup Final, it was after his acrimonious departure to France to sign for Marseille that Franck Ribéry's career really started to take flight. His unmatchable speed and dribbling made him a hit and before the end of his first season at the club there was a growing clamour for him to be included in the French team for the 2006 World Cup.

Earning his first cap as a substitute against Mexico in the days before the tournament, he was in the starting line-up by the time France kicked off their campaign. He played in every game and picked up a runners-up medal after France lost the penalty shoot-out to Italy, by which time he had been substituted.

After being linked with many of the top clubs of Europe, Ribéry signed for Bayern Munich in 2007 and won the German league and cup 'double' in his first season, repeating the feat in 2010 when he scored in the 4-0 cup final defeat of Werder Bremen. Never far from controversy both on and off the pitch, he missed out on the 2010 Champions League Final through suspension, despite attempting to overturn his severe three-match ban at the Court Of Arbitration For Sport.

Ribéry was voted French Player Of The Year in both 2007 and 2008, and also won the German Player of the Year Award in 2008.

ARJEN ROBBEN

Country: Holland
Born: January 23, 1984
Position: Winger
Clubs: Groningen, PSV Eindhoven, Chelsea, Real Madrid, Bayern Munich

Comfortable on either wing or playing as a withdrawn striker, Arjen Robben started his career with Groningen and was named the club's Player Of The Year in his first season. After another 12 months he had impressed enough to warrant a transfer to PSV, where he helped the club to the league championship after forging a deadly attacking partnership with Mateja Kezman (their prolific form earned the duo the nickname 'Batman and Robben').

After moving to Chelsea in 2004, he initially struggled to recover from injury but won the Premier League title in each of his first two seasons and lifted the FA Cup in his third, coming on as a substitute for Joe Cole in the extra-time defeat of Manchester United.

Below: Arjen Robben after scoring for Holland in the 2010 World Cup semi-final against Uruguay.

The cup win came at the end of a troublesome campaign that had seen the Dutchman dogged by niggling injuries and relegated to the bench, but his lack of form did not deter Real Madrid signing him in August 2007 after a £24 million deal was agreed. Despite winning the league in his first campaign at the Bernabéu, Robben never really made the shirt his own and after two seasons he was offloaded to Bayern Munich.

Proving a revelation in his first season in Germany, Robben scored a career-best 23 goals in all competitions as he helped the club to a league and cup 'double' and second place in the 2010 Champions League. He capped a fine season with a World Cup runners-up medal and was considered one of the best players at the tournament after being short-listed for the Golden Ball award.

ROBINHO

Country: Brazil
Born: January 25, 1984
Position: Centre-forward
Clubs: Santos, Real Madrid, Manchester City, AC Milan

Robson de Souza, nicknamed Robinho (meaning Little Robson), first caught the eye with Santos in 2002 when he helped the club to the first of two Brazilian league titles. Comparisons were quickly drawn with the legendary Garrincha and it was not long before a host of European clubs were alerted to his talents. Having seen his mother kidnapped for six weeks in 2004, Robinho decided to quit Brazil and he eventually moved to Real Madrid in July 2005 for a fee of £17 million. Although his three seasons were not always free from strife, he won the Spanish league title in 2007 and 2008.

His time at the Bernabéu ended after he threatened to go on strike to earn himself a move to Chelsea. However, the London club failed to match Real's valuation and Robinho surprised world football when he signed for Manchester City in September 2008 for a British record fee of £32.5 million. After an impressive first season, injuries and a lack of form saw the unsettled player lose his position in the starting line-up. After failing to establish a working relationship with successive managers, he spent the second half of the 2009-10 season on loan to Santos, having scored just once in the season for Manchester City against lowly cup opposition. His suspect temperament and City's desire to recoup their millions hindered the further development of his career until he joined Milan at a discounted price in the summer of 2010.

Robinho made his international debut during the 2003 CONCACAF Gold Cup and while his appearances at the 2006 World Cup were made largely from the bench, it was as a member of Brazil's Copa América winning team in 2007 that he really caught the attention, finishing the competition with both the Golden Ball and the

Golden Boot. He arrived at the 2010 World Cup with the weight of expectation on his shoulders but he scored only once in the second round game against Chile.

RONALDINHO

Country: Brazil
Born: March 21, 1980
Position: Forward
Clubs: Grêmio, Paris Saint-Germain, Barcelona, AC Milan

A sublimely gifted player, Ronaldinho first came to prominence with his substitute appearances at the Copa América in 1999 and although he did not play in Brazil's defeat of Uruguay in the final, shortly afterwards he starred at the 1999 Confederations Cup, scoring in every match except the final and winning both the Golden Ball and the Golden Boot.

One of the best players at the 2002 World Cup, he made headlines in the quarter-final with a free-kick that beat England keeper David Seaman from 42 yards and he helped Brazil to victory in the final, forming a spectacular attacking trio with Ronaldo and Rivaldo.

After leaving Brazil in 1998 he took time to settle in France following a protracted transfer to Paris Saint-Germain but it was when he moved to Barcelona in 2003 that he really established his credentials as one of the world's most exciting players. He was named FIFA World Player Of The Year in both 2004 and 2005, and he was also selected as European Player Of The Year after winning his first Spanish league title in 2005. Further glory came the following year with another Spanish league title, plus victory over Arsenal in the Champions League final in Paris, but he failed to impress at the World Cup that summer where he played largely in a supporting role to Adriano and Ronaldo.

In July 2008 Ronaldinho signed for AC Milan but wavering form in his two seasons at the club led to him being controversially overlooked for Brazil's 2010 World Cup squad.

RONALDO

Country: Brazil
Born: September 22, 1976
Position: Forward
Clubs: Cruzeiro, PSV Eindhoven, Barcelona, Inter Milan, Real Madrid, AC Milan, Corinthians

Once dubbed 'The Phenomenon', at the peak of his football powers Ronaldo was the closest thing to a modern day Pelé that Brazil has managed to produce. Blessed with searing pace, unbelievable skill and a razor sharp finishing ability, he could find the net from any area of the pitch, whether breaking from his own half to score alone or tapping in from close range.

Ronaldo Luiz Nazario de Lima was born in Bento Ribeiro, in the suburbs of Rio De Janeiro. On the recommendation of Brazil legend Jairzinho he was signed by Cruzeiro and he made his debut for the club in 1993, aged just 16. He was soon scoring a goal a game for the club and the following year he earned a place in Brazil's squad for the 1994 World Cup, having already made his debut against Argentina. He collected a winners' medal as a non-playing squad member and the same year he left Brazil to join Bobby Robson's PSV Eindhoven.

In two years in Holland he scored 42 goals, despite playing only 13 matches in the 1995-6 season. When Robson took over at Barcelona in 1996 he promptly spent £12 million on Ronaldo, who scored 47 goals in all competitions in his one season with the Catalan club, notching the winning goal from the spot in the final of the European Cup Winners' Cup.

He joined Inter Milan for a world record transfer fee of £19 million in 1997 and scored 25 goals in his first season. However, his world began to unravel at the 1998 World Cup in France, where the Brazil team were relying heavily on his skills. He scored four goals in the competition but on the morning of the final Ronaldo suffered a fit, which led to his name being struck from the teamsheet in the hour leading up to the kick-off. However, when the

Left: Brazil's Robinho lets fly against North Korea at the 2010 World Cup.

Below: Ronaldinho strikes the ball for AC Milan against Parma in March 2010.

Brazilians took to the pitch Ronaldo had been reinstated. Patently unfit and fresh from the hospital, he played in the final but Brazil lost the game and his pallid performance gave rise to numerous conspiracy theories.

Wear and tear after years of playing top-level football from a young age resulted in a serious knee injury in November 1999. Five months later he made his return in the final of the Italian Cup but he collapsed in agony without being touched after just seven minutes. Critics wrote off his chances of returning to football but he fought back after extensive rehabilitation and proved his fitness in time for the 2002 World Cup. The tournament proved his redemption and he scored eight goals, including two in the

final against Germany, as Brazil lifted the trophy. Ronaldo won the Golden Boot and he was also named FIFA World Player Of The Year for the third time. However, his subsequent transfer to Real Madrid for £23 million in September 2002 caused bitterness at Inter Milan, who had stood by him while he was injured for long periods of his contract.

Carrying extra weight he struggled to convince Real Madrid fans that he merited a place above favourite Morientes but he eventually proved his worth, twice winning the Spanish league with the club and scoring in the 2002 World Club Cup Final victory over Olimpia. At the 2006 World Cup his performances were criticised but he nevertheless netted three goals to become the

competition's all-time top scorer with 15 goals. He spent two seasons with AC Milan dogged by a recurring knee injury and after his contract was not renewed in 2008 he began to wind down his career back in Brazil with Corinthians.

CRISTIANO RONALDO

Country: Portugal
Born: February 5, 1985
Position: Winger/Forward
Clubs: Sporting Lisbon, Manchester United, Real Madrid

Whether playing on the wing or in a more central attacking role, Cristiano Ronaldo is a sublimely gifted footballer admired throughout the world game for his unmatchable dribbling skills and his accuracy with the ball. His artistry has helped him to a host of honours. In 2008 he was voted European and World Player Of The Year after a season when he had finished as the Premier League's top scorer with 31 goals in 34 games, a tally that also earned him the European Golden Boot, an amazing feat achieved while playing primarily on the wing for Manchester United.

Having been developed through the youth ranks at Sporting Lisbon, Ronaldo made his debut at 17 but spent just one season in the first-team before a transfer to Old Trafford. He won the FA Cup in his debut season with United, scoring the first goal of a 3-0 defeat of Millwall in the final, and he went on to win three consecutive league titles. In 2008 he also scored United's only goal of the Champions League final against Chelsea and although he missed from the spot in the deciding penalty shoot-out, he still collected a winners' medal.

Linked with a move to Real Madrid for the best part of two seasons, Ronaldo finally defied the wishes of coach Alex Ferguson and transferred for a world record £80 million fee in July 2009, with Real Madrid fans packing the Bernabéu Stadium just to welcome him.

For all his talents, the criticism that has been levelled at Ronaldo is that he has failed to shine on the biggest stage when it really counts. He had an anonymous Champions League final for Manchester United in 2008 when leading the line against Barcelona and he scored just one goal in each of the 2006 and 2010 World Cups and the 2008 European Championship.

WAYNE ROONEY

Country: England
Born: October 24, 1985
Position: Forward
Club: Everton, Manchester United

Wayne Rooney became England's youngest international when he debuted as a substitute against Australia in 2003, aged just 17 years and 111 days. He has since become one of the biggest stars in English football, although he has yet to

Below: Cristiano Ronaldo on the ball for Real Madrid against Mallorca in August 2010.

show the full range of his talents on the world stage. He signalled his arrival in the Premier League with a fabulous late goal for Everton that ended Arsenal's 30-match unbeaten run and made Rooney the youngest goalscorer since the beginning of the Premier League era.

He impressed at the European Championship in 2004, netting four goals. However, a serious foot injury in the quarter-final clash with hosts Portugal ended Rooney's tournament and without him England were knocked out on penalties. A lucrative £27 million move to Manchester United followed and he began his career at Old Trafford with a stunning hat-trick in the Champions League against Fenerbahçe. He has since won three Premier League titles with the club and he partnered Carlos Tevez in attack as United beat Chelsea on penalties in the 2008 Champions League Final. He also scored a late winner in the FIFA Club World Cup the same year and was voted the Man Of The Match.

Towards the end of the 2005-6 season a broken metatarsal in his foot seriously affected his plans to take part in the World Cup. In the run up to the tournament his medical reports fascinated the nation and although not fully fit he was included in the England squad. His impressive powers of recovery saw him defy the odds to return for the second group game but although England reached the last eight, Rooney did not perform at his best. He was sent-off against Portugal for violent conduct and had to look on as England went out on penalties again.

In the build up to the 2010 World Cup Rooney enjoyed his most prolific season. Having scored 26 league goals by the end of March, he was the leading scorer in the Premier League when an ankle injury unsettled his season. Making a premature return, he failed to regain his form and he did not score again that season. As a consequence he was pipped to the Golden Boot by Didier Drogba and without him United slipped up in the title race. He was also a shadow of his best at the World Cup.

TOMAS ROSICKY

Country: Czech Republic
Born: October 4, 1980
Position: Midfielder
Clubs: Sparta Prague, Borussia Dortmund, Arsenal

In 2001 Borussia Dortmund paid a Bundesliga record of £18 million to Sparta Prague for Czech Republic international Tomas Rosicky. A lively midfielder with an impressive range of passing and a tendency to get forward, Roskicky had been given the nickname 'the Little Mozart' for his abilities to orchestrate the Sparta midfield and he had won three successive league titles with his hometown club.

Dortmund had been impressed with the player's performances in the Champions League and were looking to replace the recently

Above: England's Wayne Rooney weaves through Switzerland's defence in September 2010.

transferred Andreas Möller. Rosicky helped Dortmund to the league title and the UEFA Cup final in his first season but he would win no more honours during his five years at the Westfalen Stadium as Dortmund were beset by financial problems. With Rosicky's own loss of form and injury problems, a sale was inevitable.

Arsenal paid £6.8 million for the Czech midfielder just prior to the 2006 World Cup. He had scored seven goals while helping propel the Czech Republic to the tournament, including the winning goal in the deciding play-off, and he scored twice more in three games at the finals but his team were eliminated in the group stage.

After an injury midway through his second season at Arsenal, Rosicky was left on the sidelines for 18 months. The injury caused him to miss Euro 2008 and he did not return to the game until September the following year, scoring on his Arsenal comeback as a substitute against Manchester City.

JAVIER SAVIOLA

Country: Argentina
Born: December 11, 1981
Position: Forward
Clubs: River Plate, Barcelona, Monaco, Sevilla, Real Madrid, Benfica

Javier Saviola was just 19 when Barcelona paid £18 million for him in 2001 but by then he had already cemented his reputation as a gifted footballer and prolific goalscorer. He was only 16 when he made his debut with River Plate and just 18 when he was voted South America's Footballer Of The Year in 1999. In 2001 he was Player Of The Tournament at the World Youth Championships and he finished as top scorer in

the competition as his 11 goals in seven games helped Argentina to the trophy.

Under coach Louis Van Gaal he scored 17 goals for Barcelona in his first season, finishing fourth highest in the league. However, he fell out of favour with successive bosses and was loaned out to Monaco and Sevilla by coach Frank Rijkaard. The season with Sevilla rehabilitated his reputation as he won the UEFA Cup with the club in 2006 and secured his place in Argentina's World Cup squad, making three appearances at the finals.

The following year Saviola signed for Real Madrid and spent two frustrating seasons at the Bernabéu before moving to Benfica in the summer of 2009. He started to enjoy regular first-team football again and in his first season in Portugal he helped the club to the league title.

PAUL SCHOLES

Country: England
Born: November 16, 1974
Position: Midfielder
Club: Manchester United

Paul Scholes may not get the same attention as some of his Old Trafford team-mates but there are few players who are as effective on the pitch. His fantastic runs into the box, and his incisive shooting and heading abilities, have resulted in an impressive goalscoring record for both club and country, yet there is a discipline to his game that is rarely found in attacking midfielders. Never one to neglect his defensive duties, Scholes is a terrifically hardworking and tough-tackling player.

Coming through the Manchester United youth ranks with a generation of players that

Above: One of the world's best players, Andriy Shevchenko (right) chases the ball for Ukraine against Greece in 2009.

included Ryan Giggs, David Beckham and Gary Neville, Scholes made his first team debut in September 1994 against Port Vale. The following year he collected his first major honour, coming on as a substitute in the FA Cup final as United beat Everton.

Honours have been plentiful during his career at Manchester United and Scholes has collected nine Premier League titles, three FA Cups and a world club title. He was an important part of United's 1998-9 'treble' winning squad, scoring in the FA Cup final against Newcastle. However, he missed that season's Champions League final through suspension, finally picking up a winners' medal in the competition in 2008 after United beat Chelsea in Moscow.

His international career began in 1997 against South Africa at Old Trafford and he went on to play at two World Cups, in 1998 and 2002, and the European Championships of 2000 and 2004. However, to accommodate Steven Gerrard and Frank Lampard he was often selected out of his usual position by coach Sven-Göran Eriksson. After 65 appearances and 14 goals, Scholes announced his international retirement following Euro 2004, aged just 29. Successive England managers have tried to entice him back to no success, although the player did later admit to a sense of regret at not accepting Fabio Capello's invitation to join the 2010 World Cup squad.

BASTIAN SCHWEINSTEIGER

Country: Germany
Born: August 1, 1984
Position: Midfielder
Club: Bayern Munich

Since he first caught the eye at the Confederations Cup in 2005, midfielder Bastian Schweinsteiger has enjoyed a rollercoaster career in German football. Joining Bayern Munich as a teenager, he made his debut in November 2002 and celebrated the German league title in his first season. He went on to win it a further four times in the next seven seasons, along with three German Cups. He scored in the final of the

2010 German Cup and picked up a runners-up medal in the Champions League final later the same month.

His international debut came in June 2004 and two years later he was one of the stars of Germany's World Cup, proving most influential in the third place play-off game when he scored twice and provided the cross for the third goal in the 3-1 victory over Portugal. Comfortable on either flank, he is at his best on the left but after initially losing his place in the starting line-up at Euro 2008 he was back for the knockout stages, operating on the opposite flank as the Germans finished as runners-up. He was utilised in the centre of the midfield at the 2010 World Cup in place of the injured Michael Ballack.

ANDRIY SHEVCHENKO

Country: Ukraine
Born: August 29, 1976
Position: Forward
Clubs: Dynamo Kiev, AC Milan, Chelsea

Andriy Shevchenko is one of the biggest stars in the history of Ukrainian football. In 2004 he was given the Hero Of Ukraine award by the country's president and he has been voted Ukrainian Footballer Of The Year on six occasions. Brought through the youth ranks at Dynamo Kiev, his first trophy was presented to him by Ian Rush at an Under-14 tournament in Wales. He went on to win five Ukrainian league titles in his five seasons in the first-team. He also formed a lethal partnership with Sergei Rebrov in Dynamo Kiev's spirited Champions League campaigns of the late Nineties, scoring a first-half hat-trick away to Barcelona in 1997-8 and reaching the semi-finals the following season.

Shevchenko was signed by AC Milan in 1999 for £16 million. During his seven years at the San Siro he was a prolific marksman, finishing his first season as the league highest scorer with 24 goals in 32 games. By December 2003 he had scored his 100th Serie A goal, going on to finish the season as the league's top scorer as Milan won the league title. For his efforts he was rewarded with the 2004 European Footballer Of The Year Award.

Much of Shevchenko's career has been defined by his performances in the Champions League. Three times the top scorer in the competition, he scored the decisive spot-kick in the penalty shoot-out victory over Juventus in the 2003 final. However, two years later he was a part of the team that surrendered a 3-0 lead to Liverpool in the final and his failure to convert his penalty in the shoot-out handed the cup to 'The Reds'. He remains one of the leading scorers in the history of the competition.

Just before the 2006 World Cup he signed for English Premier League champions Chelsea for a British record fee of £30 million. He had long been a target of the club's Russian owner Roman Abramovich but the transfer caused

a dispute with manager José Mourinho, who had not been consulted. Even after Mourinho's departure, Shevchenko only made the starting line-up infrequently and a frustrating two seasons at Stamford Bridge were rewarded with just a League Cup winners' medal in 2007. Although Luiz Felipe Scolari loaned him back to Milan for the 2008-9 season, this second spell was less than successful and in August 2009 Shevchenko returned to Dynamo Kiev.

Since making his debut for the national side against Croatia in April 1995, he has been the team's driving force and has become the nation's all-time leading goalscorer. He also captained the side and helped guide them the 2006 World Cup for their first major tournament.

WESLEY SNEIJDER

Country: Holland
Born: June 9, 1984
Position: Attacking midfielder
Clubs: Ajax, Real Madrid, Inter Milan

Comfortably two-footed, Wesley Sneijder made his debut for Ajax at just 18 in February 2003 and he soon impressed with his playmaking abilities and his accuracy with free-kicks. His nine goals from midfield helped the club to the league championship in 2004, while his most prolific season came in 2006-7 when he scored 18 goals as Ajax lost the title on goal difference. Shortly afterwards he left for Real Madrid and despite picking up a league winners' medal in his first campaign at the Bernabéu, injury unsettled him the following season and he found it hard to regain his place in the team.

A surprise move to Inter Milan in August 2009 saw him return to form and by the end of the year he had won the league, cup and Champions League 'treble'. He carried this form into the World Cup in South Africa and ended the tournament as joint highest scorer, awarded the Bronze Boot after 'assists' were taken into account. He also picked up a runners-up medal after Holland's defeat in the final and he was voted second best player of the competition.

LUIS SUÁREZ

Country: Uruguay
Born: January 24, 1987
Position: Striker
Clubs: Nacional, Groningen, Ajax

One of the stars of Uruguay's run to the 2010 World Cup semi-finals, Luis Suárez is a prolific goalscorer who came to prominence as a part of the Nacional team that won the Uruguayan championship in 2006. His performances gained him a move to Dutch club Groningen but just one year later he had impressed enough to sign for Ajax. An evermore influential member of the team, his 35 goals in just 33 games saw him finish the 2009-10 season as the league's top scorer and he was rewarded by being crowned Dutch Footballer Of The Year.

At the 2010 World Cup he was the cause of a controversy after his goal-line handball denied Ghana victory in the last seconds of the quarter-final but the resulting red card meant that he was unable to play in the semi-final. He was also sent-off on his international debut in 2007.

JOHN TERRY

Country: England
Born: December 7, 1980
Position: Defender
Clubs: Chelsea, Nottingham Forest

A strong, no nonsense centre-back with inspirational leadership qualities, John Terry has enjoyed a long and successful career with Chelsea, captaining both his club and country. The Barking-born defender was spotted by 'The Blues' playing Sunday League football and he worked his way up through the club's youth and reserve teams before eventually making his senior debut in October 1998. After a spell on loan with Nottingham Forest, Terry became a first-team regular under Chelsea boss Claudio Ranieri and he was quickly installed as club captain when José Mourinho took the reins at Stamford Bridge in the summer of 2004.

The following season saw him named PFA Player Of The Year as he led Chelsea to their first league title in 50 years, conceding only 15 goals as they did so. He has won two further league titles, in 2006 and 2010, and three FA Cups. He also captained the club to the 2008 Champions League Final but in the penalty shoot-out he missed the spot-kick that could have won the trophy for Chelsea and after having to settle for a runners-up medal he was reduced to tears.

He made his England debut against Serbia and Montenegro in 2003 and was an integral part of the side that made it to the quarter-final stages of Euro 2004 and the 2006 World Cup. Succeeding David Beckham as England captain after the 2006 finals, he was the undisputed leader of the side until a tabloid scandal saw him stripped of the responsibility by Fabio Capello in February 2010. His performances at the World Cup that summer were erratic and his stock fell even lower after he gave an interview during the tournament that was judged to have been critical of the England manager.

CARLOS TEVEZ

Country: Argentina
Born: February 5, 1984
Position: Forward/Midfielder
Clubs: Boca Juniors, Corinthians, West Ham United, Manchester United, Manchester City

It is little wonder that Carlos Tevez was dubbed the 'new Maradona' after winning a hat-trick of South American Player Of The Year awards

between 2003 and 2005. An ingenious dribbler of the ball, he boasts a powerful and accurate range of shooting, making him just as deadly inside the box as out of it. Signed by Argentine giants Boca Juniors from youth side All Boys, he was part of Boca's all-conquering team that claimed the national championship, the Copa Libertadores and the World Club Cup in 2003, and the Copa Sudamericana in 2004. However, it was at the 2004 Olympics that he shot to world attention, scoring eight goals and finishing as the tournament's top scorer as Argentina won gold.

After an 18-moth spell with Corinthians of Brazil, Tevez signed for West Ham in August 2006 in a controversial third-party deal that saw his economic rights remain with an independent company. Although he had a significant impact on the pitch and helped the club to avoid relegation in his one season at Upton Park, the legal case concerning his eligibility to play while owned by a third party rumbled on, long after he had been loaned to Manchester United in a similarly complicated move.

He proved an instant favourite at Old Trafford, winning the league title twice and scoring the opening penalty in the shoot-out that helped him to a Champions League winners' medal in 2008. However, a stormy relationship with manager Alex Ferguson after the arrival of Dimitar Berbatov ultimately led Tevez to leave for Manchester City in July 2009 rather than extend his deal with United.

FERNANDO TORRES

Country: Spain
Born: March 20, 1984
Position: Striker
Clubs: Atlético Madrid, Liverpool

With a blistering turn of pace Fernando Torres has the speed and ease on the ball that can leave defenders for dead, qualities that have seen him develop into one of the world's great footballers since coming through the ranks at Atlético Madrid. He made his debut for the club in the second tier of Spanish football at just 17, earning the nickname 'El Niño', or 'The Kid', and he went on to become a prolific goalscorer for the club after promotion back to the top flight in 2002.

A transfer to Liverpool in 2007 proved a success and despite the pressure of inheriting the number 9 shirt from club legend Robbie Fowler, he scored 24 goals in his first season in the Premier League, placing him joint second in the race for the Golden Boot.

After debuting for Spain in September 2003, he hit three goals in four appearances at the 2006 World Cup. While he is still revered for scoring the goal that won Spain the 2008 European Championship, he was deemed a failure at the 2010 World Cup. After a misfiring run he was dropped for the semi-final and only made a fleeting appearance as an extra-time substitute in the final as Spain lifted the trophy.

FRANCESCO TOTTI

Country: Italy
Born: September 27, 1976
Position: Midfielder/Forward
Club: Roma

Francesco Totti made his debut for AS Roma in March 1993, aged just 16, but did not become a first-team regular until two years later. In 2001 he captained Roma to the club's first Italian league title in 18 years, scoring 13 goals in 30 appearances during the campaign.

Preferring to play as an attacking midfielder or deep-lying forward, Totti made his first appearance for the Italian national side against Switzerland in October 1998. He went on to impress at Euro 2000, scoring a superb goal against Romania and converting a crucial penalty in the semi-final shoot-out with Holland. He was Italy's best player in the final defeat to France but his red card against South Korea in Italy's disastrous 2002 World Cup campaign, and the ban he received at Euro 2004 after spitting at Denmark's Christian Poulson, put Totti under the microscope for the wrong reasons.

Although not on top form and playing with metal plates in his leg, he collected a World Cup winners' medal in 2006, starting in the final tucked behind Luca Toni.

His most prolific season came when he scored 26 league goals in 2006-7 as Roma finished runners-up in Serie A, a position he has achieved

Below: John Terry gets stuck in for Chelsea during the 2010 Community Shield match against Manchester United.

with the club on six occasions. In that season he not only finished as the top scorer in Serie A but he was also awarded the European Golden Boot and captained the side to a 7-4 aggregate win over Inter Milan in the final of the Italian Cup, scoring in the first minute of the first leg.

Famed for his goal celebrations, he was voted Serie A Footballer Of The Year in 2000 and shared the award with Pavel Nedved in 2003.

KOLO TOURE

Country: Ivory Coast
Born: March 19, 1981
Position: Central defender
Clubs: ASEC Mimosas, Beveren, Arsenal, Manchester City

A powerful defender with outstanding tackling abilities, Kolo Toure was discovered by Ivory Coast's most successful club ASEC Mimosas and enjoyed a spell in Belgium with KSK Beveren before signing for Arsenal as an attacking midfielder in February 2002. He was an established international at the time, having made his first appearance for the Ivory Coast against Rwanda in 2000 but he did not make his first-team debut for Arsenal until the beginning of the 2002-3 season.

Toure was turned into a world-class central defender by Arsene Wenger and the highpoint of his seven seasons with the club was winning the Premier League title in 2004 as a member of Arsenal's unbeaten 'Invincibles'. He also won the FA Cup in 2005, having earlier sat out the 2003 final on the bench.

Below: Kolo Toure on the ball for Ivory Coast at the 2010 World Cup.

In latter seasons he formed an effective defensive partnership with William Gallas but a bust-up with the Frenchman proved to be the beginning of the end of Toure's career at the Emirates Stadium and he signed for Manchester City in the summer on 2009. He was joined at the club a year later by his brother Yaya Toure.

On the international stage he helped the Ivory Coast to the 2006 African Nations Cup Final, where he scored a penalty in the shoot-out defeat to Egypt, and he played at both the 2006 and 2010 World Cups, captaining the team in the absence of Didier Drogba for their opening game at the 2010 finals.

EDWIN VAN DER SAR

Country: Holland
Born: October 29, 1970
Position: Goalkeeper
Clubs: Ajax, Juventus, Fulham, Manchester United

An incredibly reliable and consistent goalkeeer, Edwin Van Der Sar's biggest asset is his calmness under pressure, which has helped him to win a host of honours since first debuting for Ajax in the 1990-1 season. He won four Dutch league titles and three Dutch Cups, including a league and cup 'double' in 1998 but the highlight was the Champions League triumph of 1995, when he kept a clean sheet against Milan in the final in Vienna. After 226 league appearances with Ajax, and having scored one goal (a penalty in an 8-1 defeat of De Graafschap), he moved to Italy for two seasons to play for Juventus.

It was a shock to many that after his time at the biggest club in Italy, Van Der Sar chose to sign for unfashionable Fulham for the start of their English Premiership adventure in 2001 but it was an excellent acquisition for coach Jean Tigana. The Dutch keeper proved an instant crowd favourite in West London, helping Fulham to an FA Cup semi-final and to top flight survival with some inspirational performances during his four seasons at the club.

He struggled with injuries in 2003 but still remained enough of dominant force between the posts to attract the attention of Manchester United, who were desperate for a reliable and settled keeper. In June 2005 Van Der Sar signed for United for a reported £2 million fee and established himself as first choice goalkeeper, helping the club to win the league title three times. He also earned a second Champions League winners' medal after United beat Chelsea in the 2008 final, making the decisive save from Nicolas Anelka after the penalty shoot-out had entered its sudden death phase.

He has played at six major tournaments with Holland, three times reaching the semi-finals, and on three occasions – the European Championships of 1996 and 2000, and the World Cup in 1998 – has suffered elimination by the lottery of the penalty shoot-out. He captained

the side to the quarter-finals of Euro 2008 before retiring from international football. However, he was talked into making a two-match comeback during the 2010 World Cup qualifiers when the Dutch suffered a goalkeeping injury crisis. His tally of 130 appearances makes him Holland's most capped international player ever.

RUUD VAN NISTELROOY

Country: Holland
Born: July 1, 1976
Position: Forward
Clubs: Den Bosch, Heerenveen, PSV Eindhoven, Manchester United, Real Madrid, Hamburg

Strong, fast and with a killer instinct for goal, Dutch striker Ruud Van Nistelrooy first made his name with PSV Eindhoven and after winning the Dutch league title in 2000, he attracted the attentions of Manchester United. A proposed transfer fell through after a medical revealed a weak right knee. The knee was to rupture two days later but after a lengthy spell on the sidelines, Van Nistelrooy signed for United for £19 million in April 2001.

A prolific striker, he scored 150 goals in all competitions during his five seasons at Old Trafford, winning the Golden Boot and the Premier League title in 2003. He finished as the top goalscorer in the Champions League on three occasions and he hit the net twice in United's defeat of Millwall in the 2004 FA Cup Final. After a training ground altercation with team-mate Cristiano Ronaldo, the Dutchman was overlooked for the 2006 League Cup Final and he remained out of favour with coach Alex Ferguson until he was sold to Real Madrid at the end of the season.

He scored freely during two good years at the Bernabéu, helping the club to the Spanish league title twice, but these were followed by 18 months that saw him dogged by injury and in January 2010 he was transferred to Hamburg.

JUAN SEBASTIÁN VERÓN

Country: Argentina
Born: March 9, 1975
Position: Midfielder
Clubs: Estudiantes de La Plata, Boca Juniors, Sampdoria, Parma, Lazio, Manchester United, Chelsea, Inter Milan

The son of striker Juan Ramon Verón, 'Seba' was born in Buenos Aires and joined his father's team, Estudiantes de La Plata, before moving to Boca Juniors in 1996. He transferred to Sven-Göran Eriksson's Sampdoria the same year and stayed two seasons before a £15 million move to Parma, where he was a member of the team that won both the Italian Cup and the UEFA Cup in 1999. He rejoined Eriksson at Lazio for £18 million and in his first season was at the creative heart of the team's league and cup 'double' of 2000, earning himself a reputation as one of the Lazio's greatest ever stars.

A player in demand, he transferred to Manchester United for £28 million in July 2001 and despite question marks over his impact, in his second season at Old Trafford he became the first Argentinian to win the English league title. A £15 million move to Chelsea in 2004 was not a success as first-team appearances were restricted by a back injury and after the arrival of José Mourinho as coach, Verón was deemed surplus to requirements. He was loaned to Inter Milan, where he inherited a Serie A winners' medal in 2006 after Juventus had their title revoked. He was also a member of the Italian Cup winning team of 2005, although he only made the briefest of appearances as a late substitute in the second leg of the final.

Returning home to Argentina in 2006 to sign for Estudiantes once again, it proved to be the move that revitalised his career. Verón was twice voted South American Footballer Of The Year, in 2008 and 2009, and with the veteran playmaker pulling the creative strings, the club won the 2009 Copa Libertadores. In lifting the trophy as captain 'Seba' was following in the footsteps of his father, who had won the trophy three times with the club.

Famous for his tattoo of Che Guevara, Verón made his debut on the international stage against Poland in 1996 and he was an important member of the team that reached the World Cup quarter-final in 1998. However, four years later he captained the team to a shock first round exit in the competition and it took many years for fans to forgive him for his part in the dismal showing. Overlooked for the 2006 World Cup, he spent a time in the international wilderness but played in the final of the 2007 Copa América when Argentina lost to Brazil and was recalled again by the time of the 2010 World Cup.

PATRICK VIEIRA

Country: France
Born: June 23, 1976
Position: Midfielder
Clubs: Cannes, AC Milan, Arsenal, Juventus, Inter Milan, Manchester City

Born in Senegal, Patrick Vieira's family moved to France when he was a child and he started his career with Cannes. He was impressive enough to earn a transfer to AC Milan but the move was short-lived as he spent much of his time in the reserves until Arsene Wenger enticed him to Arsenal in September 1996.

Vieira's nine years at Arsenal coincided with a period when the club seriously challenged the supremacy of Manchester United, winning the Premier League title on three occasions. The first of these was as part of a league and cup 'double' in 1997-8, with the success largely built on Vieira's midfield partnership with Emmanuel Petit. After three seasons as runners-up, Arsenal repeated the 'double' in 2002 with Vieira as captain. He missed Arsenal's 2003 FA Cup Final victory through injury but by the time he led the team through an unbeaten season to the league title in 2004, the £3.5 million that Arsenal had paid for his services seemed a bargain indeed.

The following season he scored the winning penalty in the shoot-out that decided the 2005 FA Cup but it proved to be his last kick in an Arsenal shirt. Lured to Juventus in a £13.5 million deal, he helped the Turin club to win Serie A in his first season, although the title was later revoked after the club's involvement in a match-fixing scandal. With Juventus punished with relegation to Serie B, Vieira jumped ship and signed for Inter Milan. He won four consecutive Serie A titles with the club, although he had signed for Manchester City midway through the last of these winning campaigns.

Vieira's successes in club football have been mirrored by his achievements on the international stage. He was part of the France team that won the World Cup in 1998, beating Brazil 3-0 in the final. He had started on the substitutes' bench but came on with 15 minutes remaining and was involved in creating the third goal. In 2000 he was on the field from start to finish as France beat Italy 2-1 with an extra-time 'golden goal' to win the European Championship and the following year he was voted French Footballer Of The Year. In the 2006 World Cup he held his place despite suggestions that he should be dropped and he twice scored vital goals that helped France reach the final. Injury forced his substitution in the second-half of the final itself and he was on the bench by the time the cup was lost on penalties to Italy.

DAVID VILLA

Country: Spain
Born: December 3, 1981
Position: Striker
Clubs: Sporting Gijón, Real Zaragoza, Valencia, Barcelona

A natural predator with an eye for goal, David Villa has been Spain's most consistent striker of the modern era. Starting his career with Sporting Gijón, Villa gained his break in the Spanish top flight when he signed for newly promoted Real Zaragoza in the summer of 2003, winning the Spanish Cup in his first season and scoring a penalty in the 3-2 final defeat of Real Madrid. A big money move took him to Valencia in 2005 and he finished as the club's leading goalscorer in each of his five seasons at the Mestalla, winning the Spanish Cup in 2008 before moving to Barcelona for £34 million at the end of the 2009-10 season.

Villa made his international debut against San Marino in February 2005 and he scored twice in Spain's opening game of the World Cup the following year. Although he finished the 2008

Above: Spain's David Villa (right) celebrates with Xavi after scoring against Chile during the 2010 World Cup.

European Championship as the tournament's top scorer, he was ruled out of Spain's victory in the final because of injury. Two years later he finally got his reward when Spain were crowned world champions. Villa did not score in the final itself but his five goals were enough to see him finish as the joint highest scorer, tying with Wes Sneijder, Thomas Müller and Diego Forlán. After 'assists' were taken into account, he was awarded the Silver Boot.

XAVI

Country: Spain
Born: January 25, 1980
Position: Midfielder
Club: Barcelona

After a stint in the lower divisions of Spanish football with Barcelona B, Xavi made the step up to the first-team in October 1998 and finally established himself as the side's key playmaker the following season, a position he dominated at the club for much of the 2000s. For all of his creative skills and pinpoint passing, Xavi is a hard working midfielder who rarely wastes possession and is famed for ability to set the tempo of play from the centre of the pitch.

He has won the Spanish title on five occasions with Barcelona and although injury caused him to miss much of the 2005-6 season, he returned to fitness in time to make the bench for Barcelona's victory in the Champions League final. Although he failed to make it onto the pitch, three years later he was voted Man Of The Match as Barcelona beat Manchester United to lift the trophy again.

A vital part of Spain's Euro 2008 winning side, he not only set-up Fernando Torres for the only goal of the final but he was voted Player Of The Tournament. He scored in Barcelona's victory in the 2009 Spanish Cup Final and was at the heart of Spain's 2010 World Cup win.

S CHAMPIONS

ÉENS

GREAT MANAGERS

Above: Manchester United manager Matt Busby enjoys his team's 1968 European Cup victory.

CARLO ANCELOTTI

Born: June 10, 1959
Management: Reggiana, Parma, Juventus, AC Milan, Chelsea
Major honours: Club World Cup 2007; Champions League 2003, 2007; European Super Cup 2003, 2007

An experienced midfielder with Roma and Milan, Carlo Ancelotti is one of only six managers to win the Champions League as both a player and a coach, having twice lifted the European Cup as a player with Milan. He began his coaching career with Reggiana, inspiring the team to promotion to the top flight but the following season he took over at Parma, helping the club to the runners-up spot in the league in 1997.

He earned himself a high profile move to Juventus in 1999, winning the Intertoto Cup almost immediately. However, it was only after returning to Milan in 2001 that he really built his reputation. Inheriting a team struggling to fulfil its potential, he tinkered with the side and inspired players such as Paolo Maldini, Dida, Gennaro Gattuso, Filippo Inzaghi and Andriy Shevchenko to beat his former club Juventus on penalties in the 2003 Champions League Final.

Milan won the Italian Cup the same year and he took them to the league title the following season. Despite leading Liverpool 3-0 in the 2005 Champions League Final, his Milan team crumbled and lost the game on penalties but they gained a degree of revenge two years later when they beat 'The Reds' to lift the trophy once again. The 2007 FIFA Club World Cup proved

to be his last trophy with the team and after his contract was terminated in 2009, he moved to Chelsea, winning the club's first ever league and cup 'double' in his debut season.

LUIS ARAGONÉS

Born: July 28, 1938
Management: Atlético Madrid, Real Betis, Barcelona, Espanyol, Sevilla, Valencia, Real Betis, Real Oviedo, Mallorca, Spain, Fenerbahçe
Major honours: European Championship 2008; World Club Cup 1974

A striker who failed to make the grade at Real Madrid, it was at city rivals Atlético Madrid that he scored the majority of his goals, finishing the 1969-70 season as the Spanish league's joint highest goalscorer. He became the club's coach after hanging up his boots in 1974 and would enjoy four separate stints in charge at the Vicente Calderón Stadium in the next 30 years, earning the nickname 'the wise man'. He won the World Club Cup soon after taking charge and the league title in 1977, while he lifted the Spanish Cup on three occasions with Atlético and once more with Barcelona in 1988.

It was as coach of Spain's national team that he enjoyed his greatest moment, introducing the beautiful, short-passing 'tiki-taka' style of play to the team and winning the European Championship in 2008. The final was his last game at the helm of the national team and after the tournament he spent the following season in Turkey, coaching Fenerbahçe.

ENZO BEARZOT

Born: September 26, 1927
Management: Prato, Italy
Major honours: World Cup 1982

Enzo Bearzot was the mastermind behind Italy's first World Cup triumph since 1938. As a player he gained just one cap in 1955 but after hanging up his boots he joined the coaching staff of the Italian football federation in 1969, initially with responsibilities for the Under-23 team. After a spell working alongside technical director Fulvio Bernardini, he eventually became sole manager of the senior team in 1977, taking them to his first World Cup the following year.

Little was expected of his team at the 1978 tournament but Bearzot's commitment to teamwork and a more adventurous approach meant they finished fourth. However, the 1982 World Cup campaign began badly and he stood by his players in the face of media animosity, which resulted in a squad boycott of the press. His loyalty was rewarded when he stuck by out-of-form striker Paolo Rossi, who went on to bag the goals that won the trophy.

His ageing side failed at the World Cup in 1986 but that should not devalue his reputation as a shrewd tactician and superb man-manager.

RAFAEL BENÍTEZ

Born: April 16, 1960
Management: Real Madrid B, Real Valladolid, Osasuna, Extremadura, Tenerife, Valencia, Liverpool, Inter Milan
Major honours: Champions League 2005; UEFA Cup 2004

Despite starting as a player at Real Madrid, Benítez never made the first-team and a knee injury cut short his career in the lower leagues at 25. His early coaching days were far from distinguished, as he was sacked by Valladolid with just two wins from 23 games in 1995-6 and was shown the door the following season at Osasuna. However, he led Extremadura to promotion, and he achieved the same feat for Tenerife in 2000 before guiding them to a third-placed finish in the top-flight. Courted by Valencia in 2001, he led the club to two league titles and UEFA Cup success against Marseille in 2004, before joining Liverpool.

At the end of a mediocre first season in the Premier League he led the club to Champions League glory with an epic final victory over Milan in Istanbul, with his team coming back from 3-0 down to win on penalties. He took 'The Reds' to another Champions League showdown with Milan two years later but this time lost out. Although he won the 2006 FA Cup, his achievements in domestic football with Liverpool were limited and he left the club in June 2010. He moved to Inter Milan shortly afterwards.

FULVIO BERNARDINI

Born: December 28, 1905
Management: Lazio, Vicenza, Fiorentina, Lazio, Bologna, Sampdoria, Brescia, Italy

Fulvio Bernardini was an educated and elegant centre-half who earned the nickname 'Il Dottore' (the Doctor). However, he built a reputation as one of the best coaches in the Italian game after taking a series of modest clubs to success. In 1956 he guided Fiorentina to their first Italian championship and followed it by taking them to the 1957 European Cup Final. In 1964 he took Bologna to a first title in 23 years. In the mid-Seventies he took charge of the national team, helping Italy through the World Cup qualifiers before handing the reins to Enzo Bearzot.

MATT BUSBY

Born: May 26, 1909
Management: Manchester United
Major honours: European Cup 1968

Revered at Manchester United, Sir Matt Busby remains one of the greatest post-war British managers, a man who built a succession of great teams and forged a dynasty. Like Jock Stein and Bill Shankly, Busby hailed from Scottish mining stock. Born in Orbiston, Lanarkshire, he escaped a life at the coalface through football. He played at half-back, winning one international cap for Scotland in 1933 and an FA Cup winners' medal for Manchester City the following year before finishing his career with Liverpool.

His first managerial appointment was at United, and although just 36 years old, he quickly asserted his authority, demonstrating a tough disciplinary approach and a ruthless streak belied by his amiable exterior. When he took over in 1945 the club was in disarray. Old Trafford was being rebuilt following severe bomb damage, money was short and the team was struggling in the league.

Busby began his own rebuilding process, setting up a coherent youth policy at the club and reorganising the scouting system. The first sign of progress was the 1948 FA Cup win, which was followed, after a couple of close calls, by the 1952 league title, United's first since 1911. His team scored prolifically that season but Busby was not content and began rebuilding immediately, bringing in talented youth squad players. The era of the 'Busby Babes' was born, with Bobby Charlton, Duncan Edwards, Dennis Viollet, Tommy Taylor and Jackie Blanchflower.

Two successive championships followed in 1956 and 1957 before Busby defied the Football League to enter Manchester United into the European Cup, making them the first English club to take part in the competition. The decision rebounded with tragic consequences when the team plane crashed on a Munich airfield in 1958 en route home from an encounter with Red Star Belgrade. Eight players were killed and Busby himself was severely injured.

He recovered and began rebuilding the team with an iron determination, unearthing major international talents like Denis Law and George Best. Two more league championships followed before Manchester United finally triumphed in Europe, beating Benfica 4-1 in 1968 to become the first English team to win the coveted trophy.

Busby's retirement in 1969 did not sever his influence on the team and a succession of managers, including Wilf McGuinness, Frank O'Farrell and Tommy Docherty, struggled to fill the vacuum he left and deal with the influence he continued to wield in the boardroom. It took another Scotsman, Alex Ferguson, to restore the club to its former glory. Busby lived long enough to see the club win the league again before dying, aged 84, on January 20, 1994.

FABIO CAPELLO

Born: June 18, 1946

Management: AC Milan, Real Madrid, Roma, Juventus, England

Major honours: Champions League 1994; European Super Cup 1994

Before moving into international football with England, Fabio Capello was one of the most decorated coaches in club football, winning league titles with Milan, Roma, Real Madrid and Juventus. A no-nonsense and fiery character who rarely hides his emotions, he has often had disputes with opposition players and coaches, as well as top officials at his own clubs. He controversially quit Milan in 1996 after winning the Serie A title four times in five seasons, plus the 1994 Champions League, but his record speaks for itself and his hard-working teams often play in his own image.

He won the Spanish league in each of his two stints with Real Madrid, with ten years separating the triumphs. Back-to-back titles with Juventus in 2005 and 2006 kept him in Italy until a match-fixing scandal saw the team punished with relegation and stripped of both the titles he had won for them. He became England manager in 2008 and led the side to the 2010 World Cup in South Africa, but despite qualifying impressively the tournament ended disastrously.

An excellent player in his own right, Capello won 32 Italian caps between 1972 and 1976 while playing for Juventus and Milan.

HERBERT CHAPMAN

Born: January 19, 1878

Management: Northampton Town, Leeds City, Huddersfield Town, Arsenal

One of English football's great managers, Herbert Chapman was a visionary who, in his career, advocated numbered shirts, European football, white balls, floodlit matches and attempted to keep pace with the best of foreign tactical developments.

Chapman had an undistinguished playing career, spending time with, among others, Northampton Town and Tottenham Hotspur. Despite planning to go into engineering after hanging up his boots, he returned to Northampton as player-manager in 1907 and soon demonstrated his ability by leading the club to the Southern League title in his second season.

He moved on to Leeds City, finishing fourth in Division Two in 1914. However, he was suspended for life in 1919 over allegations of illegal payments made to guest players and he quit the game, only returning in 1920 when his appeal was upheld. He took over at Huddersfield Town and began a golden era for the club, winning consecutive league titles in 1924 and 1925 with limited resources.

He moved to Arsenal and sparked a revival in the club's fortunes, introducing the much copied WM formation in the wake of changes to the offside rule in 1925. The reversal of north-south power was demonstrated when Arsenal won the 1930 FA Cup, beating Huddersfield 2-0. With some bold transfer coups, including signing Alex James and David Jack, Arsenal embarked on an era of dominance that included five league titles. Sadly Chapman did not live to see them all: he died in January 1934, with the club on the way to another title, after contracting pneumonia while watching his third-team play.

JAVIER CLEMENTE

Born: March 12, 1950

Management: Getxo, Baskonia, Athletic Bilbao, Espanyol, Atlético Madrid, Spain, Real Betis, Real Sociedad, Marseille, Tenerife, Serbia, Real Murcia, Real Valladolid

Injury ended Javier Clemente's playing career at the age of 23 and he went straight to the coaching staff of the club he had played for: Athletic Bilbao. He quickly rose through the ranks, eventually leading them to the Spanish title in 1983 and the league and cup 'double' in 1984. His next job saw him move to Espanyol, and although he failed to win trophies he reached the 1988 UEFA Cup Final before returning to Bilbao for a short but unsuccessful spell in 1991.

Taking charge of the Spanish national team in 1992, he coached the side to three successive tournaments before his sacking in 1998, following an embarrassing defeat to Cyprus. He took on successful relegation battles at Real Betis, Real Sociedad and Marseille, but was unable to do the same for Tenerife in a three-month spell with the club in 2002. He returned for his third stint at Athletic Bilbao in 2005 before re-entering the world of international management with Serbia, who he failed to take to Euro 2008.

BRIAN CLOUGH

Born: March 21, 1935

Management: Hartlepool United, Derby County, Brighton & Hove Albion, Leeds United, Nottingham Forest

Major honours: European Cup 1979, 1980

Brian Clough was a free-scoring centre-forward before injury ended his playing days. Aged 30, he embarked on one of the most interesting managerial careers in history. At Fourth Division Hartlepool he forged an enduring partnership with Peter Taylor. The pair moved to Derby and

Below: Nottingham Forest's Brian Clough poses with the European Cup, a trophy that he won twice.

in five seasons rebuilt the club, taking them from 18th in Division Two to their first league title. The duo left after interference from the board and brief and eccentric sojourns at Brighton and Leeds United followed. Clough lasted only 44 days at Elland Road before player-power had him removed but Nottingham Forest proved to be similar challenge to Derby and offered him the chance to mould a club in his own way.

This time it took four seasons to go from Division Two to the league title. He cemented his reputation as England's foremost club boss by winning the European Cup in consecutive seasons, against Malmö and Hamburg. League Cup victories followed in the Eighties but in 1993 his final season was marred by relegation from the newly-established Premiership. Always outspoken, he knew how to motivate ordinary players, but was not afraid to buy big either, making Trevor Francis the first million-pound player in British football. He believed football was a simple game but his teams always played it skilfully and wholeheartedly.

JOHAN CRUYFF

Born: April 25, 1947
Management: Ajax, Barcelona
Major honours: European Cup 1992; European Cup Winners' Cup 1987, 1989; European Super Cup 1992

One of the game's greatest playing talents, the three-time European Footballer Of The Year proved to be almost as gifted in the manager's office at Ajax and Barcelona, the clubs that had seen his best as a player. Without any coaching qualifications, Cruyff guided Ajax to the title, two Dutch Cups and the 1987 European Cup Winners' Cup before returning to Barcelona.

Two years later Barcelona defeated Sampdoria to lift the Cup Winners' Cup at the start of what was to be a golden era for the Catalan giants.

Below: Spain coach Vicente Del Bosque, on the touchline during the 2010 World Cup semi-final.

Playing sumptuous, attacking football, his team won two Spanish Cups, four consecutive league titles and, in 1992, the European Cup. Again Sampdoria were the victims as Ronald Koeman's stunning extra-time free-kick gave Barça the one trophy they most desired.

Two years later Barcelona again reached the European Cup final, only to find themselves on the receiving end of a 4-0 thumping from Milan. With his side's success waning, Cruyff was forced out in 1996 and serious heart problems make a permanent return to football management unlikely. However, in 2009 he took on the less than onerous responsibilities for the Catalonia national team.

VICENTE DEL BOSQUE

Born: December 23, 1950
Management: Real Madrid, Besiktas, Spain
Major honours: World Cup 2010; Champions League 2000, 2002; World Club Cup 2002; European Super Cup 2002

Opinion is divided on Vicente Del Bosque. Some class him as the luckiest coach ever, a man who has won the biggest trophies in both club and international football with teams that he inherited from others. He took over a young and talented Spanish team immediately after victory in the 2008 European Championship and led them to a World Cup trophy within two years, while at Real Madrid he had players of the calibre of Luis Figo, Zinédine Zidane and Ronaldo bought for him in successive seasons to add to a squad already packed with talent. With such teams how could he fail?

There are others who rate him highly and think that he was terribly unlucky to be sacked by Real Madrid in June 2003 after delivering two Champions League triumphs and two Spanish league titles in four years. When he desperately needed to bolster a failing defence, he was instead given more of the world's finest attacking stars and he did magnificently to smooth over the super-egos of the dressing room and fashion a style of play that fitted his attack-heavy side.

His playing career began with Cordoba and Castellon but it was at the Bernabéu that he enjoyed his greatest successes, collecting five league titles, four Spanish Cups and 18 caps. When his playing days came to an end he stayed with the club and filled a variety of roles, initially as manager of B-team, Castilla. Having stepped in as Real Madrid's first-team boss for an 11-game spell in the 1993-4 season, and for one game during the 1995-6 campaign, he did so for a third time during 1999-2000, a season that culminated in victory over Valencia in the Champions League final.

Asked to stay in the role, he delivered another Champions League victory, two league titles, the European Super Cup and the World Club Cup, but when Madrid lost to Juventus in the Champions League semi-finals in 2003,

the writing was on the wall. Offered a role as technical director, Del Bosque instead decided to finally sever his ties with the club.

After being linked with the Spanish national team after Euro 2004, Del Bosque instead settled for a move to Besiktas in Turkey but lasted just eight months in the job before being sacked after a run of poor results. He turned down the chance to coach Mexico in 2006, finally returning to the game as coach of Spain after Euro 2008. He led a talented Spanish side to glory at the 2010 World Cup, beating Holland in the final.

SVEN-GÖRAN ERIKSSON

Born: February 5, 1948
Management: Degerfors, Gothenburg, Benfica, Roma, Fiorentina, Benfica, Sampdoria, Lazio, England, Manchester City, Mexico, Ivory Coast, Leicester City
Major honours: UEFA Cup 1982; European Cup Winners' Cup 1999; European Super Cup 1999

After an unremarkable playing career, Sven-Göran Eriksson proved himself one of the game's most successful coaches, with his ice cool, intellectual approach rubbing off on his players and his teams often performing with confidence and intelligence. Eriksson made his name in Sweden, winning a league, cup and UEFA Cup 'treble' with Gothenburg in 1982, before taking Benfica to the league title and the UEFA Cup final in his first season in Portugal.

After retaining the title Eriksson quit Benfica for Roma, where he won the Coppa Italia. After a spell with Fiorentina, he returned to Benfica, losing the European Cup final to Milan in 1990 and winning another league title in 1991. After more success in the Italian Cup with Sampdoria in 1994, he won the trophy twice more with Lazio, along with the Cup Winners' Cup in 1999 and the Italian league title in 2000.

Taking charge of England's national team in 2001, Eriksson became the country's first foreign manager and the best paid international coach. With David Beckham as his captain, he led England to three tournaments but despite initially constructing a team capable of winning, he failed to inspire his players at the moments that really counted. His team threw away a 1-0 lead over Brazil in the 2002 World Cup quarter-finals and he oversaw a penalty shoot-out defeat to hosts Portugal at the same stage of Euro 2004.

Eriksson found himself at the centre of a series of tabloid newspaper exposés that proved too much for the Football Association and he led England to the 2006 World Cup knowing that he would leave his post after the tournament. However, England again lost to Portugal on penalties in the quarter-finals and his tactics were even criticised by FIFA president Sepp Blatter. He has since coached Manchester City, Mexico and led the Ivory Coast at the 2010 World Cup Finals in South Africa, but he has yet to rediscover the magic touch.

ALEX FERGUSON

Born: December 31, 1941

Management: East Stirlingshire, St Mirren, Aberdeen, Scotland, Manchester United

Major honours: World Club Cup 1999; Club World Cup 2008; Champions League 1999, 2008; European Cup Winners' Cup 1983, 1991; European Super Cup 1991

A handy but limited player with a string of Scottish clubs, most notably Rangers, Alex Ferguson got his chance in management with Scottish minnows East Stirlingshire. There he began to develop the motivational skills that would make him one of the world's most successful coaches, before moving to St Mirren and winning the First Division title in 1977.

Offered the manager's job at Aberdeen, Ferguson seized his opportunity to shake up Scottish football and break the 'Old Firm' duopoly. At that time Rangers and Celtic had won 14 successive league titles between them but driven on by an extraordinary hunger for success, Ferguson inspired Aberdeen to the 1980 Premier Division title. Two further championships followed, along with four Scottish Cups and victory over Real Madrid in the 1983 European Cup Winners' Cup Final.

In 1986, Ferguson led Scotland at the World Cup finals (and through the qualifying play-off games) after the sudden death of Jock Stein, and three months later Manchester United asked him to become their manager. After decades of underachievement, England's biggest club were desperate for success but for four years Ferguson struggled as he sought to revolutionise United, cutting out the dead wood and shaping the club in his image.

Above left: Ferguson at Aberdeen in 1983. Above: Lifting the 1999 Premier League trophy with Manchester United.

As results dipped the pressure on Ferguson intensified but he finally kickstarted a golden era for United with his first trophy, the 1990 FA Cup. The Cup Winners' Cup and League Cup followed, before the league title finally returned to Old Trafford in 1993 for the first time in 26 years. United went on to add seven more league titles and three FA Cups in the next ten seasons, including their first league and FA Cup 'double' in 1994. However, it was the historic 'treble' of 1999 that really established Ferguson in the pantheon of great managers.

Faced with serious challenges in the league, FA Cup and Champions League, Ferguson brilliantly juggled his resources and exhorted his team to play thrilling, attacking football, none more so than that seen at the conclusion of the Champions League final against Bayern Munich, when two goals late in injury-time saw

United crowned European champions for the first time since 1968.

Knighted for his achievements, Ferguson announced his intention to retire at the end of the 2001-2 season but as United faltered he could not resist another challenge and extended his contract, leading his team to another league title in 2003. Free-spending Chelsea made success harder to achieve in the early years of the new millennium but Ferguson led United to victory in the FA Cup in 2004, rebuilding his team to lift the league title three more times between 2007 and 2009.

A penalty shoot-out victory over Chelsea brought another Champions League triumph in 2008 but defeat to Barcelona in the following year's final proved a disappointment. As of 2010, his haul with United includes 11 league titles, five FA Cups and two European Cups.

1964: Signs on as a professional at Dunfermline.

1967: Signs for his boyhood heroes Rangers for £65,000.

1969: Briefly player-coach at Falkirk.

1975: Appointed manager of St Mirren.

1977: Led St Mirren to promotion as First Division champions.

1978: Joins Aberdeen as manager and breaks up Old Firm dominance.

1983: Wins Cup Winners' Cup, beating Real Madrid.

1984: Completes hat-trick of successive Scottish Cup wins.

1985: Wins Scottish Premier League for third time.

1986: Manages Scotland at World Cup finals.

1986: Joins Manchester United but success is initially elusive.

1990: United win FA Cup – Ferguson's first English trophy.

1991: United win European Cup Winners' Cup, beating Barcelona in Rotterdam.

1993: United win English league for the first time in 26 years.

1999: United win European Champions League, Premier League and FA Cup to complete unique 'treble'.

2006: Wins first of three successive league titles.

2008: Wins Champions League for second time.

Above: Pep Guardiola is thrown into the air by his team after Barcelona win the 2009 Champions League Final.

JOSEP GUARDIOLA

Born: January 18, 1971

Management: Barcelona B, Barcelona

Major honours: Club World Cup 2009; Champions League 2009; European Super Cup 2009

A defensive midfielder with Barcelona's European Cup winning side of 1992, after hanging up his boots, Josep 'Pep' Guardiola returned to the club where he had spent the majority of his career to coach Barcelona B, and after impressing he was promoted to replace Frank Rijkaard as manager of the first team just a year later. He immediately shook up the side he inherited, encouraging the departure of many star players, such as Ronaldinho, Samuel Eto'o, Deco, Gianluca Zambrotta and Edmílson.

In his first season in charge, Barcelona won the Spanish league championship, the Copa del Rey and defeated Manchester United to win the Champions League. However, for fans the most significant match was a 6-2 away defeat of Real Madrid, achieved shortly before wrapping up the title. By the end of the year he had added the European Super Cup and FIFA Club World Cup to his trophy haul, securing the latter after beating Estudiantes in extra-time.

Employing a thrilling brand of 'Total Football', Guadiola's team won the Spanish league again the following year and were everyone's favourites to retain the Champions League, until a shock defeat by José Mourinho's Inter Milan in the semi-finals ended their run in the competition. However, in just his earliest days as a coach Guardiola has shown the ability to have his teams play the most fluid and beautiful football.

BELA GUTTMAN

Born: March 13, 1900

Management: SC Enschede, Újpest, Kispest, AC Milan, Vicenza, Honvéd, São Paulo, Porto, Benfica, Peñarol, Austria, Servette, Panathinaikos, Austria Vienna

Major honours: European Cup 1961, 1962

A hugely respected coach, Hungarian Bela Guttman enjoyed a 40-year management career that began in the early 1930s. He coached several teams in Eastern Europe, took the reins of AC Milan in Italy, and was one of the first coaches from Europe to work in South America, where he led both São Paulo and Peñarol. The main highlights of his career came at Benfica, when he took the Portuguese club to European Cup glory in 1961. He was fêted for taking the trophy away from Real Madrid for the first time after beating Barcelona in the final, and he retained it the following year after a 5-3 defeat of Real. Guttman won numerous national titles during his trek around the globe, including the Mitropa Cup with Újpest in 1939. He died in 1981.

ERNST HAPPEL

Born: June 25, 1929

Management: Den Haag, Feyenoord, Sevilla, Club Brugge, Holland, Harelbeke, Standard Liège, Hamburg, Swarovski, Tirol, Austria

Major honours: European Cup 1970, 1983; World Club Cup 1970

One of the world's most successful and disciplined coaches, Happel won a staggering 17 trophies, including the league titles of Austria, Belgium, Holland and West Germany. He was the first manager to win the European Cup with two different clubs: Feyenoord in 1970 and Hamburg in 1983. He was also in charge of losing finalists Club Brugge at the 1978 final. In that same year he almost won the World Cup with Holland but Rob Rensenbrink's shot late in the game hit the post and the Dutch went on to lose to Argentina in extra-timne. After his death in 1992, the Praterstadion in Vienna was renamed in his honour.

JOSEF 'SEPP' HERBERGER

Born: March 28, 1897

Management: Tennis Borussia Berlin, Germany, West Germany

Major honours: World Cup 1954

Josef 'Sepp' Herberger was coach of Germany from 1938 to 1963 without ever really managing a club side of note, yet he proved tactically shrewd and a great motivator. Pragmatic and adaptable, he built foundations that allowed West Germany to become one of the strongest teams in the world. In 1954 Herberger's strategies earned West Germany a surprise World Cup triumph. The late call-up of winger Helmut Rahn was a stroke of genius, as was the bold gamble of fielding a second-string side against the mighty Hungary early on in the competition – the 8-3 defeat helped them take an easier route to the final, where a full strength Germany beat the Hungarians 3-2 with two goals from Rahn.

HELENIO HERRERA

Born: April 17, 1917

Management: Puteaux, Stade Francais, Real Valladolid, Atlético Madrid, Malaga, Deportivo de La Coruña, Sevilla, Belenenses, Barcelona, Inter Milan, Spain, Italy, Roma, Rimini

Major honours: European Cup 1964, 1965; World Club Cup 1964, 1965

In terms of trophies, Helenio Herrera's record is impressive enough but the impact of the man they called 'Il Mago' (the Magician) cannot be measured in silverware alone. Herrera was a revolutionary manager and a well-paid control freak who dominated his club and whose use of man-management techniques was way ahead of its time. His tactical innovations can still be felt in the game today, most notably his role in the development of the highly-defensive system of 'catenaccio', with which Inter Milan enjoyed such success in the mid-1960s.

Herrera used tough man-for-man markers supported by a sweeper, asking his team to focus primarily on defence, pressing their opponents hard and then hitting them on the counterattack at pace. So successful was this approach that Inter won three league titles and successive European Cups and World Club Cups in 1964 and 1965. However, it would be wrong to remember Herrera merely as the godfather of defensive Italian football.

Born in Argentina but raised in Morocco, Herrera played his club football in France and it was there that he began his managerial career with Puteaux. After a spell with Real Valladolid, he guided Atlético Madrid to back-to-back league titles before embarking on a tour of the clubs of Spain that ended with a championship with Barcelona. Far from being defensive, at Barcelona Herrera earned a reputation for coaching an attacking team, often playing forwards in defensive positions and encouraging them to push forward in search of goals.

He was at the helm of the Spanish team at the 1962 World Cup, although he could do nothing to stop them finishing bottom of their group. After the glorious successes of 'Il Grande Inter' Herrera was snapped up by Roma but he could only add an Italian Cup to his list of honours. He also had another spell coaching the Italian national team in the late Sixties, finally ending his career in 1981 while back at Barcelona.

MICHEL HIDALGO

Born: March 22, 1933
Management: Menton, France, Marseille, Congo
Major honours: European Championship 1984

Michel Hidalgo had a distinguished playing career, scoring a consolation goal in the European Cup final of 1956 for Reims against Real Madrid. He also played for Monaco, where he won two league medals before taking over at RC Menton as player-manager. He later became president of the UNFP, the French players' union, before his appointment as coach of the French national team in 1976.

Having succeeded Stefan Kovacs, he helped develop the talents of a young Michel Platini as the team reached the semi-finals of the 1982 World Cup, dramatically losing the decisive tie with West Germany despite having led the game. Two years later, on home soil, he guided France to victory at the European Championship, winning the final against Spain. After the

victory he became France's technical director, before returning to full-time management with Marseille in 1986, where he won two league titles. In 2004 Hidalgo came out of retirement to manage Congo for a short period.

GUUS HIDDINK

Born: November 8, 1946
Management: De Graafschap, PSV Eindhoven, Fenerbahçe, Valencia, Holland, Real Madrid, Real Betis, South Korea, PSV Eindhoven, Australia, Russia, Chelsea, Turkey
Major honours: World Club Cup 1998, European Cup 1988

Guus Hiddink rose to prominence during his time at PSV Eindhoven, where he won the league and cup three times each, and topped his reign by claiming the European Cup in 1988. His attractive, free-flowing football won many admirers and after spells at Fenerbahçe and Valencia he took charge of the Dutch national team, with only a penalty shoot-out preventing his side reaching the final of the 1998 World Cup. A move back to Spain followed to take charge of Real Madrid, with whom he won the World Club Cup in 1998, and then Real Betis. However, he may well be best remembered for his outstanding achievement in taking co-hosts and underdogs South Korea to the semi-final of the 2002 World Cup, even though they had never previously won a game at the finals. After the tournament the stadium in Gwangju was renamed in his honour.

Returning to PSV, he won the league and cup 'double' in 2005 and the Dutch title in 2006, while in his spare time guiding Australia to the 2006 World Cup Finals. Despite being linked with the England manager's job on several occasions, he took charge of Russia's national team and then Turkey, with a temporary spell at Chelsea resulting in an FA Cup win in 2009.

OTTMAR HITZFELD

Born: January 12, 1949.
Management: Zug, Aarau, Grasshoppers Zurich, Borussia Dortmund, Bayern Munich, Switzerland
Major honours: World Club Cup 2001; Champions League 1997, 2001

Composed, determined and steely, Hitzfeld was the first coach to win the new format of the European Cup with two different clubs following its reinvention as the Champions League in the early 1990s. Not much notice was taken when he took over at Borussia Dortmund in 1991 but within four years the club were dominating the Bundesliga and then Europe, with a Champions League win in 1997. However, he had been promoted out of the coaching job by the time the side won the World Club Cup later that year.

Poached by Bayern Munich in 1998, his authoritarian style was just what was needed. He

Left: Helenio Herrera, whose defensive tactics brought him success with Inter Milan.

transformed the club in his own image, winning four league titles in five years, as well as the Champions League in 2001 when his side beat Valencia on penalties. After six successful years with Bayern, Hitzfeld was sacked in May 2004 and subsequently turned down the opportunity to coach the German national side on health grounds. He returned to Bayern for a second spell in 2007, again winning the German league title, before taking over as coach of Switzerland and leading them to the 2010 World Cup.

ROY HODGSON

Born: August 9, 1947

Management: Halmstad, Bristol City, Orebro, Malmö, Neuchatel Xamax, Switzerland, Inter Milan, Blackburn Rovers, Inter Milan, Grasshopper, Copenhagen, Udinese, UAE, Viking, Finland, Fulham, Liverpool

Roy Hodgson has been one of the most successful English coaches abroad. He made his name in Sweden with the championship winning sides of Halmstad and Malmö. With the latter he reached the 1979 European Cup Final before losing to Nottingham Forest. He went on to manage clubs in Switzerland, Italy, Denmark and England. He succeeded Uli

Below: Aimé Jacquet of France lifts the World Cup after victory over Brazil in 1998.

Stielike as Switzerland's national team coach, taking the Swiss to the 1994 World Cup, their first major tournament in 28 years. He also helped them qualify for Euro 96 but quit before the tournament to take over at Inter Milan, with whom he reached the 1997 UEFA Cup Final.

In 2002 he became coach of the United Arab Emirates and in 2006 took over as coach of Finland. Joining Fulham the following year, he saved the unfashionable London club from relegation and in 2010 he led them to the first ever Europa League Final, beating Juventus and Hamburg en route, an achievement that saw him voted England's Manager Of The Year. Soon after he was appointed manager of Liverpool.

JIMMY HOGAN

Born: October 16, 1882

Management: Holland, MTK Hungaria, Young Boys, Switzerland, Austria Vienna, Racing Club Paris, Fulham, Aston Villa

Moderately successful as an inside-forward for Burnley and Fulham, Jimmy Hogan was enticed to coach in Vienna in 1912 by Hugo Meisl. He failed to get his message across to the educated university students, but the unwavering support of Meisl encouraged Hogan to persist with the principles of ball control and intelligent passing that was to be the hallmark of the sport in Austria, Germany and Hungary in that era. The emphasis on skill encouraged by the so called 'Vienna School' of football led to the 'Wunderteam' of Austria, the rise of West Germany as a football force after the war and the 'Magical Magyars' of Hungary. By way of acknowledging his influence on Hungarian football, Hogan was the team's guest of honour when Hungary memorably defeated England 6-3 at Wembley in 1953. He died in January 1974.

AIMÉ JACQUET

Born: November 27, 1941

Management: Lyon, Bordeaux, Montpellier, Nancy, France

Major honours: World Cup 1998

Aimé Jacquet led France to their greatest-ever sporting triumph: victory on home soil at the 1998 World Cup. A decent player in his time, he picked up five league titles and three French Cups at Saint-Etienne in the 1960s and 1970s. He had a brief international spell, playing twice for France, before turning to management at Lyon, where his talent was quickly spotted.

He took over as coach of Bordeaux in 1980 and led the club through the most successful period in their history. Under Jacquet, Bordeaux won three titles, two French Cups and starred impressively in Europe, reaching the semi-finals of the European Cup and the European Cup Winners' Cup, confirming his reputation as France's foremost club manager. A meticulous

planner, he prided himself on knowing his players well and he paid rigorous attention to detail, all qualities that would serve him well during international tournaments.

After leaving Bordeaux in 1989 he took a Montpellier side that included Eric Cantona to an unexpected French Cup triumph. However, a downturn in fortunes followed when he left for Nancy. He was sacked and moved into the French Football Federation set-up, working as assistant to Gerard Houllier before taking over the national team in 1993 and leading a side built around a solid defence to the semi-finals of the European Championship in 1996.

Despite facing enormous press criticism at home, he held on to his job to deliver the ultimate prize in 1998, masterminding France's victorious World Cup campaign on home soil. He quit immediately after the final.

ROGER LEMERRE

Born: June 18, 1941

Management: Red Star, Lens, Paris FC, Strasbourg, Espérance, Red Star, France Military, Lens, France, Tunisia, Morocco, Ankaragücü

Major honours: European Championship 2000; Confederations Cup 2001; African Nations Cup 2004

Lemerre is the only coach to have won both the European Championship and the African Nations Cup. He guided the French Military to the Military World Championship in 1995, he was Aimé Jacquet's assistant when France won the World Cup in 1998, and on taking over as coach in his own right, he celebrated victory at Euro 2000 after beating Italy 2-1 in the final, thanks to an injury time equaliser from Sylvain Wiltord and a David Trezeguet 'golden goal'. He also won the 2001 Confederations Cup but was sacked after a disastrous first round exit from the 2002 World Cup.

Taking over as Tunisia's coach, he guided the North Africans to a 2-1 win over Morocco in the 2004 African Nations Cup Final, with goals from Santos and Ziad Jaziri, and he also led them to the 2006 World Cup. He was sacked following the team's quarter-final exit from the 2008 African Nations Cup and he subsequently had a short but disappointing spell with Morocco.

MARCELLO LIPPI

Born: April 12, 1948

Management: Pontedera, Siena, Pistoiese, Carrarese, Cesena, Lucchese, Atalanta, Napoli, Juventus, Inter Milan, Italy

Major honours: World Cup: 2006; World Club Cup 1996; Champions League 1996; European Super Cup 1996

Just one glance at Marcello Lippi's list of Serie A titles confirms his managerial greatness but he has worked hard to attain that level of success.

After being in charge of a succession of minor Italian clubs, it was not until he finished seventh and sixth with Atalanta and Napoli respectively, on shoestring budgets, that his talents were recognised. His achievements earned him a chance to take over at the helm of Juventus, where he delivered the Champions League after beating Ajax on penalties, the Italian Cup and three Serie A titles in four seasons between 1995 and 1998. He spent a brief period at Inter Milan before returning to Juventus to pick up the title in both 2002 and 2003, and he also led the team to defeat in the 2003 Champions League Final.

He took charge of the Italian national side in July 2004 and led them to the 2006 World Cup in Germany after a two-year unbeaten run. Despite the distraction of the ongoing match-fixing scandal dominating domestic Italian football, Lippi was much praised for his tactical acumen and the building of an indomitable team spirit as he guided the country to a fourth World Cup win, beating France 5-3 on penalties after a 1-1 draw. Three days after the final Lippi decided not to renew his contract but he returned to the job two years later and took the team to 2010 World Cup in South Africa. He had always planned to give up the job after the tournament and he stepped down after Italy's premature exit.

VALERY LOBANOVSKY

Born: January 6, 1939

Management: Dnipro Dnipropetrovsk, Dynamo Kiev, Soviet Union, UAE, Kuwait, Ukraine

Major honours: European Cup Winners' Cup 1975, 1986

Notorious for his solemn expression and for ruling teams with an iron fist, Valery Lobanovsky was the man responsible for making Dynamo Kiev a force in European football. As coach he took the club to victory in the European Cup Winners' Cup in both 1975 and 1986, and to the semi-finals of the Champions League in 1999.

He also had three stints as coach of the Soviet Union, reaching the final of the 1988 European Championship before defeat to Holland.

A left-winger as a player, he won the league and cup with Dynamo before moving to Chernomorets Odessa, but it was as a coach that he made his name, starting in the late Sixties. Teamwork was the cornerstone of his sides but he also brought through outstanding individuals, such as Oleg Blokhin and later Sergei Rebrov and Andriy Shevchenko. He died on May 13, 2002.

HUGO MEISL

Born: November 16, 1881

Management: Amateure, Austria

Hugo Meisl developed the famed 'Vienna School' of football, alongside Englishman Jimmy Hogan. A highly educated man and a believer in 'pure' football, he was an admirer of the British game and his recruiting and encouragement of Hogan not only had a profound effect on the game in Austria – notably with 'Wunderteams' of the 1930s and 1950s – but also on football in Hungary and Germany. Under his leadership, Austria finished fourth at the 1934 World Cup.

Having played for Vienna Cricket and Football Club, he started coaching with Amateure (later to become FK Austria Vienna). He was an advocate of FIFA and as a champion of the international game, he was the driving force behind the creation of the Mitropa Cup, a forerunner of the European Cup. He died in 1937.

CÉSAR LUIS MENOTTI

Born: November 5, 1938.

Management: Huracán, Argentina, Barcelona, Boca Juniors, Atlético Madrid, River Plate, Peñarol, Mexico, Independiente, Sampdoria, Rosario Central, Puebla

Major honours: World Cup 1978

A decent player in his day, it was not until chain-smoking César Luis Menotti went into management that he became a football legend, reviving the fortunes of Argentina. 'El Flaco' (The Thin One) was a highly-strung coach who had already enjoyed a short but successful spell as manager of Huracán when he took over the national team after the 1974 World Cup. He went on to coach Argentina at the 1978 finals and he cultivated an attacking style, with creative players such as Mario Kempes and Osvaldo Ardiles at the heart of his teams.

After beating Holland in the World Cup final, he stayed loyal to many of his ageing stars at the tournament four years later. However, despite having Diego Maradona in the line-up this time his team did not have the stomach for a campaign contested at the tail-end of the Falklands War. After leaving the job Menotti was particularly critical of his successor, Carlos Bilardo.

He has variously enjoyed and endured short spells at many clubs, including very brief stints at Barcelona in 1984 and Sampdoria in 1997, plus a return to Independiente that lasted only nine matches in 2005.

Above: One of the great coaches of modern times, Marcello Lippi lifts the World Cup in 2006

Left: Valery Lobanovsky with Dynamo Kiev during the 1997-8 season

RINUS MICHELS

Born: February 9, 1928
Management: Ajax, Barcelona, Holland, Los Angeles Aztecs, Köln, Bayer Leverkusen
Major honours: European Cup 1971; European Championship 1988

An Ajax centre-forward who won five caps for Holland, it is as the coach who pioneered 'Total Football' that Marinus 'Rinus' Michels will always be remembered. With Johan Cruyff as its heartbeat, Total Football – a philosophy dependent on versatility, adaptability and all-round ball skills – was first developed with Ajax in the late Sixties, and then with the brilliant Dutch team of the Seventies.

The football may have been pleasing on the eye but 'Iron Rinus' was no soft touch. For him, playing beautiful football was a serious business and he demanded a high level of professionalism from his players. That combination of silk and steel took Ajax to a first European Cup final in 1969, and although they lost to Milan, the foundations for future success had been firmly laid. Ajax went on to win three successive European Cups and, while Michels left for Barcelona after the first victory, he could still claim much of the credit for the trophies won without him.

At Barcelona he initially found progress hard but after taking Cruyff to the Nou Camp, he celebrated league success in 1974 and lifted the Spanish Cup in 1978 during a second spell in charge. He also found time to lead an outstanding Holland team to the 1974 World Cup Final, captivating fans around the world with the side's stylish play. Unfortunately his talented team threw away a 1-0 lead against West Germany and finished as runners-up.

In 1978 Michels joined the Los Angeles Aztecs in the NASL before going back to Germany for a successful spell with Köln. He returned as coach of Holland in time to mould individuals like Ruud Gullit and Marco Van Basten into a disciplined Dutch unit good enough to win their first international trophy, the 1988 European Championship.

After a spell with Bayer Leverkusen, he led Holland to the 1992 European Championship but when they slipped up on penalties to surprise winners Denmark, he called time on a glorious career. In 1999 FIFA named him as the Coach Of The Century. He died in March 2005, aged 77.

Above: Rinus Michels capped his return to managing the Dutch national side by coaching them to victory at the 1988 European Championship but he retired after defeat to Denmark in the same competition four years later.

BORA MILUTINOVIC

Born: September 7, 1944
Management: Pumas UNAM, Mexico, San Lorenzo, Udinese, Costa Rica, USA, Nigeria, MetroStars, China, Honduras, Al Saad, Jamaica, Iraq
Major honours: CONCACAF Championship 1989; Gold Cup 1991, 1996

Bora Milutinovic was the first person to have coached five different countries at the World Cup: Mexico (1986), Costa Rica (1990), USA (1994), Nigeria (1998) and China (2002). He also started the 2006 World Cup qualification campaign with Honduras but he resigned in June 2004 after just ten games in charge. The Yugoslav-born coach has the ability to get teams to exceed expectations and his sides have been responsible for a number of World Cup shocks over the years, including Costa Rica's defeat of Scotland in 1990 and Nigeria's win over Spain in 1998. His best World Cup performance was taking hosts Mexico to the quarter-finals in 1986. His career began in Mexico with Pumas UNAM in 1977 and between international appointments he has coached clubs in Argentina, Italy, the United States and Qatar.

JOSÉ MOURINHO

Born: 26 January 1963
Management: Benfica, Uniao de Leiria, Porto, Chelsea, Inter Milan, Real Madrid
Major honours: Champions League 2004, 2010; UEFA Cup 2003

José Mourinho is an outspoken and controversial figure but even his fiercest detractors would be hard pressed to criticise his exemplary record in club management. He first cut his teeth in the game as Bobby Robson's translator at Sporting Lisbon and Porto, and then as Robson's assistant coach at Barcelona. His first job as head coach came at Benfica in 2000 but it ended with Mourinho walking out after only nine games, frustrated at problems in the boardroom.

He next guided Portuguese minnows Uniao de Leiria into the top five before jumping ship in January 2002 to coach Porto. It was there that he really made his name, guiding the team to an extraordinary trophy 'triple' in 2003, winning the league, cup and UEFA Cup. He trumped that achievement the following season with victorious campaigns in both the league and the Champions League.

Mourinho took over at Chelsea in 2004 and won back-to-back league titles in his first two seasons with a club that had not won the championship in 50 years. However, after an acrimonious falling out with chairman Roman Abramovich, Mourinho's departure in September 2007 shocked the English game.

After a season's sabbatical Mourinho joined Inter Milan and despite not endearing himself to the Italian media and football authorities, he again won back-to-back titles in his first two seasons. He also became only the third coach to lift the European Cup with two clubs following victory in the 2010 Champions League Final. It may have been Inter's first triumph in the competition in 45 years but it proved to be his last game for the club, as a much predicted move to Spanish giants Real Madrid followed in the days after the final.

MIGUEL MUÑOZ

Born: September 15, 1924
Management: Plus Ultra, Real Madrid, Spain, Granada, Hercules, Las Palmas, Sevilla
Major honours: World Club Cup 1960; European Cup 1960, 1966

Miguel Muñoz was arguably the greatest manager that Real Madrid ever had. During his 14-year reign, Real won the Spanish league title nine times and the Spanish Cup twice. Of greater significance were the European Cup wins of 1960 and 1966. The 1960 victory was the classic 7-3 triumph over Eintracht Frankfurt at Hampden Park in Glasgow, regarded as one of the best matches of all time. It was Real Madrid's fifth successive European Cup triumph, with Muñoz having captained the side in the 1956 and 1957 victories (he was the first person to win as both a player and a coach). Inevitably, Muñoz became coach of the Spanish national team, taking them to the final of the 1984 European Championship and the 1986 World Cup quarter-finals.

BILL NICHOLSON

Born: January 26, 1919
Management: Tottenham Hotspur
Major honours: UEFA Cup 1972; European Cup Winners' Cup 1963

Bill Nicholson guided Tottenham Hotspur to a host of domestic and European trophies in a 16-year career as manager of the club. He was appointed to the job in October 1958, and although Spurs were not far off the relegation zone at the time, the team famously beat Everton 10-4 in his first game in charge. However, his most famous and enduring achievement was winning the 1961 league championship and FA Cup 'double', the first time the feat had been achieved in the 20th century.

Nicholson won the 'double' after spending more money than any British manager and with a team playing outstanding and attractive football. His Spurs side, featuring Danny Blanchflower and the skilful John White, began the season with 11 straight victories and ended up winning 31 games, including 16 away. In 42 league games that season they scored 115 goals. The 'double' was successfully completed by defeating Leicester City 2-0 in the FA Cup final.

Under Nicholson Tottenham became the first British club to lift a major European trophy, beating Atlético Madrid 5-1 in 1963 to win the Cup Winners' Cup, and nine years later he took the club to glory in the UEFA Cup after beating Wolverhampton Wanderers over two legs. He resigned shortly after Feyenoord defeated Spurs in the final of the 1974 UEFA Cup but later returned to the club as a consultant, working with them until 1991. He died in October 2004.

BOB PAISLEY

Born: January 23, 1919
Management: Liverpool
Major honours: European Cup 1977, 1978, 1981; UEFA Cup 1976; European Super Cup 1977

Bob Paisley began his playing career with the famous amateur side Bishop Auckland in his native North East but from 1939 until his retirement from the board in 1992, he was Liverpool through and through. Few football professionals can have been a player, coach, physiotherapist, manager and director of the same club but Bob Paisley fulfilled all of these roles during his career at Anfield.

He forged his 'odd couple' partnership with manager Bill Shankly in 1959, and for 15 years was happy to play second fiddle to the extrovert Scotsman. Shankly relied heavily on Paisley's shrewd judgment of a player's strengths and weaknesses, and when the manager suddenly resigned in 1974, the unassuming Paisley was reluctant to take on the mantle. With the support of his senior players, he agreed to the challenge, continuing to develop the football philosophy that he had helped to formulate.

His teams played a simple, fast, passing game with the players working tirelessly for each other, and soon Paisley's Liverpool were surpassing the achievements of the Shankly era. After a first season without trophies, his Liverpool side went on to win the league the following year and a 4-3 aggregate victory over Club Brugge gave them the UEFA Cup too.

In 1977 Liverpool won the title by a point from Manchester City and four days after an FA Cup final defeat to Manchester United, they outplayed Borussia Mönchengladbach to win the European Cup in Rome. As a member of the British Army in World War II, Paisley was able to joke that the last time he had visited the city he had helped liberate it. That was Kevin Keegan's last game for the club but in keeping with his reputation as a good judge of a player, Paisley replaced Keegan with Kenny Dalglish, who went on to score the winner against Club Brugge the following year as Liverpool retained the European Cup. Other useful investments included Alan Hansen, Graeme Souness and Mark Lawrenson, as he strove to renew his incredibly successful side.

Under Paisley, 'The Reds' continued to dominate the league, winning four of the five titles between 1979 and 1983. 'I've been here during the bad times too – one year we came second,' he would famously joke. In that year off, 1981, they added a third European Cup after beating Real Madrid 1-0. He also managed three League Cup triumphs in his final three years, before he called it a day in 1983, staying on as an advisor to Joe Fagan and then Kenny Dalglish.

CARLOS ALBERTO PARREIRA

Born: February 27, 1943
Management: São Cristovao, Ghana, Asante Kotoko, Fluminense, Kuwait, Brazil, UAE, Saudi Arabia, Bragantino, Valencia, Fenerbahçe, São Paulo, MetroStars, Atlético Mineiro, Santos, Internacional, Corinthians, South Africa, Fluminense
Major honours: World Cup 1994

In charge of Brazil on three occasions, to many people the man known as 'The Professor' is modern Brazilian football. He is famous for combining modern coaching techniques with the exciting tradition of his national team. Parreira was not a distinguished player himself, arriving instead from a background of physical preparation, having been on the coaching staff when Brazil won the 1970 World Cup in Mexico. He married the attacking and exciting

Below: Liverpool manager Bob Paisley celebrates winning the league title.

play demanded following that success to a more pragmatic, match-winning approach.

For his 1994 World Cup-winning side he was blessed with stars such as Bebeto and Romario, enabling the team to claim Brazil's first World Cup win for 24 years. After leading South Africa at the 2010 World Cup Finals, he became the only man to coach at six World Cups: Kuwait (1982), United Arab Emirates (1990), Saudi Arabia (1998) and Brazil (1994 and 2006). Despite his triumph in 1994, the tournament four years later ended unhappily for him as he was sacked before Saudi Arabia had even completed their games.

VITTORIO POZZO

Born: March 2, 1886
Management: Torino, Italy, AC Milan
Major honours: World Cup 1934, 1938; Olympics 1936

Many believe Vittorio Pozzo only won the World Cup in 1934 because the all-powerful Mussolini 'arranged' for it to happen, while others see him as a managerial genius. He is certainly still the only coach to win the World Cup twice and he was the first man to lead Italy in a competitive game. He also won Olympic gold with Italy and lifted the Central European International Cup.

The Second World War broke up his career, and 'Il Vecchio Maestro' (the Old Master) never really rediscovered his touch, despite remaining manager of the national team on and off from 1912 until 1948, and continuously so from 1929. Part of the problem in his latter career was that Italy was largely ignored by the footballing world after the war but Pozzo had already done enough to earn his reputation.

ALF RAMSEY

Born: January 21, 1920
Management: Ipswich Town, England, Birmingham City
Major honours: World Cup 1966

Though he never coached a major club, Alf Ramsey was one of the game's top managers for his success at both ends of the spectrum: in piloting a relatively minor club to the First Division championship and in guiding the English national team to World Cup triumph.

A high grade fullback who played for both Southampton and Tottenham, Ramsey was a natural leader and an instinctive reader of the game, winning 32 caps and captaining both club and country. Retiring at the age of 35 in 1955, he took up management with Ipswich, then in the Third Division South. Playing with a deep-lying striker and his wide players tucked, the club embarked on an extraordinary seven-year run of success, moving swiftly through the divisions until they secured the First Division title in 1962.

An enigmatic character, he was unflappable, pragmatic and iron-willed. His clipped vowels concealed a working-class upbringing in Dagenham but while he was never close to his players, he commanded their utmost respect. It was these characteristics that led to his appointment as England manager in 1962. Soon after taking the job he announced that England would win the World Cup but in his first match in charge they exited the European Nations Cup with a 2-5 defeat to France.

Ramsey set about building a team with the ability to take on the world, shoring up the defence with the addition of goalkeeper Gordon Banks and gradually refining his 'wingless wonders' system. England's World Cup victory in 1966 was a triumph for Ramsey's preparation and planning. He drafted Geoff Hurst into the squad late but when injury ruled Jimmy Greaves out of the confrontation with Argentina, Ramsey put Hurst in and then played him in the final, with match-winning consequences.

A knighthood did not go to Ramsey's head and his preparation for the World Cup in 1970 was even more meticulous. Bad luck played its part in undermining an even better squad but the quarter-final defeat to West Germany raised questions about his cautious tactics.

Two disastrous results against Poland in 1973 led to failure to qualify for the 1974 tournament and to Ramsey's eventual dismissal. He had a brief spell at Birmingham as caretaker-manager in 1977 and was later technical director with Panathinaikos in 1979, before retiring from the game completely. He died on April 28, 1999, but will always be remembered for his role in England's greatest sporting achievement.

GEORGE RAYNOR

Born: January 13, 1907
Management: Sweden, AIK, Atvidaberg, Juventus, Lazio, Coventry City, Skegness Town, Djurgardens, Doncaster
Major honours: Olympics 1948

Englishman George Raynor took Sweden to Olympic gold in 1948 and to the 1958 World Cup Final. Chairman of the FA, Stanley Rous, first noticed Raynor when he was coaching in Iraq during the Second World War and later recommended him to the Swedish FA, who tempted Raynor away from Aldershot reserves. In his first game in charge he made his mark by devising a strategy to outwit Switzerland's revolutionary 'Swiss bolt' system.

He established a series of training camps to improve the skills of young players. The scheme was a roaring success and by 1948 he had helped Sweden to gold at the Olympics with a team that included Gunnar Gren, Gunnar Nordahl and Nils Liedholm. It was only the amazing Brazil team of Pelé and Garrincha that prevented him from lifting the World Cup ten years later.

OTTO REHHAGEL

Born: August 9, 1938
Management: Kickers Offenbach, Werder Bremen, Borussia Dortmund, Arminia Bielefeld, Fortuna Düsseldorf, Bayern Munich, Kaiserslautern, Greece
Major honours: European Championship 2004; European Cup Winners' Cup 1992

Above: Vittorio Pozzo leads the celebrations after Italy's 1938 World Cup win in France.

Otto Rehhagel's playing career at Hertha Berlin and Kaiserslautern was less than distinguished. Having cut his managerial teeth at Kickers Offenbach in 1972, a run of 12 games without a win in the hot-seat at Dortmund suggested another unassuming career in the making, with the team even losing by a record 12-0 in one game. Yet 14 years at Werder Bremen spawned such players as Rudi Völler, Karl-Heinz Reidle and Andreas Herzog, as the club won two league titles and the European Cup Winners' Cup. One poor season at Bayern Munich followed in 1995-6, where he failed to command the respect of big name signings such as Jürgen Klinsmann. He was sacked just weeks before Bayern won the UEFA Cup but he restored his reputation by taking Kaiserslautern to the league title in 1998.

His greatest triumph came at the European Championship in 2004, when he pulled off one of the greatest shocks in the history of international football, guiding outsiders Greece to the title. His team beat host nation Portugal in the final but gained few admirers for their defence-first policy. He also led the Greeks at Euro 2008 and at the 2010 World Cup but never again managed to match the success of that one incredible night in Lisbon.

Opposite: England's World Cup winning manager Sir Alf Ramsey on the training pitch with players Tommy Smith, Chris Lawler and Gordon Banks.

Above: Bobby Robson displays the UEFA Cup after Ipswich Town's victory in 1981.

DON REVIE

Born: July 10, 1927
Management: Leeds United, England, UAE, Al-Nasr, Al-Ahly
Major honours: Fairs Cup 1968, 1971

Between the mid-Sixties and mid-Seventies, Revie turned Leeds into the fiercest contenders in British football, winning six major trophies and finishing as runners-up to a further 11. Revie had been a decent centre-forward for Leicester, Hull, Manchester City and Sunderland before joining a broke and demoralised Leeds in the Second Division as player-manager in 1958.

By 1965 he had taken the club from the relegation zone of the Second Division to the runners-up spot in Division One and to the FA Cup final, where they lost to Liverpool. The following ten seasons saw Revie construct a team renowned for its win-at-all-costs attitude, and win they did: the league in 1969 and 1974; the FA Cup in 1972; the Fairs Cup in 1968 and 1971; and the League Cup in 1968.

In 1974 Revie left Leeds to replace Sir Alf Ramsey as manager of the England team, but he could not recreate the same magic on the international stage. Midway through the qualification campaign for the 1978 World Cup he caused consternation when he resigned to take up a £340,000 four-year contract to manage the United Arab Emirates.

Revie subsequently coached Saudi side Al-Nasr and had a short spell in Cairo with Al-Ahly, before returning home in 1984. After his resignation from the England job, the FA had banned him from the English game for ten years. The ban was overturned but, despite brief negotiations with QPR, Revie never returned to club management in England. He died in 1989.

FRANK RIJKAARD

Born: September 30, 1962
Management: Holland, Sparta Rotterdam, Barcelona, Galatasaray
Major honours: Champions League 2006

On taking charge of the Dutch national team in 1998, Frank Rijkaard had no previous coaching experience but took his team to the semi-finals of the 2000 European Championship, playing some of the most thrilling football of the tournament. In a shock decision, he resigned just minutes after his team had been knocked out of the competition on penalties by Italy. He spent one unsuccessful year at Sparta Rotterdam, overseeing the first relegation in the club's history, before rebuilding his coaching career with Barcelona.

At the Nou Camp he succeeded in turning around the fortunes of the club, winning back-to-back league titles in 2005 and 2006. He also managed to win the Champions League in 2006, making Barcelona champions of Europe for only the second time in the club's history. Perhaps more significantly to the fans, he became the first Barça coach to win twice at the Bernabéu, home of rivals Real Madrid. However, he was unable to sustain this level of success and after a disappointing season Rijkaard left the club in May 2008, with the announcement coming soon after a 4-1 defeat to Real. Following a year out of the game, he joined Galatasaray in 2009.

BOBBY ROBSON

Born: February 18, 1933
Management: Vancouver Royals, Fulham, Ipswich Town, England, PSV Eindhoven, Sporting Lisbon, Porto, Barcelona, Newcastle United
Major honours: UEFA Cup 1981; European Cup Winners' Cup 1997

Bobby Robson started his coaching career in 1967 with a brief spell in Canada before returning to coach Fulham, where he had spent much of his distinguished playing career. He was sacked after less than a year in the job and in 1969 he began his long and successful stint at Ipswich. He turned the small town club into one of the country's best and most attractive sides, winning the FA Cup in 1978, the UEFA Cup against AZ Alkmaar in 1981, and twice finishing second in the league.

Robson was rewarded for his achievements in 1982 when he was offered the England job. His side lost to Argentina, and to Maradona's dextrous subterfuge, in the quarter-finals of the 1986 World Cup. They performed badly in the 1988 European Championship but were only a penalty shoot-out away from the World Cup final of 1990. Robson then began his decade-long journey around the European continent, winning numerous domestic trophies in Holland, Portugal and Spain, plus

the European Cup Winners' Cup in 1997 with Barcelona. Returning to England in 1999 he helped breathe fresh life into Newcastle, the team he had supported as a child.

His stay at St James' Park cost him the opportunity to take charge of England once more after the resignation of Kevin Keegan in 2000. He was controversially sacked by Newcastle in 2004 and became a consultant to the Republic Of Ireland team in 2006. He died in 2009.

ARRIGO SACCHI

Born: April 1, 1946
Management: Rimini, Parma, AC Milan, Italy, Atlético Madrid
Major honours: World Club Cup 1989, 1990; European Cup 1989, 1990; European Super Cup 1989, 1990

Having never played the game professionally, Arrigo Sacchi's big break came after his up-and-coming Parma team knocked AC Milan out of the 1986-7 Italian Cup. The following summer Milan president Silvio Berlusconi moved to bring Sacchi to the San Siro and within a year he had created a brilliant, attacking team. Winning the Serie A league title in his first season in charge, he then took the team to successive European Cup triumphs in 1989 and 1990 before he was tempted away to coach the Italian national side.

He guided Italy to the 1994 World Cup Final in the USA, where his team were beaten on penalties by Brazil, but he resigned after the 1996 European Championship and returned to Milan for a brief, unsuccessful spell. He then had a short stint at Atlético Madrid, and an even shorter one (just 28 days) back at Parma before leaving for health reasons. He resurfaced at the club as general manager in December 2001 and he subsequently became director of football at Real Madrid before resigning in 2005.

HELMUT SCHÖN

Born: September 15, 1915
Management: Saarland, West Germany
Major honours: World Cup 1974; European Championship 1972

Helmut Schön scored 17 goals in 16 international games before the war forced him to flee his native Dresden. His first national coaching job was with the postwar limbo state, Saarland. From 1955 he was West Germany's assistant manager, taking over the reins from Sepp Herberger in 1964. Schön's fine, undervalued team nearly upset England in the 1966 World Cup Final, eventually losing in extra-time. In the 1970 quarter-final the Germans exacted revenge, beating England and eventually finishing third.

Schön's natural inclination, as an inside-forward, was to produce ball-playing teams. His truly great 1972 European Championship winning side, boasting Franz Beckenbauer, Gerd Müller and Gunter Netzer, epitomised the spirit of 'Total Football'. Despite arguments with the players over money – which depressed the benign, erudite Schön deeply – his flexible, powerful 1974 World Cup team pulled through to beat Holland and win the ultimate prize.

West Germany lost in the final of the 1976 European Championship before faltering at the 1978 World Cup. However, that performance cannot devalue Schön's many achievements in a long career. He died in 1996.

LUIZ FELIPE SCOLARI

Born: November 9, 1948.

Management: CSA, Juventude, Brasil de Pelotas, Al-Shabab, Gremio, Goiás, Al Qadisiya, Kuwait, Criciuma, Al-Ahli, Júbilo Iwata, Palmeiras, Cruzeiro, Brazil, Portugal, Chelsea, Bunyodkor

Major honours: World Cup 2002; Copa Libertadores 1995, 1999; Recopa Sudamericana 1996

Scolari led Brazil from the doldrums to a record fifth World Cup in 2002 but his style is different to many Brazilian coaches. With a reputation for making tough decisions and sticking by them, especially over selection, Scolari preferred home-based stars to some playing in Europe. He placed an emphasis on a workmanlike midfield and a strong defence, putting the team before all individuals. His playing career was hardly sparkling as he was a defender for a series of modest Brazilian teams but when called upon by his nation as a manager, he transformed their fortunes from Copa América strugglers to world champions in just over a year.

He coached hosts Portugal to the final of Euro 2004 but lost to outsiders Greece. He subsequently led the team to the 2006 World Cup semi-final, before enduring a short and unsuccessful stint in England with Chelsea. In South America he has won the Copa Libertadores twice, with Grêmio in 1995 and with Palmeiras in 1999.

BILL SHANKLY

Born: September 2, 1919

Management: Carlisle United, Grimsby Town, Workington, Huddersfield Town, Liverpool

Major honours: UEFA Cup 1973

Bill Shankly was the founding father of the great Liverpool dynasty of the Sixties, Seventies and Eighties. After a long playing career, which included five caps for Scotland and a long stint at Preston North End, he spent a decade as manager at various lowly clubs that failed to match his drive and vision. In 1959 he finally alighted at Liverpool, then languishing in Division Two. He dispensed with the services of 24 players but was canny enough to retain two members of the coaching staff: Joe Fagan and Bob Paisley. Together they would go on to form the legendary Anfield 'Boot Room'.

With their help, and through his own willpower, charisma and native intelligence, he transformed the club, taking them to promotion to Division One in 1962, and to the league championship in 1964. He emphasised a neat passing game, with constant movement and indefatigable teamwork, hallmarks that stayed with Liverpool teams through the decades.

The FA Cup was collected in 1965 after beating Leeds United 2-1, and the league title was won again in 1966, although they failed at the final hurdle in the European Cup Winners' Cup against Borussia Dortmund the same year.

As the team built around Ron Yeats, Ian St John and Roger Hunt began to fade, Shankly set about rebuilding. His enthusiasm was embodied on the pitch in the shape of new signing, Kevin Keegan. The pocket-sized powerhouse helped 'The Reds' to another Division One title in 1973. That year they also achieved one of Shankly's much-coveted ambitions, a European honour, in the shape of a UEFA Cup victory over Borussia Mönchengladbach. After the 3-0 FA Cup final trouncing of Newcastle in 1974, Shankly unexpectedly announced his retirement.

He left behind a powerful legacy at Anfield, and will be eternally venerated by the club's fans for his passion for the game, his commitment to good football and his witticisms. ('This city has two great teams: Liverpool and Liverpool reserves,' he once famously quipped.) He died on September 29, 1981.

JOCK STEIN

Born: October 1, 1922

Management: Dunfermline Athletic, Hibernian, Celtic, Leeds United, Scotland

Major honours: European Cup 1967

Jock Stein announced his arrival as a manager by guiding unfancied Dunfermline Athletic to the Scottish Cup of 1961, beating Celtic – the team Stein had captained to the 'double' of 1954. 'The Big Man' moved to Hibs for a spell but by

Above: Bill Shankly with the UEFA Cup trophy after Liverpool's aggregate victory over Borussia Mönchengladbach in 1973.

1965 he was in charge at Celtic Park. With a determination born of his background as a miner, he quickly built one of the best British club sides ever. In 1966 he won the first of an unprecedented nine titles in succession. His team's exuberant and skilful victory over dour Inter Milan in the 1967 European Cup Final was a victory for football, and they nearly repeated the feat in 1970, losing narrowly to Feyenoord.

Celtic tried to move Stein into a more senior role after his final title in 1977 but he decided instead on a new challenge at Leeds. This lasted mere weeks before he returned north to manage the Scottish national team. He steered them to the 1982 World Cup Finals but they failed to progress beyond the first round. Tragically he died of a heart-attack immediately after the game that ensured Scotland a place in the play-offs for the 1986 finals in Mexico. His balance of honesty, intelligence, steel and likability marked him as one of the very greatest managers.

GUY THYS

Born: December 6, 1922

Management: Cercle Brugge, Racing Lokeren, Wezel Sport, Herentals, Beveren, Union Saint-Gilloise, Antwerp, Belgium

When Guy Thys, a club manager with no real success, was appointed national team coach of Belgium in 1976, he inherited an old team from his predecessor Raymond Goethals. Thys embarked on a policy of developing young

Left: Luiz Felipe Scolari coaches Portugal from the touchline at the 2006 World Cup.

players and went on to build one of the best national sides in the history of Belgian football. Thys's team proved to be the surprise package of the 1980 European Championship, only losing the final with West Germany after a goal two minutes from time. Playing exciting and open football, Belgium also reached the World Cup semi-finals under Thys in 1986. He left the job in 1989 but returned less than a year later to take the side to the second round of the 1990 World Cup. He died in 2003.

GIOVANNI TRAPATTONI

Born: March 17, 1939
Management: AC Milan, Juventus, Inter Milan, Bayern Munich, Cagliari, Fiorentina, Italy, Benfica, Stuttgart, Salzburg, Republic Of Ireland
Major honours: European Cup 1985; UEFA Cup 1977, 1991, 1993; European Cup Winners' Cup 1984; World Club Cup 1985; European Super Cup 1984

Italy's most successful coach won two European Cups as a player with AC Milan but it was as coach of Juventus that he really made his name, winning all three major European trophies, plus the European Super Cup, the World Club Cup, six Italian league titles and two Italian Cups. He added another league title and UEFA Cup with Inter Milan before succeeding Franz Beckenbauer at Bayern Munich. He struggled with the language in Germany but after a spell at Cagliari he returned to Bayern and became the first foreign coach to win the German league.

Appointed coach of Italy in July 2000, he took the national team to the 2002 World Cup and to the 2004 European Championship but he could not replicate his successes in club football. He subsequently won the Portuguese league with Benfica and the Austrian title with Red Bull Salzburg, before taking the Republic Of Ireland to the World Cup play-offs in 2009, losing to France in controversial circumstances.

PHILIPPE TROUSSIER

Born: March 21, 1955
Management: INF Vichy, Alencon, Red Star, Créteil, ASEC Abidjan, Ivory Coast, Kaizer Chiefs, CA Rabat, FUS Rabat, Nigeria, Burkino Faso, South Africa, Japan, Qatar, Marseille, Morocco
Major honours: Asian Cup 2000

Paris-born Philippe Troussier started coaching in France but only found success after moving to Africa, where he led ASEC Mimosas Abidjan to three consecutive league titles. He gained a huge reputation with spells in charge of the Ivory Coast, Nigeria and Burkina Faso, who he led to fourth place in the African Nations Cup on home soil in 1998. Nicknamed 'The White Sorcerer', Troussier took South Africa to the 1998 World Cup Finals but switched to Japan after the tournament. He revolutionised the Japanese team, winning the Asian Cup in 2000 and reaching the last 16 of the 2002 World Cup. He spent just two months in charge of Morocco in 2005 before he was sacked. He and his wife converted to Islam in 2006 and he changed his name to Omar.

LOUIS VAN GAAL

Born: August 8, 1951
Management: Ajax, Barcelona, Holland, AZ Alkmaar, Bayern Munich
Major honours: World Club Cup 1995; Champions League 1995; UEFA Cup 1992; European Super Cup 1995, 1997

A fine, creative midfielder in the 1970s, Louis Van Gaal became head coach of his former club Ajax in 1991. Putting his faith in youth, he created a fast, accomplished, ball-playing side who peaked with their 1995 Champions League triumph over AC Milan. Having lost the 1996 final, and having seen his best players leave the club, Van Gaal headed for Barcelona in 1997, winning back-to-back Spanish league titles. However, he proved unpopular with fans at the Nou Camp who resented his preference for Dutch players in the Barcelona team.

He resigned in 2000 to become Holland coach but failure to qualify for the 2002 World Cup forced him out and he returned to Barcelona for a short, unsuccessful spell. After a brief period as technical director of Ajax he took charge of AZ Alkmaar in 2005, leading them to Dutch league title in 2009 before moving to Bayern Munich. In his first season with the German club he won the league and cup 'double' but lost out in the final of the Champions League to Inter Milan.

ARSENE WENGER

Born: September 22, 1949
Management: Nancy, Monaco, Nagoya Grampus Eight, Arsenal

An average player with Strasbourg, Arsene Wenger joined the club's coaching staff in 1981, going on to become head coach at Nancy. He moved to Monaco in 1987, where he won the league, the French Cup and reached the European Cup Winners' Cup final before departing for Japan. Having transformed Grampus Eight from also-rans into title hopefuls, Wenger took over at Arsenal. He arrived in England in September 1996 to newspaper headlines of 'Arsene Who?' However, in 1998 he became the first foreign coach to win the English championship, throwing in the FA Cup for good measure. After a series of near misses, a second 'double' followed in 2002. He brought the league title back to Highbury again in 2004 and the FA Cup in 2005 and although he finally took the club to their first Champions League final in 2006, his team lost 2-1 to Barcelona.

MARIO ZAGALO

Born: August 9, 1931
Management: Botafogo, Brazil, Fluminense, Flamengo, Kuwait, Al-Hilal, Vasco da Gama, Saudi Arabia, Bangu, UAE, Portuguesa
Major honours: World Cup 1970; Copa América 1997

Famously spelling his surname 'Zagalo' as a player and 'Zagallo' as a coach, he was a vital member of Brazil's World Cup winning teams of 1958 and 1962, scoring in the 5-2 defeat of Sweden in the 1958 final. He began his coaching career as youth team boss at Botafogo before becoming manager in 1967. He won two Rio State Championships before his big opportunity came just three months before the 1970 World Cup Finals, when he was asked to take charge of the national side. He allowed his team to play with such freedom and panache that many regard their performances as the greatest ever seen. Continuing as national team coach, he also led club sides Fluminense and Flamengo to State Championships before a fourth-place finish with Brazil at the 1974 World Cup.

He worked quite often in the Middle East, with Kuwait, Saudi Arabia and the United Arab Emirates, who he led to the 1990 World Cup Finals. In 1991 he became Brazil's technical co-ordinator, teaming up with coach Carlos Alberto Parreira to win the 1994 World Cup in the USA, and becoming the first man to be involved in four World Cup victories.

He again took over as Brazil coach later in 1994 and came close to winning another World Cup four years later but his team stalled in the final of the 1998 tournament. After winning another State Championship with Flamengo, in autumn 2002 he returned for one last crack with the national team, again working as technical director alongside coach Parreira at the 2006 World Cup.

Opposite clockwise from top left: Philippe Troussier lifts the Asian Cup in 2000; Arsene Wenger parades the Premier League trophy in 2004; Giovanni Trapattoni during his stint with Red Bull Salzburg; Louis Van Gaal enjoys Ajax's 1995 European Cup win.

Below: Mario Zagalo hoists aloft his fourth World Cup as Brazil's technical co-ordinator in 1994.

WOMEN'S FOOTBALL

THE HISTORY OF WOMEN'S FOOTBALL

Above from left to right: Sun Wen of China scores at the Olympics in 2000; a women's football match in Treharris, Wales, in 1951; Briana Scurry, Mia Hamm and Brandi Chastain celebrate gold at the 2004 Olympics.

Opposite top: Dick, Kerr's Ladies in their England kit in the 1920s. Lily Parr holds the ball.

Opposite bottom: Sweden's Malin Andersson is congratulated after scoring against Brazil in the 2003 World Cup quarter-final.

Below: The women's football team of Welshpool munitions factory, pictured in 1915.

Women's football may not have come to the public's attention until the last decade of the 20th century but its history began in Europe 100 years earlier. The first recorded women's football match was staged in England at Crouch End Athletic Ground on March 23, 1895. The game saw a North London team convincingly beat a side from the south of the city 7-1.

The match was organised by educated middle class feminist, Miss Nettie Honeyball, and her British Ladies Football Club. The team had advertised in the *Daily Graphic* for women to play 'a manly game and show that it could be womanly as well'. The fixture proved a qualified success, although reports indicate that the ladies forgot the rules and failed to change ends at half-time. 'When the novelty has worn off, I do not think that women's football will attract the crowds,' wrote a 'Lady Correspondent' in the *Manchester Guardian*. This idea of football for the middle classes indeed failed to take off. It took the Great War to really kickstart women's football, this time as a sport for the working class.

The development of women's football in the early 20th century happened with work teams at the munitions factories during World War I. After the war, the popularity of women's football continued to grow in England and crowds of up to 53,000 watched teams such as Dick, Kerr's Ladies from Preston play matches to raise money for charity. However, the FA banned women from playing on league grounds in 1921 and this destroyed the game in England for more than 40 years. The Dutch and German federations followed suit in the 1950s, although they were to adopt the women's game 20 years later.

The sport continued to develop in other European countries, most notably in Italy and Scandinavia. By the early 1970s the Italian women's league, run by the amateur women's football association, was attracting players from across Europe and offering to pay living expenses, while some of the better homegrown players were earning weekly wages.

A key step forward in the development of the game came from UEFA in 1971. Dismayed that its member nations had participated in two 'unofficial' World Cups in Italy and Mexico between 1970 and 1971, UEFA held a vote of its member states and an overwhelming majority voted in favour of national associations taking over the governance of women's football. Most European nations did this, although Italy (1986) and England (1993) left it until much later. Germany, Sweden and Norway, whose associations did take control of the women's game in the 1970s, are three of the top teams in the world today, while Italy and England have struggled to qualify for World Cup competitions with any consistency.

This change allowed for official international competition to begin, albeit limited to just friendly matches at first. A UEFA women's committee was established in 1971 (composed entirely of men) but folded seven years later, having failed to successfully create an official championship tournament for nations.

Across the Atlantic, another political decision was being taken that would help to shape the future development of women's football. The US government introduced an equity funding programme, Title IX, which ensured that the same investment would be put into women's collegiate sport as men's. The entire North American sports structure relies on competitive college sport, from which the country's top leagues draft their talent. While the men's scholarships were centred around basketball, baseball and American football, the minority sport of 'soccer' soon began to emerge as the preferred women's scholarship sport.

Numerous colleges in America provide soccer scholarships, drawing on the best young players from across the world to supplement the country's own talented players. This programme has helped drive the participation rates to more than eight million and it also enables the national team to cherry-pick a world-beating squad. It was not until 1985 that the USA first took part in an international fixture but by playing so many competitive games each year, with funding most

Above left: Dick, Kerr's Ladies represented England against France in Paris in 1920.

Above right: Pohler and Carlson of Germany celebrate winning Euro 2005.

national women's teams across the world could only dream of, the side became the world's first official champions just six years later.

With the growing number of national teams and competitions, FIFA followed up UEFA's call to member associations in 1983 with an announcement three years later that a Women's World Cup would be established, the first one to be staged in China in 1991. An official world tournament would not only give more credibility to the women's game, but it would have an impact on the development of the sport through elite competition. It was to be an occasion where the USA, and star striker Michelle Akers, would stamp their mark on the game. The potential of women's football as a serious spectator sport became apparent when 65,000 attended the final to see USA beat Norway.

At the 1995 World Cup FIFA president Sepp Blatter outlined that, 'the future of football is feminine'. The sentiment turned out to be more than just lip service because following the 1995 World Cup in Sweden, the next two major women's tournaments ensured that the game could live up to those expectations. Women's football was launched at the 1996 Atlanta Olympics, with the host nation sweeping all before them to take the gold medal from China in front of 76,000 cheering fans. However, while a section of the American audience was being won over, it was the 1999 World Cup that launched women's football across the world as a sport in its own right – a sport that could

complement the men's game, rather than be forever regarded as its poor relation. Over half a million fans packed into stadia to watch the games, while a global audience of 40 million tuned in to watch the tournament on television.

It is a valid question whether the cup would have left such a legacy had the United States not triumphed on home soil. However, triumph they did, giving rise to a wave of enthusiasm across the country that enabled the successful formation of the world's first fully professional women's league, the Women's United Soccer Association (WUSA), launched 18 months later to modest, yet encouraging audiences.

Despite average crowds of 6,000 for the eight WUSA teams, in Autumn 2003, on the eve of the World Cup, the league announced that it was to close. The darlings of the 1999 tournament – Mia Hamm, Kristine Lilly and Julie Foudy – may still have been fronting TV advertising campaigns, but sponsorship income was not hitting targets and the world's only professional league collapsed. Players were forced to join semi-pro sides in the USA, China or Europe.

The 2003 World Cup did not have the same impact in the USA as it did four years earlier, largely due to a late switch from China, caused by the SARS outbreak. It also suffered because its September scheduling clashed with the American Football and basketball seasons. Still, the USA team regularly sold-out smaller venues but only finished third after a play-off with Canada, paving the way for an all-European final

for the first time. That shift in power highlighted the advances made by the North European nations. Although USA beat Germany to the 2004 Olympic crown, it was the Germans who retained the World Cup in 2007.

The professional game finally returned to America in 2009 with the launch of Women's Professional Soccer (WPS), and once again many of the most talented players in the world were recruited. However, in some continents the sport still needs major development, as many countries do not operate a national league or a national team and the opportunity for girls to play organised football is limited. FIFA's introduction of both Under-17 and Under-20 World Championships has helped to encourage associations to appreciate the value of developing the women's game and a significant improvement has been seen.

In 2000 a major FIFA survey showed that there were 22 million girls and women playing affiliated football across the world. A similar survey by FIFA in 2006 demonstrated that this figure had grown to 26 million, an indication of how fast the sport has been developing. However, the biggest numbers are still concentrated in the North Americas, Europe and China.

Of the 207 FIFA member nations, more than half are now actively competing on the international stage in women's football and feature in FIFA's rankings, while more than 120 nations started the qualification campaign for the 2011 World Cup, to be held in Germany

DICK, KERR'S LADIES

Dick, Kerr's Ladies were pioneers of women's football. At a time when women had barely secured the right vote in Great Britain, this team of Lancashire factory workers were attracting crowds as large as 53,000 and were deemed to be a genuine threat to the men's game.

The firm of Dick, Kerr and Co Ltd was the leading British manufacturer of light railway equipment, but in 1917 the needs of a country at war necessitated that the production lines of the Dick, Kerr factory were converted to the manufacture of munitions and a new workforce of uniformed women was recruited. It was felt that these young women needed some kind of sporting release to run off their excess energy, and lunchtime workyard football games proved popular. The women were even playing against men, a practice that had been officially banned by the Football Association in 1902. Factory teams sprang up around the country, often with the aim of raising money for charity.

At the Dick, Kerr factory, the women had already played one match against the men of the plant in a game organised by factory worker Grace Sibbert, whose husband was a prisoner of war. Office administrator Alfred Frankland joined with Sibbert in a plan to stage a charity match on Christmas Day 1917, the intention being to raise money for the local hospital for wounded soldiers at Moor Park. Frankland brought his organisational skills to bear on the challenge and, for the princely sum of £20 (£4,000 in today's money) he hired Deepdale, home of the legendary Preston North End.

By staging the game at Deepdale, Frankland was putting women's football on a level playing field with the men's game. It was a gamble that paid off as 10,000 spectators passed through the turnstiles to watch Dick, Kerr's beat Arundel Coulthard Foundry 4-0. 'Dick, Kerr's were not long in showing that they suffered less than their opponents from stage fright, and they had a better all round understanding of the game,' reported *The Daily Post*. 'Their forward work, indeed, was often surprisingly good, one or two of the ladies showing quite admirable ball control.' With the match raising a much needed £200 for the hospital (about £40,000 today), Frankland immediately booked the stadium for a further three matches and prepared to build the team into a force to be reckoned with.

Charitable causes were benefiting greatly from these games and women's football was flourishing, but although Dick, Kerr's started as a part-time project for factory workers, after the armistice it was obvious that there was still a need for charitable donations and Frankland continued to bring a level of professionalism to the team. Pushing back the boundaries of football again, in December 1920 he staged one of the first floodlit matches in England, getting

special permission from Secretary Of State For War, Winston Churchill, to borrow two anti-aircraft spotlights to illuminate the proceedings. He also had the brown leather footballs white-washed to enable them to be better seen.

After dominating women's football in England in the immediate post-war era, the only way that Alfred Frankland could offer his team a fresh challenge was to go international. In the years after the war France was a country in need of rebuilding and Dick, Kerr's Ladies extended a hand of friendship to the Federation Française Sportive Feminine, inviting them for a series of exhibition games. Frankland would eventually bill the team as Dick, Kerr's International Ladies, dressing them when required in the white shirts and blue shorts of England, but for the first international clashes with France, his team would keep their traditional black and white striped shirts and caps.

The four-game series kicked off at Deepdale, with captain Alice Kell leading Dick, Kerr's to a convincing 2-0 victory in front of a crowd of 25,000. The following day they repeated the feat with a 5-2 result in Stockport, before the French finally hit their stride, securing a 1-1 draw at Manchester's Hyde Road. One of the French players even indulged in the most outlandish of goal celebrations for the time: she performed a full somersault, landing gracefully on her feet.

The final game of the tour was at Stamford Bridge in London, but Dick, Kerr's suffered an early blow when Jennie Harris was knocked unconscious by a shoulder charge. With the team reduced to ten women, Florrie Redford's sole strike for the English was not enough to prevent a 2-1 defeat.

In the wake of these games, the popularity of Dick, Kerr's Ladies soared. Players like Lily Parr became minor celebrities, featuring regularly in the newsreels of the day. They played to some of their biggest crowds: a record 53,000 saw them beat St Helens 4-0 at Goodison Park, with a reported 14,000 turned away; 35,000 spectators watched them take on Bath at Old Trafford; 25,000 people turned out to witness them destroy a Rest Of Britain team 9-1 at Anfield; and 22,000 watched the return fixture with the French in Paris before a pitch invasion ended the game at 1-1 five minutes from time.

Those within football who felt threatened by the women's game campaigned for it to be banned, perpetuating a myth expounded in newspapers by 'medical experts' that football was a dangerous game for women to play. The FA finally succumbed, citing unsubstantiated rumours about the legitimacy of the charitable fundraising as the main excuse. In an FA decree of December 5, 1921, it was concluded that all women's games should be banned from the grounds of its member clubs.

Dick, Kerr's rescheduled the club's games at Rugby League grounds, but the FA ban was more damaging to their weaker rivals who

Above: The first picture of Dick, Kerr's Ladies in October 1917.

found they were unable to compete in the new environment. Dick, Kerr's best days would soon be behind them, but in September 1922 the team embarked on their most ambitious challenge, a North American tour.

Problems beset the trip. On arrival the team found that the Canadian leg of the tour had been cancelled after pressure from the FA. Worse still, their US fixtures were to be played against men, including immigrants from England and Scotland who had turned out for teams such as Chelsea, Blackpool, Kilmarnock and Morton, plus at least one local who would go on to represent the USA at the 1930 World Cup Finals. Dick, Kerr's acquitted themselves well, losing just three out of nine games, and even in defeat they proved tough opponents. 'I played against them in 1922,' recalled Paterson keeper Pete Renzulli. 'We were national champions and we had a hell of a job beating them.'

In the years after the US tour the climate changed. Dick, Kerr and Co Ltd had become English Electric and were less tolerant of sponsoring the activities of a football team that no longer carried the company's brand name. In 1926 they parted company with Alfred Frankland and severed all ties with the team. Frankland persevered, rechristening the side as Preston Ladies, but they would continue to be known as Dick, Kerr's for many years.

The team outlived the 1957 death of Alfred Frankland, but eventually ran out of steam – and fixtures – in 1965. Lily Parr, possibly the greatest woman footballer of all time, continued playing until 1951, scoring over 900 goals. Not a bad return for a winger. She died in 1978.

With the huge growth of the game in recent times, it seems that history has finally caught up with the pivotal role played by the team in the history of women's football. 'It is fast becoming a world sport,' concluded Tom Finney in the early Nineties. 'Perhaps this is due in some way to the determination of Dick, Kerr's Ladies, who played on after the FA ban and helped lay the foundations for today's game.'

LEGENDS OF WOMEN'S FOOTBALL

BRANDI CHASTAIN

Country: USA
Born: July 21, 1968
Position: Defender
Club: Shiroki FC Serena, California Storm, San Jose CyberRays, Gold Pride

Brandi Chastain's victory celebration in the 1999 World Cup Final made her the most recognisable player in women's football. After scoring the winning penalty in the shoot-out against China at the Pasadena Rose Bowl, in front of a TV audience of 40 million Chastain dropped to her knees and whipped off her shirt to reveal her sports bra – 'momentary insanity' she claimed in the subsequent press conference.

Chastain started her career as a striker, making her international debut in 1988. Three years later she came off the bench in a World Cup qualifier against Mexico to score her first goal for her country, going on to score four more times in the same match. She moved to Japan to play for a season in 1993 but after a two-year injury-enforced break she returned to the game in defence, the position where she earned the majority of her 192 caps.

Along with Mia Hamm and Julie Foudy she played her last international game in December 2004, in a 5-0 victory over Mexico. The match was planned as a farewell for Hamm and Foudy but it had been Chastain's intention to carry on. However, the following year she was controversially dropped from the USA squad by new coach Greg Ryan, and although she harboured hopes of a call-up for a number of years, she would not play for her country again.

She made a short-lived comeback with Gold Pride in the Women's Professional Soccer league in 2009, aged 40.

DORIS FITSCHEN

Country: Germany
Born: October 25, 1968
Position: Central defender
Clubs: FC Hesedorf, Eintracht Wolfsburg, TSV Siegen, SG Praunheim, FFC Frankfurt, Philadelphia Charge

Fitschen was the first great star of women's football in Germany, helping to lead the team from defence and turning the traditional also-rans into a leading nation of European football. Playing an important role as sweeper for the international team, she managed to achieve an outstanding four European Championship triumphs and a bronze medal at Sydney Olympics in 2000.

At club level in Germany she picked up three league titles, three German Cups and a Super Cup, before switching her career to the United States early in 2001. She had the honour of scoring the first ever goal in professional women's football, a penalty for Philadelphia Charge on the opening day of WUSA in 2001. However, before the end of her first season as a professional, Fitschen was forced to retire from the game due to injury. She played her final international for her country earlier the same month when winning the 2001 European Championship.

JULIE FOUDY

Country: USA
Born: January 23, 1971
Position: Midfielder
Club: San Diego Spirit

For many years the captain of the all-conquering USA team, Julie Foudy made her debut in 1988 as a 17-year-old and went on to play for her country until December 2004. In her 16-year international career Foudy made 271 appearances and scored 45 goals. An attacking midfielder, she showed a desire to win every ball and every game.

Aged 20 she played every minute of the USA's victorious inaugural World Cup campaign in 1991 and she helped her team to win the gold medal in the first women's football event at the Olympics in Atlanta in 1996. She was also part of the 1999 World Cup team that captured the attention of the American nation, winning the trophy in front of 90,000 fans and a huge television audience.

Although she was unable to lead the United States side to victory as captain at the 2003 World Cup, when they finished in third place, she ended her career on a high after winning a second Olympic gold medal in 2004. Among a team of high profile and successful players, including Mia Hamm and Kristine Lilly, Julie Foudy's achievements have sometimes been overlooked but her record speaks for itself.

MIA HAMM

Country: USA
Born: March 17, 1972
Position: Centre-forward
Club: North Carolina Tar Heels, Washington Freedom

Mia Hamm is one of the most famous players in women's football history. After helping to shoot the USA to World Cup victory in 1999, she was the most-requested world footballer – male or female – on Internet search engines. Her profile was such that she fronted a campaign to promote milk, signed a multi-million pound sponsorship deal with Nike (who named the largest building at the company's headquarters after her in 1999), wrote a best-selling autobiography, and even had a high profile marriage to LA Dodgers baseball star Nomar Garciaparra.

Being an out-and-out striker, she scored more international goals than any footballer in the world, male or female, which certainly helped endear Hamm to the American public. She was the player recruited to launch WUSA, the world's first professional

Opposite: Mia Hamm, the most famous footballer in the women's game, takes a shot at Denmark's goal in 2004.

Right: Germany's Doris Fitschen at Euro 2001.

Above: Renate Lingor scores from the spot against France during Euro 2005.

league, and she attracted the league's highest attendances wherever she played with her team, Washington Freedom.

Born in Alabama, Hamm did not have much time to call it a home, being dragged halfway around the USA with her soldier father. She began playing football, as many young girls did at that time, and at 15 she became the youngest player to debut for America, in what would be the first of many important career matches against China. Four years later she was the youngest member of the squad that travelled to China for the inaugural World Cup, playing in five of the six matches as the USA won the trophy. She was a part of the unsuccessful World Cup squad in 1995, when she even stepped in as keeper for the dying minutes of the game against Denmark after the sending-off of Briana Scurry. She also netted the opening goal of the 1999 World Cup.

After recovering from a series of injuries to be fit for the 2003 finals, Hamm's team went out in the semi-finals to eventual winners Germany, with America settling for a third place play-off victory over Canada.

It was the 2004 Olympics that provided a suitable epilogue to her fantastic career, as the USA again triumphed in the competition she had first won in 1996. Hamm was voted World Player Of The year in both 2001 and 2002, and was runner-up in the following two years. She retired in December 2004 with 275 caps and 158 goals, finishing her career with a farewell tour of America with the USA team.

CHARMAINE HOOPER

Country: Canada
Born: January 15, 1968
Position: Centre-forward
Clubs: Rockford Dactyls, Chicago Cobras, Atlanta Beat, New Jersey Wildcats

Hooper was never a particularly fast or skilful striker but she had an uncanny ability to score goals, something that she did with regularity. At one point she held the record for the number of caps and goals scored by a Canadian international until surpassed by Christine Sinclair, and she was voted Player Of The Year for Atlanta Beat in the first two seasons of WUSA, America's professional league.

Hooper travelled to play in the best leagues in the world, having semi-professional contracts in Italy, Norway and Japan, and she regularly topped goalscoring charts. She played in her third World Cup in 2003, scoring twice and making a breakthrough for Canada as the team reached the semi-finals of the competition. Hooper's side missed out on a place in the final after defeat to Sweden and then lost a pulsating third place play-off match with hosts USA in Los Angeles, but there was some small consolation when she found herself named in the World Cup's All-Star Team.

She played her last game for her country in 2006, having scored 71 goals in 130 games. Her older brother Lyndon Hooper was also a very experienced Canadian international.

STEFFI JONES

Country: Germany
Born: December 22, 1972
Position: Defender/Midfielder
Clubs: SG Praunheim, FSV Frankfurt, Niederkirchen, FSV Frankfurt, SC 07 Bad Neuenahr, Washington Freedom, FFC Frankfurt

Born to an American soldier father and a German mother, Steffi Jones was a regular in the German defence between her debut in 1993 and her international retirement in March 2007, making 111 appearances for her country. In a period when the Germans battled their way to the top of the FIFA World Rankings she won numerous honours, including two Olympic bronze medals in 2000 and 2004, and three European Championships. However, she missed out on playing in a World Cup final after rupturing a cruciate ligament in a group game against Argentina at USA 2003. She was flown home immediately to have surgery and, alongside eight million other Germans, watched her team-mates lift the World Cup live on television.

Jones won numerous domestic honours in a seven-year stint with FFC Frankfurt, including the German league and cup 'double', and the UEFA Women's Cup in 2002 and 2006. She also won the WUSA Founders Cup in 2003 with Washington Freedom. She finished her career with FFC Frankfurt and after retiring in December 2007 she became president of the organisation committee for the 2011 Women's World Cup.

RENATE LINGOR

Country: Germany
Born: October 11, 1975
Position: Midfielder
Clubs: SC Klinge Seckach, FFC Frankfurt

For many years Renate Lingor was one of the key players at the heart of the Germany team and she contributed hugely to the country's success, making 149 international appearances and scoring 35 goals.

Despite starting her Bundesliga career at the age of 14, she did not play for the national side until she had succeeded at Under-20 level, winning the Nordic Cup with Germany in 1995 and ending the competition as its top scorer. She made her international debut against Slovakia later the same year but she was initially only regarded as a fringe player. Even though she made the 1999 World Cup squad, she was limited to just three substitute appearances, scoring once against Mexico after coming on for Maren Meinert.

The Sydney Olympics in 2000 presented her with the opportunity to establish herself as a regular first team player and win some recognition for her country. She scored the opening goal in the third place play-off victory against Brazil to win the bronze medal and she was a regular in the side that won the 2001 European Championship Final on home soil, retaining the title four years later in England. The crowning moment of her career came with back to back World Cup wins in the USA in 2003 and in China in 2007, and as her profile increased, she was voted third in the 2006 FIFA World Player Of The Year award.

In club football Lingor started her career in the German Bundesliga with SC Klinge Seckach. The club reached the German Cup final in 1996 and Lingor scored a ninth-minute equaliser, although her team eventually lost 2-1 to FSV Frankfurt in front of a 40,000 crowd at the Olympic Stadium in Berlin. She then joined SG Praunheim and stayed with the club as it became FFC Frankfurt in 1999, helping to win the inaugural UEFA Women's Cup in 2002. In her first season at the club she secured a league runners-up medal, but she went on to win the league title and the German Cup seven times each with the club.

HANNA LJUNGBERG

Country: Sweden
Born: January 8, 1979
Position: Centre-forward
Club: Sunnanå SK, Umea IK

Hanna Ljungberg made a name for herself at the 2001 European Championship. A fast and tricky striker, she starred up front as Sweden reached the final, losing to hosts Germany. She saw heartbreak again in October 2003 when Sweden were once more on the losing end of a final to Germany, this time at the World Cup in Los Angeles. Back home in Sweden 3.8 million people watched the final and the team were treated to a triumphant welcome home, with two jets accompanying their landing.

Ljungberg also played a major role in putting her club side on the map, winning the Swedish league title with Umea IK on seven occasions. In 2002 she scored a record 39 league goals in one season and she virtually put on a one-woman show as Umea IK won the 2003 UEFA Women's Cup, netting two goals and setting up two more in the first leg victory over Fortuna Hjorring. She added another goal to her tally in the return leg but missed the final the following year after being ruled out of the game for six months with a cruciate ligament injury.

Ljunberg underwent knee surgery but battled back to fitness in time for the 2004 Olympic Games in Athens, eventually helping Sweden to finish in fourth place. She pulled out of the 2008 Olympic squad through injury and retired the following year. She had scored 72 goals in 130 internationals.

Along with her international team-mate Victoria Svensson, she featured on a set of stamps issued to commemorate the 100th anniversary of the Swedish FA, alongside stars of the men's game, Henrik Larsson, Freddie Ljunberg, Thomas Ravelli and Nils Liedholm.

MAREN MEINERT

Country: Germany
Born: August 5, 1973
Position: Centre-forward
Club: Rumeln-Kaldenhausen, FCR Duisburg, FFC Brauweiler Pulheim 2000, Boston Breakers

The biggest compliment that was ever paid to Meinert is that teams would regularly change their defensive tactics when playing against her, often employing a man-marker in the hope of stopping her finding the back of the net.

After she picked up winners' medals at the 1995 and 1997 European Championships, Meinert became the sixth overseas player selected to join the WUSA league in 2000, a month after Germany had won the bronze medal at the Sydney Olympics. A season later she shot her country to the Euro 2001 title but then surprised the women's game by retiring from international football.

She was tempted out of retirement to help Germany win the 2003 World Cup, scoring the equalising goal in a 2-1 win over Sweden. She continued playing club football for Boston Breakers until WUSA was wound up in August 2003, winning the Player Of The Season award that year. At the end of her career she showed in the 2003 WUSA All-Star Game that she was still one of the hardest players to defend against in the world.

DAGNY MELLGREN

Country: Norway
Born: June 19, 1978
Position: Striker/Winger
Clubs: Klepp, Bjornar, Boston Breakers

Dagny Mellgren was from a footballing family and it always seemed likely that she would play the game. Her father played in Norway's top flight and her brother and sister also played the sport. A short but tricky forward who had an aptitude for playing the offside trap and getting into the space behind defenders, she played 95 times for her country and scored 49 goals.

The best moment of her career was scoring the 'golden goal' that helped Norway to a 3-2 victory over world champions USA to win a surprise gold medal at the 2000 Olympic Games in Sydney, Australia. She was also in fine form at the 2001 European Championship but this time the Norwegians failed to overcome hosts and eventual winners Germany in the semi-final. At the tournament four years later she scored against the Germans in the final but Norway were already trailing and she picked up a runners-up medal.

Mellgren was among the first of the overseas stars to join the American professional league, WUSA, where she was a key player for Boston Breakers. After the collapse of the league in 2003, she returned home to Norway to finish her studies as a radiographer and rejoined Klepp. However, she retired at just 27 in December 2005, announcing that she longer possessed the motivation for the game.

Below: Hanna Ljungberg of Sweden celebrates scoring against Nigeria at the 2003 World Cup.

Right: Marinette Pichon celebrates scoring against Brazil at the 2003 World Cup.

CAROLINA MORACE

Country: Italy

Born: February 5, 1964

Position: Striker

Clubs: Spinea, Belluno, Bardolino, Trani 80, Lazio, Reggiana Zambelli, Milan, Sassari Torres, Agliana, Verona Gunther, Modena

Morace was a prolific goalscorer in the semi-professional Italian women's league and finished the top scorer for 11 consecutive seasons from 1988 to 1999, helping eight different clubs to a combined 12 league titles and scoring more than 500 goals. She made her international debut at just 14 years of age in 1978 against Yugoslavia and went on to hit 105 goals in 153 appearances. She played in two European Championships.

After finishing her playing days, she pursued a coaching career and attracted mass media attention when she became the first woman to manage a professional men's team, Serie C1 side Viterbese, but she resigned after two games due to the press attention. She then became the manager of the Italian national women's side but resigned after the 2005 European Championship.

LILY PARR

Country: England

Born: April 26, 1905

Position: Left-winger

Clubs: St Helens, Dick Kerr's Ladies, Preston Ladies

Lily Parr was the undisputed star of Dick, Kerr's Ladies, a team of factory workers who formed in 1917 to play charity matches, raising money for wounded soldiers. The team was already well established when 14-year-old Lily Parr was poached from St Helens, and in her first season with the club (1919-20), she scored 43 goals. A six-foot left-winger with quick feet, a fierce shot and a sharp eye for goal, Lily Parr fast forged a reputation for scoring, or setting up, many of the team's goals.

In the early 1920s Dick, Kerr's Ladies started playing international matches and before a tour of France *The Daily News* described Lily Parr as 'a 15-year-old girl back who is said to kick like a

Left: Lily Parr, a pioneer of women's football and star of Dick, Kerr's Ladies.

First Division man'. She went on to score over 1,000 goals in a career that lasted until 1951, long after the Football Association had tried to extinguish the growing popularity of women's football by banning it from Football League grounds. By the time Parr retired, Dick, Kerr's Ladies had become formally known as Preston Ladies and she was playing at left-back.

She died of cancer on May 24, 1978, but she was recognised for her contribution to women's football when she was inducted into the National Football Museum's Hall Of Fame in 2002.

MARINETTE PICHON

Country: France

Born: November 26, 1975

Position: Centre-forward

Clubs: Saint-Memmie, Philadelphia Charge, New Jersey Wildcats, Juvisy FCF

Pichon was a strong forward who made up for her lack of height with a great presence in the penalty area. She played two seasons of professional football in WUSA for Philadelphia Charge, initially stepping into the boots of the injured fans' favourite Kelly Smith to shoot Charge to the semi-finals of the 2002 Founders Cup. She was the second highest scorer in the league that season and was voted the Player Of The Year and also Striker Of The Year. After the closure of WUSA she played alongside Smith for the New Jersey Wildcats, before returning home to her native France.

At international level Pichon's biggest achievement was helping France to qualify for the World Cup for the first time in 2003, netting a goal in the first leg of the UEFA play-off against England. However, Pichon's talents could not help the team to get past the group stage in that World Cup, or at the 2005

European Championship. She announced her retirement after France failed to qualify for the 2007 World Cup, having scored 82 goals for her country in 112 games.

HEGE RIISE

Country: Norway

Born: July 18, 1969

Position: Midfielder

Clubs: Nikko Securities, Asker, Carolina Courage, Team Strommen

Riise had the two biggest attributes required to make the ultimate player: strength and superb technical ability. She helped the Norwegians to the 1991 World Cup Final, losing to the USA, and lifted the European Championship in 1993. She was voted the best player at the 1995 World Cup and was the tournament's second highest scorer with five goals, including one in Norway's 2-0 victory over Germany in the final. At the inaugural women's football event at the 1996 Olympics in Atlanta she won a bronze medal, and in 2000 in Sydney she added the gold to her collection when Norway beat USA.

After a spell as a professional with Nikko Securities in Japan between 1995 and 1997, with whom she won league and cup titles, she was voted Player Of The Year in Norway for her performances for Asker in 2000. She was signed by Carolina Courage in October 2001 and continued to impress in America, winning the club's Player Of The Year award for the first two seasons and leading them to victory in the 2002 Founders' Cup.

Riise made her last appearance for Norway at a major tournament at the 2003 World Cup Finals in America, recovering from a serious knee ligament injury to make four appearances from the bench. She retired from international football in 2004, having made 188 appearances for her country. She joined Team Strommen the following year and finally hung up her boots in 2006.

SILKE ROTTENBERG

Country: Germany
Born: January 25, 1972
Position: Goalkeeper
Club: Grun-Weiss Brauweiler, TSV Siegen, Sportfreunde Siegen, FFC Brauweiler, FCR 2001 Duisburg, FFC Frankfurt

In a sport where female goalkeepers are often derided for their lack of height and presence, Rottenberg commanded her penalty box and was the rock on which Germany's international success was built. Renowned as the greatest women's keeper ever, she first played for her country against the USA in 1993 and went onto make 126 international appearance before her retirement in 2008.

She was voted the best goalkeeper at the 2003 World Cup in the USA after helping Germany to defeat the hosts in the semi-finals and Sweden after extra-time in the final. She had already picked up winners' medals in the European Championships in Scandinavia in 1997 and on home turf in 2001, and was in fantastic form during the 2005 tournament in England, conceding just twice on the way to lifting the trophy for a third time.

During her long career Rottenberg has also won two Olympic bronze medals in 2000 and 2004, four German league titles (twice with TSV Siegen and twice with FFC Frankfurt) and three German Cups. She lost her place as Germany's first choice keeper after tearing cruciate ligaments and had to watch from the bench as Nadine Angerer kept goal when the team won the 2007 World Cup in China. She retired the following year, having been voted Germany's Women's Player Of The Year.

SISSI

Country: Brazil
Born: June 2, 1967
Position: Midfielder
Clubs: San Jose CyberRays, Sacramento Storm, California Storm, Gold Pride

A veteran of three World Cup tournaments and two Olympic campaigns for her native Brazil, Sisleide do Amor Lima was regarded as one of the most entertaining players in the world in her day. She took up the game at seven years of age and when she was a young girl she would tear the heads off her dolls to kick around. Her obvious hero was Pelé.

Formerly a teacher, she was one of a handful of foreign stars integrated into the WUSA professional league at its launch in 2001 and for three seasons she was virtually ever present for her club side San Jose CyberRays. She won

the inaugural WUSA league title with the club in 2001 when it was still called the Bay Area CyberRays.

Although she was more likely to set up goals for others, free-kicks became her trademark and along with China's Sun Wen she was joint top scorer at the 1999 World Cup. She was also voted the second best player at the tournament.

PIA SUNDHAGE

Country: Sweden
Born: February 13, 1960
Position: Midfielder
Clubs: Ulricehamn IFK, Falkopings KIK, Jitex BK, Osters IF, ROI Lazio, Stattena IF, Hammarby IF

For many years Pia Sundhage held the record for the most international appearances in the history of women's football, scoring 71 goals in 146 games. She kicked off her glittering international career at the age of 15 in 1975 and ended it at the 1996 Atlanta Olympic Games.

She scored Sweden's last penalty to beat England on spot-kicks in the unofficial 1984 European Championship Final after two legs had failed to separate the sides. She was also a part of the side that finished as runners-up in the unofficial 1987 World Cup, and she played in the 1991 and 1995 World Cup tournaments.

During her club career in Sweden's top flight she won four league championships, four cup competitions, and she also enjoyed a year as a semi-professional in Italy with Lazio.

Sundhage continued her career in women's football after her playing days had ended, beginning coaching at club level in Sweden. She subsequently coached in the American professional league with Philadelphia Charge (as an assistant coach) and with Boston Breakers, where she was voted the 2003

WUSA Coach Of The Year after winning that season's league title. In 2008 she became coach of the USA national team.

SUN WEN

Country: China
Born: April 6, 1973
Position: Midfielder
Clubs: Shanghai, Atlanta Beat

Regarded by many as the best player in the world on her day, Sun Wen first took up the game as a small child, encouraged by her football fan father. She grew to possess all the qualities that you would expect from a world-class star: pace, vision, accuracy of passing and the ability to score, not only on a regular basis but often spectacularly so.

Sun made her international debut at just 17. A year later she was China's main striker at the 1991 World Cup and she was a member of the side that finished fourth in 1995. She was joint top scorer at the 1999 World Cup, sharing the Golden Boot with Sissi of Brazil, and was also voted the tournament's best player, but this was small consolation for losing the final to hosts USA on penalties in front of a crowd of 90,000.

Sun was hugely successful in China when playing for her hometown side Shanghai, and moved to America in 2001 to play for Atlanta Beat in the WUSA professional league until the demise of the competition in 2003. She retired soon afterwards but following two years out of the game she returned to the Chinese women's team in December 2005, at the urging of new head coach Ma Liangxing. However, injury got the better of her and she hung up her boots for good in August 2006.

A well known face and star of chat shows in her homeland, she was voted FIFA World Player Of The Century in a poll conducted on the FIFA website.

Left: Sissi parades with the flag after Brazil draw with Germany to finish top of their group at the 1999 World Cup.

Below: China's Sun Wen beats Germany's Sandra Minnert to the ball in 2003.

GREAT WOMEN PLAYERS OF TODAY

NADINE ANGERER

Country: Germany
Born: November 10, 1978
Position: Goalkeeper
Clubs: 1 FC Nuremberg, Wacker Munich, Bayern Munich, 1 FFC Turbine Potsdam, Djurgårdens IF, 1 FFC Frankfurt

Angerer made her international debut in August 1997 against Holland but for ten years she was unable to hold down a regular place in the German national team due to Silke Rottenberg's dominance of the position. However, at the 2007 Women's World Cup it was Angerer who kept Rottenberg on the bench and she went through the tournament keeping a clean sheet, picking up a winners' medal and setting a World Cup record for the most consecutive minutes without conceding a goal. She even saved a penalty from Marta in Germany's 2-0 win over Brazil in the final.

She subsequently kept her place in the national team and helped the Germans to win the 2007 European Championship and the bronze medal at the 2008 Olympics. She had been a squad member for Germany's three previous European Championship victories and for the Olympic Games of 2000 and 2004.

Angerer started off as a striker before realising her potential as a goalkeeper. She has played the majority of her career in Germany, having turned down the opportunity to play in the American college game in the Nineties. However, she spent a season in Sweden with Djurgårdens. She won the UEFA Women's Cup with Potsdam in 2005.

SONIA BOMPASTOR

Country: France
Born: June 8, 1980
Position: Midfielder
Clubs: La Roche ESOF, Montpellier HSC, Lyon, Washington Freedom, Paris Saint-Germain

Although Sonia Bompastor began her football career at La Roche ESOF, it was after a move to Montpellier in 2002 that it really took flight. She twice helped the club to the league title before winning it twice more with Lyon in 2007 and 2008. A move to the newly formed Women's Professional Soccer league in the USA proved a great success and she started every game for Washington Freedom in her first year, before spending the close season on loan to Paris Saint-Germain.

An attacking midfielder by nature, although Bompastor's key strengths are her turn of pace and her deadly left foot, she has also been utilised in defence by both club and country. A regular for France since her debut against Scotland in February 2000, she made her 100th international appearance eight years later. She made the shortlist for the FIFA World Player Of The Year Award in 2009.

SHANNON BOXX

Country: USA
Born: July 29, 1977
Position: Midfielder
Club: Boston Renegades, Saarbrucken, Ajax of Los Angeles, San Diego Spirit, New York Power, Los Angeles Sol, Saint Louis Athletica, Gold Pride

Boxx was suddenly catapulted into the big time in Autumn 2003 when she received a call-up for the United States squad for the 2003 World Cup, despite never having played an international. After impressing national coach April Heinrichs playing for San Diego Spirit in WUSA, she featured in two warm-up games and went on to score in the opening World Cup match against Sweden and in the third place play-off victory against Canada. Just a year later she was an ever present in the team and helped her side win the gold medal at the Athens Olympics.

A defensive midfielder who likes to get forward, she has over 100 caps to her name and has become one of the world's finest players. She captained the World All-Star XI that beat world champions Germany in 2004 as part of FIFA's Centenary celebrations and she was voted third in the 2005 FIFA Player Of The Year Award behind Birgit Prinz and Marta.

After missing most of the 2006 season through injury, she bounced back to star at the 2007 World Cup. However, her first-half red card in the semi-final with Brazil contributed to a crushing and unexpected 4-0 defeat for the Americans. Revenge was to be had the following year when she played every minute of America's campaign at the 2008 Olympics in Beijing and ended up with a gold medal after a satisfying but closely fought defeat of Brazil in the final.

CRISTIANE

Country: Brazil
Born: May 15, 1985
Position: Striker
Clubs: São Bernardo, Clube Atlético Juventus, 1 FFC Turbine Potsdam, VfL Wolfsburg, Linköpings FC, Corinthians, Chicago Red Stars, Santos

An outstanding player for club and country, Cristiane Rozeira de Souza Silva first started playing football on the streets of her hometown when she was just seven years of age. The progress of her career has certainly not been harmed by her seemingly telepathic international relationship with serial World Player Of The Year, Marta. Together they forged a lethal strikeforce, scoring many of the goals that turned Brazil into a force to be reckoned

Below: Sonia Bompastor of France outpaces Germany's Britta Carlson at the 2005 European Championship.

with in women's football in the first decade of the 21st century.

Cristiane first played for Brazil's Under-19 side at just 15, finally making her full international debut in 2003, but it was at the Olympics the following year that she made her surprise breakthrough. Starting the competition on the bench, she hit a hat-trick in a 7-0 hammering of Greece and scored twice more in the quarter-finals against Mexico, winning a silver medal after losing in the final to the USA and finishing as joint top scorer alongside the legendary Birgit Prinz.

She was an established first-team regular by the 2007 World Cup, hitting the net five times as the Brazilians upset the odds to reach the final. She scored five more to pick up a silver medal at the Olympics a year later, again finishing the competition as its top scorer. Her campaign featured a hat-trick scored against Nigeria and two against the Germans, helping her to third place in the FIFA World Player Of The Year Award for the second year running.

In her club career Cristiane has won the Copa Libertadores and the Copa do Brasil. She struggled to adapt to the game in Germany, often appearing as a substitute, but she won the league and cup 'double' with Turbine Potsdam in 2006. She moved to the USA to join Chicago Red Stars in 2009 and scored the first ever hat-trick in the newly formed Women's Professional Soccer League.

DANIELA

Country: Brazil
Born: January 12, 1984
Position: Midfielder
Clubs: Kopparbergs/Göteborg, Saad, Linköpings, Saint Louis Athletica

Daniela Alves Lima, better known as just Daniela, finished in the top ten of the 2007 FIFA World Player Of The Year Award, having spent most of the decade at the heart of Brazil's midfield. She was an ever present member of the team in three consecutive Olympic campaigns, winning the silver medal – and getting on the scoresheet – in both 2004 and 2008. She also played every game as Brazil finished as runners-up at the 2007 World Cup.

In South America she played her club football for Saad and was the top scorer in the 2007 Copa do Brasil as her club picked up the trophy. The following year, along with international team-mate Cristiane, she signed for Linköpings in Sweden. She moved her career to the USA in 2009 to play for Saint Louis Athletica, joining up with former Brazilian head coach Jorge Barcellos. Although she made an early impact for Athletica, a dreadful career-threatening tackle by Washington Freedom's Abby Wambach curtailed her first season four games into the campaign and she has struggled to recover.

MARIBEL DOMINGUEZ

Country: Mexico
Born: November 18, 1978
Position: Centre-forward
Clubs: Kansas City Mystics, Atlanta Beat, Barcelona, Indiana, L'Estartit

Maribel Dominguez had been a closely guarded secret in the American amateur W-League for Kansas City Mystics but her consistent good form in 2002, when she was named as the league's Player Of The Year, caught the eye of several WUSA teams. As a result she was signed by Atlanta Beat in 2003. A small and fast forward who regularly hits the back of the net, Dominguez made an immediate impact in the professional league in America and became popular with fans.

After the collapse of WUSA in 2003, Dominguez returned home to Mexico to prepare for the 2004 Olympics, where she helped her team to the quarter-finals. She has a fantastic goalscoring record at international level and has captained her country. She also captured headlines around the world in 2004 when she was set to sign for Celaya, a men's side in the Mexican Second Division. However, FIFA stepped in to reiterate their policy that men's and women's senior football should be kept separate.

In 2005 she took her career to Spain, living

Above: Cristiane celebrates scoring against Ecuador at the 2007 Pan American Games.

up to her 'Marigol' nickname with a hat-trick on her debut for Barcelona. She subsequently stayed in Spain with L'Estartit, and plans to move into coaching when her career is over.

JULIE FLEETING

Country: Scotland
Born: December 18, 1980
Position: Centre-forward
Clubs: Ayr United, San Diego Spirit, Ross County, Arsenal

Julie Fleeting was born into a footballing family. Her father Jim played for Ayr United and Norwich City and like many British girls, Fleeting's early footballing years were served playing alongside boys until she followed in her father's footsteps by signing for Ayr United, where she won several honours. She caught the eye of US scouts in 2002 and after the end of the Scottish season she made the switch to San Diego Spirit. A tall striker who is both comfortable running at defenders and good in the air, her typical British-style of play helped her flourish in the American professional league.

When the WUSA league closed in 2003, Julie returned home to Scotland and Ayr United but she was soon tempted to try her luck in the English Women's Premier League, with Arsenal flying her down to London every Sunday. She made an immediate impact, helping Arsenal to a league and cup 'double' in 2004 and scoring a hat-trick in the FA Cup final just a day after playing an international match for Scotland.

Undoubtedly the star of the Scotland team since her debut at the age of 16, Fleeting ended the 2009-10 season with 111 goals from 111 international appearances. However, with the Scotland team struggling to compete in qualification campaigns, it seems unlikely that Fleeting will ever grace a major tournament.

She was awarded an MBE for services to women's football in June 2008 and took a sabbatical from the game the following year to have a baby. While at school she also represented Scotland at basketball.

INKA GRINGS

Country: Germany
Born: October 31, 1978
Position: Striker
Club: FCR 2001 Duisburg

A prolific goalscorer for club and country, both must be thankful that Inka Grings did not have a chance to pursue her childhood ambition to play tennis. Spending the majority of her career with FCR 2001 Duisburg, she has enjoyed great personal success with the club since joining in 1995. Twice voted German Player Of The Year, first in 1999 and again ten years later, she also topped the league goalscoring charts six times in 12 seasons.

Grings set a German league record in 2000, scoring 38 goals as Duisburg won the title. She stayed with the club despite a very public falling out with coach Dietmar Herhaus in 2006, and although her career has been dogged by injuries, causing her to miss some key international tournaments, she has continued to perform at the highest level.

Debuting for her country as a 72nd minute substitute against Finland in May 1996, she would not score her first international goal until two years later, achieving the feat in her tenth game for Germany. She picked up winners' medals in both the 2005 and 2009 European Championships, finishing as the top scorer in both competitions. She scored the opening goal in the 2005 final against Norway and she also hit the net twice in a 6-2 defeat of England in the final four years later. Despite her successes, her career for Germany has been slightly overshadowed by that of her international team-mate and strike partner, the great Birgit Prinz.

SOLVEIG GULBRANDSEN

Country: Norway
Born: January 12, 1981
Position: Midfielder
Club: Kolbotn, Stabæk, Gold Pride

Solveig Gulbrandsen made her international debut in 1998 and her performances for Norway have won her much acclaim over the years. She won gold at the Sydney Olympics in 2000 at the age of just 19, but the Norwegians struggled to maintain their form over the next few years, losing to Germany in the semi-finals of Euro 2001 and going out to hosts USA in the 2003 World Cup quarter-final.

It was Gulbrandsen who helped to secure Norway's rise back to the top of the women's game, first scoring a hat-trick in a 9-3 aggregate annihilation of Iceland in the play-off to reach the 2005 European Championship in England. Despite carrying an injury going into the finals, Gulbrandsen was undoubtedly the star of the tournament, helping Norway to perform beyond expectations and reach the final. By this time Gulbrandsen had become the darling of the English fans and was cheered on by much of the 21,000-strong crowd at Ewood Park, where they lost a tough game to Germany. She had already scored twice in the semi-final victory over Sweden and earned a yellow card for lifting her shirt over her head in celebration after scoring the first goal.

Gulbrandsen gave birth to her first child in June 2006, but just a year later she was part of the Norway team that reached the World Cup semi-final before losing to Germany. Later the same year she won the Norwegian Cup with Kolbotn. She has spent most of her career in Norway but in 2010 she briefly moved to the USA to play for Gold Pride in the WPS league.

KARA LANG

Country: Canada
Born: October 22, 1986
Position: Forward
Club: Vancouver Whitecaps, Pali Blues

An inspirational playmaker for her country, Kara Lang made her breakthrough on the world stage at the age of just 15, scoring three goals in six games at the inaugural FIFA Under-19 World Championship, staged in August 2002 in her homeland Canada. Her height, combined with her deadly pace when running onto long balls and the ability to shoot from seemingly anywhere in the opposition's half, was enough to see Canada through to the final, where they lost to the Americans on penalties in front of a crowd of 48,000.

She made the transition to the senior national team with ease, notching a brace against Wales in her second international while still a 15-year-old student, setting a record for the youngest international goalscorer. The signing of a semi-professional contract in February 2003 with W-League side Vancouver Whitecaps further added to her potential, and at just 16 she was an ever-present member of Canada's team at the 2003 World Cup. She scored a memorable free-kick goal in the World Cup semi-final to give her team a 1-0 lead over Sweden, but they lost the game and eventually finished in fourth place.

She played her college football with UCLA and returned to Vancouver Whitecaps in 2010. Although her career has been dogged by a couple of serious cruciate ligament injuries, she reached the quarter-finals of the 2008 Olympic football tournament and continues to add to her many international goals and appearances.

SIMONE LAUDEHR

Country: Germany
Born: July 12, 1986
Position: Midfielder/Left-winger
Clubs: Bayern Munich, FCR 2001 Duisburg

After starting her career with Bayern Munich, Simone Laudehr moved to Duisburg in 2004 and helped the club to second place in the German league for four consecutive seasons. She made her international debut in July 2007 and just two months later she scored in the dying minutes of the World Cup final to help Germany clinch the trophy with a 2-0 defeat of Brazil. She picked up an Olympic bronze medal the following year and was a member of her country's European Championship-winning team in 2009.

Most at home on the left wing, Laudehr's talents have also been utilised in attack and in midfield, where she played in the final of Euro 2009. She won the German Cup and the

Opposite clockwise from top left: Arsenal's Julie Fleeting lifts the Premier League trophy; Norway's Solveig Gulbrandsen on the ball at the 2003 World Cup; Canada's Kara Lang in 2003; Simone Laudehr celebrates scoring in the Euro 2009 semi-final.

Opposite: Possibly the best women's player of all time, Germany's Birgit Prinz in the 2007 World Cup Final.

UEFA Women's Cup in 2009 with Dusiburg and soon after she was shortlisted for the FIFA World Player Of The Year Award.

KRISTINE LILLY

Country: USA
Born: July 22, 1971
Position: Winger
Clubs: Tyresö FF, Boston Breakers, KIF Orebro

Kristine Lilly's finest moment in a long and glittering international career was undoubtedly the 1999 World Cup Final: a speedy winger and an occasional forward, she jumped to clear a goalbound header from China's Fan Yunjie in the last minute of extra-time to force a penalty shoot-out. Lilly then netted the USA's third spot-kick to put the Americans ahead, leading them to a 5-4 win. Like fellow legends Julie Foudy and Mia Hamm, it was her second World Cup win following victory over Norway in China in 1991.

A year after that famous second World Cup victory Lilly became the first player in football history to reach the 200-cap mark. She has currently made 347 international appearances, a world record for both men and women, and she has scored 130 goals for her country, a testimony to the influence this midfielder has had on the success of the American team.

At club level Lilly captained the Boston Breakers in the WUSA league for three years and after a stint in Sweden with KIF Orebro she is once again playing for the Breakers in the newly formed Women's Professional Soccer league. She played in every game of the league's inaugural season in 2009, scoring three goals.

One of the fittest players in the game, she can dictate the pace of play and is a prolific creator of attacking moves. Nicknamed the 'Iron Woman', Lilly also runs her

Below: The amazing Marta of Brazil in 2004.

own soccer academy, while her former school named a football pitch after her.

She captained the USA team from 2005 to 2007, and won gold medals at the Olympics in 1996 and 2004, only missing the 2008 competition after taking a year off for the birth of her daughter. She has played in five World Cup tournaments, winning twice, but a recall to the national team in 2010 means that a sixth World Cup remains a serious possibility.

MARTA

Country: Brazil
Born: February 19, 1986
Position: Striker
Clubs: Vasco Da Gama, Santa Cruz, Umea IK, Los Angeles Sol, Santos, Gold Pride

Voted FIFA World Player Of The Year an unprecedented four times before reaching her 24th birthday, Marta has already made such a significant mark on the world game that she has been described as the female Pelé. A quite extraordinary talent, she offers the kind of lightning speed and natural ball control that can turn even the tightest of games. She has also played her part in transforming Brazil into an influential power on the international stage.

Marta started her career playing in boys' teams as a youngster and was discovered by Vasco Da Gama when she was just 14 years old, but her skills were first brought to the attention of the wider world at FIFA's 2002 Under-19 World Championship. She soon helped the senior team to the quarter-finals of the 2003 World Cup and just a year later the Brazilians proved the surprise attraction at the 2004 Olympic football tournament, reaching the final only to lose in extra-time to the USA.

Before winning the silver medal at the Athens Olympics, Marta had made her name on the club circuit after joining Umea of Sweden in March 2004. She came in as a replacement for the injured Hanna Ljungberg and made an immediate impact, helping the team to the UEFA Women's Cup and a hat-trick of domestic league titles.

She finished as a runner-up in the FIFA World Player Of The Year Award in 2005, winning it a year later and retaining it for the following three seasons. The seven goals she scored at the 2007 World Cup fired the Brazilians to the final where they lost to Germany, but Marta finished the tournament as both its best player and its top scorer.

She signed a three-month loan contract with Santos in 2009 to play in the Copa Libertadores and in the Copa do Brasil, enjoying victory in both competitions, the most emphatic of which was a 9-0 defeat of Universidad Autónoma in the final of the Copa Libertadores. The same year she had begun her career in America's WPS league with Los Angeles Sol, transferring to Gold Pride for the 2010 season.

TIFFENY MILBRETT

Country: USA
Born: October 23, 1972
Position: Forward
Clubs: Shiroki FC Serena, New York Power, Sunnanå SK, Vancouver Whitecaps, Linköpings, Gold Pride

Tiffeny Milbrett's unfaltering touch in front of goal has made her one of America's most prolific strikers, scoring 100 goals in just over 200 internationals and at times forging a deadly strike duo with Mia Hamm. Short of stature, at her best she could always rely on an incredible turn of pace and was most comfortable with the ball at her feet.

She started her professional career playing club football in Japan but was back in the US to become a founding member of New York Power in the Women's United Soccer Association in 2001, becoming the league's Player Of The Season in her first campaign. She also scored the first WUSA hat trick, when the Power beat Boston Breakers 3-1. When women's professional football returned to the USA in 2009 she was signed by Gold Pride to play in America's new Women's Professional Soccer league, scoring on her debut at the age of 36.

She made her international debut against China in August 1991 and she scored three times for the team that finished third at the 1995 World Cup in Sweden. She picked up a gold medal after hitting the winning goal in the 1996 Olympic final against China and won a silver medal four years later. She was also a member of the team that won the World Cup on home soil in 1999.

BIRGIT PRINZ

Country: Germany
Born: October 25, 1977
Position: Centre-forward
Clubs: FSV Frankfurt, FFC Frankfurt, Carolina Courage

Birgit Prinz is possibly the best player to have graced the women's game. A tall, strong and athletic figure, Prinz dominates matches from her centre-forward role, often tracking back in order to win the ball in midfield, before creating as many opportunities for her team-mates as for herself.

Voted FIFA World Player Of The Year for three consecutive years, she fired Germany to international success at the 2003 World Cup and collected the Golden Boot with seven goals. She was also voted Player Of The Tournament. She scored another five goals as Germany retained the trophy in 2007, and she played a significant part in helping her country to dominate European football, picking up winners' medals at the European Championships of 1995, 1997, 2001, 2005

and 2009. She has made more than 200 international appearances.

A European champion for her club as well as her country, she lifted the inaugural UEFA Women's Cup with FFC Frankfurt in 2002. That victory brought her to the attention of America's professional league and in the summer of 2002 she signed for Carolina Courage, making her mark by scoring the winning goal in the Founders Cup final to secure the 2002 WUSA title.

Prinz has won numerous domestic honours in Germany, where she returned for her second stint with FFC Frankfurt. She was also a part of the team that won the UEFA Women's Cup in 2006 and 2008, scoring in the second leg of the 2006 final. The one title that has eluded her career is the Olympic gold medal and she has had to settle for a hat-trick of bronze medals.

KELLY SMITH

Country: England
Born: October 29, 1978
Position: Centre-forward/central midfield
Clubs: New Jersey Lady Stallions, Philadelphia Charge, New Jersey Wildcats, Arsenal, Boston Breakers

Scouted for a soccer scholarship in America while playing football in Watford, Smith went on to break college and league goalscoring records and was so highly regarded at Seton College that they decided to retire her number

Below: Kelly Smith, doing it for England in 2007.

six shirt when she left. She stayed on in the United States for a year, coaching young girls, in anticipation of the launch of WUSA in 2001, the world's first professional football league for women. She impressed with Philadelphia Charge and soon became a fans' favourite, running a series of successful soccer camps under her own name.

United States national coach April Heinrichs voted Kelly Smith as her world player of the year after the England striker debuted in WUSA's inaugural year, but her four seasons were blighted by injury.

Smith joined the New Jersey Wildcats after the collapse of WUSA but further injury curtailed her time with the club and she returned home to sign for Arsenal and to begin the long preparation for the 2005 European Championship in her home country. While she was not 100 per cent fit for the tournament, she was easily England's best player and captured the imagination of the new found home audience for women's football.

A welcome injury-free season followed, along with the league and cup 'double', and she was also crowned both Players' Player and England International Player Of The Year. In the 2006-7 season, Smith's 30 goals in 34 games helped Arsenal to win the 'quadruple', although she missed both legs of the UEFA Women's Cup Final through suspension.

Smith had a good 2009, signing for Boston Breakers and returning to the States to play in the WPS league. She also helped England to finish as runners-up in the European Championship, scoring in the 6-2 final defeat to Germany, while she finished third in the annual FIFA World Player Of The Year Award.

Smith is at her best with the ball at her feet, taking players on and carving out opportunities from the tightest of angles. She plays as an out-and-out striker for England, but she performed in central midfield for Philadelphia Charge, enjoying being able to track back deep into her own team's half to fetch the ball before trying to dribble it past a full defence and shooting for goal.

HOPE SOLO

Country: USA
Born: July 30, 1981
Position: Goalkeeper
Clubs: Philadelphia Charge, Kopparbergs/Göteborg, Lyon, Saint Louis Athletica, Atlanta Beat

Recognised as one of the best players in the women's game, Hope Solo was a highly prolific striker in her teens, only becoming a goalkeeper during her university years. However, her height and athleticism lent itself well to the position and she made an instant impact in college football with the Washington Huskies, becoming a formidable shot stopper.

She began her professional career with the Philadelphia Charge, where she played one season. After the collapse of the Women's United Soccer Association, Solo moved her career abroad, first playing in Sweden and then France, before continuing in the newly formed Women's Professional Soccer league in the USA, joining Saint Louis Athletica in 2009. In her first campaign she was voted the WPS Goalkeeper Of The Year and after the club folded she joined Atlanta Beat in May 2010.

Making her international debut in 2000, Solo finally became the first choice keeper ahead of the 2007 Women's World Cup in China. After helping the United States to reach the semi-final, Hope was extremely critical of coach Greg Ryan's decision to replace her for the match itself, after he controversially selected 36-year-old veteran Briana Scurry, who had not played a full game in three months. Without Solo the USA were comprehensively beaten in the semi-final, losing 4-0, and she was subsequently dropped from the squad for the third place play-off. She did not feature for the national team again until the following year, selected again after the departure of Ryan.

By the 2008 Olympics she was once more the USA's first choice keeper, producing a series of impressive saves against Brazil as the Americans won the gold medal.

CHRISTINE SINCLAIR

Country: Canada
Born: June 12, 1983
Position: Forward
Clubs: Vancouver Breakers, Vancouver Whitecaps Women, Gold Pride

Christine Sinclair was introduced to the game at the age of four and has since forged a highly successful career as a footballer, following in the footsteps of her uncles, Bruce and Brian Gant, both of whom played in the North American Soccer League. At just 26 years of age she became Canada's most capped player, while she also holds the record as her country's leading goalscorer.

A tall and prolific striker, she was just 16 years old when she made her international debut in the 2000 Algarve Cup. She continued to play youth football and finished the 2002 Under-19 Women's World Cup as both its best player and its top scorer, with a record ten goals. The following year she was part of the full international team that reached the semi-final of the World Cup, scoring one of her three tournament goals in the third place play-off defeat to the USA.

Voted Canadian Player Of The Year on five consecutive occasions from 2005 onwards, soon after her first award it was announced that together with international team-mate Tiffeny Milbrett she would be playing in the English league with Chelsea, but work permit problems scuppered the move. She continued to play in Canada and eventually relocated her career to the USA in 2009 to join FC Gold Pride in the Women's Professional Soccer league. She was shortlisted for the World Player Of The Year Award in 2008.

INGVILD STENSLAND

Country: Norway
Born: August 3, 1981
Position: Midfielder
Clubs: Donn, Athene Moss, Kolbotn, Kopparbergs/Göteborg, Lyon

It was perhaps inevitable that Ingvild Stensland became a footballer. She grew up with a father who coached the game and with older sisters who also played. Since then she has grown into a respected and creative midfield general, an international captain, and has featured in the world's top 20 women players on several occasions, thanks to repeated nominations in FIFA's World Player Of The Year Award.

Stensland made her international debut against the USA in March 2003 and soon became a vital part of the Norwegian midfield, winning a runners-up medal in the 2005 European Championship after losing 3-1 to Germany in the final. She played in every match of the 2007 Women's World Cup in China, finishing fourth after the Norwegians were heavily defeated by the United States in the third place play-off game. She was also an ever present member of the side at the 2008 Summer Olympics and she was later named Norway's Player Of The Year.

VICTORIA SVENSSON

Country: Sweden
Born: May 18, 1977
Position: Forward
Club: Jitex BK, Alvsjo, Djurgardens

Victoria Svensson was undoubtedly the star of the Sweden team that reached the 2003 Women's World Cup Final, only to see her team lose out to an extra-time goal from Germany in Los Angeles. In fact it was Svensson who was harshly adjudged to have fouled a German player, with Nia Kunzer scoring the winner from the resulting free-kick.

Shortly after returning from the World Cup finals, Svensson made headlines when Italian men's club Perugia approached her to play for them, but in response to their offer FIFA once again set stringent guidelines that disallowed women from playing for men's football clubs.

She made her international debut against Italy in October 1996 and has gone on to make over 150 appearances for her country, a Swedish record. She was voted Sweden's best player in 1998 and 2003 and she has finished as the league's top scorer on three occasions.

ABBY WAMBACH

Country: USA
Born: June 2, 1980
Position: Striker
Club: Washington Freedom

One of the greatest strikers to ever pull on the USA shirt, Abby Wambach sits alongside Mia Hamm as one of the national side's legends. Winner of a gold medal at the 2004 Athens Olympics after scoring four goals in the competition, including the extra-time header that beat Brazil in the final, Wambach's speed, skill and dominance in the air was used by her country to devastating effect.

Earlier that year she scored all five goals in the second-half of a game against Ireland – levelling a USA record – and added to her accolades by winning the Footballer Of The Year award for the second time in a row. The previous year Wambach secured a surprise place in the 2003 World Cup team, scoring three times, including a goal in the memorable 1-0 victory over Norway in the quarter-final.

She was the joint second highest scorer at the 2007 World Cup, hitting two goals in the third place play-off victory over Norway. Unfortunately, a broken leg during the last warm-up game before the 2008 Olympics ended her chances of competing in Beijing.

Wambach's career in professional club football began in 2002 with Washington Freedom, having already become the University of Florida's all-time leading goalscorer in college soccer. In 2003 the number 28's stunning strikes helped the Freedom win the Founders Cup and she was voted the Most Valuable Player in the final. She also earned the WUSA Goal Of The Year Award for a sensational diving header. After the demise of WUSA she continued to play for Washington Freedom in the amateur W-League, and she stayed with the club for the formation of America's new professional league in 2009.

She has scored over 100 goals for the USA national soccer team. Not bad for a girl who was once a high school basketball star.

Above: Abby Wambach celebrates scoring as the USA beat Brazil to win gold at the 2004 Olympics.

THE HISTORY OF THE WOMEN'S WORLD CUP

Above from left to right: Mia Hamm kisses the World Cup in 1999; Brandi Chastain's famous celebration at the 1999 World Cup; Germany's 2003 World Cup victory.

Below from left to right: The USA do a lap of honour in 1999; action from the 2003 World Cup final at the Home Depot Stadium.

The inaugural women's World Cup in 1991 came 20 years after women had first contested an official international match. In the early Seventies the women's game had taken its first steps on the road to recognition, with numerous national federations taking the running of the female game under their own governance, or at least forming links with amateur women's associations to allow national sides to be established. This move was widely encouraged by FIFA, the world governing body, which had issued directives to its member states to run the women's game alongside the men's.

As an increasing number of national sides emerged, international games became more competitive, with the Scandinavians' technique and fitness proving to be a generation ahead of their peers. Indeed, Denmark had the honour of being champions at the first unofficial world cup held in Mexico in 1971. The Americans also exploded onto the world football stage in the early Eighties and competed twice in the 'Little World Cup' held in Italy in 1985 and 1988, with both tournaments won by England.

With an increasing number of unofficial world championships, and with UEFA having already staged a European Championship, FIFA felt under pressure to launch an official Women's World Cup. FIFA President João Havelange announced at the 1986 Congress in Mexico City, prior to the men's World Cup, that a women's tournament would be launched and that it would take place every four years in the year following the men's competition.

In November 1991, 12 nations arrived in China for the first official Women's World Cup. The host media swarmed to see the home side thrash Norway 4-0 in the opening match. The Norwegians returned to form to reach the final, where they met new kids on the block, the United States. The Americans had benefited from a significant investment in female 'soccer' scholarships, making US colleges a hotbed of football development. Their forward line of Michelle Akers, April Heinrichs and Carin Jennings – labelled the 'Triple-Edged Sword' by local journalists – hit 18 of the team's 23 goals in just five games to reach the final.

Even without the home nation competing (China had lost to Sweden in the quarter-finals), an unexpected crowd of 65,000 witnessed the

first World Cup final. Akers hit two goals to take the trophy to America for the first time, snatching a 2-1 victory late in the game. The move to have an official women's competition on the world stage had been fully justified.

The first Women's World Cup had been a unanimous success and the second tournament had a great deal to live up to. Staged in Sweden, where participation rates were high and where there was a culture of acceptance of women playing football, it gave the European sides a chance to show a superior tactical awareness.

More than 14,000 packed into the national stadium for the opening match, only to see Brazil steal a surprise 1-0 victory against the home side. After that defeat Sweden had to battle hard to progress to the final eight, where they were knocked out by China on penalties. In the semi-finals Norway avenged their 1991 final defeat by securing a tight 1-0 victory against the USA, before Hege Riise and Marianne Pettersen netted a goal each to beat Germany 2-0 in the final in front of a 17,000 crowd.

While the 1995 World Cup had been a step forward in terms of performance, it was the 1999 tournament in the USA that would change women's football forever. The American media was highly sceptical that the tournament could be a success as football was a minority sport and the women's team had previously attracted minimal crowds. However, the Americans had a potential audience of seven million female players to draw upon and tickets began selling out as early as Mia Hamm and her team-mates began their preparations.

As the tournament gained momentum, the interest spiralled. With 90,185 supporters in the stadium, and another 40 million homes around America switching on to watch, the final was a success, with USA's Brandi Chastain creating headlines when she whipped off her shirt in celebration of her winning penalty against China. Spectator figures for the tournament reached 660,000, around six times that of the 1995 tournament in Sweden, while images of the winning team adorned *Sports Illustrated* and even the illustrious *Time* magazine.

The World Cup played a vital role in the development of the women's game. The stars of the 1999 tournament became household names in the USA and the first professional women's league was launched in America.

The 2003 World Cup was initially awarded to China, but FIFA made the decision in early 2003 to move the tournament due to the outbreak of SARS in the host country. The United States pitched for the finals and the World Cup returned to North America four years after the huge success of 1999. With a short lead time to organise and promote the tournament, smaller venues were used, but despite the USA team not progressing to the final, a sell-out 26,000 crowd at the Home Depot Arena, Los Angeles, saw Germany beat Sweden 2-1.

The Swedes had taken the lead in the 41st minute of the final, with Hanna Ljungberg scoring on the break, but Germany equalised through Maren Meinert just one minute after the interval. Both teams squandered chances

to finish off the tie, and early in extra-time the Germans secured their first world title when Nia Kuenzer headed in a 98th-minute free-kick from Renate Lingor. The result made Tina Theune-Meyer the first female coach to triumph in the competition.

Television audiences in the USA may have been focussed on the gridiron season rather the Women's World Cup this time, but the viewing figures in Sweden were even higher than those achieved by the men's team's appearance in the quarter-finals of the previous year's World Cup.

In Germany eight million had watched the team's victory in the final and an even larger domestic TV audience of 12 million tuned in to the final four years later to watch the Germans become the first team to retain the title. They had been heavily tipped from the outset and even beat Argentina by a record 11-0 scoreline in the opening game. However, the 2007 World Cup was not without its surprises. With a side boasting Marta and Cristiane, the Brazilians caused a major upset when they scored four times in the semi-final to eliminate a USA side unbeaten in 51 games.

In the final Brazil took the game to reigning world champions Germany but missed a penalty and lost a gripping contest to second-half strikes from Birgit Prinz and Simone Laudehr. Healthy worldwide viewing figures for the competition have shown the growing importance of the Women's World Cup and as competitiveness has increased, each tournament has raised the profile of the game and has driven interest in women's football as a spectator sport.

Above: The Germans are crowned world champions in 2007.

THE WOMEN'S WORLD CUP WINNERS	
1991:	USA
1995:	Norway
1999:	USA
2003:	Germany
2007:	Germany

INDEX

EVERYTHING YOU NEED TO KNOW

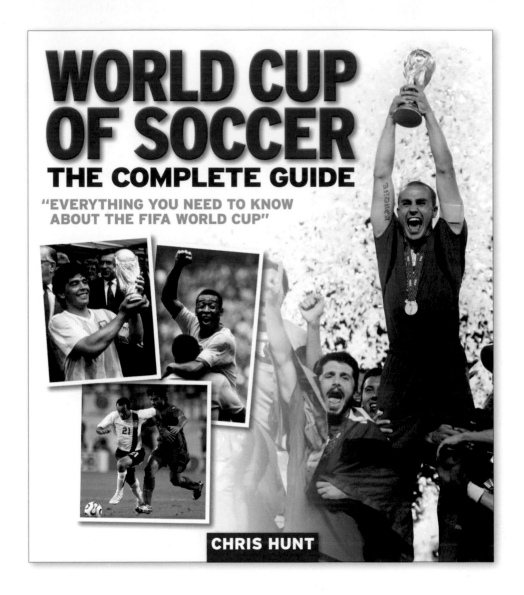

COMPANION TO
THE COMPLETE BOOK OF SOCCER

AVAILABLE WHEREVER BOOKS ARE SOLD

ABOUT THE EDITOR

A magazine editor and journalist, Chris Hunt has written about football and rock music for many years. He is the author of *World Cup Stories: The History Of The FIFA World Cup*, which was first published in 2006 to accompany a BBC television series. His encyclopedia *World Cup Of Soccer: The Complete Guide* was first published in 2010 and is the companion to this book, while his experiences in Japan for the World Cup in 2002 were documented in another BBC television programme, *Beckham For Breakfast*. He took weekly football magazine *Match* to record-breaking circulation heights in the 1990s and he has also been the Editor of many of the acclaimed special editions of leading music magazines *Mojo, Q, Uncut* and *NME*, covering subjects as diverse as The Beatles, U2, Kurt Cobain, Oasis, punk rock and mod. **For more information:** www.ChrisHunt.biz

Contributors: Nick Gibbs, Luke Nicoli, Hugh Sleight, Andrew Winter, James Eastham, Gary Tipp, Kevin Hughes, Paul Robson, Mike Pattenden, Joe Cushley, Steve Cresswell, Tim Hartley, Matt Allen, Richard Adams, Alistair Phillips, Bev Ward, John Plummer, Sara Hunt, John Glover.